Weary

Weary

The Life of Sir Edward Dunlop

Sue Ebury

Viking

VIKING
Penguin Books Australia Ltd
487 Maroondah Highway, PO Box 257
Ringwood, Victoria 3134, Australia
Penguin Books Ltd
Harmondsworth, Middlesex, England
Viking Penguin, A Division of Penguin Books USA Inc.
375 Hudson Street, New York, New York 10014, USA
Penguin Books Canada Limited
10 Alcorn Avenue, Toronto, Ontario, Canada M4V 3B2
Penguin Books (N.Z.) Ltd
182–190 Wairau Road, Auckland 10, New Zealand

First published by Viking Australia, 1994
10 9 8 7 6 5 4 3
Copyright © Suzanne Ebury, 1994
Illustrations Copyright © Ray Parkin, maps of Burma–Thailand
Railway, 1963 and 1993, other maps Australian War Memorial,
Canberra

Typeset in 10/12 pt Garamond Euro by Midland Typesetters
Made and printed in Australia by Australian Print Group, Maryborough, Victoria
Edited by Linda Ristow
Designed by George Dale
Index by Russell Brooks

National Library of Australia
Cataloguing-in-Publication data:

Ebury, Sue.
Weary: the life of Sir Edward Dunlop.

Bibliography.
Includes index.
ISBN 0 670 847607.

1. Dunlop, E.E. (Ernest Edward), 1907–1993. 2. Burma–Siam
Railroad, 3. Surgeons – Australia – Biography. 4. World
War, 1939–1945 – Prisoners and prisons, Japanese. 5. World
War, 1939–1945 – Medical care – Burma. I. Title.
617.092

CONTENTS

Maps & Line Drawings

For Patsy Adam-Smith
Who introduced me to 'the subject of War'

PART ONE

1907 – 1939

'He held his rifle above his head so as to prevent any water running into the barrel . . . and swam with his other arm and his feet. For a portion of the way he trod water apparently with the same ease as he walked upon solid earth. So he overcame the powerful current and emerged almost directly opposite the point where he had entered . . .

'That he would not dally long enough to hunt out the more convenient crossing place was another illustration of Deerfoot's indifference to his own comfort. What though his garments were dripping when he stepped upon solid earth again, and the air was almost wintry in its chill, he cared naught.'

from *Deerfoot in the Mountains* by EDWARD S. ELLIS

ONE

Beginnings

WHEN WEARY DUNLOP emerged from his 'long dark night of captivity' in the prison camps on the Burma-Siam Railway in August 1945, he carried with him a tattered packet of papers. Discovery by his former Japanese captors of any one of those closely written sheets of paper would have led to his execution, so detailed and damning were the contents. These papers formed his medical diary, 'maintained simply as a military duty . . . in no sense designed for publication . . . ', and on his return to Australia that October they were consigned to a desk drawer.

For the next forty years, the little pile of folded pieces of paper, exercise books and notebooks was concealed from all but a few. Marriage, a busy surgical practice and an increasingly full public life eased the pain of his war. But the attitudes of successive governments towards returned soldiers and the gradual whittling away of pension benefits from survivors, began to cause him grave disquiet. The diaries' time had arrived: surely their publication would focus attention on an aging and increasingly incapacitated group of Australians – former prisoners-of-war of the Japanese in the Second World War.

Since the publication of his *War Diaries* in 1986, there has been a tidal wave of interest in their contents and in the man who wrote them amidst the appalling conditions of Allied prisoner-of-war camps in South-east Asia. He was the spokesman for that dwindling band of men and women who spent long, lost years as prisoners of the Japanese between 1942 and war's end in August 1945. And he was the tangible reminder – a survivor – of a ghostly company who suffered and died to build a railway.

In 1939 Ernest Edward Dunlop was eager for war, like others of his generation. Yet initially his attempts to enlist in either the British Army or the AIF met with inflexible opposition. Since the beginning of September he had been the leader of an operating team in the West

London sector of the Emergency Medical Service, based at St Mary's Hospital, Paddington. His request for release from these duties in order to join up was firmly rejected. Weary resorted to urgent letters and, finally, Sir Thomas Dunhill sent a cable for him to his old Children's Hospital chief in Melbourne, Major-General Rupert Downes, who was now Director of Medical Services for the Australian Imperial Force. Eventually, the desired reply arrived and he accomplished what everyone had insisted was impossible: enlistment in the Australian Army without returning to Australia.

By 13 November he had been sworn in by Lieutenant-Colonel William Bridgeford at Australia House and was Captain Dunlop, VX259, of the 2nd AIF. Three weeks later, his passport to war arrived by telegram: 'Ascertain if Captain E.E. Dunlop . . . available appointment Overseas Base.'

Weary's considerable achievements to date had been academic and sporting, but with the onslaught of war, his ambition was to work as a surgeon as close to the front line as possible. His hatred of fascism, shared by many in that depressed and turbulent decade leading up to war, and his intense dislike of the policy of appeasement pursued by Neville Chamberlain, propelled him towards the rôle for which he had yearned during his childhood at Stewarton, when he absorbed stories of the great-grandfather who fought in the Punjab, and watched six men of his family march off to that Great War which was going to end all wars. Yet, ironically, he would spend most of the next two years as a staff officer. It was not until he reluctantly agreed to be Medical Liaison Officer between the AIF and the British Troops in Greece that we begin to see the mettle of the man emerge before the apprehensive gaze of those who worked with him.

His official war diary as Medical Liaison Officer is suspended abruptly amidst the confusion of 21 April 1941, when retreating Allied troops choked the narrow Greek roads, and Weary had to abandon his wrecked staff car on the precipitous edge of the Brallos Pass and hitch a ride back to Athens on an artillery wagon. Communications between Headquarters and the forward areas had collapsed, and he was constantly on the move between various medical units and Athens, and No. 5 Australian General Hospital at Kephissia. Weary acquired a new car and Private 'Blue' Butterworth as a fresh driver (the previous one had broken an arm in the accident which put paid to their vehicle), and took them straight back into the action. As far as Blue was concerned, it promised to be a rugged assignment, but very quickly he decided that Weary led a charmed life and he could do much worse than be attached to him.

Three days later, they were returning to the hospital at Kephissia with two wounded Kiwi lieutenants in the back seat and a Stuka shadowing them along a twisting mountain road. Blue recalls nervously checking and re-checking the rear vision mirror and noticing that the two Kiwis 'were very het up. We all were . . . I'm wanting Weary to say, Stop! Pull over under a tree – any old thing – I was no brave bloke'. The Stuka stayed with them. When they reached the railway siding, Weary quietly told Blue to pull up, and he walked over to the ambulance train parked there. The other three tumbled out of the car and took to the nearest cover. Three Stukas now screamed down and opened up with their machine guns. Weary himself remembered that 'I was just having a look and saying good-day to some of the wounded on board, when suddenly we were attacked. But the planes very generously shut off their machine guns as they went over the train marked with a red cross . . . They were strafing their way up to it, then they shut off, then they started up the other side . . . In the middle of this, I noticed that the Greek train driver had shot through. I picked up a rifle and bayonet, and chased him. By this time, the planes had wheeled round and started their attack again and were on their way back, so I thought it prudent to fall on my face and make myself as small as possible. Suddenly, I became aware of the Greek train driver striking an heroic posture: "We Greeks have no fear!" I rather sheepishly got to my feet.' Blue and the amazed Kiwis were flat on their faces the whole time. 'The blokes said, "Who is this fellow?", and I said, "I don't know much about him." "He's bloody mad! He's got no nerves! *Who is he?*".'[1]

Major Edward Dunlop, as he now was, had been born half a world away from Greece in the north-eastern Victorian town of Wangaratta. In his veins mingled the blood of independent Lowland Scots Dunlops and the English Walpoles. The former gave their name to a cheese and to the pneumatic tyre. The latter wrote 'gentleman' after their name, for in the eighteenth century their family had provided Britain's first effective prime minister, Sir Robert Walpole, transformed by his monarch from a commoner to a Knight of the Garter.

Sir Edward Dunlop was the first descendant of his mother's family to be knighted since 1726. By the time he was born on 12 July 1907, the branch of the Walpoles from which he was descended had come down in the world.

Young Ernie's mother and aunts were immensely proud of their connection with such distinguished ancestors. Aunt Violet and Aunt Lily, particularly, seldom failed to impress on their nephews how it was their duty to improve the family's standing from the low point to which it had fallen in Australia. 'I remember [them] solemnly telling my brother and me that it was up to us to restore the honour of the family'.

But Ernie preferred to have his pulses quickened by tales of Scottish knights, and to daydream about his Scots forebears or imaginary adventures in which he performed heroic deeds, than to listen to romantic stories of his family history. There were plenty of them, however, and their message sank deep in the young boy's brain.

Almost a century before his great-grandson opened his blue eyes on the Antipodean world, Henry Nagle Walpole was born in London in 1810. The East India Company offered opportunities to adventurous young men with neither means nor influence. At the age of 26 he was sent out to Madras as a schoolmaster sergeant with the 2nd Battalion of Artillery and, shortly afterwards at St Thomas's Mount Church, he married Matilda Sophie Bathe on 27 July 1836.[2]

By 1837, he was a warrant officer in Burma, where his son, Thomas Richard, was born in Mergui, but not to Matilda. The mother was Maria Angelina Jackson, a widow who had witnessed his marriage just thirteen months earlier. A year later, they had Thomas baptised in Moulmein, where the East India Company garrison was housed on the Salween river, 250 kilometres as the crow flies from the broad River Kwai Noi, where Henry's great-grandson would suffer as a prisoner-of-war just over a century later.

When their daughter, Catherine Marie, was born at Fort William in Calcutta on 29 November 1840, Henry was no longer a non-commissioned officer but a private in the No. 1 Troop of the Bengal Artillery.[3] It took him four years to regain NCO status and the post of assistant overseer,[4] but in another three he was once more in the ranks. This time, he wore the dark blue coat with scarlet facings of the 1st European Fusiliers, the pick of the Company's troops with a ferocious reputation. In 1848, they were sent into battle in the Punjab against the even more ferocious Sikhs.

This second war against the Sikhs was a savage and bloody business; Henry must have been tough – and lucky – to survive the battles of Mooltan and Gujarat, for in the artillery regiments the casualties outnumbered the suvivors. By the Sutlej Campaign of 1850 he was fortunate to be an apprentice surgeon in the subordinate Medical Corps and back behind the lines: for every gunner in the 3rd Brigade of Horse Artillery was killed.

In 1855, Henry arrived in Melbourne with Catherine and Thomas, a new wife and two more children. They made their way to the gold diggings but colonial Ballarat was not to Mrs Walpole's liking: taking her two small children and all Henry's papers, she disappeared back to India about the time of the Mutiny in 1857. Only her reputation as a 'spiteful and vindictive' woman survives, undoubtedly the judgement passed by her step-daughter, Catherine Marie.[5]

Catherine never forgot India; she told stories and wrote poetry about it, and passed onto her daughters recipes and a taste for 'stinging' curries. A century after her departure from India, Weary found an affinity with the Sikhs in the Punjab which he could never explain. He referred to himself as an 'honorary Indian'.

Money was short; but Henry's time on the diggings was 'fairly remunerative'.[6] He selected a small parcel of land at Devil's Creek. His surgical experience enabled him to practise in Australia without mishap, and he derived a slender income from 'those who knew him'.[7] By 1868, both Henry and Thomas claimed they were surgeons, Henry signing himself: 'Surgeon & apothecary, H.E.I.C.S [Hon. East India Company Service].[8]

In 1866, Catherine married Edward Payne against her father's wishes. Strong-willed, and a match for Henry, she refused to eat until he agreed. She was now 25. Edward, a neighbour, was 38 and had been at sea before becoming a 'splitter' or 'woodman', a not uncommon occupation in that part of Victoria, where the ringing of axes and the rasp of the crosscut saw marked off the daylight hours. His portrait shows an imposing face with a high forehead and strong cheekbones; hers, taken at around the same time in later life, displays regular features, a clear-cut brow, the strong 'Walpole eyebrows' and a firm chin.[9] The purpose in the face suggests that no one would trifle with Catherine.

Henry thought his articulate and well-educated daughter was marrying beneath her – he had not forgotten those distinguished forebears – but sawmilling settlements did not attract the more eligible bachelors. Thomas married Grace Richardson that December, another neighbour whose family ran one of the sawmills. Accounts of Henry, Thomas and Catherine agree that they appeared markedly superior to their fellow settlers. Catherine spoke French, Italian and German; she read Latin, played the piano and painted in oils and watercolours.

Catherine and Edward moved their family to Pine Lodge in 1873, where their fifth child, Weary's mother, Alice Emily Maude, was born in 1874, along with three more girls (Catherine, and the twins Violet and Lily May) and a son, Ernest. After the birth of the last, they moved to land not far from Baddaginnie in the Benalla Shire, then, around 1889, they selected land at Whorouly which they called Sunnyside.

Henry divided his time between Catherine and Thomas, both raising families and continuing the Walpole tradition of teaching other people's children. Catherine's teaching must have been of a temporary nature (apart from her own brood), since she complained of the small sums she earned, but Thomas was by now head teacher at Upper Everton. It was while living with him that Henry died in 1889 and was buried in Tarrawingie Cemetery.

Catherine Payne dominated her children's lives. The steely resolution which enabled her to defy her father and marry a man thirteen years her senior also made her determined to educate her daughters as young ladies in the humble environment of a selector's wooden cottage. Catherine didn't know the meaning of the word 'compromise'.

She made a profound impression on her grandchildren: Alan, Weary and their cousin Jess Gillies all spoke of her imperious and dignified manner. 'Bossy,' Jess called her. 'Too bossy to brush a fly off her face!' Jess saw her grandmother most during the First World War, when Cath, her own mother, cared for the old lady while Violet and Lil were nursing in Salonika and on the Western Front. The Dunlop boys did not see too much of Catherine, for long journeys from the farm were difficult when there was livestock to be tended and 40 kilometres was a considerable journey in horse and buggy days. But Weary never forgot the 'awesome sort of invalidism' that hung like a pall over the place, where Catherine spent most of her time in bed, crippled and deformed by advanced rheumatoid arthritis. His most vivid memory was when his Uncle Ernest encouraged him to dare-devil feats on the back of a cow, and Catherine screamed from her wheelchair: 'That boy will be killed! That boy will be killed!' as he flew over its head onto a fence post.

She demanded attention from all her daughters and was reluctant to let any of them roam too far, but by the time Edward died in 1897, Edith had escaped by marrying a well-to-do Wangaratta widower, Jacob Vincent, and Alice had been working as a governess in New South Wales for some years. Any daughter of Catherine's had a well-developed sense of duty, but Alice had no intention of becoming a martyr to Mother, like the younger ones. When she returned to Victoria after her father's death, she took a new post as governess with the Davis family at Stewarton.

A few miles down the road at Major Plains lived James Dunlop, a young bachelor whose mother had recently died. He had a house, a good livelihood as a share-farmer and reasonable prospects. James was a first generation Australian, raised in a Scots Presbyterian household founded on the virtues of thrift, hard work, early rising and doing one's duty by one's fellow man. His grandfather, the Rev. Walter Dunlop or 'Our Wattie', as his parishioners of thirty-five years had called him, had been a well-known minister in the Scottish border town of Dumfries.

Weary was proud of being descended from the Dunlops of that Ilk, claiming kinship with all those who legitimately bear the old Celtic name. He identified much more with his 'Scottishness' than with his English inheritance, yet, of the four grandparents, only James's father, Archibald, was born in Scotland.

Archibald was 21 when his father, 'overtaken by age and infirmity', reluctantly yielded up his pulpit. Walter died twelve months to the day later, on 4 November 1846. (Had the decision been left to him, undoubtedly he would have died in harness.) After lingering three more years, Archibald packed his goods and took ship for Australia.

Harriet Ann Stuart also arrived in 1850, as an assisted migrant on the *Maitland*, and went into service in the Port Phillip District. Archibald and Harriet met, Archibald proposed, and the two were wed on 18 September 1851 at Merri Creek. They set up house at South Morang on the Plenty River.

We don't know what Archibald did for a living in the early days, but he may have tried his hand digging for gold, for an Archibald Dunlop invented 'a dry mining shaft' in 1854. South Morang is not far from the Caledonia Diggings at St Andrews (near Smith's Gully, where Weary farmed), an area in which many Scots settled and mined for gold. Latterly, he worked as a carpenter, building simple wooden houses for selectors and often walking great distances in the course of his endeavours.

Harriet bore him nine children, and the Dunlop name figures prominently amongst the pioneers of Devenish, Stewarton and Benalla, where many of their descendants still live. But prosperity eluded Archibald, who owned a restless and independent spirit. When the desire to escape the bush settlements struck him, he thought nothing of walking to Melbourne and back; and it was on one of these long walks home from the city that he suffered a stroke, dying a week later in 1877, when James – the youngest – was three months short of his fifth birthday.

Luckily, the three older boys had all selected land and were working, although Harriet had to take in sewing to feed and clothe the six children still at home. When young James left school and needed a job in 1886, his elder brother, Walter, employed him in his creamery at Duck Ponds, Major Plains.

It was hard and heavy work for a fourteen-year-old, hauling cream and milk cans, keeping old boilers, steam engines and separators working. Industrious, quiet and steady, James didn't intend to spend the rest of his life in the creamery where, each night, after washing the machinery and mopping the floors, he made up his bed on the still damp bricks. His first investment was the purchase of five shares in the Goorambat Butter and Cheese Factory following the collapse of the land boom in the 1890s. Despite the Depression, he found work as a bread carter and labourer, acquiring skills at horse breaking and building, ploughing and sowing and animal husbandry. The passing of the black-clad widow-queen, and the birth of a bright new Commonwealth of Australia in 1901 rang in a new era for James, who by now could afford a team of horses, a wagon and a gig.

James and Alice were married in the spring of 1904 from Jacob and Edith Vincent's imposing house in Wangaratta when James was thirty-two and Alice two years younger. Their wedding photograph shows a tall, slender young woman with beautiful eyes and a cloud of dark hair standing beside her broad-browed husband, who has been seated by the photographer in the custom of those Edwardian days. After a honeymoon in Ballarat James took his bride back to the quiet farm at Major Plains. Life had gained new lustre and purpose.

James's limited education denied Alice the intellectual stimulus she would have liked, but otherwise they were well enough matched, enjoying the security of a warm and loving relationship which weathered the stresses of bad seasons and Alice's pregnancies.

The birth of their first child, Alan, in November 1905 was an ordeal. While James was away fetching a woman to attend Alice, the baby was born. When husband and midwife arrived, she had delivered her own son. She was much shaken by the experience, but recovered her health and resumed the routine of cleaning and cooking and caring for the small baby.

Around the end of 1906, she discovered she was pregnant once more.

TWO

Friday's Child

ERNEST EDWARD DUNLOP was born very early on the morning of
Friday 12 July 1907. During her second pregnancy, Alice had thought
often and anxiously about this child. The memory of the trauma
surrounding Alan's birth twenty-two months previously, and the
twenty-eight kilometres separating them from the nearest doctor, made
her determined that this time, matters would be better handled.

Some time before the baby was due, James harnessed up the horses
and buggy and they drove along the three-chain roads to the railway at
Benalla, then took the train to Wangaratta, where she was to spend
some quiet winter days at Edith's home before her labour pains began.
The best doctor in the district was to attend her. Alice would then
recover comfortably in the private hospital they had chosen, with
members of her family close by.

Alice's wish that Dr McArdel be present was granted, but thereafter
everything went sadly wrong. Disaster attended the birth in the person
of the midwife who ran the imposing brick structure that advertised
itself as a hospital. Her habit of going from bed to bed without washing
her hands or taking any hygienic precautions had the inevitable result:
Alice contracted puerperal fever, then a common infection of the lying-
in room which, until the discovery of sulphanilimide and antibiotics
later in the century, killed numbers of women.

After some days, she was brought back to the farm sick, confused,
heedless of everything around her and unable to care for her newborn
son. One of the maiden aunts came to Major Plains to nurse them both
and a kindly young neighbour took Alan into her home, where he was
to stay for the next seventeen months.

Alice's condition deteriorated severely three weeks after her return
from Wangaratta. She wandered in a no-man's-land, knowing neither
time, nor place, nor persons. In desperation, James accepted advice that
she should be cared for in Kew Asylum and he accompanied her to

Melbourne, where she was admitted on 16 September, nine and a half weeks after her confinement.

The casebooks of Kew and Beechworth asylums reveal puerperal psychosis as one of the common illnesses then affecting women patients. There was little treatment – only time, and sedatives to quieten her during bouts of acute restlessness. The photograph taken by the hospital at her admission shows the vulnerable face of a hopelessly depressed young woman from whom all emotion other than intense sadness and despair has been wiped. Although the doctors assured him that there was every chance of Alice recovering completely, James scarcely recognised his once-pretty, dark-haired wife in the distraught, emaciated figure with close-cropped hair whom he visited. He never expected to live with her at Major Plains again.

But by January she had improved a little and James requested that she be moved to Beechworth, closer to home, where he could visit her more frequently. It was another eleven months before she was reunited with her family.

Weary counted it his great good fortune that he had 'three mothers' – Alice, Violet and Lily – but it is 'Aunt Lil' that he singled out particularly as his foster mother; it was she who he believed had most to do with looking after him during Alice's illness, and the bond between the two was strong.

Lil cherished a more than usual love and tenderness for her younger nephew. She married late and had no children of her own to supplant Ernest in her affections; and although he boarded with his father's sister, Belle Simons, during his first year as a student at the University of Melbourne, it was Lil who was his fond benefactress during those impoverished years. (By then, Violet was nursing in isolated mission hospitals in Tanganyika.) She closely followed his activities in England and the Middle East, was as devastated as Alice when they learned of his imprisonment by the Japanese, and proudly wore a locket containing a portrait of her 'dear boy' which Alice gave her in 1943. She thought of him – and in private called him – her 'son'.

Because of their training, Violet at the Children's Hospital in Carlton and Lil at the Melbourne, the twins were the logical sisters to assume care of the baby. Probably, they took it in turns. It is difficult to work out exactly what occurred between September 1907 and the time of Alice's return. People in the district knew what was wrong, but adults dropped their voices when discussing mental illness, or did not mention it at all in front of children. Many years elapsed before the boys were told, such was the stigma of confinement in Kew, and even Weary was uncertain about all the details of his mother's illness until in 1990 he read the reports from the casebooks.

In spite of Violet's experience with children, not too much was known about infant nutrition in those days, and baby Ernest was raised on Robertson's Groats in the absence of mother's milk. He suffered from rickets as a result, but once he began taking solid food – his first spoken word was said to be a ringing demand for 'Meat!' – he grew quickly, and by the time Alice was ready to return to her family, he was running everywhere and eating heartily.

Almost a year after her transfer to Beechworth, the doctors pronounced Alice cured. At the beginning of December 1908, James collected her and took her home to an ecstatic welcome from the overjoyed Alan, who 'rushed upon her with an eager cry, never having forgotten her'.[1]

But it was to seventeen-month-old Ernest that Alice turned first, captivated by the plump, blue-eyed baby with his brown curls, and over the succeeding months, under the sober, watchful gaze of the elder boy, she appeared to lavish more attention on her younger son. Alan believed that Alice favoured Ernest and, in his later years, he spoke of this to their lifelong friend, Gert Hutchins. 'Underneath, I think, Alan felt that Ern was more of a favourite and [he] got a bit of a complex. When his mother came home, Weary was the one she went to and made all the fuss of. Alan felt it.'

The homecoming must have been doubly difficult for the three-year-old, separated from his mother for half his lifetime, unable to understand why she had disappeared so totally. Miraculously, she was back and he was safely reunited with the centre of his existence. But he no longer had her undivided attention; instead, she lavished it on an unknown rival whom he was told he must love as his brother. He brooded over this cuckoo in the nest named Ernest, feeling jealous and rejected. It was many decades before he came to terms with these feelings and transformed them into an immense pride in Weary's achievements.

As the summer of 1908 became 1909, Alice gradually took over the household. In his memoir of their childhood, *Little Sticks*, Alan conjured up a vivid picture of Major Plains, the aunts, and his mother 'at work in her detached galvanised iron kitchen upon which the hot summer sun had beaten mercilessly all day, and though the sun was low in the western sky as she bent over the wood-fuelled kitchen stove to prepare an evening meal for us, the whole interior was an inferno. The stove was at the far end of the primitive structure, where not the slightest puff of cool air could reach Mother, from whose face a stream of perspiration ran down. Two aunts fluttered about . . .'

Alan's description of the aunts as 'moths about to be engulfed in flame [with] Mother . . . the unassisted high priestess of the kitchen' places them firmly in supporting roles, and rather ineffectual ones at that. But Weary's recollections were of two extremely capable women – who saw it as their duty throughout their lives to 'look after Alice', the frailest of the sisters – and it is more than likely that Alice insisted on taking charge.[2]

All five sisters were strong and independent personalities, and their niece, Ruth Lack, remembers this as characteristic of 'Walpole women': Catherine Marie's heritage. Weary agreed.

Weary's 'earliest recollections were [of] my mother being an ordinary sort of housewife . . . she seemed able to work extremely hard in those days'. She needed to: cooking and cleaning and looking after two babies of eighteen months and three years in those conditions, even with a local girl coming in to do the heavier work, and occasional help from her sisters, would sap the energies of the strongest.

Alice's health broke down periodically, with what the family called 'bilious attacks', which persisted long after Ernie left school at 16. Reflecting on her behaviour almost three-quarters of a century later, Weary considered her to have been 'very highly geared', needing to push herself beyond the limits of her endurance. Occasions requiring vast amounts of extra effort, cooking and entertaining, harvest-time, the annual Royal Show at Benalla, ended with Alice retiring sallow and ill to her bed, sometimes for a week at a time. She would finish up prostrate, 'vomiting her heart out . . . after such intense mental and physical activity [she just] keeled over'.

Alice had an inner restlessness. Weary often quoted an old adage of his mother's: 'I must mix myself with action, lest I wither with despair', and this is precisely how Alice attempted to counter the frustrations of a life lacking the companionship of intellectual equals with whom she could share a world of books and ideas. But those periods of intense activity always exhausted her capacity to deal with the conflicting emotions which motivated her. Migraines and physical prostration followed inevitably.

None of this was obvious to baby Ernest, who was quickly renamed 'Ernie', the diminutive he answered to until high school and working days in Benalla shortened it further to 'Ern'.

The adventures of his first three years were circumscribed by the wire-netting fence which surrounded the little house set squarely in its home paddock. Twelve feet high, it efficiently penned in the two small boys and kept out the hens which scratched in the dust by the back gate, ever vigilant for an opportunity to dart through if an unwary visitor took a moment too long to enter the yard. Alice hated them near the house. This back gate was a pulley-operated contraption which fascinated first Alan, then Ernie, until they patiently worked out how it closed of its own accord.

Amusements were simple and toys few. The rhythm of life at Major Plains was marked by the changing seasons and their accompanying rituals of ploughing, sowing and harvest. In summer, the sun dazzled on the iron roof and trampled earth, while the rains of winter and spring turned the dusty tracks and yard to a quagmire of squelching mud which encrusted their boots and made the weekly wash a nightmare.

Harvest-time was signalled by the arrival of a team of men on bicycles and the great threshing machine, powered by the noisy, black malevolent force of a giant traction engine. The boys clung to the round wooden fence posts by the front gate and watched this feared and fascinating monster, which seemed to shake the very foundations of the earth as it slowly chugged along the road and up the farm track, steam belching from its tall chimney, the great rear wheels crushing shrubs and grasses in its path, the smaller front ones gleaming and swinging about as it was steered.

That was as close as the boys got to it, although it disturbed their dreams. Alice kept them well away from the workmen, so that they wouldn't hear any 'bad language'. (Later on, at Summerlea, they would be sent off on their ponies to slash thistles in another part of the farm for the same reason.)

Weary recalled little of the time at Major Plains and admired Alan's more detailed recollections, for he was too young to remember anything earlier than an incident which occurred when he was around two years old. There was no pump or well close to the house: water came from a bore sunk in the far corner of the home paddock and had to be hauled up to the cottage in cream cans on a horse-drawn sledge made from the Y-shaped bough of a tree. James was rushing up water to put out a small fire, the boys perched on the sledge alongside the cans, when Alan's horrified cry alerted James to the fact that Ernie's leg was twisted over the side and caught underneath one of the runners. He cried out neither then, nor later, when Alice staunched the bleeding and bathed and dressed the badly mangled foot. A quantity of sticking plaster and the passage of time saw it healed.

This stoic attitude probably began in response to her admonition, 'Be a brave boy and don't cry', which so many children have heard from their elders, but Ernie came to see it as a desirable trait to be adopted at all costs, so that he could be more like the characters in the popular children's books Alice deemed suitable reading.

By the age of nine or ten, he was much taken with a storybook hero, a young Red Indian brave called Deerfoot of the Forest, who inspired him to invent ever sterner trials for Alan and himself in order to test their endurance. During one of their 'Indian' games, Alan applied a red-hot poker to Ernie's bare foot – his resentment of his younger brother often assumed aggressive forms – but he was not always a keen participant in the schemes which were dreamed up. He hovered on the periphery of Ernie's private, make-believe world, an occasional but not essential companion. From very early on, Ernie initiated, Alan followed, in these adventures.

They would take off their boots and, slinging them from one hand by the knotted laces, walk barefoot across the surface of a paddock baked hard and hot as an oven under the more-than-century heat of a midsummer's afternoon. Ernie was determined to do it without flinching and strode boldly across, Deerfoot to the backbone, whilst Alan hopped nervously from one clump of flatweed to another. When the clods of recently harrowed ground were white with frost early on a winter's morning and the air crackled with cold, the endurance test would be repeated until, after almost a kilometre, the younger brother would announce that they could put stockings and boots back on their numb and blue-blotched feet.

On moonless nights, when the booming of the bittern had him shivering under the blankets, imagining unspeakable horrors down by the Sheepwash Creek where the rumoured Bunyip lurked, he would steel himself to creep out of bed – 'I was scared as hell, but Deerfoot *couldn't* be scared' – and walk stealthily towards the eerie cries, turning in his feet in imagined Indian-style so that they would make no sound or mark in the grass.

What began as a game, just one aspect of a highly imaginative and intelligent child's fantasy world, had become a rule of life by adolescence and second nature by adulthood. Blessed with a high threshold of pain anyway, he trained himself not to flinch or show fatigue, and by the time he was in the prison camps, he was mostly indifferent to intense cold or heat, and could distance himself from pain, clinically observing both himself and its inflictors. To the last, he made no concessions to pain, and it was a rare occasion when he consented to take analgesics of any description. His almost pathological fear of being hospitalised caused him publicly to deny injuries. In March 1987, he consented to having only his right wrist x-rayed because his doctor would have put him straight into hospital if he had realised, as Weary did, that a bone in his left hand was also broken. 'People die in hospitals,' he said laconically, after that accident.

Only a few of those closest to him knew the agonising pain he suffered after that fall down the stairs in his home. And on the one occasion that he quietly asked for pain-killers, none could be found in the house at Smith's Gully.

Weary attributed his remarkable ability to recuperate quickly from all kinds of ills to good genes and an iron constitution developed in those far-off farm days. Alice had a fear of tuberculosis (one of her sisters-in-law and a niece both died of it) and for much of the time at Stewarton, the whole family slept out-of-doors in all weathers. James put up a two-roomed tent over a smooth cement floor. The canvas sides could be rolled up in summer, making cooler bedrooms than the close and stuffy house with its corrugated iron roof; in winter it was cosy and windproof, even when freezing rains drummed on the canvas and a furious southerly whipped the nearby box trees into a frenzy.

This bred-in-the-bone toughness stood by him during the war years in Thailand, particularly during the terrible wet season of 1943 when he was lucky if he could snatch an hour or two's rest at night after the last of the men crawled in from the line.

In the spring of 1910, a little procession turned out of the farm gate at Major Plains and moved off slowly towards Stewarton. The great farm wagon, piled high with beds, bedding and other household goods and drawn by some of the farm horses, led the way. James walked at the head, a riding hack was hitched to the tailboard, and bringing up the rear was the gig, driven by Alice and containing Ernie and Alan, wriggling with suppressed excitement. Between the two vehicles plodded the rest of the Clydesdales, the two dogs ran backwards and forwards, and under a clear blue sky, willie wagtails darted out from the grass verges, hawking for insects in the warm sunshine.

It had been obvious the previous day that something extraordinary was afoot, as the little boys watched their mother emptying drawers and cupboards. Knowing better than to pester their parents with questions, they remained in a state of wondering anticipation until the journey, when James and Alice told them that they were moving to a farm six and a half kilometres distant.

About an hour later they crossed the culvert over the Sheepwash Creek and turned in through a cyclone gate onto a 'short, hard-surfaced track' overhung by spreading yellow box trees, 'the falling blossom of which perfumed the air and showered the driveway like confetti at a wedding'. The name on the gate was Summerlea. On a slight rise ahead of them was a cottage, its striped cream and brown iron roof curving elegantly down to form a shady verandah, the whole enclosed behind a low paling fence.

Alice lost no time going indoors, and James led the boys round to the shady south side of the house, where he sat down with them on the edge of the verandah. A second track wound towards the road and they saw beyond that a line of huge red gums marking the course of the Broken River.

James was now the owner of 235 hectares of prime farmland, his reward for industry, skilled management and some good seasons. Overnight, the horizons of their world had expanded mightily.

Weary looked back across more than eighty years to this move as the beginning of the golden age of his youth, when 'life at its fastest moved at the pace of horse or bicycle' and 'the spirit of Australia Felix shone in the eyes of country people'. This romantic view, frequently articulated by him in speeches or articles dealing with his background, is selective but nonetheless true. And he never abandoned the firm Victorian values that regulated the lives of those pioneers amongst whom he grew up.

'Like most Australians of my time, I was reared in a world in which the map was quite substantially coloured with imperial red denoting the British Empire, and our proud attitude could be summed up by "*Civis Britannicus sum*",' he declared in the Newman Address delivered at Monash University in 1987. This attitude was firmly reinforced by his parents and the educational system, which extolled those very virtues that had enabled James to acquire his farm and told the young readers of the *Commonwealth School Paper* that deep down in their hearts they loved England and their king, and their system of government, and held that there was 'no better system on all the earth'.

Very much a product of the nineteenth century, he inherited Wattie Dunlop's Scots Presbyterian values and the empire-building energies of his Walpole greatgrandfather, whose experience in British India imparted a tough edge to the English gentility of those other Walpoles who retreated to their country vicarages.

Since the 1960s, Australians have cast aside the imperial blinkers that distorted their view of nationhood, and in the process focussed almost obsessively on the strengths of their colonial past. Descriptions of heat, hardships and heartbreak come dangerously close to sounding clichéed when thrown into almost any contemporary examination of rural life. But when Weary spoke of the 'fierce heat of summer', and the 'rough roads and tracks' and 'arid brown landscapes in which a smudge of dust in the distance [is] slowly transformed into sweating horses with a cloud of attendant flies . . . [surrounding] the gig, cart or buggy', he was speaking from actual experience about a time when 'Life was full of heartbreaking work and . . . menaced by floods, droughts and pests'.[3]

His uncle, Archibald Dunlop, whose farm was only a few kilometres from Summerlea, drowned in front of his aunt's eyes in the 1916 floods, when he and his horse were swept into a 'wash-away' and carried downstream for some distance before a neighbour risked his life to pull the dead body from the water.

That September nine-year-old Ernie had watched the rising flood-waters as anxiously as everyone else. Sheepwash Creek was an anabranch of the Broken River, and whenever it rose, the waters swirled in a maelstrom across the low-lying land between their house and the road, marooning the family on the rise and endangering the lives of their stock, as well as that of James, who could not swim. Nonetheless, he always managed to move the sheep to higher ground and reach home with minutes to spare before the waters spread out with frightening speed across the southern reaches of their property.

The experience of years in the district meant that James always had his sheep safely on the northern part of their land when melting snows and heavy rain in the Victorian Alps poured a colossal volume of water into the headwaters of the Broken River some ninety-five kilometres away and floods threatened each spring.

The sour smell of the retreating waters in flood years reminded both boys of death and loss, and they no longer played so carelessly on its fringes.

The drought of 1913–14 which preceded those worst floods since 1870 had threatened the health of both stock and farming community – 'I recall . . . seeing my father sharing a meagre ration of potatoes to keep alive starving beasts'. The great rabbit plagues, which ate the paddocks bare, were dealt with by James, Ernie and Alan at Summerlea by laying bait of poisoned apples in a long, shallow, ploughed furrow. The unpleasant task of throwing the stiff carcasses into the farm dray fell to the boys. Mouse plagues they fought 'with poison, sunken kerosene tins of water and ordinary traps'. And Joker, their dog, did his bit. 'We just managed to keep them out of the house.' They were lucky. But the smell in the sheds was frightful, and the floors a heaving mass of grey bodies.

James and Alice kept to the middle of the road in their politics. They took the *Argus* and the two local newspapers: it would not have occurred to them to subscribe to the *Lone Hand* and the *Bulletin*. James was a bushman through and through, but his Bible was the one his Covenanting ancestors had lived by, and a well-read copy of Edmund Burke's political speeches stood on the bookshelves. There were no heated debates about Labour *versus* Capital round their dinner table.

Alice was better read than James, but in spite of James's limited education, Weary recalled that 'he wrote in a beautiful copperplate hand, mapped and drew well, and was quick with mental calculations . . . As a boss he worked harder than his employees, and had no labour problems'.

Unionism was not part of his creed; Ernie's parents were behind the Liberals and later the Country Party. They gave no support to the Labor Party, which represented a challenge to the existing social order. They were surrounded by tangible evidence of their very recent reward for years of thrift and hard labour, confirming a universal belief that Australia was a country where a man could start out with nothing but his two hands and his wits, and end up owning his house and a sufficiency of land to pass on to his sons.

James was a gentle, shy, undemonstrative men, well-liked by his fellows, and the Rev R. S. McConachy extolled these virtues in his address at the memorial service for him in 1948.[4]

Alice had style: everyone in the district recognised that. 'My mother was a very gracious sort of person . . . Deportment was important in those days and she moved with a rather ladylike gait . . . if she sat down [it was] with a straight back.' But they loved her most for what Gert Hutchins, who grew up on the farm next door, has remembered down the years as 'her receptive warmth . . . something I've never experienced from anybody else, although I think it rubbed off on Weary . . . '

Lilian and Ben Steen were neighbours, their farm on the Broken River an easy distance from Summerlea. Gert's aunt often used to put the little girl up behind her on her horse and ride over to visit Alice. Gert wasn't sure whom she admired more then: Alice or young Ernie. 'I always used to tell my mother, I'm not going to milk cows. I'm going to grow up and be a lady like Mrs Dunlop.'

Alice also stood out from other women in the community because of accomplishments none of her good-hearted neighbours had had the opportunity to acquire. 'My mother painted quite well, she sang pleasantly, she wrote enthusiastic letters to the paper . . . and she was able to assume some leadership in local affairs.'

Although 'in those days . . . there was never a period when there wasn't help in the house, a Flo or an Emily', and there was always someone to share the farm work with James, there were no luxuries and holidays for the boys were a few days spent with relations. James was out in the grey light of dawn and Alice and the boys turned out shortly after.

There were no more children. 'I understand from my father that [Alice's illness] was the finish of their sex life. In those days, with no sort of contraceptive devices, it was difficult to avoid pregnancy.' James loved Alice deeply and had no wish to endanger her health or the happiness of the family. 'The doctors warned them off the course, I think.'

Ernie and Alan were stood in front of a photographer and told to 'watch the birdie' shortly after moving to Summerlea. Ernie is half a head shorter than Alan, but already shows that he will outgrow him: his head and hands are larger and the features not so finely drawn. The angelic, blue-eyed child with soft brown ringlets, who more than once caused Alice to reflect fondly that he would have made a very pretty girl, leans nonchalantly on a photographer's balustrade beside his more slender brother, both boys immaculate in their starched white, frilled dresses and looking as if butter wouldn't melt in their mouths.

When first they moved to Summerlea, Ernie and Alan were given the simplest tasks, such as gathering the 'morning wood' – the twigs and small sticks that lay on the ground under the yellow box trees in the home paddock – used to start the kitchen fire under the porridge pot and the heavy black kettle. Each morning, one of them stirred the porridge pot so that the oatmeal didn't stick or burn; and after breakfast those hens and their rooster who were not allowed to range freely were fed. Before the sun went down, the boys were sent out to gather the eggs from various favoured spots around the machinery and shearing sheds.

They were five and a half kilometres from the nearest school, so there was no question of a formal education for either boy until he could ride well and handle the long day. Alice put her skills as governess to work and gave them their first lessons. Ernie insisted on joining in when Alan began to sit down at the long kitchen table with their mother – 'I remember a certain amount of arithmetic and spelling, c-a-t, cat' – and after the exceptionally good season of 1911, there were music lessons at the big Faber piano which arrived one red letter day and had to be taken in through the window when it was discovered that there was not enough space to manoeuvre it through both front and sitting-room doors.

Alice played well, both parents sang, and the boys loved listening to them, but as far as Ernie's practical progress was concerned, 'I was very resistant – Alan may have learned to play a bit, but he didn't persist.' Years later, Weary wrote: 'We should all be exposed to some music training – an instrument, a choir or [some] musical discipline . . . ', regretting a dimension he could never hope to experience. He could rarely resist humming and tapping and beating time to music which had a pronounced melody or beat and he had a strong and tuneful baritone voice, but he had no understanding of classical music. He prefered opera and ballet with their visual distractions to orchestral or chamber music. His one appearance on the stage was in the minor singing part of the Lord High Chancellor when Benalla High School put on a musical, *The Court Jester*.[5]

Lil Steen was the opposite of Alice. A tall, big-boned, strong countrywoman who could expertly butcher a sheep or skin and joint a rabbit, she was renowned as a crack shot and a strong swimmer who had swum the Broken River in full flood. When Alan began school at the beginning of 1913, Ernie lost his companion during the week and increasingly sought her out.

Lil Steen taught Ernie to ride. Weary believed that James asked her to, partly because he had no time and possibly because Alice and he thought it would help her adjust to the loss of her two older children from diptheria within a few days of each other. She taught him to swim, too, and later to shoot and fish and relish a wide range of country pursuits. At the age of five, 'I had a passion for her – I was totally in love with her at that stage [and] in terror lest I should be seized by some fever in which I should rave, and give it all away!'

'I think she was madly in love with him, too,' says Lil Steen's daughter, Gert Hutchins, who was born when Ernie was five and a half. 'He was so much like her . . . he may have taken the place of the son she lost . . . she had something special for him.'

As he grew older, she took him fishing and rabbiting – she made her own nets, and they used to set out with her two ferrets – and then taught him to shoot, and they would go off after possums.

Ernie and Alan narrowly escaped drowning in the Sheepwash Creek in 1914, when Alan slipped from a mossy log and Ernie fell in trying to rescue him. Lil took Ernie into the water and showed him how to swim. Alan watched from the bank, then the two boys practised their strokes and their kicking in the creek all that summer. By autumn, both could swim.

There was a dare-devil streak in her, a delight in taking up a challenge, that sparked off a response in young Ernie. Lil would set her horse at any log or fence in her path – and so did Ernie. Alan joined in sometimes, but it was Ernie with whom she identified, and for whom she predicted a bright future.

On 12 July 1914, Ernie turned seven and was enrolled at Stewarton School No. 2094. The little weatherboard building was stoutly built of oregon, its small-paned windows looking onto the pepper trees which surround so many Australian country schools and giving their teacher, Coleman Fury (or 'Dillon', as everyone called him), a clear view of the fenced-off section of the paddock where the pupils' ponies grazed until home-time.

Memories of that first day were vividly imprinted on Weary's mind almost eighty years later. 'I rode my horse into the saddling paddock and had a long and satisfying pee against a tree – and had my bottom spanked!'

He was not a docile pupil, and 'it was corporal punishment if you put a foot wrong'. Ernie Dunlop often felt the force of Fury's hand and broad leather strap, for he was pugnacious and quick to respond to schoolyard provocation. 'In those days there were schisms between certain elements in the community: the Irish were a bit apart, and straightforward Brits and Scots like myself were apt to [be] involved in fights fairly regularly . . . which usually terminated in someone getting a blood nose or a black eye.'

The angelic three-year-old with the luxuriant brown curls had toughened up in the four years since he posed for the camera in his starched dress and buttoned boots. He quickly earned a reputation as a fearless fighter who preferred taking on boys older and bigger than himself.

Ernie now rode Toby, the old pony, and Alan had graduated to his new horse, Star. Ernie knew all Toby's tricks, and the Shetland's lazy ways were promptly dealt with by his energetic new master, who kept up with the others in the school party by constantly flailing his legs and heels against Toby's ribs. They nicknamed him 'Ornie Windmill'.

His first weeks at school were overshadowed by the growing menace of war and the newspapers they collected with the mail on their way home from school in Stewarton were scanned by James and Alice with increasing anxiety. Alice's forty-second birthday on that fateful 5 August was a sombre occasion. By the time the boys rode in the gate that afternoon, the word that Great Britain was at war with Germany had flashed like a crown fire through the district.

'How passionately British we were!' Weary wrote many years later. 'The day has gone by since the British Command could call upon soldiers to sacrifice themselves in such hopeless gallantry.'

But in 1914, few had qualms about their duty to King and Country. Every day of their lives, Ernie and Alan saw the colour print of a battle scene from the Boer War which hung on the wall above the wood-burning stove in the kitchen. The grim, khaki-clad soldiers, the terrified horses rearing amongst the figures of the living and the bodies of the dead, the brilliance of star shells exploding in the sky amongst the rolling smoke from the guns – all made such a profound impression that neither boy felt the need to discuss its awful implications.

Storybooks exalting the heroism of soldiers and the glory of defending the Empire; family tales about their great-grandfather's days in India; the picture on the wall: they saw war as a forum for illustrious deeds, adventure and high honour. 'It was in the very air in my boyhood . . . we kids pined impotently [at] the lack of opportunity to go and die in "some corner of a foreign field".'

All the able-bodied members of the family who could be spared volunteered: four Dunlop men – cousins Alex, Archie, Hugh and Percy – and four of Alice's relations, unmarried Uncle Ernest and cousin John Ambrose and the nursing twins, Violet and Lil. Cousin Victor was rejected and submerged his disappointment in farm work for James.

Ernie sighed for the chance to do something. His heart 'stirred to the romantic chivalry of the Anzacs . . . who poured from the bush and farms', as Alice read aloud the letters and postcards from Violet and Lil, who had sailed off to play their part in history. But all that was possible was enrolment in the Young Gardeners' League and leech collecting in the Sheepwash Creek.

The boys coaxed a few vegetables out of their garden before the summer heat shrivelled the last of the carrots and lettuces and handed the shillings James and Alice paid them over to the League; and they collected leeches for the war effort by dangling their bare legs in the creek and flicking the leeches into a jar before they fastened on too firmly.

The early progress of the war was followed on a large map James pinned up on the wall. Each evening, after they had finshed their homework at the kitchen table, Ernie and Alan moved the tiny flags marking fronts and battles according to that day's newspaper. Postcards and letters arrived from Egypt, from Salonika, where Aunt Lil had gone, and from France, where Uncle Ernest and John Ambrose were infantrymen and Aunt Violet was nursing the wounded. German rifle bullets were exclaimed over and treasured. Postcards showed cathedrals behind protective sandbags and French villages near where their aunt was.

But the war dragged on in the nightmare of the trenches, and James needed the boys to help Victor and him with the farm work. The map was abandoned.

They did heavy work for young boys before they left for school each morning. 'Very early I developed into the character who rounded up the horses.' Riding bareback and accompanied by a couple of dogs, 'it was quite a ceremonial [sic] getting up all those Clydesdales and half-draughts and carriage-horses . . . ' Then, leather schoolbags containing their homework and lunch of jam or mutton sandwiches bumping on their backs, they rode off to school.

Ernie hurled himself enthusiastically into school life. He already showed greater stamina than Alan, who was a conscientious student, hard-working, but a worrier. By mid-morning, the latter was often feeling rather dreamy, 'but young brother seemed to be always alert, taking in everything eagerly and readily as though not given to day dreams'. Their early grounding in the three Rs had been thorough and, although it was his first teacher's 'impetuous Irish temper' which Weary recalled best, 'I must have redeemed myself in some way, because I had prize books given to me by Dillon Fury.'

He also passed through at least two grades in that first year – more a tribute to Alice's teaching, perhaps, then to diligent study under the red-haired Mr Fury's eye, for Weary believed that he was 'a reluctant and rather perverse pupil'.

Ruby K. Wilson succeeded Fury for a short spell, then 'the ace in the pack . . . a very superior lady named Vera Alice Cecilia Hilliear' arrived in Stewarton: 'magnificent in deportment and composure [she took] control of the school'.

Every Monday morning during term time, until Ernie completed his primary education in December 1920, Vera Hilliear arrived on the pillion of her boyfriend's motorbike. During the week, she boarded with a local family and rode her bicycle to school. In wet weather it was Ernie's duty to unbutton her boots ('she wore something like spats') which were frequently sodden after wading along the flooded roads, wheeling her bicycle. He may have been a terror in the schoolyard, but he was painfully shy with adults, and Alan describes this task as 'one of the funniest . . . sights imaginable . . . the devoted young slave kneel-ing [and] timidly undoing one button after another, pausing occasion-ally to gaze up out of innocent blue eyes as though serving a goddess'. Alan didn't laugh out loud, however, as Ernie was swift to defend his dignity against any slights.

Vera Hilliear recited Tennyson, Coleridge and Fitzgerald's *Rubaiyat of Omar Khayyam* in her expressive voice and encouraged her pupils to memorise much poetry.

Seventy years later, Weary could quote stanzas of 'In Memoriam' and 'Omar Khayyam' faultlessly, and his love for poetry stayed with him throughout his life. He preferred Keats to Shelley, but knew them both; he found pleasure and beauty in the Victorian romantics; he read and memorised Masefield. But he discovered a passion for A. E. Housman in prison camp, where he discussed the poetry endlessly with his Canadian physiologist friend, Jacob Marcowitz.

He often quoted from *A Shropshire Lad*, particularly 'When I was one-and-twenty . . . ' and the richly descriptive 'Reveille'. Housman's scepticism, even perhaps the blasphemy permeating the cutting irony of his work, struck a common chord in Weary. He recited the love sonnets of Shakespeare and Michelangelo just as readily, slipped odd lines into his letters, and ruefully shook his head at his own efforts, none of which measured up to his ambitions. He worked carefully over one effort for some years, finally attaching it to the introduction he wrote for the memoirs of his great friend Rowan Nicks.

Vera Cecilia Hilliear's imaginative teaching brought fresh meaning and enjoyment to history, geography and nature study; she drilled them well in arithmetic, grammar and spelling. To the accompaniment of a small organ, she joined her fine voice with theirs and the little schoolhouse rang to the sounds of the 'Marseillaise' (in English), the Russian national anthem ("God the All-terrible') and other stirring songs of a martial nature in keeping with the times. 'Scots Wha' Hae' was a favourite.

But Ernie showed no more than an average interest in his school-work – 'I just did what was necessary' – and over the years he became only too familiar with Vera Hilliear's 'rather lethal ruler that smacked your hand if you misbehaved'.

He preferred to practise circus tricks on his pony, Jock, who had replaced Toby; to gallop like the wind across the countryside, clearing fences, logs and ditches; to go hunting with Joker, the dog. To his family and friends, he appeared to have a head for heights, but his apparently cool determination to conquer the tallest or most difficult trees was actually motivated by a height-giddiness reaction – which was why he fell out of them so often – and an intense desire to overcome it.

Sometimes, his activities had Alan holding his breath, sweaty-palmed, as the younger boy slithered 'out, like some kind of tree snake . . . till he reached the outer limits of a limb with the end branches bobbing up and down as though caught in a whirlwind'.[6]

Once, he had a tremendous fall from the pepper tree next to the house, landing on a piece of timber which smashed his head and blackened an eye. Alice doctored the injuries and he rode off to school next day, uncomplaining but with an almighty headache.

The family thought that Zubah, their buggy horse of uncertain temper who more than once caused a serious accident (bolting, or once rolling on Ernie in the water so that he narrowly escaped drowning), had thrown him. Ernie said nothing to disabuse them of this notion. It was years before he told Alan that later, as a medical student, he learned that he had fractured his skull. The dint could still be felt, more than seventy years later.

He had a compulsion to test himself against every possible situation. He never lost it. He would never give in. Why else, at 82, would he insist that stitches be put in his face, on the spot (without an anaesthetic), and his broken nose pushed back into place after dazzling spotlights caused him to miss his footing on a catwalk and fall onto a steel truss supporting the platform? He refused to miss the dinner in honour of the visiting British Lions and their ANZAC rugby opponents in Brisbane that night in 1989, and he was quietly proud that he was able to take his seat, unbowed and no longer quite so bloody, in time for the main course. Once again, he had an almighty headache for days.

Ten days later, Babara Todd, a hospital sister who was working as his housekeeper at the time, removed the stitches in his kitchen.

The football jersey which was presented to him then became a much-loved piece of clothing, worn in private whenever he donned his 'ratting togs' at weekends or when he was cold. He was wearing that jersey on the night of his death, and the ambulance men who attempted to resuscitate him on the way to hospital had to cut the left sleeve from wrist to shoulder.

Most people who knew Weary well can tell stories like the Brisbane one; anyone present at a gathering of those men who were closest to him during the war can find the occasion turning into a 'Do you remember when . . . ' session, if it is realised that the outsider wants to hear their choicest Weary stories. It is interesting that the majority of these anecdotes show Weary in relation to the teller – they are about an incident or memory shared with Weary by the person telling the tale, not often about the group, for each believes that something special happened between him – or her – and Weary.

Weary would sit there, smiling, occasionally chipping in. He never thought of himself as a hero; yet for the survivors of Dunlop Force, hero is too small a word for him. In their darkest hours, he put his life on the line for them. They would die for him. And they say so. He is the Ulysses who brought some of his men home to their quiet hearth, unlike the subject of Homer's epic poem which they read and discussed so passionately in the prison camp in Java in 1942 and which he quoted for the remainder of his days.

Ernie Dunlop's obsession was reading. 'I used to read night and day when I wasn't doing anything else.' The bookshelves at Summerlea were better stocked than those in most houses in the district and he graduated from the moralistic nursery stories which his mother selected, through *Tales of Scottish Knights* and his early hero, Deerfoot, to

Fennimore Cooper, Kingsley, Dickens, J. M. Ballantyne and Sir Walter Scott. Stodgier fare, such as the political speeches of Edmund Burke so admired by his father, and 'improving' popular religious works, was useful to conceal romances by Marie Corelli and Ernie's particular favourite, Ethel M. Dell.

For a time, he spent precious pocket money on *The Gem* and *The Magnet*, comic papers which showed life through a range of stereotypes. He reminisced in 1993 how 'Augustus . . . would never [fail to] use a paperknife to open a letter and would regard with horror anyone who used a thumb'. (Weary obviously absorbed these lessons: he always used a letter opener when opening his post.)

There was no library in the district, but the school's collection of around a hundred volumes offered adventure stories, tales of explorers and heroes and the sixpenny 'Rewards' beloved by church and school as prizes. The plums in this literary pudding were the historical romances of A. Conan Doyle, Bulwer Lytton and H. Rider Haggard and he saturated himself in *The White Company*, *King Solomon's Mines* and *Ayesha or the Return of She*. Ernie roamed far and wide in the golden realms of imagination, but confided these riches to no one.

Labour was scarce during the war and Ernie and Alan began to undertake tasks usually performed by full-grown men. Working in tandem, they could load the wagon with bags of wheat weighing two hundred and ten pounds each, after taking their turn at bag-sewing while James guided the harvester up and down the paddocks from morning till dusk. Harvest-time coincided with the summer holidays, and the long hours in the hot sun toughened their bodies and developed their strength.

By the time the farm was sold and they moved to Benalla in 1923, the Dunlop boys were renowned for miles around for tossing a sheaf or hefting a bag of wheat with the best of them. Weary is still proud of his ability at the age of 15 to lift a two hundred and ten pound bag of wheat in each hand. (He was only outdone by someone, he recalled, who could simultaneously lift a third bag with his teeth!) By the time he was at Ormond College and playing rugby football for Australia, he could carry the entire scrum on his back.

At one level, he revelled in the rough and tumble life on the farm: the wild riding, shooting, fishing and dare-devil antics, the long hours and hard physical labour in all weathers. Yet his early affinity with Alice meant that he also saw through his mother's eyes much that was harsh and crude in their existence, and he hungered after the wider world 'out there' which existed in the books he read, in his mother's stories and in his private dreams of the future. Only Aunt Lil, Alice – and, perhaps, Vera Hilliear – glimpsed this secret side of his character and the sharp intelligence which informed it.

The news that the war was over reached Stewarton late at night on 11 November 1918. Next morning, when they arrived at school, the pupils were given a half-day holiday. Leaving Alan to make his own way home at lunchtime, Ernie galloped Jock off to Dookie to join in the celebrations there, his pony flying before the hot north wind which he remembered scorching the spring grass and whirling the dust and leaves in his hair and eyes.

Of the thirty Stewarton men who had enlisted, one of the Davis boys whom Alice had taught would not come home, and another had lost a leg. One cousin had died of meningitis before he had a chance to fire a shot, but the other Dunlop cousins would return; the aunts would come back to take turns at minding arthritic Catherine Marie and give Aunt Cath a rest; and Uncle Ernest Payne and John Ambrose would farm at Sunnyside once more.

There had been a succession of good seasons since the drought broke in 1914, and throughout the war James gathered in record crops of wheat and oats. Their flock of Border Leicesters had done well, and dairying and fat cattle were profitable. But there was not a living in it for both boys. James's health was beginning to fail, and when the time came to plan the future, it was decided that the more studious Alan should go on to Benalla High School, and Ernie should be the farmer once he had passed his merit certificate. A primary school education had been sufficient for James; it would be adequate for Ernie.

Alice recalled her recurrent day dream during her second pregnancy when she hoped that, if this child were a boy, he might one day study medicine, and trusted that they had made the right decision.

Vera Alice Cecilia Hilliear had other ideas.

She saw how effortlessly big, shy Ernie learned his lessons. No one had suggested to him that there could be more to life than hard work on the land he was already helping to farm, and it had not occurred to him to reject his parents' announcement about his future. 'I was determined to fit myself to cope with it by an Indian stoicism.'

One evening Vera Hilliear rode her bicycle over to Summerlea and was conducted into the cool front sitting-room. The door shut firmly behind James, Alice and their determined caller. Alan hovered in the hall, straining his ears to catch the voices. Something momentous seemed to be in the air. He overheard her pleading with Alice. 'You are going to send Alan, so why not send Ernie, too?'

That visit by the discerning young teacher decided the future: both boys would go to Benalla High School.

In 1920 Ernie gained his Merit Certificate, one year earlier than most, and discarded his religion. He was 13. 'I decided this heaven and hell approach to life seemed a bit illogical. Saints, sinners, cardinals, popes – who really knew about these things? I'd better make up my own mind.' He had been working up to it for some time, but he kept quiet about this change of heart as there seemed no point in causing unnecessary trouble.

James and Alice had built their household on the firm foundation of their religion. There being no Presbyterian church within easy distance of Summerlea, they turned instead to the Methodists, whose little chapels were scattered throughout the district.

Alice had been brought up in the Church of England, but she happily adjusted her beliefs to accommodate James's stricter, non-conformist views. 'Her faith was firm as a rock . . . to her, awareness of the spiritual was essential to the welfare of people and nations. She conveyed these ideas to us with missionary fervour'.[7]

Over the years, Alice's influence has been more potent than all the stern homilies of Brother Perkins, the Methodist Home Missionary from Devenish who was a regular visitor to Summerlea, and his band of lay preachers. She was more tolerant than most, eschewing the 'narrow suspicious church relationships of my boyhood' that Weary described to his wartime padre friend and Redemptorist priest, Gerard Bourke.[8] 'The hours I spend with you, dear heart, are like a string of pearls,' sang Alice to a shocked Brother Perkins and the Quarterly Tea Meeting, then firmly rebuffed Brother Perkins's criticism of 'The Rosary' as unsuitable with the short reply that 'all music was good'.

It was inevitable that the religious differences in the community would be part of the boys' lives, and Ernie was not above schoolboy tricks like putting silver nitrate in the holy water in a Roman Catholic church, or squaring up to schoolmates from the other side of the religious tracks over some argument that required him to defend his Scots' honour against the taunts of the Irish and their conviction that all Protestants would burn in hell.

James saw no virtue in these activities: he gave Ernie a hiding just the same, no distinction being made between carving initials and caricatures on the pew in church, or bloodying the noses of the Heaney boys. Gentle his nature may have been, but transgressions were promptly and conventionally punished.

The proximity of the wooden church at Duck Ponds ensured that some part of every Sunday was spent in rapt attention before whichever preacher was bringing that week's Word to the tiny congregation. Sin hovered over the assembled brethren like a tightly stoppered genie, and only unrelenting vigilance would protect them from temptation and backsliding and popping the cork. Alcohol was an abomination before the Lord.

James and Alice were teetotallers; although Presbyterians have always enjoyed their whisky. Weary believed that grandfather Archibald had had too great a fondness for the bottle and even if James had been too young to see much of its effects, his mother probably encouraged him to turn away from drinking for life. He was a temperate man by nature. Weary remembered his father giving up his one pipe of tobacco a day as a contribution to the war effort.

This was fundamentalist Christianity of a kind which threatened hellfire and brimstone and very uncomfortable punishment at the seat of divine judgement.

Yet not even the fieriest efforts of these well-meaning prophets intimidated Ernie and the 'admirable but very rigid faith of my near-Calvinist parents' satisfied him neither spiritually nor intellectually.

After church, while the grown-ups gossiped round the door, the boys retreated to a safe distance on the banks of the billabong which gave the area its name, and Ernie would mimic whichever portion of the morning homily appealed most to his sense of the ridiculous. Thus, said Alan, 'purging our minds and souls of fears, making the whole thing a joke ending with hearty laughter'.[9]

The Scots observance of Sunday was restrictive. James had modified slightly the Dumfries traditions handed down by Archibald, so that they drove the few miles to Duck Ponds, but only essential tasks were carried out on the farm and if Ernie and Alan felt like livening up the day with some rabbiting or fishing, they had to slip away secretly. James encouraged an early knowledge of the Bible by awarding a penny for each verse accurately memorised and recited, and only 'improving' books were regarded as suitable Sunday reading. Ernie easily got round this, as he did most things which didn't suit him. Alan was more bothered by his conscience and timidly inclined to knuckle under.

But despite Ernie's developing scepticism, he did not rebel openly until they were living in Benalla and James and Alice were teaching Sunday School. 'I did go to church, but I drew the line at going to Sunday School . . . I think it hurt my parents very much when I preferred to . . . play golf . . . or swim.' The church he chose to attend in Benalla was not the Methodist one of his parents: he and Alan became Presbyterians. Nonetheless, those early lessons were well learned, and the same values that shaped their parents' lives 'remained with us . . . inspiring us to seek to be of service to our day and age', wrote Alan sixty-five years later.[10]

It would take twenty-three years and another world war before Ernest Edward Dunlop would arrive at the Articles of his faith amidst the Golgotha of the camps on the Burma–Siam Railway.

THREE

The Philosopher's Stone

IN FEBRUARY 1921, Ernie entered the gates of Benalla High School and was duly enrolled in D form, the middle rung of the ladder which would take him to B form and his Leaving Certificate.

The single-storeyed, red-brick building in Barkly Street was a testament to the determination of the district that those young people whose parents could not afford to send them away to private schools should enjoy a sound, if rather limited, education beyond Merit Certificate standard. During Alan's first year, in November 1920, the school had been upgraded to 'Class A' status, and it could now accredit the Leaving Certificate to those students who were judged to be of pass standard, qualifying them to matriculate at university.

During the week, both boys boarded in Benalla with one of James's sisters, Ann Guppy, peddling the twenty-two kilometres from Stewarton to Barkly Street every Monday morning, and returning to the farm on Friday afternoons.

After Ben and Lil Steen moved to Mokoan Park, a new farm closer to Benalla, Ernie and Alan escorted little Gert home from her primary school each Friday. 'I've never understood how they had the patience . . . I had a 26-inch wheeler and they had the big twenty-eights . . . they'd peddle along very slowly and I'd stop every now and again . . . horses used to throw their shoes, and I'd have handlebars full of shoes by the time I got to the gate.'[1]

But they were good-hearted country boys, and Gert was their honorary 'little sister' with whom they had played since she was a baby. When Ernie outgrew Toby the Shetland, he lent him to Gert for a year and taught her to ride, when she was four years old and he was nine and a half. He repeated the lessons the way Lil had taught him and rewarded her with the riding pad when she showed that she had learned them well. Now they watched over her tolerantly on their weekly journeys.

At school, Ernie now answered to 'Ern'. Only with family and

34

schoolfriends was he free of the agonising shyness which reduced him to inarticulate embarrassment in the presence of strangers. A group photograph taken in 1920 before he left Stewarton School shows a tall boy who has turned away from the camera, but glanced obliquely at the photographer just as the shutter clicked. Shoulders hunched and chin dropped into his chest, Ernie stands a little apart from his companions, isolated in the middle of the back row and uneasy in the formal situation. (Even then, his size and fiercely independent air gained him personal space.) The likeness between Weary and his elder son, Alexander, at the age of thirteen is marked.

Despite this, his likeable nature, sense of fair play and natural ability on the sports field made him popular with the other boys, but academically, 'It was the same old problem: I liked to read prodigiously, but I wasn't very interested in schoolwork'. Nonetheless, he topped his class consistently in all but mathematics, algebra never coming easily to him, although geometry lost its ability to mystify.

Summerlea was a haven to which the boys escaped each weekend and swung their backs into the farm work, relieved to be away from the constraints of town life. Without their help during the week, James had given up the profitable dairy herd, the fat cattle and the vealers that had augmented his income from cereals and sheep. Now the severe form of contact dermatitis which afflicted him turned every spring and summer into misery, and made harvest-time almost unbearable.

Record crops in 1921 swelled the farm bank account to a healthy level. It seemed that the future for both boys would lie away from the land and James decided in 1922 that he must sell the farm.

All the district gathered at Summerlea for the auction and clearing sale, wandering round the sheds and house, peering into doors and drawers.

James was a good farmer, so the land was in top condition, the livestock fit, and the implements and harness well cared for. The land, the team of horses and the great farm wagon were knocked down to the highest bidders. Even the dog kennels painstakingly made by the boys from odd scraps of timber and hammered-out kerosene tins fetched five shillings apiece; and an 'old, muzzle-loading pirate pistol', which had figured in many childish games, and the boys' precious, wartime souvenirs were snapped up by an eager bidder when Ern and Alan were too distracted by all the excitement to remove them to safety.

Seventy-two years later, James's building skills were still evident in the long machinery shed with its smoothly adzed slab walls, the grain storage sheds and the chaff shed next to the old stables.

The track from the main road passes close to the dark waters of the Sheepwash Creek, and late on winter afternoons, mist swirls above the still surface under the massive red gums. No wonder Flo, who helped Alice in the house and whispered spooky stories about the Bunyip rising out of the waters to a wide-eyed Ernie, succeeded in scaring herself as well as the little boy and insisted that Ernie escort her to and from her assignations late at night. He would settle down under a tree some distance from the lovers until summoned to see Flo back to the sleeping farmhouse. Ernie was known for his discretion – 'I was always on good terms with the lower decks'.

Ben Steen bought Star, for Gert had outgrown Toby. There would be no more wild rides for Ern on Zubah, who would play his wicked tricks on a new owner. (Not that Ern was attached to him. 'I don't think he was particularly fond of horses,' said Gert Hutchins many years later; but Weary smiled at the memory of his exploits and retorted: 'It wasn't that – I was hard on them, always urging them on to . . . go faster, jump higher, or further . . . ' He would drive his surgical teams in the same fashion, thirty years hence.)

Most of the stock had already been disposed of at the saleyards at Nalinga, minus James's prize ram, which had been discovered in its paddock one day, dead from mysterious causes. Ernie never confessed to his part in what happened. 'It will be on my conscience to my dying day . . . chasing my father's prize ram, on horseback, wielding a stock-whip' until it dropped dead from exhaustion.

Jack Ludeman's peaches, pears and apricots would now be safe from Ernie's lightning raids on the way home from school.

Joker had earned his retirement. Luckily, neither boy realised what an ignominious end he would suffer at the hands of the farm's new owner, clumsily hanged on the banks of the creek where he had often sat while the boys fished for blackfish and Ernie caught the only cod ever taken from the Sheepwash Creek.

Even the farm's name was changed: its new owners, the Ballintines, called it Ballantrae.

The old way of life had gone.

'In my boyhood in the Victorian countryside, I never saw anything admirable at all. I was only half in love with [it] . . . I saw all the shabby confinement of our lives, even in our best clothes.' This view contrasts strongly with Weary's publicly expressed love for the Australian landscape and his admiration for the virtues of the pioneers: 'What men and women they were, whose oxen and horses trod those plains . . . strong, enduring and kindly, with the courage, fortitude and resourcefulness that characterised our . . . fathers.'

It took time, and absence from the land which nurtured him, to awaken his senses to the 'strange beauty' of the Australian countryside.

Ernie departed the farm with scarcely a backward glance, unlike Alan, who took a while to adjust to changed circumstances and preferred the security of a familiar base. Jock and the buggy conveyed the four Dunlops to Belle Vue, the weatherboard house at 56 Barkly Street, Benalla, which James had bought from the District Inspector of Schools.

Away from the farm and the grasses which caused his painful allergies, James's health recovered. He spent the first few months restoring the Victorian villa and its garden to freshly-painted suburban tidiness, then he turned his mechanical abilities to good account by forming a partnership to install carbide lighting in isolated farmhouses.

Benalla suited Alice. James and she quickly became involved in the local Methodist church and taught Sunday School. The more active life and a wider circle of friends allowed her a fulfilment formerly denied her.

She had communicated her inner restlessness to her younger son, however. Town life to Ernie meant that he must now channel his abundant adolescent energy into sports instead of riding, hunting and farmwork. He had become a powerful swimmer: at 14, he swam the River Murray at Yarrawonga, and collected the Victorian Education Department's Senior Certificate in swimming, diving, life saving and resuscitation, and that December earned the Royal Life Saving Society's highest award. In winter there was Australian Rules football and in summer he enjoyed tennis 'very early in the morning on . . . very fine grass courts just across the river'. The five o'clock start allowed him plenty of time to swim afterwards in the Broken River.

The school was only a short distance from Belle Vue, and Ernie polevaulting the chest-high gate into the paddock where Jock grazed was soon a familiar sight at lunchtime.

He dashed off his homework by the bright light of the gasoliers that had replaced the soft glow of the farm's kerosene lamps, his study habits as casual as ever. Alan, a conscientious student, resented Ernie's *laissez-faire* attitude and the ease with which he absorbed his lessons; he nagged him habitually about reading novels when he ought to be poring over the textbooks Alan was learning. His photographic memory enabled Ernie to catch up with the elder boy and pass his Intermediate Certificate examination in English, geometry and trigonometry, physics and chemistry after two years and reach the appropriate standard in algebra, drawing, history and civics and French. Both would now sit their Leaving Certificates in 1923.

Six feet tall and physically strong, he was fed up with what he now saw as Alan's 'unreasonable bullying', which he had endured ever since he could remember. Alice was aware of this friction: 'I have always contrived to help the dear boys to keep up a friendly relationship,' she wrote, much later.[2] But one evening when James was away, the elder boy's needling provoked Ernie into throwing him violently to the floor. For some reason, Alice did not intervene.

The final confrontation came at school when Ernie's simmering resentment exploded in a fight well out of sight of the teachers but before an eager audience of fellow students. Alan tried to avoid it by suggesting that they wait until they got home, 'but I was having none of that, because we would be separated'. Ernie's longer arms enabled him to keep just out of his brother's reach, whilst jabbing with his right at the other's eyes until Alan could no longer see his opponent. Both eyes closed, blood streaming down his face, Alan retreated painfully to Belle Vue.

James took one look at him and decided grimly that he had been punished enough, then he gave Ernie the belting of his life.

Ernie didn't care. He had made his point. Alan never bullied him again.

Ernie had not paid too much attention to his teachers' warnings about the difficulties of passing the Leaving Certificate until shortly before the examinations, when he was jolted into action by the senior master telling him bluntly that his work was not up to scratch and he would fail in every subject. The prospect didn't please him. In a remarkably short time, he mastered all his subjects – for, when he chose, he could memorise entire pages with no apparent effort – and passed brilliantly.

In December 1923, at the age of 16, he left Benalla High School with no clear idea of what he would do next.

Not only had James and Alice misjudged his ability: there is nothing on record to show that his teachers at high school saw any special potential and no one took much notice of the fact that he had completed his Leaving Certificate in three years instead of the usual four.

Vera Hilliear had recognised the signs of the gifted child to whom learning comes effortlessly, but such students have no difficulty in maintaining a place at the top of the class with only brief bursts of activity, and Ern's energies appeared to be directed more towards sports. Although a few Benalla boys had competed successfully for scholarships in the past, nobody suggested Ern Dunlop was a suitable candidate.

When James heard that one of the local chemist's shops needed a lad, Ern was quite compliant about fitting in with his father's proposal. He had no ambitions. 'I was a bit footloose . . . [and] there was a vacancy in the local pharmacy . . . So I duly became apprenticed to a man named W. McCall Say . . . ' On 1 February 1924, James paid over the sum of £52 for the privilege. Uncle Henry Guppy was a JP, so he witnessed the documents.

Ern's head was stuffed full of romantic notions about alchemists and their hunt for the stone which would change base substances into gold, so he exchanged his school uniform for a white coat and went to work behind the counter as a junior apprentice for fifteen shillings a week. At their meeting that May, the Pharmacy Board of Victoria exempted him from sitting their preliminary examination after sighting the Leaving Certificate which bestowed entrance to university.[3]

The Victorian brick building in Nunn Street with its high, pressed metal ceilings and leadlighted plate glass windows, where he spent the next three years, is now a health food shop with a nice sideline in tea, coffee and home-made cakes; but in 1924, the two apprentices made up mixtures and ointments, ran messages, rolled pills and stirred up innumerable potions with pestles and mortars.

William McCall Say had qualified as a pharmacist in London and gave his employees a first-rate training, but he had his doubts about Ern Dunlop and eventually confided them to James. 'He was a bit dubious . . . decided I was too shy to be a successful pharmacist.'

Selling condoms was bad enough, but requests by female customers for various intimate items sent him blushing and confused in search of his employer or the senior apprentice. The latter was a socially assured Tasmanian who drove a small sports car and prided himself on having a way with the girls. Seventeen-year-old Ern was an admiring and amused audience for his stories.

He enjoyed his own rather tame social life. He played cricket for

Benalla and, in winter, Australian Rules with the local team. There was time for golf on the rather primitive course. Also, 'I was fairly solidly in love at that stage . . . but much too long in the legs to do anything very significant', except take Evelyn Scholes to films, concerts and local dances. Evelyn had been a year ahead of him at Benalla High School and was the only other candidate in 1922 for the Education Department's Senior Swimming Certificate. Ern remained 'shyly devoted' to her for some years.

He had learned to dance at 14 when Marjorie McGawlick, a local dancing instructress, had steered him round the floor chanting, 'Can't you hear the beat, can't you hear the beat', while Ern stumbled painfully in her wake, 'so busy being shy that sometimes I *didn't* hear the beat'. But by the time he took Evelyn to his first Bachelors' Ball in 1924, he was proficient enough not to worry about tripping up his partners.

'My first major ball . . . became a great scandal [although] . . . I had little to contribute . . . It shocked some elements of the town and one of the ministers preached a jeremiad. From that, it flowed into *Truth* . . . They said we'd "out-Sodomed Sodom and out-Gomorrahed Gomorrah".'

Benalla's respectable citizens disapproved furiously of the drinking – and, worse, the love-making and petting – which went on in the back seats of cars; of riotous groups walking the streets in evening dress when the rest of the population was getting up to go to work; and of one party in particular which bought strings of sausages and wore them festooned around their necks.

It must be the immoral American films which were to blame for these goings on, the older generation decided, titillating the young with daring new dances and permissive popular songs. For the 'Jazz Age' had burst upon Australia. People were crowding into the picture palaces as never before and emulating free-and-easy Hollywood behaviour. Even country youth was not safe from its pernicious influence.

The year 1925 passed uneventfully. Alan had spent 1924 as a student teacher at Healesville and in 1925 he returned home to work as a student teacher at Benalla High School. In 1926 he was to go to Melbourne Teacher's College. He had a motorbike; he had lived away from home; he would shortly be leading an independent life in the city. Apart from a visit to Melbourne with the school football team in 1923, when he saw the sea at Williamstown for the first time and in the excitement lost his train ticket, Ern's life had been confined to the towns and countryside of north-eastern Victoria. He was becoming increasingly restless, ensnared in the 'small prison of the chemist's shop' with no goals and no money other than his wages (now one pound a week). The prospect of spending the next fifty years or so behind the counter filled him with panic.

'About this stage I suddenly saw yawning before me a life as a nonentity . . . if I didn't bestir myself and start working.' At the beginning of 1926, he enrolled in the correspondence course of the Melbourne Pharmacy College and 'became a very keen student . . . I taught myself the discipline of study'.

In the examinations that December, he topped his year: the reward was the first H. T. Tompsitt Scholarship, which credited £10 towards the course fees for his Intermediate year, and a handsome medal. Alice wondered if Vera Alice Cecilia Hilliear might be right after all, and Ern was brighter than Alan. She cut out the announcement of his results from the newspaper and added it to the clipping announcing the boys' success in the Leaving Certificate examinations of 1923.

Will Say was still doubtful about young Dunlop's vocation in what was 'essentially a shop-keeping game', but he was pleased to arrange for his apprentice to transfer to the employment of a Melbourne colleague, J. Garrick, of Smith Street, Collingwood, and to assist him in finding a room in a boarding house not too far from the shop.

The closeness Ern had enjoyed as a child with Alice had dissipated during adolescence, when he struggled to break free of her domination. By the age of 17, he 'felt like a boarder in a very nice house', well cared for but with little in common beyond the ties of family. For his father he had a profound respect, but no love.[4] The bond was severed finally the day he left for Pharmacy College in the new year of 1927, when he leaned out of the Melbourne-bound train and waved to the receding figures of his parents on the platform.

'I first lived in Nicolson Street, very close to the Exhibition Building, in a boarding house with an old girl named Mrs Dalzeil.' His single room with its tiny fireplace, iron bedstead and washstand was midway down the side of the two-storeyed brick terrace house and looked across the neighbouring houses towards the leafy greenness of the Exhibition Gardens. Cable trams rattled past the door. The other boarders at Number 31 were a fairly rough lot who took little notice of the quiet nineteen-year-old. One of them, a New Zealander who, like Ern's Tasmanian colleague in Benalla, believed himself irresistible to women, liked to have an appreciative audience for the explicit tales of his conquests, although he regarded the boy 'as rather a pansy type because I didn't get mixed up with girls'.

To reach Garrick's Pharmacy, Ern plunged through Fitzroy down Moore or Bell Street to Smith Street. Gangs waged warfare all through that district and Squizzy Taylor was a legend in those parts. It was unwise to linger. Prostitutes lounged in the doorways of the little houses and Ern's path lay past an establishment called Blenheim's Leading Ladies that was to achieve even greater notoriety some years later through its popularity with Chief of Police Tom Blamey and his boys. 'I was one who minded my own business and said "Good morning" sweetly as I tipped my hat to the prostitutes – I never had any trouble.'

But after a few months, Mrs Dalzeil's health failed, and she and her daughter had to sell up. Ern sought lodgings elsewhere, eventually moving into 174 Moore Street, Fitzroy, where the Williams family ran a very downmarket establishment catering for rough and ready types from Mount Isa (where Mr Williams worked) or those like himself whose budget was a pound a week full board and lodging. Garrick paid his fourth-year apprentice thirty shillings a week.

'Moore Street was drab and drear', his dark little inside room looking down into a mean back yard where the sun shone only fleetingly. A photograph taken at the time shows a cheerfully smiling Ern, with the Williams's cat on his shoulders, posed against a rusty corrugated iron fence.

The house is on the corner of Wood Street, one short block from the boomtime architectural extravaganza of the Fitzroy Town Hall and Public Library. Now, it is clean and newly painted, renovated like many of the houses in the vicinity by a generation of Melbourne home-owners for whom Fitzroy has become an acceptable suburb in which to live. But in 1927, its waist-high railings dividing the front door from the footpath would not have protected the bow window from a stray bottle hurled by a passing drunk leaving the pub on the corner of Napier Street.

Its only advantages were that it was close to Smith Street and Garrick's Pharmacy and he could just afford the rent.

He had scarcely rid himself of the notions of alchemy and its medieval scientific mysteries, when he found himself in the curiously antiquated surroundings of Garrick's Pharmacy. Great carboys of jewel-coloured water gleamed in the gloom of the long, narrow shop; old-fashioned bottles lined the dark shelves and tier upon tier of polished wooden drawers with faded Latin labels opened to reveal old drugs, dried leaves, herbs and roots. 'Garrick did a lot of primary dispensing in which he made his own infusions and tinctures . . . the place was a sort of museum . . . He was a very extraordinary old boy, one of the cries of Smith Street.'

He also had a very special soda fountain and made his own drinks – orange, raspberry, sarsparilla – which were popular with the locals; and the windows displayed threepenny, sixpenny and shilling bargains to compete with Coles, which had recently opened in Collingwood. Behind the counter was Miss Humphreys, a 'good old bustling soul who dropped her aitches and chattered away in the Collingwood vernacular', and with Ern in the dispensary was a smart Sydney boy, rather older, who was a 'mine of information on sin'. Clatworthy dressed in fashionable suits and drove a car, but although he 'was at a more advanced stage of training, he hadn't done any exams'.

From Monday to Friday, mornings were spent at the Pharmacy College in Swanston Street opposite the Royal Melbourne Institute of Technology. Each lecture lasted about an hour, with a break of twenty minutes or so while the next lecturer filled up the blackboard with his notes for the day. These would have to be copied down by the students. Three textbooks were prescribed for the entire course: one each for chemistry, botany and *materia medica*. The first subject was the most difficult in the Intermediate year; the last involved a prodigious amount of memorisation.

Dean Ellis, a Tasmanian who was in the same year, remembers that most of them slipped next door to the Oxford Hotel for a quick beer during the mid-morning break between lectures. But Ern neither drank nor smoked: he could not afford it. Even a ride on the cable tram that clanged up Gertrude Street to the College was an extravagance that gave him constant bother: 'I never was quite sure whether it was worse to take it out in shoe leather, or to get a twopenny.'

The shop claimed him until six o'clock. After dinner, there was no time to read novels or browse through the shelves of the nearby library. 'I worked like a dog – I used to study very hard. I led a very austere life at that time.' Occasional parties and playing Australian Rules on Saturday afternoons were his recreation and 'on Sundays I usually worked'. All for thirty shillings a week.

'I was poor as a rat.'

On 19 December 1927, he opened a letter from A. T. S. Sissons, the Director of Studies and head of the college, and read: 'You have been awarded the following prizes: The Gold Medal of the Pharmaceutical Society, the Silver Medal for Botany; Certificates of Honour in Chemistry and *Materia Medica*.' His average mark had been ninety per cent.

Sissons, also lecturer in chemistry and dispensing, enclosed a personal letter of congratulation with the official one, adding: 'It is most reassuring to know that men of your ability and personality are entering pharmacy.'

His peers regarded him as quiet and studious, although 'I can't say that I had the image of a swot'. Mollie Woodhouse, a friend from those days who went out with him to pharmacy functions and dances, recalled that 'he was a very shy country boy'.

At the opening ceremony of the 1928 Session on 1 February, Ern Dunlop received his medals and certificates and the plaudits of Dr Tonkin, on behalf of the College, for his 'patience, courage, integrity and honesty of purpose, which went well with his scholarly qualities'.

Alice added two more cuttings to her little pile of memorabilia. Folk in Benalla decided Ern Dunlop might be a young man to watch.

Yet by now he thought he was 'in too narrow a channel'. The old restlessness was plaguing him. The theoretical work of the previous year had balanced out the tedium of shopwork and dispensing. 'It didn't interest me so much. I never was frightfully wrapped up in making pills.' But the final year included a great deal of practical pharmacy and he brooded constantly on an ambition that he had not yet confided to anyone. For he had a new hero: 'Sir Thomas Dunhill . . . surgeon to four monarchs . . . an Australian from the bush who'd only had a bush education . . . who'd done pharmacy and turned to medicine . . . '

He had no money; his wages were barely enough to live on and it had been impossible to save. There was nothing to spare at home in those Depression years, so he could not count on help from James and Alice.

Also, there was Evelyn. They were still going out together, for she had come to Melbourne to work with the Education Department as a swimming instructor and their feelings for each other became more intense as Ern's final year advanced. Alan was already married – Ern had been Best Man – and there had been plenty of teasing at the wedding from guests who asked when the younger brother was going to take the plunge. He would have a Diploma of Pharmacy by the end of the year and, although nothing was said, there was no doubt that marriage was on Evelyn's mind when she invited him to spend the holidays with her family.

Ern was devotedly in love, but with frightening clarity he saw that marriage would close off his chances of going to university. Medicine took six long years of study and two years as a resident in one of Melbourne's teaching hospitals. The alternative was too depressing to contemplate: a lifetime in a pharmacist's shop in the suburbs or a country town, a wife, a mortgage and children. He could not do it. As gently as he could, he refused her invitation.

That year, he fulfilled all the College's expectations in the final examinations, earning Sissons's 'hearty congratulations on the splendid success you achieved. It was a fitting termination to the work you have always done at the College. We are all delighted that you have won the Medal and have the distinction of being the first to win the Tompsitt Prize for the Final Course'.

He had also been the first to win the Tompsitt Scholarship in 1926. Two gold medals: he had found the philosopher's stone within himself.

Sir Edward Dunlop is one of Benalla's favoured sons, after whom they have named a street and a building for the use of their elderly citizens. He returned to the district frequently, at first to visit his parents, but increasingly after the war to attend official functions, often as the guest of honour.

North-eastern Victoria has claimed him as its own and he acknowledged this debt to the region in interviews, speeches and forewords to books. The further he distanced himself from his rural and small-town upbringing, the more he identified his roots, casting a benevolent eye (sometimes veering towards the sentimental) back to that time before the Second World War when an uncomplicated life in a country town and a schoolgirl sweetheart were the last things he wished to embrace.

Stewarton and Benalla gave him his values, but they were also the grit in the oyster, the irritant which impelled him to pack his bags eagerly and launch himself out into the wider world. 'I never had any great enthusiasm for country town life . . . subconsciously, I just wanted to get away.'

FOUR

Men of Ormond

UNTIL HE TOPPED his final year, 'it was not evident to his fellow students that he had an outstanding brain,' commented Mollie Wood-house many years later when discussing the years at Pharmacy College. Dean Ellis did not recall any obvious academic brilliance, either, though he remembers Ern Dunlop being 'bright' and both of them were good 'pill-rollers' because of their years of practical experience before coming to Melbourne. His fellow students were surprised by his triumph.

Ern was well-liked and everyone was pleased at his success, but none of them – students, lecturers, the family – had realised that his lodestar was Sir Thomas Dunhill and that he had no intention of settling for a humdrum life behind a shop counter.

Immediately he learned his pharmacy results in December 1928, he applied to study medicine at the University of Melbourne. Since the most pressing problem would be money, there was no time for the luxury of a holiday to celebrate his success before beginning full-time work at Garrick's Pharmacy. But at least, as a qualified pharmacist, his wages would now allow him to save something each week towards the expenses of the academic year that would begin in March 1929.

The family rallied round: James's older sister Belle and her husband Tom Simons offered him bed and board at their house, 9 Hampden Road, Armadale; and Aunt Lil, who after Catherine Marie's death in 1923 had married Arthur Dutton and now lived at a farm called The Pelican on the King River, suggested she could help out now and again with a little money.

On Wednesday 6 February 1929, Garrick gave Ern the morning off work to attend the graduation ceremony and official opening of the Pharmacy College's 1929 session and to accept his gold medal and the certificate listing his credentials as a registered pharmaceutical chemist. Alice proudly added the various newspaper articles and photographs of the medallist to her store. Nearly as proud as Alice and James was William McCall Say.

In March, alongside the number 14742, Ernest Edward Dunlop matriculated as a student in the University of Melbourne, signed his name in the University roll book and 'made the declaration required by the statutes'.

'That year was just a grim nightmare . . . I went up to the university feeling that there I would find a new world with people to whom I could relate, and instead I found a lot of overgrown schoolboys . . . I felt the difference that the two or three years made with fellows just coming up from school.'

Ern's peers were mainly 'public school types' for whom he felt no affinity and he did little but 'swot miserably'.

Then, around May, the university discovered that somehow they had overlooked Ern's lack of Latin, a prerequisite for medicine, and informed him that he must pass at Intermediate standard by the following November. In despair he went to Taylor's College who were quite unconcerned: 'Ah, don't worry about that – we'll get you through, son! Just come here once a week.'

Term time was a miserable grind of travelling by tram from Hampden Road and later Tintern Avenue, Toorak to Flinders Street (the end of a tram section), then, to save the cost of the extra section, covering on foot the remainder of the distance to the university in Grattan Street, Carlton. Most of the journey was spent learning Latin: 'I could reel off whole pages of Virgil, but the grammar I found a bit more worrying.' Alan described his brother as spending a good deal of one brief holiday in Benalla marching up and down the hall reciting Caesar's *De Bello Gallico*. He could not afford to fail – 'I was dead serious about whether I could make the grade' – and he also found natural philosophy intimidating, since his great dislike for mathematics at high school meant he had not applied himself as conscientiously as he should have done.

Nonetheless, when the end-of-year results were published, Ern had first class honours in chemistry, zoology and botany, with a shared exhibition in chemistry, having topped the year in chemistry and zoology and come second in botany. Natural philosophy was the only subject in his entire course for which he failed to sit – and gain – honours. (Later, he regretted not having done so, for he believed that he probably would have succeeded.) As for Latin, 'I wasn't too pleased with my examination', but the required pass was his.

His ambition now embraced gaining a scholarship to Ormond College, which Dunhill had entered as a third-year medical student. Hoping that his 1929 results would be considered good enough to put that neo-Gothic seat of Presbyterian learning and privilege within his reach, Ern immediately sought an interview with the Master of Ormond and applied for a scholarship.

Meanwhile, the long summer vacation dragged out interminably behind the counter in the dark and stuffy shop while he awaited the decision, the only consolation being his wages from the holiday job.

The Master of Ormond was the formidable Dr D. K. Picken, a grave Scottish mathematician who, Weary later recalled, 'saw through mathematics to the fundamental principles of ultimate reality, and somehow or other mathematics and Christianity merged together . . . David Kennedy Picken thoroughly believed that in Ormond College's Christian medical college [sic] there was something that was terribly important to the world'. He lived somewhat austerely in the lodge with Mrs Picken and their daughters and nothing went on that the omniscient Master did not know about, as in mortar board and black gown he loped purposefully about the College.

At the beginning of February 1930, David Kennedy Picken wrote a crisp note from his summer holiday beside the sea at Rosebud, congratulating Ern 'most cordially' on his results and requesting a reply 'at once' if Ern had a 'serious intention of coming into residence' that year.[1]

Indeed he did. Eleven days later, Dr Picken offered him a full residential scholarship to Ormond College, insisting that he 'wire' his decision, for 'the competition for scholarship funds has been very severe this year'. The Depression had begun to bite more cruelly and unemployment continued to rise; not only were its effects all too obvious amongst the poor in the streets of Collingwood and Fitzroy adjoining the university suburb of Carlton, but the shock waves from the collapse of the American stockmarket in Wall Street on 22 October 1929 were also hurting businessmen and property owners. The wool and wheat cheques which paid the fees of many an Ormond student were diminishing.

When the academic year began in March, Ern had a major scholarship worth, he recalled, about £60, his savings from the holiday job, Aunt Lil's promise of assistance and around £30 from the chemistry exhibition. He hoped it would be enough to see him through the year.

He entered Ormond College full of purpose and cherishing a romantic vision of emulating two scholar athletes whom he had ranged alongside Dunhill: former Ormond medical student and Rhodes scholar L. T. 'Ginger' Ride, (who became Professor of Physiology at the University of Hong Kong and then its Vice-Chancellor) and C. B. Fry, the British athlete who captained Oxford at cricket, equalled the world record for the long jump, was a football international and captained England against Australia and South Africa in the 1912 Triangular Tests.

Frank Raleigh, the diminutive and elderly College porter, escorted him along the high-ceilinged corridors to his room and Ern then sought out his ground-floor study in the eastern corner of the building, where he met the 'wife' with whom he was to share for the next five years.

'I found myself paired with another stray piece, a grave, responsible youth with tow hair even more bleached by the North Queensland sun, clear, frank blue eyes and a shy, flashing smile . . . .His most profane exclamation was "Strike"!'

Charles Hopkins was another romantically inclined young second-year medical student who played the violin. Weary's first impression was of an 'incarnation . . . of an impeccable character in English schoolboy literature called David Blaize'. Charles, too, was something of an oddity, having been educated partly at an English public school, and he had completed his first year of medicine at the University of Queensland. When Ern walked in the door, Charles was so delighted to find someone who would talk to him, he almost overwhelmed his new companion with conversation. Arriving at Ormond a week earlier than most of the students, he had been dismayed when none of the residents deigned to speak to him or take the slightest notice of his existence until Ern introduced himself.

They soon discovered the reason for this curiously anti-social behaviour: Ormond College's complicated and protracted initiation rites. And unlike the majority of their year, they had not come up to university as part of a group of schoolmates with a shared sense of identity from Scotch or Geelong College. Quite soon in those first weeks, Ern and Charles found a friend in another second-year medical student who had entered Ormond with them and who did not fit in with the public school mob: E. C. (Mick) Wilson from Western Australia. Wilson's elder brother, a fourth-year medical student at Ormond, was far too conscious of his senior status and role in the initiations to spend his time with 'scum', so Mick had to fend for himself.

'Life really began for me at Ormond College,' said Weary. But he also considered that he was 'an unconventional selection to a club of some 120 resident students', mainly drawn from Victoria's Presbyterian public schools. 'I was different . . . older . . . a country boy [and] I felt very sensitive as to the impression I would make.' Other boys had a country upbringing but of a contrasting kind: their fathers and grandfathers counted their broad acres in thousands and their flocks in tens of thousands. And he was a state school boy.

The memory of those differences lingered for more than sixty years and awareness of his less privileged background never entirely left him. Weary was an outsider. Maturity and professional success, easy acquaintance with heads of state and other community leaders, membership of a number of clubs, including that preserve of the rich, the landed and the powerful, the Melbourne Club, never took away his ingenuous (and amused) 'Gee-whizz' amazement at the way the media promoted him as one of Australia's heroes and tribal elders.

At the back of his mind, there was always an element of surprised gratitude at the way in which Dr Picken awarded him a scholarship and 'Ormond College . . . showed a comforting tolerance of my poverty, and dependence upon academic success.'[2] One wonders why. Picken would have winkled out of him the information that he was the great grandson of a well-known Lowland Scots minister; his ability to work hard and achieve results was demonstrated by coming out top of his years in Pharmacy College. Later, his prowess at sport made him conspicuous at a time when Ormond saw the rise in popularity of Rugby Union. His academic success allowed him to realise his goal of emulating the scholar athletes he so admired and who had been held up as the ideal by imperialists and empire-builders. Picken was a great believer in the last.

Yet he did not merely set out to fulfill the popular image of success that dominated society's thinking at the time. Dunhill, Ride, Fry, and the Rhodes scholars whom he regarded so highly personified excellence. And it is excellence which was always his first aim: not fame, not material success – although a modicum of both was his dividend and he thoroughly enjoyed them.

Most of his fellow students appeared to possess an in-bred confidence bestowed by money and all the advantages of their broader, public school education. They moved easily in society – or so it seemed – and their willing acquiescence in childish initiation rites surprised him.

Unlike Graham Thirkell, another freshman and a bursary holder who entered Ormond that year from Scotch College and became a life-long friend, Ern was not prepared for the realities of initiation; his only acquaintance with it had been second-hand, in books dealing with English public school life, such as *Tom Brown's Schooldays*. He found being addressed as 'scum' (Students' Club Uninitiated Member) and fagging for 'gentlemen' younger than his own 22 years intimidating, and the first of these trials, the 'Inquisition', the most intimidating of all.

The freshmen, each wearing a 'dead meat ticket' bearing name, faculty and other personal details, stood in line until they were called one by one. After a 'medical examination' by members of the Students' Club, Ern was hooded and led by one of the Trial Committee into the Common Room where other members of the committee crowded round, each with his designated role such as judge, jury member, policeman and so on. The Book of Doom was opened with a rattling of chains and he heard for the first time the nickname which third-year law student D. J. Nairn selected as suitable for him – and by which he would be known for the rest of his life.

Based on the association of his surname Dunlop with tyres (and, by extension, tires), he was solemnly christened 'Weary' and condemned to a nightly display of 'pneumatics'. Weary was not explicit about these, vaguely describing them as pumping himself up, 'circulating' and deflating 'and it's pretty hard to produce some variation in displays of pneumatics, night after night . . . any deficiencies, you had your bum tanned with a knotted towel [which] you wore round your neck, like the merchants of Calais'. 'Senior gentlemen', fourth-year men or greater, administered chastisement to erring freshmen, who humbly allowed themselves to be flicked on the buttocks with the wet end of their knotted towels. Charles Hopkins recalled that 'They used to have great fun with Weary . . . they were always on to [him]'. The 'pneumatics' involved Weary deflating himself, then squatting down on the floor before pumping himself up and rolling round the room. Weary found this disconcerting and juvenile but performed with his customary good humour.

That same evening, after undergoing the humiliation of the medical examination, the blindfolding, the bright lights on the face and other 'intimidating techniques', he was marched out to the dumpty –

Ormond parlance for the latrines – and there, a fifth-year medical student and footballer, 'Bob Officer . . . dressed as a policeman, was to . . . put my head in a dumpty' for some alleged crime. That, Weary was not prepared to tolerate. 'I said: "You know, this is one thing, my boy, you're not going to do!" Fortunately . . . we didn't come to blows.' Bob Officer's strength and physique were impressive, but Weary was more than equal to him – although he never mastered the former's trick of driving a tack into the wall with his thumb, a feat Weary described admiringly more than once when discussing initiation and the Ormond years.

Undoubtedly, the others had plenty of fun with the freshmen. There was a scatological and ' blood-spattered undergraduate comedy about everything' and some tasteless elements, such as firing a gun behind someone's head while they were blindfolded, but the second-year men particularly must have felt a certain relief that such things were behind them and a new generation was being subjected to the scrutiny of the College.

He found the trial particularly difficult because of his sensitivity about being different. 'Their prestige and place was without question, but you were a grub from the outer circle and uncovered for the scum you were.' The Lord High Executioner and his associates knew exactly how to humiliate a shy state school boy from the country: 'Dunlop, is Benalla High School proud of you?' and similar searching questions about his origins were asked, while all around him clustered young men sure of their place in the Establishment.

Over sixty years later, this may seem of no great moment, but at the time a state school boy was very much an outsider, and as a member of a minority, he had to conform to the rules which would eventually fit him into the system. Ideally, initiation resulted in the freshmen being gathered into the circle of Ormond men where there would be 'no distinction of birth, of possessions, of class or of creed'.[3] But while 'Such was the expectation . . . practice sometimes differed.' In 1936, for example, the only freshman to come from a state school was told that his state school education was a 'crime'. Weary forgot his crime, but when addressing the Ormond College Club forty years later, he described how the Inquisition and the Wake 'laid your tortured soul bare'.

During the weeks leading up to Easter, Weary memorised (and along with the other freshmen was examined on) the history of Ormond and its chief benefactor, Francis Ormond; details about the men resident in

Ormond, 'exactly what room they were in, who they roomed with, their skills, records and peculiarities'; and then sat 'one terrible examination, in which the mathematics were just beyond human ken, about different rates of growth of grass in the College grounds, with applications of manure and stimulants and how then the sheep came in and ate at a certain rate . . .'

The procedures were carefully designed: Weary singled out R. S. Hooper and A. H. McGregor, medical students a year ahead of him, and Don Nairn, as having a special talent during his years for making these mock-Masonic rituals sound 'terribly formal and import-ant . . . pretty rough and ready stuff, but . . . amusingly designed. We finally had a wake, in which stark bollox naked, you thronged around the College in an endless sort of stomp, stomp, stomp, singing a terrible dirge . . . Miss Brown went by last week, the worms are eating her damson cheek . . . the worms crawl out and the worms crawl in and so on . . . when you finally reached the Common room . . . you had to lie down, people took your candle and bombed your navel with molten wax . . .' Sir Archibald Glen, a fellow Ormond student, recalled that this was designated a 'naval engagement without loss of seamen'.

But whereas he had an imperfect memory of some aspects of initiation, he forgot nothing about the nightly ceremonies and duties, at the end of which he and his companions became 'Ormond men', no longer scum but permitted to mix on an equal basis with their fellows in an atmosphere of muscular Christianity and camaraderie.

Ormond College's initiation ceremonies were examined by Stuart Macintyre in a book published to mark the centenary of the College.[4] There is no doubt in his mind, nor was there in Weary's and the majority of his contemporaries who endured the ritual, that the procedures forged close bonds between freshmen and imbued them with what was known as 'the Ormond spirit'.

'We were welded together,' said Charles Hopkins, 'and mixed with no one else outside our year.'

'I shrank from many aspects . . . but I have to admit I finished up by knowing an awful lot about the College and . . . the inmates,' Weary emphasised. 'Being examined by people in this way, you get to know a lot about them. It was all summed up by old Bert Coates . . . those who examine are themselves examined . . . you either had a high opinion of the fellow that was putting you through or you didn't think much of him!'

On occasion, some freshmen were so threatened by this rite of passage from schooldays into manhood that they left the College, preferring to board elsewhere, and although Weary later acknowledged that the benefits outweighed the disadvantages, driving freshmen together in their misery, at the time he was obviously ambivalent about this aspect of Ormond and confessed that he was most anxious about the impression he made on the other students. Any humorous elements only became apparent with hindsight. When it was his turn to initiate freshmen in subsequent years, he didn't particularly enjoy the job – 'wouldn't think I was a very harsh inquisitor'.

Weary's memories of his first term in Ormond focussed on initiation. Commencement activities for 1930 do not rate a mention and no programmes or papers connected with the ceremonies were saved from either 1929 or 1930: all else paled alongside those evenings spent earning acceptance into the student body.

Besides, he was always driven by the necessity to work and even if he had not retained lingering Calvinist qualms about alcohol that first year, there was no money to spare for the traditional student drinking sessions in local pubs such as Johnny Naughton's in Sydney Road, frequented from the first by some of their better-off peers like Thirkell. Charles Hopkins emphasised how hard-up they both were and how great was the self-induced pressure to pass examinations. His parents gave him a pound a week for expenses; Weary had even less, but at least he had his own bedroom. In order to save money, Charles shared with Keith (Bennie) Rank, another second-year medical student who had come to Ormond on a scholarship in 1929.*

By Easter, initiation was behind them and the pattern of lectures and College life in this predominantly masculine society was well established. No longer was Weary required to supply a more senior man with hot shaving water or cups of tea in the morning, but he took turns with the other new men to sort the post and answer the telephone for the whole of his first year. The medical students' full timetables did not allow them to lark about like the arts students; lectures began at 9 am – sometimes earlier – and ended around 5 pm. A great deal of the first two years of the medical course was spent in the dissecting room amidst the stench of formalin. In the hour and a half before dinner there was

---

* Now Sir Benjamin Rank Kt, he was the protegée of Sir Harold Gillies, the eminent New Zealand plastic surgeon, and was the first Australian to practise this speciality at Heidelberg, Victoria, after training in London in the 1930s.

just enough time for some tennis, athletics and suchlike in the summer and football practice or a run on the oval in the winter.

The solid work habits developed earlier on held up and one of Charles's enduring memories of their years at College was of Weary, wearing dressing gown and slippers and wrapped in a rug, at his desk by 6 am each morning, 'a fine example of cheerful fortitude' no matter how late he had gone to bed.[5]

Once again, the regime paid off: the 1930 examinations saw him equal first in physiology and gaining third place in anatomy after Rank, his neighbour in the next-door study: 'Only thing I ever beat him at!' Edward Gault tutored them in physiology and their lecturer in anatomy was a little man with a fine brain and ability for surgery named Albert Coates, who had been a postman and studied at night school in order to qualify to enter medicine.

There were no honours as such in the second year of medicine: instead the six best students in anatomy were appointed prosectors and the twelve top physiology students, apostles. Weary learned that he was both head apostle and a prosector when the examination results came out at the end of the year. Henceforth, Rank (who was also a prosector, but not an apostle) would vie with him for academic honours each year.

For most of 1930, Weary was still finding his own level in the Ormond community, in which sports played a major rôle. He was persuaded to begin boxing as a heavyweight; and when he turned up for a practice game of Australian Rules that April, his speed on the field, his height of 6 foot 4 inches and his splendid physique ensured his selection for the Ormond team which took part in the two intercollegiate matches that July. For the first match he was put on the forward line, despite being a natural ruck, and the *Ormond Chronicle* lists him as kicking one goal in the match versus Queen's. Subsequent games saw him with the ruck. But apart from the brief mention in the football, his name is not the feature in the *Chronicle* that it would be in future years.

He had grown used to the architectural scale of the buildings and the elitist atmosphere that was so overwhelming to some new arrivals. The attentions of the domestic staff were in marked contrast to the boarding houses of his pharmacy college days and an important component of the students' education – 'Not only were they essential to the privileged routine of the undergraduate, their presence helped to fix his sense of class relations.'[6] He was being shaped in a new mould, but his childhood empathy with the 'lower decks' never left him. The values of a Caledonian and pastoralist elite which ruled at Ormond only reinforced that solid code by which Alice and James had raised him.

Here, at Ormond, Weary felt he was breathing the rarified air of academia, and before him stretched an exhilarating prospect.

Weary was beginning to make his presence known off the sports field as well, and he had started to put behind him the shy insecurities of a bush-bred boy.

'My first year or two . . . I was a fairly noted "ratbag",' he explained on being shown a copy of Miss Amy Johnson's reply to an invitation to the College issued by some of the Ormond gentlemen. That June he was one of a 'Council of Six' that planned a notable rag to coincide with Amy Johnson's triumphal visit to Melbourne after her solo flight from the United Kingdom to Darwin. The idea only occurred to them when she declined their politely offered hospitality – and they decided to go ahead with the visit anyway. On Tuesday, 17 June, they installed 'Miss Johnson' in a hired car, together with a chauffeur and two 'aides', and stationed groups of cheering students at key intersections. Despite the loss of a wheel and the official party having to transfer from the open tourer to a closed car, 'soon hundreds were gazing with admiration at the "lone flyer" in her chariot. The climax was reached when the policeman on point duty in Swanston Street saluted and cleared the traffic to allow "Miss Johnson" to cross.' The hoax was not exposed until the next morning's newspapers came out.

By the time he was a second-year Ormond man, a prosector and an apostle, his real talent for ratbaggery began to emerge. When Commencement kicked off at the start of the new university year at 'The Shop', Weary rode downtown on a Carlton United lorry drawn by a team of great Clydesdales. The citizens of Melbourne needed all their tolerance on Commencement days: students ran riot in the streets and the pubs all over town, selling their magazine in aid of 'charity' and getting up to all manner of tricks.

Dressed in a cloud of tulle and tight satin and waving a wand, a bow tied firmly round his brow and with two bob wrapped in a handkerchief and tucked in his bathing trunks under the fairy costume for emergencies, he hovered round a cenotaph 'erected in memory of the fallen old girls of the university . . . made possible by the Lord Mayor's Sex Appeal'. The photograph in the *Chronicle* for 1931 shows a very hefty fairy.

Weary deserted the lorry when it reached The Block in Collins Street in order to have a drink in the bar of the Australia Hotel and he created such a stir, wandering up and down the bar, that everyone wanted to buy drinks for the sixteen-stone fairy with the wand. He was far too late to catch the lorry's return trip. 'I had to get myself back to Ormond by tram . . . me trying to entertain the whole tram, eternally sick of waving wands, children and one thing and another and . . . the wretched conductor insisted on my paying a fare . . . It was humiliating, finding the money . . . '

After the grind of 1929 and the rather wobbly first term in 1930, he had entered joyfully into the corporate life of the College.

Weary's sheer zest for life and willingness to be involved in all manner of fun and games ensured his popularity. When he described some of the memorable pranks in which he was involved, his pleasure at recalling these days was very evident; his eyes lit up and his attention sharpened in the same way as when he reminisced about his rugby-playing activities. Weary's participation in rugby, boxing and athletics brought friendships which crossed over to other years and academic disciplines.

He was part of a group behind a number of escapades whose scope and inventiveness increased as they gained in confidence. Weary's superior in the art of ratbaggery was Ross McOmish, the son of a Baptist minister and a first-year medical student in 1930 who 'came up to Ormond with the highest scholarship in the place' and that year failed in every subject. Geoff Hudspeth and Graham Thirkell were another two invariably mixed up in any wickedness. Hudspeth, an engineering student from Tasmania, rowed in the Second Eight which defeated Queens that year and played football in the Ormond team with Weary in the 1931 match against Newman College, whereas Graham, in addition to his Thespian activities in the Ormond play, fancied himself as a Noël Coward and entertained his fellow undergraduates to a succession of ribald songs he had written, like 'The Joys of Copulation' and 'She Wears her Pink Pyjamas'. He was a good pianist and accompanied Charlie Hopkins's soulful violin items at Common Room concerts.

Hudspeth's abilities lay in another direction. He could mimic anyone to perfection, including the Warden of Trinity and his own College's Master, and used his talent on the telephone to confuse these august gentlemen on at least one occasion. His most memorable public performance with Weary featured the two of them in a Commencement play, with Weary as the Strongman, Professor Hechenstein, and the nuggety Hudspeth, half his size, as his trainer. With an incredible display of strength, Weary bent iron bars and lifted huge weights – which Geoff then nonchalantly straightened out. At a critical moment, as he was posed with the 'weights' above his head, Weary accidentally shed his tiger skin immediately in front of the delighted and apprehensive young ladies from Janet Clarke Hall who filled the front rows of the audience. Weary was 'not happy' about this but Hudspeth, equal to the occasion, hurriedly announced: 'The professor is now taking off his tiger skin!' But this was only the official face of their clowning.

Not for Weary, Geoff and Ross the mundane schoolboy pranks of 'water-bagging', or lowering a chamber pot containing a set alarm clock out the window of the floor above so that it went off just as an amorous young man was about to score with his girlfriend on the study sofa. Their schemes were more ambitious.

They organised invitations to an 'At Home' at Number Nine Darling Street, South Yarra, for the Old Girls of the very proper school of Clyde, to take place on the same evening as a fashionable wedding reception. The replies were to be sent to Weary's old schoolmate Tom Thornburn, masquerading as Miss Isobel McKay, and Weary pinned all of them up on the notice board in the Students' Union Building. The furious wedding party and the former Clyde pupils and their guests never knew who had arranged it.

Their most ambitious scheme was perpetrated on the night of a University ball, when everyone was decked out in white tie and all the finery they could muster, Weary evolved a plan whereby the two of them would snib all the Yale bedroom locks while the majority were celebrating. Spreadeagled against the soaring stonework of the College, he crawled limpet-like along the narrow stone ledges, entering by the windows. He fixed the locks so that each was firmly snibbed shut when he walked out the door and pulled on the attached string. He successfully completed all the unoccupied rooms on the first and second floors.

As a final gesture, he snibbed Geoff's door and strolled back to his own room, feeling very pleased with himself, only to discover that Geoff, anticipating this treachery, had hammered matchwood into Weary's lock and cut it off flush so that he, too, was locked out.

Shortly after, the main body of the undergraduates returned and all hell broke loose when they found themselves locked out of their rooms. Graham Thirkell, splendid in opera cloak and silk hat, found a ladder and broached the first storey, to be greeted by an irate J. E. Clarke. The latter – who had not been at the ball – was in bed and, when he saw Thirkell looming outside his window, decided he was being raided and tipped a bucket of water on his attacker. A drenched and furious Thirkell challenged him to a fight but Clarke prudently declined to emerge from his locked bedroom. The rest of the night was taken up by irate Ormond men alternately trying to gain access to their rooms and discover the identity of the criminals who had locked them out of their beds. It was years before the truth emerged.

Ormond had been without its Master since his illness and departure for convalescence in England and Europe during second term in 1930, and the sight of his crisply-pleated black gown swirling down the corridors or across the vestibule to the dining hall had been replaced by the shabbier, donnish garb of the pipe-smoking Vice-Master, Barney Allen. Dr Picken's absence made only a slight difference to the corporate life of the College, which had its own rhythm – Barney Allen's eye was just as sharp, but he 'paid [the students] the compliment of assuming [they] knew how to behave themselves . . . [and] kept the twinkle behind his severity'.[7]

Dr Picken re-entered the life of the College in the second term of 1931, when on 3 May he 'leapt off the Adelaide train' and strode up the aisle of Scots Church in Collins Street to take his place at the Jubilee Service of thanksgiving for the fifty years of Christian and Presbyterian education given to more than 2000 students at Ormond.

That year's *Chronicle* records the impression Weary was making on the athletics team and in rugby and boxing. Placed first in the shot putt in the inter-collegiate athletics competition that May, he also came in a respectable fifth in the 880 yards. Weary is the tallest member of the 1931 athletic team in the official photograph and although standing squarely in the centre of the back row, he has ducked his head in the old way and looked up diffidently at the camera as the shutter clicked.

It is a different matter in the unofficial photographs taken on the day of the Morrison Fours: this tallest member of the 'Richmond Razzberries' crew (which lost out to the 'Knights of Temperance' for the 'Sir Francis Raleigh Pot' that October in a light-hearted finale to the rowing) is draped convivially round the necks of some shorter members of the crew. All eight had enjoyed plenty of Richmond beer from Mrs Disney's – at elevenpence a bottle, a penny cheaper than Johnny Naughton's. Weary had lost his inhibitions about alcohol and was as eager as the next one to assist the 'serpent' in raising its head.

Ormond had been 'dry' since 1915 when the Students' Club

voluntarily decided to 'abstain from alcohol for the duration of the war' and although it was not the Club's intention to make this a firm rule, 'Digger' Picken was instrumental in having the ban on alcohol made permanent.[8] He was wont to harangue the men in chapel and after dinner when it came to his notice that some of them had been on a bender, or when their rowdiness during meals suggested that they had overdone the hospitality dispensed in the local pubs. Alcohol was 'the Serpent' and, as Graham McInnes describes it, Dr Picken would proclaim: 'Men, Ah'm sorry to have to obsairve that once again The Sairpent has raised its ugly head in the College. I'll not tolerrate it and will make an example of those men who desairve it . . . '[9] They were not deterred.

Invitations to official drinking sessions were mock-masonic in tone. 'Brother Dunlop' received 'the call' to attend a function at the Victoria Palace in Little Collins Street one December Monday at 7.30 pm. from the 'Priests of the Temple of the Serpent'. Stewards were appointed to collect money and acceptances. The language was, as usual, undergraduate, even though four of the stewards were senior men already working at the Alfred Hospital, the Melbourne Hospital and in offices in the city.

The Serpent raised his head regularly during Weary's time at Ormond, although lack of funds prevented too much indulgence, and unfailingly provoked the Digger's wrath until the changed attitudes of the post-Second World War years prevailed. Certain traditions hung on, but the Serpent's annual awakening from hibernation after examinations were over lost its importance once alcohol was allowed in the College.

The third-year medical course was also devoted solely to anatomy and physiology. In 1931, the Royal College of Surgeons travelled to Australia for the first time to conduct the examination for the Primary FRCS England, the first part of the Fellowship examinations. Rank and Weary, as the top two anatomy students and prosectors to Professor Wood-Jones's Department of Anatomy, were appointed Prosectors to the Royal College of Surgeons of England and, under the direction of W. A. Hailes, 'entrusted with the preparation of suitable anatomy examination dissections'.

Both took great delight in preparing some thoroughly difficult examples which Hailes had shown them and it was to be a useful experience: they discovered a loophole in the regulations which made it possible for them to sit this examination as final year medical students in 1934 when next the examiners travelled out to Australia. Both Weary and Sir Benjamin Rank believe they were the last two Australians ever to do so, the gap in the regulations being firmly closed afterwards.

Weary topped the physiology class in 1931 and shared the exhibition with Charles, but in anatomy he ran second to Rank.[10] Rank, who admired Wood-Jones as 'eminent' amongst his teachers and who, in turn, was regarded by the professor as his 'boy', believes that the competition between Weary and him was well-balanced: his particular strength was an excellent visual memory that eventually led him to specialise in plastic surgery, whereas Weary was stronger 'on the functional side of things', in chemistry and physiology, for instance.

Despite that second place in anatomy, he topped his year with the best aggregate marks and first class honours in each subject. Alice told the *Benalla Standard* and the editor told the district, announcing the achievement at the head of the 'Personalia' column.

Weary had always been handy with his fists: Tom Thornburn well remembered the monumental fight when Weary and he disagreed over the method of appointing the captain of the Benalla High School football team. Weary thought the captain should have been elected by the team – and if so, there was a good chance he would have been first choice; Tom resented his remarks and, though the bout began in a trivial enough fashion as they were leaving the football ground, they ended up pounding each other for twenty rounds before agreeing to shake hands. But it had never occurred to Weary to take up boxing as a sport until the university approached him in 1930. They were short of heavy-weights and someone of Weary's size and weight, who was also quick and light on his feet, was snapped up as a promising prospect.

Eddie Miller, a former Australian light heavyweight champion, trained the students in his gymnasium downtown amidst an atmosphere of sweat and punching bags and nostalgic photographs from Miller's past. In these, he looked like a Greek athlete, 'a clean-limbed fellow with a sculptured face', but Weary remembered him as 'an old, shambling gorilla, with one eye that would hardly open . . . terrific cauliflower ears and a flattened nose. He was very, very hard to hurt, Old Eddie, and every now and again he'd give you one to go on with . . . just the picture of the old punch-drunk boxer who still had the instincts and reflexes in the ring and probably could hardly read the paper when he got out.'

Nonetheless, he trained Weary well enough for him to win the inter-collegiate boxing in 1931 and go on to represent Melbourne University unsuccessfully in the inter-varsity boxing that August against J. C. McGilvray of Sydney University, 'not . . . an extremely powerful fellow . . . but with his experience he was too clever for me'.

By 1932, Weary's technique in the ring had improved enough for a newspaper to comment that he 'used his weight and reach to advantage . . . quicker to attack and smarter in his footwork'. Lucky for Ormond that he displayed such improvement: Newman College was fielding a tough Irishman, Emmett McGillicuddy, in the inter-collegiate boxing tournament on 2 August, and they appeared in force, expecting their candidate to flatten 'the great bear over at Ormond'.

'The whole of Newman turned up to see McGillicuddy dispose of me . . . he came rushing at me like a wild boar, right at the beginning of the first round, and I pushed out this left and, dear me! . . . his teeth sprayed out all over the ring.' Emmett McGillicuddy was led away, and Weary prepared to represent Melbourne at the inter-varsity boxing in Sydney.

He gained the title, despite a gargantuan five-hour luncheon with Graham Thirkell and the latter's uncle, Sir Hugh Poynter. By the time Weary rolled amiably into the stadium in Rushcutter's Bay, full of steaks, strawberries and cream and red and white wine followed by six large tankards of black and tan, 'everybody was flicking off the last ounce and working on punching bags'.

Watching Melbourne lose the first two bouts, both in the first round, and contemplating his opponent, Humphries, who was said to run miles every day and to sleep 'hard' on the floor in order to retain his reputation as a 'knock-out' king specialising in devastating attacks during the first round, helped sober him up a little.

With some trepidation, he entered the ring, shook hands with Humphries and retired to his swing-out seat in the corner; but when the bell rang, he ambled out good-naturedly to shake hands again, and 'something hit me like a thunderbolt in the midriff. I had two body blows then got smacked under the chin back into my seat'.

Feeling dizzy and sick, he fought merely to survive the next two rounds, although by the third round, he had recovered sufficiently to break Humphries' jaw. 'It was a real slugging match.' Intense rugby training throughout the winter of 1932 had made him particularly fit and tough – that was the season when he could carry the entire scrum

1 *Ernie (l.). Pretty enough for a girl with his ringlets and frills*

2 *A travelling seamstress made the boys' tussore sailor suits and Alice's dress*

3 *Everyone at Stewarton wore boots and shabby clothes. Ernie third from right, back*

4 *On Sundays, they went rabbiting with the dogs secretly*

5 *Ernie (l.) emulated his hero, Deerfoot, and Alice made their fancy dress*

6 *James and Alice at Belle Vue, Benalla, 1922*

7 *Summer in Benalla. Ernie (r.) swam early in the morning before work*

8 *Cpl Dunlop (with Bren gun) saw himself as a gunner, like his great-grandfather. Continuous military training, Seymour*

9 *The pharmacist's apprentice (l.) and schoolteacher Alan*

10 *The Gold Medallist. Graduation, Pharmacy College, February 1929*

11 *Muscular fairy, Melbourne Uni Commem, 1931*

12 *He had a new hero:*
    Sir Thomas Dunhill

13 *With 'wife', Charles Hopkins*

14 *Picnicking on deserted beaches during that never-to-be-forgotten*
    tropical summer

15 *Senior men: (from l.) Charlie Newman, Graham Thirkell,
[unknown], Geoff Hudspeth, Weary*

16 *Edgar King, pioneer in
oesophageal surgery at the Royal
Melbourne Hospital, won three
Jacksonian prizes*

on his back – otherwise, it is doubtful whether he could have prevailed by the end of the bout. The world was still spinning when their team manager 'Huck' Hamilton escorted him back to the dressing-room as Australian Universities' Heavyweight Champion.

Earlier that winter he had measured himself against 'Young' Stribling, nicknamed the 'Georgia Peach', when he visited Australia and boxed at Eddie Miller's gym – a newspaper publicity photograph shows the two of them in smart suits squaring up to each other, surrounded by an admiring crowd. 'I trained with 'Young' Stribling rather nervously . . . on one occasion I achieved a . . . good straight left and knocked him down. I just waited to be murdered.' But Stribling 'got up and danced around me, and hit me very lightly from every angle to show what he could do. There was no . . . retribution about it.'

Stribling could afford to be magnanimous: he was the up- and-coming world heavyweight champion. Perhaps he sensed, too, that medicine and rugby took precedence with Weary: boxing was only another means of exploring his prodigious strength, seeing how far he could push himself. Sporting reminiscences may dominate Weary's accounts of the Ormond years, and the great stack of newspaper cuttings Alice saved is almost exclusively about rugby and boxing, but these activities were always secondary, a necessary and exhilarating counter-balance to the long hours of study.

As he became increasingly involved in hospital work and his final year loomed, Weary exposed himself less and less to situations where his hands might be seriously injured.

Weary rarely used his speed and weight to advantage in the ring. He should have beaten McGilvray 'to a pulp', but 'I never had the killer instinct'.

Ever since witnessing Weary's form at Australian Rules in the winter of 1930, Charlie Hopkins had endeavoured to recruit him to Rugby Union. Though slight and light in weight, Charlie was a good 'hooker' who became secretary to the Melbourne University Rugby Club during his first season.

Weary broke an ankle during an Australian Rules practice match at Scotch College early in the 1931 season and, with his leg in plaster most of that winter, he was not available for selection for the Ormond football team. But towards the end of second term, fourth-year medical student and Australian representative player Gordon Sturtridge combined with Hopkins to persuade him to join the university fourths for a game of rugby.

Four games later, he had scored so many tries, the Melbourne University Rugby Club's selectors put him straight into the firsts for the inter-varsity carnival that August and, following Melbourne's win, he was picked for the Combined Universities' team.

The many photographs which show him leaping to a tremendous height in a line-out disprove Jack Pollard's contention that he 'found trouble jumping in Aussie Rules and played Rugby' after he broke his ankle.[11] Weary himself denied it and confirmed Pollard's statement that he was a line-out specialist. He continued to play in the football team, but rugby now absorbed him totally. When Ormond challenged Trinity to a rugby match during third term, winning by 11 to nil, Weary was singled out as one of the College's three best players. Trinity regarded itself as being top of the tree at rugby, and was somewhat disconcerted at losing this inaugural match when the cup had been presented by one of their own men, Cumbrae Stewart.

At the annual ceremony in Wilson Hall in April 1932, both Weary and Charles received half-blues for their performance on the rugby field the previous year (Weary also collected a half-blue for boxing). A month later, on a wet Saturday at Middle Park, Weary was singled out as one of the 'most noticeable' players, and the following weekend, as lock in the 'Probables' team at the Amateur Sports Ground on 8 May, he was selected to represent Victoria in the match against New South Wales.

The Melbourne University Athletics Club complained that because of the popularity of rugby it was 'losing potential stars'. Weary was not one to let them down: on 18 May he helped Ormond win the athletics for the fifteenth successive time, managing a third in the shot putt, before boarding the overnight train for Sydney with the rest of the Victorian rugby team and the Melbourne University teams, which were also on their way north for the inter-varsity carnival. Brisbane was host during that May vacation.

They were all tired out when they reached Central Station. To save money, the teams jolted north sitting up and packed into second-class carriages. Betty Willmott's most abiding memory of the trip (she continued on to Brisbane for the women's hockey) is that whereas the boys all bagged the luggage racks to sleep in, Weary was too large to fit and he spent the night on the floor in the corridor. Anyone wishing to use the lavatory had first to step over Weary.[12]

The press seized on this willingness to forego comfort as the 'real sporting spirit', particularly when the match showed an unprecedented profit of £20 for a Victorian–New South Wales match. New South Wales supporters had a low opinion of Victorian rugby and only 6500 turned up to watch the match on 21 May: those who did were rewarded with a game which put the southerners 'on the map'.[13]

No Victorian team had ever received such a reception in Sydney. 'Victorian Forwards are Giants!' blared the *NSW Rugby News*. 'The Victorian team to meet New South Wales today is easily the most powerful that has ever represented the State. It includes three Australian representatives, and a number of players who will be closely watched by the Australian selectors . . . Six of the visitors are over six feet . . .'

New South Wales beat them by 26 points to 19, but only, said the press, 'because luck . . . was on their side . . . The Victorians [gave] . . . a display of honest forward work and straight running back attacks'.

After a riotous night at John Ball's Aaron's Exchange Hotel down near the quay, Weary, Gordon Sturtridge and N. Wilson caught the train to Brisbane. Three days later, Weary was one of those 'showing plenty of initiative in their forward raids' on the Exhibition Oval, when Melbourne met Queensland University in the first match of the carnival, 'Dunlop . . . being equal to any forward on the field'. Queensland won 5–0, but only just – the Victorian forwards had made it difficult for their opponents to score.

Sydney University trampled on Melbourne's hopes in the second game, also, but 'Dunlop and Pearson played a fine forward game for the losers' and Weary narrowly missed scoring at the end of the match, when 'the big Dunlop was held up right on the Sydney team's line'.

Fellow medical student Charles Marks had arranged for Weary to stay with his family. Charles's father, a leading Brisbane obstetrician and gynaecologist, and two sisters, were only too happy to join the rest of the university rugby club in fêting the visitors. There were dinners and parties and a memorable expedition in a Black Hawk Stutz to a Surfers Paradise boasting only one hotel and grazing kangaroos, before Melbourne and the new winter term reclaimed the southerners.

One wonders how much time that term was spent on the fourth-year subjects of public health, therapeutics, R & A (surgical) anatomy and pathology (he had already satisfied the course requirements in *materia medica* and pharmacy through graduating from Pharmacy College). It must have taken concentrated effort after the finish of the rugby season to produce 1932 examination results of first class honours in public health and pathology, with second place in pathology, and the required passes in therapeutics and surgical anatomy.

In July, Newman defeated Ormond once again at Australian Rules, despite all the team's efforts and Weary kicking the first goal. Weary regretted that in all his time at Ormond they 'never succeeded in winning the football'. They did better in the rugby, vanquishing both Newman and Trinity. Then, on 19 July, a week after his twenty-fifth birthday, the selectors announced the team to play for Australia in the third Test against the All Blacks: Weary, considered by the Sydney *Sun* 'unlucky to miss the lock place' in the first Test, was in at last. And none too soon, thought the *Sun*: 'His form against New South Wales was brilliant.'

FIVE

Dunlop of Benalla

AFTER A LAST TRAINING RUN on the oval and an exuberant send-off at Spencer Street Station, he boarded the Monday express for Sydney. Overnight, in the local newspapers, he had become 'Dunlop of Benalla', the first Victorian-born rugby player to represent his country. The other three Victorians awaited him in in Sydney, G. L. Sturtridge who played for University with Weary, D. L. Cowper and O. Bridle. None of them had been born in the state.

Weary's rapid rise to International status after only two seasons of rugby union made him 'the "find" of the season'. He had played only fifteen games of rugby in first grade since moving from the fourths in August 1931 to the university team in the inter-varsity carnival. His sixteenth game would see him in the Wallabies' green guernsey, facing the legendary All Blacks.

All the newspapers were full of praise beforehand; but after the Wallabies were defeated by 21 to 13 on 23 July, Alan Hulls hurled brickbats at them from the pages of *Truth*. 'Australian forwards lifeless . . . Dunlop obviously has the makings of a fine lock, but he is very crude.'

'I've got many sad thoughts about that Test,' mused Weary. The Sydney Cricket Ground where they trained was on Bulli soil, which caused cuts and abrasions to develop into very nasty infective running sores. In Weary's case, it was more serious: he developed a 'sort of brawny cellulitis' at the shin and was sent to Howard Bullock, surgeon/ doctor to the Union. This former player for New South Wales fully understood the intense disappointment Weary would suffer should he be pronounced unfit and deprived of his first cap. Despite a temperature of around 39.5°C. and a horribly sore leg, Weary was allowed to take the ground for Australia.

'I remember one or two things very clearly. Once, coming out of the scrum, Syd Malcolm, our half-back, put the ball right on my chest and

67

it just bounced off, I wasn't able to run . . . I also remember getting off-side rather badly, showing my inexperience . . . it wasn't an awfully good Test.'

Why did rugby union appeal to him so much more than his own state's game of Australian Rules football? A reporter encouraged him to discuss this just after his selection in July 1932. It was the team aspect of rugby which appealed to him, he explained. 'The whole team gets into action at one time, and moves like one man in great dashes down the field, striving to defeat the opposing side and put the ball over the line . . . ."Tackling" is more thrilling than anything in the Australian game.'

At the age of 25, Weary discussed the game pragmatically. Sentiment was not universally admired in a tough young Australian student; a romantic approach to so ruggedly masculine a subject as football was too private even to be admitted to one's closest friends. By the time he was in his eighties, he had no inhibitions about describing his almost mystical attitude towards it – 'It was as if I'd played the game in some previous life' – and how the ball would 'find' him, how he was always in the 'right place'. 'I used to really live on a Rugby football field . . . My time of greatest supremacy was the first match [Victoria] ever played versus Queensland. Shortly after the game started, from the kick-off, I ran through the Queensland team and scored in the corner. I'd just taken the ball and gone through the entire team. I scored three times in that match.'

Wherever he was, the ball would 'find' him: he emphasised this point several times. What he did not mention is how he analysed each game and his performance in it; his constant revision of moves and passes and tactics; his rigorous training in the ring and on the field; his powerful physique coupled with a quickness and lightness of foot; his ability to position himself and make very rapid decisions.

Finally, there is one aspect of his play which every team he belonged to knew about and neither Weary nor a newspaper has mentioned: what his rugby-playing contemporaries Colin ('Kiwi') Lowndes and Charles Hopkins called his 'mad elephant act'.[1]

When things were not going well for their team, the other players knew that Weary could be goaded into superhuman effort which would often bag them a try or knock out their opponents. If the opposing side failed to provoke him sufficiently, they understood exactly how to do it – members of his own team have kicked him in the shins to let loose that explosive concentration of energy or, as Colin Lowndes put it, 'we had to "word" one of our flankers to give him a bloody nose'.

Lowndes remembered 'seeing him in a Vic./NSW Interstate match . . . soar up to take the kick off at his fingertips and do his "mad elephant" feat, heading straight for the posts, leaving scattered bodies like chaff laid out cold either side of his path to ground the ball under the posts'.

The term 'mad elephant' is something of a misnomer; anger might fuel the behaviour, but his mind always remained in total control. When he was playing at his peak during the years 1932 to 1934, his superb physical condition, strength, intelligence and will combined with an intuitive grasp of exactly what should happen.

That August, captained by Gordon Sturtridge playing five-eighth and with Weary as lock-forward, Melbourne defeated Sydney University and Queensland University at the Inter-varsity Rugby Union Carnival for the first time.[2] It was Gordon Sturtridge's last year. In 1933 Weary would be captain; by the end of the 1934 season, he would have led his team through the greatest season of rugby the University of Melbourne had known since the club played its first competition game in 1909.

'My treasured memories . . . include my presidency of the Ormond College Students' Club [and] my first Australian Cap for Rugby Union' Weary told a packed auditorium at the University of Western Australia in 1989.[3] Towards the end of 1931, he was elected a member of the 1932 Club General Committee, which played a central role in the regulation of College life and wielded considerable power. It was the voice of Ormond and, inevitably, because of the length of the medical students' course, dominated by that faculty. Of the eight committee members, six were medical students: Weary and Ronald McK. Rome being in their fourth year (although Rome had one more year's residence than Weary), and the other four in their fifth year. The remaining two men were third-year law and commerce.

From 1932 to 1934 Weary was a member of this select group: 'Dunlop of Benalla' had come a long way from the uncertain state school boy who wasn't sure how to reply when asked in 1930, 'Is Benalla High School proud of you?'

'The Club was a microcosm of professional life,' wrote Don Maddocks in his review of the College, 'a place in which the medical student might practise importance and prepare himself for the long task of achieving recognition in the hierarchies of medicine.'[4] It was also exclusively masculine.

College social life generally excluded women, although the Common Room dances each term, the Dramatic Society's play and the annual ball brought the non-residential female members of the College, sisters and girlfriends and Dr Pickens's daughters into the arena. The Women's College was known to Ormond men as 'The Dumpty' (male students also used this word for the lavatory) and, traditionally, men and women strolled around its perimeter path on Sunday afternoons after lunch. Custom decreed that female students tread the path in the opposite direction to the men and that neither sex acknowledge the other. They called it 'triggling'.

The College was the core of their existence and the backbone of the year was the calendar of hearty all-male celebrations common to both university and public life, beginning with the presentation of blues in Wilson Hall each April which heralded the football season.

During the May and August vacations Victoria, New South Wales and Queensland took turns to act as host to the inter-varsity tournaments; second term was busy with the inter-collegiate football and rugby matches in June and July which culminated in the annual Sports' Dinner; and each October third term brought the Ormond Regatta and the Valedictory Dinner. Not very serious rowing competition in the Morrison Fours was followed by the challenge eights, an excuse for the four teams, including Weary's Richmond Razzberries, to mess about in boats in one last glorious burst of tomfoolery before settling to the deadly serious business of examinations.

The Club 'flowed into the network' said Don Maddocks. The network was important: it eased the career path of its younger members. Each year's top graduates left Ormond's halls for work as junior residents in the wards of the Melbourne Hospital, where they had completed their clinical training under the critical eyes of its eminent specialists before graduation. Many of the latter were also Ormond men, and until the honorary system was abolished in the 1970s, they taught without payment as part of their responsibilities.

Weary trod a well-worn path: committee member in 1932, President of the Club in 1933, junior resident at the Melbourne in 1935 and not only senior resident in 1936, but relieving Medical Superintendent during the occasional absences from the hospital of John Bolton. When he arrived in London to prepare for the second part of his fellowship examinations at the Royal College of Surgeons in 1938, he carried with him a sheaf of letters of introduction from old Ormond men to eminent English surgeons and academics and to his hero, that former pharmacist and Ormond man, Sir Thomas Dunhill.

Sporting victories and defeats feature prominently in the pages of the *Ormond Chronicle*. Despite the presence of theology students, religion is relegated to odd corners, and serious interest in music, literature and the classics emerges only intermittently.

Weary might read poetry for his private pleasure and Charles Hopkins play his violin, but the overwhelming impression is that whilst Ormond acclaimed its Rhodes' Scholars, it was not a College which exalted intellectual activities. The latter implied a dangerous and idealistic acquaintance with left-wing politics – which, in that troubled decade, could mean Communism – and few Ormond men were attracted to a doctrine preaching bloody revolution and the overthrow of the existing social order.

Even the acknowledged *literati* who inhabited study I 40 were pretty conservative, although one of their number in 1932 was responsible for bringing Dr Herbert Vere Evatt to speak to the Labour Club and thereby triggering the debate some weeks later which culminated in a near riot.[5]

The Depression held Australia in an iron grip, stirring the unemployed into riots and strikes and causing suffering such as had not been seen since the 1890s. University colleges appeared to be islands of privilege and plenty amongst the slums of Carlton, Fitzroy and Collingwood.

Weary was attracted by neither Communism nor Fascism, but shared with others at Melbourne University the conviction that noisy 'Reds' should not be allowed to besmirch the university's reputation. Given Weary's upbringing and his determination to succeed in a conservative profession, radical ideas were unlikely to appeal to him.

Not surprisingly, socialist doctrine found a ready sympathy amongst some of the theology students and 'Communism was making a distinct impact' on a few. But the Labour Club's noisy politics attracted a good deal of attention in the community and stalwart types like Weary were furious that 'a very small minority of Communist sympathisers . . . used to achieve tremendous publicity about the red university'. Eventually, this caused so much comment that 'the Chancellor [said] that the public needn't be too concerned: the university was well able to look after itself – and there was always the university lake!' he recalled. 'Who could resist a challenge like that?'

The students had already been enraged by the Labour Club meeting at which 'Doc' Evatt treated a capacity audience to a jeremiad against 'Honest Joe' Lyons's desertion to the capitalists as leader of the new United Australia Party. In addition, a resolution that Communism should not be discussed at the university had been carried at a meeting of the Students' Representative Council.

Defiantly, the club invited a noted Communist academic from Sydney, Professor John Anderson, to speak. Then, the University Debating Society gambled on repeating that success with a debate on the merits of Communism versus Fascism and booked the huge public lecture theatre in the Arts building. Usually, these events were sparsely attended only by members, but with such an emotional subject, they expected a good turn-out. They were right. On Monday, 3 May, the lecture theatre overflowed with a crowd baying for blood.

A key speaker for the Left was to be a young left-wing firebrand named Sam White.* Anticipating provocation, the champions of the Right made their dispositions: Weary, with a group from the university boxing and rowing fraternities, was strategically placed in the first row in front of the speaker's lectern. At a signal from Trinity College's Vin Youngman, they were to seize Sam White and convey him immediately to the lake.

But the crafty apologists for Communism saved him until last, employing their lesser fish, Geoff Vellacott (an Ormond theology student) and Ingwerson (nicknamed the 'Baron') to speak outrageously of a Union Jack dripping with the martyred blood of workers and similar heresies calculated to arouse the ire of their listeners. The impatient audience sat there, grinding their teeth, and the strong-arm crew controlled their wrath with difficulty until White stood up to speak.

To their amazement he put forward arguments so innocuous, they were hard pressed to find anything provocative enough to justify a ducking. In desperation, Youngman gave the signal when the word 'Communism' was uttered, and Weary and his crew seized White and bore him swiftly down the aisle towards the door.

---

* Sam White became a journalist and the Paris correspondent of the London *Evening Standard*.

Great was their consternation when they forced their way into the open air to find a crowd of more than a hundred Carlton unemployed, waving broken bottles and life preservers. 'In no time, the only two left on their feet were Berris Butcher and I using Sam White as a shield, battering our way through. Even Sam White was yelling at that point.'

They broke away from the mob, still heading for the lake when they ran into a squad of police. But on putting White down and explaining sheepishly that it was only a university prank, they were bemused to hear the police suggest that they could 'get on with it' once the unemployed had been seen off the grounds.

It had become too serious for that, however; the three of them decided that retreat was more prudent.

Meanwhile, Professor Agar, the President of the Professorial Board, had restored some order with an impassioned plea for freedom of speech and fair play, turned the mood of the audience and reconvened the meeting. Where previously there had been a united desire to vanquish those speaking for Communism, schism now prevailed. Sam White was allowed to regain the platform and finish his speech.

Half the room howled for action; the other half for toleration. At the end of the evening, the crowd erupted into outraged violence. Fights broke out; one of Weary's party, a strong rower named Jock Adam, was knocked down the staircase as they left the room and Weary ran a gauntlet of stony stares, although his size and reputation in the ring obviously dissuaded any would-be assailants from attacking him and he regained his bedroom without further ugly scenes.

Scarcely had he dropped off to sleep than a thunderous knocking on his door announced an ordinarily quiet, pleasant theological student who shouted that he wished to fight Weary at 6 am the following morning, bare-fisted. 'You goddam fool,' growled Weary. 'If you want to fight me, you'll fight at a respectable hour and with gloves. Get yourself a second.'

Before the rest of the College were out of bed next morning, Geoff Hudspeth accompanied Weary to the university pavilion, gloves were provided, and Weary tapped the theolog around gently for four rounds. Then, honour satisfied, they shook hands.

Many years later, a friend teased Weary about being a Bulldog Drummond in his younger days; but incidents like this one scarcely justify comparison to such a stereotype. There was no bullying; they were animated by pride in the reputation of their university; and they were children of an era which continued to hold up empire builders as heroes.

That same day, a group besieged the offices of *Farrago* and threw Sam White, Geoff Vellacott and a third man, John Harris, in the lake, but Weary refused to take part: 'Not in cold blood,' he said.

Weary's seniority in 1932 and 1933 did not release him from the pressure to achieve high marks in examinations and keep his place at or near the top of his year. When he was offered a place in the Australian Rugby Union team that was to tour South Africa in 1933, he refused: 'as a scholarship boy' he could not afford to take a year off and he referred to this as one of two hurtful decisions he had to make while at Ormond. The other was when he decided not to aply for a Rhodes Scholarship on the advice of Dr Picken, who thought it inadvisable for Weary to go back to junior status at Oxford.

No one in Ormond was unaffected by the Depression, but scholarship holders, particularly, balanced on a knife edge of uncertainty. The high value attached to membership of the Ormond brotherhood was given an even keener edge by the realisation that times were hard, money short and scholarship places eagerly sought. Picken did not give too many a second chance if he believed that they did not perform to the required standard in examinations, and there were plenty of clever students waiting to take the place of someone found wanting.

That summer, when examinations were over, Weary did not work for Garrick or McCall Say: with Charles Hopkins, he caught the train to Queensland. From Brisbane, they trundled up to Townsville, dividing the best part of two days and nights between a poky carriage and their second-class sleeper. The Hopkins's sprawling bungalow on The Strand was to be their base for the next six weeks.

Charles took him up the coast to Cairns and then inland to stay on the Heale family's property on the Atherton Tablelands. Weary has never been able to resist a challenge, especially one involving extraordinary physical effort, and he accepted a bet that he couldn't swim across Lake Eacham and back, a distance which he calculated to be about a kilometre and a half. His ambition almost outstripped his capabilities. These lakes were popularly said to be 'bottomless', and although a metre or so down it was icy, the hot sun had warmed the surface of the water until the temperature was almost unbearable. He only just managed to reach the shore on the return journey; no one realised how nearly he had not made it until he doubled up, streaming perspiration and suffering from severe cramps and heatstroke. This was the third time he had come close to drowning: once in the Sheepwash Creek, once in the river at Benalla during an underwater swimming competition when he became entangled in a fallen tree and now in Lake Eacham.

A day or so later, after everyone dined unwisely on a boiled tongue which had gone off in the heat, Weary and Hazel Heale had to drive at speed to the local bush hospital and borrow a stomach pump, stopping frequently along the way as the effects of acute food poisoning brought on vomiting. Weary helped the local doctor pump out the stomachs at the homestead and then washed out his own. The effects did not disappear for two or three weeks. For months, he could summon up the sound and feel of the seawater slapping beneath him when he had to hang himself repeatedly over the stern to cope with persistent diarrhoea, as later they sailed steadily up to Dunk Island then zig zagged from island to island and out to the Reef back south to Townsville.

It was the longest holiday he had ever had, a 'magic vacation tour' on which Charles 'sailed us up the coast, handling the navigation and the kerosene marine engine with skill and experience' and back again. Magnetic Island, Palm Island with its Aboriginal settlement (where Weary was photographed with an old Aborigine nicknamed 'King Tiger'), Hinchinbrook Island and on to the 'scented paradise of an almost uninhabited Dunk Island', owned by the Hopkins family, for Christmas: he had never been to sea before, never seen anything to compare with it.

'Unforgettable, unforgotten, the unbelievable violet, cobalt, green and opalescent sea and the magic night phosphorescence of glowing silver as the dark water was stirred by the leap of gleaming kingfish, or dipped to bright flaming rings by successive strokes of the oars in the dinghy.'[6] The memory was as vivid when he described it over half a century later as it was when they celebrated the bright new year of 1933.

Wilson Hall overflowed with students that 7 April in 1933 when Weary walked onto the platform to receive a Full Blue for Rugby. It was Commencement, and as President of the Club, his evenings were monopolised by initiation activities; as a member of the Students'

Representative Council, he was involved in broader issues affecting the whole of the student body; and as a Representative player for the Victorian Rugby Union, he had already begun training more intensively than any other year. Medicine, Surgery and Obstetrics and Gynaecology, the final year subjects, had to be fitted in as well.

Weary's tendency to collect more than 'his fair share of injuries' was well known to the sporting press, who mentioned it at intervals. His enthusiasm for boxing was waning. As a fifth-year medical student, he was now spending more time in the hospitals and was reluctant to injure his hands in any way that might jeopardise a career in surgery. Nevertheless, when the adrenalin was flowing during a match, at times he showed a reckless disregard for his own safety.

The rugby season opened with a match at Middle Park in which Weary played for the Victorian 'Probables' team against the 'Possibles', so that the selectors could decide the positions for the match against Australia in May.

During that first term, he was completing the required spell of obstetrics at the Women's Hospital in Grattan Street, Carlton, and on the first Friday in May, Weary had his first delivery. It was twins. Such an euphoric occasion for both mother and doctor made him late for football practice. Borrowing Charles Hopkins's bicycle, he peddled furiously up Grattan Street, the late afternoon sun full in his face. Weary did not notice the car coming straight for him until it was too late. He applied the brakes. They failed. And he found himself flying over the car and landing face down in a rockery.

Charles's bicycle had been reduced to a heap of crumpled metal on impact and Weary, blood streaming down his face from a broken nose, was helped up by a very worried driver. Never willing to confess to feeling pain, Weary made light of the accident and he recalls saying, 'Oh, don't worry – it was my own bloody fault!' (This rash honesty was rewarded by the car's owner sending him the repair bill, which he had great difficulty paying.)

He was diagnosed as having a compound fracture of the nose and concussion. Someone took care of the nose and lectured him on the foolishness of his ways. Weary did not listen: he was due to play for Victoria against Australia in four days time.

At the Motordrome the following Tuesday, when the Victorian Representative team ran onto the ground to do battle with the Wallabies, the crowd greeted his appearance with a rousing cheer.

Victoria fielded its strongest team ever against the full might of the

Wallabies to draw the match at 12–all, the Australian team's last-minute try saving them the ignominy of defeat. The 3000 spectators and the sports writers were in ecstasy. It looked as if the southerners might vanquish New South Wales, despite the absence of three Victorian Representative players in South Africa.

That night, the Victorian Rugby Union exuberantly farewelled the Wallabies at a ball in Leonards' Café in St Kilda. Weary then put in a full day's work at the Children's Hospital and left it to the diehards to wave to the *Ulysses* as it steamed down Port Phillip Bay at 4 pm on its outward journey to Cape Town. Charles had persuaded him to see the physician, Sidney Sewell, about his concussion, but apart from a lingering headache and throbbing pain in the centre of his face – which he was determined to ignore – it was work and play as usual.

In their last match before leaving for New South Wales, Victoria played 'The Rest'. Weary was breakaway and, with Phelan, 'was spectacular in the loose and line-outs . . . after the first ten minutes, Dunlop gave his best game to date'.

When the Victorian team drew out of Spencer Street Station that Thursday evening, bound for the first interstate game of the season, its reputation was already being discussed in the Sydney newspapers: 'there is now a definite menace from the south to the . . . supremacy of New South Wales'. And on the billboards at Central Station next morning, the sporting headlines warned, 'Win not certain. Victoria Ready for Fray'.

On Saturday 3 June, the rugby faithful paid their one and sixpences to watch New South Wales play Victoria on the North Sydney Oval. 'When the teams filed onto the field, there was a gasp from the crowd. The Victorian forwards might have formed an All Black pack, so big were they. Dunlop, Perrin, Lang and Arnold are magnificent specimens . . . New South Wales seemed flustered by the All Black tactics . . .'

They had been training for seven weeks, even undertaking a 'special course of physical culture'. Playing with the forwards was the New Zealander and former All Black hooker, Jessep, one of Weary's adversaries in the third Test the previous year. Throughout that 1933 season, commentators and sports writers repeatedly would liken the eight to an All Black pack. 'Jessep has done wonders with them. They are big and fast and can ruck like the devil.' At 16 stone 6 pounds and 6 foot 2 inches, Tom Perrin as lock-forward was the heaviest; Weary, at 6 foot 4 inches and 14 stone 10 pounds was next. Weary and Perrin were both Internationals. With Dewar they formed a formidable front row.

The forwards carried the game. Jessep had trained them well. It was a 'new era', said the *Sunday Observer*, 'the rise of Victoria to a power . . . capable of football in a manner that would not disgrace the high traditions of the home State'. The official programme displayed photographs of Jessep, Dunlop, Perrin and Ward. They did not disappoint the crowd.

The North Sydney Oval was covered with the same Bulli soil which had caused Weary such problems during the third Test. Iron-hard, and 'with great cracks about an inch across', the Victorians attributed to it the large number of injuries they sustained that day. Scarcely a man did not limp off when the whistle blew. Perrin and Burke had sprained ankles; Jessep an injured thigh; Weary's face was badly battered; and two others were doubtful starters for Monday. Dr Ward, the team's manager, summoned two extra players from Melbourne.

Bruce Judd – 'Dinty' to his mates – was a great, tough Irishman, over 16 stone in weight, and the only forward in the New South Wales pack who performed well in the match. Weary and he were old rivals from interstate games and the third Test. Not long before the final bell, Weary had the ball and was breaking through when someone caught his foot in a tackle and Dinty 'jumped on the back of my shoulders and neck and skidded my face for about two yards' along the compacted Bulli soil. 'I still remember Dinty Judd saying in slow, measured tones, "Well, Weary, you're down and you're down to stay".'

Streaming blood, the skin and flesh stripped from the bone and Bulli soil ground in its place, Weary's nose was a mess. He 'never had a sound skin' on his nose again.

Next day, the Rugby Union took them to Bulli for an outing. On Monday, at Manly Oval, the 'bandaged giants' trounced New South Wales 14 to 8.

Photographs of the match show Weary's face partly obscured by strapping which failed to protect him from further provocation by the opposing team. Ron Walden, also a forward and the New South Wales boxing champion, persisted in putting his hand out and rubbing Weary's nose whenever he was nearby. When Weary warned him off, he took no notice, so the next time the hand came out, Weary swung his arm up savagely. Unfortunately for Victorian team-mate Tom Perrin, Walden ducked adroitly and Tom's eyebrow was split open by the force of Weary's blow. 'Ron Walden kept away from me after that.' The referee did not notice.

Weary's revenge was victory. At the final bell, 'the Victorians jumped gleefully into the air and their manager ran on to the field to congratulate them'. They celebrated through the night at Aaron's Exchange Hotel and, in the early hours of the morning, polished off dozens of oysters in Dinty Judd's great mobile oyster bar. He was a generous loser.

'All Black in physique, All Black in mode of play!' said Alan Hulls in that week's *Truth*. This time there was no criticism of Weary's crude play – Hulls singled him out as one of the stars of the forward pack, praising the massed attacks of Dunlop, Perrin and Dewar.

The Victorian team returned jubilantly to Melbourne, having made history by defeating New South Wales for the first time on their home ground. It was only the fifteenth game between the states: competition was just forty-four years old, and Victoria's previous wins occurred in 1894 and 1929. What greater praise could be bestowed than a Sydney journalist's parting remarks: 'more essentially Rugby Union even than the All Blacks.'

The winter term was no different from any other: training in the early evening, football or rugby on Saturdays, playing either for his college or his state. Weary passed on all he learned from Jessep's coaching to his Ormond team, for now that Sturtridge had gone, he was captain.

That August the inter-varsity rugby union carnival was in Sydney and Adelaide University took part for the first time. Melbourne beat inexperienced Adelaide by 28 points to 6, but despite their hard training, Weary's fifteen was defeated in its matches with Queensland and Sydney.

Weary was chosen to captain the Combined Universities' team which played Metropolitan, led by his old arch-rival in the New South Wales forward pack, Dinty Judd. The newspapers seized on this as another historic occasion: the first time all four universities were represented in an Australian Universities' team. They named Weary as the outstanding forward and, as usual, commented on his prominence in the line-outs. His entire allegiance was to rugby this vacation and he did not fight in the inter-varsity boxing championships held in Melbourne that August.

He returned to the lengthening spring days of third term, and his duties as Club Chairman at Ormond's Annual Ball, held for the first time in the College, and the Valete Dinner. The Club gave him his earliest experience in public speaking, but his soft voice and quiet delivery, not much changed over the years, prompted Sir Benjamin Rank's comment that 'what he has to say is much better than the way he says it'.

Many years of practice and a microphone improved his style, but he did not start out as a naturally talented speaker. Nonetheless, he presented written addresses well. Experience and love of a good story taught him when to drop something into the narrative and he developed various techniques over the years in order to catch and hold the wrapt attention and good humour of his audiences.

That night, his speech farewelling the leavers and proposing the toast to the College and its Master was described as 'somewhat metaphysical' by the *Chronicle*'s reporter – and one suspects that he may have rambled, a fault which occurred if he did not have time to prepare a speech carefully.

After this dinner, Weary handed over the Chairmanship for 1934 to Jock Adam, although he agreed to stay on the committee for a further year when Dr Picken was not enthusiastic about the change. The Digger considered Adam to be 'a bit of a wild man' – Sir Archibald Glen pointed out that in the context of the times, this merely meant a capacity to play harder than his peers – whereas Weary was always amused that the Master regarded him as a 'sober, responsible character', better at controlling undergraduate affairs. But Weary was adamant: the past two years had been rather too full of extra-curricular activities for comfort.

Despite his good results in 1932, with first class honours in both Pathology and Public Health, his 1933 subjects would be a heavy load and he had no intention of doing poorly. Weary's record card in the University of Melbourne Archives gives him second class honours in Pathology and second place in the class in 1932: Weary insisted that this was a clerical error, as after his first year his marks were never less than first class honours.[7]

Examinations for the final year medical students were not held in November 1933; Henry Searby had changed the timing and structure of the course, so that for a few years from 1934, finals were held in March and the months until August taken up with special subjects in various hospitals, stretching it out to six years.

Sadly, Weary declined the captaincy of the Combined Universities Rugby Union tour of Japan the following February in order to study through the long summer holidays. He resented greatly not being able to enjoy what would have been a consolation prize for missing the Wallaby tours of South Africa and New Zealand.

Two months swotting with Charles Hopkins in The Nook, Aunt Lil's house in Elsternwick, did not improve his mood. By Christmas he was so 'browned off' that when the Superintendent of the Ballarat Base Hospital offered him a job as a resident, he took it. He admits it was an unusual appointment, but 'they were desperate for residents and I wasn't far from being qualified'. Until now, his role in the operating theatre had been that of an observer; overnight, his superiors turned him into an assistant surgeon who was detailed to perform under supervision simple, routine operations, such as tonsillectomies, and straightforward obstetrics.

Off-duty hours were spent studying. Never a gambler, Weary resisted becoming part of 'a fiendish poker club' run by other hardened characters in the hospital until the night before he was to return to Melbourne, when they persuaded him to join a 'grand binge'. They raised the stakes to horrendous heights and he lost every penny of his wages. It was a gloomy financial start to his last academic year.

When the results of the final examinations were announced in late March, Weary had first-class honours in medicine, surgery, and obstetrics and gynaecology, coming second in his year and winning the Fulton Scholarship in Obstetrics and Gynaecology. The last was worth a welcome sum of some £30. Rank carried off the Jamieson Prize in Clinical Medicine, but only Weary and Medwyn Hutson achieved first-class honours in every subject.

There are some interesting parallels between the early academic careers of Weary and Thomas Dunhill. Both were 21 when they graduated with their diplomas of pharmacy; and being the products of country schools, each had to cram the equivalent of a matriculation Latin course in order to study medicine. Dunhill was also one of only two in his year to gain first class honours in the Final examinations; and both men carried off the top award in Obstetrics and Gynaecology – in Dunhill's case, the Exhibition, which by Weary's time had become the Fulton Scholarship. Now Weary would follow Dunhill by entering the Melbourne Hospital as a resident.

Benalla and his parents claimed him for a few days' holiday. Alice made sure that the *Benalla Standard* told the district of her younger son's latest success, and she proudly added one more clipping to her store. Alice, James and devoted Aunt Lil were always in the background; love, pride and admiration were uncritically lavished upon him and he could always count on their encouragement, though he had moved beyond their understanding.

Not everything was approved, however. They were greatly disturbed one 'swot vac.' when he smuggled home a human pelvis and finished its dissection before his anatomy examinations, agreeing that he should bury it deeply and secretly in the back garden immediately he had finished with it.

On one of Weary's holidays in Benalla, indulgent Aunt Lil provided her Standard car and the wherewithal for driving lessons. Shrewdly, he sat his test there rather than in Melbourne and thereafter, he drove as if he had a country road to himself.

Weary plunged back into the hectic sporting life of second term. Even a cursory reading of Alice's book and the yellowing newspaper reports of his 1934 activities shows that he lived life at the gallop. Inter-collegiate athletics were a minor distraction from rugby training with the other Victorian representative players and his work as captain of Melbourne University's rugby team.

That June, Sydney was less remarkable for rugby than Weary's gambling successes. Early in the train journey, he acquired the bank in an all-night game of *vingt et un* and he held it all the way to Albury. 'Even the conductor was £5 down to the bank'. When the train pulled into Central Station, Weary had pocketed winnings of £20. He had recouped his Ballarat losses.

It was fortunate for the producers and cast of J. M. Barrie's one-act play *Shall We Join the Ladies?* on 31 July, that this event preceded the finals of the university boxing championships, otherwise their butler, Edward Dunlop, might not have cut such a 'graceful figure'.[8] Peter Jelbart, 'a big, strapping oarsman' a good deal younger than Weary, had challenged him for the heavyweight title and the championships took place in the university pavilion later that week. Before the bout, Jelbart's father came up to Weary to wish him luck and suggested that his son was not quite up to the title-holder yet, which Weary interpreted as a hint not to knock the younger man about too much.

By the end of the second round, he 'had him cold and could have knocked him out', but he felt diffident about doing so when the father was sitting in the front row. He decided to coast along. With thirty seconds remaining in the fourth round and Peter, rather sick and dizzy, in a clinch with his head down low on Weary's chest, 'he suddenly shot his head up like a battering ram and completely smashed my face'. The final bell was about to go and Weary, ahead on points, knew he could last the few seconds easily, but Sid Sherrin, the referee, took one horrified look at the blood gushing down and awarded the decision to Jelbart on a technical knock-out.

Weary was furious and disappointed that he had not been allowed to finish the round; in professional boxing, this decision would have been disqualified and he would have retained his title, but in amateur boxing there is no disqualification and therefore no point in appealing. Jelbart was now Melbourne University heavyweight champion.

Weary had yet another broken nose, this time a central facial fracture with a broken upper jaw which required immediate and expert attention by the surgeon Tom Miller. The All Blacks were already in Australia, they were playing New South Wales the following Saturday, 4 August, and Weary had been selected to play in the first Test in Sydney a week later.

The Sydney *Telegraph* photograph shows him with a swollen and pudding-like face when he appeared in a practice game on the Sydney Cricket Ground just over a week after the boxing. Every time he bent down, the pain was excruciating.

Along with other interstate Australian team members and the mighty All Blacks, Weary was put up at the Wentworth Hotel. 'It was an awesome sight when you walked down to breakfast . . . two great tables of All Blacks sitting there like Achilles and his band. And no one would lift his head from his plate.' Each morning Weary greeted this 'soundless phalanx' and walked on until one of their number, Beau Cottrell, caught him up in the hotel corridor to explain that Geddes, the manager, had forbidden them to fraternise with the opposing side. 'You'll find us very friendly after the match,' he said.

Weary shrugged. 'O.K. Beau. You go and tell your manager that the fact I say good morning to you doesn't mean that I won't try to knock your bloody heads off on Saturday.'

The New Zealanders were planning to deprive him of the chance. Many years later in the Auckland Club, the 1934 captain and half-back, Frank Kilby, confessed to Weary how he had arranged for Australia's dangerous line-out forward to be removed. Two All Black forwards, Don Max and A.(Bubbs) Knight, were lined up; and fairly early in the match Don Max pinned him at two points, 'somewhere behind the shoulder and the hip', and Bubbs Knight let fly expertly with his elbow. Weary's nose was knocked flat once more and streaming blood. Alec

Ross, the Australian team captain, tried to persuade Weary to go off. 'Do me a favour,' said Weary. 'I don't want to leave this ground until I've settled a score.'

He was allowed to go on playing; but every time he bent down in a scrum, his nose gushed blood and, upright, his breathing caused bubbling and frothing and his vision was obscured. Bubbs Knight was a giant seventeen-stone abbatoir worker with cauliflower ears and a battered face displaying his own record of broken noses. At last Weary marked his man and moved in. He put his hands behind the back of his head and kneed him in the face – 'a pretty vicious thing to do. I'd never done anything like that before, but when you've had your nose broken as an exercise . . .'

When the injured forward refused to leave the ground and play resumed, Weary found, to his horror, 'it was a decent old pork butcher named Jacky Hore. I'd got the wrong man.'

The press called this first Test a 'grim tussle' and described the 'new, grimmer intensity about the wedge-like drive of the forwards' during the second half.[9] There was more than one private battle in progress that day: J. D. Kelaher (NSW three-quarters) and his opposite number amongst the All Blacks, G. Hart, 'resumed their private war, where they left it at armistice time last Saturday' (when New South Wales was beaten by the All Blacks). It was 'one of the dirtier matches' Weary ever played in.

When he returned to the dressing room after the match he cleaned up his face and set his freshly re-broken nose by inserting a toothbrush up each nostril – after draining the usual two bottles of beer awaiting him on top of his locker 'by way of an anaesthetic'. He had no alternative: he didn't dare go near his surgeon, Tom Miller, who had forbidden participation in 'rough sports'. (Later in the year, it took a further, fifth, battering when a football thrown by another Ormond rugby player, Jock Frew, accidentally hit him full in the face. A photograph taken afer the Rugby Premiership shows a very crooked profile indeed.)

By Monday Weary was back in Melbourne and leading the university team in their first match of the inter-varsity rugby carnival against Sydney. They lost that day and again on Wednesday against Queensland, but were victorious in the Friday fixture against Adelaide.

Their reward was the Kanematsu Cup, which had been donated to the Australian Universities' team when it won at Koshien on its tour of Japan earlier in the year. Kanematsu Limited presented it for 'perpetual competition between the universities of Adelaide and Melbourne', and the competition would seem richly ironic a decade later. Weary was unable to lead the Combined Universities' team against Victoria at Olympic Park on Saturday 18 August; he was anxious to give his nose an opportunity to heal before taking the train to Sydney for the second Test, which was to be played on the Sydney Cricket Ground the following Saturday.

But on the evening before the Test, Weary was running a high temperature and shivering with infuenza. Even a rub down with vinegar and water by the team's trainer and a present of a bottle of overproof Jamaica rum from Gordon Shaw, the President of the Rugby Union, failed to revive him. Huddled miserably in a greatcoat, he watched from the sidelines while Australia drew the match 3–all to win the Bledisloe Cup.

Next day, he was well enough to share the rum with Bubbs Knight and Don Max, who then had to be 'practically carried on stretchers' when the time came for the All Blacks to sail. The two teams roared out 'Now is the Hour' while the ship slipped away from the docks, then Weary caught the Sunday night express back to Melbourne in time to begin his last, short third term and lead the university rugby team into the final phase of the competition for the Dewar Shield.

One of the team's vice presidents and its self-appointed, unofficial 'coach', was bookseller A. H. Spencer of the Hill of Content bookshop in Bourke Street. Spencer believed passionately in the British Empire, rugby, and the ability of Weary to lead his team to victory. He wrote letters of advice and encouragement to Weary almost weekly and spoke to him often on the telephone throughout the rugby season. Weary was a favourite of Spencer's, who was as generous with books as he was with advice on University's performance when Weary dropped into the shop on Bourke Street hill.

'You must stir your lads up to win,' he had exhorted Weary that July. 'I would give my best shirt and boots, yes, and singlet, to see "Varsity" win the competition.'

The grand final took place that 29 September on a damp and dismal Saturday at Middle Park. Weary played a conspicuous and 'hard-working game' as breakaway, particularly in the line-outs. At one stage he brought down two dangerous backs, the Miller brothers, in the same tackle. His one attempt at a try was disallowed when the referee ruled a forward pass, and the Queenslander, Minnis, was the only team member to score. But it was as an inspirational captain, a born leader capable of motivating his team to victory, that Spencer most admired him.

To the intense delight of the team and their supporters, University beat Melbourne 5 nil. Spencer's joy was expressed in boyish, two-inch high letters in his congratulatory letter: 'HOO-RAY, HOO-RAY, HOO-RAY, HOO-RAY'.[10]

'That you were able to command their *affection* to the extent that you did, augurs well for your future in life,' he wrote. 'Gain the affection of those around one . . . and success comes with it.'

It was only the second time University had won the Premiership since 1910; they would not win it again until 1959.

For most of the university, final examinations began in late September that year, but the sixth-year medical students, who had spent the months between their finals in March and the end of August working in Melbourne hospitals, regarded the rather perfunctory *viva* examination they sat as a gesture only. Whilst they were now free to do as they pleased until January, when the lucky ones would be appointed to residencies in the Melbourne and Alfred hospitals, few could afford to be idle. John Adey, psychiatrist and Superintendent of the Receiving House at Royal Park, came to Weary's rescue with a temporary job as a resident.

Adey was a excellent teacher and Weary found the work interesting, observing almost every kind of insanity under Adey's guidance. He was installed in a house and given a paraphrenic housekeeper who could be kept fairly sane providing Weary ate and appreciated her food. Unfortunately, the more he ate, the more she cooked, and often he had to dispose of it secretly once she had gone to bed. This, the sickly, penetrating stench of the paraldehyde administered each night to knock out the patients and ensure quiet wards full of still figures under red coverlets, and John Adey attempting to teach him hypnosis were the more abiding memories he had of this locum at Royal Park.

All Melbourne was *en fête* in October. They celebrated a century of European settlement with fireworks and bunting and illuminations in the presence of a royal duke.

They had the Poet Laureate, John Masefield, to tell them how fortunate they were to be part of such a glorious Empire and to read to them in his fine English voice his tribute to the 'Men of Anzac', to talk of sacrifice and blazing heat.

Masefield was lionised by all sections of society, with receptions and lectures in the Town Hall and at the university, where an honorary degree was bestowed on him. He visited its colleges, and Weary folded up his more than six foot length on the floor near the white-haired poet's chair, remembering the words of 'A Consecration' from *Saltwater Ballads* so vividly down the years that he would quote from this poem when he returned from his own war of sacrifice.

The bells of St Paul's Cathedral peeled out on 18 October when Prince Henry, Duke of Gloucester, arrived on a state visit to Australia; he was entertained lavishly at dinners and functions and a State Ball at Government House.

Not half a mile from its gates, on Armistice Day, he solemnly dedicated the Shrine of Remembrance to the memory of those who served and died in defence of freedom in the Great War. It must have been uppermost in the minds of some who stood there that morning and heard the silvery notes of the 'Last Post' drift across the parkland and the watching crowds that another war was slowly brewing, and that Billy Hughes had reason to cry out to the people that 'the dove of peace has fled'.

Professor Buckmaster and Mr Gordon Gordon-Taylor, the English examiners from the Royal College of Surgeons, returned to Australia in November 1934 to conduct the written and oral primary examinations in physiology and anatomy for the fellowship of the Royal College of Surgeons of England. Weary and Rank presented themselves as candidates, exploiting the loophole in the regulations which they had tumbled to when they were prosectors in 1931.

Forty-five sat the written papers on 29 November and the *viva* four days later, and of the twenty-two who were successful, 15 were from Melbourne. Weary 'enjoyed, so far as a fox enjoys a hunt, the meticulous . . . examination' by Gordon-Taylor and Professor Buckmaster.

By passing the primary examination, they also achieved the primary fellowship of the Royal Australasian College of Surgeons and the first part of the MS (Melbourne). Rank, John Bolton and he celebrated their success with the remains of the Jamaica rum that had been the downfall of Bubbs Knight and Don Max. Whereas Weary was untroubled by the binge, Rank was so ill, that when he accompanied his father – who had come to Ormond for the first and only time in order to thank the Master for having his son – to Dr Picken's study, he 'could see the carpet rotating and waves of nausea' swept over him.

On 22 December, Weary graduated MB BS. The Depression and the extended course had taken its toll. His year was the smallest number of medical students to graduate, just thirty-eight filing up to bow before the Deputy Chancellor, Sir James Barrett, and receive their certificates embellished with the seal of the University of Melbourne.

He was through. He had worked so hard, for so many years, that the end of his course gave him no great sense of achievement: and graduation lacked savour. He was twenty-six and had been studying since he was seventeen. There were four more years in hospitals before he would be eligible to sit his fellowship. The Primary results had given him more pleasure.

Time to spend a teetotal Christmas in Benalla, to work off Alice's vast meals with slashing games of tennis, go to the 'talkies' and idle away the days before 1935 summoned him to the Melbourne Hospital.

Six

'Nulla Vestigia Retrorsum'

IN JANUARY, WEARY WAS appointed a junior resident medical officer to the Melbourne Hospital for an annual salary of £50 plus full board. Eighteen graduates, the best in their year, were assigned to the Melbourne, the next twelve to the Alfred Hospital. Here, under the supervision of the hospital's honorary surgeons and physicians, they would gain further practical training in their chosen fields.

'When I first went to the Melbourne [in 1935] . . . I chose a chap named William Hailes . . . ' As one of the two top students, Weary was able to request the honorary for whom he wished to work, in this case the Senior Surgeon to In-Patients and head of the unit, W. A. Hailes. It was he who had devised and supervised the dissections Weary and Rank prepared as prosectors to the Royal College of Surgeons in 1931.

The relationship between an honorary and his resident, teacher and pupil, was a very personal one, 'strong and helpful', with a resulting pride and a continuing interest in furthering the younger doctor's career.

The honorary system of hospital management evolved when hospitals were charity institutions; top surgeons and physicians attended the poor for nothing, whilst their private patients paid fees and were treated in private hospitals. The resident medical staff gained valuable post-graduate training in the various specialties, but this proved to be an inadequate management system when the charitable institutions ceded their responsibilities for funding medical care to the State after the Second World War.

Now, teaching is divided between the university medical departments and the consultants, who are paid both to attend patients in the public hospitals and to assist with teaching the students.

When Weary was at university, Wood Jones, W. A. Osborne and Marshall Allen were the only persons with chairs in the Faculty of Medicine; from his fourth year all clinical work was taught in the hospitals by the honoraries, outside the university. Now, public hospitals house the universities' undergraduate and post-graduate teaching units and each specialty has its own chair.[1]

In 1935, for the first time, an associate assistant surgeon was appointed to Hailes's unit, interposing another layer in the hierarchy between the honoraries and their residents.[2] Surgeons could be generous mentors, however, trusting their residents to perform many of the minor operations under supervision, and Weary was allowed to execute a range of procedures that year.

Edgar King was Hailes's corresponding Surgeon to Out-patients. Weary became particularly interested in King, who was his former anatomy and surgery tutor, an early thoracic surgeon and the only person ever to win three Jacksonian Prizes of the Royal College of Surgeons.

King was regarded as one of the finest teachers in the medical school. Weary had found him an 'extraordinarily pithy, wonderful teacher'. His technique of replying to one question with another was effective; but his patience was not great. If the student still had not grasped the point by the third question, King would move onto something else. This first year, during which he worked with King beyond the four months in Hailes's unit, was to shape Weary's future surgical career.

'Oesophagectomy was his particular interest . . . I had to prepare his cases . . . if he operated on one of those, I wouldn't go out of the hospital for three weeks until the patient either survived or . . . '

In the 1930s, before modern anaesthetic techniques, the lung on the side of the operation had to be collapsed over a period of days so that the patient became accustomed to using only one lung. One of Weary's jobs was to do a pneumothorax, that is, collapse the lung.

King performed the first successful oesophagectomy in Melbourne. The outcome of major surgery was uncertain in areas such as King's; the mortality rate from cancer was high, and with oesophageal cancer in particular there were few survivors. The intensive care unit had not yet been devised.

A warm working relationship developed between the two men, and the reference which King wrote at the end of the year praised him as 'one of the best resident medical officers with whom I have been asociated'.

Work with Hailes could be much more humbling. During Weary's four-month stint in the surgical unit, he assisted with a good number of prostatectomies. At the time, Hailes was very keen on a procedure that involved using what is called a Harris boomerang needle, and Weary was ordered to kneel on the floor by the operating table where, concealed by the drapes, he had to push up the patient's prostate gland, thus giving the surgeon a better view.

But he was also allocated more responsible duties: his first operation at the Melbourne was to remove an appendix, assisted by Edgar King, and he performed some thirty operations in 1935, including appendicec-tomies, the removal of small lumps and tumours and other straight-forward procedures.

A resident's day was long. Usually, a six o'clock start allowed Weary to spend an hour or two visiting patients in the wards before breakfast in the residents' dining room and, if it was a morning on which Hailes or King was operating, he would be in the theatre in time to scrub up for the first operation at eight o'clock. 'It was an enormously busy year – I loved it.'

He had to write up all his notes on the cases and prepare any questions he wished to ask his chief. Most nights it was ten o'clock when he made his final round of patients. Residents were on call twenty-four hours, so there was only a dim prospect of enjoying an unbroken night's sleep.

Weary remembered his quarters as being surprisingly comfortable: he returned each night to a spacious first-floor room above the main entrance to the hospital. In addition to a bed made up with hospital precision, there were a couple of armchairs, a chest of drawers and a wardrobe. A capacious wooden drinks cupboard housed glasses, beer and any other alcohol he could afford. Tall glass doors led onto the wide grey stucco balcony overlooking Lonsdale Street at treetop level. It was splendid for entertaining, the only snag being its location next to the Superintendent's room and opposite the boardroom. 'My great worry was that if I invited an attractive woman up for a drink before going out, we had to pass the [boardroom's] open door, and they all stopped in their deliberations to look at us.'

In many ways residency was a vastly more earnest continuation of college. Both Weary and Rank saw the tradition of living in this almost exclusively masculine society as a great strength which worked to their advantage.

'You never thought of . . . hours of work – you were up by day and up by night,' he said. And as for the dedication of the sisters: 'You could never get up early enough in the morning that you'd be there before them,' said Weary. 'They knew all about every sick patient . . . they wrote all the notes on [them] in a copperplate hand and they looked after the students and your allocation of patients . . . whenever any doctor came in, they always went to see the patient with him'.

One of Melbourne's most famous matrons, Jane Bell, ruled the hospital in the stern tradition of Florence Nightingale. Tiny, bespectacled and wearing a little lace cap, she would appear at the head of a covey of nurses in the wards, where the great rows of beds, thirty-four inches apart and exactly parallel, had their coverlets folded at the corners with an icy precision. 'Just fair in the middle of the patients, *exactly* symmetrical, were the hospital crests', remembered Weary, whose own voice rose to a falsetto as he imitated the sound of hers calling her staff to order: 'No, no, nurse, not that way, no, no . . . '

Jane Bell could be an intimidating champion of her nursing staff's welfare. Not even the great Mr (later Sir) Alan Newton escaped Matron Bell's censure when he upset one of the ward sisters by persistently criticising her work. Rank, who was Alan Newton's house surgeon at the time, was accompanying his chief on his rounds one Saturday morning when Matron Bell swept up as they were leaving. 'Mr Newton! I'd like to speak to you.' 'Yes Matron?' 'I'd like you to know I will not have my nurses spoken to as you have spoken to Sister O'Donnell. You have upset her very much so that she can't sleep at night. You will apologise to her!' Which he did.

These were the days before antibiotics, when nursing skills quite different from those of the post-war era were required, when applying leeches was a recognised procedure and people sweated out their fevers until a crisis signalled that either death or recovery was imminent. Patients had to be nursed through pneumonia, rheumatic fever, typhoid, chronic bronchitis and emphysema in the medical wards.

But the real horror area tucked away in some shambling buildings in a corner of the hospital was the 'seps wards', where in order to minimise the risk of cross infection, patients suffering from gross sepsis were kept well apart from the medical and surgical cases. Frightful skin conditions, amputations, gangrene, venereal disease – 'Looked like the Middle Ages,' Weary said.

He never grew used to it, although the urge to 'drown . . . in disinfectant' – what he called the 'unclean complex' – left him. 'I've seen people . . . whose condition was such that just the pressure of their bedding had opened both knee joints so that you were looking into their knees.'

It was lucky he had a strong stomach. His first week at the Royal Melbourne in 1932 as part of his medical course had impelled him to tell James and Alice that 'I've seen more horrible sights in three days than I've seen in my whole life . . . My poor partner got all "swimmy" in the head after looking over a few cases this morning and hurriedly left'.[3]

It was 'big needles' which affected Weary and made him weak at the knees.

Later in 1935 he spent two depressing months in those wards, filled with despondency about the inmates' chances of recovery, before beginning two months as casualty surgeon in November.

Four months in the medical wards as the house physician for Sidney Sewell were comparatively relaxing compared to the previous four with Hailes and King, and the last four in the seps ward and in casualty. He found some spare hours to study for the first part of his MD and, towards the end of his time with Sewell (who was one of the examiners), the latter suggested he go on to complete the examinations. 'He has great ability, initiative & decision of character', wrote Sewell, '& a thorough knowledge of his work. At the same time he is a charming & courteous colleague.'[4]

Weary realised that he was regarded as a 'favoured son', but his sights were fixed on a Master of Surgery and he planned to sit the finals in 1936. Sir Sidney was not impressed: thereafter he referred pointedly to Weary as 'Mr Dunlop' whenever he conducted his team on its rounds.

It was lucky for Weary that his tour of duty as a house physician overlapped with the rugby season, otherwise it would have been impossible for him to play that winter. Despite having only one Saturday off in three, he persuaded someone to stand in for him occasionally at the hospital, and played for Victoria against New South Wales on the North Sydney Oval on 1 June 1935.

'That Dunlop is a tough 'un,' said the press, and a New South Wales player, McLaughlin, would have agreed: he was unfortunate enough to collide with him and the impact fractured three of his ribs.

One week later, Weary played such an aggressive game against the intimidating Springboks (who were back in Australia in 1935 and whose publicity rated their forwards at 'ten to a ton'), that he was selected provisionally to play for the Wallabies in the first Test on 26 June. But after New South Wales beat the South Africans 17-6 on a wet ground, the selectors were reluctant to drop any New South Welshmen and he missed out.

'Great blocks of the veld,' he called them, 'very large and very intimidating.' They dwarfed all the Victorians except Weary and made most of them nervous, according to the *Age*, the exceptions being 'those doughty forwards E. 'Weary' Dunlop, Lang and Baker'. On the field they spoke only in Afrikaans and this, plus their fierce attacking style, created a hostile atmosphere which quickly communicated itself to the opposing team.

Weary recalled that the only English he heard their captain and forward, Phillip Nel, speak was: 'If you lie on the ball, we'll kick your ribs in!'

The South African pack included half-back Danie Craven, full-back Gerhard Brand, forwards 'Boy' and Fanie Louw, Freddy van den Berg . . . men who became part of the history of rugby union.

At one stage he tackled Phillip Nel (who weighed around seventeen stone) at full speed and remembered the 'humiliation of shivering on him like a spear', making no impression until he got his legs on the ground and hauled the other man over.

The Victorians took a hammering in the first half, but Weary rallied the forwards in an attacking game during the second half and they managed to score another eight points in a match which ended in a win to the Springboks of 45–11.

Just sixteen years previously, it had been necessary to advertise in the press in order to muster fifteen players to represent Victoria; the team which played on 8 June was drawn from a large pool of players and 12 000 spectators turned up to cheer them on.

The Maori All Blacks were also on tour and played Victoria on Carlton Oval on 3 August. Weary scored the first try, just managing to touch down as he was tackled at the ankles, but despite Victoria's fierce attacking game, the Maoris won 28–16.

The Maoris were to play a Test match against the Springboks, but before that took place in Melbourne, it was decided to arrange a kicking contest between Gerry Brand, then said to be the 'the best rugby custodian in the world' and renowned for tremendous long-distance punts, place and drop kicks, Nepia, captain of the Maoris and a world figure, Weary and H. 'Soapy' Vallence, a well-known League forward for Carlton.

On 30 August, 'Soapy' led off with superb kicking, four drop kicks which split the posts from the halfway mark; but 'Gerry Brand decided he wouldn't compete against a professional unless he got into trouble and lost his amateur status, Nepia was slightly injured in one leg and kicking with his left foot and . . . it was just slaughter'. Weary got a few over, as did Nepia, but the honours of the day went to 'Soapy' Vallence.

Weary joined the Old Boys team that season and captained it. They were a hard-drinking crew in love with the atmosphere of the game and, according to Weary, 'liked grog rather than rugby'. One rowdy evening in the old London Hotel, Weary sketched a rampant unicorn on the tablecloth when it was decided that they should have a badge and a motto. Underneath, he scrawled *'Nulla vestigia retrorsum'* – never a step backwards. Thereafter, the unicorn adorned their blue and white ringed sweaters and he played with them in the first grade for the next three years. Melbourne adopted the unicorn badge when Old Boys eventually amalgamated with them.

Earlier that winter, Old Boys had beaten Powerhouse, and were furious when, after the match, Powerhouse appealed against one of their tries and the decision was reversed, giving them the game. At dinner with the other forwards that evening, Weary suggested that they should adopt a battle cry; whenever it was shouted by one of their number, all should fling themselves into the game 'with bared teeth and nails' and refuse to leave the field defeated. The Irish element in the team carried the day and they settled on the Gaelic battlecry of the Fitzgeralds, *Cru mà buagh*.

All went well for Old Boys – despite their partiality for alcohol they were not bad players – until they faced Powerhouse again at the end of the season. They lost the toss and during the wet and horrible first half were battling into the wind, but managed to prevent Powerhouse scoring until mishandling gave their opponents a three-point lead.

When they changed ends in the second half, the wind dropped and the advantage was lost. With only five minutes to go until the whistle, Weary suddenly remembered the battle cry and roared out *'Cru mà buagh'*!

'Everyone streamed madly down the field and I found myself in possession of the ball, went charging through and gave someone such a tremendous hand-off that I broke my finger.' He was tackled just short of the line, but someone else managed to touch down. Three all. They were undefeated.

His injured left middle finger became the most celebrated and over-treated in the hospital. 'Everyone was giving advice and following [its progress] with bated breath.' Rugby finger is a well-known pattern injury, and this one was stubbornly difficult to mend, with thickening of the middle joint and a lot of pain. Eventually, Charles Littlejohn operated on it enthusiastically and unsuccessfully. Never again was Weary able to straighten the finger.

Weary's success in the FRCS primary examination allowed him to participate in March 1935 in the massed magnificence of the Australasian Surgical Congress.

The *Argus* splashed out with an extravagent forty-seven column inches.[5] The President of the Royal College of Surgeons of England, Sir Holburt Waring, came from London with messages from the King and from the Council of his college, plus the senior college's gift of a great mace for its colonial cousin.

On the warm opening night, Professor Wood-Jones delivered the George Adlington Syme Oration to an audience which spilled out from Wilson Hall into the grounds, some more agile guests risking damage to their tail-coats and academic gowns by perching in the branches of a Moreton Bay fig tree to secure a better view, others standing in the doorway throughout. As a former prosector, Weary was seated in the hall.

Wood Jones's oration, 'The Master Surgeon', spread before him a prospect as romantic as his earlier ideas about pharmacy. Rank and he were inspired by the possibilities of surgery, exhilarated by the distinguished company all round them; being numbered in this gathering of power and influence was a heady experience for the two young men.

Alice cut out all the newspaper reports and circulated them to anyone who showed the slightest interest. 'Return please – Alice' she wrote crisply in the margins in her elegant hand.

Debate about war and Australian lack of preparedness in defence matters continued to rumble on in the press and in the circles in which Weary moved. Hitler introduced conscription to Germany that March; and 'Albatross' published a pamphlet which told thinking Australians, if it had not already occurred to them, that Japan might not limit her territorial ambitions to Asia. That perennial spectre of invasion by the yellow hordes was hovering once more.

Some months later in Swanston Street, Weary ran into Major-General R. M. (Rupert) Downes, a senior neuro-surgeon at the Children's Hospital. More importantly, Downes had become the Director-General of the Medical Services of the Army in 1934, and he was keen to recruit young doctors. He seized Weary by the hand and prompted him to rejoin the militia.

Undoubtedly influenced by Downes and the pulse of the times, he joined up on 1 July, becoming 'an officer in the Active Citizen Military Forces of the Commonwealth'. In September he was commissioned as a captain in the Royal Australian Army Medical Corps, attached to the Coburg-Brunswick Battalion.

He had been an enthusiastic cadet in Benalla at the age of 14 and passed his sergeant's examinations, but abandoned his ambition to be a machine gunner when he moved to the city to finish his pharmacy diploma and transferred from the Goulburn Valley Battalion to the City of Melbourne. 'Tommy White was my colonel . . . in the 6th Battalion. We marched through Melbourne with fixed bayonets.'

Not enough hours remained in the day for the drill hall and the battalion after pharmacy lectures, shopwork and study. He reverted to the ranks and deserted to the Medical Corps, until Scullin's Labor Government honoured their election promise to abolish compulsory military training and released him from army routine in 1929.

But he had thoroughly enjoyed the annual camps at Seymour, where he learned to fire a Lewis gun and to sleep under canvas on a straw palliasse, boots under his head, without too much grumbling. The camps, the route marches and the training one night each week gave them only slight grounding, but it 'brought all classes of society together' and made the job of turning them into soldiers when war came 'easier'. Now he returned to the militia with renewed enthusiasm.

Weary showed an easy-going face to the world and was popular with most of his contemporaries, but there was constant friction with Leon Rothstadt, the Superintendent of the Melbourne during his junior resident year. Weary had found Rothstadt difficult to deal with in the wards and particularly obstructive about him working with King's oesophagectomy cases once the four months attached to Hailes's unit had passed. Grudgingly, he had agreed that Weary might continue to assist King with his private patients outside the hospital.

Relations between the two men came to a head during the last quarter of 1935, when Weary was summoned to a continuous military training camp shortly after gaining his commission.

He requested leave to attend; Rothstadt refused. There was a stand-up row. Finally, Weary announced that he would appeal to the hospital committee against Rothstadt's decision.

Realising that the vote would go against him, Rothstadt backed down. Too many senior members of the medical profession were convinced of the importance of training doctors for the war that was coming, and Weary could also drum up support from Rupert Downes. He was on even better terms with Downes now, since he had escorted Rosemary Downes that September when she came out at the ball given during the British Medical Association's centennial meeting. Weary attended the camp.

Their antagonism flared up again at the end of the year when Weary was working in casualty. He had arranged for a colleague to take over his duty while he attended a farewell lunch for another doctor who was leaving the hospital. Late that afternoon, they rolled back from the tavern near the old Menzies Hotel in Williams Street 'full to the gills', and tumbled up the stairs to Weary's room to sleep off the effects of too much Bisquit de Bouche. Someone had failed to show up for the lunch, and Weary had polished off a double ration of French brandy. Leaving the bed to his companion, he stretched out on a chair on the balcony.

Unknown to Weary, his substitute had decided to go off duty and that evening Weary was a bit sluggish answering the bell. Rothstadt stormed over to the residents' quarters to find out what was causing the delay. He missed Weary, but someone had not managed to reach the bathroom and vomited in the corridor. Assuming that Weary had a woman there, he demanded that he open his room when he returned from the ward.

Weary refused; and Rothstadt suspended him from duty.

The implications were serious. Luckily, John Bolton – who had also been at the luncheon and knew the identity of the doctor Weary was protecting – was able to convince Rothstadt that he had been mistaken, and Weary was reinstated.

The year 1935 ended amiably, and although there was no lessening of animosity between them, when Rothstadt was leaving in 1936 it was Weary who insisted that they give him a slap-up farewell dinner at which the doughty ex-Trinity rower, Vin Youngman, delivered endlessly eloquent speeches dedicated to real and imagined absent friends. The residents had clubbed together and bought a desk set – 'the sort of thing you give your maiden aunt' – to present to the man Vin hailed as 'Dr Rothstadt over there – the most absent friend of all'.

Their revenge was too subtle for Rothstadt (whose ward rounds later as a clinician were described as 'shifting dullness'), and he joined in the gales of laughter amidst the banging of glasses on the tables.

Weary was appointed the senior surgical resident in 1936. As registrar he was responsible jointly to John Bolton, who replaced Rothstadt as Superintendent and moved into the room next to Weary, and his honoraries. His salary doubled to £100 a year, but the hours and conditions did not change.

Roy Chambers oversaw two months of gynaecology; then, for a further two months, Weary worked with John Tait, the urologist. (He remembered this last chiefly for the tedium of watching the other man peering down an endoscope, then a recently introduced electrically lit instrument which made life easier for the surgeon but was scarcely enthralling for his assistants.) Charles Littlejohn's four months of orthopaedics spanned the rugby season.

As surgical registrar in the general surgical wards, residents called on him for help and advice when they felt uncertain about procedures they were undertaking in the absence of their honorary. He continued to assist King with the occasional private case outside the Melbourne – Bolton was more co-operative than his predecessor – and he had responsibilities to his own honoraries' patients. During Bolton's absences from the hospital, he was Acting Superintendent. And he was preparing for the finals of his Master of Surgery.

Orthopaedics were dismissed by Weary as 'inspired carpentry', but the hysterectomies performed by Chambers, then the leading gynaecologist in Melbourne, he found much more absorbing. Despite this, neither Chambers nor the university's Professor of Obstetrics and Gynaecology, Marshall Allen, was successful in recruiting him to their speciality. Dunhill was still his man, and hearing him deliver the Stawell Oration during a visit to Melbourne the previous year for the BMA Meeting had merely increased his determination to do general surgery.

In September, he moved into the casualty flat. The entrance to Casualty was on the ground floor facing Swanston Street, and often at night the staff had to thread their way amongst the derelicts sprawled on stretchers on the floor. They shambled in off the street to recover from binging on 'metho' or the crude alcohol known as 'threepenny plonk'.

The four months as the senior casualty surgeon were to be 'a killer';

soon he felt there would never be an end to the trying business of directing 'the sheer masses of people' into the right channels. Because of this pressure, despite most of the procedures being minor ones, 'you never seemed to do anything quite to your satisfaction'.

They had one night off in three. Whenever the longed-for night arrived, he was usually too tired to do anything but go to bed.

More than a year in the hospital had trained him to drop into a deep sleep instantly he hit the pillow and to stumble out and dress immediately the bell drilled into his dreams. He was through the door and on his way down the corridor before he was fully awake.

'We had a lot of intrinsic fun in the institutions themselves,' said Rank. It was free from the Presbyterian control exercised at Ormond. They could entertain women in their rooms; there were parties both in and outside the hospital, plenty of opportunities to gather round a bar or in cafés like Mario's in Exhibition Street and clubs, cards and some modest gambling. Rank remembers chess, although Weary never cared for the game, and there were the inevitable pranks.

Fatigue could be a disadvantage when his rugby-playing friends dropped in. His room's proximity to the street was too convenient. One night, Weary had crawled into bed 'dog-tired'. He accepted a tankard of beer and dropped off to sleep with it balanced on his chest, while the party crowded into the room around him.

He awoke much later with the feeling that something was wrong to see a naked and unconscious (but not unknown) woman slumped on the floor. He leapt out of bed and, with John Bolton's help, tried to bring her round. When wet towels and face-slapping had no effect, they put her in Weary's bed and he spent a few uncomfortable hours in an armchair in Bolton's room until it was light.

They dressed the now semi-conscious girl in a raincoat and scarf and frogmarched her down the long, silent corridors and out of the hospital into Bolton's little car to drive her home. 'A noble act of friendship.'

Rank was the victim of a particularly succcessful prank and clearly enjoyed recalling it. He was the senior resident in charge one evening when both Bolton and Weary were off duty and away from the hospital. It was his first time, so he took it very seriously.

Around eight o'clock he received a telephone call from a Melbourne *Herald* reporter enquiring about a rumoured case of leprosy. Rank wasn't sure – he thought he'd heard it mentioned – so he took down a copy of Price's *Textbook of Medicine* and read out a description of the disease to the reporter, who asked some curly questions (which

Rank answered satisfactorily) and eventually rang off.

Somewhat uneasy, he decided to go down to the seps ward and see the case for himself, and was surprised when the staff there knew nothing about it. Rank became increasingly agitated as he did the rounds of the other wards and discovered no leprosy case. He ended up in Casualty examining the Admission book. Still no trace of a leper. Now very alarmed, he rang the *Herald* to tell them that no leprosy patient existed in the hospital.

'My God! *What? What? What case of leprosy?*' They got all excited.[6] It seemed only minutes before a reporter was on the doorstep, clamouring to talk to Dr Rank. Later in the night, worried and suspicious, he suddenly recognised the voice on the telephone when there was a second call for him: this time it was John Bolton, who was not as clever as Weary at disguising his voice. The game was up.

Next day they faced the consequences uncomfortably. The hospital authorities were extremely displeased at an article in the *Herald* headed: 'The Lost Leper'. But that was not all: the story had spread rapidly through Mrs Orr's pub, where all the reporters drank, setting the bar abuzz, and eventually even the Victorian State Health Officer became involved. The three of them were given a dressing-down: there were to be no more jokes about leprosy, and speaking to the press was forbidden.

Weary turned 29 in 1936. He never regretted a minute of the ten years spent away from Benalla and felt increasingly remote from the aunts, uncles and cousins and friends who filed up the path at Belle Vue to see 'Cousin Ern' when he was home. Alice was too avid for confidences and eager to show off her clever son.

The older Dunlop relations never quite came to terms with the most celebrated member of the family; they were uncomfortable with him, tied by blood but estranged by education, fame and a lack of family feeling on Weary's part. He kept them at a distance. 'I never had much in common with my relations.'

If Weary was in Benalla on a Sunday he walked to morning church, but Alice and James wisely shied off enquiring about his religious activities in Melbourne. James was now the circuit steward of the Benalla Circuit of the Methodist Church and President of the Benalla Dads' Club. Menopause had suffused Alice with energy and brought to an end the crippling migraines of earlier years.

Even Alan was not entirely at ease with him and could never bring himself to use Weary's nickname; nervously pedantic in the letters he wrote to Weary, even in old age, he would begin 'Dear Brother', 'Dear E. Edward', or even 'Dear E. E.'. Anything to avoid imagined offence by using the baptismal name, but uncomfortable with both the nickname and, later, the second name adopted professionally in London.

Living apart had driven a wedge between the bush schoolmaster and the surgeon and his awe of his younger brother grew as the years passed. Inspectors found him 'too earnest and hard working', and Alice acknowledged him to be 'highly strung': 'he lives and works . . . at high tension.'[7]

When Weary was Best Man at Alan's marriage to Winifred Erlandson, he turned aside questions by the curious about his plans for settling down, pleading the need to establish himself professionally first.

There was never a shortage of girlfriends, but pride and ambition forbade the development of anything too serious. He had discovered his tastes to be heterosexual very early on, when a Benalla scoutmaster suggested that if young Ern Dunlop had some doubts about whether he would grow up to be a normal man or not, he was willing to give an expert opinion. All Ern need do was unbutton his flies and submit to a simple examination.

Ern didn't like the sound of this: he beat a hasty retreat and told no one.

Early fumblings on the sofa in his Ormond study – 'doing it' – progressed to more experienced petting. But those twin fears, pregnancy and venereal disease, discouraged experiments until, one night, a more experienced girl fervently initiated him. From thereon, he enjoyed a number of affairs, but his head was always firmly in control. He was determined not to be diverted from sitting for his fellowship in London.

Weary met Helen Ferguson during his days at Ormond. Those who knew her then say photographs did not do justice to the high cheekbones, beautiful eyes, translucent skin and mass of dark hair. Margaret Gibson (or Peggles, as she became to the Fergusons) thought Helen 'most beautiful'; James Guest sat near her in lectures and said she was the sort of girl 'you wished you could get to know better'. She had been Captain of Morongo, where she had survived almost ten years of a Presbyterian education, and could regard those she met with a cool, quizzical look. Her reserve attracted. Helen intrigued Weary greatly, but she shied away from any involvement. Besides, she was often overseas with her parents and led a life cushioned with money and far removed from that of a hard-up, would-be surgeon.

Weary escorted her home from an evening at Picken Lodge when she was 'not much more than a schoolgirl', and 'she . . . bang[ed] the gate and scoot[ed] in very quickly'. That was the only time he took her back to Falkirk, her parent's house, although he remembers dancing with her at common room dances and other functions at the college.

The Fergusons lived in a vast Italianate stucco villa at 461 Royal Parade, Parkville. Helen's grandfather, Mephan senior, had built and furnished it in a style appropriate to a successful nineteenth-century engineer and ironmaster whose works had manufactured a number of Victoria's railway bridges and the great iron pipes used to carry water across the long dry miles in India and Western Australia.

They drove large, handsome motor cars – Mephan junior had a yen for speed and the Buicks they drove in the 1930s had been preceeded by an exotic Isotta Franschini; the rooms were filled with solid expanses of gleaming cedar and ornate Victorian buhl. The dining table seated eighteen with ease and expanded to banquet dimensions; and after dinner the women of the household withdrew to a drawing room hung with placid Australian pastoral scenes and fanciful oils of romantic ladies in trailing dresses gazing out over almost improbably blue Italian seas.

Grandfather Mephan was a big, boisterous, white-bearded man, who delighted in teasing the women and younger members of the family. The housekeeper, Mrs Muldoon, also used to terrorise Helen when she went to live there with her parents after they moved from Adelaide, forbidding her to go anywhere or do almost everything. Boyd, younger than Helen by two years, was less affected. Helen would eye Falkirk's two intimidating figureheads like a frightened rabbit.

When his father died in 1919, Mephan junior bought out his brothers' interests in Falkirk. The birth of their youngest child in Melbourne, Mephan James William, had taxed Mary Ferguson's health; she summoned her unmarried sister, Leydon Balmer, to her side and handed over Jamie's early rearing to her. Thereafter, Aunt Leydon was a stable presence in the household.

The firm's most prosperous decade was in the 1920s. All three children were sent to boarding school at an early age, Helen to Morongo, the boys to Geelong College, for Mephan and Mary – or 'Tossie', as she was called – were often away for weeks at a time on business in Sydney, Brisbane, Adelaide and Perth.[8]

Helen kept Weary at a distance. He would have liked to see more of her, but at home in Melbourne her world revolved around weekends of golf at The Peninsula, tennis at Royal South Yarra, luncheons and parties and dances. Their paths continued to cross occasionally at the latter.

She had not yet enrolled at university to study science. At school she had resigned herself to matriculating in English, music and history when her request to undertake a science course was dismissed by both her mother and the school as an unsuitable ambition for a well-bred young woman.

Tossie was intent on raising Helen to be a gracious hostess and the wife of an important man. Invergowrie, Melbourne's closest institution to a finishing school, and a Grand Tour of North America, Europe and the United Kingdom were to impart a final polish to this adored only daughter, who might catch the eye of some rich and eligible young man in the 'old country' and make a brilliant match.

Mephan and Mary Ferguson liked to travel. In 1934, at the age of twenty, Helen was removed from Melbourne for most of the year to accompany them on the first of her overseas trips. She returned smartly dressed and prettier than ever but heart-whole and unattached, and busied herself with tennis, golf and parties once more.

Mephan emphatically vetoed Helen's suggestion that she should study pharmacy: no daughter of his was going to stand behind a counter and serve the public, little better than a shop girl. Domestic science at Invergowrie had not satisfied her earlier ambitions. She persuaded her parents to allow her to enroll for the first year of a B.Sc degree course at the university in 1937.[9]

Weary's two years in his resident's room below the Melbourne's grey-tiled pepperpot towers ended in December 1936. He applied successfully for a job as a resident at the Children's Hospital and in January 1937 he moved into the residents' quarters in Nicholson Street, Carlton. Thanks to the Depression, there was a shortage of doctors and not long after arriving there he was promoted to assistant registrar.

Weary found working amongst children a happy experience – despite the treatment he received from his first patient. 'There I was in a white coat with a stethoscope round my neck and there arrived a lusty youngster from . . . Fitzroy who no doubt had been told by his mother that if he didn't pull himself together she'd take him to the doctor. So that he greeted me by screaming "Bastard! Bastard! Bastard!" and he pulled my stethoscope apart and kicked me under the chin.'

A newspaper article about rugby-playing doctors published that year shows a carefully posed photograph of an urbane, smiling Dr Dunlop listening to the chest of an angelic girl with the large eyes and blonde curls of a Shirley Temple. Weary has tamed his own abundant head of hair: he has abandoned the slightly off-centre part for a side one, and has polished his natural waves close to the scalp with hair cream.

His bedside manner with the young might have improved rapidly, but his social life took a dive when it was realised where he was working: 'Everywhere you went, people were dead scared . . . if you came from the Children's.' In the summer of 1937 an epidemic of poliomyelitis swept Australia and entire wards in the red brick buildings in Nicholson Street were crowded with the victims of this viral disease which predominantly affected children – hence its former name, infantile paralysis.

Such was the atmosphere there, that when Weary caught German Measles, the early symptoms of sore throat, enlarged, painful glands, stiff neck and a slight temperature were feared initially to herald polio.

Medical, surgical, baby wards, out-patients – he found all aspects of his work satisfying. Surgical work at the Children's was quite different from the Melbourne. In orthopaedics Weary worked with John Colquhoun and Eric Price; Harry Douglas Stevens, a general surgeon not much larger in stature than his small patients, introduced him to surgery on hare lips and cleft palates; but he found cerebral surgery with Rupert Downes depressing. There was no successful way of treating the various childhood malignancies, such as brain tumours or leukaemia. The infective fevers – scarlet fever, diphtheria, rheumatic fever – and intestinal infections could be fatal. None of this would change until the introduction of antibiotics.

Overall, he remembered his year at the Children's for its bright, pleasant atmosphere and the comparative ease with which children accommodated to sickness, buoyancy and high spirits triumphing over crippled lives and terminal disease.

In September Weary graduated Master of Surgery. The only other to gain the degree that September of 1937 was John Hayward, a lecturer in pathology at the university who had graduated MB BS the year before Weary. Both men were educated at Benalla High School (Hayward's father had been a headmaster there) and both were protegées of Edgar King's.

The insurance policy which James had taken out for Weary matured on his thirtieth birthday and Weary added £300 to his bank account. He could sit for his London fellowship in November 1938 if the College would agree to accept him as a candidate with slightly less than the required four years hospital experience following graduation. The reply was in the affirmative.

Towards the end of the year, the Fergusons sold Falkirk and bought a newer, more convenient house in the fashionable suburb of Toorak, for 'Tossie wanted to be at a better address'.[10] Weary carelessly misread the date on the invitation to the housewarming party and rang the front door bell at 605 Toorak Road a night early. An amused Mary Ferguson suggested he stay for dinner and questioned him about his plans for the future. Acquiring his fellowship was the most immediate goal and he was to work his passage to England on one of the Orient Line ships the following May.

Next evening Weary donned his dinner jacket and black tie once again and spent rather more time at Helen's side than was politely possible. He returned to his room at the Children's and wrote to Helen 'in a pained effort of nonchalant restraint' on an Australian Army Medical Corps Christmas card, asking if he could ring her 'some time before leaving the Southern Hemisphere'. He had found her 'gorgeous as ever'.[11]

The increasing attraction that had swept across him at the dinner table two nights before was obviously returned: Helen's 'small, neat Xmas card' pointed out how far away May was – why not come and see her sooner? Weary's card with its brown satin ribbon was carefully kept – most unusual behaviour for Helen, who had a reputation throughout her life for destroying letters.

They went out together for the first time on New Year's Eve. After the parties and the sirens and the streamers and the joined hands of 'Auld Lang Syne', Weary wrapped Helen's purple cloak around her, and they walked hand in hand along St Kilda Beach lapped by a pewter sea, the sky overhead suffused in flame and gold. For Weary, it was 'the morning of the world'. Helen had never been in love before. She was timid, uncertain and restrained, but just once, when they were seated on the kitchen table back at 605 eating peaches later in the morning, she leaned deliberately towards him and rested her cheek against his. From that moment, he worshipped her.

When Weary wrote to Helen from London on New Year's Day 1939 he reminisced about the first and only time before 1938 that he had taken her home. By now they had a private joke about their changed relationship; from 1 January 1938, he referred to the Helen he danced with at Ormond and saw home from Picken Lodge as 'your sister'.

There was no time for holidays. His small store of capital would have to last five months of London living until the fellowship examinations in November. More money, as much as possible, was needed, and three locum tenens were to be the means of earning it.

The first was a busy general practice in Coburg with a preponderance of obstetric cases. Weary found the Coburg–Brunswick area awkward, the main streets congested with traffic, and the directions given him by patients confusing. The locum was memorable for one of his mothers beginning a prolonged labour over which he agonised for days, listening to her heart, doing tests, finally calling in the more experienced partner. He provided no comfort, and breezed out the door saying, 'Mother's all right, Baby's all right. Just hang on, hang on . . . ' while the husband stood silently by and a succession of sisters, grandmothers and ancient female relations stared at the new boy 'with stern, accusing faces'. During his obstetric training as a student there had always been an experienced midwife at hand. Now he was on his own.

Then the doctor for whom he was filling in returned and did a high forceps delivery, 'dragging the baby out against all opposition. You can imagine the attitude of the family . . . this creep's done nothing for days and as soon as doctor came home he . . . produced the baby'.

Weary was relieved to move out to Mordialloc, where the obstetrics, daily surgery and house calls were uncomplicated.

The Austin Hospital for Incurables was a vastly different environment. Hugh Trumble, one of the early neurosurgeons to the Alfred Hospital and a notable cricketer, was operating there on a series of depressing tubercular and cancer cases. 'I remember him more keenly than anyone else out at the Austin . . . [for]surgery of tuberculosis and some very innovative operations which bore his name. One of those was tuberculosis of the hip joint in which he put a strut of bone across from the pelvis to the trochanter of the hip.' Weary prepared patients for Trumble and the other surgeons, assisted them and, towards the end of the locum, operated under Trumble's supervision.

The Austin was in suburban Heidelberg some distance from town and Weary was hampered by not having a car. Apart from Saturdays, which from autumn were sacred to rugby, he saw Helen whenever he had a few hours off-duty. Occasionally she would drive him in the family Buick. A small cheap diary survives from 1938 and, in amongst Helen's almost daily jottings about lunches, dances, tennis, bridge and golf with girlfriends, Weary's name features three times only. They saw each other often and Helen did not bother to note down their meetings: there was never any risk of her forgetting their arrangements.

In amongst the almost nightly cocktail parties and dances at the end of first term, Helen gave a dance on Saturday 21 May. It would be odd if Weary had not been there, given the intensity of their feelings for each other, but he had no recollection of it. Memory gave pride of place to the epic send-off given him by the Old Boys and assorted 'rugby characters' after a Saturday match. It turned into a mammoth beer drinking contest.

Old Boys had won their game and celebrated at their Melbourne pubs before drinking their merry way in various establishments along the road to Healesville. They were to stay in a large boarding house at Nyora Estate kept by a relation of Phil Allen's.

Dinner was eaten very late, 'a gross of bottles' was put on the towering mantlepiece and the evening jogged along until a hefty South African member of the Old Boys, Kennedy 'Flash' Gordon, stood up and accused Weary of 'piking': he was to 'stand up like a man and drink with him'.

Ten huge tankards of cold beer were called for and set five on each side of the table. Weary found it demoralising that Gordon could open his mouth and pour the beer down his throat without any perceptible movement of the larynx, whereas he took two and a half gulps to each tankard. Gordon then said triumphantly, 'I call for ten.' They drank ten each. ('I think I probably gained a little on that ten.') 'I call for five.' Gordon was growing weaker. He drank two of his five, 'his eyes fell down like a blind, he walked into the wall and to the floor. So I drank three and . . . went out and was violently ill.'

'Flash was unconscious until about 5 o'clock next day.' Weary ate breakfast as usual.

SEVEN

Journey to the Promised Land

'FOR MANY YEARS I JUST had an agonising desire to travel . . . whenever I went to Sydney, down there to the quay . . . [it was] anguish to think of the world lying out there . . . so much more exotic and exciting.'

The great Australian ambition was to take a trip 'home'. Australia was where they were born, where they lived and worked and saved up for that glorious day when they could wave goodbye, for 'Australia wasn't in the real world . . . that was all those exciting places overseas'.

Many friends had already gone: Bennie Rank, John Colebatch, Bob Officer, Colin MacAuliffe, Jack Horsfall.

Weary had joined in singing 'Now is the Hour' as the All Blacks departed, he had bidden farewell to the Wallabies before their tours of South Africa and New Zealand, and cheered from Station Pier when the Australian Universities' Rugby team sailed for Japan. Each time he had been asked to go; each time he decided painfully that he was not available for selection: 'It fair broke my heart.'

The Manager of the Orient Line gave him a favourable hearing when he enquired about a job on one of their ships. There would be a vacancy on the SS *Ormonde* in May: his earnings as an assistant surgeon were to be only the token shilling a month, but it was the best way possible for an indigent young doctor to travel. All he need supply were his uniforms and spending money for the voyage.

James and Alice, Aunt Lil, Alan and Winifred and various friends crowded into his cabin on B deck on Empire Day, 1938. They admired the flowers someone had sent and stole sidelong glances at a self-possessed Helen who chatted pleasantly to everyone, showing no special partiality for Weary and causing him some private chagrin. The family wondered about her presence. Weary was not given to confidences, although lately Aunt Lil had begun to suspect Helen's significance.

It was the first time James and Alice had come to Melbourne to see

Weary. They had not attended his graduation from Pharmacy College in 1929, nor the two degree conferral ceremonies in Wilson Hall in 1934 and 1937. (He had not thought to invite them and they never asked why. After all the years of study, graduation was an anti-climax. Besides, suggested his cousin, Ruth Lack, the expense of coming down to Melbourne would have bothered them.) His departure for England, to the headquarters of Empire, was a different matter.

'Edward sails' wrote Helen in bright blue ink alongside Tuesday 24 May 1938 in her tiny diary. She kept track of the ship's progress: and three minutes before the *Ormonde* sailed from Fremantle, Helen noted on the back of a snapshot she sent to Weary: ' . . . between Echuca & Deniliquin. I was learning German verbs in an endeavour to forget that the *Ormonde* was sailing for London in approx 3 mins.'

The ship's Medical Officer was Kenwin Harris, a bachelor physician (with a fiancée awaiting him in Ceylon), who informed his assistant surgeon that in addition to holding daily surgery, Weary was expected to keep the female passengers happy, to chat and dance with them and be an entertaining dinner partner. A nursing sister, Susie Dunn, completed their team, and Weary sent photographs of the three of them standing on deck outside the surgery back to Helen. She stuck them all carefully in an album, including one of Weary clowning in the children's sandpit.

The voyage across the Bight was uncomfortable. Before Weary had a chance to unpack his suitcase, he had to give up his assistant surgeon's cabin to a passenger, and the purser buried him deep in a cabin on F deck.

In Melbourne he had been charged with searching out someone's cousin and being kind to her. Eventually he ran his rather plain and shy quarry to earth, danced conscientiously with her each evening and did his best to draw her out. When she left the ship in Fremantle, he was stupefied to discover that he had been lavishing attention on the wrong girl.

Amongst the passengers who joined them there was a theatrical company which had been performing in Perth. By dint of nagging the purser, Weary had managed to work his way up to D deck and, all the way across the Indian Ocean, he found himself surrounded by showgirls and dancers. There was little surgery and a 'flower bed' of pretty girls.

Even the captain had consolation on board after Ceylon: his 'sea wife' joined him there and was cosily installed in a cabin. The six-week voyage was to be 'a moving mass of ship's madness love affairs'.

As the weather grew warmer, he exchanged his double-breasted blue serge for tropical whites. Ship's officers were pampered beings: Weary's clothes were laid out for him each morning and evening, even the studs and sleeve links being put in for him.

They reached the equator and, with fuss and ceremony, Neptune appeared with his trident to order a ducking for all those passengers crossing the line for the first time, including the assistant surgeon. Almost immediately, the ship sailed into a typhoon, and for the next few days the heat and humidity stifled all activity behind the tightly sealed portholes, while torrential rain cut visibility outside to less than 200 metres.

Those passengers who were not confined to their bunks sprawled listlessly in chairs in airless public rooms. But the winds died down as they neared Ceylon, and once more the seas flattened out to sparkling tropical blueness.

Weary was determined to cut a dash in Colombo. 'It was the right thing to do' to hire a car for shopping and sightseeing, so he laid out the princely sum of £5 for a Bentley and driver, and was driven to various shops where he bought cigarette cases and souvenirs and gifts. He was delivered up to an ingratiating shopkeeper called Chandi Ram, whose emporium supplied him with a magnificent dressing gown which hung in his wardrobe until his death. He drove to Mt Lavinia and admired the view, before returning to the ship in a stately fashion with his driver and guide. 'I subsequently found that I'd been overcharged and this rascal got a percentage of everything I'd bought.' New chums like Weary were a soft touch for the wily Sinhalese.

Once out of Colombo, more bad weather blew up and for five days across the Arabian Sea Kenwin and Weary attended to passengers and crew in a 'shambles of seasickness', while the ship was buffeted by gales of 'over a hundred miles an hour'. Then Kenwin's fiancée developed severe abdominal pains and began to haemorrhage.

Weary discussed emergency procedures with the captain. The ship would have to change course and turn its bow into the gale so that it would be as steady as possible. He prepared to operate, although he was concerned that the available instruments were inadequate and the rough seas would make surgery hazardous. Luckily, the bleeding stopped and it was decided that any treatment could wait until Aden.

The ship dropped anchor at Aden at 1 am. Shouting Somali boys rowed Weary, Kenwin and his fiancée ashore where they transferred to a car amidst a 'clamorous, babbling mass of Egyptians, Arabs, Jews and Somalis'. The driver hurtled recklessly along the moonlit narrow streets and roads, cursing shrilly in Arabic and honking the horn at the camels, donkeys, dogs and people which, even at that hour, ambled across their path.[1]

They saw their patient admitted to the British hospital in the centre of town and returned to the ship, which steamed out into the Gulf of Aden as dawn broke. Weary stood on deck until the houses glowing with fluorescent brightness in the early morning sun were a distant jumble of boxes caught between the water and the towering rocks at their back. 'Everything was fantastic and unreal.'

Weary was an enthusiastic tourist and ready to be enchanted by every port: Fremantle, Colombo, Socotra, Aden, through the Bab-el-Mandeb up the Red Sea to Suez, Naples, Toulon and Gibraltar. He was sailing through scenes from the postcards which Lil and Violet had posted back to Australia in 1915, and his letters made even barren Socotra sound romantic, when he wrote of the wild cave-dwelling Bedouin and the aloes and dragon-blood trees in a landscape of sand and limestone cliffs. By day the blazing sunlight bleached out all colour; but when the sun dropped down, passengers and crew revived in the slight breeze and cooler darkness of night.

The social duties of a ship's officer granted him a licence to enjoy the company of all without commitment. It was fortunate for Helen's peace of mind that she knew nothing of his involvement with one of the French showgirls, Yvette. Weary found her good company, but not everyone approved of her. Gabrielle Wood, daughter of an English bishop and sister to a future Archbishop of Melbourne, Frank Wood, thought her commonplace and more than once took Weary to task for this shipboard liaison.

A number of the passengers together with Weary and Kenwin disembarked at Suez and went sightseeing 120 kilometres away in Cairo – again, 'it was the thing to do' – while the *Ormonde* sailed up through the Canal. They spent a night at the Oriental Hotel; they gazed out over Ibrahim Pasha Street while drinking tea on the shady terrace at Shepheards; and they rode out in horse-drawn gharries to explore the Great Pyramid.

Despite the heat, Weary and Kenwin had exchanged their uniforms for tweed jackets with collars and ties and pith helmets; Aileen Macarthur sported the trousers made so fashionable by Chanel in daring contrast to Gabrielle in her print dress. An Egyptian photographer captured them for posterity with the mandatory camels and their white-jacketed and be-tarbooshed guide posing poker-faced beside them. Then they boarded their train and rattled across the desert to Ismailia and on up to Port Said, where Weary bought a Cyma gold watch from Simon Artz before rejoining the ship and sailing out into the Mediterranean.

The June days were cloud-free, the sea calm, and when another ship of the Orient Line appeared on the horizon, Weary captured on his Box Brownie the customary exchange of visits when the ships hove to.

By night, the sea was black, mysterious, and when they steamed slowly towards Naples early one morning, Weary saw Capri 'glowing like a jewel' and towering Vesuvius shrouded in haze. He took 'Ailes' sightseeing. In his letters home, he decided prudently to call her a patient.

Fog in the North Atlantic replaced the shining blueness of Toulon and Gibraltar and delayed their arrival in England. For twelve hours they were fogbound off Cape Finisterre. At night, the mournful sound of ships' foghorns all around intruded in Weary's restless sleep like the eerie booming of the bitterns of his childhood.

The *Benalla Standard* was eager to print Weary's impressions of 'arrival in the Motherland' and ran his letters in serial form whenever Alice handed one over to the editor. All the district was privy to where he was and what he was doing.

Weary's first sight of England was early on a cold morning, the clouds parting to allow long shafts of sunlight to highlight 'trim, respectable English trees' on their grassy slopes and pick out some of the Fleet at exercises near Portsmouth. Near Dover they stood out into the Channel to await their pilot and, as Weary drank in the sight of 'the white cliffs . . . and a lovely greenness', he admired the 'ordered land [and] quaint old houses . . . the charm and character exhaled by this soil explained to me the hitherto not understood reason why we exiles term England "Home".'

It was late in the day when they docked at Tilbury and not even the warm afternoon sunshine enhanced the view from the train window of London's drab industrial suburbs. It was a subdued journey: the *Ormonde*'s captain had persuaded them to escort his abandoned mistress up to town.

He placed Jane in their care before they docked and she disembarked
discreetly but tearfully when his wife came on board. Weary and Kenwin
parted from her at Charing Cross Station, piled their luggage in a taxi
and drove to Bloomsbury. Suddenly the London he had read about
materialised; 'in . . . glorious sunshine and under a soft blue sky I first
saw St Paul's Cathedral, the Strand, Fleet Street . . . and many familiar
sights'.

England to colonials of previous generations was not a foreign
country: when they finally reached her shores, they recognised the
buildings, the pattern of the streets, the landscape. Weary had arrived
in the city he learned at school was the centre of his cultural being, the
place from which Harriet Dunlop had set sail only eighty-eight years
before. Even his voice was not particularly Australian: quite quickly he
slipped back to the same accent that Alice, Violet and Lil learned as
small children at Catherine Marie's knee.

Weary's room at London House had been arranged before leaving
Australia. For the next nine months, he would be part of a constantly
changing population of postgraduate students from all over the Empire,
housed in heavily subsidised comfort reminiscent of a university college.

They longed to shave and bathe in fresh water after six weeks of
saltwater baths and Jane offered the use of her flat. After dropping their
luggage, their taxi bowled down Oxford Street and Bayswater Road,
past Hyde Park and Kensington Gardens, fetching up in Notting Hill
Gate. 'Incredible in London to lie full length in a large tub, looking out
[at] . . . sunshine bathing a garden with the soft green of plane trees,
elms, poplars, and the thrushes singing'. English birds sang sweetly in
the ears of new arrivals from Mother England's far-flung colonies.

Light of heart and full of energy, despite an abominable sore throat
which had been plaguing him for the past few days, he sallied forth for
a night on the town with Kenwin and Jane. 'Hyde Park, Rotten Row,
Regent Street, Pall Mall, Piccadilly, Soho, all in one gulp. It really was
a grand night.' The two of them plied Jane with food and drink at the
Café Royal, while she continued to weep between courses, black
mascara running down her cheeks.

His night out aggravated the aching throat, which developed into
laryngitis and bronchitis that sent him to bed for a few days. Through
his open window, Weary could hear the score being called in a mixture
of colonial accents from the tennis courts in the square.

London House is just off Gray's Inn Road. It occupies a block
fronting onto Mecklenburgh Square, with its tennis courts and gardens,

adjacent to the open spaces of Coram's Fields and St George's Gardens. Doughty and Guilford streets form the other two sides of the block.

Before the buildings were bombed in the Blitz, they formed a hollow square of stone-built, nineteenth-century houses. The old foundling hospital of Great Ormond Street is a few blocks away and just down Doughty Street at number 48 is the four-storeyed house where a young Charles Dickens wrote *Oliver Twist*.

He was within easy walking distance of the British Museum or, if he chose to cross Gray's Inn Road in the opposite direction and wander down between Holborn and the Thames, he could explore the narrow streets of a much older London which soon had him in its thrall. 'I've lost myself innumerable times,' he wrote to Alice and James. He was in the midst of Dickens's London, and once he was east of Ludgate Circus, under his feet lay Roman London. History was all about him.

The establishment was presided over by a retired naval officer, Commander Crofton, and his wife Hilda, assisted by Elizabeth Mimms as secretary and Major Freddy Drumond, who had served in a Guards regiment until the loss of an arm forced his retirement. The study bedrooms were pleasant enough, and although Weary found the food indifferent, the occupants dined in style in a beautiful hall under a great clock, which showed the time in whichever country a diner called home. In the 1930s, dinner consisted of five courses, served by stewards in white jackets.

Nothing had been spared for these young men: they were regarded as the bright hopes and future leaders of the Empire by those to whom these ties were important. There were common rooms and a magnificent library, tennis and squash for recreation, parties and dances attended and given by political leaders and the aristocracy. The Duchess of Gloucestor visited more than once while Weary was there; and he was much impressed by a conversation with Lord Lloyd, although perhaps not quite in the way Lloyd intended.

He found Lloyd's proud account of how the world was viewed by viceroys and of Curzon's power when he was in Egypt 'unbelievable'. It was evident to Weary that the glories Lloyd related would never be seen again. But more interesting than Lloyd's views on colonial government and Egypt were his forcefully held anti-appeasement beliefs, which accorded with Weary's own.

Weary's interest in politics intensified after arriving in London. For the whole of that 1938 summer, the eyes of Europe were trained on Czechoslovakia and the problem of her Sudeten Germans.

Golden afternoons lengthened into long summer evenings. That July, Londoners lolled in hired deck chairs in the parks or sprawled on grass of a deep, velvet greenness almost unbelievable after harsh Australian lawns. With daylight lasting around eighteen hours out of twenty-four, Weary embarked on an enjoyable exploration of London. Lyons Corner Houses offered cheap meals or there were substantial snacks and good English beer on tap at a different pub around each corner.

He tracked down various Melbourne friends. At Trinity College Cambridge was the former Australian sprint champion, Jack Horsfall, and Dickie Latham, the Ormond Rhodes Scholar, was at Oxford. Colin McAuliffe was married and living in London. John Colebatch was studying for his Membership of the Royal College of Physicians; Ben Murray was at London House; Keith Rank and John Hayward, like Weary, were anxious to pass their examinations at the College of Surgeons in Lincoln's Inn Fields and Bob Officer (who had assisted at Weary's initiation so many years ago) was already FRCS.

All the major teaching hospitals offered courses of study, but he decided to go to St Bartholomew's Medical School, and prepare for the November examinations. Two other Australians at London House enrolled with him: Frank Mills, and a congenial Queenslander, James Yeates, who had both been in London for some time. The course would begin in September.

A fellow resident at London House passed on a locum job as acting resident surgical officer at the Woolwich Memorial Hospital's alcove on Shooter's Hill in Kent, and this relieved him of London House expenses for three weeks. Three honorary consultants, Cecil Rowntree, Lawrence Abel and G. S. C. Milligan, came down once a week to operate, but between visits the residents had to carry on as best they could. Weary enjoyed it for, with the senior degree, he found himself in charge, doing 'most of the surgical work . . . as many as six major operations on some days'.

At the conclusion of the locum, Weary collected his first English testimonial from Milligan, who rated his abilities 'much above the average', and moved back to London House. He had turned down a job at a children's hospital in the hope that some adult surgical work would eventuate, but August looked barren of opportunities until he was offered a locum at Sidcup.

Sidcup was a London County Council hospital for long-term convalescents, the hospital of the First World War where Sir Harold Gillies, the plastic surgeon, pioneered his reconstructive work on the shattered bodies of men wounded on the battlefields of Europe. Its superintendent, Elleringworth, was a 'lean, stringy, typical Australian with a suntan' harbouring an interest in Wagner and pictures.

By Weary's time there, no surgery was allowed. 'No one must ever die here,' Weary was told, when he asked Elleringworth's permission to do a tracheostomy on a cancer patient who was choking to death.

'It's no more complicated than lancing a boil!' Weary retorted. 'You put this man in an ambulance and he'll die on the way back to Bart's.' Luckily for the patient, the superintendent did not know enough about surgery to realise the extreme danger of doing a tracheostomy on a man 'blue as a plum [and with] . . . a great swollen neck'. With outward *sangfroid*, but really desperately scared that the man would die on the table, Weary performed a tracheostomy. The patient survived.

Weary had arrived in England armed with letters of introduction and references. Professor Marshall Allen, who had not given up hope of attracting him to obstetrics and gynaecology, recommended him to Fletcher Shaw, one of the outstanding obstetricians of the time: 'one of the best of our younger men . . . [and] one of our outstanding student leaders'.

Sir Alan Newton, John Bolton as Superintendent and the Committee of Management all spoke for his years at the Royal Melbourne, and Vernon Collins, Superintendent of the Children's Hospital, testified to Weary's 'brilliant' career.

Weary sent off Sir Alan Newton's letter of introduction to Sir Thomas Dunhill that July and he had already been invited to call on 'the great goitre surgeon of his day', and observe him operating at Bart's. Everything this fairly small and very precise man did was done deftly and well – and after an operation, 'if there was a little blood on the drapes, he'd roll them up himself'.

His meeting with Sir Gordon Gordon-Taylor was less orthodox. Weary's dancing had improved out of sight since the early Benalla 'Can't you hear the beat' days and he was never one to creep around the floor. A particularly vigorous spin during a 'grand' evening at the Savoy catapulted his partner and he into the spare, distinguished figure of Gordon-Taylor, who enjoyed a reputation as one of the great ballroom dancers in England. To Weary's embarrassment, when he turned to apologise, he noticed puzzled recognition on Gordon-Taylor's face.

Gordon-Taylor was a great friend to visiting Australians. Weary was promptly invited to his operating sessions at Middlesex Hospital and, when he discussed his future plans, Gordon-Taylor suggested working either at St Mark's, which specialised in colon-rectal surgery, or the British Postgraduate Medical School at Hammersmith. Professor Grey-Turner at Hammersmith was a close friend; he could also put in a word for him at Mark's. Weary must come and see him when he had made up his mind what he wanted to do.

Those consultants Weary saw in action made a profound impression on him. 'They think nothing of starting a list of 9 or 10 major cases at midday and working straight on until 10 pm without stopping to eat; then go off to see some private cases.'

September brought the consultants back to town from their summer holidays. The course began at Bart's 'auspiciously' on 31 August 'with Mr McGovern on orthopaedics'.[2] The hospital was deep in the East End, between the noise and reek and bustle of Smithfield Market and the restoration splendour of St Paul's Cathedral.

'The triumvirate', as Mills, Yeates and Weary were christened, struck out on foot each day down Gray's Inn Road to Holborn, across the end of Hatton Garden with its dealers in gold and diamonds, and up Giltspur Street to the jumble of buildings that forms London's oldest teaching hospital, founded by the Augustinian canons in 1123.

For ten weeks he attended lectures in the classrooms at Bart's, studied cases in the hospital and was cross-examined about them by the consultants who were his teachers. At night and weekends, he took out his books and pored over them until the early hours of the next morning. 'It was a pretty condensed and busy course.' Amongst his teachers were Sir Thomas Dunhill, Naunton Morgan (specialising in surgery of the colon-rectal area), Roberts, the thoracic surgeon from the Brompton Chest Hospital, and the man whom Weary regarded as a 'superb teacher and very sound operator', general surgeon John Hosford.

Bart's reputation drew students from all over the world, amongst them a contingent from India, Ceylon and Africa. (He never forgot a story current at the time of two Englishmen allegedly shaking hands while one said to the other: 'Dr Livingstone, I presume'.) His happy experiences in this international community at Bart's and London House exerted a significant influence on Weary's outlook on education and the form in which aid should be extended to Asian countries in the post-war years.

Meanwhile, he read about the situation in Central Europe with growing concern and an increasing contempt for the appeasement policies of Chamberlain's government. It was not that he believed England should fight a war for Czechoslovakia's sake: but that if Hitler and Nazi Germany were not contained now, their power would spread like a cancer through Europe.

In the midst of the Munich crisis, when Chamberlain had flown to Germany for the third time and the world waited to hear if once again England and Germany were to be swept into war, the Dean of the Medical School, Girling Ball, called together the staff and students of Bart's and assured them that should war come, classes would continue as usual. ' . . . if Bart's had stopped teaching in the last show, there'd be no doctors now! Whatever happens, we carry on. We will teach here in Bart's.' Weary was amused by this dramatic faith that only Bart's trained the doctors of the future.

Newly-dug trenches slashed across London's green parks and garden squares. The appeasers won the day and there was no war that September.

By November, this grimy district of narrow courts and lanes and smoking chimney pots fed the 'pea soup' fogs through which they walked each morning and evening. 'You could hardly see your hand in front of your face.' It was dark by 4.30 in the afternoon.

It was bleak weather for weddings, but the sun broke through on the first Monday in November when Weary was best man at Rank's wedding at All Hallows, the Toc H church close by the Tower of London. Examinations began that week. Politics were forgotten. Weary was working harder than he had ever done before, days and nights a 'sleepless, unreal and intolerable' blur. He cared far too much about the outcome even to write to Helen in his customary lighthearted fashion.

Friday 11 November, Armistice Day, plunged him into deep gloom. He had not been entirely happy with the written papers the previous day and now he faced the clinical examinations and surgical pathology. In the clinical examination, an encounter with his examiner, a 'rugged, ruddy, white-haired, bulldogged old man' called Milne left him 'just about speechless and incoherent', but he recovered himself sufficiently to fight back.

He correctly diagnosed the attractive woman presented to him with her x-rays as being syphilitic, a case of Charcot's joint, but Milne attacked him over his suggested treatment for the second patient, who had a cyst in the humerus, the long bone of the upper arm. Thereafter, his confidence faded and, as he prepared to leave the room with a glum face, even Milne's final words – 'I want you to know, my lad, that my bark is worse than my bite' – brought him little comfort.

Operative surgery with Norbury and Mitchener was even worse, although he felt his operation on the dead subject went well. Mitchener never poked his head out from behind a copy of *The Times*, and the precise and articulate Norbury chose to savage Weary over his Latin when he was dissecting and ligating the lingual artery. Mitchener, appealed to by Norbury as to what he would do with such a candidate, drawled from behind his newspaper, 'I'd plough the bastard.'

The last session began badly. Recently Weary had read a very convincing Canadian paper on head injuries and he began to propound these new and unconventional theories when presented with a skull with a trefined hole in it. He could see from the growing impatience on the faces of his examiners that they were not happy, as they interrupted his heretical diagnosis, and he quickly recovered himself to say, 'However, as Wilfred Trotter says . . . ' before drawing a deep breath and quoting a page of Trotter's classical theory from Choyce's *Textbook of Surgery* which he had got off by heart. His photographic memory had come to his rescue. The examiners sat back and the tension eased as he reverted to the established British school of thought. He was relieved at the close of the examination when they told him he had done well, but doubted his success in the others.

That night, Weary put aside his textbooks – he decided that nothing now could influence the results – and went to the theatre with a Canadian friend who was also smarting from a skirmish with the examiners. Weary was brooding over his performance that day, depressed that despite being 'crammed with information', he had been reduced to feeling like a 'blushing schoolboy'.

John Bolton had arrived from Melbourne and was now at London House working for his MRCP. Jim Yeates and he mounted a concerted campaign to raise Weary's spirits, John proffering 'psychological aid' and Jim (who was feeling even less sanguine than Weary about his own prospects), taking him off to the country that Saturday in his little Austin, nicknamed Penelope, to visit friends in Bedford and go sightseeing in St Albans. Even an impressive performance of *Pygmalion* that evening failed to cheer him up and he continued to brood all Sunday under London's leaden skies.

The autumn leaves in Lincoln's Inn Fields which he had admired were now just so much 'sere and brown rubbish' as he walked to Queens Hall on Monday for his two pathology vivas. Each lasted about twenty minutes, but to Weary's surprise, he felt much steadier during the first and responded every time to the often sarcastic and difficult examiner who 'haggled and fought me over every word'. The second session with the rather less trenchant Mr Souttar of the London Hospital and Professor Pannett of St Mary's Paddington raised his flagging hopes when they informed him that he had done particularly well.[3]

But despite their assurances, Weary still felt badly shaken. He required a pass in every section, written and practical; failure in one would mean re-sitting the fellowship after further months of study, and any future attempt would have to be from a job in a hospital. He could not afford to continue living at London House. He was 31 years old: it was exactly ten years since he sat his pharmacy finals and applied to the University of Melbourne to study medicine.

The results were to be announced later that afternoon. For two hours, Weary wandered restlessly and aimlessly through London, almost certain that he had failed. In desperation, he went into Westminster Abbey, hoping to find some comfort. When he reached the Embankment, he stood by Cleopatra's Needle and stared into the Thames, briefly wondering what it would be like to throw himself into icy oblivion.

Fifty-six candidates sat for the fellowship examinations in November 1938; they gathered at the College in a room at the bend of the beautiful Regency staircase and waited in subdued silence.

One by one, their names were called and they approached the member who was to inform them of their fate. 'One passes out, seemingly walking backwards, and with a motionless heart you come to . . . the stairs – one path down to the cloakroom, the other up to the boardroom . . . . At this point you are informed as to your [result] and . . . either pass up to meet the assembled [Council Members of the] College of Surgeons . . . or [go down] into outer darkness.'

When Weary's name was called, he was so convinced of his failure that he marched determinedly on down the staircase and was stunned to hear his name repeated more loudly. 'Dunlop, I have pleasure in stating that you have been approved.'

Weary passed. So did Frank Mills. Jim Yeates was among the forty-four who failed. Weary raced off through the swirling mist and fog to send telegrams to Helen and to Aunt Lil. The world seemed 'a much more rosy place . . . when one is MS, FRCS'.

On Tuesday morning he went to the ES & A Bank in Gracechurch Street and drew out his last £5, leaving a shilling in the account to keep it open. He invited a girl he knew out to dinner, booked a table at the Rembrandt and took off with James in Penelope for a pleasant drive in the country.

They arrived back in good time for Weary to soak in a leisurely, hot bath before changing into his dinner jacket. But on returning to his room, he discovered his clothes still laid out neatly on the bed where he had left them, but his wallet empty: all his money had been stolen. Ben Murray came to his rescue with another fiver and Weary celebrated his success in style.

Next morning, with a severely aching head, he went to County Hall, but was dismissed curtly when they looked at his qualifications. 'No jobs for surgeons.'

'Who said anything about surgery?' replied Weary. 'I said a job.' Nothing immediately. He could have a locum at St Stephen's Fulham Road in the New Year.

The rest of the week was an orgy of sleeping late, sherry parties, dinners and shows. He visited 'Pansy' Wright in his laboratory in Oxford's painfully new Nuffield research building,* he played tennis in thick fog and swam in an indoor pool. By the weekend, 'stone, motherless broke', he faced up to looking seriously for work.

---

* Later Sir Douglas Wright, Vice-Chancellor of the University of Melbourne.

EIGHT

Mr E. E. Dunlop MS, FRCS

ON MONDAY, HE PUT ON his pin-striped trousers, black House of Commons coat and homburg hat and called on his friends in Harley Street to discuss the future. Sir Gordon warned him off applying for the next vacancy at St Mark's, because he was obliged to sponsor the son of an old friend, although he offered to put in a word for him with Professor Grey-Turner. But Weary hesitated to ask favours of an already busy man and decided to approach Grey-Turner himself. Sir Thomas provided him with 'a rattling good letter'.

The man who answered the door to the rooms at Hammersmith was 'small, slight, stooped . . . rough hewn and dressed in a drab suit and flannel shirt with a soft, unmatching collar'. About to enquire if the professor was in, Weary suddenly noticed the 'commanding authority of that large head with its deep-set eyes'. It was the Master Surgeon himself.

He conducted Weary into the museum-like surroundings of his sanctum, where he retreated for morning and afternoon tea. The walls were lined from floor to ceiling with specimens in jars, photographs – 'You'd see photographs of a fellow holding his excised jaw . . . and some sort of great tumour from elsewhere in his body' – and trophies, the subjects of his extensive articles and books. He liked to put his bowler hat over the teapot as a cosy, and there he would sit, chatting and dipping ginger biscuits in his tea.

Weary spent that week 'hounding people for a job' and dared not leave London. Helen would have derived no comfort from his letter which insisted that: 'Alas, I must try and do something worthwhile in this old town first, and it seems possible that even a long beastly year might elapse before I see you again.' Research jobs at the British Postgraduate School paid very badly, but could lead to better things and the experience would enhance his chances of worthwhile work when he returned to Melbourne.

Weary's financial exigency was relieved by a summons to a general practice locum at Guildford. He arrived at very short notice to find only the scantiest patient records and frequently he entered a house with no idea of why he had been called.

The practitioner (who had been rushed off to hospital) did his own dispensing, which well suited Weary with his pharmacy experience, but the main source of revenue was obstetrics. Weary felt faintly uncomfortable; it was evident that the good sisters at the hospital would have preferred the Irish Catholic mothers to be delivered by someone in the faith.

Surrey shivered under a blanket of hoar frost when he arrived. A week later, the locum was cut short when he wrapped the car around a tree in a treacherous lane while driving across the Hog's Back during the first snow of the season. Weary had to be prised loose, suffering from a fractured sternum and some broken teeth. He struggled on for a day, but when he began to cough blood, he took himself back to London House.

John Bolton welcomed him with an invitation to help drink a case of Hardy's wine which had just been delivered. Next morning, after much drinking and very little sleep, he awoke with pneumonia. Bolton called in a Harley Street specialist: x-rays at the Royal Free Hospital down the street revealed that he had crushed his chest and damaged a lung. Only his tough frame had saved him from more serious mauling.

The Croftons pampered him in their flat with huge fires, comfortable sofas, quantities of China tea and sherry. They sat him in a chair, wrapped in a bearskin rug, and brought in Commander Crofton's niece to play the piano to him. Hector MacQuarie, a New Zealand writer and long-term weekly boarder at London House who worked at publisher Angus & Robertson's London branch, supplied books, fruit, and even a sprig of mistletoe which Weary put in an envelope and sent to Helen with a note. 'Re specimen my angel regret berries too squashy to enclose.' Helen tucked it away in a drawer with her letters.

The Christmas season began on a gloomy note. Helen wrote that she had failed chemistry and would be sitting supplementary examinations. Her science course was taxing for someone who had not studied it at school and her confidence suffered when friends suggested that careers were not for women and examinations were a 'masculine pursuit'.

Then Weary's hopes for a resident's job were dashed by a brief letter from Professor Grey-Turner; as a Master of Surgery and a fellow of the London College, Weary was too senior and over-qualified. But Jim

Yeates, who did not have a senior degree, received an unexpected present by the same post: he was offered the appointment denied to Weary as house surgeon at the Hammersmith Hospital.

Weary flung off the mantle of convalescence on Boxing Day and launched into an energetic programme of hospital dinners and dances, pub crawls, films and shows. New Year's Eve 1938 could not have been a greater contrast to 1937, spent with Helen in a boy-girl dream of love. Normie Cust and Weary sang uproariously round the piano at a tavern near the Middlesex Hospital. They danced round the snow-encrusted statue of Eros in Piccadilly Circus and joined with the crowd in singing 'Down by the Old Mill Stream', while in nearby Trafalgar Square the unemployed marched with 'a black coffin containing the message "Unemployment – No appeasement".'[1]

From New Year's Day, a locum for three weeks at St Stephen's Hospital in the Fulham Road empowered him to decide which of the old age pensioners in his care should receive free condensed milk and extra vitamins; and he earned sufficient money to realise a long-cherished ambition to go to the rugby at Twickenham, where England played the Rest on 7 January.

His damaged chest had wiped all prospects of playing rugby that season. He settled for being a spectator and spent the evening with the two teams at a tavern called the Lotus in Blackheath, airily promising to play for London Scottish, Harlequins and Blackheath, depending on who was drinking with him. A fortnight later, Colin MacAuliffe and he were among the 80 000 enthusiasts who watched England beat Wales 3 nil.

'This general surgery is a man's job,' he wrote to Helen after a week at The Mayday Hospital, Thornton Heath, near Croydon. 'Often in the last two years I've been sorely tempted to seek some lucrative surgical specialty with less dizzy heights and nervous strain, but the fascination somehow defeats me.'

First Marshall Allen, then Allen's London friend Fletcher Shaw and other consultants he spoke to suggested that obstetrics and gynaecology would make Weary's fortune and reputation by the age of forty. He rejected the idea, having no desire to 'belong to the common run of shrewd shopkeepers', although occasionally, when depressed about the length of their separation and the difficulties of building a practice when he returned to Melbourne, he wondered if Helen might not be happier married to a thriving practitioner in a country town, than a 'striving . . . surgeon nursing prospects of a somewhat dubious nature'. He discerned a 'strange restlessness' in her and was convinced that her gentle nature should be protected from 'distress or alarm'.

But this 'cutting job' at The Mayday enabled him to expand his surgical repertoire very satisfactorily. On one occasion in February he did twelve major operations in twenty-four hours, including his 'first Cholecystectomy, Prostatectomy and a major gastric operation'.

No job lasted long enough to free him from the constant search for employment. He had turned down a two-month locum in Bristol to take The Mayday job, because it would keep him close to the centre of things. Towards the end of the month he spent all his spare time calling on some thirty members of the West London Hospital council and writing to 'some 50 people associated' with the hospital, only to see them appoint a previous house surgeon.

On one of his days off he had called on John Hayward, who was working in Chelsea at the Brompton Chest Hospital where the great thoracic surgeon, Tudor Edwards, held sway. Jack Lovelock, the New Zealand Olympic miler, was also a house surgeon there. Weary arranged to do a locum in March for Hayward, who had planned a skiing holiday in Germany, but when he left The Mayday on the last day of February, there remained eighteen days to fill in.

He had no difficulty killing time for a week, for 'London is full of things to do for those with idle hands'. Hector took him to a rather grand cocktail party in Harley Street, he played golf, watched various surgeons operating, tapped Hilda Crofton's chest and diagnosed obvious influenza, drove round Surrey in the March sunshine with James and drank sherry beside the fire at Hammersmith Hospital.

Spring had officially arrived, according to *The Times*. On the spur of the moment, he bought himself a cheap excursion fare to Paris.

The trees in the Champs Elysées were a film of green against a blue spring sky when Weary walked from the Jardin des Tuileries to the Arc de Triomphe. He strolled by the lake in the Bois du Boulogne and wished Helen were with him to see the swans, to wander through the Louvre and admire 'the glowing marble of Venus de Milo, the famous Mona Lisa', to sit on the pavement of the Café de la Paix and sip a *picon et grenadine* amongst the crowds milling round the Place de l'Opéra.

He decided that the French were 'the most marvellous people . . . so wise, so witty, so charming . . . I had romantic ideas about the French.'

He found himself a small hotel, the Bellevue, near the Gare St Lazare for 35 francs a day, and rang up Lorna O'Riley, whom he knew from rugby days in Sydney. Lorna introduced him to her fellow students at L'Ecole Normale de Musique de Paris, and Weary joined them in the cafés in Montparnasse, talking politics and nonsense and drinking with them deep into the night. Everyone was preoccupied with the prospect of war.

Weary's schoolboy French, at first barely adequate, improved rapidly in their company, although his accent never lost its Australian twang. He found himself in the midst of an international student population and good-naturedly let a Swedish boy who had missed the last train doss down on his sofa one night. Next morning he was in trouble with the pretty young receptionist: Marie suspected the worst of men who invited handsome blonde boys to their room and she coldly demanded to see the Swede's *carte d'identité*. She remained distantly polite to Weary until the end of his stay.

Weary did not tell Helen of the holiday until he was on his way back to England. The uncertainties of work; the possibility of a war which would enforce an even longer separation from the girl he wanted to marry; the disappointment of missing the job at the British Postgraduate Medical School with Profesor Grey-Turner had made him feel 'blown on by chance . . . a bit chilled and reckless'.

Weary was always goal-directed; yet often in London he felt at the mercy of forces outside his control. In Paris he let off some of the steam which had been building up over the past six months.

He never wavered in his love and adoration of Helen. Yet in the way of his generation, he was able neatly to separate his goddess on the pedestal, the girl he wished to make his wife, from other women eager to be bedded. Some knew the score; others, girls who were caught up in the feverish atmosphere of approaching war, fell in love and went to bed with him because the future was grey and uncertain.

He felt bad about his lapses, however, and now and again replied to some reportedly sweet letter from Helen with protestations of his unworthiness and promises to repair his faults.

He tried to write to Helen several times from Paris, but his conscience inhibited him until he was aboard the *Côte d'Argent*, with the cliffs of Dover looming in the distance. He never wrote about the students in the Latin Quarter; dwelling instead on 'a nice French family' he visited, the wife a cousin of President Lebrun, and 'meals . . . a collection of grandparents, governesses and odd relatives'. He avoided mentioning his friendship with the very pretty daughter, who was a student at L'Ecole Normale de Musique de Paris, and the sharp-eyed grandmother questioning him closely about his financial status and prospects. The French girl was broken-hearted when he left and his second visit left her sadder than ever. '*Je suis si seul, je suis si seul,*' she lamented in a letter to him. '*Un moment! J'ai du courage . . .* ' The phrase haunted him.

Both Weary and Helen deplored the futility of life apart. But she was dependent financially on her parents, who vetoed her idea of travelling to England when the storms of war were blowing up in Europe; and his iron-clad determination to succeed in a difficult field took precedence over his private longing. Pride dictated that he not go back until he could support a wife. Always able to put other responsibilities ahead of his emotional fulfilment, this trait became more marked as he grew older.

Perhaps being 'bound on the wheel of life' became an excuse for not taking action in his private life. It was as if he was impotent in regulating his emotional life; he trained himself rigorously to put patients before all else, so that eventually they came before his own family.

That he was not alone in this, was revealed one day when Dunhill briefly dropped his guard as they were walking back to Harley Street. 'There are so many demands made upon us', he said, 'you can find you've got right away from your family and your home, and it's terribly hard to get back.' It was a warning that often echoed in his mind down the years.

Tragically, Helen and Weary's relationship was to become the first victim of this pattern of behaviour.

His friends always knew about this this single-minded streak. Arch Glenn remembers Weary reading aloud to a group of them on holiday at Lorne during the 1930s and refusing to waver from his objective, even when the others lost interest and turned away, chatting and laughing. He read on to the bitter end.

Weary's professional attitudes were formed during these years: the long list; the individual attention to patients and their families – whatever the day or hour; the sacrifice of personal needs to the demands of his profession. The example set by his distinguished mentors in London confirmed his belief that nothing less than total dedication would do.

The Brompton Hospital for Consumption and Diseases of the Chest in 1939 was 'quaint, old and extremely famous'. Jack Lovelock, an 'entertaining fellow with gregarious colonial instincts', showed him around. 'Most of the equipment and hospital planning belongs to an antique shop . . . there isn't any real facility for research work, or progress . . . yet any dictum of this hospital is regarded by the Empire as the word of God.'

Weary was to work with the First World War chest surgeon, Roberts, his peppery teacher from Bart's with a great knowledge of wine. Roberts's famous colleague at the Brompton was Tudor Edwards, one of the first thoracic surgeons and a handsome man with a grand manner. Nurses swooned when he made his ward rounds.

Weary did little surgery himself. For a fortnight, he assisted Roberts in the theatre and with the management of his cases, once more performing pneumothoraces as he had done in Melbourne for Edgar King. Most of the patients were volatile and tubercular. He was fascinated to watch lungs and portions of lungs being removed 'after the fashion of appendices', and he was able to observe some cancer surgery.

He made some useful friends, but his prospects seemed as precarious as ever. At Christmas, when London had nothing to offer and he was feeling particularly depressed and desperate to get back to Helen, he had cabled Melbourne about a promising university job said to be vacant, but was too late. He had written to Hailes and others about work; both Hailes and King thought he should return and take a chance on setting up in consultant practice despite his lack of capital. Bob Officer had secured a job at Melbourne's Alfred Hospital, and was to work his return passage as surgeon on the SS Ormonde at the end of March. But 'London . . . is a sort of El Dorado and one is lured on by the thought of stupendous luck which might so exalt life.'

That luck changed with the arrival of an envelope from the British Postgraduate Medical School. Professor Grey-Turner was pleased to offer Edward Dunlop Esq., MS, FRCS, a six-month position as house surgeon. Salary: £105 per annum, plus board, lodging and laundry. Scarcely enough to marry on and support a wife, but it might lead to greater things.

Earlier, when Weary told Gordon-Taylor that he had been found too senior for the houseman's job that was given to Jim Yeates, Gordon-Taylor was insistent that Weary must try again. He would speak to the professor first. 'I'm sure he would take you.' Weary unburdened himself to Dunhill at the same time. Dunhill also promised to put in a word for him and wrote a further reference immediately.[2]

Armed with introductions from these two illustrious patrons, Weary again called on the Master Surgeon, requesting that he be considered for a future vacancy. Two months later, he was successful.

'It is an excellent place for one who wishes to work with furious concentration,' he wrote, from the wretched little room he had been allotted. Next to the hospital in Du Cane Road, Shepherd's Bush, loomed the forbidding structure of Wormwood Scrubs Prison.

He was bitterly disappointed when a naval surgeon snatched the job he coveted with Professor Grey-Turner, because of the policy of giving preference to the Services, and he was handed the consolation prize of working for Arnold K. Henry. Henry was a Northern Irishman who had held the Chair of Surgery in Cairo before coming to the British Postgraduate Medical School and was an authority on long bones.

The professor was a master anatomist, but Weary decided privately that although he was a 'superb surgeon at exposing bones' he was not 'very fluent' when it came to operations generally. He spent too much time on meticulous preparation rather than the bold surgical measures a case might call for. 'He was too much of an anatomist.' However, Henry was more generous to his housemen than Grey-Turner and Weary had plenty of surgery during his time at Hammersmith.

This was some compensation for being deprived of the opportunity to work with 'probably the best all round surgeon in England', but it did not prevent him feeling 'an itch for a stilletto [sic] when I see my naval colleague assisting the great white chief'.

He found it even more galling that the other man found Grey-Turner intimidating and would have preferred the milder Arnold K. Henry – except that he did not 'dare say so lest he offend both the Professor and the Admiralty'.

In time, Weary developed a high regard and great affection for Professor Henry. He was impressed by many of his original ideas and his vast knowledge of the French anatomists, whom he read in the original.

When Henry took holidays in April, Jim and Weary found they had not a great deal to do; they attached themselves promptly to 'the rival professorial camp'. Weary now enjoyed unlimited access to one of the world's leading surgeons, whose reputation attracted visits by famous medical demigods from all over the world.

In his early days in Northumberland, lecturing in the College of Medicine at the University of Newcastle and operating at the Royal Victoria Infirmary, George Grey-Turner gained extensive experience in 'hillside and table surgery which enabled him to work single-handed with great self-reliance. As an example, it is related that on one of these same kitchen tables he successfully resected 10 feet of gangrenous bowel in a young woman so advanced in pregnancy that he first gained access to the abdomen by emptying the uterus. He did this without blood and without the help of modern relaxant anaesthesia'.[3]

It was as an assistant to Edgar King in 1935 that Weary first observed the pioneering techniques for oesophagectomy devised in Vienna by Denk and practised by Grey-Turner in the early 1930s.

Now, Weary was at the fountainhead. Teacher, writer, lecturer, compassionate doctor, surgeon: this third mentor's influence on the young, idealistic Australian surgeon was profound. He was a bank of inspiration on which Weary would draw in his subsequent professional life.

'The simplicity of his methods remained to guide me during six years of war surgery in the desert, in the jungle, in the prisoner-of-war camps and later in South Vietnam. How simple and bloodless it was to divide a colostomy by tying a rubber tube across the exteriorised bowel.'

Grey-Turner operated all day. He specialised in no one branch of surgery, but 'excelled in many activities now claimed by specialists'. Operations moved with 'planned precision – unhurried, undramatic and unremarkable'.

By 1939, when Weary heard him give the Macewen Memorial Lecture, he was a legend, 'his face magnificent in its lines and hollows and his shoulders bowed like Atlas under a world of experience. He explained to me – "It is best to wear out than to rust".'

May Day was marked by Mr Henry's return to the hospital and Weary moving his belongings to a more comfortable bedroom on the third floor under the clock tower. Each Sunday his letter to Helen was written by the wide double-hung sash windows overlooking Shepherd's Bush. Until now, apart from a few brief and often oblique references to the uncertainties of the political situation in Europe and in England, he rarely discussed politics. He cherished a poetic belief in Helen's 'mystic detachment . . . from the hard, sophisticated commerce of life'. None of Helen's correspondence from this period survives, but Weary's weekly letters to her suggest that her preoccupations were personal and loving, sometimes uncertain about him 'staying the course', often anxious about their future, but there was no intellectual interest in the world at large. She wrote of her science course, holidays with girlfriends, films and plays and the kind of feminine occupations which fill her little diary: tennis, bridge, cocktail parties, dances, golf, swimming, dress fittings and hair appointments.

Distance and separation probably accentuated his reading of her character. Theirs was a courtship by correspondence, the personal, day-to-day contact interrupted by his departure and extended by his pride and ambition to be worthy of asking her to marry him. He tailored his letters to the Helen he discovered with such overpowering happiness in 1938 and adored her with all his romantic imagination. But politics began to intrude during the spring and summer of 1939.

It was to his friends and colleagues, other men, that Weary articulated his disgust at the appeasers, his hatred of Fascism and the actions of the Axis powers. Earlier, he had contemplated joining the Republicans in Spain, either as a doctor or to fight. 'Rabid' arguments ensued between the various factions.

Conscription was introduced on 26 April, the first time in England's history that such a measure had been taken in peace time. Three days later Weary learned that he had been appointed head of a mobile surgical unit in the Emergency Medical Service. On his team would be an anaesthetist, Algie Jackson, and an assistant, Ronnie Kilgour. Typically, he told Helen that he was 'somewhat amused' to learn of this, since he had 'no definite base as yet – and am grouped along with other units run by [such] men as . . . Sir Thomas Dunhill and Victor Bonney – so war will make me as eminent as Hitler'.

He found it incredible that Chamberlain might lean towards appeasement again after Hitler's speech in the Reichstag on 28 April, when he demolished the Polish–German treaty of 1934 and denounced the Anglo–German Naval Agreement of 1935. 'There is a fever about existence here now . . . you hurry to the morning papers in an almost pleasing state of tension as to whether war will occur that day.'

Despite the unsettling atmosphere, Weary was keen to become involved in some research: the problem was finding a subject. Grey-Turner, Henry and Dr Janet Vaughan, clinical pathologist-in-chief at the medical school, all suggested various lines of investigation. Mr Henry also entrusted him with an increasing amount of major surgery as demonstrations to post-graduate students.

Professionally, it was a happy and satisfying time. Jim Yeates shared the wards with Weary, and they were good companions outside working hours. Off-duty time was rostered. Apart from seeing their patients, they were free to do as they pleased at weekends.

Hector MacQuarie showed him a side of England which was a comfortable contrast to the institutional atmosphere of an LCC hospital. Hector had a cottage in Buckinghamshire, a little green sports car and hospitable friends within an easy drive of London. Weary enjoyed a number of weekends with him, playing darts in the village pub on Saturday evenings, going to luncheon and drinks parties.

That May, Jim and Weary arranged to spend the whole of the Whitsun Bank Holiday weekend off duty. At midday on the Saturday, they jumped into Penelope and drove out of London on the Oxford Road. By 12.30 am on the Tuesday morning, when they turned the Austin into Du Cane Road again, they had travelled 1450 kilometres to Scotland and back.

Weary's letters are breathless with the beauty of spring. Never before had he seen such a 'dream of loveliness': the glowing burgundy of copper beeches and mile upon mile of hedgerows dripping bridal white blossom; the broom glowing golden on the hillsides and the silvery, silken green billows of new barley in fields rolling up to the horizon. 'James and I react to it by taking refuge in all the poetry we know.'

Quoting poetry aloud, they sped north. Through Lancashire and the wild broken peaks of Cumberland and Westmoreland, stopping to gaze and declaim Wordsworth at Windermere and Ullswater, until at 2 pm on Sunday they drove across the border into Gretna Green.

Weary noticed 'a measure of coldness' in the first shop he entered: he was dressed in his formal London *tenue de ville* of short black coat and striped trousers, an odd costume for a holiday weekend. But on confessing that he was Australian, the atmosphere 'immediately unfroze'.

He bought a postcard of the smithy and wrote to Helen: 'If you won't come to anvil – anvil must come to you – so bringing the jolly thing home.' Then he stuck a red penny stamp on it and put it in the postbox.

They ate lunch in the midst of 'a jolly motley crowd of Scots', the sound of the pipes and laughter and cursing in the 'same language as the familiar Australian'. He felt at home immediately.

Edinburgh was more than he had imagined, with the castle on its great rock towering above Princes Street and the gardens gay with wallflowers and tulips, punctuated by fountains in bronze and marble. Weary made a pilgrimage to the bronze war memorial of the kilted Highlander designed by Hector's sculptor friend; but it was the Royal Mile, sloping down from the great cobbled square at the castle gates to the Palace of Holyrood House, which 'quite dumbfounded' the two Australians.

Weary wrote to Helen from the hotel at St Boswells where they ate a 'tremendous late dinner and [drank] . . . Scotch ale until full to the eyes'. The moon hanging over Scott's Melrose Abbey was almost full. Finally, they crawled exhausted between cool Scottish sheets at the Duke of Buccleuch Inn. Neatness everywhere in this 'Land of brown heath and shaggy wood' and whitewashed cottages, Weary noted. And no fawning for tips. They felt much more comfortable.

Scotland and the Scots spoke to Weary out of some deep well of race memory. He responded to the lowlands immediately, instinctively. Here lay his origins, whereas calling England 'home', when first he saw its shores, was a loyal response to the ideal of Britain and the Empire on which Australians were nurtured.

On Monday they drifted down to London through the Cheviots and Yorkshire, halting that evening to sit for a while in the soaring Gothic nave of Lincoln Cathedral and listen to a violinist playing Bach, Mendelssohn and Beethoven.

Next day, Sir Thomas asked Weary if he was considering Constantinople for the next Bank Holiday – their wild, careless jaunt was regarded as 'quite a feat' by others at the hospital.

Weary was best man to John Colebatch when the latter married Betty Hillier that Friday in All Hallows by the Tower. Two weeks later they were gone – home to Australia via the USA. John had passed his MRCP examinations while he was working at Great Ormond Street and was returning to Melbourne to try his luck as a consultant paediatrician. John Bolton was also able to add MRCP to his name; he had celebrated his success by going to a good tailor and ordering some suits and was planning a research project at the postgraduate medical school.

Jim Yeates left Hammersmith on 24 June, dissolving the 'All Australian team' to Weary's sorrow. He was replaced by one Billimoria, a Parsee and a Cambridge man who had trained at Bart's. Together, they wrote a paper on 'Intramuscular Administration of Fluids' and submitted it to *The Lancet* for publication. Weary had conquered his queaziness at the sight of large needles.

With Jim's departure, Weary was appointed assistant to Dunhill for the rest of his time at Hammersmith and the 'dynamic knight' was to keep him on his toes.

Weary's interests were focusing increasingly on the gullet. His knowledge of oesophageal cancer was extended in contact with Grey-Turner; with Dunhill, he became interested in the diaphragm and oesophageal hiatus, or 'Congenital Short Oesophagus'.[4]

Weary was best man again in July, when Kenwin Harris married Susan Donnan from Sydney: 'all previous engagements off!' Marriage was on his mind. But ordinarily articulate with Helen, he always had difficulty discussing such a private dilemma as lack of money through 'choosing the will of the wisp medicine and not for gain . . . .you don't really know anything about being poor, and it might hurt you cruelly that work by its very urgency would always seem to have first claim on me'.

After he had written the letter, he gazed out on the dark, streets, wet and gleaming with rain, and 'the whole damn, dreary vista of this war to come settled . . . like a pall' on him. It was too late to escape.[5]

He had been doing some surgical research on white blood corpuscles for Janet Vaughan, who was willing to find him a grant. For some weeks he busied himself counting blood platelets, using himself as the control and taking off his own blood each morning. But he decided that there was no future in it, since the allowance would keep him 'in just about the magnificence of a dustman'.

He was contemplating seriously a project which would delay his return to Australia for some years: research into the relationship of the vagus nerves and vagotomy to peptic ulcer. He could use the animal operating facilities at the Royal College of Surgeons' Buxton-Brown Farm.

To this end, Professor Grey-Turner recommended him for a senior appointment to the Postgraduate Medical School. At the end of two years at Hammersmith, Grey-Turner would arrange for him to continue his work in the United States.

Weary did not discuss any of these details with Helen, asking merely: 'Darling, do tell me whether you want me to stay in England a little while longer whilst you come and visit . . . or that you think you are not coming in which case I shan't get mixed up in any more long jobs here and will come home soon.'

Professor Grey-Turner left for the United States early in August, taking with him the surgical life and half the post-graduate school for three months. Sir Thomas was fishing his favourite stretch of water in Scotland and would not return before Weary's expected departure from Hammersmith at the end of September.

Weary spent the last sunny weekend of peacetime rolling in the sea at Shoeburyness on the Essex coast. He returned to London on Sunday night in a train where the usual bright bulbs had been replaced by dim blue ones, and found the same blue bulbs lighting the hospital corridors and the windows draped in heavy blackout curtains.

The last Navy, Army and Air Force reserves were mobilised on Thursday, 31 August. A little before 5 am on 1 September the German army crossed the Polish frontier. Later that day, the evacuation of London's children began. Two thousand special trains moved over a million children with their escorts and teachers to the country.

Weary sat in his bedroom in the Lindo Wing of St Mary's, Paddington on Saturday and wrote to James and Alice. 'Sandbags are everywhere . . . and the balloons overhead are nearly as numerous as the stars. Blackout conditions prevail from sunset to sunrise, which means a city in darkness . . . there is something in it all reminiscent of the life of a rat in a hole! . . . It is a comfort to have no close relatives on this side of the world. As for me, I am as happy as a sandboy.'

PART TWO

1940 – 1942

On the idle hill of summer,
  Sleepy with the flow of streams
Far I hear the steady drummer
  Drumming like a noise in dreams.

Far and near and low and louder
  On the roads of earth go by,
Dear to friends and food for powder,
  Soldiers marching, all to die . . .

from *A Shropshire Lad*, A. E. HOUSMAN

NINE

War by any Means

'THE BALL WAS KICKED OFF today by Mr Chamberlain to the relief of all,' wrote Weary on Sunday 3 September to Helen. But the letter did not catch the weekly airmail post this time, and turned into a diary of the first week of war. 'It is somehow good to be living at this moment, and to feel that there may be big things to do requiring endurance & sound nerves, even for a non-combatant who . . . envies the fighting men.'

Preparations for dealing with terrible civilian loss had been going on for some time. Back in April the Ministry of Health issued over a million burial forms to local authorities, who also began to stockpile collapsible coffins made from papier mâché or stout cardboard. Someone had calculated that 'in the first three months of a modern war the traditional means of burial would require some 6 000 000 square feet of coffin timber at a cost of nearly £1 million', hence the decision to use an unconventional material.[1]

In the same month the Ministry formed the Emergency Medical Service to cope with the expected casualties. The Air Ministry, using the Spanish Civil War as a basis for their projections, advised the civil authorities to expect 600 000 dead and 1 200 000 injured in the first sixty days of war.[2]

The London hospitals discharged their patients to make room for the expected casualties and set up huge operating theatres where a number of tables would be in use at one time. The large Lewis Loyd Ward at St Mary's Paddington was converted to contain six tables. Courtney Gage, principal radiologist there, photographed Weary, Porritt and Cokinnis operating: four of the six tables are in action. All three surgeons are gowned and masked, but Weary's height dictates that he stoop over the table: the young man's silhouette at thirty-two is no different from when he was in his eighties.

The Dean of St Mary's, Sir Charles Wilson,* was in charge of the West London sector of the EMS. 'He was a quite remarkable man,' said Tom Kemp, who was a student at St Mary's and went on to become a consultant physician there. Arthur Porritt was team leader. 'We had a merry gang of fellows': Alec Bourne, Arthur Porritt, perhaps three registrars, four or five house surgeons and around a dozen students. As well, there were the teams, like Weary's, which joined Mary's from outside.[3]

Weary expected to be transferred within days to the base hospital at Harefield Sanitorium, the hospital at Sidcup where he had worked in August 1938. Patients were admitted but not kept in London: twice a week buses took them down to Harefield and similar establishments.

Within seconds of hearing Chamberlain declare war, the first air raid warning sounded over London. At the wail of 'Mournful Mary', Weary and a few others 'rushed up on the roof hoping to see some action'. Nothing – it was a false alarm.

They worked twelve-hour shifts, their sleep broken by air raid sirens, but 'nary a casualty. Imagine London with provision for from 30 000 to 100 000 casualties a day and nothing transpiring'. Weary was also responsible for two afternoons a week in out-patients and he acted as surgical tutor to the students. Otherwise he heaved sandbags, played tennis and sunbathed on the roof. 'Already I've got an impressive coat of tan.'

The nights were for parties, poker, talking and hard drinking in the Fountains Abbey, the pub on the other side of Praed Street, for hospital lights were too dim to read by. The surgeons used to 'drink a vast amount of beer and solve the problems of the world' in the house surgeons' study off the hospital entrance hall.[4] The hall itself was filled with debris and stone dust, as workmen erected an impressive memorial doorway and porch to the previous war's Lord Gough and the Fifth Army.

The blackout was more dangerous than the enemy. Even groping one's way to the pub on the corner of Norfolk Place could be hazardous. When quickly it became plain that there would be no flood of bomb-damaged victims for the moment, Mary's began admitting patients again. Numbers of people were injured in the blackout, particularly in traffic accidents and falls, and there were many fractures. After

---

* Later Lord Moran, Churchill's physician.

the farewell party at the Park Lane Hotel for the ill-fated Wallabies, who came to England and never played a match, Weary took his old team mates Andy Barr and Stan Bissett out on the town. While driving down Pall Mall, their taxi bowled over a pedestrian rather the worse for drink, and Weary decided to escort him to his home to check his injuries.

An astonished butler opened the door on a magnificent flat in Chandos Street: their casualty was a Belgian baron with the best-stocked bar Weary would see for many years. After cleaning up some superficial scrapes and bumps and a mouth bleeding from a few chipped teeth, they settled in for the rest of the night. It was a revelation to Barr and Bissett, whose naïve questions about the sources and size of his income, shocked the baron. He was not used to Australians.

Algie Jackson, Weary's anaesthetist, was married a few days after the war began and again Weary was best man. Everyone had been ordered to carry their gas mask with them at all times: 'I thought it . . . funny the way the bride and bridesmaid seemed reluctant to leave their gas masks in a pew while the ceremony took place.' The vicar took great pride in giving the wedding party a tour of the air raid shelter in the crypt.

St Mary's had a reputation as a 'ruggery' place. Sir Charles Wilson believed in excellence and recruited outstanding men to St Mary's. 'He filled the Medical School with the equivalent of Rhodes' Scholars,' Kemp recalled. 'What he wanted to avoid was mediocrity . . . you could be a scholar, an athlete, a good musician, an actor – but you had to bring something into the Medical School. When I went there in 1937 . . . they were the most vigorous group of young people that I have ever met.' Wilson was the most outstanding dean Mary's ever had. Weary felt very comfortable in this atmosphere of the scholar athlete.

The New Zealander Arthur Porritt came down from Oxford with a rugby scholarship. He was a fine sprinter who won the bronze medal for his 100 metres at the Paris Olympics in 1924, and by 1939 was Consultant Surgeon to the Royal Household.*

Tom Kemp, a Cambridge man and medical student at Mary's in 1939, had played for England at rugby and was captain of the Mary's rugby

* Arthur Porritt was knighted in 1963. He was surgeon to HM's Household, 1936–46, Surgeon to HM King George VI 1946–52 and Sergeant-Surgeon to HM the Queen 1952–67. In 1973, on the eve of his appointment as Governor-General of New Zealand, he was created Baron Porritt of Wanganui NZ and of Hampstead, Greater London.

team and of England after the war. He remembers some very informal tutorials when he was about to take his finals in December 1939: Weary taught him the technique of sewing bowel together by demonstrating on a pair of Tom's old socks. 'He was as capable of getting onto the student level as he was capable of getting on to anybody else's level.' Many of the tutorials took place with the participants leaning on the bar in the pub, for the surgeons and registrars who gave them did not have a great deal to do at the time.[5]

The first rugby match of the season was to be at Richmond on 16 October against London Scottish. When Weary asked if he could come out and train with the firsts, Kemp looked at him. 'Have you played this game before?' 'Oh yes, I have a bit,' said Weary laconically. They won handsomely.

On 21 October they played the Wasps, and it was the only time while Weary played with Mary's that they did not win: it was a draw, six all. Weary went along to Kemp after the match and told him, tongue in cheek, that the Wasps had asked him to join them. Would that be all right with Kemp? 'No bloody fear,' he replied.

Weary probably played seven more matches as a member of St Mary's rugby team before leaving England. They were unbeaten that season and Weary earned his sobriquet of 'One-try Weary', through his average of one try a match.

They beat Aldershot Command twice. After the second defeat, the Commander took Weary aside and asked him what sort of training programme they followed. There wasn't one, but he hated to disappoint them when Aldershot had pulled in seven Internationals in an all-out effort to beat the doctors.

'Oh well, we're up at four o'clock in the morning doing road work, and we work in the gymnasium . . . a very tough programme indeed,' he replied. In fact, their training consisted of going for a run across Hyde Park. They had 'marvellous talent. The thing that always amazed me was that Friday night was . . . regarded as PU night – piss-up night – so that was the Mary's training.'

Weary believed that he played better rugby in England than he did in Australia. 'Rugby in England . . . delighted me – something in the air and turf that seemed to make the bounce and flight of the ball more predictable than the fiery grounds of Australia.'

The Times called him an 'outstanding forward' and doubted 'whether there is a better side in the country than this hospital team . . . '[6]

Tom Kemp also knew how to exploit the 'mad Elephant act' known to Weary's Australian team mates. Weary's bursting through for a try in the match against Bart's resulted in an injury that threatened to keep him away from the ground for a few weeks. ' . . . In the closing minutes of the game . . . I elected to expose myself to tackle, cutting in to score between the posts. The tacklers came each way, one rolling thighs to the right and the other legs to the left. Result: torn ligaments and probably cartileges and a knee full of blood.'

That night, the team had the PU in Weary's room and 'kept giving my bed a "psychic", all lifting with one finger towards the roof and letting go. The head end of the bed collapsed and eventually I was left in a sea of beer bottles.'

In the morning, Arthur Porrit went past the door and Weary called to him from his collapsed bed amidst the bottles. Weary insisted that he aspirate the knee. Porritt reluctantly did so, drawing off nearly 100 cc of blood. '. . . With a firm bandage [on] I went to the Common Room and said "Who's for squash?".' Algie Jackson thrashed him soundly.

He played against Cambridge ten days later. 'Mary's gave me the palm for record recovery. I guess I am intolerant of disability affecting myself.' The Cambridge players had their revenge eventually: thirty years later, the knee 'gave out smartly', while he was surfing at Jan Juc on the coast of Victoria.

Politics were a universal topic of conversation amongst staff and students; and some of those who shared Weary's hatred of Fascism decided to take action in a practical way. 'I felt so strongly about it I used to take some rather strong-armed rugby and boxing characters out to pick quarrels with Mosley's Fascists.'

The meetings were noisy demonstrations with much heckling and ugly scuffles broke out frequently. But Weary's main memory of them was of how cockney humour turned the mood of the crowd one day when, in response to Mosley's one-armed salute at the start of the meeting and the crowd's answering roar, a cockney voice rang out: 'Yes, Sir Oswald, you can leave the room!'

'It makes one's heart ache to be in the Services – small fun in patching up humanity – when the world seems bent on destruction.' No sooner was the Empire at war than Weary talked about 'squeezing back into the AAMC, deserting this civilian life'.

He became increasingly impatient with the lack of work at St Mary's. But rugby and the 'rattling good fellowship' of his 'charmed circle' of companions in the hospital alleviated the demoralising idleness as the Phony War advanced into October and more of the old staff returned to London to take over the surgery.

Weary 'never had a more pleasant few months than I spent at St Mary's'. It was akin to membership of a very good club, bringing him shooting in the Midlands, golf at Royal Mid-Surrey and Sandy Lodge, swimming in the heated indoor swimming pool and squash on the hospital's court. There were the surgeons and their teams; Jack Lovelock with his cool miler's mind; Algie Jackson and Ronnie Kilgour who worked for Weary; bacteriologist Alexander Fleming; neurophysician Sharpey-Schafer; consultant surgeon to Mary's Dickson-Wright of the mordant wit; and of course, Porritt and Bourne. The cardiologist Paul Wood became a good friend through drinking sessions at the Fountains Abbey; he had a poor head and found it impossible to keep up with Weary and Sharpey-Schafer, but was always game to try.

Through Weary's friendship with Porritt, he began to move in very different social circles and occasionally escorted Molly Porritt's friend, Lady Burghley, to dinners and dances. Hilda Crofton was quite devastated one evening when he took Mary Burghley (the sister of the Duchess of Gloucestor) to a London House dance and overlooked introducing her to Commander Crofton.

Throughout October, Helen and he discussed the possibility of her coming to England. Only the difficulties of getting a ship seemed to stand in the way of her leaving before Christmas. But cold, practical reality reasserted itself in Weary's letters in November. He did not tell her how intensely he was chasing a job in either the AIF or the British Army (although he mentioned at the beginning of October that he had written to Major-General Downes); but he listed the 'horrid difficulties' and, as usual, his complete lack of remunerative employment dominates.

First, he tried the navy by calling on Sir Gordon Gordon-Taylor – who in this war was a Rear-Admiral in the Royal Navy – and then the British Army. The latter offered him a posting to India as a subaltern, but Sir Charles Wilson refused to release him from the EMS, and cunningly emphasised how little activity there was, even on the Western Front, particularly for surgeons. 'People are just sitting there in *estaminets* . . . If you were my own son, I would give you this advice – stay here, doing this useful work at St Mary's.' Weary had had his first formal operating list on 9 October. Sir Charles was not nicknamed 'Corkscrew Charlie' for nothing, and had half-convinced Weary with his silver-tongued eloquence when the punch line came:

'Oh, and by the way, we do appreciate all that you're contributing to the St Mary's rugby team.'

He had put his name in for a registrar's job at the Freemason's Hospital, one of the plum appointments for young surgeons, but by the time he was called for interview in November, he was fretting at the lack of response to his determined efforts to be sent away to war.

The interview was conducted by Sir Charles Wilson, wearing a House of Commons coat and striped trousers, and D. C. L. Fitzwilliams, who was in full morning dress with his topper parked on a nearby chair. Weary walked through the door looking the epitome of the Awful Australian, unshaven and dressed in a grubby pullover, sports jacket, carpet slippers and 'bags'. He greeted them in a broad Australian accent. 'You should have seen the look on old Fitz's face as he poked his monocle in his eye and surveyed me!' He had successfully wrecked his chance of an appointment to the Freemasons.

He intensified his efforts. Sir Thomas Dunhill cabled Downes on Weary's behalf when there was no news; and in the week of 11 December there was a hoped-for reply.

Downes would have received Weary's letter shortly after he arrived back from the United States on 3 October, and possibly his concern at the 'slowness of response of medical officers for duties in the new force', the 6th Division then being raised, influenced his decision regarding Weary's posting and the unusual form it took.[7]

Lieut-Colonel William Bridgeford, the Military Liaison Officer working out of Australia House, received a radiogram from the Director-General Medical Services: 'Ascertain if Captain E. E. Dunlop, St Mary's Hospital available appointment Overseas Base. If so should proceed overseas in time meet base on arrival. Meantime should contact Medical Directorate War Office.'

By the following Saturday, 16 December, when he played with the Mary's team and they trounced United Services at Portsmouth, matters had begun to move. All he could tell Helen was that 'by an unexpected turn of events I may be leaving soon to serve with my old show . . . all rather confidential and not fixed'. The streets of Portsmouth were full of men in uniform: his sensitivity about being in civilian dress was about to end.

On 15 December, fifty Australian officers and sixty other ranks had embarked on the *Strathallan* for Palestine: Brigadier Basil M. Morris

commanding an advance party of an Australian overseas base, and
Colonel George Vasey as the senior officer with a group of 6th Division
men. They were to 'reconnoitre a training area and prepare for the
reception of the remainder of the force', the first convoy of which was
to follow them in January 1940.[8]

As Assistant Director of Medical Services, Downes had appointed
Colonel H. Clive Disher. Disher had tutored Weary in anaesthetics at
the Royal Melbourne, had served in the First World War and was
known to Weary as having commanded a teetotal Field Ambulance in
the militia. Before he sailed, Disher had been told by Downes to expect
Weary in mid-January.[9]

Weary's date of enlistment is given as 13 November on his service
record, but he was not aware of this date until after the war. He had
no official communication from the Australian Army until the cable
ordering him to report to Bridgeford at Australia House in The Strand.
His response to the cable was immediate and affirmative.

On 23 December a cable marked 'urgent', 'official' and 'secret' was
handed to him. 'It seems that I am to proceed in a few days to the
Australian Overseas Base and start life all over again at a place I
can't . . . divulge yet.' He was wanted in Egypt by 15 January to take
up an appointment as Medical Officer, Headquarters, Australian
Overseas Base.[10]

Five shopping days remained before his departure on 1 January, and
two of those would be taken up with rugby matches. He had three days
to outfit, wind up his affairs and pack his bags. Weary was not always
good at selecting the appropriate dress for an occasion. Putting on the
militia uniform which he had carefully brought to England, he set off.
The appearance of a digger in emu feathers and breeches in The Strand
caused a near riot. He fled down Shaftesbury Avenue to Morris Angel,
the tailors, and ordered more conventional garb: one complete uniform
with barathea cap, shirts and shoes and a magnificent officer's greatcoat.
British Army officers wore shiny brass buttons, Australians did not: so
they painted them over.

The guineas for the tailor came from the 'massive cheque from the
Ministry of Health' which had arrived, after an anxious wait, in
November. A day and a half after being measured, he was fully outfitted
in a uniform 'of such magnificent cut that I'm credited with looking
rather like a guards' officer' rather than a member of the Australian
Expeditionary Force. Secretly, he enjoyed it.

No sooner had one offer been made and accepted, than the means of marrying Helen was handed to him. 'I leave England with the most deep regrets and turn my back on the most glorious opportunity which is likely to come my way. They are just reorganising to open Mary's with a full teaching staff and giving me a staff job as assistant surgeon.' Weary was offered a contract from the Ministry of Health, £900 per annum and 'permission to go into the army as a surgical specialist when required'.

Why did he reject the Mary's offer? When the cable arrived from Melbourne, he made an impulsive decision. Partly motivated by sentiment – he had held an Australian commission for two years – and with a feverish impatience to quit civilian life, he snatched at the Australian appointment, with no idea of what his rôle would be.

Weary had 'never quite got over as a boy that the war had finished before I could enlist . . . When the war started, I had no feeling but utter relief that here was a great, big, wonderful war to get involved in – I was sorry that it should have had to happen, but it was just my cup of tea . . . '

Weary wrote sadly to Helen on Boxing Day, in the midst of arranging uniforms and the storage of his possessions at London House: 'If you think I am a fool to rush away from my excellent opening here . . . I hope you will forgive me. I've been rather miserable about it, but am quite resolved.'

Once he had committed himself to something, Weary always had great difficulty with his conscience about changing his mind. 'What I say, I do,' he replied, many years later, when asked why he had not reversed a decision which could only cause personal difficulties.

On Boxing Day, in fog and seeping rain, he played in a benefit match for the Red Cross with the United Hospitals against Nondescripts. Doctors drawn from several hospitals did not form as single-minded a team as the Mary's men, and they lost that day at Richmond by six points to thirteen. His last game in the United Kingdom was to be with the Barbarians at Cardiff Arms Park on 30 December.

On 28 December he had his medical examination and took the oath of enlistment. He was 32 years of age, '6 foot 4 inches in height and weighed 200 pounds'. Classification was unquestionably class I, as Major Henry Trethowan wrote on the medical history sheet. They would meet again in Egypt.

Weary packed one small suitcase and delivered the rest of his belongings to the basement of London House. The large framed photographs of Helen, whom he playfully called 'your sister' in his letters, were left behind.

Fog and a frozen ground caused the game in Wales to be cancelled. His disappointment was only slightly mollified by a telephone call from the president of the Barbarians: at the next meeting of the Barbarian Club, he intended to propose that Weary be made a member, one of only two members in the Club's history to be elected this way. Weary wore his Barbarian's tie proudly throughout his life.

Weary accompanied the Porritts and Mary Burghley to a slap-up New Year's Eve party given by an Argentinian millionaire at the Savoy. As Big Ben tolled the last of 1939 across an icy London, he slipped out of the great dining-room and strolled back to St Mary's. He was on his way to war.

Ten

Unholy Holy Land

WEARY SPENT NEW YEAR'S DAY dejectedly at Tilbury 'cowering in a refreshment room' with the other passengers destined for the SS *Mantola*. Raw, penetrating cold seeped up through the concrete floors of the Customs' sheds; depression and melancholy replaced his earlier excitement at being in uniform. 'My heart feels about as bleak as these cold, wind-swept docks, and the grey sea blanketed in fog.' He mourned for Mary's and the now vanished possibility of seeing Helen in England.

Around 8 pm a tender took them out to the ship. He was the only soldier amongst the 'whisky-bitten colonials . . . with their grubby children' returning to Kenya and Tanganyika, a few journalists and some Royal Navy Reserve officers bound for Malta and Aden. The AIF footed the bill of £38 for his first class saloon cabin on the top deck but provided nothing else; London had received no instructions about salary or allowances, had issued him with no pay book, so Weary had to pay his own way.[1]

They ran aground a few miles out of Tilbury and stood off Southend all next day. The slow old British India Line vessel was equipped for war with a 4.7 rear gun and an AA gun; and had pride of place as the flagship of the convoy with a rear admiral on board as commodore. Prevented the previous day from joining their convoy by snow and sleet, now they had to wait nearly nine hours for the tide.

They finally assembled on 3 January and the long line of ships, attended by two watchful planes and a destroyer, threaded their way past the wrecks with 'funnels and masts acting as tombstones' and through the mine-swept Channel.

It took five days to clear the Channel and steam far out into the Atlantic (by then most passengers and the ship's doctor, Seamus O'Shea, had influenza), and another four to reach Gibraltar. Weary clung to his bunk in Gibraltar; his influenza had become pneumonia. Those who were still on their feet were curious about him: as he had no idea where he was going or what he was to do, his reticence rendered him even more mysterious.

O'Shea appeared with a bottle of whisky – he ascribed the complications to a lack of 'the crature' – and wanted to put him ashore to recover in hospital, but Weary refused and continued to swallow sulphanilamide.

By Malta, he was well enough to go ashore, where after blundering into a bar where officers were not welcome and being redirected to a hotel, he fell in with 'two fantastic bearded Australian officers of the RN, wild devils both'. They proceeded to 'beat up' the town. Their cure for the ferocious hangover he had next day was a 'Prairie Oyster', a blistering concoction of egg yolk, Worcestershire sauce, cayenne pepper and mustard. 'It baffles me often why I . . . should have something of a flair for attracting hell-bent company,' he complained to Helen.

When Weary reported to the embarkation officer on the docks at Port Said on the morning of 21 January, he found a British sergeant major awaiting him with a 13-cwt truck and a 3-ton lorry. Accustomed to the bulky wardrobe trunks, valises and campaign furniture that usually accompanied officers, he flicked a surprised gaze over the modest suitcase. 'You'll not be needing the three-tonner then,' he said.

Headquarters in Melbourne had under-estimated the time the voyage from England would take; Downes, expecting Weary to be in Egypt before the advance party arrived and in need of an escort and accommodation, had alerted Major-General Tomlinson, the British Director of Medical Services in the Middle East, to that end.[2]

There was no hoped-for opportunity to explore Cairo; Weary's destination was revealed as Palestine, where he was to join the Australian Overseas Base in Jerusalem. After giving him two days to see the sights and while away an evening at La Cygale, the NCO delivered him to the railway station at Port Said in the late afternoon. He left him with explicit instructions to disembark from the Cairo train at the Canal, take the ferry across to Kantara and board the next Palestine-bound train. Weary kicked his heels on the platform until it arrived at 3 am on the twenty-third.

Some hours later, in the chilly light of a brief Palestine dawn, he was looking out on the orange groves of the Plain of Sharon.[3]

After an eight-hour crawl across the Sinai Desert, he jumped stiffly down onto the platform at Lydda to be greeted by the tall, spare figure of his new boss, the Assistant Director of Medical Services Colonel Clive Disher. 'Upright as a lance' and 'piercingly blue' of eye, Disher and he had last been together in the operating theatres of the Royal Melbourne Hospital, Disher as anaesthetist, Weary as an embryo surgeon in Hailes's team. They were the first two Australian medical officers to arrive in Palestine.

Weary, privy to many stories about the teetotal field ambulance which Disher had run in the militia between the wars, was dumbfounded to hear him order two gimlets in the bar at the Hotel Fast, where they sat down for a drink after driving up through the barren, stony hills to Jerusalem. It was some time before he discovered that Disher had an understanding with George, the barman: 'Sir *Tabeeb's*' drinks never contained gin.

Disher was delighted to have him. Despite the tactful supervision of the British Deputy Director of Medical Services in Palestine, Colonel D. T. M. Large, he was feeling the strain of meeting the punishing schedule for preparing hospital and camp sites agreed to by Australian Headquarters before his departure from Melbourne.[4] But 'what is [Dunlop's] proper capacity here?' asked Disher of Downes: in the rush of appointment and departure, no one had defined Weary's job. 'Variously described on paper as MO to Base HQ and DADMS to Base HQ; as each other service has a Deputy assistant I am calling him acting DADMS – matter of prestige for the AAMC.'[5]

He was issued with a Colt .45 (for which no ammunition was available at first) and installed in a bedroom at the Hotel Fast, overlooking the Tower of David and David's Gate.

Weary learned he was to be a 'paper doctor'. No surgery, nor any prospect of it. And not much pay, either, compared to what his counterparts in the British Army received: his full drawing as a captain was 21s 0d a day. He joined Disher in the two offices allotted them at base headquarters in the hotel. The day after his arrival, Disher wrote to Downes that his new assistant was 'keen as mustard . . . and of use already'.[6]

Weary had been as delighted to find that he was to work for Disher, as Disher was relieved to see him. He had a profound respect for his former teacher in anaesthetics. Also, he was thankful that he need not accommodate his commanding officer's previous insistence on a 'strictly non-alcoholic mess' and quickly found himself part of a congenial group of drinking companions. 'Gets on very well with everybody. An ideal comrade to work with,' commented Disher to Downes.[7]

The site at Gaza Ridge for the 2/1st Australian General Hospital was to be ready for the arrival of its Commanding Officer, Colonel J.

Steigrad, and his hospital staff with the first AIF convoy in the middle of February. Disher and he put in long hours on the medical arrangements.

Palestine was a British Protectorate and the British Army was everywhere. They had the overall command of Dominion troops throughout the Middle East, and initially in Palestine the Australians were under the command of Lieut-General M. G. H. Barker. The advance party of Australians, which Weary had joined, was led by Brigadier Basil Morris, with Lieut-Colonel George Vasey in charge of administration as Assistant Adjutant and Quartermaster-General and Major Ronald Irving, General Blamey's GSO2. There were more officers than other ranks: sixty to fifty of the latter.[8]

The Australians worked harder than the British, who devoted their afternoons to tennis, riding – even polo – and other sports before resuming work in the evening, and they needed to be available during British working hours as well. From 8.30 am until 8 pm, with not much more than an hour for lunch and a brief siesta, Weary plunged into an examination of maps, camp and hospital sites, regulations and vast piles of documents. Some days, he felt he did little more than move a mass of paperwork between his in and out trays.

Disher sent him across to Colonel Large's offices at Force Head-quarters in the King David Hotel for an extensive briefing about the medical aspects of the camps, for they had accumulated a mass of information abut health conditions in Palestine during the inter-war years; and there were innumerable people to meet. But he did not receive the formal training which officers who arrived with the first and second convoys were to experience.

Disher's correspondence with Burston and Downes shows that the two Australians at base operated a 'seat of the pants' system driven by Disher's First World War experience in a field ambulance and as Regimental Medical Officer in the 4th Field Artillery, his inflexible sense of discipline and a hearty dose of commonsense.

From the first, Disher and Weary enjoyed a most cordial relationship with Large and his staff, who did all they could to push ahead the building of the medical facilities to serve the chain of camps being prepared by the British and base staff for the accommodation of the Australian troops.

The 2/1st Australian General Hospital at Gaza Ridge, near Gaza, was to provide 600 beds, with an additional 200 beds in the 2/1st Australian Casualty Clearing Station at Qastina. This, together with the 2/1st

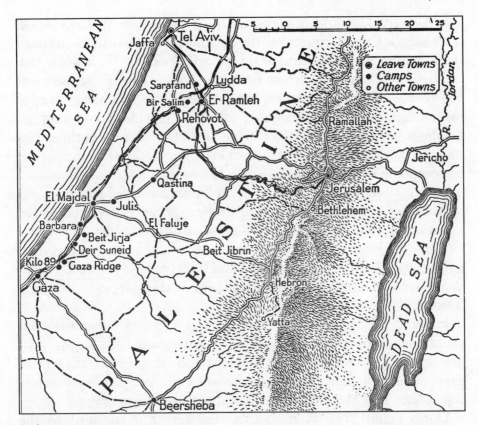

Palestine camps

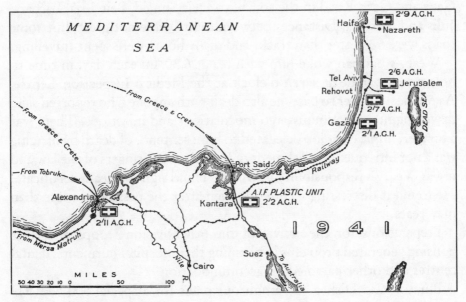

Hospitals, Middle East

Convalescent Depot to be commanded by Lieut-Colonel L. G. Male, was thought to be adequate for the Australians' immediate needs until the establishment of the 2/2nd AGH under Colonel W. W. S. Johnston.

There were a million details to settle, from assessing the merits of concrete as against canvas tent bottoms and tracing missing cases of medical equipment, to designing an operating block and hospital buildings.[9] Weary was allotted this last task. 'I spent most of three days sweating out designs . . . with furnishings,' he wrote to Helen, when at last outgoing mail was allowed on 31 January.

Weary could be a forthright critic, as Disher informed Headquarters in Australia, 'scornful of the calibre' of the expected hospital personnel and wanting to know if Downes 'had forgotten the calibre of Medical Corps'.[10] Colonel S. R. Burston, still desk-bound in Melbourne, himself compared the staff of the 2/1st AGH unfavourably with the 2/2nd in a letter to Disher, but hastily scribbled in the margin of the page: 'Don't tell No. 1!'

He need not have worried. Downes was well aware that the 2/1st could not compare with the hospital to accompany the second flight, that boasted twelve holders of English fellowships, Australia's most eminent bacteriologist, a surgeon who had won three Jacksonian prizes and at least two Members of the Royal College of Physicians.

Disher's and Weary's responsibilities were not confined to the hospital site at Gaza Ridge; they ranged across all seven camp areas from Gaza and Gaza Road in the south, to Deir Suneid, Beit Jirja, Barbara, Julis and Qastina. Distances between camps were not great, but some roads were no better than tracks and many hours were spent travelling.

Weary's batman woke him with tea at 6.30 am each day, in time to hold a sick parade at seven o'clock at the Medical Inspection Centre. As Medical Officer to base, he also dealt with anyone who reported sick, day or night, and administered inoculations and injections. There was a further, unpleasant job delegated to him: sentence of death by hanging was a not infrequent punishment of Palestinian infringers of the law and it was Weary's responsibility to witness it and sign the death certificate. He found it distressing to discuss, even after the passing of more than fifty years.

Preparations for the arrival of the 6th Division troops and their housing generated problems in planning their hospital hutments, dental centres and other paramedical accommodation.

Burston and Disher had ambitious plans for a special 500-bed VD hospital. In the meantime, Weary's pet project, over which he toiled for many hours, was the VD treatment centre. Under the tutelage of his opposite number on Large's staff, Captain Tony Scott, Weary planned buildings containing rows of irrigation cubicles to deal with the expected flow of infected soldiers.

Neither the British nor the Australians realised that sulphanilamide (M & B 693) and penicillin would revolutionise the treatment of venereal disease, and soon render obsolete his neatly drawn and measured plans and detailed lists.

But there was also time for sightseeing, and over the weeks he explored all of Jerusalem, slipping through the Jaffa Gate and wandering in the old city's maze of narrow streets and 'tortuous passageways of steps and stairs', along the *Via Dolorosa* to Calvary and the Church of the Holy Sepulchre. 'I feel like a tripper,' he told Helen, after cramming the Wailing Wall, the Mosque of Omar, the Tower of David, the Tomb of Kings, the Mount of Olives and the Garden of Gethsemane into one day.[11]

While he explored the stone-paved streets, Bible verses and their place names, which he had learned by heart and recited to James for pennies each Sunday at Stewarton, flooded into his head.

He climbed up through the twisted olive trees in the Garden of Gethsemane to the old Russian church on the Mount of Olives. The stillness was broken only by the faint voices of the sisters singing their daily office in one of the chapels, as he gazed out over Jerusalem. Beyond was the immense rift in the earth's surface that made up the Valley of the River Jordan, with the mountains of Moab and the Dead Sea shimmering far off like a 'small lake'. It was 'a lost world of tortured, domed hills, bare and brown', startlingly clear in that thin, keen air under the intense blue of the winter sky. It became one of Weary's favourite places, somewhere he could enjoy 'a great detachment and sense of peace'.[12]

A cable from Helen's mother had arrived in a packet of long-delayed mail on 2 February, wishing that he and Helen might enjoy some happiness in the coming year. As he sat in the cool green shade of the cypresses on the very top of the mountain, he decided to suggest to Helen that they announce their engagement.[13]

Jerusalem 'nearly kills us with evening parties,' wrote Weary. Whereas Disher regarded the nightly social activities as a 'blasted nuisance but . . . part of the job', which he avoided when possible, Weary accepted every invitation. By the time he had been in Jerusalem a month, he confessed ruefully to Helen that 'he could not recall a day in which he did not go out in the evening to a local bunfight'.

'Scarcely an eligible girl in the place,' Weary told James and Alice. Of the few that were there Sir Harold MacMichael's daughter might intimate to Weary that she would like more than one dance with him, but a strict protocol ensured that no officer have more than his due. British and Australian officers competed for partners among the nurses and masseuses, and the wives and daughters of the British officers and civilians.

Most, amongst them Mann, Weary, Norris, Moore and Vasey, drank steadily in off-duty hours; all, including Clive Disher, indulged in energetic horse-play and wrestling matches in the mess after dinner.

Within a fortnight of his arrival, he experienced the lavish and alarming hospitality of a local, pro-British Arab. Sheik Hanna Bey Bisharat and his brother, Shiblee Bey, from Transjordania, had ridden with Lawrence, had known Allenby, and delighted in reminiscing about the previous war's campaigns. The group of staff officers, including Morris, Milne (the camp commandant), Vasey and Weary, lunched rather too well on a whole roasted sheep stuffed with pilau, dripping with grease, and presented as a 'mountain of meat and . . . immense foothills of vegetables' on a gigantic metal dish. When they protested they could eat no more, the Sheik and his family 'walked around pulling delicacies from the depleted sheep with their bare hands and pushing them into our mouths'.

To the admiration of all, Weary swallowed an eye, and his host – who, according to custom, would not eat until his guests had finished – enthusiastically thrust the other into his mouth.[14]

Stuffed full of mutton, rice, sweets, fruit and alcohol – Hanna Bey Bisharat served whisky and gin in pint glasses to these unbelievers – they were driven back to base. Disher, who prudently had declined the invitation, noted in some amusement that a number requested indigestion remedies. Weary felt slightly queasy but was not as affected as some of his fellows; they all retired to their beds for what remained of the afternoon.

On 12 February, the first flight of the 2nd AIF arrived in Egypt. The New South Wales-raised 16th Brigade and the first contingent of the New Zealand Expeditionary Force, who had travelled in convoy with them, were met by an unusually eminent reception committee. Anthony Eden, Secretary for the Dominions, had flown out from England and greeted Brigadier Allen and his staff on board the *Otranto* flanked by the slim figure of General Sir Archibald Wavell, Commander-in-Chief of the Middle East military forces, and Sir Miles Lampson, British Ambassador to Egypt.

Weary was up at 4.30 am on Tuesday 13 February to drive into Gaza with Disher and Vasey to meet the troops. Morris was already down at the Canal; Irving had left the previous week to meet the ships at Aden. For two days, between 6.30 am and 2.30 pm, a train arrived every two hours and disgorged the khaki-clad men into the wintry weather for a hot meal and tea before taking them on to El Majdal Station and the buses which conveyed them to Julis camp.

It was Weary's job to hand out the paperwork to the medical officers, arrange for the sick to be evacuated to hospital and deal with any problems. Until their own hospital was established, Australian cases were to go to the British No. 12 General Hospital at Jerusalem and Sarafand.

The second train that Tuesday contained the hospital personnel, who were transferred to buses and driven to Gaza Ridge. Disher and Weary drove Steigrad to the camps and to British Force Headquarters, then took him back to Jerusalem for the night. Disher reported to Downes that Steigrad's reaction to the hospital site was unfathomable: 'possibly it doesn't look too complete.'[15] ('God what desolation!' Weary had written after his first visit to Qastina and Gaza Ridge on 27 January.)

Roads were well made, kitchens, ablution blocks and mess huts were up, but before the ploughed soil on which the tents were to be pitched could be rolled, rain had turned it into a sticky morass, and latrines and sullage pits were far from satisfactory. There was still a great deal of construction to be completed and the camp was overrun with native contractors touting for washing and suchlike.

The nurses reactions were not recorded. Weary, anxious to make the camp more welcoming, had enquired of Force HQ what he should put in their tents (they had been told to bring their own beds). Once they had picked their way through the mud to their hastily erected accommodation, they found an iron and ironing board had been provided for their use, and in each tent was a looking glass and a vase of flowers.

Yet the views were marvellous, especially at Julis, where one could sweep one's eyes across the wide valley from the blue Mediterranean to the mountains of Moab. And at this time of year, all was green.

After sleeping and working at the Hotel Fast for the first few weeks, the base staff were turned out on 14 February in order that it might become an Australian soldiers' hostel. Disher, Weary, Staff Sgt E. Cunningham and their Jewish stenographer moved to three offices in the Russian Compound. The mess was in Silberstein House, a short walk away.

Scorning a billet at Silberstein House, where most of the others were, Weary moved to Mea House in Julian's Way with Colonel Guy Moore and engineers Colonel Joe Mann and Captain Ellesmere ('Mac') MacCausland. Mac, who was involved in billeting arrangements, suggested that it would be a snug 'home away from home'. They were a hard-drinking quartet. Their brother staff officers promptly christened it the 'Tomcats' House'.

Weary found the winter of 1940 'one of the coldest . . . I've ever gone through, as far as sleeping was concerned'. From his window he looked out on the gaunt walls and the houses of the old city, their outlines softened under a thick covering of snow. The single oil heater in his room was ineffective against the bitter cold of the highlands and he slept in his clothes with his greatcoat piled on top of the blankets.

Thieving Arabs had stripped the house bare before they moved in: there was no hot water service, no furniture, carpets, light fittings or curtains. Each man slept on a camp stretcher and kept his clothes in a travelling trunk that did combined duty as wardrobe, chest of drawers and dressing table.

Lindsay Male was temporarily attached to the hospital until a suitable site could be found for the Convalescent Depot, but for some months, Male's main problem was that no one would agree on one. Force HQ's attitude to this was an ever-nagging annoyance to the Australian medical and engineering staff. A great deal of time inspecting all possible locations was expended by everyone, including Disher and Large, the latter strongly recommending the cooler air of the Judean Highlands.

But Large's friendly co-operation was not paralleled by other British staff officers, who could be arrogant and patronising to the Australians. Weary's months in England had armed him against such behaviour; others, less experienced, were baffled by the overt rudeness. Shortly after his arrival in February, Male was amazed at the treatment he and Weary received when they called on Brigadier G. S. Brunskill and Lieut-Colonel Forestier-Walker to seek approval for the Convalescent Depot to be established on the site near Jerusalem.

Brunskill was tall and powerfully built with a black patch over one eye, a regular soldier who had won a Military Cross in the First World War, and he towered over the small, neat figure of Male with his carefully-parted hair and quiet Australian voice. It was obvious to the two Australians that they were held in contempt – as also was Large – by this brigadier who had been in charge of administration in Palestine and the Transjordan since 1937. He had no intention of allowing the Australians to take over any first-class accommodation anywhere in Palestine.

When Weary introduced Male, the latter was ignored and neither man was invited to sit down – even though Male was a lieutenant-colonel and Weary was representing the head of the Australian medical staff. By then, Brunskill had removed himself to his office next door, and a three-way conversation ensued, with Forestier-Walker calling out to his superior officer through the wall.

They were turned out shortly afterwards, no further ahead. Male was now angry, as well as frustrated. Weary was fuming. 'My pet enemy,' Disher called Brunskill in a fit of irritation.[16]

Everyone on the medical and engineering staff participated in the search, which took them over much of coastal Palestine. Eventually, it was sited at Kafr Vitkin, a pleasing oasis compared to Jerusalem's bare, stony hills.

Neither Jews nor Arabs involved the Australians in the political unrest which simmered constantly: the British or the police were the main targets. All Australian officers had to carry pistols, however, and outside the city, they must be accompanied by an armed escort as well as a driver and be out of the hills by 5.30 pm.

Weekends were lively with parties, dinners, picnics and expeditions into the wilderness of Transjordania. On one occasion, they ran into an Arab caravan on the outskirts of Jerash. 'All . . . hell broke loose, with pots and pans and chooks raining down on the desert and screaming Arabs and ladies in heavy purdah pulling their veils across.'

The car stalled. Only Weary had remembered to bring sidearms, and the little .25 which had replaced his unwieldy Colt was useless, as it always jammed after one shot. Their Jewish driver nervously kept his head well down, fiddling with the starter, while in front of them loomed Arabs trailing carbines, knives and pistols, eyes flashing from their blackened eye-pits. One, more threatening than his fellows, screamed at them as the driver engaged first, then second gear and pulled away. Weary asked the driver what he had said. It was not as terrible as it had sounded: 'Slower, brother, slower!'

In Jerusalem, small shops were out of bounds and an even earlier 4 pm curfew was in force at one time. This limited movement between camps later in the day, and both Weary and Disher found that official duties often kept them out after curfew.

Jews stayed well away from Arab towns and villages, particularly on the Moslem holy day, but one Friday very shortly after Weary arrived he ordered his Jewish driver to take him into Gaza after he had been inspecting the hospital site. Weary was armed, so reluctantly the driver agreed.

The Arabs moved out of their path unwillingly, most of them spitting at the car. The driver slowed down to pass Gaza's great red water cart which was rumbling along the main street with a fellahin walking in front hosing filth off the road. As they drew level, he casually swung the nozzle round so that a jet of muddy water came through the open window and struck Weary in the chest.

He sprang out of the car, seized the man by his baggy trousers and the scruff of his neck and 'solemnly lifted him in the air and walked to the side of the road' where he put him across his knee and walloped his backside with his stick. A crowd of decidedly hostile Arabs gathered. Weary pushed the fellahin off and straightened up. Suddenly, someone laughed, and the whole scene broke up. They had realised he was Australian, not British: 'I suppose it was an unprecedented act for a British officer.'

The Arabs remembered the Australians in the last war only too well. Weary was well aware that he should never have insisted on going there on a Friday. His quaking driver could scarcely wait to move off.

Palestine was quiet when the first flight of Australians arrived in mid-February, but a fortnight later, when the British White Paper of 1939 limiting the purchase of land by Jews to particular areas was enforced, the Jewish population erupted with demonstrations almost daily, street riots and bombs.

Leave was cancelled and cordons of police obstructed the streets near the Russian Compound. From the roof, Weary watched a company of the 2/Black Watch led by their colonel, Hamilton, waving a chair leg, with his men close behind bearing circular riot shields like dustbin lids on their left arms and brandishing wooden clubs and baseball bats, clear the protesting Jews from the streets of Jerusalem.

'All the permanent forces stationed here are on quite a peace footing with their wives . . . and one has to study the newspaper hard to convince oneself that anything warlike is really going on.'[17] Weary believed that the hills of Judaea were a backwater in the world's eyes; he scanned the war maps in the *Daily Telegraph* and the *Daily Express* in vain for a mention of their presence, and feared he would be there for months.

But there was one advantage to this. Helen was not only eager to be engaged: she wrote about joining him in Palestine. Weary rushed to the telephone when he received Mephan Ferguson's letter containing his blessing for the engagement, and was bitterly disappointed to discover that overseas calls were forbidden. 'Oh darling, so much easier to talk about many things difficult to write.'

Jerusalem was the only place suitable for her to stay in, and he was 'simply crazy' for her to come, but pride made him sound cautious and inarticulate at first. After writing in one letter, 'I tried hard last week to tell you that my salary is horridly inadequate . . . for an officer's wife', he was stricken with worry lest she had misunderstood him, and pleaded: 'Beloved, if you have set your heart of coming out to me . . . don't wait . . . just come *soon* . . . Let us try the mad thing for once. I fear very much that if we wait for a peaceful and sensible world to be happy in that we will have to spend long years rather miserably.'[18]

The important matter of buying the ring was delegated to Aunt Lil. 'I've picked you out for a very special task involving a ring . . . there will be approximately £50 . . . You could either yourself or after conversation with the lady in question select a jeweller, and I suppose the least embarrassing way would then be to have him to show a selection.

'In case you think in view of all this that I'm being extravagant . . . I have been saving very carefully . . . it is the one thing one cannot be too small about . . . I feel small enough as it is.'[19]

The announcement was to be made in June.

There were precedents for Helen coming to Palestine. Apart from some Australian civilian wives, Brigadier Allen's wife was living in a flat in Jerusalem, and MacCausland's wife, Cynthia, was expected on 25 February. Weary, Disher and John Wilson accompanied Mac to Lake Tiberias, 'that placid sheet of water ringed by the great hills down which plunged the Gadarene swine', to meet the flying boat from Sydney. When it failed to arrive, Disher commandeered two boats on the lake and challenged Weary and MacCausland to a race. Wilson had rowed for Melbourne Grammar and earned a blue at Cambridge, Disher for Melbourne's Scotch College and Ormond College, as well as stroking the victorious AIF crew which won the King's Cup in the Royal Henley Peace Regatta. The other two spent most of the time splashing round in circles, while the Arab boatmen flapped up and down on the shores of the Sea of Galilee and cheered.

'Best trip . . . ever,' said Disher, who proclaimed his crew 'Head of the Lake'.[20] The Australian press heard about it and around ten days later, Helen read an exaggerated account in the *Argus*.

Weary did not share his boss's taste for playing Chinese checkers when off-duty. He preferred hockey, squash at the Jerusalem Sports Club with Geoff Norris, tennis, boxing with anyone who would square up to him, and rugby in the scratch team he started and called 'Jerusalem'. It included a few civilians, 'one or two army characters that played rugby', a fellow medico whom he knew from the Brompton Hospital and anyone else Weary could recruit to play on the slopes of Mount Scopus.

By their third match on 9 March, he had them playing a better game. This Saturday, they were facing the Black Watch. Weary had not yet modified his style of play to the stony conditions and he tackled one of their subalterns, Captain Hamilton, so fiercely that the two of them went down in a shower of stones. Both men 'got up bleeding from every pore – elbows, knees, hips, chin . . . and he said, "You know, old boy, we don't play quite like that here!"' It was the first game Jerusalem had won.

But the Black Watch harboured no ill feelings and occasionally he borrowed some of them to make up the numbers in the rugby team.

His romantic love of all things Scottish drew him strongly to their company. Amongst all the entertaining in Jerusalem at the time, Weary's greatest delight was dining with the Black Watch: first, the ceremony of the Retreat and then, the formal dinner in the mess, with a bottle of Drambuie placed beside each officer's elbow towards its end. He thrilled to the wail of the pipes, the regimental piper preceding his colonel into the mess and standing behind him to play throughout the evening.

'They were nights to remember, dining with the Watch after Retreat . . . People would dance reels on the tables and sing . . . ' His memories of the 2/Black Watch were made more poignant by the fate of so many of the officers and men who became friends in Jerusalem.

It was almost annihilated during the evacuation from Crete and in the Western Desert the following year. 'It was very distressing . . . all those beautiful young men killed in war.'

His letters to Helen express a loneliness of spirit and a deepening longing for her and surgery and the kind of life which he did not dare admit he might never regain. He endeavoured to overcome his depression in the wild round of hard work – ' . . . A whale for work,' wrote Disher to Melbourne Headquarters, 'and when I can't supply it . . . he finds it for himself'[21] – and even more desperate play.

It was months before Weary confided to her: 'Some happier day perhaps I will tell you about it all . . . the moody gaiety, and deep, deep drinking. Perhaps it is all part of the training which brings a little soldierly quality even to those rather remote from the field – the ability to trample down personal longings and busy oneself with a job.'

Although Weary never discussed his frustration at being confined to staff work, Disher was well aware that he longed for an appointment as a surgeon, and suggested to Downes: 'I hope it can be arranged for Dunlop to get some surgery somewhere . . . Must find a better job for him . . . Too good a man to be chasing drunken, vomiting troops at all hours . . . '[22]

Inevitably, there was trouble with troops on leave in Jerusalem. Brigadier Morris was angry and worried, Disher reported to Downes. ' . . . One feels ashamed especially on meeting the local Britishers here. Most of the Regimental officers and some COs . . . treat it as a joke and say it is only high spirits & that they will fight well. Perhaps they will but that is no excuse for men lying drunk in gutters and sometimes fighting mad.'[23] It was one of Weary's jobs to patch up the injured. The men of the 6th Division did not impress him, either.

The British were prepared to think the worst of the Australians, and Disher was sensitive to criticism, especially since he thought it was justified. 'If the present mob is a fair example of what the Division is to be then I don't know that one would feel very proud of being in the Div.'[24] Vasey – who christened himself 'the bloody housekeeper of the 6th Division' and issued a stream of instructions about the behaviour of troops – complained in a letter to his wife that they behaved on leave like guttersnipes, indulging in 'endless larrikinism, thefts and . . . general nuisance'.[25]

In March, with Julis occupied and almost complete, and the hospital settled at Gaza Ridge, the Australians intensified their efforts at preparing the other camps for the second flight. There were shortages of almost everything, including tents, heaters, stretchers and the flywire needed when the hot weather arrived.

Camp inspection with the engineers absorbed a great deal of Weary's time. Mann, who 'looked rather a sleepy little character . . . had an extraordinarily alert eye for anything . . . not on schedule'. Both Julis and Qastina, where 6th Division Headquarters was, had twenty-bed camp hospitals staffed by field ambulances; and each of the other camps was to have a medical reception centre run by the medical officer attached to the unit. Everything was to be ready for the second flight in mid-May, but they were thwarted at every turn by Brunskill and Force HQ, who could be 'desperately slow when they want'.[26] The other sites were even further behind the 2/1st AGH.

Weary became acting ADMS Australian Overseas Base on 18 April, when Disher moved to Gaza with 6th Division Headquarters as their ADMS, 'so until the new ADMS Base arrives, I am Medical Pooh-Bah Jerusalem'. He had plenty of help: Ted Cunningham remained as the staff sergeant, the Jewish stenographer who spoke six languages and was a Doctor of Philosophy would continue to type and take dictation, and there were two orderlies to run errands.

Weary was still recovering from sandfly fever, which had seized him suddenly on the morning he left for Petra, fortified with APC tablets. It might be his only chance to go there, so he stowed his shivering form in the large car lent them by a civilian friend. Their two drivers, one Bulgarian and one Russian, were fluent in Arabic and knew the road.

They drove through tracts of country bright with great, black iris and scarlet poppies, hollyhocks, tulips, anemones and vivid blue campanula. Herds of goats and fat-tailed sheep grazed around the sprawling, black tents of the wild Bedouin. Beyond Amman in Arabia, there were no formed roads, just desert tracks across endless stony miles. By 11 pm, when they reached Ma'an, Weary was chilled and shivering with a high temperature, his head pounding, and he was suffering recurrent bouts of vomiting.

All was forgotten next day when they rode their hired ponies down through the Wadi Musa into Petra. As they suddenly turned at a sheer wall of rock, Weary lifted his aching head to face the 'incredible cleft' called the Siq.

They wound on for nearly twenty kilometres in almost perpetual twilight and warm, stale air, the sheer sandstone walls at times barely three or four metres apart. 'Suddenly through a gash in the mountain-side, there is a startling flood of light and beauty, and where the way opens out . . . you are looking directly at the rosy marvel called El Khazueh or the Treasury, a huge temple carven out of the lower half of the precipitous rock with slender, graceful, Corinthian columns, rich sculpture, sphinxes and a statue of the Goddess Isis.' He marvelled at the achievements of the ancient Nabataeans, forgetting his fever in the excitement. The memory of that moment never left him.

At the end of the three-day journey, stiff with dust and fatigue and still aching with fever, Weary fell thankfully into bed. Scarcely able to sit up, he wrote page after page to Helen.

Next day, he had recovered sufficiently to take part in the rugby union trial match at Julis, where a team was picked to play against the French in Syria. On 20 April, still feeling rather weak, he captained the AIF in Tel Aviv when they played The Rest as a preliminary to their match against the French Army of the Levant. The AIF team won 8–3, 'on a terribly hard ground which cut one's feet about'. Weary realised that he was not up to his English form, but hoped to improve after training with the team the following week down in the camp at Gaza. He was to be their coach and vice-captain.[27]

That week, he had inoculated several hundred soldiers, and when Disher came up to Jerusalem on Sunday, they spent the day tidying up the paperwork. A relief medical officer, Major Salter, was to fill in for him and instructed to consult Large daily.

By Anzac Day, Weary was installed in a 'nice hot little circular tent' with his team on the Plains of the Philistines. The army had exchanged its winter uniform for drill shirts and shorts, and he missed the cool Jerusalem nights. Whilst most of the camp departed at 3 am for the Dawn Service, the 'lords of the football squad' lay abed and then enjoyed a late breakfast at seven o'clock.

By the time their bus left for Beirut on Saturday 27 April, they were footsore after three days' training on the stony ground, which removed a good deal of skin during each morning's PT and the afternoon's two-hour run. Weary enjoyed the break from medical routine: 'I like the Australian soldier . . . more in these camps than when he is letting off steam in Jerusalem and razing the town to the ground . . . ' And there was the pleasure of 'tumbling in the surf in perfectly nude condition too full of tingling life to worry about the ghostly spectre' of war.

The match that Sunday before 7000 spectators was a lively affair, serenaded by a massed brass band of French colonial troops and attended by the picturesque army of the Levant: French zouaves, coal-black Senegalese with sharp-filed teeth, slender Indo-Chinese and Algerian spahis with huge cavalry swords. The French had done their best to wreck the Australians' form by keeping them out of bed most of the Saturday night at *Le Cercle des Officiers* and heaping food and wine on them at luncheon before the game.

The Australian newspaper men all turned up for the fun. John Hetherington reported to his Melbourne *Herald* readers that a 'more spectacular setting . . . could not be imagined. The white roofs of the city shimmered in hot, bright sunshine beyond the walls of the stadium and the snow-capped peaks of the hills of Lebanon were visible in the distance . . . French officers and men wearing brilliant képis . . . and fashionably dressed women [were] . . . reminiscent of an Australian race meeting'.[28]

It was a tough contest. The French had eight Internationals in their team and 'played an absolutely foul game', determined to keep their place as the champions of the Middle East.

'. . . They were fairly strong thugs, really . . . in defence, they took a firm grasp on the trousers or tunic of the fellow ahead . . . and raised . . . [an] elbow to hit you in the teeth when you tried to break through.' The French referee ignored these illegal tactics. The ground looked green enough, but the thin crust of sand hampered heavier players like Weary. 'Large buffaloes like me were breaking through the crust as we ran.'

The Australians made no headway during the first half and Weary twisted his ankle in the loose sand. They were all heartily tired of the French by now. Weary gathered the forwards together just before they went on again: 'Look, chaps, just for now, let's forget about the *entente cordiale*!'

'I went up to tackle a fullback with a high kick, and a Frenchman deliberately fouled me by getting in my way very near tackling . . . I hit him with my fist and the palm of my hand so fiercely that he rolled over and over at the feet of his general . . . ' General Humblot, Commander of the French forces in Syria, burst out, '*Magnifique, mais très féroce*!'

Weary's mad elephant act started things happening. 'We won the game, all right,' by 11 points to 5. The French scored only one converted try, the AIF two tries, one converted, and a penalty goal.

That night the Kit Kat Club was awash with champagne when the French entertained their victorious brothers in arms to dinner, then took them on to The Lido for cabaret and glamorous hostesses. Weary managed only a few hours sleep in his room in the Hotel Royal.

Later on the twenty-eighth, while they continued their celebrations, in Europe British and French troops prepared to withdraw from Norway. Two days later, Hitler received the news that the German troops which had landed at Oslo and Trondheim at the same time as Weary was driving to Petra had now linked up. Weary's hopes of seeing Helen dimmed. 'I've long known . . . that it might be very hard for you to get out here . . . things are looking black . . . '

No sooner did he arrive back in Jerusalem that Tuesday, feeling thoroughly jaded, than he was summoned to the hospital at Gaza Ridge. Steigrad's hospital was still unfinished and they struggled to function efficiently. The operating theatre was nowhere near complete and the advance depot medical stores building was not started. Large had been critical when he inspected it in mid-April, but he had no influence with Brunskill and his staff. Force HQ might be in charge of the grand plan, but 'all the hack work' had to be done by people like MacCausland, Mann and Weary in the face of British obstructiveness.

At dawn on 10 May, Hitler's army swept into Belgium and Holland: Operation Yellow had begun. General Karl Student's paratroopers of the XI Air Corps parachuted into Leiden, The Hague and Rotterdam. Glider-borne German troops captured Belgian bridges over the Albert Canal and attacked the fortress of Eben-Emael. The first of the German Panzer divisions crossed the River Meuse.

In London, Chamberlain resigned and Winston Churchill took his place as Prime Minister and Minister of Defence.

'War on the Western Front at last. Oh how I should like to be there instead of rusting and souring in this out of the way corner . . . ' Weary felt as remote from action as the poverty-stricken old Russian nuns shut away from the world at the church he visited in John the Baptist's village of Ain Harem. 'Was another war actually going on?' they asked. 'Was Russia in it, and if so, fighting with whom – Australia? *Nous ne comprenons pas.*'

The Command were worried about the proximity of Italy and her Air Force. Steigrad organised a trial blackout exercise at the hospital on 13 May; and the medical service drew up plans for the treatment of casualties in the event of bombing raids. Disher told Colonel Cunningham of 2/1st Field Ambulance to look for a site in the back country for an emergency dressing station; and sent Weary off on a shopping expedition for quinine.

Both the second and third convoys were at sea; the second was to arrive in a few days and the malaria season would soon be upon them. The artillery and rifle ranges, to which troops were sent for training, were in potentially malarious areas.

Holland surrendered on 15 May; three days later, as the news from Europe became blacker and the British, French and Belgian armies were in retreat, the second convoy of Australians arrived in Palestine.

Each day, Weary's new batman, George Reid, woke him at 3 am to drive down to Gaza to meet the trains. The troops disembarked at the station into the swirling dust and grit of the *khamsin* and a furnace blast temperature of 40 degrees Celsius. They all looked 'browned out' after the crawl across the Sinai.

Most of the personnel of the 2/2nd AGH arrived on 18 May. Weary recognised many of those who jumped down from the high wooden box carriages onto the platform. Only one of his contemporaries, Bob Officer, arrived with Colonel W. W. S. Johnston and his hospital, but many familiar, older faces from the Royal Melbourne were there: Ian Wood, Leon Rothstadt, Eric Hughes-Jones, Julian Orm Smith, George Swinbourne and his old friend from the Receiving House at Royal Park, Colonel John Adey. Edgar King had remained at Port Said to supervise the unloading of the hospital equipment.

The journey up the Red Sea had produced the usual crop of upper respiratory tract infections: Weary dispatched Rothstadt, Orm Smith and Swinbourne with the rest of the sick to hospital, and delivered medical instructions to the regimental medical officers as they went through.[29] A dusty and clammy John Colquhoun gave him brief news of Helen, promising a longer bulletin when he visited Jerusalem.

For three days the trains disgorged Australian soldiers. He knew none of the new base staff and there was no sign of the ADMS who was to replace Disher there. 'It seems my definite fate to hang on here in charge of the show until . . . the colonel who has been appointed turns up.'

Daily liaison with Disher by telephone and dispatch rider continued; and when Weary went down to Gaza, the two men often snatched time for a swim in the Mediterranean. 'We have all begun to work a little harder . . . my days are invariably rather full . . . '

Weary remained 'the unlucky ugly duckling of the AAMC so far as surgery goes', but his administrative rôle was 'some scant consolation', for it allowed him to be of use to his old friends. Disher and he had been planning for the arrival of the medical staff of the 2/2nd AGH since February, when Downes suggested that 'there is a great period of boredom and semi-idleness in front of . . . 2nd AGH officers . . . '

They were distributed over camp reception stations and the British hospitals at Haifa, Sarafand and Jerusalem. John Adey was installed in the hospital housed in the beautiful Kaiserina Victoria Augusta palace on Mt Scopus, as was John Colquhoun; King, Orm Smith and Rothstadt were to work at Sarafand. And a busy programme of courses, demonstrations and clinical meetings began. Disher had agreed with Burston and Downes that the expertise of Colonel Johnston's unit should be tapped for training Australian Army Medical Corps personnel in the Middle East.

At the beginning of June Disher sent Weary an assistant, Captain Carter. Officially, Brigadier Morris complained that Weary would never conquer the 'paper war' if he also had to act as medical officer. Quietly, Disher was told that Weary had been too busy even to get drunk, and, given his previous record, this was interpreted as a sign of overwork.

Of his former companions, only MacCausland remained. Mann, Moore and Geoff Norris had gone to Gaza and the 6th Division at the same time as Disher; Tony Scott had been promoted to major and transferred to Force HQ in Egypt, removing simultaneously his 'excellent German cook' and Weary's 'best meal ticket'.

With the arrival of the second flight of troops, he had added a daily parade at the detention barracks to his duties. Head down against the force of the *khamsin*, he walked past the Tower of David to the Pool of Silom and a 'fantastic, antique . . . building. It had marvellous murals and ceilings and beautiful mosaic floors'.

As the troops were led in one by one to this beautiful 'glasshouse',* he used to wince at the crashing of iron-shod boots on the fragile, colourful tiles. 'There would be a clang, clang, clang, clang, *bang!* as they halted, then a screaming sergeant major: "On the command, enter! You will take two paces forward through the door, drop your trousers below your knees, and say – All correct, or not, sir!" Whereupon there'd be a clang, clang! and some poor, dejected wretch would drop his trousers and quaver, "All correct or not, sir!" '

Weary owned two Sam Browne belts. A punishment meted out in the

---

* British military term for a prison.

barracks was that one be polished for twenty-four hours until he reappeared the following day.

Vasey and Disher at divisional HQ and Steigrad at 2/1st AGH had other problems. 'Blast Force HQ and their continued obstruction,' exploded Disher, when there was no progress on buildings to accommodate the additional staff of the second convoy. At the hospital, Steigrad had to move his tented wards while workmen began to pour concrete floors at a time when it contained over two hundred patients. When the second flight arrived, 430 were in his care. Tents and patients had to be moved, then moved back again once the concrete had dried.

Blackout was imposed on Palestine on 4 June and made letter writing difficult; the atmosphere in the mess did not put Weary in the frame of mind for writing love letters, whilst heavily screened windows in his room created an airless fug, and torchlight attracted the mosquitoes.

Weary and Helen's engagement was announced in Melbourne on Thursday 6 June 1940. Helen placed the small, square-set diamond on her finger herself. Together with her mother and Alice, she had been caught up in a whirl of newspaper announcements, photography, and plans for the engagement party. Alice and James were to be part of the excitement and planned a 'flying visit' of four days in Melbourne.[30]

Alice had prepared a 'write-up about "Ern" or "Edward", the more professional name & equally dear to me' for the Melbourne press and *Table Talk*. 'I . . . did not quite realise what Edward had accomplished till it was concisely pieced together . . . ' In a long postscript to the letter, she asked if Mary would mind inviting Alan and his wife, Winifred. There had been a rift between them and his parents and brother and Alice, as ever, 'contrived to help the dear boys to keep up a friendly spirit & keep in touch'.[31]

Weary spent the day of his engagement with MacCausland, inspecting progress at the convalescent depot site at Kafr Vitkin.

That evening they took Weary's batman with them to a little restaurant at nearby Natanya, ordered a good dinner and drank Helen's health. A lone and interesting looking woman entered during the evening, and Weary sent George Reid over to her with a note explaining that they were two Australian officers having a celebration: would she care to join them? He returned looking stunned. 'She says she's the Duchess of Roxburgh!' The two men laughed and continued their dinner.

17 *Australia beat NZ 25 to 11, 11 August 1934. Weary third from left, back row*

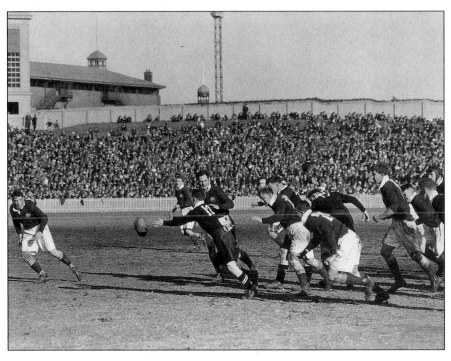

18 *About to collar the All Black scrum half, 1st Test 1934*

19 *Senior resident, Royal Melbourne Hospital, 1936*

20 *Alice Dunlop had a frail beauty – lovely eyes and a memorable warmth*

21 *On board SS* Ormonde. *Winter serge uniform was expensive*

22 *Egypt 1938 with Gabriel Wood (l.), 'Ailes' Macarthur and another passenger*

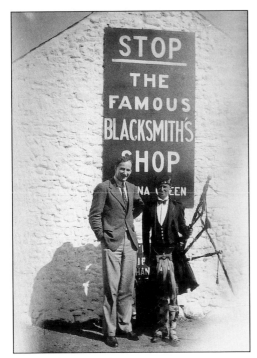

23 *Scotland was best of all, 1939*

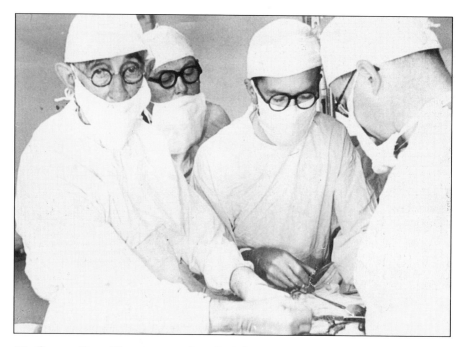

24 *George Grey-Turner operating. 'It is better to wear out*
than to rust.'

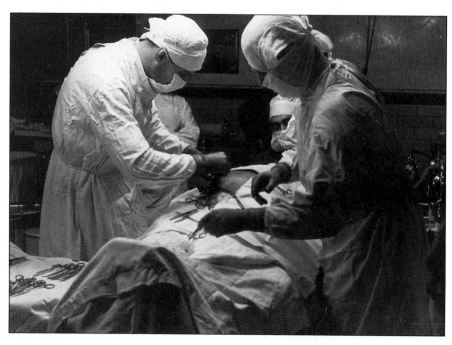

25 *War took Weary to St Mary's Paddington. They put six tables*
in the Lewis Loyd Ward for emergencies. Weary (l.) operating

26 'Why do you want to join the army?' asked Gordon Gordon-Taylor

27 Captain Dunlop VX 259, in superb barathea uniform and magnificent 'guardee' coat, on board SS Mantola

28 *Australian Overseas Base party arriving Jerusalem, 1940. The Fast Hotel became the Australian Soldiers' Club*

29 *Raising the first Australian flag of the Second World War, February 1940, Jerusalem*

30 *Watching Lt-Gen Barker were (l. to r.) Brig. Morris, Capt Dunlop, Brig. Brunskill, Maj. Gee, Col. Vasey, Capt Dale & Capt Tinley*

31 *Col. Clive Disher ADMS and his DADMS*

Much later in the evening, as they left the restaurant, Weary said to the head waiter as an attendant handed him his hat and stick: 'She says she's the Duchess of Roxburgh.'

'She is.'

He was very impressed. His second duchess.

Four days later, at midnight on 10 June, Italy entered the war. On the ground and in the air, the Italians greatly outnumbered the Allies in the Middle East and Africa: less than 700 kilometres separated the Italians in Libya from the Suez Canal, and ships steaming up the Red Sea with Australian troops on board would be within striking distance of the Italian Air Force.

Throughout the day of 11 June (when Aden was bombed by the Italian Air Force and Longmore sent out the RAF to bomb all Italian aerodromes within range), and in the mess that evening, the atmosphere was electric: ' . . . People in these parts are behaving as though war is only . . . a matter of time in reaching here.' They wanted one thing – 'the chance to justify our being here in uniform'. Surely, Weary thought, he would be allowed to 'retreat to the field'.[32]

Tents were hastily smeared with mud for camouflage and the floors of those housing the men were sunk two feet below ground and revetted with earth; hospital tents and hutments were surrounded by sandbags or with mud bricks; slit trenches were dug; red crosses were marked on the hard hospital ground.

Blackout was more hazardous than the Italians: to the common medical complaints of dysentery, upper respiratory tract infections and sandfly fever, were added sprained and broken limbs from tripping over guy ropes or falling into slit trenches.

The brilliant full moon mocked attempts at blackout. Throughout June the sky was cloudless and clear. Even on moonless nights, Weary could distinguish colours in the desert: the red of the nurses' capes was clearly discernible as they moved between the tents. And a report from an aerial reconnaissance noted that the dew on the yet unmuddied hutment roofs glistened in the moonlight and their light-painted windows stood out. Worst of all, the bright ribbons of roads in the camps were visible, even three to four miles out to sea, spoiling all attempts at camouflage.[33]

But Weary felt as far from the war as ever. He was brown and 'slim as a stick', a stone lighter than when he left England. Each morning,

Reid woke him at 6 am with orange juice and they boxed for an hour before breakfast on the flat roof of Mea House. Carter, his assistant, had inherited the sick parades.

Base threw a cocktail party to entertain 'as much of Jerusalem as we can pack within our doors'. Disher drove up with Colonel Johnston. Part of his Acting ADMS's duties was to act as minder to Johnston 'for a week or so', releasing Disher to more pressing tasks.

Leaving Carter to the routine, Weary escorted his visitor to Sarafand and to Haifa to visit the scattered staff of the 2/2nd Hospital; and they went sightseeing in Jerusalem, that 'holy city' whose other main occupations were drinking and eating.

The realities of the evacuation from Dunkirk and the fall of France hung sombrely over them all. Mails were erratic: a plane would appear out of the blue, and Weary would hurriedly scrawl a few pages to catch its return journey. He longed to hear how the engagement had been received: 'I find it so hard to talk about something so close to my heart that I'm sure I shall surprise everyone . . . '

General Sir Thomas Blamey arrived in Palestine on 20 June. With his staff was Colonel S. R. 'Roy' Burston, DDMS 1 Australia Corps, but no colonel to become ADMS overseas base. 'I am thus faced with the prospect of administration *ad nauseum* . . . '34

Disher and Johnston, both old friends of the DDMS, drove up to the highlands to welcome him and congratulate him on his promotion to brigadier. It had been decided that Burston should enjoy higher rank, for nine colonels reported to him. Disher gladly yielded up overall responsibility for medical affairs.

Burston stayed the night in Jerusalem. Nicknamed 'Ginger' for obvious reasons, the South Australian with the puckish face and pointed ears was at 6 foot 3 inches only an inch shorter than Weary, who was impressed to learn that he had been a full colonel at the age of 29 in the last war. Weary found him very well informed. He lost no time taking Burston aside and volunteering for 'the most active service available', but he was ignored.

Helen's birthday cable 'set the seal' on 12 July, when Weary returned to base late that Friday afternoon after an excellent luncheon to await Burston's arrival from Nazareth. He had celebrated his thirty-third birthday as Carter's guest with some of the last Münich beer in Jerusalem and much very expensive but 'rather dubious' Napoleon brandy.

Burston informed Weary that he was to be promoted to major and become DADMS to Corps. But he was not entirely deaf to Weary's pleas: he agreed to appoint him to 2/2nd AGH as a surgeon, the job with corps being merely attachment – a temporary matter.[35]

For once, he found himself 'an object of envy' with his fellow officers, for he would be living 'cheek by jowl with the GOC and his staff' and his brigadier.

Friday was the first of 'three Sundays' in Jerusalem, 'the Muezzin's call to prayer of the Moslems falling musically on the sleeping air' long before dawn. In the evening, horns blown from the ramparts of the city heralded the Jewish sabbath which extended from sunset to sunset. Moslem and Jewish sabbaths were 'inviolate, unlike the Christian Sunday when one packed up for expeditions somewhere – such as swimming and drinks at the Jaffa Club or a picnic in Transjordania'. That weekend was spent introducing Burston to the pleasures of tennis and swimming at the sports club at Jaffa.

General Blamey was fully aware of the problems the Australians had experienced with some sections of Force HQ, and he had decided in May that Overseas Base should be moved closer to the port where Australian troops disembarked and AIF headquarters would be better situated away from Jerusalem.

Weary and MacCausland did not know of these plans when he summoned them to a briefing over lunch in Jerusalem. Brunskill and Forestier-Walker had thwarted all their efforts to acquire suitable buildings for headquarters in the Judaean Highlands. Weary and MacCausland 'were absolutely shocked at the prostitutes' quarters being cleaned out for the Australians . . . ' and said so.

As Weary was speaking, Blamey gave a 'sly sort of self-satisfied smile [and] said, "That's the last thing I want . . . the HQ up here in Jerusalem with those people. I'm making arrangements to be down in Gaza".'

By the end of July, Weary was 'quite delighted with [my] new boss in every way' and preparing to leave his rose-strewn cream curtains and elegant room for what he imagined would be a 'real army atmosphere with camp stretchers, flies, mosquitoes and, heat, heat, heat . . . '[36]

The arrival of his crowns was celebrated in the mess. 'Somehow my shoulders feel rather bare and the mute holes made for the familiar pips rather stare at one. Of course, I am still victimised by anyone meeting me for the first time since the event.'[37]

Throughout July and early August, Overseas Base was dismantled and moved to Gaza. At the same time Weary was packing his possessions. 'I came to Palestine with one suitcase and have already expanded by one large wardrobe trunk, odd bags and valises.' To these he and Reid added mosquito nets, respirators, tin helmets, camp beds, sleeping bags and anything else stocked by the Jerusalem shops which might be useful in their new life.

The last week was an orgy of farewell dinners. By Thursday 15 August, Weary was installed in Gaza.

ELEVEN

Scarlet Major at the Base

GAZA WAS AN UGLY, DUSTY, sprawling Arab town. Weary was billeted in a white stucco house whose top storey had been abandoned by its builders and never completed. Its up-and-down battlemented silhouette against the sky reminded him of a child's drawing of a castle.

By night, with the curtains across, perspiration streamed down his face and neck while he wrote to Helen and his family in the feeble light. When, in desperation, he flung back the heavy curtains, clouds of insects crawled and flew in. His camp bed sat in the middle of the tiled floor under its mosquito net, wardrobe trunk and valise against the walls.

The heavily barred window looked out across the deep valley, where was crowded 'a veritable jigsaw puzzle' of flat-roofed mud houses, while beyond reared the high ridge captured from the Turks in the last war only after bitter fighting. Reid continued to coax him out of bed for an hour of boxing on the roof before breakfast.

Weary enjoyed the accoutrements of being an officer: the well-cut uniforms and the guardee coat from his London tailor, Sam Browne belt and shoes immaculately polished, stick tucked under his arm, a batman to lay out his clothes and brush him down. But he tipped his cap at the same rakish angle over his right eye that had provoked Blamey, when inspecting the Goulburn Valley Battalion in the 1920s, to pause in front of Weary and bark: 'Won't someone tell that bloody corporal how to put on his hat!'

Reid kept him in order. He had 'an eagle eye for deficiencies in . . . kit [and] the heels of socks' and was 'one of those . . . who seem to exist usually in fiction . . . a great treasure . . . prepared to offer advice on life, philosophy and morals'. Weary had never looked so well turned out. So 'Pommie'-like did he look, that when he was boarding a troopship full of Australians of the 6th Division at the Canal, the shaven-headed soldiers greeted the officer in the guardee coat with clinking bottles, raucous cat calls and a shower of pennies. Their chiacking petered out when Weary roared back at them: 'Don't you fellows know a chap from Boomanoomina when you see one?'

Minutes later, the ship's medical officer hustled him into his surgery with the words, 'Oh God! We've done some trooping, but these . . . I used to have "Ship's Surgeon" on the door – they took it off!'

Weary pushed his cap with its Australian badge under the chair as he sat down. Plainly, he should continue to look like a British officer for the moment.

For some days, it was impossible to settle down to work efficiently. The office assigned to him was still occupied by a very senior army official and most of Weary's books, files, papers and office furniture were scattered in the dusty yard outside.

'The little garden of my office building viewed from the roof looks like the garden of Allah. There is a high sand wall, some trees, a large goldfish pool, and . . . Jasmine heavy with perfume.' From his desk each evening, he heard the blind Muezzin call loudly to the faithful from the tall minaret which towered above them. Three Australian soldiers with shovels appeared one day, stripped to the waist, and dug a slit trench in the dry rocky soil amongst the scrubby trees.

No sooner had he secured possession of his office, than he was turned out of his bedroom by an elderly colonel and reduced to sharing with Geoff Cohen 'of brewery ilk', whose father, Colonel Harold Cohen, was Australian Red Cross Commissioner in the Middle East.

Burston was away for days at a time, moving around the camps, inspecting hospitals, driving down to Egypt to British HQ and out into the desert near Beersheba to observe field ambulance and brigade exercises. Disher was now under canvas at dusty Helwan with the 6th Division, twenty-six kilometres from Cairo.

Weary spent most of August and September at headquarters. There was no time to regret the sudden change in his social life and the lack of dinners and dances. Setting up the medical administration of Corps was taxing. He worked back until late at night 'sweating to get the new . . . routine running' and dealing with the ever-mounting piles of correspondence.

In Gaza, as in Palestine, Weary continued to hold his unofficial 'clinics' for the little Arab boys, dressing sores and feet and eyes. They called him 'Fel Mish Mish', from 'Bukra fel mish mish: Tomorrow, when the apricots fall,' because that was his invariable reply when they asked him for money.

It was one way of learning the language. 'My Arabic steadily increases . . . but my small mentors are becoming a pest. Today a high officer caught me playing marbles . . . ' It was of little moment to him what the other officers thought; but his troop of ragged companions would appear from nowhere whenever he put his nose out the door and they trailed after him, 'reminiscent of the Pied Piper of Hamelin'.

As a staff officer, Weary was entitled to his own transport. The Humber Snipe 'had a utility sort of shape in which I could put a stretcher' and when work allowed, he used to drive to Tel Aviv or even further for dinner. At the end of the evening, he would climb into the stretcher, his batman would drive home and wake him in the morning with tea.

Surfing, and tea on sandy Gaza beach afterwards, became a regular Sunday afternoon activity. There was a good swimming beach only two kilometres from the town, with a team of life savers equipped by Sydney surf clubs. Weary was a strong swimmer. Apart from days when choppy seas and cross currents made it unsafe, he found release from tension 'and claustrophobic symptoms . . . by swimming well out into the Mediterranean'.

Weary and Burston found time to ride most afternoons and 'it felt decidedly good to have a decent horse under one again'. Blamey, a keen horsemen, had some of the very few military horses in the Middle East for his use. Access to them was an unexpected benefit of working for Burston, one of the privileged members of Blamey's staff who could borrow a mount. He, too, was a 'great horse lover and racing enthusiast'.

The race meeting at Barbara to entertain the troops on 7 September was 'almost the greatest show on earth'. Two days beforehand, Arabs began to ride in from the desert on sleek riding camels whose extremely rapid, smooth gait contrasted strongly with the customary rolling awkwardness of pack animals, and on their small, lively horses. They gathered near the course, madly galloping up and down.

On the Saturday, a mass of 'seven to ten thousand Arabs [and] about as many Australian soldiers' milled around the track, mingling with British soldiers and civilians, the RAF, New Zealanders, members of the Polish Brigade and Frenchmen who had made their way down from Syria, even Czechs.

The stewards had difficulty ensuring that the right numbers and colours were worn by the appropriate horses and their Arab jockeys, the latter clad in brilliant racing silks and great, baggy trousers, with their 'long curly locks flying in the breeze from under their caps'.

Weary was loaned 'much the best horse' by a sheikh from Transjordania. It 'ran a great race and was just taking the lead coming into the straight when [it] galloped off the course almost into the crowd . . . '

Impressed by its form, he had plunged heavily; after paying £5 to his jockey, he had bet the same amount on the horse. The day proved 'a slight financial reverse . . . '

Weary had scarcely finished smarting over his losses when Tel Aviv was bombed, and suddenly war was on their doorstep. Burston, driving down from Kafr Vitkin, saw the bursts when he was half an hour from the city and arrived to smouldering, shattered buildings. Weary shared his opinion that it was a senseless, savage attack of 'no possible military value' and felt bitterly vindictive.[1]

At first light on 13 September, the Italian Tenth Army advanced cautiously into Egypt through gaps in the wire cut by the British 11th Hussars on reconnaissance.[2] On the ground, the highly mobile British 7th Armoured Division and the Support Group harried the long lumbering column; overhead were RAF Blenheims and Gladiators, and a few Hurricanes tangling with Italian Nacchis and Fiats.

Four days later, ninety-five kilometres inside the Egyptian frontier and 128 kilometres from the British Army at Matruh, they sat down in Sidi Barrani in a defensive semi-circle. Here they stayed throughout October and November, watched closely by the British.

At the end of September, reinforcements arrived from Australia. Weary set off for Egypt on Friday 27 September to meet convoy BN 5½, which was on its way up the Red Sea to Suez. More than 320 kilometres of road ran through Beersheba, then undulated across the Sinai on a narrow strip of bitumen to the canal and Ismailiya on the west bank. Next day in Ismailiya he finalised the evacuation arrangements for the sick with his British colleagues in the RAMC, who would supply sixteen motor ambulances, motor trucks for the patients' kits, and stretcher parties.

Embarkation Duty was no sinecure. Weary spent Sunday and Monday clambering on and off the SS *Orion* and SS *Aquitania*. He handed over instructions to the medical officers accompanying the troops, supervised the evacuation of the sick onto a large and dirty tug shuttling between the ships and Port Tewfik on the east bank, and gave explicit orders to each ship's medical officer about the medical stores. There was always trouble about these, and the *Orion*'s were no exception.

That weekend, he was also up and down the roads between Suez and the site of 2/2nd AGH at Kantara, discussing the proposed plans of the hospital with the ADMS Canal Area. Construction was about to start, and Weary insisted that the buildings had been placed too close together. Kantara East was not an ideal site. It was a certain target for enemy bombing raids, being adjacent to railway goods yards. Colonel Johnston and his staff were still scattered over various camps and becoming increasingly impatient to operate as a hospital.

His route back to Suez lay through the well-treed avenues, lawns and elegant villas of Ismailiya, where he ran into Orm Smith and Bowie Somerset, who had turned up on leave. Weary needed no persuasion to join them for dinner on the roof of the Continental Hotel in Cairo.

By Wednesday morning, after an all-night drive across the desert, he was back in Gaza.

Captain James English from the Corps medical officer pool took over some of the routine duties, so that Weary could help Burston plan the new medical organisation for Administrative HQ, Base and Lines of Communication HQ. Weary's particular responsibility was to draw up the standing orders to cover the medical side of Base and Lines of Communication commands. All this was complicated by Blamey, whose changes of mind about the reorganisation affected Burston's planned promotions and appointments.[3]

That October, work took him from Suez up to Haifa and to all the camps in between. Some nights in the office, absorbed in dealing with messy piles of paperwork and the stream of circulars which had to be written and distributed to all regimental medical officers, he lost track of time until the morning Ramadan gun signalled that dawn was approaching. But since the gun was fired 'when you can see the difference between a white hair and a black', not difficult in the bright desert night with its sky of soft, dark blue, there was still time for a few hours sleep.

Italy marched across the Albanian border into Greece on 28 October 'and we are all thinking what the answer may be to that'. Field ambulances which had been out training in the desert descended on Gaza, and there was a good deal of speculation about future moves, for 'Colonel Spiers, Charles Littlejohn, Eric Cooper and Co. have . . . joined us'. The 6th Division had been training in Egypt since September, and the 16th Brigade was now at Amiriya.

Weary's promised position with the 2/2nd AGH receded.[4] He expected Burston to release him when Major K. W. Starr, who had been appointed DADMS to Corps some months previously, arrived on 1 November with Convoy US5A from Australia. But Burston did not intend dispensing with his services as DADMS, even though Starr settled into his job very quickly and with frightening efficiency. Weary handed over the war diary to him, but the paperwork increased, for the arrival of each convoy released another flood. Personnel had to be trained in army ways and chivvied to provide their reports and requests on standard forms in approved fashion. The telephone buzzed all day. Three more hospital sites had to be inspected in one week alone in early November. Letters, orders, instructions, reports and circulars poured in and out of the office.

There was more than enough work for two DADsMS. Moreover, Burston suggested that when he became Director of Medical Services to the 2 AIF in November, Weary should go with him in a 'special duties' rôle. Sadly, he agreed, putting aside his ambition to work as a surgeon, but envying the others as they conjectured about their rôles in the battles to come. 'The truth of the matter is that once one requires the necessary knowledge and those combinations of truculence & *savoir faire*, impetuosity & patience, intolerant tolerance and sweet good-natured ruthlessness necessary to get things done by army channels, you are more or less doomed to staff work.'

Increasingly, he felt absorbed into the military machine, 'though I still feel . . . depressed about the amount I have to learn about the subtleties of higher military circles'.

Army life suited Weary. He knew the senior medical officers who arrived in Palestine, for many came from Melbourne, and he had worked with or studied under them. Downes and Disher were both Ormond men, as were a number of others. By the end of 1941 he had worked with all the senior members of the AIF, from Blamey down, and would now know 'nearly everyone who commanded the army' for years to come.

Not that his relationships were always free from friction. He was used to being part of a hierarchy: Ormond and the hospitals had taught him to manage his fierce independence, but now and again his quick tongue and impatience with fools landed him in trouble. All through his life, he had a tendency to choose the wrong moment to be outspoken, and senior staff officers are cool towards transgressors.

In Gaza, he decided that convalescent depots were 'hideous old Staff and Command' operations, badly set up with no medical element and no proper gradation between sick and well. With great enthusiasm, he undertook to write a new war establishment for them. This was complex, for in any unit in the army, every entity must be consulted, even down to chaplains: ' . . . G staff, operations staff, A&Q . . . and when you come to writing the equipment side, every chap you add, you've got to have the last cross strap'.

When it was finished, he went to Brigadier Basil Andrew and laid it reverently on his desk. Andrew was Deputy Adjutant-General in charge of administration for the AIF in Gaza. He had once given Weary a public dressing down for turning up late for the morning staff conference after being caught on the telephone.

Andrew looked at Weary 'with a rather cynical smile' and suggested that it had been a lot of bother to him. Weary agreed, handing Andrew the opportunity to say: 'You know, the trouble with you bloody medical units is that you don't have staff and command officers to command them. If you did . . . all these troubles would disappear!'

Weary thought gloomily about the record of the staff and command officers in the previous war, which was why the medical people decided to rid themselves of this complication, and flashed back: 'I sometimes think, sir, that when the Almighty created the staff and command officer, he'd not exactly exhausted his ingenuity.' Unfortunately, Andrew's sergeant overheard. 'This terrible comment . . . went all around Gaza.'

Despite his brushes with Basil Andrew, they shared meals in Cairo and drank together occasionally. He enjoyed an easy camaraderie with his colleagues, medical and staff. Tennis with Morris had finished when the brigadier was transferred to Bombay that August to become Australian Liaison Officer, but now and again Weary played golf in Cairo with Colonel John Down (ADMS dental), Disher's DADMS Major Alec Dawkins, Squadron Leader Walter Hammond or Burston.

Burston, a South Australian, had been an unknown quantity, but he quickly revealed himself as an ideal boss, who 'makes hard work a pleasure by his appreciation and never letting one down'. He secured Weary's loyalty and respect by 'a most deceptive capacity for hard work', and his friendship with a 'most excellent fund of humour'.

Weary finished compiling his 'booklet of standing orders, medical, to guide medical officers and troops' on 4 November and Burston ordered a week's holiday. 'I should like . . . to indulge in a busman's affair in the western desert fronting 'brother Ito' but I'm not quite certain . . . I will be permitted.' Instead, he planned to fly down the Nile to Luxor with Geoff Cohen, who had a private pilot's license.

Weary spent that evening with John Colquhoun and others at 'a farewell buffet supper'. They were on the move. The 2/2 Field Ambulance had taken the train to Egypt earlier that day. Julian Orm Smith's surgical team, part of Lieut-Colonel John Adey's 2/1st CCS, was also about to go. 'Nominally I belong to this unit and should be going too – but no, for me the austere joys of continued staff work.' He lacked even the compensation of leave with Geoff: the idea had to be abandoned in order to work on the 'plot for a new hospital', the 2/5th, at Kafr Balu near Rehovot in Palestine.

Kantara might not be ready to receive the 2/2nd AGH, but Johnston and his unit were 'full of enthusiasm about getting a job to do'. Until now, they had been scattered across camp reception stations (small twenty-bed hospitals) and the prophylactic ablution centres for the prevention of VD in Cairo, Alexandria and Jerusalem, and staffing the Medical Boards. (Organising the last was one of Weary's duties.) Burston, Starr, Weary and Miss Wilson, the Matron-in-Chief, attended a full dress inspection of the hospital on the Sports' Ground at the camp on 7 November. 'We had a grand ceremonial inspection . . . band, flag, Matron-in-Chief, march past and all sorts of grandeur!'

Burston took the salute and carried out an inspection, then the assembled company adjourned to the mess 'for tea and congratulations'. It was 'probably the first time in the history of the AAMC that a General Hospital has staged a show of this sort'.[5]

Four days later he was packed up, ready to drive to Alexandria with MacCausland for some leave and a little unofficial expedition to Amiriya, where his friends in the 2/1st CCS and the field ambulances of the 6th Division were assembling, when Burston and Starr decided to go to Cairo.

Starr had spent his time at headquarters in Melbourne mastering 'the whole of the equipment question'.[6] Drugs and equipment were in short supply and worries about them had plagued the Australians since their arrival in the Middle East.

Downes and Disher preached stringent economy and prudence to all medical staff. They were sensitive to the difficulties experienced by the British in supplying the Australians; drugs became scarce and expensive, as Weary discovered when Disher sent him shopping for quinine after orders in Cairo had been returned unfulfilled. Local suppliers quoted £5 a pound more than the British base medical stores price of £2.

Matters had been complicated when the third convoy was diverted to England. On board with the 18th Brigade was the Advance Depot Medical Stores with 96 cases of medical supplies, and in the depot's absence from Palestine the responsibility for equipping the camp reception stations devolved upon Steigrad's 2/1st AGH. They were hard pressed to do so at times, and Weary was dispatched on countless shopping expeditions. It had been agreed that each Australian medical unit would arrive fully equipped and their stocks would be replenished by British base depots, but some deficiencies were unavoidable.

By November, medical units in Palestine had no reserves and were dependent on the British for essential drugs and equipment such as surgical gloves, instruments and appliances, and panniers.[7]

Burston took Starr down to British headquarters for a full conference with Tomlinson and Scott on 12 November in order to sort out the situation and discover exactly what was required.[8] Weary's friend Scott and Starr were rather too efficient, and the latter's alarmist report appearing over Burston's signature as DDMS I Australian Corps contained the suggestion that Australian units should 'provide wherever possible stocks greatly in excess of their own requirements for *all H.M. Forces in Middle East*'*. It stirred up a hornet's nest of enquiries at the highest level.

Weary was relieved that Starr was an equipment enthusiast. 'Thank heaven I've finished with equipment – never did like conjuring'. He had spent frustrating hours combing the Jerusalem suppliers for everything from surgical instruments and needles to small stoves, and then pruning the 'want lists' of newly-arrived medical officers who demanded items in unrealistic quantities. Disher and he ceased to be entertained by the Australian soldier's appetite for analgesics when one medical officer ordered 10 000 APC tablets.

The 2/1st Hospital Ship *Manunda* was expected to dock at Port Said on 12 or 13 November; Weary was detailed to supervise the transfer and loading of invalids for the trip back to Australia. Leave was cancelled once again.

Weary spent 'two hectic nights and a day – rather devoid of sleep' in Egypt. Burston appeared with Tomlinson officially to wave the *Manunda* off on its voyage to Australia and Weary returned thankfully to Gaza by train. 'Transport of invalids can be a bit of a nightmare.'

---

* Author's italics. The supply of medical stores to units other than the AIF was not within the gift of even Major-General Tomlinson, DMS ME; it could only be settled on a government to government basis, and Scott had overstepped the mark in making this point to Burston and Starr, as had they in including it, albeit with the best intentions.

He brooded over the fact that his appointment to the 2/2nd AGH would have to lapse and rejected the idea of making difficulties about staying on staff. In Gaza, he had formed a trio off-duty with Jim English and Peter Row, but Jim had taken his whimsical humour off to school to train as a hygiene expert, and Peter Row, another medical officer, would probably leave the staff also in a month or two. At least 'Mac' was still around.

The dust and heat of summer were laid by the rains of November and suddenly 'the air was magically cold and clear', the houses and minarets 'clearly etched against a sky of light eggshell blue'. The railway station at Kantara was a jostling, khaki mass of Australians, 10 918 of them, pouring off the ships and onto the trains which jolted the men of Convoy US6 across the Sinai to the waiting camps. By 28 November, two-thirds of the 7th Division were under canvas in Palestine. The 6th Division was almost complete and would be up to strength by late December when the 18th Brigade, the 2/1st Machine Gun Battalion, the 2/3rd Field Regiment and the 2/1st Anti-Tank Regiment joined it from England.

By February, Blamey would have a corps of three divisions, complete in men though not in equipment, and command of the largest Dominion force in the Middle East.

Weary spent his most strenuous week yet on embarkation duty on the Canal. 'Sunk in a sea of work . . . two nights spent on trains, two travelling about by car and one snatching a few hours sleep on a ship.' Back in Gaza, troops distributed over six camps, sick tucked up in hospital, George Vasey and he sat talking over a beer in the mess.

Despite the high security enforced about troop movements – even Weary's letters to Helen told her what he was doing only in the most general way – it was plain that their business was known to every beggar, ragamuffin, informer and spy in Egypt. 'It's a funny thing with all this security that the little boys on the station say, "So many ships come today, so many ships tomorrow, so many ships the day after, so many trains come Gaza today, so many next day, so many the day after". How do they know?'

Vasey took a reflective pull at his beer and said, 'Well thank Christ, Weary, we've some fuckin' confirmation!'

Vasey was a courteous, correct, energetic and popular staff officer, his behaviour above reproach, but he was known throughout the upper echelons of the AIF for his idiosyncratic and colourful way of expressing himself. 'I don't think anyone could live long with George Vasey without being affected by his method of expression,' said Burston.[9] But 'no one ever took offence', said Weary. 'Women never minded – didn't seem to notice it, and he was well-liked by them.'

Reorganisation of the medical services was well under way: Weary and Burston had been 'snowed under with making plans and provisions for the changes' for over a month. Burston became DMS 2 AIF on 28 November, but he combined it with the duties of DDMS Corps for the present. A number of promotions and appointments in the hospitals and medical units were still to be finalised.

Lieut-Colonel F. Kingsley Norris arrived with the convoy as ADMS 7th Division, along with two field ambulances, a field hygiene section and the 2/5th AGH commanded by Colonel W. E. Kay. Kay's hospital had to be squeezed into the 2/1st AGH area, where the 2/2nd AGH and the 2/1st CCS were also camped, until the buildings on the Kafr Balu site were finished. Gaza Ridge was straining at the seams.

Norris was keen to master the details of the administration in as short a time as possible. Burston was amused to see Weary and Starr 'positively shiver when they hear his footsteps on the stairs. I imagine he is putting a sort of third degree on them'.[10] They were relieved when Norris disappeared to visit Disher: he was anxious to attend the training exercises then intensifying out in the swirling sand and bitter cold of the Egyptian winter.

Everyone was moving. Out in the desert on 9 December, General O'Connor's 'five day raid' had begun. While the 4th Indian Division were attacking the Italians at Tummar West, back in Palestine the advance party of 2/2nd AGH was entraining across the Sinai to their hospital at Kantara at last.

Weary was in Egypt on 18 December when Disher received notice to move forward the next day. Weary's friends in the 2/2nd Field Ambulance were on their way to Sidi Haneish; the 2/1st was already at Salum near the Libyan border and setting up advanced dressing stations.

Julian Orm Smith and his surgical team were about to go forward from the 2/1st CCS to join the 2/2nd Ambulance, up with the 16th Brigade preparing for the assault on Bardia. 'I feel so thoroughly mad . . . at the unpredictable turns of fortune's wheel, which somehow always reverses one's expectations . . . ' His friends from Mary's were now full surgeons with the RAMC; those from Australia were about to play their part in the first Australian action of the Second World War. He, who had been one of the earliest in, was anchored to an office desk. 'I shall get the hump completely if I can't find excuse for reconnaissance before very long.'

Weary returned from Egypt on 19 December to find a cable from Helen announcing her success in the final examinations for her B.Sc. To his amusement, her fate in the orals had depended on 'Pansy' Wright, whom he had last seen in Oxford, when they spent so much of the day drinking and talking that there was no time to explore the town. 'Simply lost in admiration, sweetheart . . . the great event has been duly toasted.'

Parcels of food arrived from Helen and his family for Christmas, as did invitations from friends to spend it in Bethlehem, in Nazareth, with the Scotts in Cairo or the MacCauslands in Gaza.

Instead of which, he felt it would be politic to attend the buffet supper party given by the general for his staff on Christmas Eve. 'Scarlet tabs blazed on all sides.' Blamey presented him, as the 'baby', with a tin cat on wheels from the tree. Weary deserted the mess for Christmas dinner with Mac and Cynthia, but late in the evening 'the mess won, and we found ourselves roaring songs around the piano with an inferno of din (piano collapsed)'.

Burston had returned 'rejuvenated with excitement' from a reconnaissance of the Western Desert right up to Bardia. Weary chafed anew at his containment in headquarters far from the fighting zone. 'I might just as well be in Victoria Barracks . . . RMO or field ambulance would be happiness.' But he was exhilarated by the successes, and celebrated with a day's operating: 'special treat by Don McCredie Senior Surgeon to 1 AGH – I felt quite odd in a theatre again and a little nervous really – but the patients seem to be behaving well.'

He spent the last Sunday of 1940 at Ramle, playing rugby 'against an RAF team in simply terrific rain', almost a year to the day since he played for United Hospitals against the Nondescripts. He vented his anger at not being at Bardia on the opposing team. 'I scored most of the points for my side, and in addition kicked a prodigious field goal which confounded the local inhabitants and myself.'

Amongst the RAF medical officers was an old friend from Ormond, Tasmanian Len Palfreyman. 'As ever, the RAF had a wonderful grip on the amenities . . . the luxury of a piping hot shower was much appreciated.' The RAF were also dispatching their wives to South

Africa and bolstered their spirits with determined drinking.

By New Year's Day, a trivial scratch inflicted on Weary's leg during the match was septic and swollen and when he turned up to work on 2 January, Burston booted him unceremoniously from the office 'to return for hot foments' and lie up in his camp stretcher.

He missed doing embarkation duty at Alexandria when the 18th Brigade disembarked and moved into camp in Egypt. Helen's younger brother, Boyd, was due to arrive from England, where he had been training for some time, and Weary was anxious to discover if he was with them. Apart from the luxury of being able to talk to Boyd about Helen, he was carrying a framed photograph as a replacement for those abandoned so reluctantly and unnecessarily in the basement of London House.

There was no news of Boyd; but Weary learned that 'all books, sporting kit, my entire wardrobe, the results of six months' research work, and a large vanity section of sporting trophies, caps, pictures etc.' had been lost when London House was hit during the air raids that autumn. The terrace houses on Caroline Place were destroyed, and with them went 'my beloved picture of your sister. Damn'.

Burston was preoccupied with the visit of Percy Spender, Minister for the Army, during the first week of January. He had a very successful time with Spender and the Chief of the General Staff, General Sturdee. Air ambulances were badly needed, but Melbourne had refused the requests. Spender now agreed immediately that two DH 83s should be 'immediately taken off their civil job, fitted as air ambulances, and shipped here complete with RAAF crews'.

Burston had also survived 'an attempt by Rupert [Downes] to do me for the main job'.

Blamey had promoted Burston to Major-General, Director of Medical Services AIF in the Middle East (although his rise in rank would not be gazetted until mid-February); in Australia, Downes had intrigued to be appointed to the same position, but the decision was not announced. Understandably, Burston was upset when he uncovered this 'sordid tale' and told Spender so, seizing the opportunity to vent his discontent about the way things were 'sat upon in Melbourne for months. I think it is quite possible now that on the Minister's return Rupert will have to show pretty good reason why he should retain his own job.'[11] Spender directed that Downes be moved sideways and appointed Inspector-General of Medical Services, and that Colonel F. A. Maguire be promoted major-general and replace him as DGMS.

Burston returned to the office resolved to send Weary to the Western Desert to report on the evacuation of the wounded and their condition when they reached hospital at Kantara or Alexandria. One glance at the jaundiced yellow complexion of his DADMS changed his mind. He bundled Weary in his car and supervised his admission to the 2/1st AGH. 'I'm in hospital with infective jaundice – thin, yellow, dyspeptic, nauseated and depressed.'

Steigrad visited Australian soldiers in British hospitals in Cairo and Alexandria and reported on them in his stead, as did Lieut-Colonel Lindon for those in Kantara.*

For the past month, Weary had been ignoring the signs that all was not well with his health: ' . . . completely nauseated at the sight of my office and unable to cope.' The symptoms were not hard to recognise, but he hoped to avoid the X list and hospital and recover in a CCS. Epidemic jaundice was a bowel-born disease of mainly the late summer and autumn. Whilst not as common as dysentery, it laid waste to numbers of men in Palestine and Syria, and during the siege of Tobruk. Arab labour in the kitchens and the swarms of flies which bred up during the hotter months made hygiene control difficult. An increase in the fly population appeared to coincide with a rise in the number of men contracting the disease.

Starr and he occupied the same hospital tent at Gaza Ridge, the former coughing and shivering with influenza and pontificating about the weeks it would take his colleague to recover from hepatitis. The rich canary yellow lining of the EPIP did nothing for Weary's complexion, to the delight of visitors who came sick-visiting and stayed to tease.

While Weary lay in bed on 11 January, gloomily contemplating his yellow complexion and the prospect of some weeks sickly convalescence, Churchill had decided that Wavell should pull troops out of Cyrenaica and direct their energies to the other side of the Mediterranean.

During Burston's and Starr's discussion of the equipment question with Tony Scott the previous November, two weeks after the Italians crossed the Albanian–Greek border, Greece was mentioned as 'a new burden of unknown magnitude'.[12]

Initially, help consisted of four and a bit squadrons of the British Air Force, and 4200 anti-aircraft gunners, air force ground staff and depot

---

* Lieut-Colonel L. C. E. Lindon, in charge of the surgical division of 2/2nd AGH.

troops who arrived in Athens to support them.[13] The air force flew regular sorties from Greek airfields into Albania. To the Italians' amazement and discomfort (and Germany's annoyance), Greece defeated the Italians and forced them to fall back thirty to forty kilometres into the rugged country on the other side of the border.

By the beginning of January, fourteen Greek divisions were ranged against the Italian Army's nineteen. The front extended across Albania for about 160 kilometres, from just north of Himare on the Adriatic to Lake Ochrid, straddling the Albanian–Yugoslavian border in the east. But Churchill expected German troops and air squadrons to move into Greece through Bulgaria; and his information was that Hitler would move in March.[14] The German army and air force were already in Rumania and Hungary. He drafted a telegram for the Chiefs of Staff to dispatch to Wavell and Longmore, which said in part: 'Nothing must hamper capture of Tobruk, but thereafter all operations in Libya are subordinated to aiding Greece . . . '[15]

Wavell and Air Chief Marshall Longmore flew to Athens and at a meeting on 15 January with General Metaxas, the Greek dictator, they offered Greece reinforcements and two or three divisions by mid March. He refused. Such insubstantial help would not markedly strengthen the Greek Army, but it could present Hitler with an excuse for marching into Greece. Wavell was then instructed to capture Benghazi with all speed. Meanwhile, O'Connor was planning the assault on Tobruk.

On 17 January, Weary was taken off the X list and told to take leave. 'I felt so thoroughly "browned off" it was an effort even to go.' In addition, Burston charged him with a mission to Alexandria, where the hospital ship HEMS *El Amira Fawzia* disembarked wounded brought from the 2/1st CCS at Mersa Matruh, and then to Amiriya.

He interviewed 'all and sundry' that Friday, with no appetite to admire the city he had looked forward to visiting the previous year with MacCausland. The aftermath of hepatitis had produced a crop of boils that made sitting extremely uncomfortable and 'took all the fun' out of jolting back to Cairo through the Delta.

They did not prevent him from going to a ball that evening, where he ran into General Wavell in the chaos of the cloakroom, searching for his own coat and cap in the absence of his aide-de-camp. 'This nonchalant and amazing soldier is a rather small man with a lined, dry, humorous looking face. The left eye is closed forever (by the absence of an eyeball I should think) and the keen flash of the other is arresting.'

Weary retreated to leave and to convalescence on the *Victoria*. When war drove away the tourists, this Anglo-American steamer suspended its cruises down the Nile to Luxor and became a hostel for convalescent Australian officers. It was moored most conveniently alongside the magnificent Gezira Sporting Club and Gezira Island.

Apart from complying with Burston's instruction to interview 'almost every colonel in the RAMC in Egypt' and paying two calls on Blamey to discuss the results, he was free to enjoy himself.

Leave was spent exploring Cairo in warm sunshine under a sky whose soft blue was broken by 'great cumuli piled in snowy heaps'. He took a picnic and sailed down the Nile in a felucca, then hired a gharry to drive the short distance to Memphis and Saqqara. At the Great Pyramid of Cheops he climbed to the galleries – 'quite a sweat for a tallish person bent double' – and shrugged off claustrophobia induced by the darkness and silence. He joined a tour of the mosques conducted by the remarkable Mrs Devonshire, a Frenchwoman who was an authority on Islamic architecture, and marvelled at the slender twin spires of the Mosque of Mohammed Ali and his old, ruined palace.

Cairo was a calming antidote to the depression of the previous weeks, but his sightseeing had to be sandwiched between bouts of frustrating immobility. Weary was unwell for the whole of January, narrowly escaping the X list for the second time and incarceration in the 15th Scottish General Hospital. His immunity was damaged and he could not shake himself free of infection.

Visitors came to sympathise: Blamey, Andrew, Burston and Colonel Hamilton Fairley, Consultant Physician to the AIF.[16] Fairley cheerfully cancelled Weary's dinner with him at the Turf Club and forbade alcohol until his liver had recovered. And the 'DMS . . . told me that I wasn't to go back to Palestine.'

Starr, promoted lieutenant-colonel and now Burston's DDMS to 2 AIF, had returned to work on 17 January fully recovered from his influenza. He turned his considerable organisational skills to supervising the removal of the office to AIF headquarters in Alexandria. Major Henry Trethowan was expected from London to be his DADMS. Thirteen months had elapsed since his medical examination of Weary during those hectic, end-of-December days in beloved London.

A week later on 25 January, Colonel Johnston took up his new appointment as DDMS I Aust Corps, with Major Walter MacCallum as his DADMS. MacCallum had preceded him to Gaza and carried on under Burston's supervision until Starr appeared. Steigrad, with a new staff, was to be ADMS Aust Base Area. At the end of the month, Peter

Row and Jim English departed as medical officers with the 7th Division for Amiriya, and Corps Headquarters moved to Ikingi Maryut nearby. The new organisation which Burston and Weary had planned was all in place.

Contemplating his circumstances, Weary felt that life was 'capable of jambing[sic] one relentlessly as a square peg into holes of all conceivable shapes for years to come'.

Weary's 'special duties' as DADMS were to concentrate his attention on the evacuation of wounded from forward areas back to Palestine and Egypt, and then home to Australia. 'Interesting enough . . . if one were not pining to be in Libya doing surgery.'

He spent little time in his cabin on the houseboat, for Tony and Marjorie Scott, who were in a 'chummery' in Abbassia with a British colonel, claimed him outside working hours.

The Rt Hon. R. G. Menzies, the Australian prime minister, arrived in Cairo on 5 February on his way to London, and Weary was bidden to Lady Blamey's party along with the rest of the staff. But in the company of the Scotts, Weary also gravitated towards a younger, faster and therefore more entertaining British set, whose parties attracted rich Egyptians and Greeks as well as British and Australian officers. Invitations from people such as Pamela Hore-Ruthven, friend of Lady Ranfurley and later an assistant of Freya Stark's in her propaganda machine, the Brotherhood of Freedom, always promised interesting nights awash with alcohol and amusing people.

'All Cyrenaica is now in the bag. I wonder what next? Possibly on to Tripoli . . . ' wrote Weary on 10 February, three days after the victory at Beda Fomm and the day before Dorman-Smith and Maitland Wilson sent a signal to Wavell asking 'permission for a further advance'.[17] The entire Italian Tenth Army had been knocked out. O'Connor believed he could 'take Syrte immediately with armoured cars, artillery and the Support Group', then advance on Tripoli on 20 February. Brigadier Dorman-Smith drove through the night to arrive in Cairo at 3 am on 12 February. When he arrived in Wavell's map room at 10 am, 'all the desert maps had gone [to be] replaced by maps of Greece'.[18]

That same day, Lieutenant-General Erwin Rommel arrived in Tripoli. The previous day, at Rommel's instigation, bombs had begun to fall on Benghazi. Originally, his suggestion that the X Luftwaffe Korps bomb the town was rejected by their commander, because a number of important Italians owned property there. Rommel had no sympathy with this view. He appealed straight to Hitler's headquarters, and the first raid was under way before Dorman-Smith reached Cairo.

The 2/1st Field Ambulance lost its commanding officer as a result of his decision. Burston had come forward with Blamey and Menzies and was in Benghazi the night of 13 March when La Salle hospital was damaged by a large mine. He urged haste with the evacuation then in progress. Lieut-Colonel Cunningham, Captain Douglas Stephens and a medical orderly were clearing up in the building two nights later when it took a direct hit. They dug Stephens out of the rubble, not too badly hurt. The other two were killed.

Burston's promotion to major-general while in the forward area was tinged with sadness. Cunningham was a skilled commanding officer, popular with everyone, men and officers. The first Australian ambulance commander to arrive in Palestine, he had spared nothing to turn his unit into the most thoroughly trained of the three in the 6th division. It worked well forward during the swift-moving advance to Bardia and Tobruk. His loss was felt keenly by Disher and Weary and those who had been early in Palestine with him.

A signal from Burston ordered Weary to Cairo to break the news to Cunningham's wife and daughter. He arrived 'feeling like an executioner', but the telephone had beaten him to it. Inarticulate and miserably inadequate in the face of their distress, he did what he could to help before motoring back to Alexandria.

Menzies returned from the desert on 13 February, where he had been visiting the forward troops with Blamey, and flew on to London. He had concurred with Wavell's proposal to send the 7th and 9th Australian divisions to Greece as part of 'Lustre' Force. Blamey, who was still in western Cyrenaica with the headquarters of I Australian Corps, knew nothing of this until he returned to Alexandria. Neither Blamey nor General Freyberg, the Commander in Chief of the New Zealand Division also included in 'Lustre' Force, were consulted.

Anthony Eden and Sir John Dill flew out to Cairo and after a meeting with Wavell on 20 February, they flew to Athens via Libya on 22 February with Wavell, Longmore and their staffs. Maitland Wilson, now Military Governor of Cyrenaica, was told to meet them at El Adem airfield near Tobruk. While the aircraft were refuelling, Wavell informed Maitland Wilson of the latter's projected command of 'Lustre' Force.

In Athens on 22–23 February, Greece accepted the British offer of three infantry divisions, the Polish Brigade, one – and possibly two – armoured brigades: 'a total of 100 000 men with 240 field guns,

202 anti-tank guns, 32 medium guns, 192 anti-aircraft guns and 142 tanks'.[19]

'Surgeon Consultant W. A. Hailes has arrived and has begun a furious campaign whirling round the hospitals, while I hang grimly on to effect the introductions.' Burston ordered Weary to slow Hailes down and fatten him up. He did not want him looking like Johnston, whose thin and pallid appearance in fact belied his vigorous health. Weary took Hailes and Starr to dine with the Scotts, whose house was rapidly becoming 'Kangaroo Point'. Weary talked incessantly to Hailes about surgery 'just by way of propaganda . . . I should imagine the motive has been noted'. He feared that Hailes still thought of him as his house surgeon and was anxious to dispel this notion.

Until he rid himself of his stubborn staphylococcal infection, he was condemned to being a 'sort of liaison officer' at AIF GHQ, north-west of the city amongst the alternating jacarandas and flame trees lining the broad boulevards of Heliopolis. He often stayed the night in Abbassia with the Scott's in their 'chummery', as shared accommodation was termed, for they were closer to his GHQ than the cabin on the *Victoria*.

In mid-February, Weary decided that he was cured and removed himself to Alexandria. When he reported to his own headquarters at the Rue de Musée, Colonel Hailes ordered him to hospital again, but over a drink in the crowded bar of the Hotel Cecil he 'relented and decided I could stay here for a couple of days'.

By March he had joined the rest of Junior Command in the mess in Alexandria. 'It is a little bit odd . . . to sleep in a massive reception room in a camp bed with a wardrobe trunk for furniture.' Steps of white marble led from the street to a lofty facade with classical columns in the same material. Inside, the eye travelled up from the cold marble of the floor and across beautiful wooden panelling to high ceilings supported by massive beams. These Alexandrian houses were designed for the heat, with vast, cool rooms. March had turned cold, with wild storms and rain. 'I had an astounding chase amongst the mud and water in the blackout trying to catch my cap in the gale.' In the winter chill of headquarters, even Burston wrapped himself in his great coat while working at his desk. Weary indulged in fantasies about warm Sunday afternoons with Helen beside a log fire with steaming tea and scones.

Instead, he dined with the British navy and his old rugby friend Athol Robertson, now a medical officer on board the *Hero*. After one convivial evening, only Weary's insistence on borrowing a pinnace from the flagship to take him ashore at 3 am saved him from putting to sea with them.

Weary plunged back into work with a new urgency. 'I've been about 200 miles most days this week', back and forth to Suez meeting ships. On a typical two-day trip between 8 and 9 March, he met a DADMS at GHQ ME in Cairo to discuss arrival and sailing dates of hospital ships; drove to Suez to arrange for the disembarkation of invalids from the convoy with the British Embarkation Medical Officer; and attempted to track down six missing cases of vaccines and sera with officers from the 2/5th AGH and Base Depot Medical Stores. After boarding the *Franconia*, sending various people to Kantara and sorting out the usual discrepancies in stores and equipment, he supervised the transfer of sick to hospital.

Next day, he drove to Kantara and fielded complaints from Lindon about medical boards and the transfer of sick without records, intercepted the commanding officers of the 3rd and 11th field ambulances on their way to Palestine and then returned to Cairo.

There was just time to make a thirteenth guest at the Scotts' luncheon party in their new flat and to have a quick drink at the Gezira Club, before leaving them (all drinking merrily) and driving across the Khedive Ismail Bridge to Grey Pillars, the apartment building which housed British General Headquarters in the Cairo suburb of Garden City.

Unwittingly, his call entangled him in some high-level sniping between the DMS ME, Major-General P. S. Tomlinson, his Consultant Pathologist Colonel J. S. K. Boyd, and Colonel N. Hamilton Fairley, Consultant Physician to both British and Australians. The 2/1st CCS were accused of grand larceny in Libya: 'quantities' of captured medical stores were missing. Weary quietly pointed out that Major Scott had arranged for this unit to transfer any such stores to Australian Base Depot Medical Stores. 2/2nd CCS was then the suggested culprit. Stores were a common source of irritation; Weary endeavoured to soothe the by now ruffled composure of all three important men, and promised a full investigation. He returned thankfully to Alexandria, only to learn that his provisional appointment as surgeon, which had been promised to him before leaving for Suez, had fallen through. He discovered why when Burston rang him on 12 March, fresh from a meeting with Blamey in Cairo at GHQ. 'It was decided that we should have an Australian Liaison Officer on the DDMS Lustreforce staff. G.O.C. approved of my nomination of Major E.E. Dunlop . . . '[20]

Weary was adamant that he had no wish to remain on the staff. When he narrowly missed leaving with Lieut-Colonel B. S. Hanson's 2/8th Field Ambulance, now in Cyrenaica with the 9th Division, he was mollified by the promise of some surgery. Now he was about to be deprived of that, too.*

During the past fortnight, Weary had gained and lost three provisional appointments: 'i Mobile Surgeon, ii Surgeon to General Hospital, iii Field Ambulance (almost left with this one and furiously swotted field work for days).' Burston had even given him a farewell dinner at the club with a fine burgundy ('becoming scarce') and a 'good deal of light chatter . . . billiards and snooker'.

Surgeons were two a penny, and those who had arrived to staff the hospitals and medical units were senior to Weary in experience. There was a greater need for medical officers experienced at carrying out general duties in the field, hence his intense study of the textbooks. He appealed to Burston, but the DMS was adept at making Weary feel an equal in professional matters and insisted that Weary was the right man for the job: he got on so well with the British, he knew their ways, he would be a 'diplomatic influence' and so on.

Weary found it impossible 'to harbour resentment about my complete professional ruin'. AIF Medical Liaison Officer to the British Troops in Greece he would be. Hamilton Fairley suggested that his 'continued incarceration in the staff world' was due to his efficiency, when Weary complained about his signal lack of success in leaving it. Weary regretted immediately his diplomatic behaviour at GHQ the previous weekend.

A further convoy had arrived from Great Britain on 8 March with reinforcements, but still no Boyd. It had taken HMT *Franconia* and HMT *Neohellas* twelve weeks to reach the Middle East. They had sailed far out into the Atlantic and then gathered in the harbour at Sierra Leone before continuing to Egypt. The Canal had been closed after the enemy dropped mines on 3 March, but a constant stream of shipping was passing through once more.

Weary sought out Trethowan on board the *Franconia* and sent him

---

* Had Weary joined the 2/8th Field Ambulance, there is a chance he would have spent the rest of the war in a German POW camp: twelve vehicles of the 2/8th were captured in a wadi on Sunday 6 April.

off to Burston in Alexandria. Then an even more familiar face appeared out of the crowd.

'The first person I met on the boat at Suez was Weary . . . ' Captain B. K. Rank arrived with a party of eight Australian nurses and a most beautiful set of luggage labelled 'Facio-maxillary and Plastic Surgery Equipment'.

Expecting to join the 2/4th AGH, he learned that it was in Tobruk, preparing to move on to Barce after recovering from shipwreck. Instead, Weary attached him to a party bound for the 2/2nd AGH, and told him not to take his eyes off his equipment until they reached Kantara. 'I must have looked stupid . . . out in the desert hospital. I had a British warm, which I wasn't entitled to wear as a field officer; I had this party of nurses; and I had this luggage which Sir Harold Gillies had organised for me. Looked very ostentatious.'

This 'fortunate young man has just stayed put on a plastic surgery unit in London, and . . . is now a valuable specialist to the AIF who will never have to squander his talents running extraordinary shows', Weary complained to Helen. Rank was the only plastic surgeon in the Middle East.

Weary had already arranged with Colonel Fraser for Rank's reception at Kantara. But Lieut-Colonel Lindon did not welcome him. 'The last thing we want's a bloody plastic surgeon!' When Hailes called and saw what Rank was doing with the early healing of wounds and burns, however, the atmosphere changed dramatically. ' . . . Then I had parties from all the hospitals coming in turn . . . British . . . New Zealand . . . they all came to see . . . '[21] Eventually, Rank had two large wards and 'worked like a stoat . . . The consulting surgeons to the British Army used to come down and see what we were doing'.

Weary had 88 invalids to return to Australia on the hospital ships *Manundra* and *Somersetshire*. But the quaysides were jammed with lighters and essential war material being unloaded from the ships after the earlier delays. They would be unable to move the sick onto the *Manundra* until the quays were cleared, and the *Somersetshire* was not expected until 11 or 12 March. He would have to return in a few days.

The 6th Division were back in Egypt preparing to leave for Greece. General Blamey had insisted that the most experienced division of fighting troops in the 2 AIF should be included in 'Lustre' Force and sent first, with the less well equipped and partly-trained 7th Division following. The 9th Division had taken over in Cyrenaica.

The pace stepped up. The first contingent of Australians disembarked at Piraeus on 8 March; the advanced party of Blamey's staff had arrived in Athens the previous day, at the same time as General Freyberg. Lieut-Colonel J. C. Belisario had taken his 2/3 CCS and was already established in the shadow of Mt Olympus when Weary tucked a note into a parcel for Helen on 19 March. Disher and he had been shopping in Alexandria 'with great abandon' one evening earlier that week, when he bought her a scarf and a Persian rug. Afterwards, over dinner, he pumped Disher for information about the experiences of the past few months. Disher had turned up at headquarters in Alexandria on 14 March in the middle of a dust storm, 'caked with dust, looking like a scarecrow with a ruddy face'.

'What a campaign – says he would not have missed it for anything'. He felt more 'bloody-minded than ever' when Disher suggested that war in the Western Desert was better suited to younger men. Weary was avid for details. Burston and he had read Disher's diaries closely, noting his solutions to the difficulties created by O'Connor's rapid advance and the need for high mobility amongst the medical units.

Some of the set-ups which had been satisfactory on the Western Front in the last war, such as the casualty clearing stations, were too large and not sufficiently mobile for the war being fought in the desert. They questioned the siting of hospitals too far forward, where they were at great risk from enemy bombing attacks.

The small surgical teams which Burston and his staff devised, such as Julian Orm Smith's, were 'purely AIF shows and have been invented by us'.[22] Burston had reminded Disher during January to nag the surgeon running each team into giving him feedback. Were they useful? Was their equipment adequate? Could they be improved? Disher praised their contribution highly, particularly Orm Smith's. But how would the Australian units fare in mountainous Greece?

As usual, everyone in Alexandria seemed to know where they were going. 'I was somewhat shocked at just how much the Greek restaurateurs knew about 'Lustre' Force. I was even given a letter or two to deliver . . . ' The Greek community were anxious to help. Extra hospital beds would be needed close to the port for battle casualties evacuated from Greece. When Weary called to assess the suitability of the Greek hospital there, its Board of Directors offered to accommodate 200 beds without cost in what was 'probably the best designed and most magnificently appointed hospital in the whole of the Middle East'. This became the 2/11th AGH under the command of Lieut-Colonel George Stening.

It looked as if Weary might be more in the thick of things this time, despite his staff appointment. Hitherto, his place had been safely on the fringe, Now, with any luck, as Medical Liaison Officer, he would be shuttling between Athens and areas well forward, where the Australians were likely to be. He had always been 'anxious to explore more of the hardships of war'. Increasingly of late he was consumed by a 'reckless impatience which makes me live as though there weren't a tomorrow', the same feeling which he had noticed amongst the airmen in the little RAF messes in the desert.

Perhaps Greece would be the adventure Burston had denied him in Libya. He waited impatiently for orders to move. 'Sending things may get more difficult or even impossible soon . . . I think this is going to be a momentous spring . . . '

TWELVE

Across the Wine-dark Seas

AFTER SEVERAL POSTPONENTS and changes of plan, Weary was suddenly ordered to leave on 26 March. There was just time to make his will, scribble a telegram to Helen and give it to Ted Cunningham, before packing his valise. Next morning he collected his new batman George Bennett and drove rapidly to the wharves. He was to sail on the SS *Brattdal*.

'Through the tortuous channels of M[ovement] C[ontrol] reported at quay 77 Capt Talbot approximately 0945 hours'.

He was so incensed at what he found there, that his anger jumps off the crumpled, water-stained scrap of paper on which, that afternoon, he scrawled a report to be sent straight back to AIF Headquarters.

'No accommodation has been provided for a medical officer. Present position Chief Officer refuses accommodation since no order. EMO cannot provide and cannot obtain an order. No one has any authority! This I think I can manage.'

It was the next point which he wanted improved – not so much on this ship, but on all the transports in this and every other convoy which would be constantly exposed to enemy bombing attacks, while sailing the thousand or so kilometres across the Mediterranean to Port Piraeus. On board with Weary were 227 officers and other ranks, mainly gunners.

'*Medical stores* arrived in an empty petrol tin and are as follows: 2 lb cotton wool; 1 pkt Khaki bandage; 1 pkt white surgical bandages . . . 1 tin elastoplast; 1 tube Tannofax . . . 1 bottle castor oil; 1 bottle iodine; 1 box aspirin; 1 box Dover tabs; 1 box Quinine; 33 safety pins . . . There are no dishes, no facilities for dressings, no medicine measure, no medicine, no anything, so why a medical officer? . . . Even a little morphia would help' should anyone be hurt.

By the time they were ready to sail at four o'clock in the afternoon, he had discovered that the situation on the other ships was no different. Weary's writing becomes progressively larger and more spaced out,

199

his pencil almost slashing through the paper.

'PS. This is not a grouch personally I don't want any stores!' he exploded at the foot in a final fit of irritation, addressing it to the immediate attention of Ken Starr.[1]

His outburst had the desired effect. Burston took it to a GHQ conference on 28 March. 'It was agreed that the state of equipment would be gone into . . . and a sufficient scale provided . . . '[2]

The *Brattdal* was a sturdy Norwegian cargo ship impressed into transporting South Australian, British and New Zealand gunners. Her decks bristled with 'small arms stuff' and each time the air raid alarm sounded, Weary dashed up on deck with his illicit camera in the hope of snapping some action. In the hold was motor transport; that night the drivers bedded down with the gunners amongst the guns on deck. Its 'rather bad-tempered' little captain's main concern was that the officers might wreck his passenger cabins. Norway had gone: all he retained of his country was his ship.

Conditions for the 217 other ranks were basic. Sanitation was merely adequate: six portable seats on deck with 'shoots' over the side flushed with sea water and separate urinals, and six washing bowls. Food was cooked over primus stoves – all the captain was obliged to provide apart from carriage was hot water. Hard tack cooked over a primus held no appeal for Weary and the other officers. They formed a mess and paid the steward for ship's food eaten in the captain's cabin. He had finally 'turned up trumps'.

The little Norwegian promised them plenty of raiding, but apart from the occasional solitary aircraft and 'an affair of aerial torpedoes', which Weary found 'not nearly as exciting as you might expect', the skies were quiet.

Not so the seas. Somewhere north of Crete, the *Brattdal* received an order to 'steam on until dusk and then reverse its course' on 27 March. With the rest of the convoy, she turned back for almost twenty-four hours, said to be because of mines. Weary now regretted refusing a passage on a destroyer and favouring the *Brattdal* because he had thought 'this old tramp with the troops better fun'.

They were unaware that a flying-boat crew had reported 'three Italian heavy cruisers and a destroyer . . . eighty miles east of Sicily and steaming towards Crete'.[3] The Mediterranean Fleet moved out of Alexandria at nightfall on Thursday the twenty-seventh.

Italian aircraft bombed the *Brattdal* on Friday morning, as the skipper had predicted. 'We are always bombed between Crete and

Rhodes.' The Italian air force lurked in the Dodecanese off the coast of Turkey.

Unknown to the men on the *Brattdal*, all that Friday and into the night, the Mediterranean Fleet sought and fought the Italian Navy in the Battle of Matapan.

Quite unwitting, Weary wrote to Helen from his comfortable, cream-painted cabin, with water colours hanging on the walls, books, a silver lamp by the sofa and a bunk 'almost to the proportions of a large bed'. Sadly, he contemplated the years lost to them and a future which held no promise of reunion. Once, fleetingly, he had thought of India, where Brigadier Morris had been posted, or of escorting the sick back to Australia on a hospital ship, but of the latter he decided, 'only weaklings and beaten men are going that way'.

'It can't be three years. I still sense your presence, the touch of your shoulder and a sweet, low voice, it's only when I face reality squarely that you are gone and I am so lonely, so lonely, and pain is my companion . . . '

They slipped into Port Piraeus at nine o'clock in the evening on 29 March, after a relatively uneventful four days across a placid Mediterranean. ' . . . Boredom relieved by frequent air-raid alarms and some gutless Italian air action.'[4] Weary watched the sun sink into the glowing opalescence of the sea, the isles of Greece at his back, 'the tumbled masses of mountains . . . rising in sombre shadow on one side, on the other surging colour vying with the crimson banners of the sky'. On docking, he learned that it was the battle which had kept them skulking off Rhodes that Friday.

They spent the night aboard ship. Early on Sunday, the men were trucked through the narrow streets of Piraeus and Athens to the corps reception camp at Daphni, half an hour away. Weary coerced an ESO into transporting him to Athens. He passed little knots of black-clad Greek women walking to the tiny stone churches crowned with dumpy, octagonal Byzantine towers. Bells were tolling and chanting drifted from the dark interiors into the fresh morning air. Old men sat reading newspapers on their balconies amongst carefully tended pot plants, children and cats loitered in patches of sun. Café owners were unlatching the tall wooden shutters and putting out tables and chairs on the pavements and in the squares. Sunday order and coolness had replaced the sand and heat and babble of Egypt.

He reported to the DDMS, British Troops in Greece, at Force

Headquarters in the Acropole Palace Hotel, Patission Street. This was his old acquaintance from Jerusalem days, Brigadier Large, who gave him working space in his upstairs office overlooking the palm-planted forecourt and the Doric columns of the Archaeological Museum. From his window, Weary could see clearly in the blue distance the fair, rounded prospect of Mount Hymettos, its slopes clothed in the bushes of sage, thyme and lavender whose pollen was plundered by the famous Hymettos bees.

A number of the faces at headquarters were familiar from Palestine: GOC British Troops in Greece, Lieut-General 'Jumbo' Maitland Wilson, his DA&QMG Brigadier G. S. Brunskill and Colonel J. B. Fulton, ADMS 80 Base Area in Athens. (Weary wondered about the effects of his reputed diplomacy on Brunskill; it had not gained the Australians any advantages in Jerusalem.) A Lieut-Colonel Crellin had been specially chosen as ADMS at British Advanced HQ up in Elasson, south of Gerania where Colonel Johnston was to join his corps headquarters, for Johnston knew and liked him.

Weary was to act as medical liaison between Corps HQ in the forward areas and the British at Force HQ in Athens. No one had spelt out exactly what the job entailed: Large and he would work it out as the days went by. Blamey had been in Greece since 19 March; Johnston and Walter MacCallum had arrived in the same convoy as Weary and were at headquarters when Weary walked in. He spent Sunday and Monday meeting staff, attending briefings and on reconnaissance. He was also summoned to see Blamey.

Eden and Dill were in town, having turned back from Malta after the coup in Yugoslavia inspired Churchill to resurrect his vision of forming a Balkan front. (This was despite Turkey having firmly rejected the idea when it was mooted in late February, and the evidence that she was ill equipped for a modern war.)

The GOC, General Maitland Wilson, had only recently resumed his military identity. When the first Australian troops disembarked at Piraeus from HMS *Gloucester* on 7 March, Wilson was masquerading as 'Mr Watt', a rather unlikely cloak and dagger star in a Balkan melodrama. He adopted this *nom de plume* – and civilian dress – at the wish of the Greek Government, in order to confound the German spies and informers everywhere in Athens (including outside the Acropole Palace), but who were none of them fooled. Germany was not yet at war with Greece, and her Military Attaché was still in residence at the embassy.

A Yugoslavian General Staff Officer, Colonel Peresitch, was an even more unlikely 'Mr Hope', when he came at British bidding on 8 March to discuss an alliance against the Axis powers. These overtures came to nothing, but the subsequent *coup d'état* by a faction in Belgrade and their rejection of Yugoslavia's signing of the Tripartite Pact with Germany, triggered Churchill's renewed optimism.

Weary was amongst the joint staffs at the Acropole Palace Hotel on 30 March when the Foreign Secretary and the Chief of the General Staff outlined the changes which would need to be made to accommodate Yugoslavia, should she agree to join the Allies and attack Albania and Bulgaria when Germany invaded Greece.

'I went to hear Eden say . . . why we were in Greece – we were going to achieve many things.' The possible area of operations would change from the present Aliakmon River–Edessa–Florina line to one covering the Struma valley and the Doiran Gap in eastern Macedonia. '[Those reasons] lasted about three days.'

He was as unimpressed as he had been at the conference in Egypt on 20 February when Eden adumbrated the reasons for fighting in Greece. If the line changed to the Struma valley, the evacuation of the wounded would be much more difficult: Salonika was not thought to be a safe site for general hospitals, and German air action would render hazardous any efforts at evacuation by sea.

At the end of the day, Weary made his way to Syntagma Square. Bennett had deposited his valise in a room at the King George Hotel, next door to the majestic Hotel Grande Bretagne where Blamey had his suite and the Greek Army its GHQ. He stood on the pavement in the heart of nineteenth-century Athens, facing the formal green gardens of the square thick with trees and seats and fountains. To his left was the bleak, former palace that was home to the Greek parliament, kilted Evzones guarding the tomb of the Unknown Soldier. Across on his right were the crowded tables and rickety chairs of the pavement cafés. Radiating from this green centre were broad streets with neo-classical facades, Vasilissis Sofias, Amalias, Stadiou and Panepistimiou. Camouflaged staff cars, motor cycles, military trucks and people converged on the streets around the square. But best of all, dominating the skyline above the city, was the Acropolis, with the soaring marble columns of Pericles' great Parthenon turning from cream to apricot in the setting sun.

Weary's first report to Burston from Greece was three impeccably typed foolscap pages: a voyage report for SS *Brattdal* and an appraisal of the medical situation gained from Large's briefing. Appended were copies of various British administrative and medical instructions, files, Johnston's first report from Greece as DDMS 1 Aust. Corps and the latest word from Force on malaria. Large was supplying excellent clerical help as well as an office.

Weary hastened to acquaint himself with the rail and road system. The main standard gauge railway line north from Athens to Salonika turned seawards at Larisa, passing through the Tempe Gorge and hugging the coast on the eastern side of Mt Olympus. Roads were primitive and narrow, yet all evacuation from Florina south to Elasson would need to be by the main road running west of the mountain with a secondary road to Katarini forking just south of I Aust. Corps HQ at Gerania. The 125 motor ambulances seemed none too many.

Greek ambulance trains had been hastily improvised from former refrigerator trucks fitted up to take twelve slung stretchers apiece, but with no sanitary or cooking facilities. Hurricane lamps would provide the only lighting.

Wounded could be evacuated from Larisa to Volos on a narrow gauge line, but the Greeks could loan only a few coaches. The same narrow gauge track ran across to Volos from the Pindus Mountains, forming a junction with the main line north, just west of Pharsala.

Only Piraeus and Volos appeared to be suitable ports. Stylis, a third possibility at the end of a short branch line from Lamia, had been reserved by the Greeks for parking rolling stock to be sent back from Macedonia ahead of a German advance. The Greeks controlled ports, railways and roads.

That afternoon, Weary and Johnston drove to Kephissia, a pleasant area on higher ground about eighteen kilometres north-west of Athens. They found the lightly wooded site Large had suggested for their hospital in a fold of the hills at Ekali, three kilometres from the railway station, looking back towards Athens. Nightingales were said to sing in the woods. Pines and scrubby bushes of sage and juniper would provide fragrant cover for the camouflaged tents and there was plenty of water.

Further on, at Marathon, Weary hoped to put a convalescent depot and, filled with romantic ideas, he gazed across the scimitar-shaped bay towards Euboea, 'spouting Byron . . . [in that] heavenly place . . . looking on that lovely sea and green woods . . . '

When they reached Vouliagmeni, a health resort 20 kilometres from Athens in the opposite direction, which Large had reserved for them,

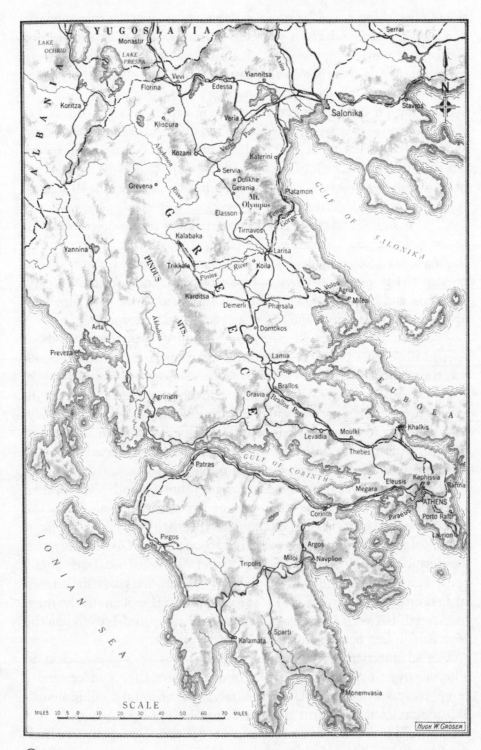

Greece

they felt nothing could be more suitable. A bracing southerly breeze blew off the sea, villas were scattered amongst pines and flowering shrubs on gently sloping ground above the sandy beach. A steep headland on one side rose to a mountain range, and across the Saronic Gulf were the blue hills of the Peloponnese.

Selecting a convalescent depot site was not to prove so effortless. He was called to see Blamey, and walked in full of enthusiasm for Marathon and Vouliagmeni, impatient to have the GOC's approval before Tuesday's conference. But Blamey 'had strong ideas . . . he didn't want his Australian soldiers . . . fouled up with British areas and lines of communication.' Vouliagmeni was too close to them.

'. . . He smiled and said, "I've seen a very good area for a convalescent depot near Megara".' Blamey's ADC, Captain Norman Carlyon told them where to find it: he had been with Blamey the previous week when he selected it during a drive round the coast to Corinth.⁵ Weary, Johnston and the DA&QMG, Brigadier W. Bridgeford (the same who had attested Weary in London), inspected it that afternoon.

They found a stretch of stony land studded with thick stands of ancient olive trees below the Corinth road. Opposite its shingly beach was the island of Salamis.

It was obvious later why Blamey had chosen it. Reached by an excellent road and a narrow gauge railway line carrying six trains a day, large enough to take a division, well supplied with bore water and backed by mountains, any number of men could be evacuated by lighter or caïque to ships waiting in the Gulf of Salamis.

The most urgent business facing Large, Johnston and Weary was to agree on policy and decide where to put five general hospitals. By the end of the Tuesday morning conference they had provisionally placed them. Of the seven hospitals expected to operate in Greece, only two were established: the 26th British and the 1 New Zealand, both of 600 beds. The New Zealanders were east of Volos at Pharsala, a little town tucked into the hills where they drop steeply to the plain on the main road north between Lamia and Larisa. And since mid-November the 26th British had been taking patients at Kephissia.

The advanced party of the 2/6th AGH was at Volos, a port in Thessaly north of the island of Euboea, where they had opened a camp reception station. Unfortunately, the hospital's equipment – 350 tonnes of it – was on the outskirts of Kephissia, where Q had transported it and where a number of its officers were quartered with the British 26th General Hospital.

Motor transport was short, and Brunskill was unwilling to move the equipment back to Piraeus in order to ship it to Volos. Why not site the 2/6th in Kephissia, and establish one of the hospitals expected in mid-April in Volos?

This would have suited both Lieut-Colonel Victor Coppleston, the surgical specialist (who did not care for the idea of operating in a hutment and wished to occupy a stone schoolhouse) and Brunskill, but Large had vetoed the schoolhouse as cramped and unsuitable and encouraged the advanced party to move up to Volos.

Weary would have to deal with Brunskill, who could be difficult. It had become obvious very quickly that one of the MLO's duties was to be a buffer between Large and the DA&QMG, who was no more co-operative in Greece than he had been in Jerusalem.

The 2/6th was a more mobile 600 beds, the expected 2/5th a cumbersome 1200-bed hospital which should be placed near the main invaliding port of Piraeus. As soon as the Australians went into action, all sick who would not be fit to return to the line in a month were to be evacuated to Egypt: another reason for siting general hospitals close to a port. But Weary's trump card was that Blamey desired a 1200-bed hospital near Athens. It was also Blamey's stated policy that Australian sick should be treated in Australian hospitals wherever practicable. Brunskill agreed to move the stores. They decided to put the 2/5th at Kephissia when it arrived on 8 April.

Weary saw Blamey before Corps HQ left Athens on Wednesday. He had no luck when he argued for the Marathon or Vouliagmeni sites against Megara, even when he produced Johnston's judgement that 'the distance from Athens is considerable', it would be 'very hot in summer and the sea breeze [was] shut off by the Island of Salamis'.[6] Blamey had been 'looking at the evacuation sites and sizing it up as to where we could all get off . . . the matter was settled very quietly with just a look from those pale, cold, blue eyes . . . and a firm "No!"'

The GOC saw its remoteness from Athens as 'a great advantage, both from point of view of discipline and security from air attack'.[7] Megara would become both a General Base Depot and a Convalescent Depot under Australian control. He approved everything else.

Venereal disease promised to march as virulently through the ranks in Greece as in Palestine and Egypt. Weary told Blamey that 'Athens at present is *dangerous* and . . . leave should be minimal'.[8] Gonorrhoea was rife amongst the Athenian prostitutes, yet the local military and civil authorities brushed it aside as trivial. General Christopoulos 'didn't feel that it should impede a fighting soldier very much', when Weary called on him to request PACs and blue light centres like those set up by the Allies in the Middle East. The Greek general looked at him in astonishment. 'But major, this gonorrhoea, it is just a cold in the nose!'

Blamey disagreed. 'GOC stated that assistance would be sought from the APM.'[9] Until something more satisfactory could be installed in the brothel quarter, the only PAC in Athens was run by two orderlies from the 2/6th AGH at a brothel in Gombetta Street – 'up to 400 clients in one night'.[10]

Even the British Army did not recognise it officially: 'Colonel Fulton is obliged to purchase condoms etc. out of his own pocket, hoping that he will be reimbursed by units . . . '[11] Large had discovered that sheaths and VD outfits in large quantities were unavailable in Greece. 'We ought to have an aeroplane across full of French Letters, but who is to pay?'[12]

'. . . Ready for war', reported the quartermaster of the 2/1st Field Ambulance to Weary on Wednesday. The following day, he would move the remaining 30 tonnes of equipment up to a spot south of Servia, where his unit was in position with Brigadier Allen's 16th Brigade. Jim English and the rest of the 2/3rd Field Hygiene Section were also to travel north with the rail party and would join corps at Gerania, a hamlet on high ground just south of the Servia Pass. Johnston and MacCallum were on their way there, also. General Maitland Wilson's advanced headquarters were to be south of them, in the village of Tsaritsani near Elasson.

At Tuesday's conference, Large had asked Weary to go to Stylis and Volos to select sites for the two 1200-bed Australian hospitals. A 15-cwt Ford utility and driver picked him up from the King George at seven o'clock on the morning of Thursday, 3 April. He was to be met at Stylis by the garrison engineer from Lamia. Weary's road lay west across a ridge of hills, along the Sacred Way through Daphni and Eleusis, birthplace of Aeschylus, then turned north to Thebes. With a quickening of the senses, he recalled the myths and legends of ancient Greece which he had devoured in the little school at Stewarton. Suddenly, they took on new form.

'My every conception of this country was wrong.' He expected green, pleasant countryside; he discovered 'wild, ranging mountains piled endlessly together and dropping . . . disconcertingly to strips of flat plain.' Stunted pines, silver firs and low, grey thorny brush clung to the slopes wherever slate-grey rock did not break through. ' . . . Great ice-covered peaks tower above.' Sky-blue and scarlet anemones flowered at their feet where Pan had roamed and the ancients had hunted bear, lion and stags in the Attica of old. 'One swelters in hot valleys.'

At Thebes they met the railway line which followed them through Levadia to Lamia. They made good time until they climbed to the Brallos Pass. 'Tortuous hairpin bends', he wrote on his sketch map about the road down to the Valley of the Sperhios.[13] It zigzagged down the mountain, sheer drops of hundreds of metres very close to the wheels where the verge had washed away in the winter rains. Tiny roadside shrines flagged past fatalities and clustered thickly on the worst patches; the larger military vehicles would need to swing right out to the crumbling edge in order to negotiate these corners. Weary's opinion of the roads during this reconnaissance appears in the official history: 'The following lesson was soon learned. Roads marked "good" in Greece are frequently deplorable. Roads marked "bad" . . . are a nightmare.'[14]

The Athens–Florina line was at its most vulnerable to air attack south of Lamia, where it ran across two nineteenth-century bridges, particularly the long and frail viaduct across the Gorgopotamos torrent. The structures would be impossible to repair quickly. If the railway packed up, they would need to bring casualties down by motor ambulances.

Second only to Weary's preoccupation with evacuating the wounded was malaria. Much of Greece was highly malarious. He had been present at an acrimonious meeting in January when General Wavell challenged Colonel Hamilton Fairley's and Colonel J. S. K. Boyd's contention that troops in Greece would be exposed to severe risk from the anopheles mosquito that summer. Wavell contradicted them, by 'quoting [Greek] authorities . . . that there wasn't any special risk'. Eventually, Hamilton Fairley convinced him that his sources were inaccurate: 'there was plenty of malaria in Greece', and Wavell accepted the strategic limitations this involved.

The British had already identified malarious areas and begun training Greek anti-malaria squads, but they would not begin work until late April. Johnston revealed that only half the Australian troops now in Greece had nets. Weary was charged with siting hospitals where mosquitoes could be controlled.

The flat plains around Lamia were watered by the River Sperhios and its reed-fringed tributaries, meandering through newly-planted tobacco, corn and barley. Numerous pools, their grassy margins fever-green, lay in the spring sunshine, clouds of insects whirling overhead. Lamia was a famous malaria research centre. 'Poor omen that,' noted Weary in the war diary.

Five hours after leaving Athens, he met the engineer in Stylis and drove a few kilometres back along the stony foreshore to Ayia Marina. Weary spent all afternoon walking over the ground. None of the three sites was ideal. Adequate cover and water were the main requirements, yet 'if there is water . . . there is malaria. If no water you cannot take the risk of putting down a hospital, which is of course needed in a hurry . . . '

At 6 pm, Weary left the engineer in Stylis and set out for No. 1 NZGH just north of Pharsala. Two hours later, as the truck was bumping down the mountain road towards their goal, a tyre exploded. 'Belching smoke and many rents . . . Driver explained two things missing from vehicle, 'One is tyre (spare) and other pump.' Weary left him morosely stuffing the tyre with grass, and tramped on over the mountains in the dark. Some twenty kilometres later, after a few fruitless encounters with shepherds and their dogs, he reached a small tavern where a policeman who spoke French materialised out of the thirty or so villagers gathered there. 'A couple of rounds for the house and the place was mine.' Everyone, including Monseigneur, the priest, gave him directions, and a friend of the policeman's set off on horseback (Weary walking alongside) to escort him to the New Zealanders' camp.

A few kilometres short of his destination the truck caught up and they rumbled on behind their guide. The hospital was not in a good site, its commanding officer, Colonel McKillop, told him: 'gushing streams and awful malaria problem.' But it was near the main line and not too far from Demerli Station at the junction of the narrow gauge line to Volos.

At noon on 5 April, a replacement tube and tyre not having appeared, Weary caught the train to Volos, where Colonel R. A. Money, the commanding officer of the 2/6th AGH, and the Volos garrison engineer had been expecting him since the previous day.

'Keen hospital planning going on,' Weary noted. Blamey had ordered all hospital personnel out of Volos on 3 April, when enemy aircraft bombed the harbour, and now their tents were pitched in lanes amongst the thickly planted olive trees overlooking sheltered Foula Bay, near Agria, five kilometres east of Volos. The site seemed ideal. The Force Malaria Officer pronounced it satisfactory, for the marshes were at least twenty kilometres the other side of Volos. Boats to take off the wounded could anchor 500 metres from the shore. Long jetties ran out parallel to a low spit of land, which formed the left-hand side of the harbour and curved round to enclose it, curled across the narrow entrance like the toe of a Turkish slipper. Through the gap shimmered the blue, distant hills of Euboea.

Weary took the train up to Larisa and spent an uncomfortable night rolled in a blanket in a railway truck. Dinner was bully beef, dug out of a tin. He was relieved to see his driver appear at 5.30 on Sunday morning, but when they returned to Foula Bay two hours later, after a nightmare ride over sixty kilometres of unfinished dirt road, he learned that the German Twelfth Army was advancing into Greece and Yugoslavia.

Operation Marita had arrived in Greece.

Blamey received other, most unwelcome news from Wavell. The 7th Division and the Polish Brigade, promised for the defence of Greece, would not be coming. The Allies had retreated from Benghazi ahead of Rommel's force, which arrived on 4 April, and Wavell had decided that the need in Cyrenaica would be greater. He sent one brigade of the 7th Division, the 18th, to reinforce Tobruk, and held the rest at Mersa Matruh.

No time could now be lost in equipping Agria for the wounded who would be brought down from the north. Weary walked across the cleared ground in front of the pretty little Byzantine church and graveyard inside their encircling cypresses and lime-washed stone walls. A large olive factory amongst the trees would make an ideal and inconspicuous surgical building, with its sixty-centimetre thick walls. Stone cottages were scattered amongst olive groves and citrus orchards on ground rising gently to an arc of steep mountains at their back. ' . . . Cover is beyond reproach.'[15] There was abundant water from four deep wells.

He called on the sea transport officers and the harbour authorities in Volos to discuss evacuation and confirm that Agria was suitable.

Volos was bombed again while Weary was driving through. He started back to Athens, driving round the coast through Almyros and Stilis to Lamia, stopping now and again on the appalling road, little better than a track, to look at likely sites for the second hospital.

Beyond Lamia, he was caught up in a tide of refugees fleeing south, choking the roads and passes with their carts and cattle. He became hopelessly lost in the failing light after the driver attempted a detour round the herds of livestock. From a point high above the track, the landscape seemed a mass of mountains tumbling sheer into 'a maze of sea and bays and islands'. By the time a village priest had pointed out the direction of the main road, it was densely dark. High on Mt Parnassus, Weary rolled himself in a blanket and burrowed into a bed of leaves. ' . . . Admired the stars and the dim ice-capped heights above and sank to sleep . . . '

Beating rain woke him some time later. 'Rest of night not so good.'

They saw the pall of smoke rising above Athens from miles off. The city stank of gunpowder and burning oil when they drove through it at one o'clock in the afternoon on 7 April.

An air raid red alert had been posted on Sunday morning immediately word of the German advance reached Athens. At sunset, just before 9 pm, all Athens heard the droning, then the throbbing of enemy aircraft. The mine-layers came in the first wave of planes, switching off their engines to glide silently in over the Acropolis and on towards the port where they dropped their mines. Close inshore a great pillar of fire rose a hundred metres in the air. Seconds later, a group of barges packed with drums of olive oil went up.

The bombers followed about an hour later. Three bombs hit the *Clan Fraser*. Shortly before midnight, the raid drew away, leaving her burning. The harbour master opposed all efforts to tow her out; a naval officer tried, for she had 200 tons of TNT in her hold, but 'she was held firmly to the wharf by the collapse of a great dockyard crane burning white hot . . . '

About 3 am, the *Clan Fraser* exploded in a sheet of orange flame, torn apart by the detonation of TNT and ammunition in her holds and 'dispersed into a vast, spreading shower of white-hot metal. The anchor was thrown a great distance inland and the port was lit by a thousand simultaneous tongues of flame. Every ship in the harbour was then on fire . . . '.[16]

Eleven ships were lost. Explosions continued all night long on an ammunition train and trucks ashore, and in the harbour. Sunday's close-packed lines of merchantmen, naval ships in British grey camouflage, lighters and caïques with their wide, curving gunwales were by the following morning twisted metal and charred wood in an oily, reeking slick. When Weary went down to look at the port, it 'was nothing but oil and bodies'.

On Monday, the harbour master was shot as a fifth columnist.

The port was closed for two days. Naïve, original plans had decreed that 'ships would cross the Mediterranean and unload civilian fashion with troops and motor transport and stores . . . comfortably in one port'. Blamey had favoured Kephissia as a hospital site because of its proximity to the port: wounded could be taken by motor ambulance cars to the docks and loaded onto hospital ships. Now the air-borne destruction wreaked on Piraeus meant that 'this had to be totally abandoned', and it 'upset the tactics and plans of how you sited your units'.

Weary's notebook for these days shows that motor transport and medical stores were scattered over Eleusis, Skaramangas, Stylis, Volos and even Khalkis, wherever cäiques or lighters could run in to jetties. Piraeus was now a most unsuitable port. Remarkably, the stores intended for the 2/6th AGH were safe; some were already on their way to Volos by sea, the remainder were retrieved from the docks and returned to Kephissia to await transport by train on 10 April.[17]

Throughout Monday night, from his bed in the King George Hotel, Weary heard 'the poor woman next door, walking up and down, up and down, wondering what had happened to her husband', the naval officer who had tried to move the *Clan Fraser* out of the harbour.

For the next four days, Weary was in Athens, preoccupied with trains, motor ambulances, medical stores and smoothing out problems encountered by the units. 'Every effort is being made to extend the scope of medical arrangements, particularly hospital beds.'[18] Air raids did little damage but gave an urgency to their preparations.

The British had stepped up their construction of an ambulance train and had borrowed one Greek ambulance train and divided it into two. These were rough enough, but each half was capable of carrying 125 lying cases. Further coaches were added for sitting patients.

The 2/2nd and 2/7th Field Ambulances were anxious to go forward but the rest of their personnel were not due to arrive until the ninth. Weary sent ten of their motor ambulances up to 1 MAC at Elasson for the casualties expected from the German advance.

On Good Friday, Johnston's first appreciation of the forward medical situation, dated 7 April, arrived in Athens: it had taken four, rather than the expected two days to reach them. Communications were poor and deteriorating; Large wanted Weary's assessment of the situation, and decided that he should go north to see Johnston at I Aust. Corps HQ.

The only transport available was with Sellick, the Red Cross Deputy

Commissioner. They reached Elasson twelve hours later, at the exact time that Blamey's message to his divisional commanders took effect: 'As from 1800 hrs 12 Apr I Aust Corps will be designated ANZAC CORPS . . . '[19]

Weary reported immediately to Johnston's HQ, only to find that he and the ADMS Dental had gone up to Perdika to the 4 Light Field Ambulance Main Dressing Station. The weather had closed in. Snow was falling in the mountains, making roads and tracks impassable in places; lower down, driving rain and mud had the same effect. At least the appalling visibility prevented enemy air action. Troops suffering from exhaustion in the freezing conditions were coming through the advanced dressing station sited near the 19th Brigade.[20]

MacCallum briefed him thoroughly on the arrangements for the various medical units. 'Our force are facing grimly terrible odds, very much alone . . . ' They were withdrawing before the advance of the 40 German Corps on the line running from the Aliakmon River up to the Veria Pass–Amindaion–Vevi line, which the Greek forces on the left flank had been unable to hold.

Johnston returned at 2330 hours to report that the 19th Aust Infantry Brigade 'were engaging the enemy in the region of Veve'. This brigade was now commanded by Brigadier George Vasey: he had achieved his much-desired field appointment. Weary wished that he could be as successful as Vasey at extricating himself from the staff. Ether, anti-malarial stores, ambulance trains and stretchers seemed banal in comparison.

Eighty battle casualties went back that night to the 2/3rd CCS at Elasson, mainly from the 2/4th and 2/8th battalions. The bridge across the Aliakmon River near Servia was to be blown up next day by the engineers once the retreating units were through; evacuation would then be difficult, either by 'hand carry' across the Aliakmon on the engineer's footbridge with a further twelve kilometres across difficult country, or by ambulance cars on a circuitous road south-west through Grevena.

Three kilometres south of Elasson, Weary found the 2/3rd CCS working to capacity with 200 patients, having already evacuated numbers to the British 24 CCS at Larisa. They were short of personnel. The nurses had been sent back to Pharsala within a few days of arriving, since the area was regarded as hazardous, and three male nurses had been evacuated sick. They needed ether, tents, blankets and X-ray equipment.

He had thirty minutes to check on the motor ambulance position (the new cars he had dispatched from Athens had arrived at the 2/3rd

CCS that morning); signal Large; and ask Crellin to requisition blankets and tents from Larissa, before reporting to the GOC.

Blamey questioned him closely about the hospital situation and the evacuation of the wounded: the 2/3rd CCS must evacuate its patients 'as quickly as possible', for further casualties were expected from the 19th Brigade area. Weary passed on the order to Longford and Belisario at his 2/3rd DDS.

Weary and Johnston sought out the 2/1st Field Ambulance who had set up an RAP on the road between Servia and Elasson. One company was still forward; the rest were awaiting orders to move to Dolikhe and open with 5 NZ Field Ambulance. Mid afternoon, they ran into Disher, 'looking most pathetically tired, but carrying on doggedly in his old good humoured way' and concerned about the roads along which the wounded from forward areas would be brought.

So far, Weary noted at 1500 hours on 13 April, only 300 of the 2/8th and 230 of the 2/4th infantrymen had turned up in the assembly area at Rodona.* Few had blankets, all were exhausted, wet and suffering from the penetrating cold. Some had no weapons – their officers had realised that they would never make it across the steep, snow-covered slopes if they had to bring out their equipment with them. 'The only immediate prospect of evacuation is by road Ellasson–Servia– Lazarades, but a considerable portion of this road is already under observation [by the Germans] and at most only 48 hours available.'[21]

Weary began the journey back to Athens by Red Cross transport. 'After two days of study and reconnaissance the whole thing is laid out before me like a game of chess played for rather inconceivable stakes, but the hell of it is I have to go back and make my reports so I lose touch with the next moves,' he wrote to Helen around two o'clock the next morning, when they stopped for some sleep.

When he reported to Large at 6 am on 14 April, he heard that Burston had arrived in Greece and was on his way forward. He was greatly disappointed at missing him on the road and puzzled as to how it had occurred: he had met the 2/2nd and 2/7th field ambulance parties just north of Thebes on the only road and outlined the developments on the northern front to their commanding officers, Lieut-Colonel Douglas Salter and Lieut-Colonel Leslie Le Souef.

---

* The official history gives the figure on 13 April for the 2/8th as 308.

'Can there be an element of panic?' wondered Weary, two hours later, when Large emerged from the morning conference with orders for the urgent evacuation of 1 NZ Hospital by rail to Athens and of all 2/6th AGH personnel from Volos by the coast road, with only 'what they can carry in their hands'.

The latter's first wounded patients had been in the camp less than twenty-four hours when the order to evacuate the site arrived. 'Stop work immediately and empty all vehicles,' read the message given to Money. 'Hospital personnel [who] cannot embark in cäiques should proceed in the empty trucks.'[22] Tents, mattresses, blankets, stretchers, equipment – all were to be abandoned amongst the olive trees at Foula Bay.

Patients and personnel from the New Zealand hospital were to be brought down by rail as soon as they could be collected from Demerli; an ambulance train being built by the British was hastily made up to full weight with whatever coaches could be gleaned from the Greeks and sent forward with stores and rations. 'Every patient which can be loaded' would return on it. 'In short it is a general clear out,' Alexander signalled to the New Zealanders from Larisa. All tents were to be 'left standing'.[23]

'Having left the forward area 12 hours ago this seems . . . unbelievable,' recorded Weary. The fate of the two casualty clearing stations, the 24th British and Belisario's 2/3rd Australian, Large consigned jointly to Johnston and Colonel Alexander, ADMS 81 Base Area in Larisa, as 'communications hopeless'.

Weary cancelled the transport which was to take the nurses from Kephissia to Volos; and endeavoured to retrieve the stores now on their way by rail and sea to Colonel Money.

'Position of British Force in Greece regarded as untenable on present line and must make a desperate retreat' to one running coast to coast south of the plain of Thessaly, from Itea through Brallos to the sea: the Thermopylae line.

Le Souef and his men got no further than Lamia; a dispatch rider brought an order from Large for the 2/7th to return to Athens immediately, and Salter's unit drove on alone to Larisa.

Weary worked through the night. He retrieved the remainder of the 2/2nd Field Ambulance party from Voulas camp and at 3.30 am on 15 April Large and he put them on the ambulance trains bound for Pharsala. By 6 pm, he had located some of the 2/5th AGH's stores on board the SS *Rawnsley*, lying off Eleusis, and arranged for them to be transported to the hospital site next day when she unloaded in Piraeus. 'All available stores to be concentrated at Kephissia from all sources.' Colonel Kay's 2/5th AGH was to 'work night and day' to set up the hospital at Ekali.

The low cloud and poor weather of the past few days had melted away, and with the clear skies in the early morning came the waves of Messerschmitts and Stukas, machine gunning and dive bombing the roads, railways and ports. Le Souef had a tricky run back over the Brallos Pass and reached Athens at eight o'clock that evening, 'full of thwarted hun hate', to be pounced upon by Weary and told to open a convalescent depot at Voulas for the patients expected from Pharsala.[24] He promised accommodation for 400 by the following day.

The eight sisters from Belisario's casualty clearing station arrived at Kephissia 'all in', after a slow trip back. Their train had attracted the attention of enemy bombers. They joined their nursing colleagues from the hospital at Kephissia in the Majestic Hotel, one of those which Colonel Fulton had taken over for the sisters' accommodation.

Both halves of No. 1 ambulance train had arrived in the Athens area by the next day. As soon as word came that they had reached Thebes, No. 2 was sent up from Athens 'and will return laden to the roof if necessary. A passenger train with 700 walking cases is also on the way down . . . '[25] McKillop thought it would be difficult to salvage stores from Pharsala. As the last patients were being loaded into the coaches, he saw Greek air force personnel looting his hospital of everything portable.

Twenty-four hours after leaving Blamey at Corps headquarters, Burston arrived back at the Acropole Palace on the Tuesday night accompanied by Brigadier Andrew, the Deputy Adjutant-General in Greece, and Lieut-Colonel Barrett. They had reached Elasson the previous afternoon just as a raid began, and had to scramble for cover under their car while the village was bombed by eighteen Stukas. After ordering his ADC to give them a stiff whisky apiece when they reached headquarters, Blamey sent them packing.[26]

Large, Burston, Andrew and Weary met early on Wednesday. Their mood was bleak. The Germans had broken through on the left and the Allied forces were in retreat. Larisa was in flames, though still in their hands, the railway line had been bombed and communications north of Thebes were in chaos.

But Burston confirmed that the 2/3rd CCS had withdrawn, without losing their equipment, to a new position well to the rear of Anzac

Corps and about fifty kilometres south of Lamia; and that he and the NZ ADMS, whom he had spoken to at No 1 AGH on his way through, believed it would be possible to salvage some of the New Zealanders' equipment if they moved fast.

Colonel Money and his road party arrived that evening, Money still fuming about the loss of his stores and equipment and the *'sauve qui peut* attitude of his senior physician, Lieut-Colonel C. G. McDonald and his senior surgeon, Lieut-Colonel V. M. Coppleston. They had refused to co-operate when he tried to save some of the hospital. Money considered their behaviour to be reprehensible: 'something near mutiny'. Weary was not impressed when McDonald and Coppleston, both loud in their criticism of their commanding officer, demanded a court of enquiry. He suggested that 'they were not likely to come out of it very well if there was . . . mutiny . . . against their boss'. They were sent out to Kephissia, as was the 2/1st Field Hygiene Section, where Fulton was to employ it however he wished.

Weary now shuttled by motorcycle between the port, where he found large quantities of medical stores lying on the coal quay, and Force headquarters, where Fulton and he arranged for these and other stores to be delivered to Colonel Kay.

On 17 April Weary suggested to Large that the 2/7th Field Ambulance be sent forward again 'with the idea of putting an ADS in the region of the Thermopylae Pass, and an MDS at the most convenient location north of Levardia'.[27] Later that morning, they got word that Belisario and his CCS had arrived at Thebes, where General Maitland Wilson had just established his Advanced HQ. Weary jumped on his motorcycle and went to Thebes immediately to check on their needs. It was the first they had heard from this unit for some time.

Le Souef was commiserating with a depressed Colonel Money at Kephissia when an urgent telephone call summoned him to head-quarters. Large spotted him as soon as he entered the Acropole Hotel, and hurried across. 'There has been a great catastrophe in the north . . . You will proceed to Brallos Pass immediately . . . '[28]

They drove off at 2 pm, taking with them a New Zealand staff sergeant who was to push on to Pharsala and salvage any drugs and stores not already pilfered by the Greeks from his hospital. In their transport were supplies of drugs, saline, dressings, chloroform, glucose, splints and ether urgently needed by the medical units falling back before the German advance.

Across the Asopos River, the ground rose gently towards Thebes on its low hills. Far in the distance, Le Souef saw 'a lone motor-cyclist approaching. To our intense surprise and pleasure it was Major 'Weary' Dunlop'.[29] Weary's comments about returning to Athens were mostly unprintable, as they chatted by the side of the road. Le Souef was sympathetic and Weary shrugged. 'Every time I get up to where our troops are in action, I am sent back to Athens. I never seem destined to get into this war.'

Before leaving for Thebes, he had attempted to persuade Burston to let him join Le Souef's field ambulance as part of the rearguard. 'It seemed improbable that all . . . would get away and many wounded would be left.' But liaison was becoming more important by the hour. Burston dubiously referred the decision to Blamey, who refused permission. 'DMS . . . says I must stay here, which nearly reduced me to tears. I felt so much happier when I was in the forward area . . . '[30] Later, when he brooded over it, he realised that he was inwardly relieved. ' . . . Afraid I am no hero.'[31]

Weary found Le Souef and his staff moving up in high spirits: 'Real job at last!' He had arranged for them to pick up one of their ambulance cars at Thebes and for others donated to the Greeks by the Society of Friends to join them. Le Souef's rear party and some tonnes of accommodation stores would follow by a train leaving Athens at ten that night.

For some reason, Weary and Large delegated final responsibility for deciding where Le Souef should set up to Crellin at Advanced HQ BTG rather than Corps: it was confirmed that one company should open an advanced dressing station on the pass north of Lamia, one company on Brallos Pass itself, with the main dressing station just south of it. 'Hellish casualties expected on passes.'[32]

Apparently, no one thought to send a signal to Johnston, who had no idea where Le Souef's 2/7th were: they should have been with Lee Force 'occupying the position across the Domokos Pass through which . . . troops would be withdrawing'.[33] Had he been able to see Salter of the 2/2nd, he would have learned that Le Souef had been plucked back to Athens to set up a convalescent depot for wounded evacuated from the forward zone, but 'There was never at any time an opportunity for . . . contacting 2/2 F. Amb . . . Their subsequent movements were, and still are obscure.'

Responsibilities were sometimes confused, particularly for the administration of casualty clearing stations. At one stage, Belisario was given three sets of conflicting orders by Johnston on behalf of Corps,

Alexander as OC 81 Base Area Larisa, and Force HQ in Athens. The British 24th CCS fared even worse. Weary noted in his diary that Brunskill had ordered them to remain open and be captured. Disher, visiting them on 17 April, 'had privately considered this to be a damn scandal'. He found it 'ready to move off, patients in M ambs of MAC . . . I told them that I had no authority in the matter but I certainly approved of their action . . . A CCS able to evacuate all its cases and told by someone [in Athens] to stay put . . . !'[34]

Later, Large told Disher, feelings ran very high when 'Brig. i/c Force HQ had said C.O. 24 CCS would be put under arrest for moving' and the commanding officer had threatened suicide. Disher offered to take the responsibility, but Large shook his head: nothing had come of it. Disher had suffered from Brunskill in Palestine and had no respect for him – 'v. excitable . . . a "no" man'.[35] Weary saw him as a 'charging rhinoceros' with 'blind, instinctive reactions'.

Burston and Andrew sailed for Egypt on Friday 18 April. The last instruction Weary was given by his DMS was that all nurses were to leave Greece. The hospital ship *Dorsetshire* was due: they could be evacuated with the patients. Weary was to 'make any decisions he considered necessary and to refer to Col W. E. Kay if he was in doubt'. Kay was now the senior Australian medical officer in Athens.[36]

Burston carried a letter from Weary for Helen which he would post in Alexandria. 'Just ever so much love dear heart – I wonder if it is possible to send enough to last the time which may be necessary . . . '[37]

Weary began to co-ordinate the evacuation to the Middle East of nursing staff and wounded. All sisters were placed on two hours notice and he specified that Coppleston and McDonald should accompany the nurses of the 2/6th. He warned Major Francis, the VD expert at Ekali, that he required information twice daily of all cases not likely to be fit in two weeks; and suggested to Large that Major J. B. Bunting, DADMS at HQ BTG should be appointed Embarkation Medical Officer and attached to Fulton. 'He is a live wire and the man for a big job.'[38]

Fulton and Weary told the 2/6th AGH to make up bearer parties, each of 50 other ranks, and Weary drew up the medical evacuation scheme. That night, he learned that the hospital ship *Aba*, due in at noon on 19 April, could take off 400 lying cases with a party of nurses and officers. Earlier on, he had been told that a transport could unexpectedly evacuate a number of medical units with their heavy equipment and vehicles the following afternoon. He hurriedly compiled lists of those who should go and those who must stay. It seemed incredible that it was only six days since Blamey announced the formation of Anzac Corps. Now, the medical scheme was 'evacuation, evacuation anywhere!'

But information in Large's office about the forward areas was scanty. When Le Souef reached the Brallos Pass that Friday, he found it deserted: not a soldier in sight. ' . . . Athens had no accurate knowledge of what was going on.'[39]

'Padres and press men returning [are the] main source', Weary complained. 'Enemy outflanking us on the left advancing region Trikkala towards Pharsolos with view to cutting off retreat – meantime strafing roads and railways. Our left flank falling back to fight a covering action on the heights north of Lamia whilst centre and right get back through Lamia to . . . cover final evacuation.'[40]

At dusk, Le Souef and his unit saw from the heights overlooking Lamia a packed column winding down the pass on the far side of the valley and along the narrow road, and 'heard the patter of feet, human and animal . . . the night long'. Greek soldiers and refugees were fleeing south. And following them across the mountain range and down the escarpment was the organised, slowly retreating Anzac column of vehicles and men. With the sunrise on the nineteenth, more than sixty kilometres of bombed road and blown bridges lay between them and the enemy.

Weary had received no reports from Johnston of the location or needs of forward medical units, but this was no fault of the Australian DDMS. Johnston and MacCallum, who had not seen Disher since 15 April, had been moving constantly by motorcycle and on foot between the medical units and relying on Crellin at Advanced HQ BTG (who knew the situation), to pass information back to Athens. They were more trusting and less jaundiced than Weary about the British staff.

Weary's confidence in Force HQ was dwindling fast. 'General "Jumbo" Maitland-Wilson's staff seemed to spend most of the time in the Club or taking afternoon tea . . . every fourth man was just so good that he would be hard to equal, but you had to carry three that were quite hopeless.'

Large was a quiet, pleasant, capable and hard-working Scot who co-operated at all times with the Australians, but 'he was up against some jungle tigers . . . like Brunskill, his AQMG [who] wouldn't talk to him rationally.' Large was in an invidious position. Despite his own experiences in Palestine, Weary could scarcely believe his ears when the British DDMS approached his immediate staff superior on the military side with a civil request and the brigadier roared, 'Get out, you little rat! Get out!'

Thereafter, he avoided humiliation by deputing Weary to deal with Brunskill, particularly on critical matters like ambulance trains and transport. Weary didn't give a damn about Brunskill, who couldn't push him around. As Australian medical liaison officer, he represented at the highest level his DMS, a major-general, and General Blamey.

The transport departed from Piraeus in the late afternoon with Sellick, the Red Cross representative, on board. He had no more stores to distribute. Everyone managed to embark except the 2/6th AGH nurses and their officer escorts, who missed it through a combination of insufficient time and muddling their directions. They attempted to leave on the *Aba* next day, but an air raid interrupted boarding, and all but the matron and twenty-four nurses had to return to Kephissia. Plans to evacuate them on the *Dorsetshire* had to be aborted when it failed to arrive.

Without consulting Large and Weary, and fully aware of the instructions regarding the nurses left by Burston, Brunskill sent a signal to Headquarters Middle East suggesting that the ship would be at risk from enemy air attack on Piraeus. Waves of Ju 88s and fighters systematically bombed and strafed the ports daily. 'Better for lying cases to fall into enemy hands in hospital . . . *Dorsetshire* should therefore not put in and walking cases and nurses cleared with troops from safest beach.'[41]

'The appalling difficulties with communications are past understanding. How can one integrate the scheme of evacuation without knowledge of where units are at any one time? As soon as car running . . . MLO proposes contact I Aust. Corps . . . '[42]

Weary and George Bennett drove out of Athens at 5 am on 20 April. ' . . . Steerage mechanism rapidly degenerated to guesswork, and radiator, in spite of repairs, leaked constantly.' They had a good run to Thebes under a clear sky, and the depression which had provoked him into writing to Helen that 'not even the most sublime optimist can see much further than the open mouth of hell in this part of the world'[43] rolled off him. They were through Thebes, climbing up the road to Levadia over one of the passes in the sunlight, when suddenly

Messerschmitts screamed down out of the milky blue sky. The two men leapt out of the car. 'I was bloody scared, but I didn't show it.'

It was the first time that Weary had been shot up on the road. 'Do you think, George, that he's shooting at us?' he asked, as the batman dived for cover.

'Oh, he's certainly firing at us,' George replied glumly, amidst what Weary remembers as 'a pleasant little rain of bullets'. Weary stood at the side of the road, filled with exhilaration on that sparkling spring morning. 'The sound of the bombs falling was like an orchestra to me . . . Everything was shades of blue . . . and I was looking up at this plane, thinking how bloody marvellous . . . At last I'd reached a point in the war at which I was worth having a shot at.' For the next forty kilometres to Anzac Corps headquarters, concealed in a valley three kilometres south of Levadia, their progress was slow and dogged by constant bombing and machine-gunning, noted by Weary as 'Pretty hot'.

He found Johnston and MacCallum persevering under 'harassing conditions of continued movement and aerial attention', and discovered why no reports had arrived in Athens: they had gone no further than General Wilson's headquarters at Thebes.

Most casualties coming through on 20 April had resulted from action in the Tempe Gorge or from the 'incessant and merciless machine gunning and bombing of troops' as they retreated from Larisa across the plains of Thessaly. On that wide, flat expanse, broken occasionally by a solitary house or the white froth of blossoming almond and pistachio trees, there was little cover and only the deep ditches each side of the straight road in which to roll away from the sputtering bullets and the exploding anti-personnel bombs. The soft earth with its spring-sown corn and tobacco absorbed the shock of many bombs. After Domokos, if they could get off the road, there were sometimes stunted pines and scrubby bushes amongst the rocks and gullies.

But such was the psychological effect, that after repeated raids, men dived out of their vehicles immediately the *Luftwaffe* appeared and everything halted until the planes pulled away. It was surprising that so few vehicles were disabled by the attentions of enemy aircraft: Weary's car was hit but still mobile, as were numbers of other damaged vehicles.

By the time he reached headquarters, most of the troops had withdrawn through Lamia, zigzagged up more than 1200 metres to the Brallos Pass and taken their places in the Thermopylae line. The New Zealanders were on the right, between Thermopylae and the sea.

Vasey's forward troops were in position on the pass.

Le Souef and his field ambulance waited with them for the German attack. His main dressing station, about a kilometre and a half south astride the main road to Athens 'now became the centre for collection and evacuation of all casualties'.

Mount Parnassus and range after towering range of the Pindus Mountains vanished into a blue haze on their left.

Evacuation was the most urgent matter, and trains the best method, in spite of the risk of bomb damage to the line. Motor ambulances, even mules and hand carrying were used locally, but now Johnston and Weary determined to overcome Brunskill and Crellin's reluctance to keep the ambulance trains running. Lines could be repaired.

Johnston would advise advanced headquarters at Thebes imme-diately he required trains, which would operate a shuttle system between Thebes and Athens. Two trains would be cut in half, so that one could be kept at Moulki, one at Thebes 'or other station', one at Athens and one in reserve, Weary scrawled in his notebook. On his way up he had watched non-hospital trains in Thebes station being bombed and strafed; and it was impossible now to bring them further forward. Motor ambulances would have to carry wounded to the trains, as well as follow Disher's directions to patrol the roads after a raid.

Weary set off towards Thebes to explain the plan to Crellin, almost immediately running into an intense air attack. 'There was nothing to do – you couldn't get through this township, the convoy just choked the road, and everyone was out lying on their bellies . . . ' The exhilaration of the morning had vanished. For the first time in his life, Weary felt 'naked fear'. He hurled himself out of the car, flattened himself into the road, trying to present as small a target as possible. Twin-engined Junkers Ju 88s were overhead, their bright orange-red incendiary bullets arcing towards the stationary column. A succession of Stukas dived over them, 'intimidatingly low', their high-pitched screaming drilling through his ears. First, strafing with the forward gun, then '250 pounds of anti-personnel bombs [dropped] on us, so there was a rain of metal about you, then a rear gun'. He could see the little froglets of dust leaping all around him, *phlip, phlip, phlip, phlip*, bullets striking the dust like rain, shrapnel and spent bullets lying in the dirt, and every time a bomb landed, it 'heaved you back and forth. There's nothing you can do . . . just sweat it out. You really feel fear . . . '

They went round, came back again, and again and again. 'I drew a long breath and thought, "Christ, this is the real thing".' He snapped his head round when he heard George Bennett yell, was aghast when Bennett jumped to his feet. His reflexes catapulted him across the road in pursuit. 'And I chased him, hit him on the back of the neck and said, "Stay down, you bloody fool, stay down!" And George said, "That's all right for you, sir – look at my seat!" '

Weary started to laugh. George had had the back of his pants shot out by an incendiary bullet.

In Thebes, he turned down the Khalkis Road to headquarters. Crellin had gone forward to Anzac Corps. They went back in search of him. They met on the road in the middle of another raid as intense as the previous one. Weary dashed over to him during a brief lull. He would send a train forward to Thebes on 21 April. He needed figures, times. Crellin was to ensure than any motor ambulance cars in the area went to 2/3 CCS by nightfall the same day. The ADMS refused to listen or even acknowledge what Weary was shouting at him above the noise of aircraft and the 'crump' of bombs. 'You can't talk here, you can't talk here . . . ' he yelled, his face white and sweating with fear.

The enemy had total control of the air. That Sunday, 20 April, air raids reached an unprecedented level and the RAF fought its last engagement in what became known as the Battle of Athens. By evening, all that remained of the RAF in Greece were seven Hurricanes.[44]

Once more, at eight o'clock that evening, he reported to Crellin's headquarters. Trains were to be loaded and move down to Athens under cover of darkness. The enemy did not fly at night. He would ring Crellin from Athens.

Weary and George set off, Weary driving, a couple of Greek soldiers in the back seat to add some ballast over the drifting back axle and give the car more stability. They crept along without lights, taking hours to cover a short distance in the torrential rain on the twisting road. Somewhere on the road, the steering packed up completely. The car did a forward somersault over an embankment and came to rest on a tree a few metres down a steep slope.

Weary pitched heavily on top of Bennett, who had been napping, and broke his arm. Somehow, amidst the confusion, he found his torch and climbed out, hastily pulling Bennett up the embankment. The Greeks scrambled out just as fast. No one had any idea how great the drop was, but in the uncertain beam of the torch, the tree looked too frail to hold the vehicle for long and there seemed to be nothing but space below it.

'Hitchhiked to Athens, arriving 0600 hours.' They finished the journey on the cold metal floor of an ammunition waggon. Weary made

Bennett as comfortable as he could, rolled himself in his greatcoat and went to sleep.

While Weary was bumping down to Athens, Wavell arrived at Levardia around 2 am to discuss the evacuation plans with Blamey. That Sunday, it had been decided in a conference with King George of Greece and General Papagos, that the British force should leave Greece. Blamey was prepared. He produced the map he had taken on his afternoon drive with Norman Carlyon on 26 March, with its plainly marked evacuation beaches.[45]

At one minute to midnight on 21 April, Blamey was to meet Rear-Admiral Baillie-Grohman and Major-General 'Jumbo' Maitland Wilson on the Plain of Thebes, to finalise the evacuation.

Weary sent Train 1A forward as far as Ipato, one station south of Thebes. It could go no further. Sunday's bombing had broken the line in three places and Train 2 was now on the other side of the block, laden with wounded waiting to come through. Only wireless telephone was working. He sent a signal to Crellin at 9 am.

Large and Weary next reviewed the medical units. 'Are they wanted?' signalled Weary to Disher about the 2/6th AGH surgical team (forward since March and now with the 2/3rd CCS at Levardia) and three British units, B Company 189 Field Ambulance, the 24th CCS and 168 Light Field Ambulance.

Throughout the day, Weary was on the move, once more by motorcycle, finding transport to take rations, blankets and stretchers back to Levardia, organising for the reception of the wounded coming down on the trains that night and for additional stores to go to Kay at Kephissia. Through sheer determination, the enterprising Money had salvaged almost half his equipment from Volos, using 'unofficial' vehicles, and handed it over to Kay.

Three hundred beds at Kephissia would be ready by evening, but only eight surgeons and six physicians remained to staff the hospital and over 200 beds were occupied already.

The field ambulances and the casualty clearing station were moving wounded through quickly. Men arrived in Athens dirty and exhausted, many having had no food for two days and some still in only the first field dressing. Air action made them very jumpy. 'Wounded who have been subjected to great strain do not stand up at all well to [it] . . . and the presence of enemy planes in the neighbourhood is sufficient to cause considerable panic.'[46]

Older men, particularly Disher, with all the responsibilities near the front line, and Johnston were showing signs of exhaustion but driving themselves on. At corps headquarters the previous day, Weary and MacCallum threw themselves into a slit trench when three Messerschmitts flew over with an angry stream of bullets and continued to discuss the evacuation of the sick.

Suddenly Weary focused on the spectacle of Bill Johnston trying to take cover behind a scraggy olive tree and shivered to see 'that courtly, wonderful old gentleman standing there with a thin olive bush [between him and] these Messerschmitts . . . for the first time, I realised what a beastly thing war was.' Johnston's reputation had been made on the Western Front in the First World War. 'He was famous for his all-round compassion.'

Disher had realised when he was in the Western Desert that it was a 'young man's war'. Older men did not weather well. The extra stress imposed in Greece by air raids rattled some of the toughest officers who had been highly decorated for bravery in the previous war. But Disher never lost his grip in the face of constant and often disconcerting changes of movement, and Johnston's medical arrangements 'remained admirably clear and complete' at all times, in contrast to the 'indecision and . . . tendency to confusion and undue haste in Base Areas'.[47]

Weary was 'terribly fit, quite tireless' and equal to these 'feverish days of strain in a Balkan nightmare', where there were 'no railways worth a damn, roads – hell, communications nil, language impossible, skies full of boche.[48]

'Night of 21/22 one of tremendous decision. Greeks ceasing fighting.'[49]

General Tsolakoglou and the Greek forces in Epirus had surrendered to the commander of the *Leibstandtarte Adolf Hitler*. Maitland Wilson told Blamey at their midnight meeting near Thebes that the Anzac troops must begin embarking from the beaches on the night of 24 April. At 7 am that morning, 22 April, Blamey issued his orders for the evacuation of Greece to his senior divisional staff officers.

Weary arranged for 800 light wounded and 366 hospital personnel to leave as soon as sea transport could be supplied by the navy. He kept back 178 officers and ORs from the 2/5th AGH and 135 of the 26th British Hospital to care for wounded coming through; later Large and he intended to reduce this group to a minimum necessary for the care of those who could not be moved.

General Christopoulos called to offer the help of the Greek medical service for those British soldiers left behind. But Weary and Large knew that the ill-equipped Athens hospitals were already full of Greek wounded. They should make their own arrangements.

At 10 am, Weary was handed a 'private letter' from MacCallum asking for 'all possible transport, train or ambulance, to be sent forward . . . to clear wounded and release 2/3rd CCS for evacuation'. It could take thirty-six hours to close a casualty clearing station of 200 beds. He located ten of the nineteen motor ambulance cars from 1 MAC which had brought wounded down overnight and ordered them forward again, then sought out the DA&QMG.

Brunskill refused, point-blank, to release the last reliable British train crew in Greece for transporting Australian wounded. He was more interested in evacuating the able-bodied. Weary, coldly angry and suspecting it would not be used at all, had a 'terrible go-in with [him] . . . and threatened him with personal complaint to General Blamey, who I was sure would refer the matter to the Australian government'.

Brunskill had no counter-argument to that, and in the middle of the day he reluctantly released the British crew to run up Train 1B to Thebes. Weary signalled Anzac Corps at 1300 hours: 'One Ambulance train now at Elion ready to move to Ioen. Should be made use of if possible otherwise return train Athens.'[50]

After leaving Brunskill, he noticed the ambulance cars parked down the street and in nearby squares. A driver protested that Large had told them to wait there until dusk. Weary rounded up the drivers and personally saw them off around 4 pm. By chance, he found out that Crellin had sabotaged his plans from Thebes. 'B[loody] F[ool] Crellin said do not send since all trains now not required. When pressed said he had last discussed this matter yesterday morning.'[51] Crellin had discussed nothing on the road with Weary on Monday morning: he had been too fearful of the deadly metal raining from the skies. While Weary had been chasing the ambulance cars, Crellin 'advised DDMS BTG that trains were not required'.

'Eventually the wounded got back by road transport.' They brought 287 casualties down to Kephissia that night.[52] The convoys moved faster now that they were allowed to drive with lights. Weary had incurred the lasting enmity of Brunskill for nothing.

His last task that afternoon was to finalise the medical arrangements for the evacuation scheme with Large before going forward to brief Johnston and MacCallum. Q had found him a car and a driver, a 'bulldog-looking redhead' called 'Blue' Butterworth who had emigrated from Yorkshire to Australia and joined the AIF.

Private Butterworth's previous driving experience had been limited to an occasional spin round Cairo in a six-wheeler Morris when he was there on leave. 'My cobber, driving the mob [would say], "Right, here's your chance!" and we'd change seats.' Now, he was put behind the wheel of a 1941 Chevrolet with a column shift which had belonged to Brigadier Allen, registration number BAR17, and Butterworth had had 24 hours to practise manoeuvring it between Daphni and Athens. Butterworth reported to the Acropole Palace and was told by Large to wait in the car across the road. Major Dunlop would join him.

Blue's confidence began to ebb. 'I'm sitting there, starting to get a bit scared . . . I didn't have a licence, and next thing I'm looking straight at the bottom of these legs, the big boots, and a greatcoat, and [my eye] started to travel up. I said to myself, "Shit! He'll never get in here! He'll never fit in this car . . . ".'[53]

Weary hopped down off the high kerb, folded himself into the passenger seat and directed Blue to the King George Hotel in Syntagma Square. It was 7 pm, rush hour, and Blue had been driving no more than five minutes before he had locked his bumper into the rear of a naval car that stopped dead in front of them. Two groups of Greeks lifted the cars apart.

Weary quietly told Blue he was pulling out of the hotel but no one was to know. He slung a few belongings in the back seat and they drove out of Athens. The night was intensely dark. They were moving against a slow-flowing stream of troops and vehicles that choked the road. Nearer Thebes, they met the covering force falling back on the Thebes Pass. Weary took over the wheel and Blue began to give directions. 'No lights, all blackout. And I'm saying, "A bit over on the right, come over on the left, over the right" – the next thing, whoof! And we're over . . . ditched.'

Weary took his coat off and grabbed Blue's trenching tool to dig out the wheel and get them back on the road. 'And I thought, who the bloody hell's this fellow, he was like – to me – he was like Hercules!'

It was 1 am on 23 April when they reached Johnston and MacCallum near Levardia. Weary confirmed that Belisario should begin closing his casualty clearing station immediately. In great detail, he went over the evacuation arrangements that Large and he had finalised late that afternoon.

They would be taken off with the troops when the nights were darkest – the new moon would rise on 26 April – from the areas of Marathon, Corinth–Megara and Argos, beginning on the eve of Anzac Day. One field ambulance was allotted to each evacuation area, with a main dressing station in the collecting area and a section at each beach. Every possible case should be manhandled to the ships; those whom the commanding officers of the field ambulances thought would be unable to make it should be left with adequate medical personnel to care for them.

The Australian and British general hospitals would continue functioning and be captured.

The 168th Light Field Ambulance would post a section at each embarkation point in the Marathon area: Rafina, Porto Rafti and Lavrion. The 4th Light Field Ambulance would open two dressing stations, one east of Megara and another eight miles east of Corinth by Ayioi Theodhoroi, where the river runs into the sea.

Weary's hand-written, official war diary ceases abruptly in Athens with an entry for 0900 hours on 21 April. From now on, his battered, brown field notebook was more than an *aide mémoire*: it was the basis of the remainder of the war diary which was not written until he arrived back in Egypt.[54] Fifty years on from those crowded spring days, some of the scribbled notes meant little when he glanced through it; but once placed beside the official document, the diagrams, figures, notes and sketches take one straight into the urgent drama of those last hours played out against the rugged mountains and the blue Aegean.

He hoped to see Blamey in Levardia. He was concerned about the nurses, for 'Admiral [Pridham-Wippell] insists on [a] hospital ship' and it was doubtful if one would arrive in time to evacuate them.[55] (No one was aware of Brunskill's signal about the *Dorsetshire* for another five days; it was thought to be arriving two days hence.) 'Expression of opinion required by GOC AIF as to sisters . . . Policy in France to leave them.' Weary was not at all happy about this latter idea, particularly in view of Burston's order. But Johnston was not so sure. He thought 'they should remain if absolutely necessary for the adequate nursing of very sick cases'. Weary was unable to see Blamey.

The sun rose on a world which was 'an infinity of beautiful blues'.

Weary had not slept. He went for a long walk and stood in their lost line 'in a cornfield ablaze with . . . poppies where worn-out soldiers slept beside their guns'. The covering force were taking up their position on the pass near Thebes. Amongst a group of low Judas trees covered in purple flowers, he saw Greek mothers bring their children to spit on the charred bodies of Germans in a burnt-out plane. He felt sad, grubby and tired. The photograph on the British Forces ID card issued to him on Sunday showed his eyes alert as ever, but his face dark with a heavy growth of beard.

Blue was woken by a Stuka screaming over and he hopped out smartly to take cover under the olive trees. He wondered where 'the big bloke' was – everyone else was disappearing – and then he saw Weary, 'sitting, I can see him now. He's got the steel shaving mirror and he's shaving . . . '

Blue had been watching Weary narrowly, puzzled as to his rôle. He had settled for Intelligence, although he had realised that Weary was a doctor from the pencil torch he handed him to direct at the wheel being dug out on the pass. It was only as they were leaving that morning, when Weary had a last word with Johnston about the hospitals in Athens and announced his intention of calling on the 2/3rd CCS, that Blue realised he was medical corps.

The casualty clearing station was a few kilometres away, east of Levardia. When Weary drove up, Belisario had only 36 walking and 4 stretcher cases left; he had evacuated all the others during the night, although he expected more to come through during the day. It would close at 2 pm and move down to Athens in ambulance trains and motor trucks on schedule at eight o'clock in the evening. Le Souef's field ambulance were still at the southern end of the Brallos Pass with all but one of the Friends' ambulance cars, which they would use to evacuate the last patients when they moved out on 24 April.

Weary put two patients in the back seat of his car and drove back to Thebes to see the regimental transport officer. As they approached the badly battered railway station at 10 am, Blue could see a Stuka shadowing them, but still a good way off. Weary paid no attention to it and directed Blue into a siding, although the two in the back seat were becoming very agitated.

An ambulance train full of wounded was sitting there, but the regimental transport officer was nowhere to be found. As Weary walked briskly over to have a word with the wounded on board, three Stukas attacked. Blue and the others were already out of the car 'making themselves as small as possible'. Weary noticed that the planes shut off their machine guns as they flew over the train marked with its red cross, 'then they started on the other side'.

It was too much for the Greek train driver. He bolted. Weary picked up a rifle and bayonet and chased him for about fifty metres. 'Get back to the train, you sonofa bitch!' he bawled. He wanted that train in Athens. While he was prodding the Greek towards the train again, he noticed that the planes had wheeled round and started their return run, machine guns chattering.

Weary settled for prudence this time and fell on his face. Suddenly he became aware of the Greek train driver, striking an heroic posture, and proclaiming: 'We Greeks have no fear!' Weary rather sheepishly scrambled to his feet. 'The tables were turned.'

He waited until the train pulled out of the station, then walked back to the car. No one said a word as Weary climbed in. 'Right,' he said, settling back in the seat. Blue let out the clutch and they moved off towards Athens.

On the road were groups of Greek soldiers, 'exhausted, starving and broken in spirit', few carrying any weapons or rations. 'Poor famished, beaten men – it is pitiable to see them plodding back . . . They had nothing left to meet the devastating Hun technique.'[56] It was a silent trip along the bomb-cratered road.

The two subdued patients were dropped off at Kephissia. Weary reported to Large at the Acropole Palace at noon.

Large greeted him with the news that since the loss of two Greek hospital ships from enemy bombing, the navy refused to bring in one of theirs, on which patients and sisters could well 'perish helplessly'. Brunskill's signal had born bitter fruit. A destroyer was suggested; but it was argued that nursing staff were 'ill equipped for bivouacking, since they are without mess tins and the usual equipment of a soldier and are unsuitably clad'.[57] How would they stand up to enemy air action on the roads and beaches, to 'landslips, sleeping on hills etc.'?

Weary was disturbed by this and regretted not having been able to see Blamey. He thought everyone greatly underestimated the women, although the risks of escape by ship worried him, and seriously ill patients left behind would need expert nursing skills. No one seemed able to make a decision. Forty-two British sisters were remaining at the 26th Hospital. 'All AIF sisters, 5 Aust Gen Hosp, volunteered to stay.' Unhappily, he agreed that 40 AIF sisters should remain. All the rest, together with the masseuses, were to go. But privately, he determined to try and evacuate the lot, even if Colonel Kay did succeed in staying in Greece with his hospital.

Kay was 'calm and confident' when he called on Large and Weary early that afternoon. He had selected those to be left at Kephissia: 9 officers and 155 other ranks; and he was 'emphatic' that he should make the tenth officer, for his second-in-command had already gone. Only fifty beds were occupied at present, practically all walking cases having been taken to the beaches. Mindful of Blamey's stricture that valuable officers could not be spared, Weary resolved to consult Johnston.

Lieut-Colonel John Rogers, the senior Intelligence officer, called Weary to a conference at 6 pm with the Rear Party, I Aust Corps, where Weary outlined his medical arrangements for the evacuation. Rogers and his staff, appointed by Blamey, were responsible for the embarkation of all Australian and New Zealand units. Weary brought up two other matters: his resolve to get the remaining nurses away if at all possible; and the Friends' Ambulance Unit. The latter had been working 'with considerable gallantry' with the 2/7th Field Ambulance and it was imperative that they be evacuated, for they were not an army unit. Should they be imprisoned, they would receive no pay. They had narrowly escaped capture during the Finnish campaign, then travelled through Sweden and the length of eastern Europe in order to give aid to the Greeks.[58] Seventeen members of the unit arrived in Athens during the night and Weary sent them off with details from 80 Base Area, who were heading for the Peloponnese.

Corps headquarters had ceased operations at midnight on the twenty-third, when Blamey received his order from Wavell to return to Egypt.

Weary also received his orders to leave Athens, but he 'couldn't do it with so many units remaining'.[59] The dates are plain in his field notebook and letters to Helen, but incorrect in the war diary, probably through the confusion reigning during the last two days rather than a deliberate attempt to conceal his disobedience.

Immediately Johnston and MacCallum arrived at Force HQ that morning, 24 April, Weary and Large described the medical situation. Johnston did not hesitate. All administrative officers of the two hospitals should be evacuated, including Colonel Kay. As to the nurses, Weary went over the whole question with Johnston once more, agreeing that even though the 'full facts probably not known to GOC and arrangements cannot now be altered', Blamey had 'informed his staff that all nurses were to be evacuated' prior to his departure at three that morning by Sunderland flying-boat.[60]

Coppleston and McDonald escorted the nurses to Nauplion.

Weary summoned Blue to drive Johnston and him to Ekali, where they called on Kay and aranged to evacuate the commanding officers and the registrars of the 2/5th AGH and the British 26th Hospital on the *Neon Hellas*, which would leave that night. Nominal rolls of the 204 staff and the 38 patients were handed over to Weary.

Colonel Popham, the commanding officer of the 26th Hospital, which was holding 315 patients, promised to give Weary nominal rolls before he embarked, when they called there to thank him 'for the devoted attention to AIF personnel by the hospital staff'.

Loading wounded onto the *Neon Hellas* at Piraeus Harbour continued throughout the afternoon. Taking them out by barge was slow, but by late afternoon around 800 wounded, soldiers, officers, and women and children evacuees were on board. All activity halted with the air raid warning, then the dive bombers struck.

The *Neon Hellas* took a direct hit and began to burn. Colonel Kay was mortally injured, Popham and the two registrars only slightly so. Kay remained conscious, despite being blinded with gross damage to the brain and paralysed down one side; out of consideration for his doctors, he begged not to be taken to his own hospital but to his British colleagues.

Weary rushed to Piraeus, where an aid post set up by men from the 2/5th AGH treated the survivors being brought hurriedly ashore. The port was still under machine-gun attack whilst people were being taken off the burning vessel and cleared to various Greek hospitals. Weary broke open kit boxes on the wharf and distributed the contents, for the civilian evacuees had lost everything.

The nurses had been embarked from the Argos area without casualties. Large, Rogers and he decided that Lieut-Colonel Odbert, the Asst Director of Hygiene at British HQ, should leave with those who remained for the Peloponnese.

Since before dawn, Weary had been driving all over the city in an attempt 'to locate all LUSTREFORCE wounded scattered about Athens in order that all capable of moving should be evacuated'.[61] It was Anzac Day. But this year, no bugle's silvery notes bade them remember the landing twenty-six years ago. The harsh reality of gravely wounded soldiers and 'refugees with their piteous bundles [and] hungry children' contrasted painfully with the dawn which greeted him along a 'road winding amongst the pines and olives'. Below gleamed 'a sinuous sweep of bay fronting the mountain ranges of Salamis, piled tier on tier, the sea the palest eggshell blue and each shadowy mountain range repeating slightly differing shades . . . I thought of [Helen] and still another dawn, that made my heart ache . . . '

Many casualties from the *Neon Hellas* had been admitted to small Greek hospitals. With two lorries and drivers and a stock of 'assorted uniforms', he spent the greater part of the day retrieving 93 walking wounded and sending them in batches to Daphni camp. Greek doctors and nurses had tended the wounded throughout the night and when those who could walk were being helped into the vehicles, forced 'their meagre supply of rations' on the men.

'This in a half-starved capital with no drugs or dressings' in Greek hands.[62] He had arranged for Lieutenant Hurford of the RAMC, whose figure on a motorcycle had become familiar to those transporting wounded as he went back and forth between the front and Athens, to fill a lorry with essential medical supplies at 26th General Hospital. Hurford took these to the Peloponnese, eventually leaving valuable morphia and other drugs with the Greek hospital in Tripolis.[63] Some men, too damaged to be evacuated, were left there.

At seven o'clock on Friday evening, 25 April, Headquarters, British Troops Greece, closed in the Acropole Palace Hotel, Athens. Weary and Blue had already left to drive out to Kephissia for the last time. 'I shall never forget . . . [the] remonstrating thousands of Greeks before British headquarters asking to leave with us and fight on – and not enough vessels for ourselves.'

For two days Greeks had been closely watching all movement around the hotel, begging to be evacuated. 'There seems to be no bitterness. If we feel that they expected so much more from us, they seem to think that they have let us down . . . '[64]

THIRTEEN

Grey Ships Waiting

'. . . As a HEADQUARTERS PERSON I determined to be amongst the last to leave.'

He could not bear to leave Athens without visiting the Parthenon. Blue drove him to the foot of the ramp in the Dionysiou Areopagitou. 'I ran up that steep incline and found myself fronting that great [Temple of Wingless] victory . . . Nike Apteros . . . and I looked at that, and I looked at the Parthenon, and I said, "What bloody irony!"' There was no one there to hear him.

While staff at the Acropole Palace hurriedly destroyed maps and papers, Weary was on his way to Kephissia in case there was 'any last service I could do for the unfortunate beings left behind'. Large and he had allowed for 'sufficient officers and other ranks to deal with 1000 casualties'.[1] They had no idea how many would be received, although 170 patients remained in the care of Major Brooke-Moore and 183 with the 26th when headquarters closed. Nearby, cared for by his British colleagues, Colonel Kay was near death.

Weary was talking to Brooke-Moore and the other officers when the telephone rang. He picked it up, and to his astonishment it was for him. Odbert – who by now should have left Athens with the nurses – said: 'Dunlop, you've got five minutes to get to Daphni!'

'I said, "Good lord, that's miles on the other side of Athens. I can't do that, Odbert." . . . [But] that's all Odbert had to say.' He repeated himself, then rang off abruptly.

It was 1910 hours. Butterworth was quietly enjoying a beer, having promised to post a last letter which an orderly was writing to his wife, when he was paged. A moment later Weary appeared with 'word that the Germans were on their way into Athens – no panic'.[2]

Weary had the car's engine running and wondered if Blue should drive ('I don't want to be killed!') but Butterworth was already shooting 'straight across the gardens, the lawn and along the Kephissia road'. The

236

sun was shining into his eyes. Weary threw Blue's cap in the back seat, took off his own peaked cap and put it on the other man's head. He insisted that they call at headquarters, where he had left maps and papers which must be destroyed. As they drove through the centre of Athens, the Greeks were putting up knife rests and tank traps. The streets were clogged with people and vehicles, they took two wrong turns and Blue spun the wheel too far round and skidded broadside on into a donkey cart. Finally, they screeched to a halt at 51 Patission Street and 'there, standing in full, pipe-clayed splendour, was a Scottish soldier, guarding the Acropole Hotel'.

Weary hopped out of the car in astonishment and said, 'Soldier, what the hell are you doing here?' And he said, 'I don't know, sir. Orders seem to be that I stay here and hand over to the Hun.'

'And I said, "You damn fool, you can't do that! Look, get in the car! . . . I *order* you to get in the car!" '

He was immovable. 'You mad loon,' said Weary. 'Is there anything I can do for you?'

'Could you take a letter to my missus?'

'I said, "Write it quickly." '

No one appeared in the echoing corridors and high-ceilinged offices of headquarters, there were no papers in his office: all his maps had been destroyed. The smell of burning paper, the smell of a retreating army, hung in the air. But he gathered up a few 'pathetic remnants of worldly goods' and dashed downstairs, picked up the letter from the soldier (who still refused to change his mind) and 'drove madly out to Daphni'.

There was no one at the assembly point; but billows of smoke led him to another part of the camp, where he found the pay corps burning millions of drachmae, while 'the gutters were running with Dewars and Haig, with these fellows smashing up thousands of bottles of whisky left in the NAAFI store' in front of the amazed eyes of Blue and wailing villagers.

Weary found Lieut-Colonel John Rogers and Major Ken Wills calmly sitting in the mess enjoying a whisky, and so, 'as nonchalantly as possible', he accepted their invitation to join them and enquired what was up. He had been feeling distinctly jittery, but he was not going to let 'these cool customers' know it. Over a couple of whiskies, he discovered that the Germans had not reached Athens yet: it would still be possible to cross the Corinth bridge by morning, although the ferries had been destroyed. Apparently, Odbert had thought Weary would spend too much time at Kephissia and lose his chance of evacuation with his headquarters – even be caught – so he had 'put on this very portentous' act before leaving Daphni.

Blue knew Daphni well. He was an experienced soldier by now, able to make the best of what was offering, find food or drink if it was there. Weary might be yarning with the intelligence blokes for a while. Mama's café was nearby. He dispatched a group of children for some beer, and when they returned with the beer but no change, sent them back for his money. By now it was dusk and the light was failing, the mountains smudged ashen against a sky suffused with the glowing, unreal, fluorescent pink-to-violet sunset which is Greece.

Weary decided it was time to go and walked over to the car. 'Right!' he said to Blue – his usual way of announcing action. But the boys had not returned with the change.

'I said, I've got to tell you this – those little bastards . . . brought the beer, but no change!'

'Do you think you'd recognise them?' asked Weary.

'So there we were, driving round Daphni, looking for change. I knew Mama . . . and when I arrived to explain to her about the beer and introduce Weary, she was ropable . . . I told them bye bye, we're on our way. Mama kissed me and the two daughters did, and then poppa grabbed me! Same with Weary. And away we went . . . '3

They had dallied too long and lost that last hour of half light. There was steady going through Skaramangas and Eleusis to Megara, but here the convoys moving down through Erithrai and Mandra joined the narrow road clinging to the coast and they became part of the column. Hewn out of the Scironian cliffs, the Greeks call this corniche *Kakia Skala*, the Evil Stairway, and along its now craterous length strewn with dead mules and wrecked vehicles, Weary and Blue slowed to a crawl.

Brunskill, carrying his terrier, Susie (whom he was determined to take out of Greece against all rules), hailed him. 'Is that you, Dunlop? The brigadier is looking for you!'

They drove on, through Agioi Theodoroi, and he wondered if George and the other wounded he had ferried to Daphni in his 'crazy ambulance service' would be taken off from the beaches, remembering uneasily that this was ancient Krommyon, where Theseus had slain Phaea, the sow which fed on human flesh. 'God knows what hardship to be endured, and what inflammation of wounds.'

Weary had been three nights without sleep. 'I had this terrible feeling,

I must keep awake, I must keep awake . . . ' He was driving. 'I kept nodding.' Then he was suddenly, sharply, awake when the car crashed down into a bomb crater and settled at a dangerous angle, leaning seawards with one wheel over the cliff. 'The only thing . . . holding the two of us from going right in was where the bitumen had blown back and formed a rim.'

The column behind lurched to a halt, then moved slowly round them. With Blue behind the wheel, Weary stood on the edge of the drop, high above two other cars upended on the rocks below. 'Put her in reverse.' The tyres merely spun and the engine revved: 'all you could smell was burning rubber'. They changed places, but Weary did no better.

A matter-of-fact English voice piped up out of the darkness: 'I'm afraid you'll have to abandon your vehicle.' Without ceasing his efforts to push the car out, Weary replied slowly: 'I don't know who you are, or what you are, but will you please fuck off!'[4]

The last of the convoy ground past them and they were alone. 'All you could hear was the wind.'

Weary refused to give up. There was more revving, more burning rubber, much shovelling and pushing and 'something like despair'.[5] Then, 'in the distance, we heard this singing, Greeks singing, and they appeared around the corner'. They were soldiers, making their way home, singing to keep up their spirits on the dark road to Athens. 'Next thing the jalopy was – whoof! – straight back on the road.' Weary emptied the glove box of Woodbines and Players cigarettes.

Around two o'clock in the morning, five hours before the paratroopers swung down from the skies, Weary was across the Corinth Canal and crossing the plains of Argos, 'several times nodding precariously over the wheel in spite of savage pinches and reminders', anxious to reach the beaches before daylight brought the *Luftwaffe* to harry them with bombs and bullets.

'Unexpectedly, at about 0400 hours recognised the car of DDMS BTG, parked by the side of the road . . . was comforted by the fact that he was lost too.'[6] He drove on, but by 5 am could go no further. Blue had been asleep for some hours. Weary pulled in, curled up under some olive trees and fell deeply asleep.

About an hour later, he was abruptly woken by a kick in the ribs. A very agitated Brigadier Large stood beside him, saying 'Get up, Dunlop, get up! . . . we've got to get on to Nauplion!' He had lost his headquarters. With Large and a naval commander transferred to his back seat, Weary hunched grimly over the wheel, they drove off, unaware that they had overshot the Nauplion turn-off by many kilometres until someone at the tail end of a convoy told them they were on the road to Tripolis.

Large was becoming increasingly anxious about his meeting at HQ Lustre force. It was 6 am. They were directed to a building which turned out to be Battle HQ. 'Kicked out.' Daylight brought the Stukas and Messerschmitts. The two in the back seat, droning on interminably about the horrors of the road and how many people were being killed on it, suddenly shouted at him to stop. 'Plane overhead! Plane overhead!'

Weary was dog tired. He watched the three men tearing across the field 'with singular amusement', then decided that perhaps he should get out. He stepped straight into a ditch 'and went up to the thigh in green, slimy mud . . . And I thought, Oh God! I'd sooner be killed in the car.'

The aircraft ignored them.

They were directed through Argos to a building near a crossroads in Nauplion and eventually Blue 'pulled into a yard and pulled a bit of camouflage net down' over the car. A bunch of Stukas which had been dive-bombing the shipping in the bay swept down. 'You wait here!' Large called to Weary, as he and the naval man rushed into the building. Weary vanished.

They had acquired a third passenger on the outskirts of Nauplion, a doctor named Livingstone, who was stretched out under the car. Two provosts were laughing at Livingstone, the yard was full of pigs squealing and fowls squawking and fluttering in alarm as the aircraft screamed back and forth, and Blue suddenly noticed Weary's tin hat on the seat. He found Weary sitting on the sea wall in the sun, notebook on knee. Blue puffed up with the helmet. Weary looked up. 'Get to bugger out of here before you get yourself hurt!'

Blue decided that this was yet further evidence of Weary's charmed life; he intended to hang on to his job as driver and batman.

Weary came under brisk attack by successive planes, but he stubbornly continued writing up his diary notes. 'They shot me up with the forward gun, and I'd hop over the wall, then they'd lam at me with the rear gun and I'd hop over . . . the other side. If more than one plane was coming, it got confusing.'

Large failed to appear and Weary was vexed to hear from a provost that the brigadier and the staff had departed by another door. 'Decided to take pot luck off the beach with the first troops I found.'[7]

The first troops turned out to be Belisario and the 2/3rd CCS, lying up 'in a pleasant little orange grove in flower. Yellow marguerites and poppies in profusion.'[8] From the orange grove, Weary looked up to the rocky headland with its great Venetian fortress, from which the stone houses of the old upper town spilled in shuttered elegance down to the harbour. Belisario provided breakfast, and Weary spent the day surrounded by the bridal scent of orange blossom, writing to Helen, reading poetry, dozing, and watching successive aerial sorties. 'It was so languorous and pleasant and I couldn't be bothered with a slit trench, even with more inquisitive planes overhead.'

At a 9 am conference of Movement Control staff in a nearby barn, he heard that the navy were doubtful of evacuating them all that night. ' . . . Reflected grimly that it had to be tonight or never.' Only a small covering force stood between them and the Germans at Corinth bridge.

All day long, in brilliant sunshine, lorries emblazoned with names like 'Dorothy Lamour', 'Hector the Great', 'Mrs Baker's Boys', moved along the road into Nauplion, raising clouds of dust which blanketed the exhausted men propped against the walls of buildings and under trees alongside the road and streets. While men smashed up the lorries, or drained the oil and water and ran the engines until they seized, Greeks scavenged amongst discarded equipment and scurried about with pieces of bedding, clothing, anything which might be of use. Rubbish lay everywhere. Figures continued to come and go around the square stone Customs House and the Hotel Grande Bretagne by the quay.[9] They fled at the sound of aircraft.

At 3 pm, Weary turned up to the second conference, where Movement Control confirmed that they were to go off that night 'unless our ships scuppered'. When the sun went down, the citadel on its headland flamed more intensely apricot than even the Parthenon on his first day in Athens. Far too close to the stone quay, the *Ulster Prince* burned, lighting up the tiny islet of Bourdzi and its pretty crenellated castle. The ships in their naval camouflage slipped silently into the harbour.

'Now the gray ships that the Germans hate are waiting . . . '

' . . . Zero hour . . . stripped of all worldly goods except one suit we stand up in and a water bottle – everything has had to be sacrificed.' They marched off in threes at 2115 hours, wounded first by ambulance, the rest walking. 'Silence and no smoking. Haversacks, Helmet steel, Resp[irator]s, greatcoats only.[10]

The *Ulster Prince* still burned, causing 'anxious moments lest the light . . . give us away'. Blue clutched Weary's valise to him, at first refusing to jettison it, and 'had a bit of a struggle' with the embarkation officer, justifying Weary's tag of 'bulldog'. A wind had risen, whipping the sea up and tossing the overloaded cäiques about, so that there was endless manoeuvring while the men climbed from the wooden boats up the scramble nets onto HMS *Calcutta*. The navy were efficient, hospitable, generous with beer. Weary 'went to sleep with the tankard still on my chest'.

At dawn, on Sunday 27 April, the two transports *Slamat* and *Khedive Ismail*, escorted by destroyers *Hotspur*, *Isis*, *Diamond* and the cruiser *Calcutta*, were steaming out through the Gulf of Nauplion on their way to Crete.

The Stukas searched for them too far south at first, and it was not until 7 am that 'Action Stations' sounded. Weary was sleeping on the deck immediately under the 4-inch anti-aircraft guns, which went off with 'the most terrible, clanging . . . noise, ear-shattering'. He shot up a companionway and found himself a job, stripped to the waist 'shovelling shells with the marines. It was great sport . . . they needed a bit of help to shift those shells. Oh, I felt marvellous.'

Calcutta's captain placed his ship between the two transports, increasing the protection he could give them, and the destroyers dashed ahead, throwing up a barrage in front of the Stukas as they dived in. *Calcutta* lurched and shuddered with the force of the guns – 'you felt you were really hitting back' – for the next two hours.

'One ship in convoy hit and on fire.' This was the *Slamat*, the larger of the two merchantmen.

Slamat went down, with the loss of almost all on board, as did the *Costa Rica*, but not before the navy had transferred the 2500 men she was carrying to other ships. *Wryneck* and *Diamond* were also sunk, going to the aid of *Slamat*. *Calcutta* would be sunk on her next voyage. The gunners told Weary that it would probably be their last. They had a weakness – they 'couldn't throw up the stuff astern' – and the Germans had found it out.[11]

The navy moved around 19 000 men from Greece on the night of 26–27 April, and it was estimated that 4250 were taken off from Nauplion and nearby Tolos that night.[12] They left behind them a defeated population of just over six million, which 'had done super-human things to fling back the Italian'.

'I like the Greeks . . . physically tough and wiry, big-hearted and loveable. There is little to soften the fibre, and a living is hardly wrung from the soil.

'I wonder if after all valour might not be the best policy – to fight to the bitter end, selling our lives dearly. I shall feel sad about this country as long as I live.'[13]

Weary's first sight of Crete was of high, snow-capped mountains. As they drew closer, there were groves of olive trees, their leaves breeze-blown silver above the squat, gnarled trunks, pencil-topped cypresses and purple-flowered Judas trees. An eight-kilometre stretch of water, sheltered by a rocky peninsula – the Akrotiri – and studded with the masts and funnels of sunken ships, spread about them in a natural harbour called Suda Bay.

Suda had suffered from the dive-bombers and only two vessels could use the quay at a time. Weary was ashore at 4.30 pm. With the 2/3 CCS and carrying full equipment, he walked eleven kilometres to camp along hot and dusty roads, 'secured a meal and one blanket' and, despite the enemy planes still overhead, fell asleep under a tree.

'I've never known anything more disorganised.' He was a lost soul, a liaison officer with no one to liaise to, no unit, no headquarters. Walter MacCallum hailed him from the midst of a jostling crowd of khaki, and Weary heard that Large's and his estimate seemed to be correct: MacCallum reported a thousand wounded in the last twenty-four hours in Greece. He ran into Lieut-Colonel Morrow in charge of the 2/5th AGH party, saw Money with his 2/6th AGH: 'only 2 killed, 1 wounded, otherwise intact.'

All day Monday, 28 April, he wandered about, trying to find somewhere to stay, someone who knew where he ought to be – Large, Odbert, Fulton, Johnston: where were they all? He heard that Force HQ was in Canea and officers were being billeted at the old post office building. He tramped off to look for it – there was no transport, so he hitchhiked – but when he arrived after many peregrinations, a brigadier turned him away. The billet 'was reserved for someone else'. He had to take his luck with the troops. Le Souef was luckier. He met Disher there, and was given sleeping space on the floor.

Weary had not had a proper meal since landing with Belisario's men. Food was dropped off to the units and he managed to scrounge some now and again when he was in the right place, but 'rations very short.' A large, rather scruffy looking party marched past, and he was told they were the captains who had lost their ships. ' . . . To my horror, there was my poor old captain of the *Bratdaal*.'

Weary had no money. Before leaving Greece, he had put on his best uniform and his Morris Angel greatcoat and spent his remaining drachmae on a camera. Now he was 'living like a dog' off the country and he did not much like being 'a completely detached soul in an army without transport and with little food'. Odbert's concern about his becoming separated from headquarters had been well founded.

John Rogers came to his rescue. He loomed up out of the unshaven, dispirited, rag-tag groups of soldiers, and peeled a few thousand drachmae from a great roll. As an intelligence officer, he had plenty. Money in his pockets once more, Weary went straight to the Piccadilly Café and walked into Disher.

Disher had left Nauplion on the *Hyacinth* with 6th Division headquarters two nights before Weary and arrived on Crete that Friday. Le Souef's 2/7th had arrived, as had 189 Field Ambulance. Disher was irritated that the British field ambulance had made 'no attempt . . . to give any mark or sign as to locations.'[14] Using borrowed British transport, he had been locating and organising his medical units, setting up regimental aid posts and dressing stations, insisting that the regimental medical officers order troops to bathe their feet and rest. He knew where everyone was, what everyone was doing.

Brigadier Vasey was in charge of the area with the 19th Brigade and most of the units around Canea were 'moving into position . . . for defence against parachutists'. Colonel Johnston had left by flying boat that day with other senior officers of I Aust Corps; Disher had no idea where Weary might find Large.

Weary foolishly became involved in an argument in the café when a colonel of artillery criticised Wavell for committing them to the defence of Greece and Crete. 'I couldn't understand how he could say that when it was known by the staff down to field rank that Wavell had opposed the whole thing, that it had been forced upon him by Churchill . . . [But] my artillery colonel said, "He should have resigned! It was his duty to resign." And I said, "Well, hardly a duty, sir, when it was required of him by Mr Churchill and Anthony Eden and the Chief of Staff."

'Whereupon he said, "I have been a soldier for seventeen years, and I wouldn't give an opinion on a bloody medical matter!" So I had to concede.'

That night, Weary rolled himself up in his blanket and again slept under the stars. Next day he continued his beachcombing existence, lying in the sun, swimming in a little horseshoe cove ringed above its rocky fringes by turf and wild flowers. 'An injudicious sneeze blocked my left eustachian tube and soon was well on my way to the miseries of otitis media.'

His feet were blistered, his socks stinking and worn to holes. He found Ordnance and the British warrant officer in the quartermaster's stores protested that he had 'no authority' to issue socks, but handed over a pair when Weary resorted to waving his .45.

Weary was still officially a straggler, but he arrived at 189 Field Ambulance the following day, Wednesday, in time to copy down their first administrative instruction, dated 29 April, to be issued on Crete. It was closing at Neo Khorion, evacuating its remaining casualties to No 7 British Hospital, and opening a CRS with a surgical team at Heraklion in preparation for battle. Large, Odbert and Fulton had departed early on Tuesday morning with Disher, he discovered.

He reported to Colonel Morrison at headquarters, with a severe middle ear infection, a temperature of 104 degrees and 'plastered with boils and carbuncles'. Morrison thought there was little point going to hospital just to be captured; there was a chance he could get away that night if he arrived in good time at the beach evacuation area.

'I felt rather disgraceful evacuating myself.'

The officer directing operations on the beach was his acquaintance from the Piccadilly Café, Lieut-Colonel Durant. He looked hard at Weary as he repeated Morrison's instruction and admitted that no authority existed for his evacuation. Blue stood nearby. There was no room.

Weary was about to turn away, but Durant stopped him. 'I've got a job for you, Dunlop. They're not exactly sick, but it might be in your line. I've got . . . [some] fellows here who are very tired. Perhaps you'd look after them.' A mob of scruffy looking men from various units were standing to one side, all in, unable to march, clad in bits and pieces of uniform and some with no boots or rifles. 'They were miserable, they were famished, and they were demoralised.'

Weary identified a sergeant-major and told him to get them into line, then announced that there would be no evacuation that night. The olive groves behind Canea were not far away; they would spend the night there. 'Their spokesman called out "That's all right for you, sir, but we're fucked!" I said, "What the hell do you think I am?" At this stage a couple of bombs fell and there was some unanimity that we go into the woods.'

They marched raggedly back across the neck of the peninsula. Units had been directed to the vast olive groves rolling down through the fertile coastal strip beyond Canea. Weary found a suitable spot, well back on rising ground, in which to bivouac. Cretan nights were cold, the peaks of the White Mountains above them were ice-capped and no one had blankets. Leaving his party under the eye of the sergeant-major – who had perked up now that an officer had appeared – Weary took Blue and a detail of the better shod back to headquarters at Canea and gained Morrison's authority to be issued with blankets, food and weapons.

They trudged back with as much as they could carry. Weapons were issued, food cooked. There was a scrap about putting out the fire – Weary angrily ordered it be done. But by then, some 'light-fingered Indians further up the hill' had noted where they were and begun to fire on them. To Weary's horror 'my wretches then started getting out their brens and rifles and returned it. Bullets . . . [were] clipping through olive bushes'; his temper was stretched to the limit with 'boils, carbuncles . . . middle ear' and hunger. 'I sat up with such a stream of profanity that I managed to stop the action.'

Weary's ear throbbed angrily, his skin under the uniform was sticky with pus from burst boils. It was not a happy night.

Food, rest and discipline began to improve their morale. Through-out the day, the men lounged under the trees overlooking fields of unripe barley and waist-high grass 'ablaze with flowers'. Along the coast were small farms, vineyards, groves of cypresses and olives, Weary, his 'otitis media pretty grim', trudged back to Canea in the late afternoon.

Lieut-Colonel Jack Barrett, who had been in charge of the Australian liaison details in Greece, spotted him and heard what he was doing with some astonishment. 'What the hell . . . Do you think you're going to become a guerilla leader or something?' He ordered him to report for embarkation that night. His new-found career was terminated. Weary brought the men into Canea and handed them over. Late that night, he and Blue were lined up on the quay at Suda Bay. Barrett shook his head at Blue. 'So dear old Weary gave me a thousand drachmae note and said to Lieutenant Macleod . . . "Look after Butterworth and I'll make contact . . . if we get back to the mainland." . . . I was left in the olive groves.'

'Evacuation *sans* batman in *Hotspur*. Hellish night trying to sleep on the deck of a vibrating little destroyer.' By one o'clock the next afternoon, they were off Alexandria, but mines laid during the night prevented their going in. They reached Port Said very late. The hospitals were full, so Weary was sent to a Canal Officers' *pension* in Ismailiya.

It was after 11 pm when he arrived to be greeted with neither surprise nor enthusiasm and shown to a room where he attempted to clean himself up. He was the only army officer amongst a group of civilians dressed for dinner and bridge. He ate a good dinner, declined an invitation to play a rubber or two and crawled into bed. Next day he felt 'damn ill.' By now very deaf, head 'expanding and contracting', Weary painfully took himself to Kantara and was admitted to 2/2nd AGH. 'Going quietly.'

FOURTEEN

'Sorry, Gone to Tobruk'

THE TELEGRAM BOY LEANED his bicycle against the stucco porch of 605 Toorak Road and rang the doorbell on Tuesday, 13 May, shortly after 9.15 am. Helen was at home with appendicitis, and Tossie took it to her immediately. 'Arrived safely love darling Dunlop.' It had taken ten days to reach her.

The letter Burston had carried back to Alexandria on 18 April arrived about the same time with his signature scribbled across the triangular censor's stamp on the envelope. In spare moments, all officers censored soldiers' letters and they censored each other's under an honour system. Weary knew that no strange eyes read his loving messages; and although he mentioned the movements of friends throughout the Middle East, he carefully omitted their destinations.

'Expensive war, isn't it?' he complained to Helen from his bed at Kantara, four days after arriving in Egypt. Once more, he had lost all his belongings. 'About £80 worth has gone with the wind.' No letters for five weeks caused much more heartache. He feared that some had gone to Greece, only to be burned, that others awaited him in Alexandria. In any case, air mails were now 'jeopardised by nonsense in Iraq', where the Arab Nationalist movement, heartened by the British defeat in Greece, was causing trouble. Anti-British feeling was encouraged by Rashid Ali, the Prime Minister; the like-minded Grand Mufti in Jerusalem was also stirring the pot, and the Germans were reconsidering their earlier rejection of his ideas for supplying arms and fomenting a revolt. German agents were already in Syria and anti-British sentiment simmered in Egypt. Iraq's pro-British Regent fled to Basra with his nephew, the infant King, to seek British protection.

Iraqi troops attacked Habbaniya, the small RAF station and flying training school eighty kilometres west of Baghdad, and the Iraqis were beaten off. When Weary wrote his first letter to Helen after returning to Egypt, Habbaniya had been reinforced by 350 British troops and the base at Shaiba, near Basra, had acquired some Wellingtons to fly to their aid, if necessary.

Britain needed Persian and Iraqi oil, which was piped from Persia to Basra, at the head of the Persian Gulf, and from north-east of the Euphrates to Haifa. An Iraqi government sympathetic to the Axis powers might encourage Germany to move through Turkey into Iraq. Not only would Britain lose her oil; with the Germans in Basra, their submarines would be able to make free with shipping in the Indian Ocean.

Weary found his fifteen days incarceration in the hospital at Kantara slightly embarrassing, for everyone else appeared to be recovering from wounds. He stayed in his room and pretended not to notice when the colonel suffering from a bullet wound in the chest, with whom he shared the room, progressed from daily exercises in front of the window to long walks and then runs in the desert 'to restore his vigour. He rather depressed me by eternally lecturing me about morale, whereas I lay in bed listlessly.'

Walter MacCallum called in on 4 May and Weary handed over the nominal rolls of personnel and patients in the 2/5th AGH which he had brought from Athens. His report to Burston and the completion of the war diaries would have to wait until his head stopped pounding and his concentration improved. He had no energy, his blood sugar level was too high (a relic of hepatitis), and fresh crops of boils and carbuncles continued to break out. At least the severe inflammation in his ear responded to sulphanilamide, his deafness gradually declined under George Swinbourne's supervision and the prospect of mastoid surgery receded.

By the middle of the month he was well enough to spend a day in the operating theatre watching John Colquhoun and Rank at work, one engaged in orthopaedics, the other in much more interesting plastic surgery, employing techniques which were entirely new to Weary.

Burston called on 15 May to congratulate him on a job well done in Greece, and also to convey Blamey's commendation. The DMS could not resist pointing out how completely his decision to send Weary as an administrative officer rather than a member of a field ambulance had been vindicated. Weary knew what was coming next: a position on the staff had been kept for him. He shook his head. Since the fall of Greece and Crete he had one idea: to go to Tobruk.

The mood in Cairo was pessimistic; Weary himself had no 'faith or expectation that the Middle East would hold out. It seemed certain that the whole Delta would go. They were talking about a box defence of Syria along the lines of Tobruk . . . falling back on the Gulf at Basra . . . ' And in the wake of the defeat in Greece and the abundant tension over Crete – which was being battered by the *Luftwaffe* ahead of the impending invasion – recriminations were thick in the air at GHQ and in every bar in town.

The loss of war material and equipment in Greece had severely reduced the army's fighting capability. The RAF, pitifully inadequate in numbers against the superior *Luftwaffe*, had been quite unable to send up effective air defence against the devastating attacks on the ports, particularly Piraeus. The number of seaworthy vessels in the Mediterranean Fleet had been much reduced during the evacuation. Now Churchill was agitating for Wavell to send troops into Syria. He seemed incapable of recognising 'how overloaded and undersustained' Wavell's organisation was.[1]

Apart from a small force fighting the Arab Nationalists in Iraq, Tobruk was the one area where morale was good and people were still fighting. Although Weary believed that the German capture of Egypt was only a matter of time, he wanted to be in Tobruk as soon as possible. He knew there was a vacancy for a surgeon with the 2/2nd CCS. Major A. W. L. Row had been evacuated on 11 April.

Burston looked at him in horror. 'Surely you don't want to go there?' He had listened carefully to Weary's ideas about the reorganisation of the field medical units; they accorded with the little he had seen himself and with Hailes's, Disher's and Johnston's thoughts. If Weary came back on the staff to the vacancy of lieutenant-colonel which Burston was holding for him, he could begin tackling the problem. But Weary held stubbornly to his intention.

Swinbourne and physician Major Ian Wood jointly discharged him on 18 May to convalesce on the *Victoria*. At breakfast with Basil Andrew one morning, he heard that his old boxing opponent from Melbourne, Emmett McGillicuddy, was in trouble. Weary saved him from the threatened court martial and had him transferred 'to convalesce' on the *Victoria*. Unfortunately, McGillicuddy's Irish temper erupted again and he threw 'Admiral' Sydney Crawcour, who commanded the houseboat, in the Nile. Weary was unable to convince Andrew that McGillicuddy should be let off this second time.

It was humid, oppressively hot, the stucco of the buildings glaring white as old bones in the sun. He went in search of the Scotts, because he had heard they were leaving Cairo, Tony bound for London following the death of his father, Marjorie for South Africa. He missed them but fell in with mutual friends and spent a riotous night in their mess with a great deal of alcohol and much broken glassware pitched 'up onto the electric fan'. Next day, he persuaded someone with a car to motor across to Suez with him, where they located Marjorie aboard her ship. She had spent a day in the train without food, so was easily lured ashore to a farewell dinner at the French Club in Ismailiya.

The next day was Tuesday, 20 May 1941.

Weary spent the day at the Gezira Sports Club with Walter Hammond and Greg Cutler, playing golf and worrying over what was happening in Crete. War correspondents might be telling Australians at home that troops 'were better equipped with AA and other guns than they had ever been before', but the men in Egypt and on the spot were under no such illusions.[2] Medical units would be suffering from shortages – Le Souef and others arrived on Crete with only the drugs they could carry in their pockets. Disher wished he had 'some knowledge of the Medical arrangements . . . during the aerial invasion . . . Lack of equipment will render conditions much worse.'[3] Over 500 patients and nurses had been taken off by hospital ship *Aba* to Haifa, but the three field ambulances and their commanding officers were still on the island.

For days, Crete had been under intense air attack. The air raids over Canea and Maleme that morning were earlier than usual, the Stukas and Messerschmitts appearing out of the cloudless summer sky to bombard the airfield and the narrow strip of flat land along the coast west of Suda Bay, then flying off again. Shortly before 8 am there was another raid, this time by twin-engined bombers, Ju 88s and Dornier 17s, and fighters of the VIII Air Corps. Then out of the sky, the smoke and the dust, came the gliders.

At his headquarters above Canea, General Freyberg and his staff heard 'a pulsation, a kind of throbbing in the air . . . when the bombing ceased', and they discerned 'hundreds of enemy transport planes, tier upon tier, coming towards us. Here were the troop carriers . . . They came in quickly and with precision . . . when they were only two hundred feet above the ground, white specks suddenly appeared beneath them mixed with other colours as clouds of parachutists floated slowly to earth.'[4]

'Madam, come and see umbrellas, umbrellas!' shouted a Cretan maid to her mistress.[5]

Weary stayed on the houseboat in the Nile for the remainder of May. The luxurious and extensive facilities of the Gezira Club allowed him to indulge in 'some swimming, much loafing about . . . ' and golf with Burston, Hammond, Cutler and Eric Hughes-Jones. Crawcour (no longer running the officers' leave house in Jerusalem and rising early to scrub Blamey's back now that he was in charge of the *Victoria*) was also a willing and not so skilled opponent.

Everyone, Australian and British, was analysing glumly and minutely the campaign in Greece. Large, Burston, Johnston, Disher and Weary all agreed that the medical units serving in forward areas were cumbersome and 'not mobile enough to meet the requirements of present-day warfare'.[6] They had planned for the remembered, static conditions of the First World War; but in Libya and in Greece, they found themselves part of a fast-moving, constantly changing campaign, not only threatened on the ground, but by 'heavy and incessant enemy air force action'.[7]

Large was most critical of the excessive amount of equipment carried by Australian medical units, particularly casualty clearing stations, which lacked the vehicles allotted to field ambulances and thus inflicted an inordinate strain on transport. The 2/3rd CCS had exceeded the normal amount by 65 tonnes, requiring twenty-two 5-ton lorries and extra railway trucks to bring it back to Athens, and many hours had been devoted to transporting equipment belonging to the 2/6th AGH from Volos to Athens. All had been lost in the débâcle of retreat.

Although all Weary's experience had been administrative, in Greece his employment on medical liaison allowed him to travel freely between general hospitals and field medical units and observe the differences between the British, Australian and New Zealand sections. That March, he had listened closely to Disher discussing how he had dealt with sick and wounded in the desert, questioning him keenly when they were in Alexandria before leaving for Greece. Now he had seen for himself how inadequate their set-up was.

His report to Burston attacked the problem by suggesting 'Forward Operating Centres . . . special completely mobile and completely independent forward operating units equipped with resuscitation and X-ray facilities and able to accommodate, feed and nurse at least 50 patients'. The large general hospitals should be moved far back from the zone of mobile warfare; and expanded casualty clearing stations 'capable of dealing with 250 to 300 patients . . . should be located much further from the front line zone in positions comparable with the more advanced general hospitals in static warfare'.[8]

Since 29 May, when *Orion* and *Dido* and their four escorting destroyers limped into Alexandria harbour, troops had been arriving from Crete. Weary heard that 103 of the 250 2/Black Watch on board *Dido* had been killed at sea in the waves of bombing after their evacuation from Heraklion. Amongst the dead were men he had dined with in Palestine.

George Bennett failed to turn up in Egypt. Weary had assumed that he had gone to one of the beaches with other 'walking wounded' when he was unable to locate him on the last, crowded day in Athens. Now he blamed himself 'for not having pushed . . . enquiries' and feared Bennett had been captured. Butterworth had not appeared, either: both batmen were missing.

Burston kept his word. Weary's priority for Tobruk was fixed and he was warned to be at Amiriya on Saturday, 31 May, to await the departure of his draft. Tony Scott was still waiting for a vessel to take him to England, so he and Weary gave each other a farewell dinner on the Thursday night, 'getting slightly plastered', and early Saturday morning he set off for Amiriya before the temperature climbed to its daily maximum of around 48 degrees Celsius. After four hours or so in a car like an oven, he felt as if he was sitting on red hot coals and over the next four days, while he awaited his departure from camp, his boils and carbuncles grew steadily worse. He decided to drop into the 2/11th AGH, the Greek hospital in Alexandria whose beds he had negotiated for the Allies on the eve of departing for Greece.

'All I wanted was for someone to dress my boils and carbuncles and give me some medicine.'

They persuaded him to get into bed – 'You can't go back to . . . that wretched camp' – and eventually he yielded to their blandishments and climbed in thankfully. Scarcely had he done so than the sirens screamed their warning as enemy aircraft approached on a bombing raid to Port Said and, some time later, announced their return. Left-over bombs were dumped on Alexandria, some falling very close to the hospital that afternoon and smashing buildings across the road and nearby. The population of Alexandria was moving out of the Nile Delta 'like a stream of ants. A train left every quarter of an hour, even the roof was covered with people'.

Weary quite enjoyed himself for a few days, cajoling the nurses into holding his hand during the raids, until Colonel Hailes appeared unexpectedly by his bed and suggested that he inspect Weary's carbuncles. He stood with a stern face looking down at the crops of angry inflamed ulcers on Weary's buttocks and back, swinging his spectacles back and forth. 'Weary, they get boils in Tobruk.'

'I said, "Look sir, you wouldn't dream of putting me on the sick list, you wouldn't tell the old man that I'm too sick to go to Tobruk?" "I don't know, I don't know! They get boils in Tobruk . . . " By the time he left, I knew the game was up.'

When he judged that Hailes had gone, he shot out of bed and went down to Matron Bennett's office. 'You Judas Iscariot, you and George [Stening] . . . you put me on the X list!* She was contrite, but firm. 'We just couldn't do anything else.' He dashed to the telephone, but his party had gone. It had been difficult to obtain space on a boat: 'you had to have pretty high priority to get up there', particularly during June, when the tonnage of supplies shipped in was lower than at any other time and only destroyers made the 'spud run', as the navy called it. Now he had no idea when he would be able to leave.

Tony Scott came over to console him, staying the night at the hospital, and Weary escaped for an evening. They began drinking respectably enough within the walls of the Hotel Cecil, but as the night wore on they progressed to the more raffish and celebrated bars of the town like Rosie's House and Mary's House. 'We drove about at a dignified pace in gharries, propelled by picturesque and avaricious ruffians . . . profoundly discussing life & morals in between screaming directions and maledictions in execrable Arabic . . . ' It was now Thursday 5 June.

'. . . Must get away next week,' he wrote the following Sunday.

On 12 June, the anniversary of his engagement to Helen, he was wandering disconsolately back to bed when he saw the slim back of Brigadier 'Roley' Pulver, whom he knew had been posted to Tobruk as AQMG, 'so I hurriedly scuttled round and put on a uniform and contrived to meet him again'. Weary congratulated Pulver on his new appointment, then dropped his voice confidentially. 'I'm in a terrible

---

* Lieut-Colonel G. G. L. Stening, OC 2/11th AGH.

hole, I had a convoy listing to get to Tobruk and frankly, I got pissed the other night and I missed my draft. Could you take me up there as a staff officer?'

Weary was to meet him at Amiriya Railway Station the following morning. 'I went back to bed and about five o'clock, I padded quietly out, leaving a little note on my pillow.

"Sorry, gone to Tobruk."'

On Friday 13 June, he boarded HMS *Waterhen* for the run in to Tobruk.

He never discovered what they thought when confronted by the empty bed. And his record of service just states: ' . . . Struck off X list. Marched out to 2/2 CCS.'

One of the petty officers on HMS *Waterhen* was Tony Edwards, an old rugby friend from Victoria who had played for the Navy and for the state. Weary began to feel queasy in the furnace heat of the engine room when Edwards was showing him over the destroyer. By the time the others were on their way to the mess for lunch, he had to dash up on deck. 'So there I was being sick over the rail with Tony Edwards holding my hand and saying, 'It would be just the same with us . . . but we're busy . . . '

It was night when they slid cautiously past the rusty Italian anti-submarine net and into the harbour of 'that delightful seaside resort . . . chiefly notable for dust, dive-bombers, derelict ships and death.'

Weary found all of these within twenty-four hours of his arrival. Every ten minutes for three and a half hours on the night of 14 June, enemy dive-bombers flew in waves over the town. At the hospital, an incendiary bomb set fire to an ambulance between two wards, others blew in all the blankets used over the windows for black-out and knocked all the plaster off the ceilings. Shrapnel hailed down from the anti-aircraft guns' response.[9]

Next day, on Egypt's western frontier, *Operation Battleaxe* began.

Tobruk was around 160 kilometres from the heights of Halfaya Pass, where Lieut-General Sir Noel Beresford-Peirse was pitting his 7th Armoured Division and 4th Indian Division against the superior armour and 88 mm guns of Generalleutnant Erwin Rommel and the German-Italian troops of the Deutsches Afrika Corps.

The garrison was warned that heavy and medium bombers would be in the Tobruk area, attacking Rommel's supply lines and any reinforcements which might be moving up. The anti-aircraft gunners were not to fire on these, nor on the Hurricanes that might also fly over that day, part of the air support provided for the 25 000 men in XIII Corps, as Western Desert Force had been renamed. Their brigadier returned a message to Egypt: 'Please send us silhouette of a Hurricane. It is so long since we have seen any friendly planes that the gunners would not be able to remember what a Hurricane looks like.'[10] There had been no combatant aircraft in the garrison since the end of April.

Inside the perimeter defences of Tobruk, Brigadier Wootten's 18th Brigade waited for the signal to move through the wire and 'execute a strong sortie . . . to join forces with the formations advancing from the direction of the frontier'.[11] From their gun positions inside the wire, the besieged put up a barrage into enemy lines with their rationed ammunition. Three days later the battle was over. The signal never came.

On 22 June, Wavell received a cable from Churchill informing him that he was no longer Commander-in-Chief of the armies in the Middle East. General Claude Auchinleck would replace him. Wavell was to go to India, to command there in Auchinleck's stead.

Weary knew nothing of this throughout Sunday 22 June. But in his cave that night, on the 9 o'clock BBC news, he heard an announcement so momentous that he shot to his feet. Troops listening to the radio in the Salvation Army Hall responded to Churchill's speech with a spontaneous cheer, and followed up by singing 'God Save the King'.

'The Germans had invaded Russia on a 2000-mile front with unprecedented heavy fighting and casualties, and I said, "God! It's a whole new ball game".'

Major-General Leslie Morshead, commanding the 9th Division from his headquarters in the bomb-shattered Town Hall, had four battalions of infantry locked up in Tobruk: the 18th Brigade under Wootten; the 20th (Murray); the 24th (Godfrey) and the 26th (Tovell). With them, Weary remembered various British units, including the 3 Armoured Brigade, the 1 Royal Northumberland Fusiliers, 1 Royal Horse Artillery and the 18th Indian Cavalry Regiment. But the men who made the strongest impression on the Australians in Admiralty House were the officers of a party of British B Battalion Layforce commandos left over from the battle plan of 15 June, who were sharing their cave accommodation. Major Lord Sudeley of the Royal Horse Guards had seven officers and 300 men, whom General Morshead found very useful. They came back in to rest up between raids.[12]

The Layforce men caused a minor sensation amongst the Australians when they appeared in the fortress bristling with guns, 'fannies' (combination knives and knuckle-dusters which came to be identified with the ME Commandos) and daggers. Weary noticed that some of the officers spent most of their time sleeping, whereas Sudeley – 'tall, fair, handsome and . . . blue of eye' – scarcely spoke for the first two days while he fussed around blowing up his air mattress to the right tension. Randolph Churchill, Weary and Jock Clarke remembered, 'wouldn't shut up, he drove us all mad, he talked all the time'.[13]

Evenings were whiled away gambling and drinking a mixture of rum and 'infuriator' (Italian cognac which quite often was used to start the primus stoves), occasionally eked out with Recoaira mineral water, vast stacks of which had been stockpiled by the Italians. Several times Sudeley and Weary cleaned up their opponents at poker.

It was the closest Weary had been to a group like this. Not until the publication in the 1950s of *Officers and Gentlemen* did he recognise his companions as brother officers of those described by Layforce's intelligence officer, Evelyn Waugh.

Despite their occasionally rather sleepy appearance, their bravery and daring was unquestioned. Sudeley's men regularly raided and patrolled through enemy lines in July, releasing Australian units for practice attacks ahead of the exercise planned by General Morshead on the shoulders of the Salient.[14]

The garrison's forward defences ran in an irregular arc about 45 kilometres in length, from a point west of the town, where the deep cleft of the Wadi es Sehel ran down to the sea, round to the eastern extent of the wire at the coastal headland of Wadi ez Zeitun. In caves and dugouts and weapon pits, sometimes in shallow holes in the ground, men crouched or lay in dust, flies and heat, looking out over a stony yellow no-man's-land thickly sown with wrecked vehicles, mines, booby traps and thermos bombs.

When Weary stepped ashore under the waning moon of 13 June, some units had been in the garrison since February, others had retreated there on 7 April.* (It was Wavell's decision to send the 18th Brigade to

---

* The 2/2nd CCS had moved into an Italian hospital by 15 February, the 2/11th Field Ambulance arrived at the end of March.

Tobruk and withhold the rest of the 7th division from 'Lustre' Force which had so alarmed and angered Blamey the day Germany invaded Greece.)

Tobruk was on a natural harbour, deep and sheltered, but by June its waters were littered with sunken ships, their masts poking above the surface in places like flooded, ring-barked forest. When the destroyers dropped anchor, loading and unloading was carried out by lighter or along the long jetty. Another little jetty ran out towards the *San Georgio*, a rusty, bombed steamer lying on the bottom of the harbour.[15] Rough planks had been thrown across its deck and in the darkness and complete silence, men filed through a gap to board vessels moored on its other side. Moonless nights were preferred for the run to Alexandria, for then the gleaming white wake that trailed the ships did not give them away to the *Luftwaffe*.

Above the docks rose the unfinished concrete of Admiralty House, one of the most exposed positions in the fortress. The road from the docks sloped gently up to the central square between the flat-roofed villas, their white walls pocked by shells and bomb fragments, and the minaret of the mosque stood tall and white above the town, its star and ice-cream cone top intact.

The 2/2nd CCS was a Queensland unit and Weary's commanding officer was Wilfred Park, promoted to temporary half-colonel when the previous commanding officer, Lieut-Colonel Wilson, was evacuated to hospital in Egypt at the end of May. The two sections of the CCS, light and heavy, were around seven kilometres apart. Weary was senior surgeon and second-in-command, living and working with the light section in the cave under Admiralty House. It was a lively spot, dive-bombed and shelled by night and day, and a popular bolthole with anyone caught under fire in the street outside. With him was a Queensland surgeon, Derek Yeates, Jim Yeates's brother.

Two medical officers, Major D. A. Cameron and Major O. E. J. Murphy, were with Park out at Sidi Mahmoud on the Bardia Road. Theirs was the more impressive set-up, in underground chambers dug into the side of a hill, lit by electricity and fitted out as a hospital with four wards and an operating theatre.

Patients who would return to their units eventually were shuttled there by motor ambulance daily from the hospital. It functioned more as a convalescent depot, most of them suffering from non-infectious medical complaints or recovering from minor surgery. The 2/11th Field Ambulance shared the complex and a dental clinic moved there in June.

Occasionally, they housed the overflow from Weary's area, but the distance between Sidi Mahmoud and the docks was inconvenient when patients had to be evacuated by sea.

Surgery did not eventuate on the scale Weary had hoped. When he arrived in Tobruk, he found that the usual rôles of the CCS and the hospital under Colonel Spiers' command had been reversed. The 2/4th AGH operated like a casualty clearing station in the former Italian barracks rather less than a kilometre from the docks, and the senior surgeon was his old orthopaedic chief from the Royal Melbourne, Lieut-Colonel Charles Littlejohn.[16] He and his team performed the bulk of the surgery in their sandbagged operating theatres.

The verbal agreement to send surgical patients down to the team at Admiralty House was rarely observed. In any case, the number of surgical cases that month was down on May, and Spiers began a series of afternoon surgical lectures for orderlies in order to keep everyone occupied.[17]

As well as being sent to the light and heavy sections of the casualty clearing station, cases were admitted, treated and distributed from the hospital to two other locations: infectious cases and patients who could not be treated underground were sent to the beach section; and neurotic cases sent back from the units' regimental aid posts as 'NYDN' ('not yet diagnosed, nervous') went to Lieut-Colonel E. L. Cooper's 'Z Ward', an underground bunker of reinforced concrete beneath the Port War Signal Station and some AA guns. From the signal station flagstaff flew a dusty Union Jack; it was a favourite target for the dive-bombers.

In May, increasing numbers of men had been diagnosed as having 'fear and anxiety states', and by July there was a growing incidence of obviously self-inflicted injuries. The claustrophobic accommodation administered by Cooper was not popular: the sound of bombing and shellfire reverberated within the bunker's concrete walls, provoking hysteria in some. But the alternative, the beach section of the 2/4th AGH some distance from the town, was not so well protected. Twenty-four bombs landed there during June.

Latterly, medical officers found that only more deeply troubled cases need be sent to 'Z Ward'. A few days rest and quiet in dugouts and caves near their aid posts was sufficient for most men, who could then return to their unit.

The 2/2nd CCS took the remainder, the docks section being largely a staging post for serious cases leaving the fortress. Since the middle of April, patients had been evacuated mainly at night. Every afternoon, between two and five, the hospital sent them down to the deep shelter where Weary worked, and here they were held until they could be loaded onto the destroyers.

Weary and Jock Clarke loaded stretcher patients with the orderlies, packing them swiftly onto the lighters that were towed out by *Eskimo Nell*, the hospital tug, and then manhandling them onto the destroyers in the early hours of the morning. They were often under heavy shellfire. On 20 July, the tug broke down. Shells were whistling into the harbour and exploding in the water all round them. They cowered miserably on the lighter's flat top, drifting out towards the boom and the harbour mouth, while a tall, redheaded orderly named Greer swam ashore through water thickly covered with oil and fetched another tug.[18]

The strain of carrying out these manoeuvres night after night was considerable. Very little time was available to unload stores and load patients so that the destroyers could be under way and within the protective orbit of the RAF flying out of Alexandria, in order to beat the *Luftwafffe*'s dawn search.

The Navy endured even greater stress maintaining the frail sea line of communication between Egypt and the garrison. Weary offered beds in the hospital to the crews from lighters and other craft whenever they put in to Tobruk for more than a quick turn-round. Camouflage nets were thrown over the vessels and the crews spent the day resting and sleeping on shore, secure from enemy action.

Weary hated being underground and spent as much time as possible outdoors. He began each day with a long swim in the harbour and a stroll around the docks area on what he regarded as an 'early morning inspection', dodging any shells which the enemy's great guns, Bardia Bill, Jack, Jill and Butch, might hurl in that direction.

Swimmers wore their tin hats to protect them from the constant hail of flack from the anti-aircraft guns' reply, but at first Weary parked his on the beach with his shirt and shorts. Jock Clarke told him he was a fool; commonsense prevailed when he realised what a wallop the nose cones of the shells could give as they fell in the water, and he soon took to wearing his helmet. Nothing deterred him from swimming. During a raid one day he decided to retrieve a rowboat adrift in the harbour and endangering one of the ships coming in. He swam out and towed it back to shore, whereupon a British captain stormed across and began to tear strips off him. Weary paid no attention: merely strolled across to where he had left his clothes on the beach and pulled on his shirt. The sight of his major's crowns stopped the Englishman in mid roar. Weary saluted smartly and moved off.

Sea bathing in the 'limpid, clear and very buoyant water' banished staphylococci, and within three weeks he was free of his hitherto stubborn boils and carbuncles. Everyone had grown lean on the diet of tinned bully beef, M&V (meat and veg.) and bread augmented by ascorbic acid tablets and Marmite.

He became notorious for his strolls in the open, although he did not scorn a handy slit trench when an attack hotted up. Major Trethowan's welcome to Tobruk gave him a taste of Weary's nerve, although Weary admitted later that on this occasion he felt the same paralysing fear which he had encountered for the first time on the road in Greece. Trethowan, having taken up his position as a DADMS on Burston's staff, came in at the end of June to assess the medical situation, and the two of them were down in the cave when they heard the sound of planes approaching.

'You ought to come up and see this, Bill,' said Weary. He took him outside towards a trench on the waterfront and into a dense smoke screen. In the dust and raining shrapnel and chatter of the Bofors guns and the noise from the sixty or so planes strafing overhead, it was impossible to find that or any other trench. 'I was quite bushed . . . with one accord we both fell on our faces and sweated it out.' Trethowan covered his face with his gas cape; Weary flattened himself in the dirt.

Weary's daily clinic was patronised by Australian and British soldiers, as well as Palestinians, Cypriots and Libyans in the labour corps and Italian prisoners. 'Symptoms largely by pantomime.' Then he made his round of social calls on units in the hospital.

The 2/2nd CCS had lost much valuable equipment at Barce, where they had taken the place of the 2/4th AGH at the end of March. But in its dash back to the safety of the fortress on 4 April, ahead of Rommel's advance through Cyrenaica, it had to abandon the autoclave, generator and lighting plant and most of the X-ray equipment. Weary spent his first fortnight examining equipment shortages and how the unit functioned, and by the time Trethowan arrived at the end of June, he had begun to overhaul the unit and make up its deficit.

Trethowan bestowed official approval on Weary's raids on 5 Advance Depot Medical Stores, who had plenty of Italian medical equipment and surgical instruments. Weary picked out sufficient for one surgical team and had everything fitted into panniers.[19] Ordnance was also co-operative. By the middle of July they had made him a foot suction pump by converting a tyre pump and were hard at work constructing orthopaedic equipment from his detailed working drawings.[20]

By the time the 2/2nd CCS left Tobruk, they were 'one of the most superbly equipped units in the army'. Weary's two years on the staff had been well spent: he knew how to work the system to his advantage. 'I could get things done.' But otherwise, life was disappointingly idle, with many social calls and much chess – seven games one day marking Yeates's and Weary's high point of inactivity. Spiers and Littlejohn were bridge players and eventually boredom drove Weary and Yeates to make up a four. They would play in the CCS cave until 2 am some mornings before the senior officers returned to their more hazardous quarters at the hospital.

Shelling intensified on 1 July, when the two storeships which brought in the first shipment of fresh meat for some time lay alongside the docks, and that afternoon a 'lucky shell inflicted 30 casualties and caused eight deaths'.[21] They rushed the victims to their cave and patched up the wounded before sending them up to Littlejohn's surgical section at the hospital. He was relieved to feel 'quite confident' when confronted by his first 'real war surgery'.

Next morning, halfway between the cave and the cookhouse, he heard the roar of a shell and decided to run for it rather than dive into a slit trench. He arrived at the door at the same moment as the shell and was sucked into the building 'as a sort of satellite' in the dust and confusion.

Weary raised himself to his knees, at first wondering why he could still see the Palestinian kitchen worker's arm, knocked off by the shell, lying in the dust. 'I put my thumb on his brachial artery and thought, my God – I'm still alive.' It had been a dud.

They were shelled so often, sometimes when ships came in, other times for no apparent reason, that they grew to know the guns very well. At night, if Weary saw the flash, he had forty-five seconds until the shell arrived; if all he heard was the roar of the shell, he had three seconds in which to dive into a slit trench. Raids could occur any time of the night or day. At night sleep was broken by a dissonant *son et lumière* of explosions, strings of bright tracer bullets, the whistling crescendos of shells and pounding ack-ack guns, sweeping searchlights and the red following glow of tracer shells. More frightening than the bombs – for one was safe from all but a direct hit in even a shallow hole in the ground – were the machine-gun bullets sprayed by the dive-bombers from their fore and aft guns.

Nothing stopped the guns, not even the choking, ever-present dust, fine as talc, that could blow endlessly off the desert for days. Tobruk was notorious for dust storms. The *khamsin* roared up to the coast from the heart of the Sahara, whirling sand and grit in blast-furnace versions of the November pea soup fogs Weary had struggled through in London on his way to Barts. Everyone looked like figures which had been standing on a shelf in a junk shop for centuries. Plumes of dust streamed from the men's feet when their boots touched the ground; a car or lorry stirred up such a cloud it was almost invisible.

With the meat ships on 1 July came the mail – more welcome to the men than anything else – and the lists of those who had been captured on Crete, 'sad reading, especially for one who has been over here with the first battalions to arrive'. Many old friends were missing, including medical officer Alan Carter from the staff days in Jerusalem and Le Souef and most of his field ambulance.

'Queer that I should have simply begged the DMS to let me cast in my lot with a general hospital that stayed with its wounded, and then in the Greece [sic] landslide to go with Le Souef & Co. for the rearguard party.'

But there were surprises. Blue Butterworth walked into the Admiralty House shelter late on the afternoon of 4 July, asking for Weary. Weary's tendency to spring out of the cave into a slit trench in order to take photographs of the raids when everyone else was rushing in, and his peregrinations about the garrison with apparently little concern for shells and bombs, had quickly gained him a reputation. The men there looked at Butterworth. 'This bloody Dunlop. He's mad . . . Where did you meet him?'22

Weary was marching along the wharf towards the CCS when he saw Butterworth. 'Where the bloody hell did you come from?' He was amazed that a private soldier could make his way from Crete to Tobruk. Blue was secretive about his methods, but they had been effective.

After Weary was taken off on *Hotspur*, Butterworth felt miserable with the corps troops and, not realising that his own 2/1st Infantry Battalion was nearby, took refuge with the Cretan family who owned the olive grove where they were sheltering. (It was lucky he did: 493 of his battalion were captured.) Here he met some crew members of a Greek ship which eventually took him to Alexandria. He then set off on a grand tour of Palestine and Syria, meeting Colonel Johnston on the way, and ending up in Alexandria in late June with a piece of paper which persuaded someone to send him in to Tobruk. It was his second time there: his battalion had been part of the triumphant march across Cyrenaica earlier in the year.[23] He was impressed by the reaction whenever he mentioned that Weary had sent for him, for immediately, he was passed along the line.

Not only the fighting men were showing signs of strain: the siege conditions of Tobruk were also telling on some of the CCS personnel. Cameron was evacuated to Base, Park was admitted to hospital on 1 July and Jock Clarke, the dental officer, managed to get Hogg onto a destroyer, where George Stening's brother was medical officer, and into the 2/11th AGH in Alexandria. Clarke recalls how after nine months in Cyrenaica, he himself was 'beginning to come apart at the seams – I'd been . . . under fire for a long time', as had his sergeant, John Ross, his corporal and his orderly.[24]

Weary took command of the unit. It was plain to him that they were inefficiently organised; neither section fulfilled its intended function. A casualty clearing station was not a convalescent depot. Since he had arrived in Tobruk, Spiers and Littlejohn occasionally gave him some surgery at the hospital so that a start could be made on training a surgical team and theatre orderlies, but in practice he treated mainly men wounded in the immediate vicinity.[25] His sorties along the docks after a raid could be fruitful: 'I picked up some casualties at times.' He was quick to admit anyone, rather than rush them straight to the hospital, but 'with a general hospital in a fairly small perimeter, there was no rôle, really, for a CCS'.

It was time for them to be reformed in one location – preferably Sidi Mahmoud – he reported to Lieut-Colonel Harry Furnell, the ADMS 9th Division, to take on some reinforcements and refit so that they could perform as a conventional casualty clearing station. Either surgical cases should be sent to them from the hospital, or a surgical team from the CCS should gain regular experience in the hospital so that other ranks could be trained in surgical procedures. Although this document is written over Park's name, it was Weary's work. Park was tucked up in bed in the 2/4th AGH.

Weary found ample time in Tobruk to consider new ways of employing a medical unit in forward areas along the lines of his earlier report to Burston. He decided that some of the 2/2nd CCS personnel, together with others serving with kindred medical units in Tobruk, could form the nucleus of a mobile field hospital. Tobruk was a god-sent opportunity for him to formulate these ideas.

For not only was Weary acquiring equipment; he had begun to gather round him a group of medical officers and surgeons with particular skills. Derek Yeates's brother, Captain James Yeates, joined them and Weary applied for his transfer from the 2/5th Field Ambulance. There were others who would fit in well: the dentist, Captain J. E. R. (Jock) Clarke, and Major E.W. Casey, radiologist.

They were an agreeable bunch in the medical corps. There were convivial dinners and cards in dugouts round the town, even one notable evening on 14 July when Douglas Stephens, the son of Harry 'Doug' Stephens for whom he had worked at the Children's Hospital in 1937, gave a dinner party for Weary at a 2/5th Field Ambulance advanced dressing station under the escarpment just behind their forward lines. 'Ron Rome piloted me in and out of the mine-fields. His driver knew the tracks.'

Stephens's eyrie, thirty steps up from the road, had a superb view of the Mediterranean. The guests were received by a corporal and 'assembled on a little shell-torn slope just at dusk [for] a pre-dinner whisky or two with gramophone music and chatter – also cheese straws!' There was no gunfire that night.

When Weary descended to the candle-lit cave, he saw a sideboard in the corner covered with a white sheet and a cupboard adorned with glasses and bottles. At the long trestle table, also covered with a sheet, their places were marked with pieces cut from captured Italian ordnance cloth shoulder tags embroidered with emblems, each bearing a carefully inked date and name. Weary's was a red Tuscan lion, which he posted to Helen. She added it to her hoard of letters and cards.

Everything came out of tins and was conveyed to the table from the kitchens below by a chain of orderlies: tomato soup, sardines on toast, steak and onions and mashed potatoes, blancmange, jelly and fruit, a savoury, raisins and nuts and cheese straws, chianti, coffee and Italian cognac. 'Doug sitting at the head of the table with his boyish charm might well have been back in South Yarra.' His batman had even provided a table bell to summon the helpers.

Music played on the gramophone, borrowed from the hospital, throughout the evening and the volume was so great that at one stage Stephens stuffed his pyjama pants into the horn to make conversation easier. In the haste of returning the gramophone to the hospital, Stephens forgot to retrieve them.

Lieut-Colonel Harry Furnell called on 21 July. 'Evacuation of the unit to Australian Base Area Palestine would occur at an early date to enable refitting, reinforcing & rest.' Each man could take a valise or kitbag and essential orderly room equipment would accompany them, but their vehicles would have to remain.

At 2230 hours on Thursday 24 July, 5 officers and 82 other ranks climbed into their lorries and drove 'under cover of darkness with strict road discipline to No 6 Jetty'. They had no sooner climbed out onto the wharf than the enemy fired a few shells across in a desultory farewell gesture.[26]

Weary lined up with the others to lug stores ashore; a hundred tonnes had to be humped along the rickety jetty to the wharf before they could leave. It was hot work, with now and again a few shells whistling overhead to ginger things up. He had just straightened up when 'a stocky sweating character with his hair falling over his face said 'How are you Weary?' and he realised it was Bill Ross who used to be in the front row of the St Mary's scrum.

It took them two hours and twenty-five minutes to unload and board the destroyer. It wanted but five minutes to two o'clock when HMS *Hero* pulled smoothly out. 'The night very dark . . . High spirits prevailing with thoughts of leave . . . ' The new moon was a good omen.

Bill Ross was surgeon-lieutenant to *Hero*. He took Weary down to his cabin and they stayed up drinking and yarning all night.

The *Luftwaffe* did not interfere. The sun came up on a glorious morning and it was smooth sailing under clear skies all the way to Alexandria. Ross and Weary drank the last bottle of champagne on the destroyer as they sailed in. They dressed ship in Alexandria Harbour exactly twelve hours and five minutes after leaving Tobruk.

FIFTEEN

The Back Garden of Allah

ALEXANDRIA SHIMMERED IN THE mid-afternoon heat that Friday. It was too early for a breeze from the sea to relieve the heat bouncing off the pavements or stir the striped awnings of the cafés along the Grande Corniche. Lorries conveyed the unit the 22 kilometres from the docks to the dusty staging camp at Amiriya, where the men were to await their move to Palestine. Weary and Park saw them into camp, then took the train to Cairo to report to headquarters.

'I found my feet again in Tobruk,' Weary reassured James and Alice.[1] Tobruk had been an unlikely convalescent camp, but an effective one. He stepped onto the docks in Alexandria fitter than he had been for eight months: hepatitis vanquished, staphylococcal infections no longer troublesome, skin burned dark brown and, though he was still lean, carrying five kilograms more weight than when he went in. But the most striking change in his appearance was that the long, thin upper lip was now masked by a clipped, military moustache. He had escaped the staff, had been in command of the unit for a full month, and now there was the renewed hope of surgery.

Most of his time was spent dashing back and forth between Alexandria and AIF Headquarters in Cairo, where Hailes, who had digested his earlier report, listened receptively to his ideas about mobile field surgical units. 'Why don't you raise one?' he suggested. Burston was up in Syria but would be back in Cairo shortly; they would discuss it again. Weary was not interested in a simple experiment; if he raised the unit, he wanted to try it in battle and he wanted to command it. When Burston returned, they agreed that he should go ahead. At some point, he would need to convince both Blamey – whose dislike of Australian units serving with the British forces was intensifying – and Tomlinson of the unit's worth in such a venture, but he pushed that problem aside for the time being.

He also had ample time to get into trouble in Cairo. Walter

Hammond had praised the Metropole Hotel's dining room and a particular prawn dish so often that Weary and two others determined to celebrate their return from Tobruk by sampling it themselves. They were given a table, ordered their prawns and, since the order would take some time, elected to stay in the bar for drinks. It was 9.30 pm. Time passed and neither their red-fezzed waiter nor dinner appeared. They summoned successively the waiter, the head waiter and the maître d'hotel. All three consorted with the kitchen to deny knowledge of the order and, since it was well past 10 pm, the hour by which house rules decreed food orders must be placed, neither prawns nor – since the Australian officers were judged so objectionable – any other dinner would be forthcoming.

Alcohol had lowered Weary's flash point and his temper flared when the maître d'- who more or less matched Weary in height but not in muscle – denied him access to the manager and attempted to put a half Nelson on him. Weary seized him by the scruff of the neck and the seat of the pants and, raising the struggling man in the air, marched across the room towards the lift, demanding the manager. Tables and waiters tumbled in their wake, the latter felled by some well-placed punches from the others.

The manager, when they found him, made some token enquiries, then firmly aligned himself with the kitchen and the waiters. With a belated sense of self-preservation, Weary decided they should disappear before the provosts arrived. They shot down in the lift, only just making it onto the street minutes before the MPs appeared. It was a sour end to the evening.

Weary's time in the Middle East was punctuated by such incidents – he had been lucky in Gaza, when the crowd had not turned nasty over his treatment of the fellahin – and he described with gusto those occasions when he used his fists to settle disputes.

Julian Orm Smith and Bowie Somerset came to his aid in a restaurant one night in Palestine, when a sergeant of the Palestine police pestered the girl Weary had taken out to dinner with unwelcome invitations to dance, and greeted her refusals with a stream of obscenities. Weary and the girl pointedly moved to another table; the police positioned themselves drunkenly at a neighbouring one. When Weary told the girl to leave quickly and swung a jaw-breaking punch at the sergeant, Orm Smith and Somerset came to his aid. The three men fought their way out of a tight spot, leaving a posse of angry police, a trail of broken furniture and some bloodied faces in their wake.

But there were other occasions during the irksome days on the staff when a craving for excitement propelled him into irresponsible episodes which he would rather have forgotten. His first sight of Libya was from the cockpit of a Blenheim with a young pilot who had lost his nerve and was flying like a madman on a reconnaissance over Mersa Matruh. Later, after an evening of heavy drinking in an RAF mess, Weary had seized the chance to join illicitly a Gaza Squadron bombing raid over Benghazi, although he sobered up swiftly once he saw the red and green tracer bullets exploding around them while they dodged enemy anti-aircraft fire. He looked down at the desert lit up by flares and searchlights and explosions and regretted risking his life 'just to be shot at' on what he had imagined would be a joy ride. It bore no resemblance to the daytime flips in a little 32 hp Taylor Cub over Palestine with Geoff Cohen. He turned down further invitations.

There was still no word of the rear party of the 2/2nd CCS when they left Amiriya on 30 July. After reporting to Cairo GHQ with Weary, it was decided that Park should remain there. In his absence, Weary accepted the camp commander's compliments on the good behaviour of the men during their stay – although not without a slight shiver as he recalled his lucky escape from the Metropole Hotel.

Blue and he had a struggle to load his great wardrobe trunk, reclaimed from the kit store, onto the train, eventually jamming it halfway in a carriage door. After giving it an extra shove for good measure, Weary found his way blocked by a bunch of grubby fellahin clamouring for payment. The train was already moving. He threw a handful of piastres in the air and ran for the nearest carriage door. (Blue tactfully held his tongue each time they changed trains, when the two of them had to heave and sweat to haul the trunk aboard.)

Kantara West was reached at one the next morning, where Park joined them; once across the Canal, it was an uneventful run from the east bank to Palestine.

Finally, four changes and sixteen hours after leaving the staging camp, they jerked to a halt in Gaza Station and transferred to trucks for the drive to their new camp at Kilo 89. Tents had been pitched for them in Hearne Lines; the 2/6th AGH fostered them in. 'The campsite is excellent and provides many amenities. Much appreciated after the Western Desert.'[2]

The barren sweep of stony, summer-baked desert with the occasional dotted line of a camel train looming through the haze, even the stifling humidity of the blackout, were bearable when there were leave passes to Tel Aviv and Jerusalem, swimming and surfing at Gaza beach, and days and nights unbroken by the sounds of bombs and ack- ack fire, the scream of shells and the searchlit brilliance of the Libyan sky.

They took in no patients. They were to rest and re-fit.

The MacCauslands and their excellent cook, Katbe, welcomed the 'major from Tobruk' back to Palestine with roast beef and ice-cold beer. And a shoal of letters from Helen awaited him. Weary lay on the beach at Gaza 'reading and gloating . . . until I was quite sure that you were occupying the adjacent hump of warm sand . . . '3

Weary's first call on 31 July was to Base Headquarters, where he consulted the ADMS, Colonel Steigrad, and the Deputy Assistant Director of Ordnance about the unit's urgent need for practically everything: medical stores, generators, lighting sets, oil stoves, tilley lamps, anti-gas equipment – even clothing. Also, he was preoccupied with retrieving some precious, specially constructed bulky items from Tobruk, which had been acquired inadvertently by the 2/5th Field Ambulance when they took over the docks hospital and a quantity of hospital stores. Weary hoped that Sergeant Gray and the six other ranks who had remained behind to bring out the unit's five trucks and heavy equipment could repossess it before Movement Control ordered them out.

When all base could suggest was an appeal to AIF HQ, he transferred his efforts to their counterparts in the 6th Division at Julis, through whom he now discovered his indents must be submitted. But no one would give him the essential priority to re-equip: the DADOS suggested carelessly that he resign himself to a delay of 'maybe months'.

In fury, Weary called on ADMS Lieut-Colonel Beare and his deputy, Dawkins, but neither was encouraging. Army procedures dictated that Weary indent nothing further until his own stores arrived with Sgt Gray's party; and when Jock Clarke turned up at Kilo 89 on 4 August, he gloomily predicted that the others would not be coming out until after 8 September.

Weary dashed off a signal to Burston immediately, requesting that the rear party's departure be expedited. 'All expendable stores were left . . . surgical instruments, panniers, X-ray . . . motor transport . . . ' He was anxious to begin training, and his plans for the mobile field operating unit were taking shape in his head since the encouraging discussions in Egypt at the end of July.

Training began despite the lack of equipment. He embarked on 'a flurry of spit and polish', daily inspection of lines and a flood of routine orders, for 'things have been a bit slack and men coming back from forward areas to standing camps take handling'.

Colonel Adey, now Burston's ADMS in charge of personnel, was more sympathetic to Weary's request for personnel to bring the unit up to strength, particularly for a quartermaster, and Captain J. D. Morris arrived the following day, together with surgeon Major A. A. Moon, transferred from the 2/4th Field Ambulance. Four days later, Major E. L. Corlette, a physician specialist, was marched in to fill the vacancy left when Major Murphy had joined the staff of the 2/5th AGH. All was complete by 18 August when, without warning, the rear party turned up with their packed lorries. And Casey rang from Kantara to announce that he had the X-ray equipment.

Belisario was now a full colonel commanding the 2/5th AGH, which included Weary's drinking companions Greg Cutler and Reg Betting-ton and John Ray, the husband of Helen's friend Peg. They shared the mess for a few weeks while the hospital awaited its move to Asmara, only vacating their lines as the last of the troops being transferred from Egypt were arriving on 26 August.

The news that these were the 18th Infantry Brigade, the first to be relieved from Tobruk, flashed like wildfire through the camp. With them were Ron Rome, Douglas Stephens and the rest of the 2/5th Field Ambulance. Lieut-Colonel Green took over from Belisario as Commanding Officer of Hearne Lines.

The decision to bring them out was known only to the highest command; even the garrison suspected nothing until destroyers dropped the Polish Brigade Group in Tobruk on the night of 19-20 August. Security in Egypt had tightened since the days when Weary and Vasey worried about troop movements being common knowledge amongst the street urchins of Cairo and Alexandria.

Weary had been disappointed when his CCS was brought out of Tobruk so swiftly. His representations to Furnell and Burston on 9 July, suggesting the unit's consolidation at Sidi Mahmoud and asking for more surgery, had not turned out quite as planned. At the time, he was unaware that Burston had advised Blamey of a decline in the garrison's physical condition, and that when Morshead saw Blamey in Cairo on 5 July, he confirmed that the troops' capacity to resist attack was declining: most men were 'a stone underweight', few escaped gastroenteritis, a number needed to be brought out of the front line for rest to combat fear and anxiety states. It is likely that Morshead's conversation with Blamey convinced him that it was time to evacuate the Australians from Tobruk and consolidate them in Palestine under a unified command.[4]

Blamey was on the docks at Alexandria to meet the 18th Brigade when it came ashore that August, 'overjoyed', his ADC, Norman Carlyon noticed, 'to see these young veterans clumping down the gangways'.[5] Within days they were at Kilo 89 enjoying their beer and leave parties.

While Weary was 'penned to camp' during the final week of August awaiting 'an inspection by two generals who won't say when they are coming', his prospects took a turn for the better. First, Hailes called to discuss the new unit; then Burston, accompanying Major-General Downes on his majestic tour of inspection of AIF units in the Middle East, asked Weary to spend Sunday with him in Gaza on 31 August so that they could talk undisturbed about his plans. Burston, 'greatly pleased' with Weary's management of the unit, was entertained by the younger man's obvious relief at being told that he was 'too junior in army standing to be given the command permanently'. During an earlier conversation in Cairo, when the DMS had promised Weary someone he 'could handle', Weary had suggested Lieut-Colonel Norman Eadie as commanding officer. Now Burston confirmed that this would occur in the middle of the month, freeing Weary to raise the new unit. Surgery was within his grasp once more.

Downes, his ADC Major Clive Fitts and the rest of their party lunched with the officers of the CCS on 1 September. Enthusiastically, Weary seized his chance to talk to Downes 'like a Dutch uncle about how the units were not suited to the type of warfare we were having and that new things were needed'. Downes's only response was a terse 'There's nothing wrong with the units, Dunlop, it's the way you use them.'[6] Burston and Hailes maintained a diplomatic silence. Weary, startled to realise that Downes was 'pretty rigid in the mind' and unreceptive to new ideas, belatedly remembered how dissatisfied Burston and Disher had been with the Melbourne administration during his time on the staff in 1940.

Downes had been sidelined when his own ambitions were thwarted by Blamey's appointment in the Middle East of Burston as DMS, and Major-General F. A. Maguire replaced him as Director-General in Australia, whilst he was given the doubtful consolation prize of being made Inspector-General of Medical Services. He had been on a grand tour of the medical services wherever Australian troops were employed since April, reaching the Middle East and East Africa during August and September, before returning to Australia via India and Ceylon. But it was unlikely that his report would affect the organisation of the medical services abroad: any impetus for change would come from men like Burston, Hailes and Fairley.

Two days later, Weary and his new quartermaster, Morris, drove to Cairo in 'a rapid chase for equipment' and personnel. With great good-humour, Burston accused Weary of 'showing all the cunning of an old soldier'. His terrier-like persistence, when joined to Burston's and Hailes's influence and commitment to the raising of the new mobile unit, resulted in an astonishing degree of co-operation by ordnance.

Weary was much gratified to hear Dawkins inform him that 'all requests are being met including . . . a car, and 15 cwt utility lorry . . . . recommended for establishment of a CCS', and wound up the day with a technical session with Hailes and Fairley. He celebrated his triumph over the system by dining and drinking with Eric Cooper, also back from Tobruk.

The following night he drove out to a British tented camp in the desert at Quassassin, three hours from Cairo on the Ismailiya road, to spend the night with Arthur Porritt and others from St Mary's. Porritt, who was in charge of the surgical division and acting commanding officer of a 1200 bed hospital there, recalls that the camp's most memorable feature was 'three taps in the middle of the sand put in by the engineers'. The oddity of this desert water point's location appealed greatly to Weary's sense of the ridiculous.[7] They 'played cards and gossiped, drinking regrettable doses from pint glasses [while] listening to enemy planes flitting overhead' in the brightness of the desert night.

At Kantara next day Morris and he secured all the items on the indent from the staff officer in charge of the medical stores, and adjourned to the mess for a drink with John Colquhoun and Eric Hughes-Jones before beginning the monotonous journey across the Sinai back to Gaza.

On 10 September they received orders to move from Kilo 89, officially because the training wing of the medical corps was to take their place, and on 13 September they crowded into Legge Lines at Beit Jirja with the 2/5th Field Ambulance and the 2/6th AGH. The CCS was almost fully equipped and staffed; it was time to concentrate on the surgical changes.

Weary wished to discuss his plans for the experimental unit with Johnston, now in Syria with I Australian Corps headquarters. In view of the DDMS's experience in all three campaigns, Libya, Greece and Syria, his input would be useful. Burston and Hailes also agreed that Weary would profit from visiting the Australian medical units in Syria.

Eadie, about to relinquish his post at the 2/1st Convalescent Depot for the new command, had been told nothing about the proposed reorganisation of casualty clearing stations, nor that his 2/2nd CCS was to be the guinea pig. It was deemed tactful for Weary to report to his new commanding officer at Kafr Vitkin and suggest he accompany him to Syria.

Early on Monday morning, 15 September, Blue slung Weary's valise and their rations into the back of the 15 cwt Ford utility. Their driver sped them up the fast coast road to Kafr Vitkin, picked up Eadie, and they were across the border in Syria and at corps headquarters in the hill resort of Aley by late afternoon. 'Lovely to be lost in mists again, and to feel cold . . . with formidable mountains clothed in pines and olives, and the blue Mediterranean shining far below.'[8]

Johnston was attracted to the idea of using both casualty clearing station and mobile operating unit in Syria, but first he would have to find them a suitable building for winter quarters similar to the school and hospital buildings used by the other medical units.

Johnston, even Eadie, might be 'very desirous' of employing them there (if nothing else offered, it would be an improvement on camp in Palestine), but Weary secretly harboured the more ambitious notion discussed with Burston, Hailes and Starr. It could only be a matter of time before the next push in North Africa, where conditions for testing the new unit would be ideal.

Next day, they called on Orm Smith, whose 2/1st CCS was installed in a mental hospital at Asfurieh. Weary was eager to discover precisely how he would organise a theatre and surgical team in the field. Orm Smith talked, Weary asked questions and scribbled in his field notebook, and Eadie listened. They discussed equipment; a theatre layout using two tables; personnel; the technique of giving the new injectable anaesthetic – Pentothal – and the size of a dose; the dangers inherent in giving blood transfusions when blood could be infected or malarious. He made a sketch of a dressing centre, stretchers running at right angles to the instrument table, and noted alongside it Hailes's suggestion of using it to treat less severe wounds that would otherwise go through with just a dressing.

Smith had led the first surgical team to be sent forward to work with the 2/2nd Field Ambulance at the battle of Bardia and, with Douglas Stephens as his assistant, accompanied the main dressing station into the Tobruk area in January 1941 as the senior surgeon. No one had had more exposure to surgery in forward areas; his field experience and sharp intelligence stimulated Weary's perception of how the unit might perform. By the time Eadie and he had spent a few hours with Gillespie, the commanding officer of the 2/3rd CCS in Beirut, a further six detailed pages had been added to his notebook. Just enough daylight remained for them to drive to Zahle and inspect a possible site before returning to Beirut for the night.

There were more inspections at Tripoli next morning when they called on Kingsley Norris, ADMS 7th Division, who sent them on to the 2/4th Field Ambulance in its snug quarters in an Italian mental hospital. Weary had had no contact with him since Starr and he had been run ragged by Norris's endless questions and enthusiasm at head-quarters after his arrival in Gaza in 1940. Now he had the experience of the Syrian campaign behind him.

Weary had promised himself a few days exploration in Syria. After parting from Eadie, he spent the afternoon looking for Boyd, whose unit was based in Tripoli, eventually tracking him down in the bar of his barracks that evening. Boyd put him up for the night and Weary relished the 'wonderful luxury [of] . . . someone who knows and loves HLRF', but felt sadly inhibited when it came to discussing her with Boyd. He wanted to hear about their childhood, about anything at all relating to Helen, but stumbled over all but the most general questions.

Next morning he drove back to Beit Jirja the long way round: across the Lebanon Range to admire The Cedars and Baalbek then on to Damascus to Shible Bey Bisharat, who welcomed him with a tremen-dous dinner party. He was back in camp on Friday evening in time for dinner in the mess. Eadie had taken command formally the previous day.

On his return, Weary discovered the real reason for their move from Kilo 89. During the moonless nights between 17 and 27 September, the Royal Navy brought out almost 6000 Australians. By the end of September they were all in Kilo 89 and Julis. With the arrival earlier of the 18th Brigade, the 7th Division had been complete; now almost the entire 9th Division was in Palestine.

Throughout September and October Blamey's objective of the relief of the Australians from Tobruk would be achieved. On 22 October, Morshead handed over the command of the garrison to Major-General

Ronald Scobie and boarded HMS *Endeavour* for Alexandria. A week later, he was at divisional headquarters in Julis.

Ten days after Weary's return to Palestine, there was still no word from Burston or Johnston about their suggested function in Syria. 'I haven't got nearly enough work to do, and am beginning to wonder if we will after all just spend the winter in billets . . . ' Training and sport were intensified to keep morale up and boredom at bay. 'Just too hearty for words,' Weary thought ruefully. 'We are going back to garrison habits – formal mess once a week with an impressive menu.' Eadie and Weary called on Steigrad to see if he knew more than them. 'Future role of unit – indefinite.'[9]

October brought cool nights, a visit from Adey and a letter from Burston, but this last ignored the CCS and dealt only with the experimental unit. Under instruction from Burston, Adey was to facilitate Weary's plans for training picked orderlies in anaesthetics and pathological techniques at the hospital in Gaza and for Ewen Corlette to disappear to Syria to gain field experience as a physician with the 2/1st CCS.

The keenly anticipated signal summoning him to Egypt arrived a week later. 'I've been recalled to headquarters for special duties,' he informed Helen. By 13 October he was enjoying evenings in a mess civilised by starched linen and vases of rosebuds on the tables and 'occupied almost entirely by brigadiers and heads of service'. Unlike Palestine, Cairo suffered from no shortage of alcohol, particularly when he dined with Burston one evening and put away 'several of the famous Turf Club gimlets, sherry, burgundy, brandy and then some'. His liver had recovered its former resilience.

Everyone agreed that mobile surgical units using their own transport were required and that casualty clearing stations in their present form needed revision, but there were individual differences about how changes should be made. Weary had listened to them all: Hailes, Johnston, Spiers and Littlejohn, Orm Smith, Edgar King, Kingsley Norris, McLorinan and Belisario. Unfortunately, Disher, the most eloquent critic of the medical service's shortcomings during the 'Benghazi Handicap' and at the time more creative at dealing with them in the field than anyone else, was now back in Australia. He missed his old boss's quiet commonsense.

The days were crowded with activity, working furiously at details of equipment and personnel, writing a complete war establishment for No. 1 Australian Mobile Operating Unit and personally negotiating its use with Auckinleck, Blamey, Tomlinson, Burston and their staffs.

Auckinleck had given the command in the Western Desert to Lieut-General Sir Alan Gordon Cunningham and, by October, Eighth Army – as the new force comprising XIII and XXX corps was now called – was limbering up for *Operation Crusader*. With Burston's full support, Weary was pushing for all he was worth to test his team with them.

Blamey was the 'unwilling horse' in the race to raise the unit and use it in the next offensive, for 'once any Australian unit gets into the command of a UK formation, it is like prising open the jaws of an alligator to get them back again . . .'[10]

Weary regretted the absence from Cairo of Hailes, his 'great surgical mentor', and Fairley, 'just at the time when I wanted [their] aid and support'. Tomlinson was no problem. But he remembered only too well being silenced by a cold stare from Blamey's pale blue eyes when he tried to contradict the GOC's choice of a site for a convalescent depot in Greece. Weary argued his case eloquently and, eventually, the opposition to dropping an orphan Australian medical unit into the British plan of battle was relaxed, Blamey 'making an exception in my case because it was . . . important . . . that this sort of unit be tested'.

In contrast to the ponderous caravans devised by Jock Monro to transport the British field surgical units, Weary's highly trained personnel would travel with their own equipment in standard transport and be ready to operate one hour after arriving on site.[11]

By 20 October, the document describing his 'suggested Establishment and Equipment Tables for Mobile Surgical Units forming Sections of a company of an Australian Casualty Clearing Station' was complete, down to the last latrine screen and Higginson syringe.

The detail packed into the thirty closely-typed foolscap pages covers everything, from the rationale for re-organising a casualty clearing station so that it includes a mobile operating company to detailed floor plans of the operating theatre and reception, resuscitation and X-ray ward. Sketch plans illustrate special items of equipment and define the precise placement of articles on the tables in the theatre.

Each pannier, table, piece of equipment and stretcher has a designated location every time the unit sets up; the panniers – in which medical stores are carried, from drugs and dressings to instruments – are meticulously described item by item, as are the vehicles and the method and order of packing them. Thirty-six personnel, 8 vehicles, 16 tents, an autoclave, generator and lighting plant, beds and bedding and 448 separate items of ordnance stores, medical and X-ray equipment, drugs and surgical instruments are listed. Even the sequence in which the vehicles travel is laid down.

Weary was thankful for his earlier practice run on the convalescent depots, even though Basil Andrew had been so condescending about his efforts at the time. He handed it over to Burston and was back at Beit Jirja by 22 October, in time to welcome Spiers and Littlejohn and the remainder of the 2/4th AGH from Tobruk.

Official approval arrived from Ausforce in a signal on 26 October. 'For Major Dunlop. Authority to raise experimental unit granted. Indents have been forwarded to T. E. K. Vehicle requirements will be delivered to you. Submit indents for medical equipment.'[12] But Eadie demurred. Where were the personnel to come from and who was to administer it? Was it part of his CCS? He had not been consulted: 'all communications have been . . . direct between DMS and Major Dunlop 2 i/c, 2/2 Aust CCS'.[13]

Next day, Weary and Eadie called on Steigrad, since the CCS was under the administration of Base Area, and Eadie handed over his official letter during what the war diary blandly called 'a three-cornered discussion'. Steigrad knew nothing, either, so he forwarded the letter immediately to Burston. Now two senior officers were put out.

Weary quietly bent his head over his equipment tables, discovered a few omissions, and tried to ignore some niggling doubts about his technical skills after being away from surgery for almost two years. His 35 chosen men continued systematically to check equipment and refine their techniques in such matters as erecting and brigading EPIP tents and packing and unpacking panniers.

Finally, on 31 October, Burston's attempt to soothe Eadie's ruffled pride with an apology and explanations arrived. 'I regret very much that in the stress of things I had quite forgotten to write to you explaining my ideas with regard to the Experimental Unit . . . We are trying to rush the thing through . . . ready to use in operations . . . likely to occur at any time . . . The new unit will be a definite unit, probably called No. 1 Mobile Surgical Unit, with its own establishment and War Equipment, so that it will be able to draw its personnel and equipment in the ordinary way. '[14]

32 *Sheikh Hanna Bey Bisharat (c.) & Shiblee Bey entertained them to a memorable lunch. (From l.) Weary, Milne, Morris, the Sheikh, [unknown], Vasey*

33 *Every two hours a train disgorged soldiers on Gaza Station, February 1940*

34 *Rugby at Beirut, April 1940. AIF vs the French*

35 *General Thomas Blamey arrived in Palestine, June 1940*

36 *'The old man', Brig. Burston (r.) arrived with Blamey. Col. Johnston, as he was then, met him*

37 *Three Australians dug a slit trench in the garden of HQ, Gaza*

38 *'Siddy' Crawcour ran the* Victoria *and sent
Weary's snapshots to him in Tobruk, scrawling:
'Trust you get all the doctoring . . . hankered for'*

39 *Surgeon Consultant W.A. Hailes arrived in the Middle East*

40 *Alexandria. They froze in their new mess that winter*

41 *Greece. Long columns of vehicles and men moved north through Lamia*

42 *Burning 9 million drachmae at Daphni. Gutters ran with Dewars and Haig. Weary talking to Fred Ordish, adjutant*

43 *'Thine academically,' wrote Helen at graduation*

44 *'Expensive war' he complained to Helen from his bed,
2/2nd AGH, Kantara*

45 *'Sorry, gone to Tobruk.' He left from Amiriya Station on
'Roley' Pulver's staff*

46 *They lived in a cave below Admiralty House, Tobruk*

47 *They crossed the Canal at Kantara West; it was an easy run from the east bank to Palestine*

48 *Back in Gaza, fit and sporting a military moustache*

49 *Boyd gave Weary the long awaited photograph of Helen*

Eadie, mollified, immediately committed himself to doing 'everything possible to make the experiment a complete success' – which success could only add 'honour' to the unit, he now realised, as he told the weekly conference of officers and NCOs on 1 November.[15] (He could be slow on the uptake.) He offered to detach those 2/2nd CCS personnel whose training Weary had already begun, as Weary had intended he would, but whose future had suddenly appeared doubtful. And that same Saturday, he and Weary embarked on a whirlwind of activity in Egypt. 'I've spent three whole days and nights travelling about on the wretched railways of Palestine and Egypt trying to draw blood from various stones in the way of equipment in a hurry.' The personnel question was settled. Burston had assured Eadie that they 'would not be lost to him', and in the meantime, reinforcements would take their places so that the CCS could move if it was required.

It was all too much for Eadie, who lacked Weary's iron constitution; on the way home, he had to be admitted to hospital at Kantara for two days.

Weary, exasperated by 'delays . . . stupid people, and the maddening vagaries of army supply' in his attempt to put surgery on wheels, took the utility and driver and ranged from Gaza to Haifa in a furious hunt to make good the deficiencies in equipment. And because their vehicles had not yet arrived, he used CCS transport to stage their first trial on 6 November to test the generator, lighting and X-ray.

Eadie and the entire unit had become absorbed in their progress – the war diary deals with little else at this time. During the first, vital fortnight of November, when they trained intensely and made ready, not even Sundays were free from unpacking, checking and classification of stores. Weary was a perfectionist. They timed the various operations and revised the packing and unpacking routines, changing the order of some. Tents were not dropped quickly enough; it took 3 NCOs and 10 men two hours to erect five EPIP tents, brigading two sets of two. With Littlejohn watching critically, they set up the theatre and reception centre and worked on the internal layout of tables and equipment.

The vehicles were delivered lacking tops, canopies and tools. Weary drove to Rehovath to secure red rubber sheeting from the Red Cross for the theatre flooring. In Tel Aviv, Peter Row found better wooden containers for the stores. And MacCausland arranged the loan of an RAE electrician. Weary's mood was buoyant: 'My team are . . . a red hot crowd, keen as mustard and willing to work like galley slaves'.

On 14 November they 'moved off in convoy with everything and every body on the vehicles and in 1 1/2 hours laid out a small field hospital with our own electric lighting and . . . technical gadgets working – had lunch provided by our own field kitchen, struck camp in under the hour and off again.

'Altogether this is the most complete job I've had entrusted to me in the army and the success or otherwise . . . is of considerable importance in our organisation.'

The exercise was viewed by the entire CCS, who came along for the show; and at the weekly officers' and sergeants' conference next day, everyone was preoccupied with fine-tuning the performance in time for their début in *Operation Crusader*. Derek Yeates was the other surgeon; that imperturbable, seasoned campaigner Peter Row was adjutant.

'. . . Best fun I've had since playing trains as a small boy – just like having your own circus.' But as Weary wrote to Helen on the night of Sunday 16 November, he was unaware that under a sky rent by lightning, the entire Eighth Army – 118 000 men – was lumbering through squalls of rain and sleet across the North African desert towards the Wire.

All he needed was the order to move. Then Taylor,* who was arranging for personnel to replace those taken from the 2/2nd CCS to staff the new unit, and Furnell pointed out to him on 19 November that neither the AIF Order confirming Weary's authority to raise the unit nor his appointment as commanding officer had been published. Weary shot off a signal to Ausforce. Immediately confirmation arrived, Weary sent a telegram to headquarters, Cairo: 'Unit now established. Ready to move.'

Later he decided that they should have moved off towards the battle immediately, rather than 'waiting feverishly for a chance to move to the field'. News began to trickle through about *Crusader*. 'Next thing I read in the *Palestine Post* the battle had started.' He sent a frantic signal to Cairo – 'Ready to move, one hour's notice', but there they stayed, in their standing camp in Palestine. They had been forgotten on the Order of Battle.

Burston was in Syria, Tomlinson was ill and Weary could prise no

---

* Lieut-Colonel Taylor, OC 2 Echelon AIF, Base Area.

satisfactory answer to his frantic questions about their movement out of British headquarters. Nothing had been so disappointing as this. 'For just about two years I've done every wretched administrative job after the other, and if ever I looked like doing any conceivable sort of surgical job, the bottom just fell out of the thing,' he told Helen after he calmed down. 'My lads are so disappointed, I can hardly face them.'

Burston scarcely knew what to say when he returned to be confronted by Weary's deep dejection, lamely suggesting that they might move up to the Western Desert later, 'when things straightened out a bit'. Through the eyes of the press, Weary watched the Battle of Sidi Resegh 'slugged out' and Auchinleck move up to take personal command, while 'we were stuck in [Palestine] . . . eating our hearts out, after all this tremendously hard work to establish'. They now experienced even more intensely 'the real horror of army life . . . idleness in fixed camps'.

Winter had arrived officially with the end of summer time on 31 October. The rains held off until mid-November, when they put an end to the swimming that had broken the tedium of their weekly route march to Hirbya, and rendered exercise on the wet roads more strenuous. Two blankets were no longer adequate at night. Everyone but Weary had changed to winter battle dress at the beginning of the month: ordnance were unable to produce anything to fit his long legs (throughout his life, tailors shook their heads at the distance between hip and knee), so he was still in summer shorts, 'which creates an impression of toughness'. He splashed out on a trench coat which gave some protection from the wind and rain.

Despite Burston's feeble assurances, Weary knew that they had missed their chance, as did everyone else at the end-of-month Saturday meeting of the officers and NCOs. No one mentioned the mobile operating unit. Eadie was troubled that the men would become restless after this latest setback, particularly now that the move to Syria appeared to have faded. Weary listened cynically to an agenda dominated by a discussion of ping pong committees, sporting equipment and leave. The decision to plant a garden seemed the final blow to his ambitions.

They stepped up the training, the nursing sisters taking part with lecture demonstrations in practical nursing, and everyone from Eadie down flung themselves into table tennis, soccer and rugby. Weary gathered a team together for the last, although practice was hampered by the lack of goalposts; and the officers' ping pong contests with the recently arrived VADs caused quite a flutter of interest, especially when the return match featured dancing after the main event. By December, the rains had turned the Palestinian desert a vivid green, and training was suspended while the troops deepened the slit trenches to improve the drainage in the sodden camps.

Meanwhile, in Asia, Japan was secretly launching a war that she anticipated would establish her as a major colonial power and secure the raw materials denied her by the United States, Britain and Holland when they clamped on economic sanctions in July. Her Greater East Asia Co-Prosperity Scheme was designed, she informed her subject nations later, to free the Phillipines, Malaya, Singapore and the Netherlands East Indies from the yokes of their European masters and unite them under Japan as overlord of the 'New Order' in South-east Asia and the Western Pacific.

In mid-February 1941, Churchill had observed to Roosevelt that 'a sudden act of war upon us by Japan might be imminent'.[16] Although he found 'disturbing' the increased Japanese naval activity off the coast of Indo-China and the Japanese government's intervention in negotiating the settlement of a frontier dispute between the Vichy French and Thailand, his anxiety waned in the face of continuing Japanese negotiations with the United States and more urgent preoccupations in the Balkans.

By May, Churchill's attention was bent on the Middle East and he discounted the danger of Japanese attack on Singapore, as it 'would be an operation far more dangerous to [Japan] and less harmful to us than spreading her cruisers and battle-cruisers on the Eastern trade routes'.[17] When, that July, Japan had refused to withdraw her troops from China and Indo-China, President Roosevelt froze all Japanese assets in the United States and cut off the oil vital for the Japanese war machine. Churchill and the refugee Dutch Government in London followed suit.

The reinstatement of oil shipments was conditional on the withdrawal of Japanese troops from China and Indo-China and this was unacceptable to Japan, perfectly positioned in the latter country to carry out the invasion of Malaya, the Philippines and the Netherlands East Indies. With Dutch acquiescence to the embargo, Japan's last source of oil had been cut off.

Malaya was rich in rubber and tin; and Singapore, her five great guns thrusting seawards, attested to the might of the British Empire. Their overthrow would destroy Britain's prestige in the eyes of the races presently under her benign colonial rule; and it would endanger the free passage of ships carrying men and cargo through the sea lanes between Australia and Europe.

Despite Churchill's faith in the United States gaining at least three months' breathing space before hostilities could begin, by August he had recognised the inevitability of war with Japan and the vulnerability of Malaya and the island fortress, whose defences were 'still considerably below standard', despite the £65 000 000 expended on them between the wars.[18]

Belatedly, Britain decided to implement a show of naval strength in the Pacific and Indian oceans by sending a 'deterrent squadron'. Force Z sailed for Singapore on 24 October: one of the new *King George V* class battleships, HMS *Prince of Wales*, accompanied by the battle cruiser *Repulse* and four destroyers. They made the voyage without air cover, for the aircraft carrier *Indomitable* was laid up for repairs in the West Indies and no order was issued for another to escort them. Once in Asia, they would have to rely for air support on the RAF and RAAF squadrons stationed in Malaya.

Since 24 November, the United States Government had warned the Allies that 'a surprise aggressive movement in any direction' by the Japanese could occur, possibly towards the Philippines or Guam.[19] Although air reconnaissance further south disclosed the movement of convoys from Formosa and Indo-China towards the Malayan Peninsula, American intelligence was unaware that the Japanese First Fleet was gathering in Tankan Bay in the Kurile Islands north-east of Hokkaido.

On 1 December, alarmed at the revelation that Japanese troop transports were sailing through the South China Sea, the British declared a state of emergency in Malaya. Next day, Force Z, the first element of the Far Eastern Fleet, reached Singapore and on 3 December, Admiral Sir Tom Phillips flew in from Manila to take command. Their arrival was broadcast to the world.

Great Britain had not attached as much urgency to boosting the defences of Singapore as had the Australians, who for twenty years cocked a nervous eye north at the 'yellow peril'. Senior army officers had been preaching the importance of fortifying Malaya and Singapore with adequate air and ground forces for some years. They held little faith in Britain's ability to send help when the fleet lay between seventy and ninety days distant. By the latter part of 1941, Singapore was informed that, in the event of Japanese attack, she would need to hold out for

180 days, the length of time it would take the fleet to reach her.

The AIF had been in Malaya since February 1941, when Maj-General H. Gordon Bennett, together with the headquarters of the 8th Division and the 22nd Brigade group, arrived and moved up the Malayan Peninsula to quarters in Malacca, Kuala Lumpur, Seremban and Port Dickson.

Air support had been promised, but this part of South-east Asia was woefully ill served by an inadequate four squadrons of American Brewster-Buffalo fighters plus out-dated Hudsons, Vildebeestes and Blenheims. Everything had been poured into the Middle East and the raids over Germany.

Within a span of seven hours on Sunday 7 December, the Japanese bombed Pearl Harbor, the Philippines, Malaya, Singapore and Hong Kong. Some, including Menzies and Curtin, had hoped that she would turn away from confrontation with the United States at the last moment. Instead, in two waves of bombing raids between 07.55 and 08.40 local time, she had seized the initiative and wiped out half of the American fleet lying at anchor in Hawaii.

In Jerusalem for a clinical meeting at Hadassah Hospital, Weary and the others were transfixed by the BBC announcement that the Japanese had attacked the American fleet at Pearl Harbor. Rather the worse for an evening spent with a large party of British officers in Jerusalem, dining, drinking and speculating feverishly about the future course of the war, Weary and Peter Row did not reach their beds at Beit Jirja until two o'clock on Monday morning. He was convinced that they would be confronting the Imperial Japanese Army in South-east Asia before too many months were out.

A few hours later, they discovered that *Operation Crusader* and Rommel's retirement to Gazala on the night of 7–8 December was 'just about swept from the *Palestine Post*', whilst the minds and eyes of the Allies focused on this more urgent danger in the Pacific and the Far East. A Japanese invasion force was ashore at Kota Bharu in Malaya, and their air force had bombed Singapore and the United States naval and air force bases in Manila.

That day they hurriedly searched maps of the Far East and the Pacific for the names of 'numerous little spots which have suddenly become significant', such as Guam, Wake and Midway, also attacked from the air that Sunday. 'Oh it is not so good to be idle . . . '

On Monday, 8 December, Britain declared war on Japan. Gathered round the radio in Melbourne that evening, the Fergusons heard a sombre Curtin announce: 'We are at war with Japan.'*

Two days later, Japanese bombers and torpedo-carrying aircraft sank the battleship *Prince of Wales* and the *Repulse* off the coast of Malaya. Phillips's decision to dash north in order to intercept the Japanese ships escorting the invading troops had been justified at first. Initially, the murky cloud cover of the north-east monsoon protected them and they were unseen by enemy reconnaissance aircraft, although he had sent the slower destroyer, HMS *Tenedos*, back to Singapore at 6.35 pm on 9 September because of her restricted range. Phillips was unaware that an enemy submarine, I58, had shadowed them during the night, torpedoes trained on the capital ship's tempered steel hull. Trusting in the superiority of his gunners, he had not called for fighter protection when he realised that they had been spotted during a detour to investigate a reported landing at Kuantan on 9 December. For just after dawn on 10 December, the two great ships with their three accompanying destroyers were revealed under a clear sky to an Ensign Hoashi in a 'Babs' reconnaissance aircraft.

At 12.40 pm, the *Repulse* went down; then, shortly after twenty past one, the *Prince of Wales* sank beneath a great pool of her own fuel oil, taking Phillips with her.

Weary shaved off his moustache in disgust: 'Awful to think that a few short sighted, thick spectacled little yellow rats . . . can hit battleships better even than Huns'. He began to doubt the corporate belief in the inferiority of Japanese war material and fighting abilities.

The phlegmatic CCS diarist ignored the shattering events of those early December days, limiting his entries to routine domestic matters: divisional exercises, leave and entertainment. Weary initialled each page and apparently saw nothing unusual in this blinkered view of their existence, yet everyone was wondering what changes the war might bring as it swept frighteningly close to Australia. Would they continue to kill time at Beit Jirja, nannying other, luckier, AIF units bound for a more active war? Even optimistic Peter Row now doubted the possibility of either the desert or Syria claiming No 1 Australian Mobile Operating Unit, but the appearance on 16 December of Colonel Hailes with the firm intention of inspecting them in action raised

---

* Australia declared war on Japan officially on 9 December.

Weary's spirits slightly. Unlike the previous day, when the only rôle for twenty of the men was as 'Hun parachutists' in a 9th Division exercise near Khassa, they would have a chance to show what they had been trained to do. That exercise had been held over two rare rainless days. While his men 'were completely annihilated in the inevitable dawn attack', Weary accompanied Eadie to the 2/3rd Field Ambulance's area to watch Doug Stephens, John Devine and their men function in simulated battle conditions.

Weary silently contemplated the irony of the younger men's wide experience compared to his endless months spent in administration and the probable detriment of his surgical skills. Stephens had now been involved in front-line surgery since the start of the Libyan campaign, first as Orm Smith's junior partner in the mad race across to Benghazi and later with his field ambulance in Tobruk. Even Devine, denied access to European patients in Tobruk by Littlejohn, had enjoyed more surgery than the better-qualified Weary, for he had operated on prisoners-of-war and native labourers.

Promptly at 9 am that Thursday, the 8 vehicles and 36 men moved out of camp in the direction of Dimra. To Weary's relief, everything went like clockwork and Hailes was full of praise, although this was scant comfort when there were no prospects of employment. Lately, Weary had felt even faint envy of the New Zealand unit akin to his, despite their uncertain fate after being captured somewhere out near Sidi Resegh. He decided there was only one word to describe his army career: futile.

The 9th Division rugby fifteen, captained by Weary, was to play the Combined Palestine Police in Jerusalem on Sunday, 21 December, and a large leave party from the 2/2nd CCS travelled up in order to cheer them on. Most of the Australian Medical Corps also congregated in Jerusalem that Saturday for the cocktail party given by Colonel Spiers and the 2/4th AGH that preceded the Sunday clinical meeting at the 2/6th.

The AIF thumped the Palestine Police. Their game the previous week against the 2/4th Anti-Tank Regiment had welded them into an efficient team. 'Only catch was that we played a fool practice match on stony ground which caused several casualties.' Weary was one of them. He was unconcerned about a couple of cracked ribs, but very disturbed at injuring a finger in exactly the same way as in 1934. This time, he refused Charles Littlejohn's offer to put it right and treated it himself with plaster immobilisation.

With his left middle finger permanently misshapen through Little-john's attentions in Melbourne and now a chip of bone loose in the middle finger of the other hand from a confrontation with a medicine ball during training, he decided to swear off rough sports.

Burston was in Jerusalem for the meeting and charmed Weary as usual. All the younger man's simmering resentment at his unit's inactivity dissipated when the general asked him to lunch 'so nicely' that there seemed little point in being ungracious and raising the subject again.

Winter sliced in an icy swathe south all the way from the Russian front (where German tanks would neither start nor fire in temperatures thirty-five degrees below zero,) to the Middle East. Jerusalem gaped at its heaviest snowstorm for twenty years and by Christmas morning at Beit Jirja, 'Oh the wind and the rain, just torrents of rain . . . and mud and cold'. Over 400 millimetres of rain had been dumped on the camps in Palestine by Christmas Eve. The darkened skies were split by lightning, the tents battered by hail and most of their blackout paint washed away, the slit trenches invisible under sheets of water.

Belisario and the 2/5th AGH returned from East Africa around 3 am on Christmas Day and later came to lunch, singing valiantly in spite of being stowed in huts at Barbara because the weather was too foul for their tents to be put up at Beit Jirja. The lights failed and the Christmas fare 'failed to turn up', but the CCS officers pooled their Christmas parcels and managed to scrape up enough Christmas pudding for everyone.

'Our flag has fallen out of the map,' Weary wrote disconsolately to Helen. They had rested, re-equipped, and been left behind. Five months after leaving Tobruk, they were still 'in a staging camp and never taking a patient'. 'My mobile operating unit raised with such travail languishes similarly. Now that the chance of operations has been lost I am to hand over its command, and on paper return to the CCS.' Surgeons were attached to such units only when work was imminent, he told Helen, but in fact the unit held no more savour for him. Burston had kept his word to Eadie and agreed to let Weary return to Eadie's command, whilst Peter Row took his place.

Weary had one consolation: at last Boyd had handed over the photograph of Helen sent out with him to the Middle East long months ago.

Three days later, on 28 December, the CCS received the longed-for signal from Burston. 'I . . . expect to be on the move again fairly soon in the direction of Boyd's battalion,' Weary suggested to Helen. The proposed transfer to Syria infused a new urgency into everyone's life and over the next fortnight, they began the general organisation for the move, checking, packing and listing equipment. Weary contemplated 1942 with renewed enthusiasm and, at Burston's bidding, sped off to Cairo on 13 January.

On 6 January, unknown to Weary, the decision made by the Australian government's agreement to dispatch I Australian Corps, including the 6th and 7th Divisions, to the Far East in early February was to pitch him into a war unlike anything he had imagined during the long months of hunger for action. What he learned, when he reached headquarters, turned all the unit's arrangements topsy-turvy: his earlier prediction that they would be fighting the Japanese was confirmed. In ten days they were to be ready to leave Beit Jirja for a transit camp at Suez. Their destination, he told Helen as plainly as he could, given the censorship restrictions, 'instead of being rather cold in the near future . . . seems likely to be hot'.

PART THREE

1942 – 1945

*Rather the scorned – the rejected – the men hemmed in
   with the spears;*

*The men of the tattered battalion which fights till it
   dies,
Dazed with the dust of the battle, the din and the
   cries . . .*

*Not the ruler for me, but the ranker, the tramp of the
   road,
The slave with the sack on his shoulders pricked on with
   the goad,
The man with too weighty a burden, too weary a load . . .*

'A Consecration', *Salt-water Ballads*, JOHN MASEFIELD

Sixteen

Fastest Ship of the Convoy

WITHIN A WEEK OF WEARY discovering that their departure was imminent, many of the 60 000 men in the 6th and 7th divisions were suffering from severe reaction to a rapidly organised TAB inoculation programme. Boyd had taken to his bed when Weary saw him next. 'English stuff and with about twice the wallop of our CSL vintage.'

Someone official in Cairo christened the movement of I Australian Corps from the Middle East 'Stepsister'. Even as these troops prepared to sail for South-east Asia, leaving behind the 9th Division to take part in future action in the desert, Kenneth Slessor, one of Australia's official war correspondents reported on 13 January that the streets of Cairo were 'full of newly-arrived Australian reinforcements in the dark blue uniform of the RAAF . . . it would seem that the time is not far distant when . . . 50 per cent of the Middle East air strength will be composed of Australians flying American aircraft, while, with the exception of South Africans, all fighter squadrons will be manned by Australians'.[1]

By now, this sort of propaganda about the successes of the RAAF against Axis aircraft held out scant comfort to fellow Australians, who would have preferred the air force's vigilance to be employed closer to home.

For the Australian airmen, with their Hurricanes, Tomahawks and the recently arrived American Kittyhawks, were needed more urgently in Singapore and Malaya. Fifty-one Hurricanes and 24 British pilots had arrived in Singapore with the second reinforcement convoy the same day that Slessor filed his report.[2] The only trouble was, the Hurricanes – not of the latest type – were still in their crates, and the pilots had no experience of flying in Asian conditions. Storms, known as 'Sumatras', blow through Singapore and Malaya with terrifying suddenness at that time of year. Hurricane-force winds roar up like an express train from their namesake island, bending the coconut palms double in a dark rush of blinding rain. Visibility disappears, the sky is black as

291

night, and a day that may have dawned bright under a burning blue tropical sky is translated to a howling, lashing confusion of wind and water.

Movement orders arrived at the CCS headquarters on 23 January. Before the month was out, they were to leave Palestine. There would be the usual nocturnal journey by rail to the transit camp at Suez, from where Weary, Eadie and the main body of the unit were to sail in the first flight with troops of the 7th Division.

A hastily assembled convoy would carry the two divisions to Bombay and Colombo for transfer to smaller ships. General Wavell, now in Java and Supreme Commander of ABDA (American, British, Dutch, Australian) Command, proposed to send them in to shore up the crumbling defence of Malaya and Singapore.

The Yeates brothers, Casey and Hutson were to act as medical officers to troops on the transports and left Gaza some days earlier with their parties. Casey was in charge of the stores and equipment that Weary had assembled so painstakingly for the CCS and the mobile operating unit.

While Weary and the others were boarding their train at Gaza Station at 11.45 pm on 30 January 1942, the Australians in Malaya were withdrawing down the road towards Johore Bahru. Just before first light, General Bennett watched them cross the causeway to Singapore Island. That day, Wavell had ordered the withdrawal of further aircraft to Sumatra. Now only six Brewster-Buffaloes and eight Hurricanes remained on the island. No longer did the fortress of Singapore seem as impregnable as everyone had believed.

The movement from Beit Jirja on Friday night was orderly enough, despite the inevitable confusion at Gaza Station and a scramble at Kantara East when it was discovered that last minute timetable changes dictated that their train leave earlier than expected. When, next morning, their train arrived at Suez, it was shunted into the oil wells siding, and here they remained until 4.30 in the afternoon.

Weary had never had a high opinion of Movement Control's organisational abilities, but this time, their performance transcended all previous shambles. The first intimations that they would fulfil his worst expectations occurred when Casey failed to meet them at Kantara and none of their war establishment stores could be located at Port Said. Weary had already protested about the order that they could take only one RAP pannier on board as medical stores for the entire unit: even officers' suitcases were to travel separately, and he noted sourly that 'the officers travelled in the usual passenger coaches amply provided with racks and . . . were of average muscular development'. Men would sail on troop transports, their baggage and equipment would follow separately on cargo ships.

Weary, as unit embarkation officer, was not idle. On the wharves he found remnants of their baggage – the RAP pannier, officers' valises, some packs and the nurses' trunks – all of which the AIF embarkation officer was determined would not travel with the unit on the *Orcades*. Wise to the ways of Movement Control, Weary was equally determined that they would, and superintended their loading onto the lighter which took him out to HMT 207 *Orcades*. At least the nurses had their belongings. The men embarked with only a side haversack apiece; Weary carried his valise and a pack.

The whereabouts of the rest of the baggage and all their equipment remained a mystery until shortly before they sailed, when he learned from Casey that their stores, carelessly dumped on top of their vehicles, had been loaded onto a cargo vessel. Casey had spent the previous three days in the dockyards at Port Said, overseeing the disposition of their equipment into the hold.

Nothing would induce officialdom to retrieve the officers' heavy baggage and the men's packs, which had been shunted into a siding at Port Tewfik and abandoned. Instead, the decision not to 'tactically load' the transports meant that they were to be accompanied by the personal belongings of those who had sailed the previous day, including that of the 2/5th AGH.

He was deeply dismayed to discover that all units had been separated from their baggage and equipment: they were to sail to the tropics in winter battle dress, without drugs, equipment or transport, or any means of caring for the sick or wounded other than the sparse resources contained in one pannier. Shades of Greece. He clung grimly to his greatcoat and few personal possessions.

Movement Control's lack of co-ordination ensured that none of these fighting troops travelled with their guns, ammunition and transport. Headquarters of I Australian Corps at Tjisaroea on Java were appalled to discover a week after the first flight sailed that no one could furnish any details of what was on which vessels, for 'practically 75% of the units being carried by the *Orcades* are not accompanied by their G.1098 or T eqpt'.[3]

The consequences of not tactically loading the convoy in an attempt to get everyone away faster meant that the 7th Division would not be 'ready for operations in Sumatra until about 21 March', General Lavarack deduced. He estimated that the 6th Division, scheduled to leave Suez in the same movement, might be in fighting order by the middle of April.

Convoy JS2 sailed on 1 February. Amongst the 3400 men on board HMT *Orcades* with the 2/2nd CCS and various advance parties (including personnel from 1 Australian Corps), were two battalions, the 2/2nd Pioneers and the 2/3rd Machine Gunners, 2/6th Field Company, 1 Light Anti-Aircraft Regiment, 5 Heavy Anti-Aircraft Battery, 105th General Transport Company and a detachment of a Guard battalion. They were to have sailed on the *Ile de France* a day later, but when the *Orcades* steamed in and disembarked the troops on board, it was decided to load her with Australians and turn her round without delay.[4]

Everyone was fairly certain about their destination. Weary told Helen in his last letter from the Middle East that 'the lads . . . [were] developing a real Jap hatred much more real than the very natural dislike of old Fritz'. No longer would they be involved in a European war. This was a new war, and a new enemy dangerously close to home; news of slit trenches being dug in back gardens, of air raid drill and black out regulations, trailed the spectre of bombing raids, even invasion, by that 'yellow peril' which had haunted the public mind throughout the past two decades. And the prospective victims were not inhabitants of a far-off country whose ties were stretched thin through distance and fading memories: they were their own wives, children, parents, sisters and brothers.

The *Orcades* was fast and she rapidly pulled ahead of the rest of the convoy, making Colombo after eight days. Eadie was made Senior Medical Officer and the CCS staffed the ship's hospital, but there were few sick and no serious cases. Weary spent congenial hours in the hospital with the ship's surgeon, 'Prince' Gardiner, and Sister Kitty Murphy. She pampered him with the daily rituals of morning coffee and afternoon tea, while Gardiner and Weary teased her about the thousands of tanned and naked potential partners lolling on the decks. 'Just look at them, Kitty, all those fine young men!' Gardiner would say, 'Why don't you choose yourself a husband?' But Kitty had eyes only for Weary.

They anchored off Colombo on 9 February to refuel, take on supplies and off-load a few sick, then sailed in company with a heavy cruiser to the Netherlands East Indies. Wavell had ordered them to southern Sumatra to defend the aerodromes at Palembang to which aircraft from Malaya and Singpore had been withdrawn during January in the face of heavy Japanese raids.

The even tenor of the days between Colombo and Java was broken by two appendicectomies performed by Weary and Arthur Moon.

They were unaware as they steamed round the southern coast of Sumatra on 14 February that Japanese paratroopers had been dropped over one of the airfields near Palembang.

Brigadier Clive Steele, Chief Engineer of I Australian Corps, had gone to Sumatra to oversee the demolition of the airfields and the nearby refineries, defended by a garrison of Dutch soldiers, some small groups of armed RAF men and British anti-aircraft detachments. While Steele was driving from P1 airfield to the refineries on 14 February, he learned of the arrival of the Japanese paratroopers. Steele was the senior Australian officer on Sumatra. Accompanied by Lieut-Colonel Walter MacCallum, who had arrived some days earlier by air from the Middle East with General Burston and Colonel Hamilton Fairly, he made with all speed for Oosthaven.

The *Orcades* steamed into Oosthaven early on Sunday morning 15 February, and dropped anchor in the harbour by noon. Steele ordered 2000 troops to be disembarked, including the 2/3rd Machine Gun Battalion commanded by Lieut-Colonel Arthur Blackburn, to whom Lavarack had given the temporary command of all AIF troops in Southern Sumatra on 11 February. They were to go up to P2 airfield, south-west of Palembang, and then to Palembang itself.

Arthur Moon and Ewen Corlette, meagrely equipped with the RAP pannier and a few medical stores that Gardiner offered from his stocks on the ship, were to take a small party of the 2/2nd CCS and set up a camp dressing station. Weary would have liked to go himself, but had to remain on the ship. MacCallum assured them that the Dutch would supply operating equipment, drugs and dressings.

They disembarked in steaming heat, confusion and high spirits during the daily tropical downpour at 2.30 pm. Not only did the machine gun battalion have no machine guns and the transport company no vehicles, but there were not enough rifles to go round and only five rounds of ammunition for each weapon. That their shortcomings in arms and ammunition had to be boosted by borrowed ship's mausers did 'not auger well for the success of the landing force'. Weary wondered how true was the rumour that those men unlucky enough to miss out on firearms were equipped only with waddies and had been told that they should retrieve any weapons from casualties unable to continue using them.

Scarcely had Steele left Oosthaven and begun his return trip up the road to Palembang before the order was received from Wavell's headquarters that no troops should disembark from the *Orcades*. Many were already ashore. Night had fallen and not a light was showing as the returning lighters drifted about the harbour unable to locate the ship, the men on their decks squinting anxiously for its looming outline. It was 2 am on 16 February before all were back on board.

The shocking signal announcing the fall of Singapore had arrived. Now, on the night of 15-16 February, after capturing the aerodrome, Japanese paratroopers had joined up with a landing force of their 229th Regiment and taken Palembang.

The *Orcades* was to sail immediately to Tanjong Priok, the port for Batavia. Sumatra was to be abandoned. Retreating troops and civilians hurried headlong down the 480 kilometres of narrow jungle road from Palembang to Oosthaven. As well as taking on the 3rd Hussars, refugees from Malaya clamoured to be squeezed into any available space on *Orcades* and she did not sail until 9.30 am. Later arrivals would have to take their chances on the flotilla of twelve craft waiting in the harbour.

By now, communications between the various headquarters had deteriorated. Telephone was not secure and I Australian Corps headquarters were relying on dispatch riders. Believing that 'nothing definite has been decided . . . [about] the personnel contained in the Orcades', the staff was unaware until the following day that Wavell had decreed that the *Orcades* contingent was to defend Java's airfields in the areas of Batavia and Buitenzorg.[5]

Those on board had 'no illusions about our fate . . . What a way it will be to finish the war . . . marooned here.'[6] The rest of the transports carrying the Yeates brothers, Casey, Hutson and Row were in the Bay of Bengal while their destination was argued out by Curtin and Churchill. Now that Sumatra had gone and Java seemed likely to suffer a similar fate, Wavell wanted the 7th Division in Burma to help keep the supply route to India along the Burma Road open. Australia insisted that they come home to defend their own people from what seemed inevitable invasion from the north.

'Confusion all over the ship – some units to disembark, others to remain . . . decided we should go and take MacNamara with us.'[7]

There was even greater confusion once they landed at Tanjong Priok, where MacCallum was frantically breaking open cases and hunting for medical equipment for the CCS. Cases marked 'medical stores', intended for a British unit in Singapore but diverted to Java when the island's chances of survival faded, and equipment which had been hurled onto ships in Oosthaven harbour when Sumatra was abandoned, were tumbled haphazardly about the docks. The sight which greeted him was no different from what Casey had described at Suez: 'cooking utensils, autoclaves, Red Cross comforts, bales of blankets, stretchers' all pitched indiscriminately on top of vehicles.[8] Around thirty ships were standing out in the roads waiting to berth and unload when the *Orcades* sailed in.

The 2/2nd Pioneers and the 2/3rd Machine Gunners disembarked in the late afternoon of 18 February, and the eighty-seven strong CCS and their eight nurses followed them ashore as day slipped into dense tropical darkness. Kitty Murphy wept to see him go and pressed her precious silver hip flask filled with whisky into Weary's hand just before he swung over the side. No sooner were they ashore, than they were ordered back to the ship for the night. Weary found the two days spent on board in the stifling heat and humidity making repeated preparations to disembark the 'least pleasant of the voyage'.[9]

Next morning, Thursday 19 February, they assembled on deck and heard which units were to disembark for the third time: the 2/3rd Machine Gun Battalion, 2/2nd Pioneer Battalion, 2/6th Company of the RAE, 2/2nd Casualty Clearing Station, a platoon from A Company of Headquarters Guard Battalion, and the 105th General Transport Company. Disembarking was lengthy and tedious. Every size and kind of ship and high-hulled native prau was tied up bow to stern the length of the quays.

They were issued with three days' rations. Lorries took them to a railway station, 'which seemed to be endless platforms', heady with the musky scent of the clove cigarettes smoked by the local people and crowded with sweating men in heavy serge battle dress and agitated civilian refugees fleeing inland to Bandoeng.

Some vestiges of Dutch efficiency still clung to the railways, and their train cleared low-lying Batavia quickly and steamed through country-side exploding with a lush, green fertility of banana trees and coconut palms, rice paddy and vegetable gardens rising in neatly carved terraces to the sky. Dramatically different from the flat treelessness of the Middle East, it was a landscape of meticulously tilled greenness cut by broad rivers, dark jungle and mountains.

Nearer Bandoeng, the air grew cooler as they climbed through slab-sided hills smoking with white dust from quarries and kilns burning the local limestone. Kampongs of attap-thatched and lime-washed matting huts and the occasional shuttered stucco bungalow belonging to some colonial Dutchman gave way to tea estates, their long neat rows of flat-topped bushes tended by stooping women in sarongs and conical bamboo hats. Weary spent much of the three hours or so learning polite and elementary Dutch phrases from the children sharing his carriage.

Bandoeng surprised Weary, with its solid, official, nineteenth-century buildings of lime-washed stucco spread out importantly around the railway station and the municipal gardens. The wide, tree-shaded streets were well paved and bright with flowers; next to the Governor's offices was Bethel church, divided from its fellow spiritual guardian, St Peter's, by the Botanic Gardens and the dazzling, white-pillared, colonial magnificence of the Bank of Java.

There were more lorries lined up to take them the short distance to the Christylijk Lyceum, a large school in the Dagoweg set back from the street, where they were to set up a general hospital. Burston, Fairley and MacCallum were awaiting them in the shade of huge trees that were alive with the liquid song and brilliant yellow of the Golden Oriels.

Weary's most immediate worry was their lack of drugs and stores, for the jumbled cases retrieved by MacCallum from the docks had not travelled with them. Burston had arranged for an NEI Army officer, Lieutenant John Disse, to be attached to the hospital as liaison officer and interpreter. Sergeant Clark and a couple of other ranks had stayed in Batavia to scavenge what they could from the docks and from Colonel Larsen at the Military Hospital. Orders had gone out that any case marked with a red cross was to be sent to Bandoeng. It would be Disse's job to help Weary procure their needs from local sources, army or civilian.

Food was not a problem: the Dutch ordnance corps fed them. And hawkers trotted up and down the streets from dawn until long after dark calling out the unfamiliar contents of containers balanced on long bamboo carrying poles; noodles, rice, soups, saté and curries were dispensed from rickety wheeled carts trailing a pungent odour of grilled fish and meat and glowing charcoal. Fresh vegetables and fruit were heaped high in the street markets.

Neither army nor civilians stood up well to the increasing Japanese air raids. 'Natives are streaming out of town . . . whole bloody population goes to earth.' The civilians were timid, the Dutch army even more so. During one alert, Jock Clarke had to serve himself in a café, even though planes were neither audible nor visible, for the entire population vanished at the crescendo scream of the siren. In another raid, when the planes were quite a distance from the centre of town, he stood outside on the footpath in the Dagoweg. 'I got quite a thrill.'

Weary was pessimistic about the Dutch officers' abilities to co-ordinate any vigorous opposition to the Japanese. Too many of them were plump, puffy, middle-aged reservists. During a meeting at NEI headquarters one day, the first warning of a raid sent them all diving under the tables. He stood by the window, jingling the contents of his pockets, until they sheepishly straightened up and resumed the conversation. To any of the CCS men, well-seasoned in Tobruk, this behaviour boded ill for any effective resistance.

The Christylijk Lyceum was modern and spacious, but behind its tall, shaded windows was an echoing, cool emptiness of desks and chairs – no beds, bedding or even messing equipment for the unit, let alone the sick and wounded. Light, temporary huts were to be put up by engineering labour in the grounds at the rear, as the hospital would hold at most only 400 patients, and a British ordnance major and architect in civilian life, John Denman, designed the operating theatre. There was a wide, round-about drive from the street to the front door for the eight ambulances allotted them by No. 1 Java Ambulance Car Unit; the hall was roomy enough for reception arrangements; and the general assembly room immediately behind it would make a very large ward, with classrooms as medium-sized ones.

Weary and Disse called on the local hospital and on the ordnance people at NEI Army headquarters in Lembang for beds, ward furnishings and cooking apparatus, but little could be done in converting the building until, a couple of days later, stores began to arrive from a British field hospital run by the RAF, previously housed in the Princess Juliana School in Batavia and now leaving Java.

On the night of 20 February Eadie announced, quite irrationally, that he wished to open a second Allied hospital in the recently vacated school, and he rejected all Weary's very sound reasons for refusing to release men from the CCS to staff it. Not only would it be in advance of their own lines in an area where attack was almost certain and fierce fighting could be expected, but it was nowhere near the projected line of withdrawal towards the mountains and Bandoeng. Not least, the CCS was already under-strength. There were insufficient personnel to staff a 400-bed hospital and Weary had no idea where he would find more. They spent the night in heated argument, Eadie quite 'cuckoo', impossible and pig-headed, ignoring all reason. Finally, Weary announced that he would go to Burston in order to scotch such foolishness.

Early next morning, before he had a chance to speak to Burston about the problem, they were summoned to the DMS's office. Headquarters of I Australian Corps were packed and moving at once, about to get into their cars, and would leave Java that day. Weary listened, incredulous, as Burston announced that Lieut-Colonel A. S. Blackburn VC had been promoted to brigadier and appointed to command the Australian forces, now designated 'Blackforce'; he, in turn, would report to HQ British Forces, Java, commanded by Major-General Sitwell. Sitwell's ADMS would be Lieut-Colonel Maisey RAMC. Eadie was to be Senior Medical Officer to the AIF, reporting to Blackburn, and Weary was to take command of the 2/2nd CCS with a promotion to temporary lieutenant-colonel.

When the hospital was established it would be administered by Sitwell's headquarters. Overall command would rest with the Dutch: Lieut-General ter Poorten, Commander-in-Chief, and Major-General van Oyen for air defence. Eadie's lunatic proposal was discarded.

Weary scribbled a few lines to Kitty Murphy, consigning Burston to her care, then wrote hastily to Helen for the first time since leaving Egypt. All that was at hand was a loose sheet of letterhead left over from AIF HQ Middle East and a pencil he had in his pocket. As in Greece, the courier was to be his departing general, but this time, there was no prospect of escape.

'You will understand darling that things are tough here and that I have little hope of seeing you for some time, if ever . . . I shall love you always . . .

'Jolly my family up a bit won't you.' Another minute sufficed to scrawl some reassurance to his parents that he was well and 'not afraid'.

Bridgeford, the man who had welcomed him into the 2 AIF during the wintry December of 1939, shook him briefly by the hand. Dazed and silent, he waved Burston, Fairley and MacCallum off and climbed into the car with Eadie. They had been driving for some time before Eadie suddenly said: 'You know, Weary, I think we could be in the bag!'

SEVENTEEN

Into the Bag

THE NURSES PROCLAIMED their bitter disappointment at yet again failing to function with the unit when Weary and Eadie reclaimed them from their billet at the YMCA, and escorted them to Bandoeng Railway Station. The senior sister, Vida Parker, protested for all of them, 'upset at being dumped. It seemed dreadful, after all we'd gone for' to be packed off home.[1] She still clutched the £30 cheque which HQ had given her to buy food more to their taste than the highly spiced meals at the hostel. But Burston had agreed with Weary that they should sail from Tanjong Priok that night on HMT *Orcades* with corps headquarters.

Weary had 10 000 guilders from Burston as an advance against his imprest account and a letter of introduction to Lieut-Colonel Maisey RAMC, ADMS to ABDA Command. He lost no time in going to see Maisey and Lieut-Colonel O'Dwyer, the Assistant Director of Hygiene, at their Lembang headquarters on the outskirts of Bandoeng, but they could promise him nothing beyond the twenty tonnes of stores coming from Batavia. These did, however, include 600 stretchers, some beds and cooking utensils. Blankets, mosquito nets and petrol cookers would have to be bought; the Dutch DMS, Major-General van Rees, might supply drugs, operating gear, dressings, morphia, plaster of Paris and all the impedimenta needed by a hospital in time of war.

Van Rees' DADMS, Captain Simone, turned out to be co-operative, energetic and efficient at arranging transport, rations, even Dutch regimental boots and clothing which could be dyed khaki. The quinine factory in Bandoeng was a local source of 5000 tablets; Colonel Grootsvald came up with sulphanilamide, Dagenham M & B 693, rubber gloves and extra beds and bedding.

Eadie formally handed over the command to Weary on 24 February, gathered up his belongings, Sgt Harrison Lucas and Private Xaviour, and disappeared to Blackburn's headquarters in Batavia. All ranks were drawn up outside the building. Weary was brief and blunt. 'You said you'd be good when the whips were cracking. Well, they're cracking now!' They had few stores, fewer drugs and little time. What supplies he could obtain were beginning to arrive by road and rail or must be sought locally and the empty building must be transformed into a hospital ready to receive the casualties which would soon be pouring in. They would have to work night and day. Leave was unlikely.

Simone found him a car and arranged a supply of petrol and oil; O'Dwyer supplied two lorries. Weary heard that a departing head-quarters clerk had left a box containing a typewriter in Room 55 at the Savoy hotel: someone was sent to snaffle it before anyone else heard about it. A cyclostyling machine also appeared in the office, and routine orders began to be cranked out. Slit trenches were dug. Colonel O'Dwyer had his eye on a Union Jack, a Red Cross flag was made and both were run up the flagpoles over the entrance facing the Dagoweg alongside the Dutch and Australian ones. They began to stockpile rations, aiming at a reserve of sixty days. Kitchens were put in and cookers hastily connected under the supervision of the engineers. Weary managed to send a telegram to Helen: 'Well love Java – Dunlop.'

At 9 am next morning, Wednesday 25 February, General Wavell dissolved the ABDA Command and flew to Delhi to resume his former rôle of Commander-in-Chief, India. Fewer than forty fighter aircraft remained on Java, cut off from reinforcement by air now that the aerodromes on Bali, Sumatra and Timor had been lost; and General Brereton had flown to India with his forty heavy bombers of the American Army Air Force the previous day. There was no effective Dutch air defence. The NEI High Command was now in charge. Java was isolated.

Weary was 'feverishly busy' establishing a hospital 'out of thin air'. He found it 'a shocker to have to start again after all those months of preparation. But it is wonderful how things are flowing in from all sides . . . all services . . . and from our Dutch allies.' Everyone, from staff officers down to other ranks, was uneasily aware of how slender their resources were and harshly critical of the arrangements which had separated all units from their equipment at Suez.

Major-General Gordon Bennett had arrived in Java, flown in from Sumatra after escaping from Singapore. That evening, Weary was bidden to dine with Sitwell and his staff. He was the only other Australian officer present (Blackburn had returned to Batavia late that afternoon) and was startled to see Bennett there, 'pretty tuckered-in' by the rough time he had endured. He gazed at the little, bald-headed man unburdening himself, the words spilling out. 'He was dehydrated and pinched, very excitable', skin drawn tight across his cheekbones, eyes fixed and starting from their sockets. Weary grew increasingly uncomfortable and alarmed at his appearance, deciding that 'essentially he was an egotist . . . [convinced he was] the only one who could save Australia by telling them about the lessons of the campaign . . . He was all burnt up with this, believed he was the one who was doing the right thing.' Everyone was tense. Sitwell, an Indian Army man, was 'deeply embarrassed' by Bennett's tirade about the poor performance of the Indian Army units in Malaya – 'the things he said . . . were highly indiscreet under the circumstances . . . he was a guest'.[2]

Weary interrupted Bennett at one stage, curious about the fate of his old teacher and surgeon to the 2/10th AGH in Malaya, Lieut-Colonel Coates, whom Bennett had ordered to leave Singapore. Coates had reached Sumatra on 15 February and set up an emergency CCS to care for the wounded, but Weary had heard no more. Bennett left abruptly before the end of the evening. Eventually he escaped by plane from Tjilatjap to Australia and noisy controversy about his ill-advised decision to leave his men.

Two Japanese forces were on their way to Java – no one knew how many men – but Major-General Sitwell considered he had only a 'token force' to pit against them: 'a squadron of light tanks, two battalions of infantry (Australian) and a number of AA units, with a conglomeration of small non-fighting administrative units for use at the base'.[3] Air Vice-Marshal Maltby commanded around 5500 RAF men, many of whom he was attempting to get away, and those aircraft flown in from Singapore and Sumatra ahead of the Japanese advance; the remnants of squadrons and machines were in need of complete reorganisation.

The NEI Army under Lieut-General ter Poorten was a weak sister, 'not yet prepared for modern war'; the ships and aircraft of the Dutch Navy and Air Force were unequal to the Japanese opposition.[4] Blackforce was 'practically the only British troops remaining in Java who were equipped and trained to fight, as the English troops . . . were mainly RA without guns and ground personnel of the RAF.'[5]

When Blackburn called at ABDA Command that morning, Wavell emphasised how 'every hour gained by resisting the Japanese invasion would be of value to the Allied cause in the South West Pacific . . . and

Netherlands East Indies: West Java

to Australia'.[6] Later, Sitwell agreed with Blackburn that his troops would be better employed as one force rather than scattered over five airfields. These were now to be defended by RAF and British anti-aircraft gunners armed as infantry. Blackburn's battalions, backed up by Major-General Schilling's NEI troops, were to operate as the main offensive force against the invasion from the west.

Blackburn transformed his Australians into infantry on I Australian Corps orders, organising his machine gunners, pioneers and engineers on a brigade footing into three infantry battalions. Into these, he absorbed some 8th Division reinforcements from Australia (diverted because of the fall of Singapore) and 175 deserters who had washed up in Batavia without any satisfactory explanation of why they were there. Blackforce lacked signals, field guns and carriers. Sitwell gave him a signal section, a squadron of light tanks from the King's Own Hussars and arranged for part of a battalion of the US 131st Artillery Regiment to be attached. He then accompanied Blackburn to NEI Headquarters, where General ter Poorten approved their plans.

The Dutch expected landings at each end of the island: near Merak in west Java, and in the east in the region of Surabaya. Admiral Helfrich, commanding the navy, had divided his ships into two squadrons accordingly. Learning of the approach of the Eastern Force, only that day he had summoned all the ships at the western end to steam with all speed to join Admiral Doorman near Surabaya. As Sitwell and the others sat at dinner in the hills above Bandoeng, Doorman was sailing out in search of the Japanese.

All in the mess that evening were grimly conscious of how flimsy their defences were against an invasion force ninety-seven transports strong moving steadily towards the coast of Java.

When Weary climbed out of the car in the Dagoweg later that night, even his first sight since 1938 of the Southern Cross blazing overhead failed to lift his spirits.

In keeping with the new command, Weary was promoted to temporary lieutenant-colonel on 26 February. His CCS was the nucleus of 'a sort of international medical brigade', for RAF and RAMC personnel began to arrive from elsewhere in Java. Quartermaster John Morris became registrar and a major, as did Jock Clarke; WOII Cameron took Morris's place as quartermaster and rose in rank to lieutenant. Six nurses were brought in from a local hospital to help the orderlies. Major Charles Moses, a member of Bennett's headquarters staff with whom Weary had played rugby for Victoria, arrived at the hospital with Lieutenant Walker, Bennett's aide. They had both escaped with Bennett from Singapore, but Moses' ribs had been broken in an accident during the blackout in Batavia and he was anxious to get away. Moses had pneumonia and was near delirious, insisting that 'he would rather be killed getting out' than be captured.

Some British sick were being evacuated by ambulance to Tjilatjap on the south coast and Weary decided to send Moses with the party. He detached an orderly, Private Thurlow, to care for him and at the last moment decided to give Chaplain Donald Macleod a chance to escape also. Macleod was ordered to get them on board a ship and accompany them.

Weary stood on the steps in the thin dawn light and watched the ambulance turn into the Dagoweg. He gave the party an even chance of finding a ship willing to evacuate them from Tjilatjap and run the gauntlet of enemy destroyers on watch for shipping. It was 27 February. Just over ten hours later, at 4.16 pm, Admiral Doorman's force engaged the Japanese in the Battle of the Java Sea.

The staff was rapidly increasing: medical officers and orderlies were arriving from all over Java. Eventually, Squadron-Leader R. A. Cumming and Flight-Lieutenant Nowell Peach brought in 72 men from the

RAF medical services, and 19 members of the RAMC arrived in dribs and drabs.

It took them four days to set up No. 1 Allied General Hospital. By 28 February, there were surgical, medical, X-Ray and pathological departments, a quartermaster's department and kitchens – but an inadequate supply of running water. A dental section was run by Jock Clarke (who also found himself with the essential but unenviable task of hygiene officer, master-minding the installation and maintenance of latrines in the back garden). There was even a library; Andrew Crighton, an Englishman from the British Consulate, installed himself as Librarian. And in the office was a miserable girl stenographer who had escaped from Singapore but failed to find herself an onward passage from Java. She had drifted in to the hospital and been put to work: Weary had no room for *bouches inutiles*.

Blackburn raised Weary's rank to temporary colonel with the establishment of the hospital.* All his energy and diplomacy had been directed to setting it up and Weary found his staff experience invaluable in circumnavigating the formalities of the several headquarters, Dutch and British. Sitwell had abolished all need for signatures and paperwork so that units might draw whatever equipment was available from the docks at Tanjong Priok, but the Dutch floundered in a welter of forms and purchase orders which must be submitted with the accounts before payment could be made from the imprest account.

Fifty patients – the first – arrived that afternoon by train and ambulance from the British Emergency Hospital in Batavia. Peach, the Senior Medical Officer there, had decided to evacuate his patients from the Princess Juliana Convent which Eadie had been so anxious to take over.[7] The climate was taking its toll: men were admitted shaking with malaria or with the griping pains and fever of dysentery. Weary called urgently for stretchers or bamboo beds – 200 of them if possible.

He divided the surgeons into two teams: Flying Officer Maurice Kinmonth assisted him, and Arthur Moon was assisted by Nowell Peach, with Ewen Corlette, Captain MacNamara and Captain Rees

---

* Weary never put up his rank, since he believed it would jeopardise his chances of staying with the hospital and his men. Blackburn's paperwork connected with his promotion, dated 8 March 1942, was not discovered until after the war, since it had been impossible to send a signal to 2nd Echelon in Melbourne.

as anaesthetists. They were rostered for duty on alternate days, freeing Weary for ever-present administrative work.

So far few wounded had been brought in, despite the daily air raids. The Japanese had been flying regular sorties from their captured bases in Sumatra, both Batavia and Bandoeng having been bombed heavily for the past week. Bandoeng town had escaped attack, bombing being confined to Andir aerodrome and various military installations, and although the hospital was directly in their flight path, no stray bullets had found victims. News of the naval battle off Surabaya had been skimpy, but the intelligence that the invasion fleet was close at hand led him to expect raids to intensify and casualties to flow in from the units defending the airfields. Both British and Dutch headquarters warned him to expect wounded from the Buitenzorg area any day, where Blackforce had moved its headquarters.

The previous night, the US cruiser *Houston* and HMAS *Perth* had withdrawn at the end of the five-hour battle and fled almost the length of Java for Tanjong Priok. Five and a half hours was all the time they needed to take on what little oil was available. There were no 4-inch shells. Both had damage to their gun turrets, *Houston* particularly, but they slipped out of Tanjong Priok just on dark on 28 February, expecting to make Tjilatchap by the next day.

Just off the north-west tip of Java, near the entrance to the Sunda Strait, they surprised a fleet of transports at anchor. They sailed straight at them without hesitation, their guns sinking four transports and damaging a number of others before the enemy's heavy cruisers and destroyers retaliated. Both ships went down, *Perth* taking four torpedoes before she tipped on her bow and slid under the black waters, her screws still turning.

Through the Battle of the Java Sea and this terrible conflict in the Sunda Strait, the navy had gained the land forces twenty-four hours – but at a tragic cost in ships and men.

On the cusp of midnight, the Japanese convoys began to land their troops at three points: the 2nd Guards Division at Merak and Bantam Bay west of Batavia; the 230th Regiment east of Batavia on the north coast at Eretanwetan; and the 48th division and 56th Regiment at Kragan, about a hundred miles west of Surabaya. Two good roads linked Batavia to Bandoeng, each with a railway line running more or less alongside. The enemy in the western sector moved fast, driving the tough little Ambonese and Menadonese in the NEI forces back, so that by six o'clock on the evening of 1 March, the northern road and railway had been captured. Now the only Allied access to Bandoeng was through Buitenzorg.*

Blackburn and Schilling had originally planned to attack the Japanese on the road running south between Batavia and Buitenzorg at dawn on 2 March, but the enemy's rapid advance made this impossible.

Between 11 pm on 1 March and 4.15 am on 2 March, Schilling rang Blackburn at his headquarters four times to convey confusing and contradictory orders from GHQ Bandoeng, twice to say that no NEI troops would be available to assist with the attack on the advancing Japanese column, twice to assure him that some infantry would remain to protect his flanks. Blackburn and his officers had studied carefully some I Australian Corps notes on Japanese tactics, realising that the training the men had received in the Middle East would be useless. He decided to hold to the defence of his position at the demolished bridge over the river at Leuwiliang, and disposed his force in depth. Two companies of the 2/2nd Pioneers were placed astride the road almost a kilometre apart, the balance 'kept mobile in armoured cars and on carriers and trucks, ready for immediate employment in a counter-encirclement role'. They were well-concealed and the artillery were ordered not to fire without 'direct orders' from Blackburn or the senior officer 'at the main defensive position'.[8]

Blackburn had no information from Dutch Intelligence about the enemy's movements – they neglected to inform him that there were no Japanese 'within thirty miles' at first light that morning – and his first sight of the Japanese was at 11.15 am on 2 March. Over the next four hours, 'a considerable force' gathered on the opposite bank and at 2 pm, Lieut-Colonel Williams ordered his men to open fire. They fought throughout the night and the next day, driving the Japanese back over the river where they had succeeded in crossing it. Morale was high and 'the Japanese attacks appeared to have failed everywhere'.[9]

Within hours of moving into position, Blackburn learned from Schilling that ter Poorten had ordered his troops to withdraw from Buitenzorg and fall back towards the Bandoeng plateau in order to prevent an advance against their capital city from the direction of Tjililitan airfield. He was proposing to launch a counter-attack against the Japanese at dawn next day. Although Schilling could tell him neither the exact position of the enemy, nor the line of the proposed counter-

* Now Bogor.

attack, Blackburn was asked to leave a skeleton force in position at the river and move everyone else across 150 kilometres of steep country in torrential rain in order to assist the Dutch.

The Dutch had not anticipated this third landing at Eretanwetan. Reading between the lines of Sitwell's and Blackburn's reports, one glimpses an unimaginative and inflexible NEI command in which morale was low, communications were appalling and Intelligence non-existent. They insisted that they were unable to operate anywhere outside the security of their Bandoeng headquarters.

By 2 March, the only effective fighting force left in western Java ranged against an enemy that Blackburn discovered later was 'a complete, fully-equipped division', was one ill-equipped brigade of 2000 men. Schilling, whose tactical abilities Blackburn respected, could do little in the face of the timid vacillation of his superiors. That afternoon, Schilling pressed for confirmation that Blackburn would send troops to counter-attack at Purwakarta. Blackburn declined, except 'under express orders from the C-in-C'.[10] Sitwell backed him up.

Matters were not going well for the Dutch. Both their counter-attacks in the centre failed miserably. Sitwell found them 'dispirited' and defeatist. Ter Poorten pressed on with abandoning Batavia and Buitenzorg and ordered all his forces to retreat to Bandoeng. Muddle and confusion reigned, with panicky rumours of parachutists landing, orders and counter-orders. Blackburn confidently agreed to hold out against the Japanese for a further twenty-four hours so that the NEI force could withdraw by road and rail through Buitenzorg.

He did everything they asked. By three o'clock on 5 March, after providing cover for the Dutch – who by then had demolished the harbour installations at Tanjong Priok and were on their way to Bandoeng – his rearguard joined him in Sukabumi.

The first air raid casualties arrived at the Christylijk Lyceum on 1 March. From then on, sick and wounded flooded in from Batavia, many having travelled down through Sumatra from Malaya. Captain Simone solved the nursing problem by arranging with the Red Cross for a party of Dutch VADs and their matron to come up from the Military Hospital in Batavia. Matron Borgman-Brouwer – Mickey – was the daughter of the second-last Governor-General of the Netherlands East Indies. Her brood of 'helpsters', as the VADs were called, were young, well-off Dutch girls much in awe of their formidable matron.

Their train finally crawled into Bandoeng Station at two o'clock on the morning of 2 March, having been delayed by Japanese aircraft bombing the line. No one met them at the station, their luggage had disappeared, and Mickey gave short shrift to the elderly and unhelpful Dutch Red Cross medical officer who at first declined to put himself out over their accommodation. Eventually, she settled her charges into beds at a local hospital, and made her way to the Hotel Homan Savoy for the few hours of night that remained.

Weary heard that she had arrived and sent a car for her. Over sherry, Mickey studied the bunch of English and Australian doctors, unable to decide who was in command. Everyone was charming and talkative. A tall, softly-spoken, dark-haired officer of much the same height as herself sat down next to her; it was not until he had been chatting to her for twenty minutes that she realised he was her commanding officer, Lieut-Colonel Dunlop.

Weary took her on an inspection tour. Two hundred and fifty patients were already in beds in wards converted from the twenty or so classrooms at the rear of the building and in the vast surgical ward behind the reception area. Ambulances 'kept driving up with new patients', who were transferred to mattresses on the floor of the entrance hall.[11] Weary left her with John Disse and the two of them spent an hour discussing the most urgent requirements. The nurses were to begin work next day. Disse disappeared to organise the repair of the water supply and find billets for the women; Mickey returned to a meeting in town with her nurses. That afternoon, she acquired forty more nurses who had been sent up from Batavia and billeted hazardously near Andir aerodrome, where they had been terrified by the constant bombing and machine gun fire.

Weary was impressed by his new matron-in-chief. Her tall, spare, imperious form seemed to be everywhere from that day on. ' . . . The taps began to run, the operating theatre was cleaned, the men unpacked [stores]; beds, mattresses, blankets, linen and all kinds of . . . gear appeared'.[12] She found Weary 'admirable' to work for, giving her autonomy over the nursing side, but always 'ready to help, no matter how busy he was'.[13]

Mickey was not used to being denied anything, and she and John Disse made a persuasive pair, wheedling goods out of merchants, even ferreting out three lights for the operating theatre from local shopkeepers.

Many of the VADs spoke little English and their sheltered backgrounds had never exposed them to the helplessness of delirious or purging men, or the menial messiness of blood, excreta, bedpans and cleaning, but the few who complained were swiftly dealt with by their peers and all buckled to under the eyes of Mickey and the orderlies. WOI Topping was profoundly impressed by their lack of squeamishness and the matter-of-fact way they would strip the wounded patients of their sarongs and set about washing them.

Casualties from the battle at Leuwiliang began to arrive in a steady stream on the night of 4-5 March. Around 150 men were cleared through the 22nd Field Ambulance and brought up to Bandoeng by rail and ambulance car, practically all of them arriving within twelve hours of leaving the field. Weary noticed that 'some . . . casualties were severe and arrived in an extremely shocked condition', yet 'none of the wounded from this battle died after admission'.[14] For the first time since the 2/2nd CCS had begun training in Brisbane twenty-two months previously, the unit was functioning as it had been trained to do. Four months ago, Weary had drilled them to a pitch of efficiency at Beit Jirja. Now his staff of CCS personnel cobbled together with army and air force medical units, swung straight into a routine of resuscitation, surgery and nursing.

They began operating about 2 am and throughout that day and the next both tables were in action continuously. Apart from an occasional brief spell, neither team left the operating theatre until all cases had been transferred to the wards. During the night of 4-5 March, 'thirty to forty casualties . . . were operated upon'. Weary recognised with a shock his old Wallaby friend and front row forward from Sydney, Denny Love, the lower half of his body damaged by shrapnel; and learned that another Wallaby, Cliff Lang, was missing with a company of the 2/2nd Pioneers. Private Eric Beverley, whose appendix he had removed on the *Orcades*, was back, 'near dead, with a great deal of his jaw and carotid artery blown away'.[15]

The lorries and ambulances continued to roll up the drive between the flower beds with their terrible cargo of 'macerated bodies', leaving him with a feeling of 'unreality about wounded men'. During a break from operating, he moved towards an ambulance. One man, leg blown off at the thigh with the artery exposed, his stretcher and clothes saturated in blood, rejected the morphia he was about to give him. 'Don't worry about me sir, I'm done for.'

Surgeons and theatre staff had had no sleep for two nights. Work was still 'hectic' on the morning of 6 March when Weary was called out of the theatre to see the British ADMS. Eyes gritty from lack of sleep, he heard Maisey say that the Dutch 'were likely to capitulate very soon'. The British forces proposed to make for the south coast and continue fighting a guerilla action against the Japanese. The hospital must 'remain functioning and be captured'. Weary told Maisey that he would stay, but 'what about the light sick patients and the bulk of the staff?'[16] The officers were summoned to Weary's office, where Maisey announced that Bandoeng was about to fall: all patients and any staff not required would be given an opportunity to leave Bandoeng that night and fall back into the hills near the south coast to continue a guerilla resistance. Weary disagreed: while Blackforce was 'still retiring on Bandoeng . . . GOC Blackforce and the RAF [should] be consulted before any change in the hospital function was made'.[17] The others were silent. Maisey made some vague gesture of acceptance and left.

While they were discussing the fate of the patients, Maisey had suggested that Weary should 'attempt to procure a hospital ship to evacuate patients and Red Cross personnel after the capitulation'. An admiral who admitted to responsibility for naval affairs at NEI headquarters looked at him in astonishment when faced with the request. His response was abrupt. 'Quite out of the question!'

Saturday hummed with 'wild rumours'. They all believed privately that there was 'no chance of escape'.[18] Maisey left Bandoeng with British Headquarters on Friday night, taking with him Captain Beadnell, an RAMC man who had helped out with administrative work for a few days. Weary did not see him again; instead, he was handed a letter informing him that, as the Senior Medical Officer for all British troops in the Bandoeng area, he must remain at Bandoeng with the entire staff and patients 'until the order to cease fire for British troops was given'.[19]

Maisey's new direction contradicting the earlier orders angered him, and since his brush with the admiral, he did not think much of the suggestion that the Japanese would agree to patients and Red Cross personnel being evacuated on a hospital ship. Very early that morning, he attended a conference of senior Blackforce officers at their head-quarters near Tjirandjan and heard that the Dutch were about to capitulate. Blackforce would begin to withdraw towards Garoet at last light that evening, blowing the first bridge at 8.30 am the following morning behind them.

The letter in his pocket, he drove across Bandoeng to NEI head-quarters and again canvassed the possibility of a hospital ship. The admiral had flown: a captain was now in charge. He was as dismissive as his superior officer had been. A Dutch hospital ship, clearly marked, had just been sunk. It was 'extremely unlikely that the governments concerned would agree to such a . . . proposition'.[20] Even if the navy agreed, opined a pompous Red Cross official whom he called on next, such a proposal would need to be ratified by all three governments, British, Dutch and Japanese.

The nearest hospital ship was the *Oranje*, then in Fremantle. Until 19 February, the *Manunda* had waited in Darwin Harbour in obedience to ABDA Command's signal from Batavia a week beforehand that she should be held 'at Darwin until further notice'.[21] She was disabled during a bombing raid and had to withdraw to Fremantle for repairs. The Military Board in Australia had hoped to turn the *Oranje* round on 4 March, but the Dutch would not concur.

Eadie called in on Saturday afternoon on his way south ahead of the force. Weary was emphatic that 'all staff over . . . the minimum required to care for patients after capture, and all patients able to march and look after themselves' must be allowed to join the rest of the force concentrating towards the south coast and the tiny port near Pameung-peuk, according to Maisey's earlier suggestion. But Eadie 'differed', and after a brief and heated exchange, he 'ordered in writing that the instruction of ADMS British troops be adhered to in detail'.[22]

Weary, 'despairing' at yet another example of Eadie's 'sheer lunacy' and intransigence (but humouring his senior officer, who was behaving 'like a fractious child') 'asked to be given leave to discuss the matter further with GOC British Forces and GOC Blackforce and to be permitted to take action according to orders given'.[23] Eadie agreed, told him where to find Blackforce HQ and left the building quickly. The Japanese were said by the Dutch to be on the northern outskirts of Bandoeng. Throughout the day, their planes swept over the city, bombing and machine gunning streets and buildings, making the 'pressure of work in the hospital . . . intense'. Wounded were coming in faster than staff could unpack and assemble beds and stretchers.

Weary leapt into his car smartly and directed the driver to a point off the main road near Tjirandjan. Sitwell was at Blackburn's head-quarters, just back from a lengthy reconnaissance of the area around Trogong, Garoet and Tjikadjang. Producing Maisey's letter, Weary asked for a ruling: he needed only four officers and sixty ORs to care for the patients. Sitwell and Blackburn 'went up in the air'. There was no time for written orders. Weary was told 'to pick out the fellows who could still walk and possibly fight and allot them to the retreating forces'.[24] It was already four o'clock. Those who could leave would need to make their way to a rendezvous with the last of the column in movement that night, and only hospital transport was available to cover the thirty-two kilometres from the Dagoweg to the rendezvous point at Tjitjalengka. He returned to the Dagoweg and 'assembled the hospital'.

The staff of No. 1 Allied General Hospital listened to his announcement that the hospital would be captured, but that only 4 officers and 60 ORs need remain with it: everyone else could go. He called for volunteers to stay from amongst the medical staff, adding that he would not be leaving. 'What would you do?' someone asked. He longed to tell them that he 'would have given [his] back teeth to be able to peel off and try to get away ', join the column, go on fighting. But he had no choice. This was his third retreat, but this time, for him, there would be no escape.

There was no more discussion, no hesitation: 'We prefer to stay here with you, Sir.' Blue Butterworth thought their chances of escaping were slim; he would rather pin his faith on Weary. The others agreed. They didn't think that anyone would get away and now that the rainy season had begun in earnest, sleeping rough in the jungle while slapping off the mosquitoes held little appeal.

Bandoeng was declared an 'open city' that evening. Jock Clarke slipped his little revolver into his pocket when he and Chaplain Tom Elliot decided to walk into town and call on the Bishop. 'Took the Biretta to pieces & threw it away on the way back.'[25] Jock had lovingly cared for the Biretta since Tobruk – it was a wrench to destroy it.

Weary drove to Tjitjalengka through the Dutch patrols. They were 'highly jumpy', waving the car down and questioning him when it pulled in. But when they learned that he 'was going to contact the British forces who were withdrawing [with] an important message', they clapped him on the back, cheering him 'to the echo'. When he caught up with the column, he was 'stuck up by sentries presenting their rifles'. Eventually, Major H. C. Greiner of the 2/3rd Machine Gun Battalion appeared and took Weary's proffered note explaining to Blackburn that staff and patients were staying at the hospital 'with the patients in their care, but expressed their complete willingness to undertake any further medical services which 'Blackforce' might require'.[26]

The return journey through the Dutch patrols and pickets was not so comfortable – 'they practically spat at me . . . [because] I was going back to Bandoeng to be captured', rather than fight.

At 9 am on 8 March, the wireless set in the hospital was turned up hastily as a solemn voice announced that 'all organised resistance having now ceased' troops were to lay down their arms. Everyone – Dutch, Australian, British – was wondering how they would be treated. People began to recall sensational details about the massacre of staff and patients at the Alexandra Hospital in Singapore – at the time, they had been 'too busy to feel much fear', but now they remembered the reports of 'rape and mass killings'. The VADs were 'very depressed'; few knew what had happened to their families in Batavia. Some had husbands with the Dutch forces.

Once more, Weary gathered everyone together. From now on, the town outside the hospital fences was out of bounds except for those on official business; the most 'exacting discipline' must be maintained. All ranks were instructed to give only their name, number and rank if they were questioned by the Japanese.

The hospital buildings were now 'grossly overcrowded with well over 600 patients and . . . staff'. Weary smelt once again the acrid odour of a retreating army as bonfires of burning paper consumed all documents likely to divulge information to the enemy, including personal diaries. Unit information on field medical cards and other medical papers was rubbed out or obliterated. 'All weapons in the hospital pack store including rifles, bren guns, tommy guns, pistols and grenades were put out of action and deeply buried or thrown into ponds.'[27] All, that is, except Weary's pair of .38 pistols, which he shoved to the back of the safe in his office.

No. 1 Allied General Hospital had been functioning only eighteen days. Ahead lay the shame and 'great misfortune of becoming prisoners of war'.[28]

They 'spent all day waiting for the Japs',[29] but all that arrived was the final order for surrender from the Dutch and a hotch-potch of news from which it was difficult to separate the rumours. The Japanese were riding their bicycles through plantations on the outskirts of town; the Japanese were in Bandoeng; yet they were nowhere to be seen. Tjilatchap was a shambles with 'frightful casualties'; there were few ships, for 'hysterical demolition' had destroyed most; boats crowded with over 3000 refugees and RAF personnel had been lost with 'no survivors', sunk by 'a Jap fleet waiting off the south coast [for] . . . everything that came out'.[30]

The town was full of civilian refugees from Batavia and Semerang and all the country in between, every house and hotel being crowded with people. A stream of wounded and dying had arrived in the hospitals after air raid shelters were hit on Saturday morning and fires had broken out all over the city. Vehicles must fly a white flag, or they would be fired upon by the enemy. Dutch patrols had snapped this at Weary on his way back from the rendezvous point during the night, but as he had not heard of the British forces capitulating, he had ignored it then.

For three days, they existed in a vacuum. Wounded and sick continued to be brought to the door, filling the already crowded accommodation to capacity, covering every spare floor space in wards and corridors. Food became more difficult to obtain, for Dutch Ordnance no longer delivered rations. Clean linen ran out when the military laundry ceased to function. Not a word was heard from Sitwell or Blackburn, although various Dutch sources insisted that they, too, had surrendered. The Union Jack, the Australian, Dutch and Red Cross flags continued to fly bravely over the door, when the streets of Bandoeng had broken out in an ingratiating flurry of Japanese bunting flapping from windows and flagpoles.

Weary stood on the steps of the hospital under 'the only Allied flags now flying' and watched the Imperial Japanese Army roll triumphal down the Dagoweg towards the centre of town. Long columns of tanks, artillery, infantry and supporting services flowed past. Some of the troops were on lorries, but the greater number were on foot, looking 'tired and worn'.[31] In the midst of this display, he could see a small car crawling up the street against the tide of tanks and khaki uniforms. To everyone's amazement, it turned into the Christylijk Lyceum drive and a Dutchwoman jumped out and dashed up the steps to Weary. 'Someone must come quickly,' she stammered. 'I need an officer to come quickly to my house. There are Japanese soldiers there and they are looting it.'

'Madam,' replied Weary, 'there are Japanese soldiers all over Bandoeng. There is nothing we can do.'

'But there are Dutch nurses there. They will be raped. I need some Dutch officers – where are they?'

The Dutch officers shrank back behind the others. She grabbed Weary's sleeve. 'You must come with me!'

He retrieved his pistols from the safe, put one in each pocket of his bush jacket, and glumly walked down the steps to the car. 'Let me come with you, Sir!' called out Gibbie,* pushing forward, but Weary waved him away. 'It's enough for one fool to get killed,' he said, as he squeezed into the front passenger seat. In defiance of Japanese orders to clear the streets, they drove back through the startled troops, Weary slapping his red cross brassard whenever it looked as if they would be stopped by surprised and hostile military police.

Two very frightened girls were in the front garden when they pulled up. There were Japanese all over the house, sprawled and slumped on sofas, chairs, beds and the floor, staring at the girls' bare legs and arms when they walked through. Weary was nervous as a cat, trying to keep his elbows over his pockets, while he was pawed and patted by attentive soldiers and, with much 'loud-voiced pantomime', he attempted to explain that he must take the nurses to the hospital. How they missed finding the pistols he never knew. The girls scrabbled together a few things and appeared in the doorway clutching their suitcases.

'I *shoko*!' roared Weary, pointing to his insignia. 'You – ', pointing at a Japanese private, 'carry suitcases!' But even a soldier who barely reached his chest could not be intimidated that easily. Weary carried the suitcases himself, and they put-puttered off before any more curious hands had an opportunity to discover the pistols.

The houses in the European quarter surrounding the hospital were large and solidly comfortable. Owners had ignored the order to provide billets for the occupying troops, so Japanese soldiers just marched in and ejected the occupants. The often luxurious surroundings were soon reduced to untidy squalor. Within a few hours, all the helpsters had fled from their billets to sanctuary in the hospital buildings.

The hospital flags were lowered prudently at sunset and hidden.

There were no more quiet moments to worry about their possible fate, and the hospital was left pretty much to its own devices. Over a thousand were now living there, even lorries and ambulances parked in the gardens being used for sleeping.

Some enemy troops wandered in seeking unofficial dental or medical care, or attempted to acquire cars or petrol. But Weary and the others refused the last two 'on the grounds of no authority'. All over the city, Japanese soldiers were 'using cars after the fashion of new mechanical toys and after smashing them in unskilled attempts at driving, merely went to find another one'.[32]

---

* Staff-Sgt Alan Gibson, the wardmaster at the hospital.

Patients were well looked after, and the surgeons and physicians grasped the opportunities for follow-up treatment, such as skin grafting by the Reverdin and Thiersh techniques. Not everyone's skin grafts took: one of the patients fell in love with a helpster and Weary raised his eyebrows when he succeeded in losing the grafts on his stomach and thighs. He knew what he had been up to; the patient looked sheepish, but was unrepentant.

Venereal disease patients were isolated from the others in the hutments run up in the gardens at the rear of the building. Syphilis, gonorrhoea, soft sore and lymphogranuloma were rife amongst the native population and afflicted troops reported sick from the time the CCS set up in Bandoeng, sometimes suffering from two or three of these diseases simultaneously. Squadron-Leader Cumming, who presided over the pathology department, took charge of their treatment. Most were already in Java when the force from the Middle East arrived, some being deserters from Singapore and Malaya 'with a most clouded military record'. The others were RAF men, whose hygiene was poor enough for the medical officer on board the *Orcades* to comment on it when he had a large group of them in his care between Batavia and Colombo.[33] After capitulation, the number of cases grew daily. A small group of these VD patients from Singapore were light-fingered and devious. Warrant Officer Dave Topping caught them selling hospital blankets through the fence to the natives. They retaliated roughly, threatening to cut his throat if he said anything, but no regimental sergeant major was going to be intimidated by that. Weary paraded the offenders and doled out solitary confinement on rice and water. They were a source of trouble for some time.

The Dutch forces began to file down from the hills on Monday 9 March, signifying their surrender with white towels round their necks, and were herded into camps. Weary knew little of what was happening outside and set off in search of the Japanese Commander.

Colonel Minnamota commanding the Bandoeng area had taken over the Hotel Preangar for his headquarters, and Weary made his way into the very grand, pillared Art Deco lobby past men of the 2nd Japanese Guards Division, who were openly interested in his height and physique whilst he awaited permission to see Minnamota. John Disse stuck close to him as he strode through the reception area to Minnamota's office and succeeded in making his case for two passes for movement about the town: one for him, one for the interpreter, valid for seven days.

The appalling reality of their situation struck Weary when a party of neat and polite little Japanese medical officers led by Colonel Minnamoto appeared at the door to the Christylijk Lyceum and announced their intention of inspecting the hospital. From now on, he must obey the orders of an enemy whose knowledge of modern equipment, instruments and methods was 'most vague'. A naîve request from Lieut-Colonel Odakura, the head of the medical service, for 'the recipe to make dried plasma from blood' so that the enquirer could carry out this process in the field – where, apparently, the Imperial Japanese Army used only saline transfusion – astonished him. But even while Mickey and he were escorting the senior officers around, Weary only narrowly concealed his amusement at how ridiculous a sight the two of them presented, bean-pole tall, rising out of the cluster of short, serious, bespectacled little men. A Japanese sentry now stood stiffly by the gate.

The inspecting officers failed to notice a portrait of Queen Wilhelmina hanging on an inside wall under the Dutch and Orange flags.

The pass gave Weary some freedom outside the hospital grounds and when it expired, Disse forged seven-day extensions for them both. It took three days of argument and negotiation to obtain a small issue of petrol to add to the stocks they had concealed; all further requests were refused.

The helpsters were still allowed to come and go and somehow food was brought in, linen was laundered and delivered. Townspeople, too, were generous with books and food, even money. Dutch officers managed also to send in a liberal supply of guilders for the patients, few of whom had any cash.

Mickey, Disse and Andrew Crichton slipped out to forage for food. Chinese merchants supplied rice and tinned goods and natives hawking vegetables were called in off the street, so that everyone had enough to eat, even if rice was not at all to their taste.

As wounded and sick began to come in from the captured troops, wards and grounds become even more cramped, taxing severely the native-style latrines. Jock Clarke's staff were constantly and unpleasantly employed taking up and unblocking pipes to keep the sewage flowing out into the open drains that criss-crossed the town. Flies were breeding up in the VD compound and the back garden where Jock's team had dug deep trench latrines. Weary's concern about epidemics grew as the number of dysentery patients increased.

He settled with the Dutch that convalescent patients could transfer to Sol Sana, a convalescent hospital run by a Dutch couple some kilometres away on the edge of Bandoeng. Using hoarded petrol, Lieutenant Smedley and his drivers ferried the fitter men out there in ambulances and in cars lent by civilians, and the Dutch – who, after a fortnight, had begun delivering food under the supervision of the IJA – shuttled their rations across. Weary concealed their transfer in his returns and the Japanese ignored them officially. By the end of March, ninety-four men had been moved there.

Eadie turned up several times, as did Maisey and his DADMS, ostensibly engaged in co-ordinating medical arrangements for the troops, and they all stayed in the Dagoweg. Their peregrinations were curtailed abruptly when the Japanese sent them to Batavia on 24 March, dangling the prospect of their opening a hospital, but throwing them into gaol instead. Blackburn, however, continued to move about the area fairly freely, arranging for sick troops to come from Garoet and Leles, where Blackforce was imprisoned.

A leading aircraftsman, Bill Griffiths, was rushed in from Garoet, both eyes shattered in a wrecked face, hands blown away, a broken leg, and his whole body 'peppered everywhere with imbedded fragments' from a mine explosion. He had lost a great deal of blood.

'Surprised that he should have reached hospital at all', Weary 'illogically' took him straight to the theatre and operated. Mickey pleaded with him not to save a life that Weary himself considered 'less than kindness to try to prolong'. Griffiths slipped in and out of consciousness over the next few days, begging Mickey Borgmann-Brouwer to let him die, to give him 'something, anything', but without Weary's permission she could do nothing. And when she confronted her commanding officer with the demand that if he would not end Griffith's life, she would, Weary looked steadily at her. 'My job is to save lives, not end them.'[34]

When it came to the point, she could not bring herself to administer the longed-for injection of morphine. Griffiths survived despite his overwhelming injuries.

Air Vice Marshal Maltby's car was smashed up on 19 March and Maltby arrived in the hospital with severe concussion and a fractured skull. A small room was turned out hurriedly and he was installed in it.

Weary felt as if they were existing in the quiet eye of a storm which would soon engulf them.

Captain Nakazawa of Minnamota's Staff and two other officers erupted into the hospital on 4 April, and the *laissez-faire* atmosphere of the previous three weeks dissolved without warning. First, they 'furiously ordered' that Queen Wilhelmina's portrait and the Dutch flag be taken down (but overlooked the Orange flag, much to Weary's amusement). Dave Topping held his breath when Weary snapped back, 'Take it down yourself!'[35] All the helpsters must be out of the hospital in a week. When Weary protested, Nakazawa grabbed Weary by the arm. 'Not used to people laying hands' on him, Weary 'threw him across the room' in a potent mix of rage, shame and exasperation. To his astonishment, although the officer 'fronted up to [him] in a very angry fashion', he did not dole out any punishment.

Earlier, although not without difficulty and a couple of days of 'tedious argument', Weary had extricated from the *kempeitai* gaol a party of sick bound for the Dagoweg but arrested on the whim of the Japanese military police and tossed into a cell as 'fit men, although several . . . had obviously been severely wounded' by bayonetting.

With the appearance of Nakazawa, his bargaining powers vanished. Medical staff officers now raged into the building at any hour, screaming 'DUNROPO!', issuing 'unreasonable' demands, such as ordering all red crosses to be obliterated, even scraped or scrubbed off walls, demanding inspections in the middle of the night, ignoring rank and proscribing all contact with the outside world. Visitors and parcels were forbidden. The single sentry was replaced by a perimeter guard of Dutch military police. Nominal rolls of all personnel and patients were to be submitted: name, age, profession, address, race, rank, and whether active or reserve. Weary consulted Maltby and they decided on only name, number and nationality.[36]

Weary chose to misunderstand the direction that all vehicles be turned in and kept back the ambulances and trucks. Nakazawa stormed back to the hospital, ordered that they also be sent and demanded the nominal rolls yet again. There were 714 patients in the Dagoweg that night, 166 at Sol Sana. They had no means of transferring any more convalescents – mercurial Japanese promises to send motor transport for the sick were broken without warning – nor of collecting sick men, who were left in railway trucks until the Japanese felt like picking them up from Bandoeng Station. Disse's wife lent Weary her bicycle. He was riding this on the day that he narrowly escaped being crushed deliberately against a wall by a lorry-load of Japanese soldiers.

The nurses and their matron were to go on Friday 10 April. It was an emotional day. They finished the gin at the party which the officers gave in the mess, then Mickey and the helpsters threw a party in the main ward for the patients with lemonade, cigarettes and cake that 'cost . . . prodigious efforts to procure'.[37] Mickey walked out of the hospital for the last time and across the road to her room in a house owned by an elderly Dutch doctor. The hospital had been remarkable for 'co-operation and goodwill between all members of staff . . . of the highest order' under a commanding officer 'respected and admired by all'.[38]

Minnamota's adjutant, 1st Lieutenant Sumiya, and four guards with fixed bayonets presented themselves to Weary the following Monday, demanding that he produce all the fit men by four o'clock for transfer to another, unspecified, place. Lieutenant Rintoul and 28 of the Christylijk Lyceum men were removed, together with 75 sent in from Sol Sana.

That week, Captain Nakazawa, who seemed to have acquired complete responsibility for the hospital, became increasingly 'trying'. Finally, early on the morning of Friday 17 April, he clashed violently with Weary over the division of patients and staff: Weary and a few staff were to stay with the more seriously ill, the rest of the patients and medical staff would be removed immediately to prison camp 'the same . . . as other soldiers'. They were to be sorted into three categories: lying, sitting and walking cases. Weary protested at the inclusion of a group 'whose lives would be endangered by movement'. Nakazawa contemptuously brushed aside the lists and stamped off with his escort to inspect some ten surgical patients in the resuscitation ward.

Weary led him across to the two boys with shattered faces who had been blinded by the mine explosion. Nakazawa motioned a guard towards Bill Griffiths. From a nearby bed, John Denman saw the guard 'put one up the spout'.

Weary moved swiftly between Griffiths and the rifle as the guard, 'yelling threateningly', thrust the bayonet towards the motionless man in the bed. Griffiths knew none of this – only sensed danger – before Weary's voice rang out: 'If you are going to do that, you must go through me first.'[39] He 'glared' at Nakazawa, who moved his gaze after a few 'tense' moments and gestured towards a paraplegic. Without taking his eyes off the Japanese, Weary placed himself between this patient and the soldiers. The ward was still, the paraplegics' eyes 'dark with fright in their sweating faces'. It seemed a long time before the staff captain moved on, striking 'contemptuously' the legs of other patients: 'Man walk'.

Griffiths was to be a sitting patient, the first blind boy a walking one. Nakazawa refused to look at x-ray film and strolled round the ward;

classifications were arrived at by throwing back the blankets and inspecting mens' legs, occasionally feeling their calves.

Weary now weighed into him about the rights of medical personnel under the Geneva Convention, but he waved this aside airily: 'Japan had signed no Conventions and the Japanese people lived their own convention.' He denied that General Maruyama had signed a letter stating that Japan would observe both the Geneva and The Hague conventions after capitulation. That Air Vice Marshal Maltby had a copy cut no ice with Nakazawa – he declined to look at it. Their conversation became increasingly heated on Nakazawa's part, steely with controlled anger on Weary's, who told Nakazawa that the British, Dutch and Australian governments would ultimately hold him responsible for such 'illegal' actions, and he had no doubt he would be 'hanged'.

'Good!' spat Nakazawa. 'Now you will lead the march to gaol.'[40]

EIGHTEEN

Singing and Games Forbidden

NAKAZAWA'S CLASSIFICATION GAMES took all day. Around six o'clock that evening, Weary was ordered to assemble his staff and walking patients outside the hospital in ten minutes, ready to move. 'Impossible,' he said. The arguments began again. Finally, Nakazawa hit on some mysterious face-saving solution not evident to Weary and conceded him one night to pack up. They were to be ready to move off at 9.30 am on Saturday; the stretcher and sitting patients would go two hours later. Some junior RAF doctors – Kinmonth, Simpson, Park, Rutherford, MacSwiney and Connolly – and Staff Sergeant Gibson would remain with the worst patients in a Dutch military hospital at Tjimahi.

Nakazawa forbade the removal of medical stores, surgical equipment or drugs. Weary, Arthur Moon and Ewan Corlette took no notice. Essential drugs and instruments were made up into small packages and 'as many instruments as possible, sulphanilamide & quinine etc. [were] spread over patients',[1] who also carried their own medical records and X-rays. John Disse risked capture by the heavy guard now in place around the perimeter and smuggled out some bulky records and valuable instruments, together with the records of patients who had been discharged.*

Weary and Arthur Moon applied plaster spicas to three men with fractured femurs. Jock Clarke spent the night in his dental surgery, finishing fillings and dentures and fitting the latter. Weary and John Morris attempted to bring all the documentation up to date: nominal rolls, the admission and discharge book, the unit diary, part II orders, promotions, burial returns, postings, and recommendations for awards. Morris audited the hospital accounts and the funds – the gulden equivalent of £3947 – were distributed for the journey between nineteen

---

* These were buried but not recovered after the war.

officers and NCOs and the chaplains, £1600 going to MacSwiney for Tjimahi.

After 'an extremely busy night practically none of staff having had much sleep', Weary marched boldly down the drive to the gate onto the Dagoweg. He had 'decided . . . to contact Matron Borgmann-Brouer to seek her help in hiding and preserving [the] war diary, part II orders recording promotions . . . citations recommending awards and a couple of special instruments'. Only bluff would get him past the sentry, and he proposed to try out an American flying officer's recipe for crises: 'Have something to recite with great emotion . . . Then brush aside any resistance and walk through.'

'When I have seen by Time's fell hand defaced/ the rich, proud cost of outworn hurried age . . . ' he proclaimed, bag of contraband in his left hand, right hand and arm describing grand motions in the chill early morning air as he recited the octave of Shakespeare's famous sonnet. With one final gesture, he swept aside the pop-eyed little sentry's bayonet and strode across the road, his back feeling 'exposed and uneasy'. By the time the sentry had discovered the initiative to call his commander for guidance, Weary was through the doorway of the house opposite. Inside stood Mickey. She had seen everything through the window. Weary told her that they were leaving for prison in a few hours and then, on an impulse, took her in his arms and kissed her. When he let her go, Mickey stepped back and said a little unsteadily in her deep voice: 'Oh, what a pity . . . '[2]

Weary called the staff together for the last time and 'complimented [them] on their devoted work'. During their eighteen days as No 1 Allied General Hospital, they had treated 1351 patients – British, Australian, Dutch and American – with only nine deaths.

The kitchen supplied breakfast. Everyone was equipped with rations, a blanket, a spare set of clothing, a full water bottle, and a book from the library. Nakazawa had cleared Sol Sana of patients, also, and they arrived at half past eight. Promptly at 9.30 am, Lieutenant Kikooka drove up.

Plainly, the brutal behaviour of the previous day was to be continued. 'Of 300 sick discharged, only approx. 50 [were] fit for such a march with all gear', yet Kikooka forbade their ambulances to accompany them to pick up those who collapsed, and refused requests for a hired cart to carry cooking gear and medical equipment. The three ambulances, medical equipment and stores remaining in the hospital were confiscated and never seen again.

All the officers carried their own baggage. Weary and Butterworth slung his valise 'stuffed with medical gear', a side haversack containing instruments, drugs and some heavy Dutch medical texts and an RAP pannier and the rest of their personal baggage on a bamboo pole – Weary, a good deal taller, took most of the burden of the 115 kilos. The heat was intense. He was streaming with sweat in the high humidity. Laden like pack mules, they trudged for seven kilometres and almost two hours; boots and bayonets dissuading anyone who fell by the roadside from staying there more than a very short time. 'Fortunately there were rests.' The streets were lined with Dutch, offering help, waving sympathetically, and being kicked by the guards for their concern.

'Bit of a *via dolorosa* for pale wilting wrecks.'

The 'formidable, walled, stone building with confining iron bars' of Landsopvoedingsgesticht was set well back from the unpaved Dandelsweg. Broad, high wooden doors swung open to admit the exhausted men, who were ordered to drop their baggage outside. Despite the fact that 'our necks and shoulders ached painfully and knees wobbled', Weary refused until a frantic sentry began to beat him about the shoulders with a rifle butt and he realised that an inspection by a visiting senior officer was to take place.

After a sketchy inspection, count and baggage search, during which cameras, gramophones, metal objects and weapons, compasses and maps were confiscated, they were hustled through a gate into 'an unbelievably small space' fenced off from the rest of the compound. In a 'pukka prison atmosphere',[3] Weary was greeted by Lieutenant Rintoul and the patients who had left them five days beforehand.

Concrete dormitories and verandahs ran round two sides of an area into which the 536 men were herded, with a dozen showers and primitive native latrines common to all, including the 60 VD patients (twenty of whom had active syphilis). Yet the 'troops were in amazing fettle, singing songs to [the] tune of an accordion', despite no food since eight o'clock that morning and no shelter for 150 of them. They would have to sleep in the open on the sodden, muddy ground between the buildings and the barbed wire if Weary was unable to arrange an alternative.

He handed over to his second-in-command, Squadron-Leader Mac-Grath, and set off to report to the Dutch commandant of the camp,

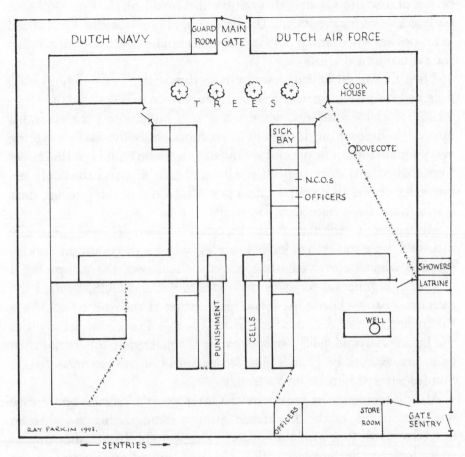

Landsopvoedingsgesticht Camp: normal accommodation 500 native boys – here 530 British troops and 700 Dutch troops

Overste van Lingham, and complain about their lack of shelter. Eventually, van Lingham persuaded the Japanese to allow a hundred of the new arrivals to spend part of the night under verandahs on the other side of the wire.

The Dutch were astonishingly optimistic: Major Sarabaer from Dutch Ordnance hailed him with the glad news that they would be liberated in 100 days according to an old Javanese legend. The Americans were already invading the islands; Tokyo and Yokohama had been bombed! In a matter of days, Weary concluded that much of the 'news' was invented. The Dutch were always full of gossip and rumours.

That night, Saturday, 18 April 1942, Weary drew a plan of their prison and wrote his first diary entry in a small black notebook that replaced, as an *aide mémoire*, the brown field notebook he had carried in his pocket since landing in Greece. It would be easier to conceal than the official unit diaries.

Their first night in prison was a miserable affair. The buildings were designed for juvenile native criminals. Seventeen officers squashed into a room 4.25 by 9 metres, while ten others huddled on the verandah outside. Wherever one looked in the compound, bodies were 'covering every square foot of floors and verandah'; men who could not find cover were soaked and shivering by reveille next morning and the proffered breakfast of one slice of dry bread per person did nothing to lift their spirits. Saturday's buoyancy had vanished.

Minnamota's adjutant, 1st Lieutenant Sumiya, was 'mortally offended' by a soccer ball kicked carelessly in his direction on Sunday evening when he arrived unexpectedly to inspect the camp. WOI Topping, regimental sergeant major for the 2/2nd CCS, hustled the men onto parade hurriedly. From his position at the rear, he could see the cocked rifles of the guard and feared trouble. He felt intuitively that the Japanese would deliberately provoke the massed prisoners and then open fire. Backed by guards with 'magazines full and bayonets fixed', Sumiya worked himself into a frenzy.

After dismissing the troops at the interpreter's instruction, Weary was unprepared for the 'haymaker' Sumiya swung at his jaw when he moved towards him and saluted. As he threw up his hands, shooting an angry look at the Japanese officer, Sumiya 'ripped out his sword and lunged' at Weary's throat 'with a deadly tigerish thrust'. His boxer's reflexes saved his life, but 'the haft of the sword hit [his] larynx with a sickening thud'. Unable to breathe or speak, he stretched out a restraining left hand towards the troops, who had begun to surge forward, muttering angrily, and gestured at the sword with his right, fixing Sumiya with a 'livid' look. 'The guards levelled their rifles and thrust their bayonets menacingly towards them.'

The lieutenant, utterly out of control and screaming with rage, swung the sword about Weary's head, 'fanning his scalp and ears' so that he felt 'the breeze horizontal rather then vertical'.* 'Too coldly furious to

---

* Weary was recalling an old saying that one feels the breeze vertically when afraid.

flinch,' Weary stood to attention throughout, until the adjutant sheathed his sword and resumed the lecture.[4] He ended with a warning that anyone crawling through the wire would be executed. And because he had not enjoyed the hymn singing led by Padré Camroux in another corner of the camp as he ducked the soccer ball: 'Singing and games forbidden.'

Later that evening, Weary found little consolation in van Lingham telling him that Sumiya had reported at Colonel Minnamota's conference that the British troops were 'satisfactory'. He swallowed his first hot food for more than forty hours with difficulty, his breathing 'still very laboured. Depression reigns'.

Overcrowding, underfeeding and calculated brutality and humiliation characterised their weeks at Landsopvoedingsgesticht.

The Dutch had more freedom than the British, being allowed to forage for food outside the prison. Corvées equipped with handcarts left each morning, and eventually, as long as Weary's lot could find the money, they shared the costs of the fruit, vegetables, sugar and dairy products brought back in.

Within three days, John Morris had drawn up rosters and typed routine orders. He was an efficient adjutant. His work before the war in the Army Instruction Unit equipped him to organise a programme of lectures for the men, drawing on the wide experiences of officers, NCOs and other ranks. Any recreation had to suit the cramped conditions: there were lectures, language classes in Dutch, French and Malay, debates, spelling competitions, contract bridge, chess and other games. Weary joined in everything, but 'what with Dutch, French and Malay classes, I find the going a bit tough'. They could kick a soccer ball around, but there was no space for a match. PT was taken by Dutch officers at first, later by their own, except when the ground became 'too utterly mucky' after the daily afternoon downpours.

'The menace of epidemics' was 'acute', yet few of the sick who lined up for Arthur Moon's parades were seriously ill. Everyone had to struggle with using a bottle of water instead of lavatory paper, as the latter blocked the native latrines, yet dysentery never reached epidemic proportions. Tinea was the most common complaint. Squadron-Leader Cumming continued to treat the VD patients with his smuggled supply of NAB and M & B 693.

According to van Lingham, the Dutch were allowed to enter the British section, but, for some unfathomable reason, the Japanese forbade the reverse. The officers formed pickets to man the gate: 'A tedious job but can trust nobody else to do it.'[5] Only men on kitchen fatigues could pass through freely to the cookhouse outside the wire, but plenty tried to do so before escape was barbarously punished.

Five days after leaving the Dagoweg, the camp was stunned and sickened by the public bayoneting of three Dutchmen caught 'escaping', although it was more likely that they were sneaking out to see their families and would have returned that night. They were 'tied to poles, troops assembled, & bayoneted to death like pigs before their comrades'.[6] The Dutch medical officer fainted and was upbraided by the Japanese for his 'unmanliness'.

When Rintoul and Weary attended *kempeitai* headquarters in Bandoeng that evening for the first time, they saw more prisoners trussed up on the floor. A dumb show with a bayonet jabbed toward's 'the CO's tummy' showed them what was in store for any offenders. If any of his men escaped, he would be executed along with the escapees – except that, as an officer, he would be beheaded. Henceforth, he was to attend at 1800 hours daily 'to hear the Emp's orders', and was lent a bicycle for transport. Orderlies were to turn up twice a day.

'Ye Gods, the difficulties of finding out what everybody is saying.' Weary was the only British camp commander and he struggled to follow what was barked at them, since the interpeter translated only into Dutch. That evening, he followed the Dutch, echoing their *'Ijo arimasen'*, but when he discovered subsequently that it translated to 'Nothing to report', he changed to *'Ijo arimas'*, 'Something to report.'

'Ijo arimas ka? Ijo arimas ka? shouted the Japanese excitedly. Weary began to complain about the lack of space, insufficient food of poor quality, no fresh fruit, and so on, until the officer borrowed a rifle and bayonet and pushed it towards Weary's midriff. *'Ijo arimasen!'* he bawled, pricking him in the stomach. Weary took the point: there were to be no complaints. But thereafter, it became a ritual. He waited until the Dutch commanders had all stated *'Ijo arimasen'*, then said firmly, *'Ijo arimas'*. The Japanese would grab a rifle, point the bayonet at Weary's stomach with much laughter, and wait for the politically correct response.

Food and its lack dominated everyone's thoughts and became the focus of deep discontent on both sides of the wire. The Dutch controlled the food: 'I think there is some bad management in this camp, as other camps report they are at least getting as much rice as they want to eat.' There had been complaints about the change from potatoes to rice at the hospital, but at least it was tempered with meat or fish and vegetables. After the first ten days of meagre and scrappy rice dishes and soup, every meal became boiled rice.

Races for whom rice forms the staple food have evolved ways of eating the large quantities necessary to satisfy hunger. Polished rice contains few nutrients (although the local Indonesian red rice is rich in them), but the thin soups spiced with chillies, vegetables and herbs which accompany it are a source of vitamins and help the dry mouthfuls down. Sauces distilled from fish or soy provide protein and enhance the flavour; sambals and pickles stimulate the appetite. It would be months before they realised the importance of these additions.

They gagged on the cold, grey, unpalatable mass dumped in their mess tins, and forced down the tasteless liquid with a few vegetables floating in it that was issued last thing at night. Some of the Dutch developed scurvy, refusing to tolerate the soup and therefore depriving themselves of the little vitamin C it contained.

Eventually, the food supplied by the Dutch kitchens became so bad and the arguments so acrimonious that Weary announced that his people would 'lay on a team for cooking for the whole camp'. The Dutch naval prisoners (who were also discontented with the cooking) set up a committee, to which Weary appointed Lieutenant Ian Cameron as his representative, and on 4 May they began a 'large-scale Dutch smuggle' of illicit butter and cheese from the town.

After his hospital reserve fund ran down too fast to continue buying these fatty extras for the camp, he appealed to the troops to raise the money on a room basis. There was a disturbing tendency for them to regard the officers as being 'full of oof' and responsible for the full cost. The hospital reserve fund would continue to provide milk, jam, sugar, condiments, fish and – occasionally – chocolate.

Everyone lost weight. 'One feels hungry all the time.' On their diet of a 'moderate amount of rice three times a day' no one had energy for exercise. There was a 'tendency to slight giddiness . . . stars flash at times when one rises to the vertical'. In three weeks, Weary dropped a further six kilos: 'Big fellows like me did badly in those circumstances.' Greece, Crete and hepatitis had knocked him about; now he was more than seventeen kilos under his normal, pre-war weight. The rice diet caused embarrassing bladder problems; after some months of star-vation, it was not unusual to see men urinating on parade, incontinent and unable to help themselves.

'The living conditions of the D[utch] contrast most favourably with ours. Infinitely more space – seats everywhere to sit on, tables, chairs etc. Every officer has a bed or mattress. Commandant has excellent office, typewriter . . . [whereas] our troops . . . are having a miserable time,' housed in muddy squalor, like cattle in a yard.

Imprisonment was difficult enough for those who went into captivity with their unit, but at least they knew an *esprit de corps* and the sturdy hierarchy of officers and NCOs with their men. The commanding officer of a hospital commands a motley force: once patients are admitted, their previous commanding officers lose all title to them and responsibility passes to the CO of the medical unit. As well, Weary had a hard core of ratbags in his charge, men with no satisfactory explanation as to how they had arrived in Java but admitted suffering from VD and malaria, and their pilfering, chiacking of NCOs and officers, breaking bounds and general insubordination aggravated the friction already existing in such a disparate group of men.

Apart from the hospital staff, all those under Weary's command had been patients, admitted from British Army, AIF, RAF and RAAF sources without their officers. But whatever their origin, they were all touchy about captivity, and the constant face-slapping, kicking, shouting and generally threatening behaviour by 'little yellow men' ignited their hatred. Only constant vigilance by Weary and his fellow officers and NCOs and fear of bayoneting kept them under control.

The petty theft continued, one compulsively light-fingered bogus flight sergeant, Leach, even stealing his AIF guard's shirt when the man removed it to take a shower and selling it before its absence was discovered. Much later, he killed the camp dog and sold it as 'steaks'.

When the Japanese allowed them to move into an adjacent area of the camp vacated by the last of the Javanese 'bad boys', Weary acquired double the area and two punishment cells. He had already appointed MPs – who were never entirely satisfactory, often throwing in their sympathies with the prisoners. The cells were no more than kennels just over a metre high and wide, long enough for a man to lie down, with a small opening covered in barbed wire at one end and a barred door at the other. Solitary confinement on a diet of rice and water was cramped and unpleasant. Mostly, malefactors were sentenced to anything from one to three days of fatigues, but sterner treatment was meted out to Leach, a persistent offender.

Everyone loathed their guards. They loathed them for being the enemy, for being Japanese, for their insistence that the lowliest private must be saluted by all the prisoners from Weary down, for their barbarous behaviour, for the daily humiliations of face-slapping and bashing. Middle-of-the-night searches disturbed men who had barely dropped off to sleep in the most uncomfortable conditions.

Red Crosses were banned on Anzac Day. Brassards were to be handed in next morning, the insignia was to be obliterated, even scraped off panniers. 'It will make interesting reading one day if someone is shot for being in possession of the Red Cross!'

Three days later, all the officers had their hair cropped; and twelve days on, all badges of rank and distinguishing badges and service ribbons were to be handed in. Weary hid one full set (so did Jock, Ewen and Arthur), amused by the consternation the order caused amongst the 'D colonel squad [who] are stricken as though fox had got into [the] fowls' roost. What is the reason? Ideas: 1 humiliation; 2 cupidity – possible sale of badges; 3 having made us all privates now easy to plunder us further'.

He found these 'petty indignities . . . very difficult to endure calmly'. Jock Clarke was one of the few from whom Weary's wild mood swings – his 'ups and downs' and passionate hatred of being a captive of a race which 'despised prisoners' – were not concealed.[7] Since the capitulation, Weary had decided, 'we should all be dead . . . it wasn't right for a great body of men to surrender'. The 'humiliation . . . was horrible.' He seethed inwardly. But he had been careful not to lose his temper since the day in the Dagoweg when he threw off Sumiya's grasp. And over the months that followed, even though 'his instinct was always to interfere' at cruelty, his companions saw 'the battle that went on in him' and admired his control. Losing his temper with the Japanese 'could have been fatal'.[8] He willed himself to endure without a flicker the face slapping that accompanied many of his exchanges with their guards.

The Japanese commander had left the Australian officers pretty much alone, preferring to spend his time gossiping with van Lingham. But in the middle of May, the *kempis* pulled in first Weary, then Cumming for questioning. Weary insisted he was a 'specialist surgeon' who had 'come straight from Australia to Java' and had 'seen nothing, knew nothing, heard nothing, and just about sunk in a pit of lies'. He was dismissed

334 | Weary 1942 – 1945

with the headings for a report which was eventually 'drafted by several officers along the lines of a schoolboy essay'. Cumming proved 'just as unfruitful'. No sooner had this been completed, than both the camp and the *kempeitai* commands changed. It was accompanied by a marked increase in brutality.

Weary had been used to snatching opportunities to buy citrus fruit, bread, jam and sugar for 'the needy' in the sick bay at shops on the way back from the *kempeitai*. In the earlier days of imprisonment, 'most of the common soldiery about Bandoeng were farmers' and, away from their officers, his accompanying guards were sympathetic enough to turn their backs while he stuffed the capacious pockets of his trench coat with illicit purchases each evening. He would return bulging with edible contraband.

The day after the change, Weary was furious when their guard prevented van Lingham and him going into a shop on the way home. Only after he was bashed and searched very roughly by the sentries on the camp gate, 'and had my coat thrown at me', did he realise that his guard had 'advance knowledge' and had done him 'a great favour in not letting me purchase anything'. Some days later, another sentry encouraged a party of Dutch to buy food, then reported them. The food was confiscated and the men were bayoneted. From now on, anyone not carrying out orders issued by Japanese soldiers could be shot or bayoneted on the spot.

Initially, Weary joined in the Dutch schemes for an 'emergency rising and commando platoon', but very quickly he tumbled to the unlikelihood of these happening. Apart from the navy, they were too 'supine' a lot to achieve anything. Individually, he found many of the Dutch 'very kind', but neither Weary nor the other officers trusted the 'shifty' van Lingham, whose half-caste origins had given him a giant chip on his shoulder.

Almost from the first day in camp, Weary conducted 'a patient war with van Lingham, putting the pressure on a little more each day' for living space and food. He suspected that it was the Dutch who prevailed in terms of quarters and food, and so, subsequently, it turned out to be. No sooner had he browbeaten van Lingham into increasing the British share of extra camp accommodation and allocating them – at last – some furniture, than he was 'informed that all troops were to move . . . to Tjimahi on foot. 17 kilometres'.

Van Lingham outmanoeuvred him yet again. To carry the baggage of their 700 troops the Dutch allotted themselves 50 handcarts;

reluctantly, they gave the British, with more than 500 men (many of whom, Weary stressed, 'had been in hospital prior to prison and . . . were unfit' and therefore unable to carry much), ten. But at least there were lorries for the sick and the heaviest baggage.

For the second time in six weeks, there was 'an orgy of packing and cleaning up. Large fires for the burning of rubbish lit this pitiful scene'. The handcarts were loaded under Jock Clarke's supervision and everyone turned in for a few hours sleep. Weary spent some of this time stowing his 'contraband' – despite the warning that anyone found with forbidden items would be executed on the spot. Since leaving the Christylijk Lyceum, he had concealed a compass by taping it behind his scrotum. (He was fairly confident that it would not be found, although he had been alarmed one day when, after entertaining the guards by imitating a kangaroo, they had commented on his size and physical strength and persistently tried to inspect his genitalia.) He sewed a second compass into the bottom of a shirt, scattered his badges of rank about amongst other clothing, and slipped his maps into a secret pocket in his valise.

The main dilemma was what to do with his 'sparks', a six-valve wireless set acquired some days beforehand from a Dutch lieutenant who had jettisoned it minutes before a *kempeitai* search by persuading Rod Allanson to take it to Weary. Its size – 60 by 53 centimetres – was daunting and it was moderately heavy.

'. . . Filled our dixies with rice and had also 4 flour pancakes for the trip (cooks having worked all night). Said farewells to van Lingham [and] John [Disse] . . . at 0935 we left behind Landsopvoedingsgesticht with no regrets but little optimism as to the other end.'

Weary tucked the wireless set wrapped in camouflage sheeting under his left arm, threw his groundsheet nonchalantly over it, and 'gave a crashing salute to the guard' as he led his men onto the Dandelsweg. All that was required, he decided, 'was a bit of cheek'.

The 'extraordinary cavalcade', escorted by sentries on bicycles (who provided him with 'comic relief' by falling off frequently), passed through Bandoeng streets lined with the families of the Dutch on the march. Women wept, guards dealt out kicks and blows to the spectators, the British and Australian troops 'sang lustily' and Japanese tempers rose, until the interpreter was forced to explain to the crowd that unless they ceased following the men, there would be shooting. Once out of the city, 'the singing died away and sweat rolled forth'.

They had marched only a few kilometres before a halt was called and they were ordered to 'strip naked whilst our effects were searched'. Weary decided that his only chance of avoiding discovery lay in appointing himself 'unofficial ombudsman to plead the innocence of various articles being confiscated', and by sleight of hand and marching up and down he managed to transfer all his incriminating baggage to the searched pile. 'During this confidence trick my original jaunty optimism fell to a low ebb.'

They straggled onto an open assembly area outside the Tjimahi camp at half past one, 'many . . . swaying in their tracks and just about all in'. It was 'hot as hell' during the interminable counting of heads, and out of the confusion of bad-tempered Japanese 'appeared an amazing specimen of the Master Race who rose . . . like Aphrodite from the waves'.

Weary had already spotted some German soldiers in swastika armbands, and met the offer of help from this vision owning a 'splendidly proportioned lithe frame poured into a superbly tailored uniform tapering to shining jackboots' with contempt. 'The humiliation of the day simmered in my blood and . . . I returned the salute carelessly and without enthusiasm, coldly sweeping my eyes from his head to his feet.' Despite the insult, he 'accomplished miracles of liaison with the Japanese . . . and brought about order to the parade at last.' It was almost two hours before they filed through the lines of Japanese barracks to their own camp.

Weary was enraged by the attitude of the Dutch NCOs and privates who escorted them to their barracks and insisted that twelve of the officers would have to share with the other ranks. Demands to see the Dutch commandant produced only a Major de Vries, who met his disgust at yet again 'being played off with the N bogey' with suave assurances that he was only following Japanese instructions.

Concentration Camp No. 4 Tjimahi was much larger than Landsop, and its patrolling sentries and three barbed wire fences, one inside the other, penned them in efficiently. A road ran in from the guardhouse at the entrance to the camp and round the perimeter of a full-sized playing field, with coffee shops and a gymnasium ranged across the top end. The camp was split in two, Dutch one side, British the other. The subdued and exhausted men were surprised to find that 'there is actually a canteen in the camp and a meal is laid on for us . . . Coffee can be purchased in the evenings . . . 4 cents. This is a very unusual privilege.'

But all eyes were drawn to a barbed wire cage on the playing field in which transgressors were imprisoned. Stripped of all but their trousers and fed half rations for anything up to three days, prolonged exposure to the fierce sun meant that most had to be put straight into hospital when they were released. Weary found it profoundly upsetting.

Next morning, Weary was 'called forth' by the Japanese commander, Lieutenant Susuki, and ordered to learn Japanese drill and commands so that he could instruct the troops. After a crash course from Susuki, and with help from the Dutch and attendant guards, Weary explained the commands and attempted to put the troops through their paces. When Susuki took over impatiently, 'his strident voice echoed all over the parade ground, but the commands as given did not sound anything like the spoken or written word'. Somehow, they muddled through.

Later in the day, Weary was called to the camp commandant's office. He was wary of Major Doornbos, who seemed a 'cold, pompous individual', but agreed to co-operate with the Dutch administration, although he thought privately that it was 'more their own idea than that of the Ns'. Weary disliked particularly the manner in which the Dutch referred to them as *Buitenlanders* (foreigners) and approached the troops directly, rather than through him as their commanding officer.

Apart from these irritations, the organisation was an improvement on Landsop, with more and better food, and the excellent canteen where anyone could buy coffee, bread, fruit and butter. Weary and his fellow officers formed a mess the night of their arrival and tasted their first fresh oranges and bananas, bread and coffee in ages.

Susuki's command elevated the *keré* and accompanying ceremonial almost to an art form. 'Drill is a frightful affair, troops being pushed about all over the place . . . ' Visits and inspections were attended by much formality and finicky instructions about cleanliness: 'Cigarette butts or ash on floor earn a kick or a smack.' But there was also 'tough, advanced' PT with the Dutch instructor, shot putting, field games, cricket and football played with 'little skill' on the central sportsfield.

On Saturday, 6 June, a party of British and Australians arrived from Sukabumi. With Lieut-Colonel Laurens van der Post (British Army) and Wing Commander Nichols (RAF), were two Australian majors, W. W. Wearne and F. A. Woods, plus some of Captain Guild's company of the 2/2nd Pioneer Battalion which had gone missing on 4 March and eventually joined van der Post's guerilla activities on the 'Mountain of the Arrow'. Weary 'at once notified van der Post and Nichols that one of them must become camp commander as senior combatant officers'.

Nichols and van der Post were both unusual men who had been

through 'a very intense and unpleasant prison experience' in the Japanese military centre in Sukabumi since April,[9] where they were 'rather badly handled and slapped about'.

Weary was astonished when they asked him to continue and accepted 'this anomalous position . . . under protest. Don't care a hang about the Ns or "the responsibility", but think that it is not correct army procedure'.

Five days later, the remaining members of the 2/2nd CCS and their charges from No. 1 Allied General Hospital arrived without warning. Japanese sentries looted their medical kit when they reached the camp but, after some detective work, Jock Clarke and Arthur Moon discovered the contents in Major Doornbos' possession. 'He did not get away with it': Jock took back the precious morphia, gentian violet jelly and a thermometer. Everyone found the Dutch difficult to understand.

They had barely finished digging the vegetable gardens Susuki was so keen on cultivating and filled in the air raid trenches (in spite of increasing numbers of aircraft overhead), than Weary discovered in conversation with a Japanese warrant officer, Doornbos and the interpreter that all British and Australian troops were to move to Bandoeng next day, 14 June. He succeeded in securing handcarts and a lorry for the sick and the camp baggage. The Dutch were generous with gulden, food and cigarettes, turned over all their canteen food to the departing troops, and gave an emotional 'farewell supper . . . with most excellent mock turtle soup, bread and onions, real butter and some tinned fruit' for Weary, van der Post, Nichols and Moon.

All camps were run on Japanese time, so after reveille at half past five, they stumbled about in the dark for the next two hours, loading the carts and eating their rice porridge. The morning was cold but 'ideal for marching, country looking lovely with mists bathing the mountains, clumps of jungle, palms and paddy fields'. The tropical trees aflame with 'great red blossoms' reminded Weary poignantly of the 'unforgettable' horse chestnuts he had admired so during spring in England.

'A much larger number of escorts than usual frisked about on bicycles with fixed bayonets & rifles loaded in a business-like way,' ultimately handing over their charges to a squad of familiar-looking guards from the Landsop days. Weary recognised Lieutenant 'Bushy Whiskers', who remembered him only too well – 'knows my name, and talks of giving me a photo of myself at the kebetei' when Weary had tried to hide behind the other officers during the official photograph of the change of command in mid-May.

They marched steadily through dreary, ill-kempt streets lined with sentries brandishing fixed bayonets. Two weeks of better food and PT had had an effect. 'I personally felt strong as a horse . . . shoulders much harder so that the pack caused little worry.' Scarcely a European was seen and onlookers were kept well back from their route. The comfortable houses in the European quarter appeared deserted, shutters closed and the gardens a green tangle of weeds. Eventually, they fetched up at Camp No. 12, XV Battalion Barracks, hard by the *kempeitai*.

The Dutch were already in residence in a neighbouring section, at Camp No. 11. Their commander, Major Linck, went 'to some pain' to help them move in to what seemed 'an enormous camp, including streets of houses' after Landsop and Tjimahi. 'Things said to be slack.' There was no Japanese drill and the 'whole place is filthy dirty'.

That evening, when the Japanese summoned the commanding officer, Nichols queried the orthodoxy of Weary continuing: he was, after all, a medical officer and Nichols was a permanent regular officer. Weary was neutral. 'That is for you to decide. I am very willing to withdraw in your favour.' But van der Post intervened. Weary should report to the *kempeitei* now and the issue could be settled at a conference of senior officers in the morning. Overnight, van der Post convinced Nichols that the unusual circumstances of their imprisonment demanded an unconventional solution: who better than a doctor and healer to take command of all the Commonwealth and English-speaking units? For this was the beginning of a new war, a battle 'for physical and moral survival . . . against disease, malnutrition and most probably a protracted . . . starvation as well as against disintegration from within by the apparent helplessness and futility of life'.[10]

The only problem, as van der Post saw it, was 'Colonel Dunlop himself, who was as modest as he was gifted in all else'. Weary was persuaded, although he felt that van der Post was 'a natural leader and diplomat . . . I wish he could take over the job'.

Van der Post and Nichols saw in Weary the qualities that would be needed to pull together the more than eight hundred demoralised UK and Australian troops in the camp. They could be sullen and uncooperative – a few were sour and disaffected, all felt profound shame at their imprisonment. On parade that morning, he was faced with 'a very nasty little demonstration at the back . . . clapping of hands and a few remarks' about the officers.

Weary and Jock were concerned that their new Dutch neighbours, whose discipline was 'non-existent will cause trouble amongst our troops, but . . . most of [ours] will play – just a very small proportion of malcontents'.[11]

At first, Weary 'felt [his] position frightfully – inspecting rows of senior British officers particularly', but within a matter of weeks, the organisation was running smoothly.

'The camp is very dirty and the latrines and showers are a nightmare.' Fatigue parties cleaned them up. Nudity was banned by order of the Japanese, as were disobedience to Japanese orders, escape and note-passing – these three being 'shooting offences'.

Two each of bicycles, armbands and typewriters were issued to Weary and Morris, as commanding officer and adjutant. John Morris typed his first routine orders on 16 June and thereafter they appeared daily. Wing Commander Nichols took charge of the British troops, with Squadron-Leader MacGrath as his second-in-command; Major Wearne and Major Woods, Duntroon graduates and former members of Sitwell's staff, were their AIF counterparts.

Rintoul and a committee took over food responsibilities from Cameron, who was relieved at no longer being 'a target for abuse' from troops at meal parades about the monotony of rice and thin soup. The diet of around 2100 calories was appalling: insufficient to support any form of energetic work or recreation, deficient in protein and every vitamin known. A small amount of coconut oil and a scrape of butter and cheese – when regimental funds could stretch to the extra expense – were the only fats available.

Meticulous maintenance of hygiene did not prevent dysentery reaching 'mild epidemic proportions' towards the end of July and, soon afterwards, Weary and the other medical officers noticed that a disturbing number of men were reporting sick with early symptoms of beri beri, pellagra and vitamin A deficiency. The Dutch had warned them to expect it, for their men had been suffering from deficiency diseases for some time, particularly the Ambons and Menados. Raw and ulcerated mouths, skin rashes and deteriorating eyesight were the first to appear, but worst of all was what they called 'Bandoeng Balls', a pellagra-type dermatitis which made scrotums raw and weeping.

It was mid-August before Weary discovered the benefits of *katjang idjoe* (bean sprouts) from the Dutch doctors, who claimed 'wonders from the . . . bean as a food' because of its vitamins C and B1. Immediately, he arranged for the entire camp to be served *katjang idjoe* soup once a week, in the hope that the symptoms of serious vitamin deficiency would abate. A month later he increased it to twice weekly and saw that each man also had one duck egg regularly.

'Nearly everyone is underweight,' he wrote in October, 'with haggard, lined faces. Burning feet is one source of terrible discomfort, the feet being most exquisitely sensitive, and sleep and rest are being lost.' 'Happy feet', the men called it. It did not respond to the treatment with yeast, although other conditions – 'Bandoeng Balls', the rashes and ulcerated mouths' – did.

At their clinical meetings, Moon observed that 'the first men to suffer in a big way were the Australians, particularly the big, burly, athletic outdoors types'. Perhaps it was because, ordinarily, they were bigger meat eaters. They decided to treat the condition with a thick, black yeast extract and one duck egg daily, boosting the diet to 2800 calories and over eighty grams of protein. After this meeting, Weary recalled that his own feet had been itching at night. He joked about it with Moon and Corlette – then realised that he was showing all the early symptoms of beri beri: lack of knee jerks and marked swelling of the legs and ankles. His eyesight was also affected.

Weary found the Japanese response to his report on the rapid and 'serious decline in the troops' health' unusual: 'a most extraordinary demand that UK group provide on paper . . . for each person, 2 small specimens of faeces, the paper to be duly labelled with the serial number of soldiers and name . . . ' What they did with this nauseous collection of papers was never revealed.

Weary heard at first hand of the fate of the *Perth* and the *Houston* when 5 officers and 7 other ranks from the *Perth* arrived in a party of 139 officers and men from Tjilatchap on 17 June. Chief Petty Officer Ray Parkin, who had steered the *Perth* during her final battle, told him how Captain 'Hec' Waller, another Benalla High School boy, had gone to the bottom of the Sunda Strait with his ship.

The overcrowded quarters and the 'almost impossible' kitchen arrangements were relieved when many of the Dutch marched out two days later. Weary was given a night 'to devise a scheme for the complete division of the camp into English and Australian'. Confusingly, the two parts were to be renumbered 3 and 4 respectively.

Next morning, he could scarcely believe their luck: the troops' barracks were roomy and well-spaced, officers were to have 'a line . . . of fine, double houses excellently furnished' in a street behind the *kempeitai*, whilst each commander and his adjutant were to share a cottage. All had been vacated by the Dutch in the usual 'very dirty' state. 'These each have a second room with a small kitchen and shower and quite a bit of furniture'. The warrant officer from the *kempeitai* who organised it all was 'even quite apologetic and asked us if they would do!'

'Am I becoming Nipponised?', Weary wondered, when more than 600 English and Australians arrived from Garoet on 22 June looking 'surprisingly untidy with long, dirty locks' and beards. Amongst them was a clutch of high-ranking officers, including two wing commanders, a group-captain, and the commanding officer of the 2/3rd Machine Gun Battalion, Lieut-Colonel E. D. Lyneham.

Lyneham chatted for a good deal of the night and produced a bottle of Doyle's Australian whisky, 'which tasted just fine' to Weary's 'neglected palate'. He seemed easier going than the group captain and some of his friends, who made 'all sorts of querulous fuss' about their house, their beds and two Bofers cases of food which they had paid some Australian soldiers to carry for them. 'Lyneham says these birds have lived on chickens and delicacies in splendid isolation by means of ample public funds'.

One RAF wing commander who had not enjoyed any comfort since the capitulation was Ron Ramsay Rae. Dark-haired, 'skinny as a heron' from living rough in the jungle with a sergeant pilot and heavyweight boxing champion called Bill Belford and several others, he matched Weary in height and physique. The Japanese had rounded them up on the south coast, while they were mending a boat in which they hoped to reach Australia, and taken them in to Garoet. Ramsay Rae narrowly escaped beheading when the Japanese colonel – drunk on whisky – fell flat on his face as he whipped his sword from its scabbard and retired in confusion at the monumental loss of face.

The Tasmanian quickly became a trusted friend, for 'he and I had a great rapport . . . [we] both felt we were in something that was foreign to our well-being'.[12] He was another whose great physical power, 'force of personality and character' impressed everyone he met.

They were well matched as athletes and their contests were enjoyed by the whole camp. Ramsay Rae always won the javelin, but Weary invariably beat him in the hop, step and jump, the shot put and the discus. The Japanese were fascinated by their size, but the more powerfully built, muscular Weary particularly intrigued them. It was plain to Nowell Peach during the sports meetings that they were curious as to whether what was concealed by his pants matched the rest of his bulk. Finally, their curiosity was satisfied on 29 August when, to loud applause from prisoners and guards, Weary lost his pants, but won the hop, step and jump with a result of 12 metres 23.

Weary decided that the other senior RAF officers were 'a bloody sight worse' than the Japanese, who – he confided to Jock Clarke – had ceased to worry him. Compared to their earlier experiences, the Japanese command under Captain Marika was almost genial, with 'a quite evident desire to please'. ' . . . They can keep it up as long as they like,' retorted Jock, 'it will not even up old scores . . . '

The Garoet party was not familiar with Japanese drill, 'and rather expect to be saluted by the Ns!' Their arrival coincided with increasing complaints about the compliments paid by troops to the Japanese, and Japanese drill was re-introduced. As the senior Australian combatant officer, Lyneham took over the command of the Australian group from Wearne. Swiftly, he organised the Australians into companies with a purely combatant basis; and the CCS returned to Weary's head-quarters' command. At Weary's first commanding officer's parade after Lyneham's arrival, the latter's Australians out-performed the English, whose other ranks were 'ghastly . . . as regards procedure and turnout'.

The machine-gunners formed a self-sufficient group, with a 'comprehensive lecture and entertainment programme and classes in book-keeping, languages etc.'. At first, they tended to think of themselves as apart from the others, but Weary soon dealt with this by expanding the educational and recreational programmes and putting them under camp control. Van der Post and Gunner Rees wrote an open letter to the camp and pinned it on a tree for all to read: and the vast educational experiment began.

Van der Post and Wearne took charge of all classes and lectures. John Morris took over the entertainment and recreation. The gymnasium, with its stage and a new name of 'Radio City', became home to variety shows, cabaret, music and church, boxing and wrestling matches; even *Julius Caesar* was produced, with three professional actors, Clephan 'Tinkle' Bell, John Morris and Alastair Campbell-Hill in the chief rôles. Campbell-Hill, a pilot, had brought a complete set of Shakespeare into captivity with him.

By August, they were publishing their own newspaper, *Mark Time*. Weary wrote the first editorial and argued for including Masefield's poem 'A Consecration' from *Salt-Water Ballads*, for he felt that the words fitted their captivity, but it was felt to be 'too depressing' and he was outvoted. Sid Scales's bold caricature of him dominated the second issue's cover. But the most idealistic experiment of all was a Commonwealth prison parliament presided over by its prison prime minister and former British MP, Squadron Leader Ian Horobin. It was therapeutic. It gave them a sense of worthwhile continuity beyond the matting-covered barbed wire and Weary supported it enthusiastically.*

The illiterate were taught to read and write by Major Pat Lancaster of the King's Hussars; those who had never completed school continued their education and sat examinations; and a 'university' syllabus was worked out. 'There is a galaxy of teachers available . . . e.g. Gunner Rees MA Cambridge . . . An immense number of languages can be tackled, history (ancient and modern), English, Classics, engineering and technical subjects, navigation, agricultural science, medical and scientific subjects.'

By September, 1207 students were attending 144 classes in thirty subjects each week, a 'terrific programme' run by forty instructors under van der Post, as senior educational officer.

Weary participated in the lectures, but it was his private discussions with van der Post that he found most stimulating, in which the latter exhibited an 'intellectual quality and depth of view beyond most of us'. He was a 'tower of strength' whenever Weary felt the need to 'pour his troubles out' about commanding a camp now numbering over 1500 men.

'Our post-war future absorbs us often, but the immediate future does not worry us much,' observed Jock Clarke, who launched an 'anti-gloom campaign' when Weary became very depressed about the news from the Middle East at the end of June. The gloomy faces were due to 'an attack of barbed wire fever', for the thought that they might be 'cooped up for years is certainly not cheering'.

Weary's only reliable link with the world outside was his radio hidden behind a wooden box cupboard at the back of his room. Each evening, he connected it to the light fitting dangling from the ceiling, praying that the sentries patrolling the line of cottages would not become suspicious at the squeal the set gave as it warmed up. Turning down the volume was tricky, and there was often a blast of 'Hearts of Oak', as

---

* Copies of *Mark Time* survived, but the minutes and reports of parliamentary proceedings, faithfully recorded on lavatory paper, did not.

he tuned into the BBC nine o'clock news. Blue Butterworth lounged outside, on watch for the sentries.

A surprise search one evening when Blue was not at his post brought two sentries into the cottage seconds after Weary heard the 'stamp of feet at the door' and shoved the radio back into the cupboard. He sat at the table, hands outspread as if meditating, 'the empty light reflector . . . swinging above'. He was 'eyed . . . off' by one sentry with fixed bayonet, while the other turned over the bedding. Weary was preoccupied with how he would dispose of the bodies after killing them, should they find the radio, and 'sought a diversion by offering cigarettes'. One accepted, the other marched him out the door and interrogated him about his neighbours.

To Weary's relief, there was no triumphant shout of discovery from inside, and they returned to find the other seated on the bed, smoking. The cupboard had not been opened. 'It was curious that they had not heard the initial squeal of the set and thunder of "Hearts of Oak", but perhaps they were not familiar with the sound.'

A Chinese merchant had supplied them with an embarrassment of mantel radio sets, five of which were now concealed about the camp. Van der Post's admiration for Weary's swift reactions and bravery reached its peak when the fifth 'dangerously large and gleaming' radio had turned up in a load of bananas, beans and sweet potato leaves that only partially concealed the red-brown mahogany cabinet. A Japanese private intercepted the handcart as it rolled through the gate before Weary and van der Post's appalled gaze and announced that he would fetch his corporal to search it. As he turned away, Weary unhesitatingly whipped the radio out from under its imperfect camouflage as 'lightly and easily as if he were merely extracting a rugby football from . . . a ruck [and] . . . tucked it under his arm'. Van der Post hurried to catch up with him as he strode past the guard and towards the prison hospital.

The accosting corporal who rudely asked what he was carrying received the ringing rejoinder, 'Medical supplies!' Van der Post found this 'so irresistible', that 'the moment I translated for the corporal, adding that he was the doctor in charge of the . . . hospital, the corporal waved us on and the incident was closed'. Had they been caught, beheading would have followed rapidly for Weary, van der Post and four others.

Smuggling goods in with returning corvées was risky; one never knew when a search would be sprung and bashing on their return was routine. Around 600 troops went out each day collecting vegetables and other rations, moving food and stores about Bandoeng, tidying streets and roads, even repairing cars and bicycles. Captain Marika had recognised the canteen officially, although the entire organisation set up for purchasing and distributing food was a racket, with both Dutch and Japanese creaming off profits.

It was a rare day that Weary was not called to arbitrate in some petty argument or other between various parts of the camp. By September, the stresses of captivity and feelings of futility foreseen by van der Post were manifesting themselves in niggling differences and bitchiness amongst the officers. 'I feel that death would be a nice release.' When Nichols calmly announced that the UK group were going to have their own kitchens, Weary decided that it was 'the last straw'. He intended 'finalising this question of camp control or getting out things are too labile for my liking'.

'I do not paticularly want the job of commander, but I will carry on providing there is clearly defined authority and absolute support,' he told Nichols, van der Post and Lyneham next morning. What was the use of a central command when officers and NCOs were slack about discipline, made no effort to co-operate with him and interfered with his staff and his decisions? No one wished to dispense with central administration. Ramsay Rae took charge of a committee to draft new orders for the three commanders and appoint an adjutant, should John Morris elect to choose his theatrical responsibilities rather than to continue as Weary's adjutant.

The command at the *kempeitai* was changed regularly. Weary's thirty-fifth birthday on 12 July was marked by the dandified Marika in his white gloves handing over to Lieutenant Sato with 'an orgy of photography'. What with the morning tea Weary gave the CCS officers and his afternoon tea for the NCOs, followed by a 'most excellent' dinner turned on by 'Moon, MacNamara, Cameron, Glowry etc. in their house . . . with an astonishing menu . . . even included some wine (sauterne), *steak* and eggs, I quite forgot about being a prisoner of war.'

Sato's mob was tougher than Marika's. 'Slapping is rather in vogue again,' and the results were painful: ruptured eardrums and broken teeth or plates. More worrying was wholesale interrogation by a group of *kempeitai* staff to identify Queenslanders and Western Australians, and an order that Weary, Wearne and two CCS privates attend the *kempeitai*.

Weary was persuaded to write a letter in consultation with other

P.O.W. CAMP 4

AUSTRALIAN · COMMONWEALTH MILITARY · FORCES

BANDOENG.

— MENU —

VIN. du. PAYS "CHRISTELŸK"

POTAGE. AUX. PETITS. POIS. "LANDS. OP. VOEDINGSGESTICHT"

CROQUETTES. "TJIMAHI"

BIFTEK. "BANDOENG."

PAW PAW "PRISONNIER"

PAIN. RÔTI "SOLSANA"

FRUITS

CAFÉ

12-7-42

'Most excellent' said Weary of his birthday dinner, 1942.
'I quite forgot about being a prisoner . . .'

senior officers to be broadcast to Australia (which he much regretted later), an essay on the 'personal feelings of a prisoner of war', and questioned at length by a smooth-voiced intelligence officer he christened 'Bird on the Bough' because of his habit of 'fluttering the eyelids in a sort of ecstatic spasm'. The interrogation continued over two days. Weary concluded that 'Bird on the Bough', who threatened him with beheading, was a 'higher formation staff officer' and more dangerous than first impressions had suggested.

Wearne disappeared. Then Lieutenant Hamilton and the two privates from the CCS were taken away and locked up. 'I do not like this . . . very worried about them.' After two days, Ambrose and Mould were returned, but Wearne was not released from solitary confinement until 4 August when Weary 'arranged' for him to be 'carried down with acute dysentery' to the Dutch hospital after three anxious weeks.

Hamilton did not re-appear for another month, 'fairly well but fat and white like something you find when you turn over a stone'. Neither would co-operate with 'Bird on the Bough', who told them 'it was necessary to co-operate or *die*'. They were both lucky: 'There was only one interrogation with very nasty threats of death.'

' . . . Bad psychological opening,' Weary decided, for someone who professed to be both psychologist and psychiatrist.

At the end of August, Sato was replaced by a lieutenant-colonel, Hideo Kawa Mura, who, on inspecting the camp, asked if the men had any money. Astonishing rumours of pay began to circulate, and of permission to wear badges of rank again. Not three weeks later, the *kempeitai* was handed over yet again, this time to 'an obvious base wallah . . . with a big pot belly and great plump face with heavy growth of black beard . . . The guard are absolute rookies . . . '

They were Koreans, and in no time it was 'Trouble! . . . All camps are complaining. Their stock in trade today . . . was smacking everyone about for reasons too obscure . . . ' As a parting gesture, the outgoing command restored the few shreds of the confiscated badges of rank that remained after the Japanese had helped themselves to souvenirs. Weary retrieved his from their hiding place and put them on.

Then, on 1 October, they learned that officers were to be paid at the same rate as the Japanese officer equivalent: 'in my case 220 yen per month, but 60 yen per month is to be deducted for food, quarters, elecric light, gas, water, etc. (NB: Our food = 10c daily!) . . . Much of the money will have to go to the troops and this should be done as a central camp scheme.'

With the pay came a different sort of 'trouble . . . Nick is supporting a scheme to take from each officer all his pay except 2 gulden weekly. The rest is to be used for the troops'.* Weary's only reservation was that such a scheme should be voluntary. Lyneham's reaction filled Weary with 'disgust'. He refused to sign such a 'ridiculous document to do with unauthorised seizing of officers' money', when Weary raised the subject at his morning conference, and charged Beaney (his adjutant) to 'hold a series of indignation meetings' at all the houses in 'Officers' Street'.

By next morning, Weary was in a 'fighting mood' and gave it to Lyneham 'straight on the chin as to the state of the camp's finances and the troops' health'. In principle, he approved of van der Post's suggestion that the officers pool all their money and 'live purely on the men's diet', but thought that the other ranks would not see the point of this 'communism'. On the other hand, it would be better than Lyneham's opinion that 'certain troops are not worth being given officers' money' and that the gratitude of 'worthy troops' should be bought individually. When Lyneham 'put the proposition that we now had sufficient money [in regimental funds] to look after the troops for 10 months . . . and therefore the officers were beautifully relieved of responsibility', Weary retaliated by summoning all the officers to a meeting in Radio City.

He took the chair. Either side were Ramsay Rae as President of the Regimental Fund and second-in-command and Moon as the medical expert. Adjutant Captain Burdon took the minutes. Two funds existed in the camp: the Regimental Fund and the imprest fund. The sources of the latter, which involved 'dangerous negotiations', were secret, for money came from loans negotiated by van der Post with sympathetic Chinese traders and other underground sources, which it was hoped the British Government would repay after the war. Money was also donated by Dutch citizens and officers.

The serious and rapid decline in the troops' health demonstrated that the existing monthly expenditure on camp purchased food of around 500 gulden was insufficient. Their captors were not at all concerned. 'We must help ourselves,' the officers' pay providentially supplying the means of supplementing their diet.

Weary recommended that the meeting adopt Wing Commander

---

* The amount troops earned on corvées was insignificant.

Nichols' sugggestion that 452 gulden could be raised each month if officers of field rank voluntarily contributed 12 gulden, and those under field rank 2 gulden, leaving each of them 2 gulden a month for their own needs. The other funds would provide the balance of the 1200 gulden required to finance extra foodstuffs. And to kick the fund off to a good start, why not donate the whole of September's pay, since it was now October?

Moon described the gravity of the medical position and Ramsay Rae explained how they would organise the extra expenditure. But when Weary invited discussion, expecting van der Post to lead strongly from the floor, Lyneham leapt to his feet and complained about the injustice of levying his Australian officers, particularly the junior ones, when their own health was impaired. Beaney then fired a few more of Lyneham's bullets by attacking the accuracy of the medical figures and the accounts, insisting that no one need donate anything for six months. Weary was dumbfounded that only MacNamara, Wearne and Lancaster lent eloquent support to Nichols' 'curt and to the point' call for everyone to donate September's pay and all above 2 gulden per week. 'Even Nicholetts hedged, although van der Post added his voice to Nichols'.

He felt he had lost control of the meeting and handled it badly. Almost choking with disgust, he stood up, flanked by the balding Moon and Ramsay Rae to close the meeting. Any senior officer who could make a better job of commanding the camp was welcome to take over, but while he was in charge, he 'would not flinch' from the decisions that needed to be made. 'I shall now write to each of you personally requesting your donations at the level we have recommended.' That Scots Presbyterian sense of duty and right-mindedness was a firm foundation.

He walked out 'in almost the lowest frame of mind imaginable and disgusted at the light in which Australian officers had been shown. Imagine, after a clear statement of the miserable health of the troops and low finances, to hear a discussion by officers to whether they would give the help required. Where is the principle "my horse, my men, myself"?' The leadership in this matter disgusting . . .

Next day he handed his letter to Lyneham, brushing aside the latter's bluster. ' . . . The principle remains the same; there is still every reason to spend money on the men.' Lyneham made no attempt to carry out the recommendations. Beaney and he continued to whinge about the 'inaccurate state of the accounts' and discouraged Australian officers in their 'immediate circle' from donating the suggested amount. De Crespigny told Weary that he was 'chipped as to having a lot of money' when he attempted to hand over 32 gulden. Jock thought 'the whole thing stank'. Weary despised both Lyneham's and Beaney's rôles in this 'deplorable affair'. From now on, he made no secret of it to either man. How could Lyneham fail to see that the principle of the exercise was to attempt to return men to their homeland one day 'without permanent damage to body & mind'? As for Weary, his only satisfaction lay in 'doing something as well as possible'.

He had been sickened by Lyneham's earlier behaviour in handing over three machine gunners to the Japanese for discipline when they had refused to guard the weapons pile at capitulation and announced that they would not deny a weapon to any men attempting to escape. It appeared that the possible death of these men did not weigh heavily on Lyneham's conscience when he decided to make an example of them. Only Ramsay Rae's searing criticism of Lyneham's behaviour and intervention with the Japanese commander had gained the men's release from the civilian prison in Garoet. This latest incident confirmed his opinion. Others agreed. 'Pretty poor material,' concluded van der Post.[13]

Weary's loyalty to those under his command was absolute. Discipline was a camp affair. One did not abdicate these responsibilities to a hated enemy. He saved both Leach and Franklin from execution, although both men threatened to turn Weary in to the Japanese about his wireless set, and its discovery would mean his death.

Over a fortnight elapsed before Lyneham handed in all his officers' share. Weary was ashamed that the smaller English officer contingent had raised 122 gulden more than the Australians. Even more shaming was their 'talk of a split in the two camps if AIF don't meet their obligations'.

Not everyone was paid by the Japanese. Some permanent duties men were employed by Weary – who announced that 'everyone must make some sacrifice' – and they must also contribute unless they had a very good reason. 'I warned them that I would not employ those who objected . . . ' The Hygiene Squad downed tools in protest. But they resumed work when they realised that their jobs would be snapped up by others. ' . . . My nickname rapidly firmed as "Dictator Dunlop".'

Moves were afoot. He farewelled with cocoa, sandwiches and sadness the British RAF doctors – Robbie Cumming and his officers, 'McGrath, Wiley, Peach and Co. They are a solid force for good in the place and so are the rest of the gang, including the ORs'. He gave a copy of Gray's *Anatomy* to Peach so he could continue studying for his fellowship.

In the dark, scented stillness just before sunrise on 13 October, he stood outside the *kempeitai* and watched them march out, an obvious hospital unit bound for some unknown camp. Weary walked back to his house, the 'soft, beautiful colour of a typical Java dawn breaking through the sombre clouds to the east'. He rolled himself up in his blanket amidst the 'brooding quietness and a sense of transparency of air washed clean by rain', and thought of Helen. She had turned 29 only six days before; he was now 35. How many more wasted years?

After the work parties had gone, Weary stood at the head of the morning parade in the grassed barrack square, tall, stoop-necked, rangy now that the weight had fallen off him. Tenko began. *Bango! Ichi, ni, san, si, go* . . . The squat Korean guards brandished their rifles, yelled – *Kura*! – slapped, bashed with a rifle butt someone who dreamed and missed his count, growled and eventually handed them all back to Weary.

Weary raised his voice so seldom that when he did, men started, stopped in surprise. Everyone heard what he had to say in his quiet, calm way. The little black Ambonese, the mischievous, chunky brown Menadonese recognised his strength. They called him *Singa yang Diam*, the quiet lion.

Donald Stuart, a rough, tough, little West Australian machine gunner who preferred to fight someone bigger than himself, a writer who takes one into the heart of the prison camps, was 'surprised by the mildness' of his voice, captivated by his gentleness when first he met him in Bandoeng.[14] For Weary 'had a great tenderness in him and he wasn't ashamed of it . . . to see Weary dealing with somebody who was really sick was very moving, [especially] when you get it in a person who is so much of a man.'[15]

He would march into the *kempeitai* at any time to protest about mistreatment. 'He was a born commander,' emphasises John Denman, whom he retrieved after a bad bashing one day. 'He could have been a first-rate officer in the field.' In Bandoeng, van der Post recognised 'an all-round quality which great leaders have, a Renaissance man . . . who led by the diversity of his character and the quality of his spirit.'

Ramsay Rae saw him stand tall, immobile, as he was bashed and slapped about, but 'you couldn't frighten him – well, he was as frightened as hell, as everyone was, but he'd never let you know'.

During his last night in the Dagoweg, Weary had stared into the future but the glass was clouded. His only certainty was that they would be governed by 'men who despised prisoners. I pledged myself to at least face them unflinchingly at all costs.'

'He has . . . the gift of courage,' noted van der Post. 'He almost thrives on danger.'

Monday morning, 2 November, was 'momentous'. He learned they were to move – to Tanjong Priok, Hoshina said. A thousand men. Jock heard it was to be Batavia: 'most . . . think it is a sea trip'. The air was thick with Dutch rumours – camps were being reshuffled because of difficulties the Japanese were experiencing with food and transport.

Nichols had lost 160 works people and drivers to Batavia on 26 October; around a thousand Ambonese followed them on the twenty-ninth. Weary had enjoyed the Ambonese as much as they admired him. Now only 87 Australian sick, 5 senior NCOs and one doctor would remain with the English and the Dutch in Bandoeng. 'Fixed as MacNamara by cutting cards with Ewen Corlette.'*

He listed priorities: money, canteen, library books, education, records, Memorial Book, sports material, tools and grave stones. He determined to relinquish the command, although it was obvious they were to function as a unit: all armbands and records were to be retained, and they were ordered to travel light. He ordered every man to carry a library book. Caution suggested that they take some of the sports equipment and a few tools.

They marked the graves of their three dead in Bandoeng Cemetery with stones and brief ceremony. Copies were made of the Memorial Book material, inspired by the *Anzac Book* of the previous war and begun by Ray Parkin, de Crespigny and other artists in the camp – 'the mirror of now . . . for afterwards'. A special issue of *Mark Time* was rushed out, containing messages from Weary, Nick and Lyneham. The

---

* Captain MacNamara drowned when the ship he was travelling on to Japan was torpedoed.

accounts were audited: Weary handed over the Australian funds to Lyneham, and camp 3's proportion to Nichols.

Wednesday was crowded with activity – the routine of the past few months, which embraced chat, sunbaking, reading and athletics, had vanished. Overste Willikens, calling to convey an affectionate farewell from the Dutch, found him 'very busy packing up' and about to preside over a conferring ceremony, at which he distributed certificates and diplomas to the participants in their educational experiment.

They had laughed at their last show in Radio City the previous evening in the unsolicited company of some Japanese soldiers, who gave money to the players, 'tried the instruments and eventually came back loaded with cakes!' Now Weary kicked off in a football match, British troops versus Menados, Ambons and Dutch, and, that evening, Nick lit candles in the house he shared with Weary and gave a dinner party as civilised as Douglas Stephens's sixteen months beforehand, with table markers, flowers and 'sergeant-brewed beer'. He signed his last routine orders as the officer commanding the British troops. Orchida and Susuka stared at him, when he went to the *kempeitai* and asked to be relieved of his command. 'Why?'

'Because I am medical; I am not the most senior officer; and I have only retained command so long because it is such a pleasure to deal with you!'

He wondered if they believed him. He had found Orchida, 'a pleasant little fellow', polite and helpful, but he would be 'glad to see the last of these guards'. They were sadistic and unpredictable. A livid bruise from a bash with a bayonet still adorned his chest and he had not taken kindly to having to sweep 'Officers' Street' a few days earlier when he was visiting there. 'Even going out for a leak at night is fraught with danger. Sudden yells and flourishes of bayonets, also many smacks.'

Departure was fixed for Friday, 6 November. After an earnest consultation with van der Post and two other 'experts', he decided to dismantle his wireless, pack it in a cocoa tin and attempt to reassemble it later. By the time he left van der Post's supper party early on Friday morning, only a few hours remained until reveille at 0315.

Heavy rain fell during the night and low cloud shut out the stars and what was left of the moon. Weary walked out of his little stucco house, snug under its steeply pitched roof of terracotta tiles, and shivered in the chill blackness, despite his English greatcoat. The dark blotted out the faces in the tide of men making their way through the low barracks and cantonments under the huge, dripping wet, kapok trees towards the prison gates, where other groups of men had gathered to say goodbye to the Australians.

In the four and a half months they spent in the Bandoeng camp, a remarkable renaissance of spirit evolved, a 'golden age' rich in intellectual development and founded on deep companionship which was to sustain them through the isolated deprivation of their prison camp lives and on down the years. Men's memories of this transcended the petty bickering and discontent arising from the 'two sources of "belly-aching" [which] always remain: the distribution of food and "the officers" . . . '

Nichols and van der Post were there as Weary moved towards them and they heard his voice, 'undismayed and even at so gloomy an hour, extracting a laugh from his overburdened men'. Van der Post had the impression that the clouds rolled back 'and in the puddles we trod underfoot were reflected the great constellations . . . and the planet Jupiter, which had newly taken over the role of morning star from Venus'.

'. . . Seeing them marching, marching out . . . was terrible . . . It was the same camp, we carried on, but we missed him greatly . . . we never had backing like that again. We had to do it on our own . . . we missed his strength . . . '

They formed up in sections of 50 on the road outside and moved off briskly at 0550. Not all the carriages had been coupled up when they reached the station just over half an hour later, but the guards let no one break ranks. They kept back the hawkers trundling their carts through the broad streets, and the tantalising scent of burning charcoal from their stoves, with the promise of noodles and rice spiced with sambals and fried eggs and crisp little *ikan bilis*, drifted across the platforms. Stomachs rumbled.

Susuki appeared with Sergeant Okomura and Hoshina to see them off, Hoshina disruptive to the last with his suggestion that they were being shipped to Australia, 'now in Nippon hands'. It was more than an hour before the thousand men and their 54 officers were stowed in the carriages, Weary sharing a third-class carriage with Lyneham and their two adjutants. 'I have given my armband to Lyneham.'

He exulted in the sight of the 'green jungle valleys full of mist, and the verdant mountain tops striking up on all sides', as the train puffed and chugged along its 'tortuous course' amongst them. 'Java is almost terrifyingly green . . . [and] succulent.' But his earlier interest in the kampongs and their inhabitants had given way to distaste, for now there was a worm in the bud: 'The one thing about imprisonment that really disgusts me is to have Javanese staring and grinning at me.' He didn't care for two of his travelling companions, either. But 'I feel perfectly cheerful and don't give a tinker's damn what happens – become a prisoner of war and see the world!'

It was mid-afternoon when they pulled in to Meester Cornelis Station.* The guards hustled them out. Weary consigned his pack, valise and medical haversack to a lorry provided for the officers' baggage, but clung to his suitcase, records and two haversacks, because of the radio parts scattered about. Their escort set a cracking pace along the Buitenzorg road and after about four miles, men began to drop out. A lorry picked them up. 'It was a sorry sight to see some of these emaciated forms and haggard faces . . . '

Rain poured down. By the time they dragged themselves into camp, everyone's clothing was soaked, their footwear thickly coated with 'tenacious red-brown mud'. 'It was an incredible sight to see the guard doing a 'hotio tutoé with one or two kilos of this on their boots'.

Camp No. 5, called by the Japanese *Makasura*, lay in a coconut grove. Down the centre of each attap-thatched bamboo hut ran a little 'rough brickwork' with a long bamboo sleeping platform each side. 'About 1 metre per person.' Officers fared no better than men. Latrines were primitive, too few and of an open drain, straddle type, draining into seepage pits. A sickly stench of raw sewage lay permanently over the low-lying area, for overflow was flushed through the green spears of growing rice in the surrounding paddy fields.

'Joy of joys! Squadron-Leader MacGrath is here . . . looking after the sick . . . ' Another RAF officer, Wing Commander Alexander, was the Allied commander. And they were lucky in their Japanese commandant, Lieutenant Tanaka. An 'intelligent fellow who speaks a little English', he was to behave well to the prisoners. Food was more plentiful. Later, the officers were issued with a special ration three times a week – cigarettes, coffee, sugar, pepper, tea, butter and a banana – 'I

---

* Now Jati Negara Station.

presume this is out of our 60 gulden a week [deducted] for food and lodging.'

Lyneham, 'happy as a sandboy' to be wearing the Australian commander's armband, was ready enough next morning to accept Weary's advice that Moon gather all the CCS and Java Ambulance Car men and officers into one company, Ramsay Rae command the RAAF and Wearne the Pioneers. Weary became SMO and put Jock Clarke in charge of a hygiene squad of 15 ORs. The Australians formed the largest group amongst the 1400 men in camp. They still thought of Weary as their commanding officer.*

Reveille was at 0700. He slept fitfully. The bamboo platform was slippery and not quite level, so that periodically he would wake to find his feet hanging over a void. Mosquito nets were useless against the bed bugs and rats, and 'all night carts with hexagon wheels roll up and down Buitenzorg Road.' He was surrounded by 'people tossing, moaning, cursing and muttering in sleep: a sort of febrile delirium'. (He did not realise that his own sleep was similarly disturbed.) Those with 'happy' feet roamed about, seeking to banish the burning pain by bathing their feet in cold water. Dreams, 'nearly always of home', turned waking into 'heavy-lidded misery'. It was a relief to walk out into the hushed stillness just before dawn, when 'the palm fronds droop more quietly, darkly and delicately than usual – and a golden radiance can be seen through the mass of fronds and hutments away to the east. Suddenly the ripe coconuts on the tall trees glow a lovely orange red and *de zon gaat op*'.† *Tenko* was at 0730.

Methodically, each afternoon, they examined their troops for avitaminosis. But the Japanese were deaf to requests for yeast for some weeks; only infectious diseases which might endanger them elicited a response, and the medical supplies issued – acriflavine for above, and creosote tablets for below the diaphragm, plus some quinine – bore no relation to their needs. There were no bandages; they tore up flour sacks to use as dressings for the tropical ulcers which began to appear.

Blackburn, Maltby and Sitwell were in a staging camp near the Princess Juliana School; the members of the RAF hospital unit which had marched out with MacGrath were scattered over the area, some in the military hospital in Batavia. Conditions for the sick there were no

---

* Years later, some insisted that he, not Lyneham, commanded the camp.

† The sun rises.

better: patients Weary sent from *Makasura* reported that there was 'damn all in the way of drugs or treatment' and it was hopelessly overcrowded.

Before Weary tackled Lyneham about the financial arrangements, Ramsay Rae, Wearne, Woods, Clarke and he agreed that they would only contribute to 'a common pool scheme with no more holding out'. Lyneham accepted the figures: 'Monthly expenditure on the camp is to be 2232 gulden approx.; medical supplies and hospital fund extra.'

Meanwhile, Weary wrote to the Japanese officer in charge of the camps in the Batavia area complaining about the diet and the increasing number of men suffering from deficiency diseases. There was no acknowledgement, but a month later, he received 'a little in the way of medical stores . . . 2 bottles of Ebios powdered yeast (about 1 lb in each . . .) and a little in the way of dressings, plus some salicylic acid'.

They fed everyone *katjang idjoe* each day and the avitaminosis cases enjoyed an egg as well. Weary's own oedema was slow to respond to vitamin B1 injections and his knee and ankle jerks never returned completely, but 'anyway, feel extremely well'.

Jock Clarke had acquired a bamboo chair – 'not a hell of a lot of use' – and steadily pressed on with his dental parades. He was limited to pulling really bad teeth and doing temporary fillings with zinc oxide and oil of cloves until the Japanese, in response to his complaints, 'promptly bought . . . cement, novocaine [and] amal. alloy'. They also presented him with a bill for ten gulden. Lyneham paid without a murmur. 'The key to his nature,' Weary concluded, 'is that he must be built up and made important.'

In the limited open space there were two parades a day, usually conducted by minor Japanese NCOs in singlets and tennis shoes ('slovenliness of dress on parade is characteristic'), PT, cricket, basketball, 'circlos' and volleyball. Mini golf was 'played with a piece of clayey soil wrapped in a piece of rag and bound tightly with string'.[16] The sticks – some quite ornate, with a blade made from a piece of curved tin – were of bamboo or palm.

The sports afternoons continued. Bill Belford still shakes his head admiringly over a memorable 440 yards battled out on Christmas Day between Weary and Ramsay Rae. 'Olympic standard.' Weary won. Ramsay Rae had been selected for the Olympic Games for this event, but an injury had diverted him. The whole camp enjoyed the athletic contests between the two men. Wearne found instructors, and educational classes began again. John Morris launched a branch of the Bandoeng Theatrical company.

The padres were busy, but some of their flock were becoming disenchanted with religion. Jock Clarke was a devout Catholic when he was captured. After eight months as a prisoner, he decided that the churches had lost touch with reality and he saw no place in their present life for the Holy Name Society, 'absurd . . . almost comical in spite of its piety', which Father Tom Elliott had begun.

There were twenty-six officers sharing Weary's hut. Unlike Bandoeng, the 'only place one can sit down is on one's bed. Consequently, spine drill seems to be the favourite pursuit.' He stopped learning Dutch but continued his French lessons with Sergeant Le Roi. Jock was amused by the hours he spent 'chuckling over some allegedly humorous French book. He would probably consider it very dull if it were written in English'.[17] But he also read Lin Yutang's *My Country and My People* and Charles Lamb's *Ghenghis Khan*. (De Crespigny was so inspired by the Lamb that he began to write his own novel on Ghenghis Khan.) Sick parades, hospital work and the avitaminosis survey swallowed up many hours, and the others became accustomed to his 'long, frequently inaudible and unintelligible monologues'.[18] He fitted in chess, volleyball, rugger passes 'running with a coconut football', reading, 'tea and chatter'. But mostly, exercise for everyone meant walking round a small enclosure. 'I sometimes feel an overwhelming sense of loathing for the camp when I see some hundred men all walking round the same little recreation area inside the barbed wire with an action as mechanical as a "merry-go-round" only with no merriment.' One day, 'to start a diversion', Billy Wearne and he walked in the opposite direction, 'triggling' Ormond-style.

Otherwise, the days under the coconut palms were hot and uneventful. He was surprised that 'many ORs under present conditions convey all the appearance of complete happiness. This no doubt is due to the fact that their lives are completely ordered . . . and there is no possibility of any advancement, hence no place for jealousy or competition'. It was 'almost impossible to keep count of time' and the diary lagged 'steadily behind'. He confided his anxieties about Helen, 'the only stable thing left in life', solely to the diary. 'If she packs up and marries an American . . . I suppose it would be best for her, but I don't know what I would do with my life then. She is . . . the only thing which enables me to see anything to look forward to in peace.'

He was not ready for peace; he had too much unfinished business.

' . . . Peace has been spoiled for me; I crave movement, adventure, new countries, variety – the strangeness of things, and shun the old life of solid endeavour amongst people who haven't suffered . . . Apart from longing terribly to see [her] . . . my one desire is . . . to be back in the war somewhere.'

A year had gone by since Pearl Harbor. He sat down to write one of the few short letters home that were permitted the officers in Java, but 'I find it impossible to say anything significant . . . feel rather like one trying to speak from the dead'.

It was Christmas. The CCS led by example: presents came in from outside, 'presumably the generous Dutch women', and 'our company and some of the others are giving the whole of this to the men . . . Cigarettes, cigars, sweets, peanuts, biscuits, clothing, few boots and shoes, some sporting material – something for everyone in camp'.

Weary's best present arrived three days beforehand. ' . . . Received per radio by means of the Batavia station and the ABC the following message from Helen: "Delighted to get your message. Splendid efforts commanding your hospital. Am happy, well and not worrying. Keep cheerful. Our future holds so much. Love Fawn."'

Donald Stuart watched the man he admired, the man he christened 'the Big Bloke', ask Lieutenant Tanaka for permission to celebrate Christmas. It was given. The Japanese even produced a piano. Weary joined in 'all the old Christmas hymns' during church parade in the morning and carols round the piano that night, 'with a splendid moon flitting amid banks of clouds and the dark palms showing delicate silvery fronds'. After hospital work, there was horseplay, 'much fun' in the RAF mess, visiting, games and 'post-prandial torpor (perhaps a little of this due to half a mug of crude white wine given me by Lt-Col. Lyneham)'. The hatchet was out of sight, although not yet buried.

The 'local old prisoner grandee', Major Anami, wished them a happy Christmas and agreed that lights could burn all night and that they need not go back to their barracks, providing everyone was on parade promptly next day. 'Huge crowds round the piano, faces vividly lit up by the cookhouse lights, all animated and very happy.' They were still singing when Weary drifted off to sleep around four o'clock next morning.

'You go Nippon,' a guard confided to men in one of the barracks next day. On 28 December the movement was confirmed by a request for specimens of stools from dysentery and diarrhoea cases and a list of those suffering from deficiency diseases. '. . . The usual battery of typists is at work on our cards and a return is required by 0900 tomorrow of troops without a blanket, footwear or eating utensils.

'. . . Our cards are marked "S", or should I say "T".' He knew nothing about either destination, but they seemed more desirable than J for Japan.

Not only the sick were told to supply specimens; everyone was to attend a parade next morning with a dab of faeces on a piece of cellophane, 'a somewhat dextrous and malodorous feat'. And when morning came, the Japanese introduced them to a new, humiliating routine: testing for dysentery by rectal swabbing with a glass rod.

That evening, in the half light provided by the cookhouse fire, he assembled his medical team and they injected everyone against typhoid, cholera and dysentery.

New Year's Eve brought some 'surprising' revelations. Tanaka, with his sergeant orderly and interpreter, called out the Australians in groups of 50, each commanded by an officer or NCO. Jock suggested that it was 'strange' that 'large numbers of officers were omitted', including Lyneham and Beaney. Weary would take command with Wearne, the next senior, as his second-in-command. 'This is a shocker to me.' He believed – and both Jock Clarke and Rod Allanson agreed – that, when approached by the Japanese, Lyneham nominated for movement those officers who had been most critical of him.

Immediately, Weary requested a proportion of the camp funds for the departing force. Lyneham shuffled a bit, then replied, 'What would you say if I said I distributed all the money to the officers and they wouldn't give it back to me?'

'. . . I would expect anything that you got to be distributed [in proportion].'

Lyneham suggested that around 1200 gulden would be available.

'I . . . turned my back on him, dismissed him . . . '

Further enquiries had failed to produce any funds. At eight o'clock on the night of their departure, Weary bailed Lyneham up and asked for a balance sheet and money. He was suspicious. When they marched out of Bandoeng, he had handed over 4526 gulden. Four days later, Lyneham had written to each officer, requesting that they 'set aside all of two months' pay over 50 gulden' and hold it for the fund, and contribute a designated amount from their retained savings – in

Weary's case, 230 gulden – on the understanding that, if the group were separated, 'the officers' contribution of each party will be added to the pro rata distribution of Group Funds'. According to Weary's and Wearne's reckoning, there should be a sum of just under 7500 gulden available for distribution on a proportionate basis. A thousand Australians and their 54 officers had marched into the camp; eighty-five per cent of them, accompanied by 15 officers, were to march out, yet they were to be allocated only around twelve per cent of available funds.

Not so, insisted Lyneham. He had decided *not* to call in this money and had told the officers so; what is more, he had given all his money to those who were leaving.

When Weary was angry he became very quiet, very still; but his words could cut painfully deep. (A Western Australian machine gunner, Bill Haskill, remembers that only his eyes used to give him away.) He was taking with him most of Lyneham's men and only five of his officers; surely, those officers remaining in Java – nearly all of them with no further commitment to their men – would not break their word and keep the money for themselves? But Lyneham, prepared for anything Weary might deal out, 'had his temper buttoned up'.

Wearne took the 1200 gulden 'and expressed after the fashion of a staff college officer of junior rank to L exactly my sentiments'.

Weary called a meeting at nine o'clock and told his fellow officers the situation 'without expressing my views'. Lyneham had been selective about whom he contacted, but one of his machine gunners, Major Hec Greiner, now in Weary's party, announced that he was told only that day that the money would not be called in.

They were all appalled and 'hot resentment was expressed'. Weary stopped them. It was neither the time nor the place for their indignation. He would like every officer to hold whatever sum he had left of the distributed money, and 'to disperse no further money on groups of men' without telling him. 'Everyone agreed . . . that as far as possible we would form a common mess with a common sum. All are fairly behind me and are disgusted.'

There were no secrets in that closed community. Various officers came up to Weary and handed over money: the two padres gave everything they had, and Ramsay Rae and the RAAF boys were especially generous. They took with them nearly 2000 gulden.

They were to move by night in their groups of fifty, 15 officers, 12 warrant officers and 868 ORs, for it was too hot to march the eight kilometres to Meester Cornelis Station by day. Major De Crespigny would lead out the first nine groups at 0130 hours. At 0230, groups 10 to 18 would follow, with Weary and the other eight officers bringing up the rear.

When he heard that there would be no food until the following evening, he saw Tanaka and gained permission for potatoes to be cooked and carried in buckets. 'Each man has 4 eggs and, if he has kept them . . . 2 buns', a full water bottle and 'as much additional rice as he can carry.'

'God knows what lies ahead in the way of hardship, short rations, disease and death before the end of the road, but the mind does not speculate much about these things.

'As for me, I am perhaps a *vrai voyageur* and hanker for new countries and new experiences . . . '

NINETEEN

Via Dolorosa

WHEN LAURENS VAN DER POST launched the English edition of Weary's *War Diaries* in London in 1989, he spoke of 'being in at the beginning of the trail', the trail which led from Bandoeng through the camps of Java and Singapore to Thailand and the building of the railway. In Weary's mind, the walk with the sick to Landsop became the first steps on a latter-day *via Dolorosa* , the way of sorrows.

Without exception, the men herded into prisons by the Imperial Japanese Army hated being ordered to lay down their arms and fight no more. Some had defied orders to surrender and taken to the hills. Others, like 'Scorp' Stuart and his two friends who were handed over by their own officers to the Japanese for refusing to guard the discarded weapons, had gone into 'the bag' humiliated and resentful, but bounced back time and again to thumb their noses at authority and practise their own independent and humorous iconoclasm.

Allied prisoners were particularly bitter about the failure of the NEI Army to offer any resistance. Rod Allanson remembers being called on parade with some of the 2/3rd Machine Gun Battalion who were to set up a perimeter around Bandoeng. Standing beside Blackburn was Major-General Schilling, who stepped forward and assured them that the Dutch would fight beside them 'to the last man and the last bullet'. This gave them 'some optimism that they would be able to withstand the Japanese', but, to his knowledge, 'not a shot was fired by the Dutch' in that area.[1]

These resentful men – some, like 'Blackforce', with a strong sense of identity, others confused and divorced from their officers and units – became more integrated during the months in the Javan camps. What particularly impressed van der Post about the Australians 'was the hunger and respect that [they] naturally seem to have for learning and . . . the ancient values of life . . . as an expeditionary force against the Japanese, they identified themselves . . . with the kind of Greek expeditionary force . . . they encountered in the pages of Homer'.

Don Gregory, a Cambridge classics graduate, introduced many of them to the *Odyssey* and *Iliad*. Others taught languages, economics, bookkeeping, shorthand – all expertise was utilised. Through this other world of the intellect, they could escape briefly the stifling frustrations and depression of being prisoners. And its therapeutic value appeared to extend beyond the prison camp years for, in discussing the medical condition of prisoners-of-war when they returned to Australia, Colonel Allan Walker noted in the medical history that there was 'some evidence that those who had been stimulated by educational amenities . . . [during] imprisonment were thinking more clearly and planning to make the most of ambition in the future'.[2]

' . . . Their intellectual curiosity, love of learning and discussion, which sometimes would continue long into the day and night as a private argument in the barracks, was endless', and for van der Post, 'one of the most marked and endearing characteristics of the Australian soldier . . . I have never met anything like it. I never expect to meet anything like it again.'

Much later, they would look back on this 'golden age' of their prison camp existence as a comparatively mild initiation into life as slave labour. The relationships formed with their fellows would soon be tried and tested amidst unimaginable conditions, for they were about to march towards what van der Post called 'a kind of hell'.

On the eve of leaving Makasura, Weary concluded that the past three years had left him 'with a nervous system as strong as an ox. I am not one of those who do not know fear, but I have learned that fear is easily trampled underfoot by self-discipline and a resolute and steadfast way of living . . . I am lucky in my constitutional toughness. Life really hasn't been too bad . . . There have been a few good books and some good fellowship.'

Promptly at half past two on the morning of 4 January, his column moved off in the warm darkness. As was now his custom, he had walked quietly up and down the line, pausing briefly to have a word here and there with some of the men, before the Japanese officer signalled for them to depart. De Crespigny's group had already gone. There was no moon, but the clear tropical sky was brilliant with stars. Marching was slow at times in the dense blackness. When they turned onto a better road and the going became easier, the long column of men began to sing: 'Jingle Bells', 'Dolores', 'Sixpence in my Pocket'. It took two and a quarter hours to cover the eight kilometres to Meester Cornelis Station, but the journey by blacked-out electric train to Tanjong Priok was short and they reached the wharf at seven o'clock after a half-hour march.

This time, Weary had entrusted his valise, a small suitcase lent him by John Morris for the medical records and papers and his leather medical haversack to Moon who, as baggage officer, had accompanied the baggage in a lorry to the station. He carried only a pack, haversack and respirator haversack.

Alongside the quay lay the *Usu Maru*, a rusty, coal-burning hulk with a single funnel so lightly loaded that her Plimsoll mark showed above the quay. Unseaworthy-looking lifeboats swung from the davits. Petty Officer Abbott, one of the men from the *Perth*, estimated its tonnage as being between six and seven thousand.

Breakfast was eaten seated on the dark quay between the ship and the looming godowns. When the sky lightened, Weary brought his diary up to date. Another party of Australians a thousand strong boarded first. One gangway only was used by prisoners and at its foot stood a 'gowned and gloved disinfecting party who lustily sprayed carbolic solution' over the embarking men and their baggage. A 'gesture' not dissimilar to the rectal swab parade, he concluded. 'Our troops must have . . . all sorts of bowel infections', yet none had been rejected as a result of the glass rod routine.

His two parties were 'drafted like sheep' down iron ladders into two separate holds aft. The centre of each, through which they entered, was partly open to the sky; below the roughly planked hatch to the deck below were empty oil drums 'to give ballast'. A sentry stood on guard above by the open hatch.

Weary's group was in an area 27 metres by 15. Crude stagings four metres deep covered with rush matting, one somewhat over a metre above the other so that there was room to lie or sit, but not to stand and ease aching limbs, ran the length of each side between decks. At night, two rows of men could lie head to foot on each. The air was foul, and fatigue and no sleep for over twenty-four hours rendered everyone bad-tempered. Rust, cobwebs, rats and cockroaches were everywhere. No one was issued with a life-belt.

At first, only one man at a time was allowed up on deck to the rows of latrines, 'foul and smelly wooden boxes' the size of dog kennels hanging over the side of the ship. Weary could only just squeeze into one. This ruling was quickly proved to be impractical – from then on, the queues to the latrines lasted all day, each day.

A little Japanese lance-corporal with his cap pulled down to his eyebrows came down to have a look at them and asked for 'a roll call parade in 4s', an impossible exercise which was replaced with calling the group rolls.

The rice and boiled potatoes they had carried in buckets from Makasura stuck dryly in their throats. They were given weak, black, sugarless tea in the middle of the day and at six o'clock the evening meal of rice and thin vegetable 'shadow' soup was dished out. Those who still had remnants of the food they had stowed in their packs at Makasura – peanuts, hard-boiled eggs – nibbled these when their stomachs were not heaving with the smell of sweat, the heat, the rolling of the vessel and the thick, fetid atmosphere.

Weary managed to make his way through to the other hold to see Moon and De Crespigny and persuaded the little *keicho* to get permission for four men at a time to go up on deck to wash their faces. Most men managed a short time 'for a breather' before lights out at nine o'clock. Weary settled himself under the canvas cover of his valise alongside six other officers just as 'the rain poured down on us in torrents' through the open hatch. No sooner had the rain stopped, than the guards closed the hatch, releasing a deluge of water caught in the folds of the great tarpaulins they hauled across. 'I just refused to move . . . ' He had not been settled long when a man cried out hysterically with pain and he crawled over to see what was wrong. 'Cramp poor chap.'

After this, he 'slept like a top in spite of the wet, but I suppose the atmosphere would drug anybody'.

They crawled up the malarious Sumatran coast and round Banka Island, never out of sight of land. Next day Weary bluffed his way forward by following 'a lad carrying a bucket . . . as though detailed to supervise' and was hailed by Lieut. 'Happy' Houston of the 2/2nd Pioneers. He failed to recognise him: he was five stones lighter, wasted by malaria and dysentery.

Houston had been in Batavia in the Bicycle Camp, as it was known, with Colonel Williams and other officers from the Pioneers, survivors from the *Houston* and the *Perth*, some of the 2/40th Battalion from Timor and odds and sods of engineers and 3rd Motor Transport men. The Japanese had tortured Williams and other officers. 'Naturally without results.'

Blackburn, Maltby, Sitwell, other senior British and Dutch officers and the Governor-General of the Netherlands East Indies had been behind a barbed wire fence in one corner. They had sailed with all their possessions, including camp beds and ceremonial swords, about a week beforehand and were 'said to be going to Formosa'.

After the first day, the Japanese were more lenient. Men were allowed up on deck a group at a time; many enjoyed a hose down with sea water; the food improved to a thickish vegetable stew with rice. There was little sickness.

The Japanese lieutenant who earlier had refused to allow the men to take exercise told Weary that the journey to Singapore would take two days. It was almost three before they dropped anchor off the east side of the island late on the evening of Wednesday 6 January amongst the many ships waiting in the roads. It was 'sweltering' below decks now they were at anchor; everyone was dehydrated, their clothes soaked with sweat.

It was Thursday afternoon before they moved off round the island, picking their way through the minefield. Weary and Wearne were on deck. 'What a place to lose!' muttered Wearne irritably as they crept into Keppel Harbour.

The ship berthed at five o'clock. Before they disembarked, No. 1 George, the little *keicho* , called Weary and Wearne to the galley and pressed on them two large steaks 'streaming with sauce'. They ate them 'under the eyes of several troops, which made us feel fearful worms' but did not lessen the 'gustatory satisfaction'.

It took an hour to disembark. Everyone formed up in their groups of fifty about a hundred metres from the quay and rice and pumpkin soup were doled out. A line of 30 cwt Ford lorries moved up.

'Loading of N transport is a revelation.' Weary and thirty-four others, a corporal, some stores and all the officers' baggage were crammed into the back of one vehicle. ' . . . Standing up, massed together and swaying about', they began a 'Cook's tour . . . in the evening light through the heart of the city': Raffles Square (with Raffles' statue missing) and Robinson's bomb-damaged department store, the Fullerton Building, the city hall, the post office, banks and the ornate, gabled Victoriana of the Cricket Club with its vista of level *padang* , flame trees and sea. Despite walls pock-marked with bomb and shell damage, most buildings appeared to be in reasonable repair and business seemed to be 'much as usual'. Chinese and Malayan civilians moved about the streets and 'some gave friendly signs'.

Once through the city and on the east coast road, they jolted through low hills rolling down to a sea fringed with lines of spidery bamboo-legged fish traps and studded with green islets. Attap-thatched huts and small roadside markets were tucked into gaps in rubber and coconut plantations. They held their breath when the lorry slowed down in Half Moon Street, but it accelerated again after Changi Gaol. Suddenly, he was astonished to see 'diggers *on guard* controlling traffic at points', well-dressed troops, 'officers with sticks and ever so much saluting'.

Away to the north, across the Straits of Johore, the sea dazzled in the dying sun. Near at hand, impressive three-storeyed barracks with tiled roofs and broad balconies were anchored in jungle green vegetation and parade grounds. British and Australian troops were everywhere.

The lorries halted in the centre of a parade ground and were immediately surrounded by officers, 'neatly dressed . . . carrying canes, blowing out puffy moustaches and talking in an "old chappy" way'. Malayan Command, he decided, looking at their red and black arm brassards. Weary had no intention of entrusting his baggage to their Movement Control. Hung about with bulky haversacks, pack, suitcase and valise, he had difficulty marching the kilometre and a half to the area set aside for units in transit. In darkness and confusion, Malayan Command allocated quarters. It took most of the night to settle in. They were now in the hands of professionals.

All Friday morning was spent unravelling the previous night's confusion and assembling the men in two adjacent blocks in Southern Area. A very early parade had already sorted them out into companies. Brigadier Blackburn arrived, 'extremely thin' but clear of skin and keen of eye, to see his boys in the 2/3rd Machine Gun Battalion. Weary and Wearne had sped across to his quarters the previous night when they heard he was there with his high-ranking companions from the Bicycle Camp.

Weary was unimpressed by the staff at the Reception Unit conference which he attended that morning with Wearne, his second-in-command. A special newcomers' conference called at noon by its officer-in-charge, Major Denaro, pleased him even less. The sight of Denaro and his fellow staff appointees, 'all beautifully dressed with appropriate little arm bands . . . swaggering along with their canes', depressed and irritated him, especially when he compared his own stained and crumpled appearance with theirs. It had taken very little time for him to feel particularly sensitive about the appearance of Dunlop Force, and he 'resented the fact that we were regarded as a rabble'.

He had not long regained his area when, without warning, a party of expanded Divisional Staff appeared. The troops moving into their new quarters ignored them: no one bothered to salute. Weary recognised only ADMS Lieut-Colonel Glyn White amongst the flock of red arm bands – no badges of rank were up – and missed hearing that the Commander of the AIF in Singapore, Lieut-Colonel Galleghan, was of the party. It was only when they were going and 'Command AIF asked if he could do something for me that I caught on'. Weary and Wearne were bidden to dinner on Sunday.

The remainder of the day was spent at the hospital amongst familiar faces. John Diver, his voluble friend from St Mary's Paddington, promised to 'see them right medically'. Jock Frew and Howard Eddey from Ormond days were there, with plenty of work – 'exactly the same vitamin trouble . . . as we had in Java'. B2 deficiency was treated with rice polishings and Marmite, but with all their facilities they seemed to have no more success in treating the men than had Weary, Moon and Corlette.

Lieut-Colonel Hedley Summons passed on a message from Helen picked up from a radio broadcast: 'All's well, Love, Helen Ferguson.'

Lieut-Colonel F. G. Galleghan, nick-named 'Black Jack', commanded the AIF on Singapore. 'He insists on a proper dress and smart turn out . . . ' Weary was on the defensive, acutely conscious of the poor impression his men made, with their prison-cropped hair and filthy, sweat-stained rags. Many were bootless, others lacked headgear, shirts or tunics. They were sloppy on parade and about paying compliments, and Galleghan had not been impressed when none of the troops had saluted his party as they left Weary and Wearne that morning.

His own attitude did not help. He was 'difficult', full of resentment, suspicion and distrust for staff who looked on them all as a 'grubby complication'.[3]

He was unprepared for the letter from Galleghan which was delivered late that afternoon. 'Comd. AIF desires following information. Name of senior combatant officer with party. Suggesting changing O.C. Pty to combatant officer. Is there any reason for not making change?'

His reply took only a few minutes to write. ' . . . Senior combatant officer . . . is Major W. Wearne. Your suggestion welcomed. Present arrangement result of Nip policy in Java of not recognising non-combatant personnel. As senior officer Lt-Col E. E. Dunlop was instructed to command the party in transit. Before making any change your further advice would therefore be appreciated. Could this matter be discussed with Comd AIF tomorrow 10 Jan. 43?'

When Blackburn appeared that evening to say goodbye, Weary raised the three issues concerning him most: the letter, his methods of raising money and discipline.

Blackburn considered Galleghan presumptuous, and pencilled an annoyed memo below Weary's reply: 'I have considered this matter & desire Lt Col Dunlop to retain command for administrative & disciplinary purposes so long as the troops brought over by him remain together as one body.'

He listened to Weary's account of his troubles with Lyneham over levying the officers and gave 'full support' to his policy and to any other methods he might employ in raising money. Discipline was at his discretion. Weary regretted that there was not time to discuss Lyneham more fully, particularly his action in retaining many of his officers and sending away other officers, such as Wearne and Woods, with his troops.

After suggesting that Weary draw up his recommendations for awards and promotions and give copies to him for 'careful burial' with the brigadier's own papers, he disappeared to finish his packing. They were to leave for Formosa early on Sunday morning.

Dinner at AIF HQ that evening was a 'much more formal and swagger affair' than either Wearne or Weary had known for some time. Early in the evening, someone ill-advisedly referred to the 'Java Rabble' and Weary shot to his feet in defence of the men under his command. He reeled off battles and places at sea, on land and in the air in which 'the troops that you refer to as the Java Rabble' had fought: the Battle for Britain, and the Atlantic, the Mediterranean, the Western Desert, Greece, Crete and Syria. 'It was like a roll of drums . . . finishing up with our battle for Java.' He was cutting, sarcastic, angry.

'And now we, the Java Rabble, salute you, the 8th Division, who have fought so gallantly here in Malaysia.'[4]

Later in the evening, Galleghan took Weary aside to tell him that it was incorrect military procedure for a non-combatant to give commands or to punish combatant soldiers. Weary casually produced Blackburn's memo when Galleghan paused. ' . . . I think that shook him a bit.'

Galleghan denied that Blackburn had the authority to give such an instruction: ' *I* am the commanding officer.' Weary, determined not to be drawn into an argument, shrugged and laughed. 'You are my commanding officer . . . Do anything you like . . . I am not even interested.' Thereafter, he turned most of his attention to Glyn White and Bruce Anderson, while Galleghan interrogated Wearne out of earshot. Wearne was intransigent; if Black Jack thought he was neglecting his responsibilities by not taking command, 'he was prepared to give his reasons against it in writing'.

Weary was cynically amused when Galleghan informed him that all criticisms had been satisfied and he would now give Weary formal authority to command the troops. It was precisely this which Galleghan had insisted Blackburn had no authority to issue since it was 'contrary to military procedure'. Blandly, he thanked the senior officer for taking such pains on his behalf.

The insult had stung him into savage rejoinder and the anger and pain stayed with him down the years. He did not record it in the diary, but Wearne and he discussed the incident with their fellow officers. It was round the barracks like a crown fire.

Ray Parkin and many others put it down for posterity in their diaries. The navy – the Senior Service – were already bitter about Galleghan. He had organised a grand march-past on Armistice Day 1942, then tried to shove the ragged remnants of an earlier party of the *Perth* to the tail of the column because they were scruffy. The Gunner in charge, twenty-five years in the Royal Navy, stood his ground, quoted King's Rules and Admiralty Regulations. He prevailed.

As they drew level with the saluting base, the Gunner roared 'Eye-s-s . . . *right* !' and snapped up 'to a real tiddley salute'. Arms straight and swinging, his forty-nine shipmates followed suit. Galleghan was furious. He accused them of giving the Japanese salute. It was a considerable time before some of his fellow officers could convince him that there was no difference.[5]

There was tension between the 8th Division and Dunlop Force.

Otherwise, it was a useful dinner. Glyn White and Captain Bennett promised help with negotiating clothing and medical stores out of the relevant depots. Weary commanded 878 men, and 178 were without boots: he was given six pairs of size 11. Many had no headgear – 20 Glengarry caps were handed over. Most socks had rotted with sweat, wear and rain: 150 pairs were available. After this abysmal session at the clothing depot, he returned to HQ to see Galleghan, who complained 'about . . . my lads – straggling on the march, irregular movements'.

Earlier, Weary had called his company commanders together and emphasised the need for 'smartness, saluting and order in movements' for 'we seasoned veterans of three services suffer the term "Java Rabble".' Galleghan had proclaimed them so to the entire camp and shamed them all. He could have insisted that they be given boots, but he did not; he denied them decency and left them in their rags. They were 'sadly handicapped' in comparison to the other troops in Changi, whom Galleghan had 'lashed verbally . . . into smartness and saluting'.

Weary persisted in his request for boots, but was unsuccessful. ' . . . The Dutch passing through [here] . . . share equally in things and have to have full information . . . must avoid any suggestion of favouritism.' He did not believe the assurances that equipment would be supplied at their destination and finally delivered a bitter little letter to the OC Southern Command personally. 'Position is: no boots – 178; unserviceable boots: 204; urgently needing repair: 304' and 'this position is fast becoming worse'.[6]

Quietly, unofficially, some of the 8th Division men took pity on the mob from Java and gave them boots and shirts when it was realised they would leave as poorly clad as they had arrived.

Money was another source of friction. Glyn White had promised medical stores and bags of rice polishings, but when Galleghan heard that Weary had almost 2000 gulden in the kitty, he countermanded the order unless Weary paid around 90 gulden for them. 'He had his own 10 000+ to look after'. Weary was quick – too quick for Galleghan's liking – with his reply. 'It is noted that on financial grounds Comd AIF Area does not approve the suggestion of ADMS AIF . . . that troops of AIF Java party who are suffering from nutritional disease be supplied with rice polishings on the same basis as other AIF troops in this area.

'The reserve sum . . . has been largely raised by a sacrifice of officers' pay on a scale apparently not considered expedient or necessary in this area . . . no Red Cross supplies have ever been available to the troops in question, and . . . at no time have they experienced conditions as satisfactory as those prevailing [here].'[7]

But the communication which caused Weary most trouble, leading to angry letters threatening later action following him up the railway into Thailand, was the one he wrote to Galleghan before they left Singapore.

'Footwear AIF Troops Java Party, S. Area. Reference my letter 15 Jan 43 . . . NO reply has been received . . . the situation remains unaltered . . . the troops are departing on Jan 20 and 21, 1943, with their footwear and clothing in the same sorry plight as that in which they entered the area.'[8]

He sent a copy to the Australian Red Cross Commissioner for good measure.

Typed on the reverse of a printed form asserting that the undersigned

solemnly swore on his honour that he 'would not, under any circumstances, attempt escape' was a furious reply from Galleghan, in which
'opportunity is taken to dissociate this HQ from the remarks . . .
herein'.

The swords were drawn. 'The tenor of your memo is NOT
appreciated . . . Communications such as you have forwarded do not
assist the difficulties of administration and in order that the matter may
be referred to later copies of this correspondence and reports are being
placed with 2 Echelon records.'9

The Commander kept his wrath warm across the years and took his
revenge at the end of the war.10

He slept on a folded blanket on the 'snug, matt surface' of a level
concrete floor, the nights cool enough for him to need a raincoat over
the canvas cover from the valise. Moonlight streamed through the
windows and the breeze brought the soft scent of frangipani and
hibiscus or the tang of the sea. Those nights, neither too hot nor too
cold, with an absence of crawling bugs and insects and whining
mosquitoes would haunt him in the jungles of Thailand.

The sports organiser, Lieut. Cameron-Smith, was a rugby player and
eager to recruit a former International for one of the Southern Area
teams. Weary hauled out his Mary's vest and captained them in a short
trial match on 13 January, and next day they played on a thickly grassed
ground down by the sea. He decided that despite his diarrhoea, which
sent him dashing into the sea every so often, his 'form did not seem too
bad – but only 20 minutes each way makes a difference'. Cameron-
Smith also played: they were picking a team for a match against the
hospital. There was no training to speak of – just a run during the daily
downpour and a swim in the local sea baths the day before the match.
He had learned from Major Denaro that morning that their first parties
would probably leave three days hence.

They played on the Hospital ground on 18 January. Another Mary's
man, A. W. Frankland, spotted the Mary's vest and Weary's massive
form amongst the forwards. The opposing backs were better than
Southern Area's, whose forwards were heavier but 'slow'. Weary
scored 'all points for Southern Area with two tries one converted',
but Frankland scored three of the Hospital's four tries, which gave
them the game: 12 – 8. 'Enjoyable,' Weary decided, in spite of the
'ragged' play.

Departure was to be spread across two days. Three parties, of 325, 300 and 225 troops, each with a medical officer, one NCO and four medical other ranks, were to go; two parties to be picked up outside the barracks next morning at 0730 and 0915 hours. Trevenna and the 2/40th Battalion men from Timor and 'Happy' Houston with his small group of Pioneers would join De Crespigny's rear party of 225. He shed as many of the sick and unfit as possible from the Force and had them admitted to hospital.

Denaro and Glyn White turned up trumps with two bags of rice polishings, some pots of Marmite, a little NAB, Atebrin and scarce anti-diphtheria serum.

Records were handed over to W/O MacKenzie of 2 Echelon AIF for burial in a 'special container'. (Sgt Brian Harrison Lucas had been typing frantically for a couple of days.) Wearne, as treasurer, worked on the finances with Weary. They changed their Java money to Singapore dollars and collected November and December's pay (in gulden, unfortunately), more than doubling their small capital. The funds were divided on a *per capita* basis, so that the men staying behind, the sick and Captain Hamilton's party, would all be provided for.

Even the Japanese were surprised by the rags the men were wearing and, after pressure from Weary, issued NEI Army clothing to a hundred of the worst-clad while they were waiting outside the barracks to board the lorries.

No one knew anything about their destination.

Drawn up alongside the long platforms in Singapore Station were twenty-two metal freight trucks, each about 6.5 by 3 metres: sliding doors, no windows, some – which had carried cattle on the previous trip – stinking and wet from recent cleaning. 'The first three to have 29 in each, the remainder 28 in each (an officer or senior NCO to each car).' The engine was British, the steel trucks Japanese.

An immaculately dressed, polite Japanese interpreter introduced the commander, then warned them against disobedience and the perfidy of the natives, particularly the Thais, who were thieves and would 'even steal our boots off our feet'. Dangling limbs out of doorways was dangerous, especially when they were passing over bridges; it was advisable to keep the door open and put a wire across the opening; and no one must leave the trucks unless the guards gave permission.

Each truck was issued with two buckets for water or rations.

Everyone had brought a full water bottle and two meals of rice in their dixies.

It was Wednesday, 20 January 1943.

They steamed slowly out at 1255. 'We crossed the Causeway in about 1 hour, noting repairs made to breach near Johore [and] . . . shattered remnants of many large oil tanks.' It was the dry season. The line ran through an endless grey monotony of rubber plantations. No prospect of a man hiding there – just dull regiments of slender, bare trunks topped by scanty crowns of leaves, undergrowth clipped close in the underlying shadows, so that the Malays and Indians working there could be seen from afar.

Kampongs of thatched houses on stilts amongst banana and coconut palms and scratching chickens interrupted the rubber, or paddy dotted with Chinese women crowned by pagoda-peaked circular bamboo hats. Otherwise, it was 'jungle, jungle, all the way to Gemas', a dense, tangled mass of bamboo, palms and vines, above which soared great rainforest trees with pale trunks running up thirty metres and more into a sparkling blue sky.

During a brief halt for lunch, the guards allowed them to buy bananas and mangosteens from the vendors who gathered by the line. 'Unfortunately we have very little Malayan currency and Java money is no good . . .'

It was eleven hours before they pulled into the junction at Gemas. Another short halt, at which they were 'given just a light issue of rice. Nothing to drink', before the doors were clanged shut one by one. Twenty-nine men with all equipment in the same box-car as Weary and Wearne. ' . . . We must try to sleep in a squatting position with a horrible aching in bent knees.' No one could sleep, of course. The best they managed to do was doze, always conscious of other arms and legs 'flopping rather horribly across one's own', and the constant stopping and starting throughout the night, with 'finally a tooth-shattering crash of your own truck'.

Next morning, everyone looked like sweeps, eyes gleaming white out of soot-encrusted faces. 'An almost incredible effort of the spine to get up – about the third convulsion achieved an aching vertical.' Kuala Lumpur brought relief with a stop for latrines, a wash under a tap and breakfast of rice and soup hot with curry.

For four days and four nights they travelled, the limestone spine of the Tenasserim range keeping them distant company all the way from Hat Yai through endless jungle, paddy and coastal plain. Curiously shaped mountains rose on their left hand, sheer and chalky-grey where the dwarf evergreen trees that clung to their sides had sloughed off. Somewhere amongst the crags was the Burmese border.

In Malaya, they could tell where they were most of the time from the English station names that remained on the platforms. On the second day, they ate their evening rice and soup at Ipoh, just on dark, at 2100 hours, and by 1515 hours on 22 January they were at the Thai border, in Padang Besar. From there, it was a steady run to the junction at Hat Yai, where their first meal in Thailand was consumed under the curious gaze of pistol-carrying Thais wearing showy uniforms of European pattern. Weary was surprised by their appearance: 'some of them would almost pass for Arabs'. The English station names were painted out and the Thai and Japanese scripts were indecipherable. But, day long, it was the countryside which held his attention – Thai cattle with great up-curved horns and working elephants in 'rough, primitive country with much jungle, little evidence of roads and many quite big rivers'.

Weary and some other officers had shaved most days 'to avoid that going-to-seed appearance', but the troops were 'so dirty and suntanned that if they were to get hold of a bunch of pisangs no one could separate them from the local inhabitants'.

They steamed on up the Isthmus of Kra, the Gulf of Thailand never far away once they passed Chaiya. Men sweated freely in the metal boxes by day, then cooled off rapidly once the sun went down. Rivulets of condensation trickled down the metal walls. He had not expected nights in Thailand to be so cold, 'with resultant shivering and the irritability of contracted bladders, in spite of the shortage of water'. Both breakfast and the evening meal were on the train, Chumphon being the only stop that day when they were able to stretch and walk about after a scanty feed of yet more rice.

It was bright moonlight when the trainload of cold, dirty, thirsty men hissed to a halt in Ban Pong Station at 0730 on 24 January. They discovered that this was the junction for a new railway which was to be built into Burma. 'Of all the rum goes – when I started this war I hardly expected to find myself a POW seated on the border of a railway in the depths of Siam.'

'God my gear is a frightful lift.' The lorries were 200 metres away. Weary clung to his baggage. Japanese Movement Control had seized the 200 kilos of rice polishings, the buckets, typewriter, clothing and other heavy articles and piled them in a corner of the station with the promise that all would be sent up five days later. 'I am pessimistic about this.' He had stowed his surgical instruments and a number of books in his valise roll. This, with a pack, medical haversack, respirator haversack, suitcase, bulky Dutch Medical Companion and water bottle, was almost more than he could carry.

Breakfast was a few hands of 'stunted' bananas thrown on the cabs of the lorries. Nothing to drink and, because they had been given no water the night before, their water bottles were half empty. They drove off packed twenty-five to a vehicle as the sun rose at 0915 Tokyo time. He shivered in the bitter cold.

The shabby little shops of unpainted wood in Ban Pong were well stocked with food and Weary could see condensed milk and other tinned goods on the shelves. Mangy dogs and pigs nosed in mounds of rubbish; skinny hens with amazingly long legs escorted broods of chicks and scratched around the buildings or scattered out of the lorries' path. Tethered cattle were grazing on the outskirts and hundreds of ducks were being led out by their duck boys to the paddy fields.

'Terrible dirt roads' took them quickly into wild jungle country where bamboo groves up to fifteen metres high, the canes as thick as a man's thigh at the base, mingled with palms and vines, teak and other trees. The thick black dust soon rendered khaki indistinguishable from NEI green. Strangling figs wound 'python-like' down the trunks and low branches brushed dangerously close to heads and eyes. Billy Wearne was side-swiped by one of these and lost his hat. As Weary was laughing at the sight of a Thai boy 'taking the catch perfectly' and racing off, Wearne reached across, took Weary's digger hat from under his shoulder strap. Later, Weary's 'rather inadequate cloth cap' also flew off, but was returned by one of the Japanese guards, which was lucky, since the diary was concealed in its crown. Vultures hung high above them on broad wings under a sun 'hot as hell.'

They were tipped out of the lorries at Wandon Bridge at two o'clock and ordered to walk what Weary remembered as a couple of hundred metres to a staging camp, while their vehicles followed cautiously across the ricketty bamboo and wooden bridge. He arrived with one shoe minus its sole, his legs trembling from the weight he was carrying. 'I looked so much like a pack camel that one of the troops . . . offered to carry my suitcase (gratefully accepted).'

Until he unrolled his valise and sat down to offer what first aid he could to his exhausted men, some had believed that his baggage was stuffed with food and 'personal gear', clothing and so on. Their criticism was silenced when they saw the instruments, the scraps of bandages and dressings, the packets of precious drugs, the medical books.

They filled their water bottles. 'No food.' The British prisoners in the camp were avid for news, their only source being other prisoners moving up-country along the roads and bridges they had built. Food was scarce, an infantry officer told him, although occasionally a Japanese guard would allow an officer to shoot a buffalo. Their latest venture was a 'ranch' they hoped to form with sixty head of cattle they had acquired. Weary listened to this with some scepticism. 'He said we were going right on to the jungle to build our own camp close to the Burmese border.'

For the past eight months, the Japanese had been moving British, Dutch and Australian prisoners from the Netherlands East Indies and Singapore to Burma and Thailand.

In mid-May 1942, Brigadier A. L. Varley had taken 'A' Force of 3000 men to Burma. For the first three months, they were employed on airfield construction; then they were moved to Thanbyuzayat and put to clearing dense forest and building embankments and cuttings. Unknown to Weary, both Coates and Eadie were in Burma with 'A' Force, caring for the sick at the other end of a railway planned to run 421 kilometres from Thanbyuzayat in Burma to Kanchanaburi in Thailand, where it would join the existing railway and give the Japanese a system extending from Burma to Indo-China.

'Dunlop' Force was the first group of Australians to arrive in Thailand. The staging camps at Ban Pong and at Tarsau, which they reached after a further two hours drive, were full of emaciated British prisoners. Huts and latrines were filthy. At Tarsau they slept the night of 24 January on the ground. A 'tow-haired, fresh, beefy-faced brainless type of Englishman' refused them water for washing . . . he insisted there was only enough . . . for bottles', although Weary discovered later that the river was only a short distance away. ' . . . Nitwits apparently are too busy to arrange [it].' He managed to shave in half a cup of water, and looked at his face in his shaving mirror 'with complete horror'.

Rice and half a cup of tea were provided and 'I slept like a top in spite of the bitter cold . . . .Thank the Lord for my policy of tenaciously holding on to my valise & greatcoat'.

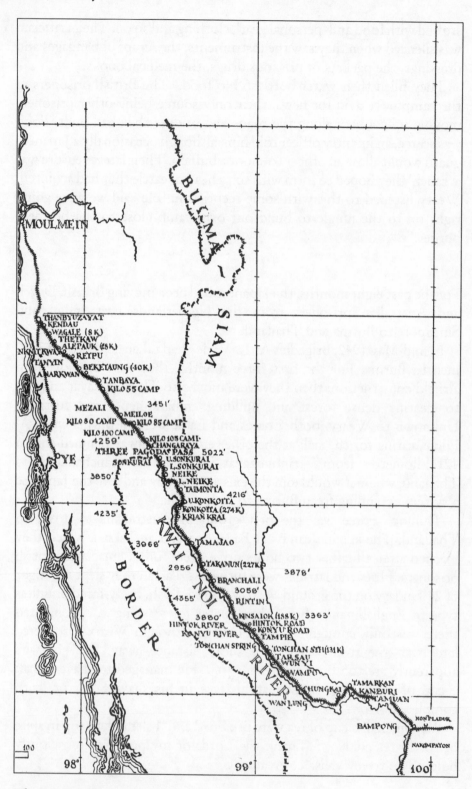

The Burma–Thailand Railway

The commanding officer of the hospital, Lieut-Colonel W. G. Harvey, showed no interest in Weary's sick. All he wanted to hear was news. The secrecy imposed by their captors meant that those left behind in Singapore were told neither the destinations nor purpose of the movements. 'D' Force began to arrive at the end of March 1943, when Lieut-Colonel McEachern brought up 2220 Australian and 2780 British prisoners. Malaya Command had issued them with more adequate medical supplies: six months supply of quinine and plasmoquine and sulphaguanidine.

When 'F' Force was sent away in April, there were not 7000 fit troops in the Changi area (the number required), but the Allies were deliberately misled by a statement that 'the reason for [the] move was to transfer a large body of prisoners to an area where food was more plentiful and the climate healthier than . . . Singapore'.[11]

The Australians, more sceptical than the British, included only 125 unfit men in 'F' force; the British unfit component was around 1000, with predictable results once they reached Thailand and were exposed to the monsoon.

They took equipment for a 250-bed hospital with them and 40 per cent of the remaining stocks of some essential drugs, but little of this arrived at their camp in Shimo Sonkurai. Japanese inefficiency and the impassible state of the roads once the monsoon hit in May, left three-quarters of the medical stores at Ban Pong. In groups of around 600 men, they marched by night in stages 'on negligible rations' to the most remote camps in Thailand.

Those who came under the control of the Japanese Malayan Prisoner of War administration were in worse case than men who were the responsibility of the Burmese end, for their food came up from Singapore and Bangkok. George Aspinall, who trekked north to Three Pagodas Pass with 'F' Force, saw nothing but a heaving mess of maggots in cases of prawns sent up from Bangkok – 'just putrified shells' – and wooden containers of stinking yak meat would be 'vitually jumping out of the box . . . The cooks used to dump the lot into big cauldrons of boiling water . . . The maggots were skimmed off the top, and after a day of stewing, the meat was fit to eat'.[12] Even smoked fish arrived blown and maggotty, Weary observed, and his camp at Hintok was much closer to the source. Food came up river to Konyu on barges and the stores were then portered by Weary, Wearne and other officers to their camps.

One of Tom Young's abiding and 'most endearing' memories of Weary is of a day during the wet season of 1943 when, from his hospital bed, he saw Weary and Wearne carrying a huge basket of duck eggs along the muddy track. 'Each had their boots on the pole which was through the basket and each was covered in mud and sweat . . . Despite the huge burden of caring for the sick and dying, Weary could spare the time to carry for miles some sustenance for the troops.'[13]

Mostly, the diet was rice, and not enough of that, with a little dried or rotting fish, a few vegetables (pumpkin, sweet potato, maybe a few onions or some cabbage or, failing that, dried Japanese radish) or the occasional small lump of yak meat. Whenever palm oil was available, rice could be made into rissoles, called 'doovers' by the men, and fried; *gula malacca* , a treacly palm sugar, was sometimes mixed with the rice, and small quantities of peanuts could be bought. But nothing was provided in the amounts laid down in the ration scale. And there was a grave shortage of fat in the diet. Had it not been for the duck eggs, which Thai traders brought up in thousands from the paddy fields, even fewer men would have returned home. The cooks – like everyone else working on the railway – became inventive at juggling the slenderest resources.

Corlette's suggestion (identical to Coates's at the Burma end) that one's 'passport back to home and mother is on the bottom of your dixie' meant that men forced down the food, no matter how disgusting it was.[14] Once, his stomach heaving at the stench and taste of the rotting fish in his rice, Weary rushed off to vomit. When he returned, his dixie was empty: Wearne had finished it off, thinking he would not want any more.

The prisoners-of-war were divided into six groups: 3 and 5 were in Burma, working south from Thanbyuzayat; 1, 2, 4 and 6 moved north from Ban Pong along a line originally surveyed by the British long before the war and re-surveyed in Thailand in 1942 by a small team of British prisoners.

Lieutenant Pringle, George Watson, Sgt Sherrin and E. W. Whincup, accompanied by a Japanese surveyer, a sergeant and four Korean guards, 'surveyed the area along which the railway would run . . . We measured relevant distances and the probable positions for rails etc., hacking our way through malodorous virgin jungle, pegged out these measured distances as far as the Pagoda Pass . . . It was a long and extremely exhausting . . . stint and walking there and back did not . . . improve our tempers or the condition of our feet . . . ' They pulled their equipment and food – two sacks of rice – in a handcart, all the way to Three Pagodas Pass.

It took the groups in 'F' Force around eighteen days to walk the 305 kilometres up to Shimo Sonkurai Camp No 1, just south of the Burmese border. The surveyors would have taken longer, although they started eighty kilometres further up the line at Kanchanaburi, where the existing railway ended.

Once work on the railway course had started, Whincup and his party 'set out [daily] to . . . fix the rail layers and straighten our previous peggings to accommodate the width of the trains . . . We were taken to the rail heads on flat open bogies pulled by a diesel engine manned by Japanese engineers . . . '15

Rather than the earlier survey, it may have been Whincup's party and their Japanese surveyor who were responsible for the error in building a bridge across the Mae Klong River at Tamarkan, rather than following the east side of the river and joining up with the railway at Tarsau, present-day Nam Tok.16

Konyu Camp was twenty-five kilometres from Tarsau along a road so rough that it took the lorries three hours to cover the distance from the staging camp. ' . . . Had to get out and push lorries uphill.' Once more, Weary shouldered his load and struggled down a steep, winding track to the foot of the mountain. When they reached the clearing, a further three-quarters of a kilometre into the jungle, 'I could feel my legs trembling and my shoulders were like hell'.

They were on the banks of a broad, deep river surrounded by thick forest of bamboo and teak, interlaced with vines and thorny rattan which tore at their skin and clothing. The Mae Nam Khwae Noi rose in the mountains near the Burmese border at Three Pagodas Pass and, for much of its length, hugged the road down which invading armies had marched south across the centuries. At Kanchanaburi, its waters joined the Meklong and flowed on to enter the Gulf of Thailand at Samut Songkhram.

Weary, along with all the other medical officers sent north, had been 'blandly informed that good hospitals and abundant medical stores were awaiting them'.17 Lieutenant Usuki, the camp commander, greeted them with the unwelcome news that there was no shelter and very little food. This 'one-pip beardless little youngster (few hairs on chin) with a face like a spoiled boy and much laughter but hard as flint' was quickly dubbed the "Boy *Shoko*".*

---

* *Shoko* = officer.

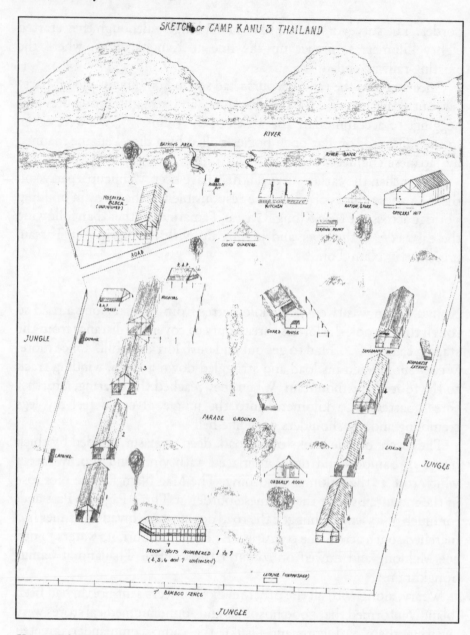

Konyu River Camp
Drawn on arrival in 1943

Weary and Wearne were summoned to his office at three o'clock, where they found Usuki with his egregious, hook-nosed interpeter, Susuki. Three hours were exhausted in devising the camp organisation and the division of the men into two works battalions, one of 438, the other of 435 men. 'All the Nips were simultaneously drawing "family trees" and none agreeing . . .'

Eventually a satisfactory chart was pencilled on a piece of paper, camp duties and a daily routine were fixed, construction work sketched out and the clerical details of returns established. 'The most sinister feature . . . was the insistence that if many men are sick we will draw less food.'

'Dunlop' Force had one dubious advantage over those later arrivals, 'H' and 'F' forces: they reached the railway course and established some sort of routine three months before the monsoon broke.

In what was left of 25 January, temporary latrines and cooking trenches were dug and bamboo fences from which to hang mosquito nets were knocked up in the company areas 'with a maze of streets and lanes'. After eating their evening rice by the blaze of huge fires, they slept on the ground.

The area set aside for the Australians was too small for the number of buildings that were to go up: nine barracks for the men and a smaller one for the officers, a cookhouse, hospital and rations' store, all to be of bamboo and thatched with attap The men's barracks were to be 50 by 6.5 metres and 3 metres to the ridge pole, every man having around a metre of bed space on bamboo platforms running the length of the building, ' . . . 100 men can make 2 houses a day approximately.'

Once it was light next morning, the sound of axes, the 'crash of timber and thud of picks and shovels' rang through the forest as they enlarged the clearing. Two men were sent off to the nearby British camp to inspect latrines, cookhouses, kitchen soakage pits and barracks so that they could be copied.

Major De Crespigny's rear party arrived in the afternoon, 'walking like men in a dream, 15 being practically right out to it including De Crespigny, who was bathed in sweat, glazed of eye and talking wildly'.

Capt. Jack Hands and Capt. Tim Godlee, the medical officer, had been split off to another camp with 375 all ranks AIF who had travelled up with De Crespigny. Weary was disconcerted to learn from Usuki that a Dutch party of 625 men would arrive next day, bringing the strength of Hands' camp to 1000 men, and that he and Wearne must also administer them. The number of men in his command would be

1875. Godlee, the only medical officer available for the Hintok Road camp, had been separated from his men, but Weary was unable to do anything about it.

Weary was appalled by the appearance of the British commander and his senior officers when he called over to their neighbouring camp that afternoon: 'all dressed in pyjamas and sarongs, unshaven or bearded, sallow and dull of eye, full of a sort of hopeless depression'. One of their number was away organising supplies: Alan Ferguson Warren, a colonel in the Royal Marines who had abandoned his escape attempt in order to stay in Sumatra and take command of demoralised troops and the sick.

Lieut-Colonel Moore and Lieut-Colonel Hill told of underfeeding, malaria, dysentery, deaths, difficulties of procuring stores and changing money and the necessity for their officers to take over camp duties such as chopping wood and hauling water. Weary was unimpressed by their reason for preferring such menial tasks to clearing jungle: 'But that is much harder work.' He did not yet appreciate the difficulties of officers working on the line, nor of how few other ranks the Japanese would allow them for camp duties.

Smedley and Moon burst into the house in the middle of this recital of woe. They were short 15 ticals for 900 duck eggs which had arrived on a barge with a load of attap. Hill promptly handed over the sum, observing wrily that they had hailed the barge themselves, but failed to stop it.

From the third day in their narrow clearing by the river, Sgt Paige's trumpet sounded reveille at 0800 Tokyo time, 'more beautiful with the mountain echoes than I'd ever believed [it] . . . could sound'.[18] They led a mediaeval existence, easing themselves stiffly to their feet an hour before the Stygian darkness lifted, and standing to at roll call in the blackness twelve hours later, when Weary could only just see the troops drawn up in front of him. The officers at the other end of the parade were 'invisible'.

There was no such thing as 'lights out', for there were none: only the brilliant stars above and the blaze from huge fires kindled for warmth and to keep off wild animals. 'Tiger fires', the men called them. Ten o'clock saw nearly everyone rolled in a blanket and attempting to sleep. Weary wrote his diary by the flickering fires of teak and bamboo.

The Dutch were expected on 27 January. Weary and Wearne reported to Usuki at 0930 and the three of them toiled up the steep mountain path through low bushes and vines dripping moisture to the

50 *Resourceful Matron*
Mickey de Jonge,
No. 1 Allied General
Hospital, Bandoeng

51 *Attap for roofs arrived on barges*

52 *Chalker drew Weary in the cholera tent during the wet, 1943*

53 *Glass rod testing for dysentery began in Java, continued in Thailand*

54 *Gimson was summoned to sketch Weary operating, Chungkai, 1/4/44. Corlette assisted*

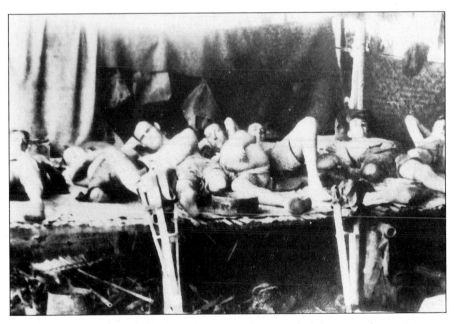

55 *Weary was horrified by the amputees' ward, Tarsau, 1943*

56 *Wet beri beri cases, Tarsau, 1943*

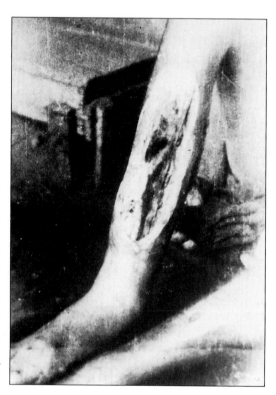

57 *At Tarsau, he looked across a hundred legs stinking with gangrene and ulcers like this*

58 *Thai houseboats moored on the Kwai Noi below the railway*

59 *POWs approach the hospital, Nakom Patom*

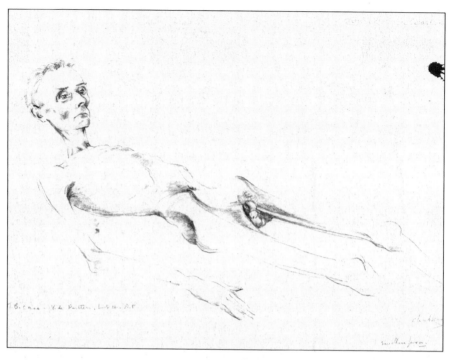

60 *Tubercular patient, Nakom Patom (Chalker)*

61 *Weary called Chalker to illustrate the medical record. Checking*
illustrations with Coates, Bangkok September 1945

62 *Weary in the dispensary, Nakom Patom, August 1945*

63 *Boon Pong recovered from the bullets*

64 *Being piped out of Toorak Presbyterian church, November 1945.
Jim Yeates at Weary's right*

65 *It was a joyous day: Aunts Ede, Violet and Lil with
Alice and James*

road junction, 'he sweating a great deal and clumping along in his top boots'. Capt. Smits' and Lieut. Toets' party, with 'a tremendous percentage of NCOs, many of these Eurasians and a lot very old', were already clambering down from the lorries. They were designated R battalion.

Hands' camp was a five-kilometre walk away. It took all afternoon to settle in the newcomers, explain the organisation and system of returns to Hands, Smits and their adjutants, and inspect the camp. 'The water supply is not good: a little trickle down the mountain with some shallow, rather stagnant pools near the camp . . . probably malarious.' Within hours, the Dutch lines looked 'like China-town, almost everyone having built a crazy hut of . . . leaves, bamboo etc.'.

There were now seven works battalions in the Konyu area: Weary's four – O, P, Q and R – in two locations on the road at Hintok and by the river at Konyu No. 3 camp; and the three English battalions. Together, they constituted 4 Group. That evening, at an officers' conference, he fixed the appointments for his battalions.

Greiner and Woods were to command two works battalions, O and P, with Piper and Primrose as their seconds-in-command, Corlette and Moon as medical officers, Clarke – the *benjo* king – in charge of sanitation and anti-malarial measures and Airey as quartermaster. Allen, De Crespigny, Smedley, Houston and Brettingham-Moore were accounts and purchasing, works, liaison and general duties respectively.

Each camp would operate its own finances and canteen along the same lines: one-third of everyone's pay was to be contributed to a regimental fund which provided food for the kitchens and for the sick, and the prices of canteen articles would be controlled, with a ten per cent profit 'to the nearest cent' going to the fund. Stocks would come from barge-loads of stores brought up the river and shared fifty-fifty with the English camp. Most sought-after were the Red Bull cigarettes at the official price of 25c a packet; the essential item, as far as the doctors were concerned, was eggs at 7c each, for these would alleviate the avitaminosis.

'It is astonishing how primitive life is here – bamboo being almost our only resource . . . not even the odd tin or petrol can or pieces of wire.' Everyone was working, most on the camp, but other parties were taken out by the engineers to make a road and bridges. The tools provided were shoddy – 'a few axes, picks, saws, shovels and knives' – and had to be repaired constantly and supplied with new handles. There were no nails; the bamboo framework of the huts and the sleeping platforms were bound together with ties made from vines or cut lengths of the inside bark from trees they had felled. Roofs were thatched with attap.

On a long sandy osier-bed by the river, men from the *Perth* wove baskets for rice from bamboo slats, willow twigs soaked until they were pliable and twine twisted from vines and bark gathered in the forest.

It took five days to build the cookhouse, and the 'ranges' dug out of solid red earth on which were balanced the *cwalis* , hemispherical metal wok-type containers well over a metre in diameter in which the rice and soup were cooked. Chimneys, even an Aldershot oven fitted with a bamboo door heavily plastered with mud, were constructed. 'Lord knows what happens to everything when the rains come.'

But it was the steady work of bustling, pragmatic Jock Clarke and his hygiene squad which earned Weary's admiration when he saw how they felled trees, and in their carpenters' shop 'split and squared good timber . . . using wooden wedges' so that they could fit the deep trench latrines with 'the most excellent flyproof seats' with sliding covers. They vented the latrines with tall bamboo pipes and alongside each were bamboo containers filled with a mixture of soap and cresol antiseptic on the Castellani bottle principle, for the Japanese never supplied enough flimsy paper for the camp's needs.

They finished the framework of the men's barracks and thatched four of them with attap before the barges unaccountably stopped bringing it up the river.

Four hundred men moved their beds onto the knobbly bamboo platforms under shelter; the others stayed on the dusty ground. The fine, alluvial dust drifted over and into everything, and it aggravated throats raw with avitaminosis. Weary nagged Usuki about the lack of attap and eventually he confessed that there would be no more. 'All transport now use to shift food for the rainy season.' Men were set to cutting reeds as a substitute.

Weary's hands blistered 'most foully' when he began working on the officers' house down by the river. More serious was a septic scratch on his leg gained one night while digging in the mud for the rubbery clams everyone sought as extra protein. He developed inflamed glands and cellulitis and had great difficulty walking. At night he hankered for Changi's concrete floor, for 'bamboo beds are diabolical, owing to their hardness, smoothness and irregularity'. Pain disturbed his sleep. Luckily it was not so cold, for he had lent his greatcoat ('worth two blankets') to a man with pleurisy.

All the officers except Allan Woods slept on bamboo sleeping frames outside the bamboo perimeter fence, surrounded by looming Gothic arches of living bamboo. Woods built himself a Heath Robinson shelter of banana leaves, bamboo and rice sacks, much to his peers' amusement. Woods was a bushman from Queensland, practical and inventive, who could make almost anything out of 'flywire and spit'.

Weary succeeded in persuading Usuki to let Jock Clarke and his hygiene squad cross the river in search of mosquitoes. Clarke discovered an abundance of stagnant pools and water lying in the cut stumps of bamboo, but his most depressing find was *Anopheles minimus*, a little mosquito striped like a tiger which bred in clear, running mountain streams with grassy edges. He knew where to seek it: the British survey team found it in 1928 and identified it as the prominent vector. It was not many weeks before cases of primary malaria began to turn up in the daily sick parade.

More obvious were venomous snakes – cobras and kraits – pythons, scorpions, huge tarantulas and centipedes, and every day men appeared with severe bites inflicted after dark. No snake or lizard had a chance if a man saw it; it was soon killed, skinned and roasting over a fire.

There was a second reason why Weary wanted someone free to rove across the river. Unlike some members of the Army Medical Corps, Jock points out, he and Weary 'never forgot we were soldiers' with responsibilities to their men beyond the obvious medical and dental ones. And if it was possible for someone to escape, it was their duty to help them. But they realised how futile any such action would be when Clarke returned. All he could see from the tallest trees he climbed was a vast, unbroken tract of narrow valleys and forest against a mountain range that ran like a row of broken teeth into the blue distance. The nearest Allies were in Yunnan, perhaps 1200 kilometres away. 'It was bloody hopeless.'

Nonetheless, seeing it was the dry season, Jock decided to start a bushfire one day in an attempt to cause their captors the maximum inconvenience. The teak and cotton trees were dry and leafless, but the undergrowth was wet and green. 'It was a spectacular failure.'

From the instant he awoke to Sergeant Paige's trumpet until he finished writing up his diary at night, Weary was rarely still. Many hours were spent reporting to Usuki (who could fuss endlessly over returns), in conference with the officers, on hospital and camp inspection, visiting the Englishmen for secret wireless news and working on the officers' hut.

He also found time to talk to the troops, individually, privately. He sought out Ray Parkin to discuss with someone else who had been there the night when the harbour at Piraeus exploded in a rush of heat and flame. 'He tells me that all his life he has been a scoffer.' But Parkin had been observing the Colonel for months now and knew Weary as a 'most kindly and gentle scoffer – except at the unrighteous. Here is a man who shoulders his own burdens so that they will not worry others, and then heedlessly piles on his own shoulders the worries of anybody who comes to him'.[19]

Weary was with Parkin at ten o'clock on 18 February, the night Corlette sought his advice about Private Jones, a man with a perforated duodenal ulcer. Moon joined them; and they decided they must operate. Weary had his 'surgical kit . . . a little chloroform and ether but no facilities whatever for operating [or] sterilising'. Dysentery patients were turned out of their circular white tent and its sides rolled up ('reflective qualities'), Smedley and Airey rapidly built an operating table from bamboo just outside Rod Allanson's tent, another man made a bamboo mask for anaesthesia and 'the CCS lads got straight on with the sterilising, boiling the set of instruments I picked out . . . towels and three pairs of gloves'.

Brian Harrison-Lucas asked the Japanese for the loan of their hurricane lamps, but they refused all but two which were added to two torches and a few candles.

More fires were lit for light and warmth. A stretcher served as an instrument table and also on it were piled sterilised towels for use as packs. Corlette was the anaesthetist; Moon assisted. 'All the Nip guard and the medical corporal were in full cry . . . resolved to see the operation.'

Grey-Turner, his surgical mentor, and the simplicity of his methods were in Weary's mind as at 0225 he carefully began 'one of the strangest operations I have ever been at . . . [before] a fantastic audience of mixed Nip soldiers, our officers and the CCS laddies'. A silent cordon of troops watched from the shadows. The sight of rice oozing out of the patient's gut was too much for one of the Japanese, who disappeared suddenly and noisily to vomit. When Weary finished, more than two hours later, he realised that he had no more noticed the spectators than he would a crowd surrounding a football field.

A Japanese soldier reached up to clap him on the shoulder. 'You No. 1 doctor.' Weary turned his back.

Rod Allanson, like Parkin and Haskell and all the others, was profoundly impressed by the emergency operation and felt proud to be one of Weary's men. 'He built up the camp morale in many cases singlehanded . . . The Japs couldn't believe their eyes when they saw this remarkable piece of surgery.'[20]

The memory of that clearing with its blazing fires and ring of intent faces, watching while the orderlies directed the beams of light from their torches onto the patient and Weary's gloved hands, is burned into Bill Haskell's mind. He has no doubt that, after the operation, the Japanese admired 'the colonel'.[21]

They packed the patient with hot bottles, wrapped him in blankets and left him tucked up on the table in the tent. Weary went to bed at half past five that morning. The Japanese were amazed. From then on they looked at him 'with bated breath' and chased him for treatment and advice. Even Corlette regarded it as a 'miracle operation'.[22]

Next day the medical corporal donated two tins of condensed milk to the patient and the basket makers wove him a bamboo back-rest 'to offset the chances of pleurisy'.

Weary was anxious when Jones's condition deteriorated, but five days on, he was obviously much better. 'I should hate to lose a case at present when the whole inspirational life of the camp seems to depend on such things,' Weary confided to his diary.

Parkin was certain that it was Weary who held 'this body of men from moral decay in bitter circumstances which they can only meet with emotion rather than reason'.[23]

Most days Weary walked ten kilometres there and back to Jack Hands' camp, leaving early while the surface of the Kwai Noi still smoked with mist and troops of White-handed Gibbons swung carelessly across the face of the cliff before dropping five or six metres into the bamboos. Their whooping and howling began well before reveille, the sound travelling vast distances.

Alone or with Wearne or one of the other officers, Weary moved between the camps without a qualm, despite 'traces of panther' and the big cat smell of tiger marking their territories. There was 'a constant flurry of life going on in the undergrowth' and one man killed a plump junglefowl with a stone. At night they heard muntjac bark, and some shivered at the cough of what might have been a tiger. By day, troops of monkeys and squirrels chattered in the trees, but the deer, wild pig and buffalo were seldom seen. He was fascinated by the birds, but could identify very few: pigeons, doves and tiny bright green hanging parrots scrambled amongst the branches, others called invisibly and monotonously from high up, 'tonk, tonk, tonk'.* Kingfishers and bee-eaters darted across the river. Once, a surprised Grey Peacock-Pheasant flew up from the path and plover picked their way delicately across the sand banks or the gravel near the hot springs. Later, he discovered that the glossy black birds with slender racket tails that swooped on insects and called like creaking doors were drongoes.

He saw beauty all about him, in the rosy fingers of Homeric dawns, the delicate fronds of bamboo in the morning light, the 'great cumulus clouds appearing over the clear rim of our mountain world'. But of all times, Weary loved the beginning and ending of each day, when beauty could 'sometimes positively hurt . . . especially the lovely quarter hour before dawn when the whole sky is aglow with brilliant crimson bands showing through the clearly etched foliage'. It was then that he thought of Helen, the memory of their lost years like a knife in the heart.

The 'terrible sick smell' of 'dirty, gaunt bodies and unmade beds' in the British barracks, and the rising dysentery rate of the Dutch R Battalion worried him. 'I am told that soldiers take their mess tins into the latrine areas (instead of the ubiquitous bottle); also they use the same tin for washing hands and face.'

Their latrines were shallow and too close to the stream; a third of the battalion was lying in the fouled area of their temporary hospital by the beginning of March. Smits blamed the age of the men ; 'we cannot work like the Australians . . . it is too hard'. In reality, discipline was poor and the Javanese had given up the struggle. Hands reported that even digging graves was too difficult for them – the dead were buried 'hardly below the surface'. Tim Godlee kept his well-run tented hospital right away from the Dutch lines.

Sick parade was held in the evening when the men came in. Weary, Moon and Corlette were ordered to inoculate everyone against dysentery, cholera, plague and typhus. (Only six weeks had elapsed since the previous orgy of inoculation in Makasura.) The number of men suffering from avitaminosis was declining on the one-to-three-egg-a-day diet, although few did not suffer from diminished eyesight or were free

---

* A species of Barbet.

Stanley Gimson drew the dysentery ward, Konyu River camp

from diarrhoea. Some men could no longer see clearly in the dark and had to be led out at night to the latrines or back to their lines. Weary had had ulcers, cellulitus and swollen legs for five weeks now.

As more cases of dysentery and primary malaria were diagnosed, Weary announced a blitz on both, insisting that everyone use the disinfectant containers by the *benjos* and clean up any areas which were accidentally fouled, that they sleep under their mosquito nets and not go shirtless after dark or wander down to the river at night. The hospital tents were full and the new structures knocked up on a low-lying and uneven stretch of ground down by the river were unfinished, 'shockingly jerry-built with no roof'.

Tadano, the *socho*,* was one of the few reasonable Japanese soldiers, co-operative and helpful within his limits. 'He talks a little pidgin English and has keen wits; always very generous with cigarettes.' He

---

* warrant officer.

responded to Weary's request for tents, providing three of American pattern with mosquito gauze lining immediately Weary showed him the inadequate accommodation. But he could do nothing about the fact that only one-tenth of the meat entitlement and a quarter of the vegetables had been supplied since their arrival, nor could he supply more tools for the hygiene squad.

His colleague, the Japanese medical corporal, was 'a rascal and trader-in-chief', up to all kinds of rackets. He never ceased attempting to buy men's watches, pens and other marketable possessions and badgered Weary constantly about selling his watch and fountain pen to him. When the much-vaunted medical supplies for the whole of Konyu – 4000 men – arrived in February, they consisted largely of a dozen bottles of Scott's Emulsion, 10 500 quinine and 1250 Plasmo-quine tablets, 8 ampoules of morphia, 300 Aspirins, a few vitamin B1 and sulphonamide tablets, ten bandages and a few other bits and pieces of iodine, tinea lotion and methylated spirits.

At the end of the month Weary was handed three questionaires to be submitted to a conference of Japanese prison camp commanders at Ban Pong. ' . . . Apparently the general will see [them] instead of coming to see us.' He discussed them with Moon and Harrison-Lucas, who would complete the other two, and they decided to fire off a salvo of complaints. Unhealthy site, inadequate rations, almost non-existent medical supplies, no containers for boiling water, no disinfectants, a shortage of tools which was delaying the construction of latrines and anti-malaria work causing malaria and dysentery; no chloride of lime or containers for sterilisation of drinking water; insufficient boots and clothing; and no letters or communication with home.

When Usuki demanded a further essay on the 'attitude of mind as to camp', Weary wondered if he was displeased at the loss of face their answers would gain him in Ban Pong. Nonetheless, he decided to write an even more 'bloody-minded' reply.

'My attitude is one of gross disquiet and fear for the lives and health of the troops placed in my care . . . The following matters worry and perplex me.

' . . . Only a fraction of the promised scale of vegetables and meat has been supplied.

' . . . Many soldiers have no house and most sleep in the open, though some have almost no clothes and blankets.

'Out of a total of 873 men I consider that only 350 are suitable for heavy work outside the camp.

'It causes grave alarm that other troops I see in the area should look like living skeletons.'

Were it not for the efforts of the medical team, he was certain that the mortality would have been much higher. 'Arthur Moon is always one of the busiest men in the camp and Jock Clarke is one of the best.'

The dry season was coming to an end. The hectic, fever-chart outline of the hills was rimmed with fire at night, while the sun rose blood-red in a mist of smoke each morning. He had expected jungle to be lush and green, but this was grey-brown and ghost-like, for teak and rosewood is deciduous. 'The vista is gaunt and cheerless, like a woodheap without end.' Picks and shovels broke as the men hacked at the brick-hard earth which then had to be piled in bamboo baskets and carried to the embankment they were building.

On 1 March, Weary was warned that he should be ready to supply 500 men a day for work on the railway and the road. Until now, the British camp had supplied most of the labour; now it was to be the Australians' turn. But there was worse news: cholera had broken out further up the river.

Weary took over the care of a tent full of patients, 'mostly malaria', for now there were more than Moon and Corlette could handle. Then on 8 March, the anniversary of the capitulation in Java, there was 'confirmation of . . . move to Kinsayok'.

When van der Post farewelled Weary at the gates of Bandoeng camp, he thought of Bunyan's *Pilgrim's Progress*, of unfashionable words like valiant, standfast, tell-true, great-heart. Weary would have grinned in a self-deprecating way if Laurens had spoken these aloud. But in truth, he had set his feet on that narrow 'King's Highway' which Appollyon trod, and now he was drawing very near to the hill Difficulty.*

---

* 'A foul Fiend coming over the field to meet him; his name is Appollyon.'

TWENTY

Valley of the Shadow

THEY HAD SPENT FORTY-SIX days building Konyu 3. Weary was reluctant to leave, for the care taken over its construction and sanitation made it superior to the other camps. Rumours had them going to Kinsayok, but Japanese Railway Headquarters at Ban Pong ordered them to begin moving to Hintok mountain on 12 March; Hands was to take Q and R battalions to Kinsayok.

To be condemned to the 'waterless bog' where Hands was at present filled Weary with foreboding. 'This news is as bloody as could be . . . the river here is the life-line and to be away from it in wet weather is too unpleasant to contemplate.'

The move to the new camp took six days. The promised lorries appeared only twice and other times men had to struggle up the hill, though the new road was easier than the steep slope with its roughly-cut steps which they had stumbled down in January. Laden with a pack and three haversacks, Weary accompanied the last group, 'perspiration streaming from every pore [and] . . . all men's lungs working overtime'.

Many were shaking with exhaustion when they straggled in. A walk which Weary, when 'legging it', could do in fifty-five minutes had taken an hour and three-quarters.

By 17 March, the majority of O and P battalions was installed in the shadow of a sheer-sided limestone hill he had christened 'Jack's Mountain'.

Hintok K4 lay in low ground between two escarpments straddling the road to Burma. Accommodation was two broken-down barracks and the drunken framework of eight others: 'no beds'. Most men now slept in tattered and leaking tents abandoned by the previous occupants, some just a single fly flung over the jerry-built bamboo frames. A shaky bamboo palisade screened them from the passing traffic.

'Shinbone Alley', the fouled area where the Dutch had bivouacked, was cleaned and incorporated in the parade ground.

There was only one route to the western portion of the railway course. At first, the men climbed a steep, zigzag path to the limestone face of the escarpment, then clambered up the last twenty metres of sheer rock wall on the trunk of a huge teak tree into which someone had hacked out steps. Then Woods built a twenty-metre ladder from stout, flexible bamboo and wire. It was slippery and almost vertical, but a significant improvement.

There was no view from the top; the jungle closed above them in a green tunnel. For three kilometres, they followed the elephant pads down a long and unstable rocky slope to the railway, cautiously threading a path between the boulders and low-growing bamboo. For men returning in the dark, there was no indication where the ladder began. The Korean guard 'Billie the Pig' used to squat at the top, using his cigarette lighter to show his working party the position of the first step.

A few Dutch details and some of their sick who remained in the camp with one doctor and another officer were marked for evacuation as soon as possible, either to Kinsayok or to hospital at Tarsau. The NEI soldiers, all light duty men, were ineffectual workers and their officers exercised no authority, reserving their enthusiasm for the canteen. 'They eat enormously.'

Weary decided that the new camp commander, Private Ikimoto, was reasonable, but his No. 2 was 'a proper little bastard' called Hiram-ura – 'the Lizard' – who fixed reveille for 0730 hours, one hour before the works battalions were to move off for the day. He was young, smooth-faced and inflexible.

Scarcely had Weary convinced Ikimoto that they should improve the water supply and dig new and deeper *benjos* on the high side of the road, than Engineer Hiroda appeared, demanding 600 men for work next day on the railway. Weary decided that his 'pug-faced, charming show-the-teeth expression' concealed a vicious nature. None were to work on the new latrines, the water scheme or anti-malaria measures. ' . . . All light duty and no duty men and all men without boots to go just the same.'

Hands came over to report that six Dutchmen had died in as many days at Kinsayok and Weary feared that the same would happen here if Hiroda's regime was not modified. 'This is the next thing to murder . . . The Ns have a great reserve of manpower here and at Singapore, and they are showing every intention of just breaking them on this job [without] . . . the faintest consideration of either life or health. This can only be regarded as a cold blooded merciless crime against mankind . . . obviously premeditated.

'I will have a showdown about this tomorrow with somebody.'

After parade next morning, Weary 'reluctantly' indicated that 12 of the 32 light duty and no duty men should go out to work, then stalked angrily over to 'the Lizard' and told him that twenty were unfit. He was non-plussed when Hiramura meekly accepted his figures. ' . . . Felt I had been a bit of a sucker not to stick out about all the other[s],' he decided, as 577 marched out with the engineer's guard.

The battalion commanders, Greiner and Woods, De Crespigny, Wearne and Weary agreed that, rather than use fit men in the duty section, they would substitute 42 no duty and light duty men and send the fit men out on railway work. Weary decided that the earlier he confronted Hiroda the better. The others went with him.

He found Hiroda about four kilometres from camp, by the blacksmith's forge at the end of the track to the railway. Weary presented him with a litany of complaints, suggesting that sending out sick and bootless men would 'crack them up and be a bad economic position'. He had added to his grievances the number of men without footwear working on 'rocks hot as hell and covered with knife-like edges', five days of nothing but rice to eat and no men available to collect

Central Thailand: Konyu–Hintok section (opposite). The whole of this area was completely covered by dense bamboo and tree-canopied jungle through which a strip 30 metres wide had to be cleared. This jungle was deciduous in the Dry Season (Nov–Mar). The mountain ridge is 1000–1500 m elevation, sloping precipitously down to the river valley through which it ran.

The Permanent Way was along a gradient cut as a ledge into the side of this steep, rocky mountainside at, roughly, the 150 m contour of elevation. This was supplemented, as necessary, by cuttings, embankments and short trestle bridges. All cuttings, except the Compressor Cutting, were made with hand drilling ('hammer and tap') and blasting. The Supply Road in this section followed, roughly, the 300 m contour. It was a dirt road, not only impassable in the Wet Season, but in many places completely swallowed up – only to be rediscovered and rebuilt after the rains stopped. The river was the only way of contact and supply then.

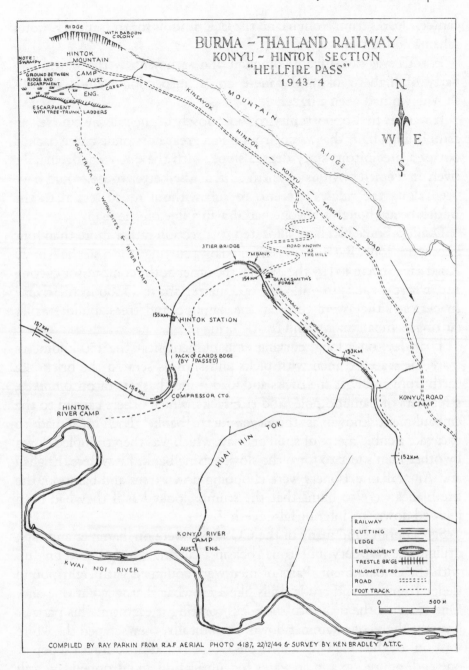

COMPILED BY RAY PARKIN FROM R.A.F AERIAL PHOTO 4187, 22/12/44 & SURVEY BY KEN BRADLEY A.T.T.C.

canteen stores from Konyu, and the lack of tools for the sanitary, water scheme and anti-malaria squads.

Hiroda was saved from comment and argument by the arrival of a party of higher-ranking Japanese on an inspection round. Weary's showdown had been a fizzer.

It was his first opportunity to look closely at the railway course, 'an astonishing affair' that swung round in a great horseshoe curve hacked out of a precipitous sixty degree slope, with the open side facing the river. It seemed obvious to them all that the better route would have been along the ridge. 'It seems to run without much regard to the landscape as though someone had drawn a line on the map!'

Dunlop Force had been allocated to a section rather more than four kilometres long. Each end was marked by a cutting: one near the Konyu Road camp occupied by the British, the other at the compressor cutting site, where a spur ran out some 600 metres above a loop in the river.[1] In between they were to clear the bamboo and trees, build smaller cuttings, embankments and trestle bridges.

That day, on a long, curving embankment near the 150 kilometre mark, he watched men with picks and shovels scratch the brick-like earth from amongst the rocks and load it into baskets or onto *tankas*, stretchers of bamboo poles and rice sacks, which others carried to the embankment known as the seven-metre bank.* Each man had to excavate a cubic metre of spoil per day, which was then trampled down by other men's feet to form the slowly rising bank. Elsewhere, English and Australian prisoners were chopping down trees and bamboo; the axe blades were so blunt that the stumps looked as if they had been gnawed down 'by inferior false teeth'.[2]

Sgt Topping and many of the CCS boys were on 'hammer and tap', drilling the powdery limestone rock in a cutting which would link up with the embankment. Pairs of men were equipped with eight-pound sledge hammers and crude drills like a crowbar sharpened at one end. One steadied the drill into the rock, rotating it each time his partner brought the sledge hammer down. Periodically, they scraped the white dust out of the hole with a long piece of wire flattened into a scoop at one end, poured in a little water for lubrication and dropped the drill back in.

The 'hammer and tap' men were plastered with white dust and sweat.

---

* It was to be seven metres high.

The heat was 'infernal: hotter than in the camp where recently the temperature at midday was 130°F. and 108°F in a tent'.

Drillers were 'hurrying like hell to put down their two drill holes of 60 cm', for they could return to camp once they had completed their quota. Weary regarded this as foolishness: 'they will soon get more work at this rate.' When the day's limit was reached – usually around lunchtime – the engineers laid the charges 'stupidly with superficial types of bore holes and do not tamp the charges . . . [so that] only a little superficial rock is blasted into the air'. Rock-clearing gangs cleared away the debris with shovels, chunkels, *tankas* and bare hands.

There were many injuries from flying drill fragments, slivers of steel which lodged in legs and arms and turned septic. No amount of probing could locate them all, but Weary and Corlette did their best by the flickering light of the slush lamps. 'No ATS.'* And no matter where men took cover during the blasting, some were hit by the stones and fragments exploding through the forest, so sharp that they cut 'branches . . . lopping bamboo like scythes'.[3]

That afternoon, the engineer - who had learned of Weary's prowess on the sports field and fancied himself as an athlete - insisted on challenging Weary to a contest in the engineers' lines. Weary won a short sprint, the standing jump, the hop, step and jump, the long jump and a few other things (despite painful cellulitis and a couple of ulcers on his shins). Hiroda's expression was dark and his petulance obvious. When only the high jump remained unfought, it seemed politic to allow him to win.

'Face' restored, he turned to Weary. 'Come to pictures!' Weary looked at him blankly, wondering what the hell he meant. After a few minutes, he realised that Hiroda was inviting him to the films being shown to Japanese troops at Kinsayok that evening. 'I accepted for reasons of propaganda and recce . . . ', for there might be an opportunity to contact Hands and Smits.

Some weeks beforehand, Smits had taken Weary aside and whispered his intention of escaping with a couple of his warrant officers. He had been a pest, winkling money out of Weary, a set of maps brought from Singapore and a precious pistol, which had been concealed since Bandoeng, having survived all the kit searches and a most thorough

---

* Anti-tetanus serum.

turning over of the camp on 10 February. Weary was not sanguine about their chances, for they had 'damn-all in the way of a plan', but decided it was his duty as commanding officer to give them what help he could. Now he doubted that Smits would attempt any action.

He was put right up by the screen, seated on the ground with Japanese pressed up against him and not another European in sight. Apart from the expected propaganda 'showing Nippon tearing Asia up into strips', he was most interested in a film featuring a Japanese admiral who had taken part in the sinking of the *Repulse* and the *Prince of Wales* – shown with cigar clenched between his teeth and a smug look on his face as he watched the ships go down – and a newsreel about Pearl Harbor. They contained footage which was probably the 'real thing'.

The Japanese around him responded with almost hysterical excitement to the triumphs of Pearl Harbor, with its 'aerial torpedoes, bombs and fires stem to stern . . . [and] systematic bombing of harbour installations'.

'*Banzai!* ' they screamed.

Weary leapt to his feet. '*Banzai! Banzai!*' he roared, cutting short the yells of those about him.

'You think good?' they asked, amazed. 'Nippon bomb-bomb, sink American and British ships.'

Weary was not going to lose an opportunity for counter-propaganda. 'Yes! Old ships no good – *taksan* [many] new ships now build – better!'

He gathered no information, had no chance to look around Kinsayok, 'so a failure as regards contacting Jack or Smits'. All he brought back to Hintok were some lice from his companions in the audience.

Next day, Weary sought out Usuki and confronted him with the same complaints he had presented to Hiroda, but he refused to intervene. There was jealousy between the guard battalion and the engineers. He returned to the mountain camp simmering and prepared for battle.

At the next morning's parade, there was a 'terrific beat up of all available labour, with none left for sanitation and anti-malaria work'. Weary fell out 46 light duty men, ordered all the others to stay where they were, and began his attack by bawling out the HQ clerk, Kanamoto. Hiroda, 'his nasty face set like a ham' ignored Weary but raged at the clerk until Weary broke in, furious that he proposed to send sick men out to work. For good measure, he added his previous criticisms about boots, rations, sanitation and medical arrangements. He heard the click of metal as the bolts on the rifles were drawn back.

'I invited him to make good his threat to shoot me.' Wearne, Weary's second-in-command, was just as tough, and after him 'you will have to shoot them all. Then you will have no workmen. In any case I have taken steps to one day have you hanged, for you are a black-hearted bastard.'

Hiroda was spitting with rage. 'You can stay here as long as you like. You will get no food and water and the sick will do the work!'

'The Lizard' then accompanied Hiroda to the hospital and cut out 46 sick men on light duties from Q and R battalions and sent them off without food or water for the day.[4]

Weary turned on Hiramura and 'had a real hate then, with S/Sgt Oliver as interpreter'. The Japanese were 'murderers and (indicating a cross on the ground) that was the fate for us'. He hurled the accusation at 'the Lizard', ending with the 'bomb . . . that if sick men were driven to work *all* would "down shovels".'

Hiroda was no longer there to hear this threat of strike action, but Hiramura 'raved at the men as if working himself into a passion to hit me (but I bet he never could if I was looking at him)'. Weary loomed over the slight young Korean, glaring, silent, until he quietened and announced that the men could work around the camp.

Weary took water out to the railway with Wearne and some light duties men; he and Hiroda 'pointedly ignored each other'; any goodwill generated by the athletics contest had evaporated.

'After that, there was nothing but war.' Weary's will had prevailed in this, the first of daily battles at each morning's parade, but Hiroda had his revenge. Next day, 'the Lizard' reduced the duty section from 144 to 80 and ordered all the officers out to work. ' . . . No consideration at all shown to sanitation.'

Weary spent an afternoon digging 'furiously' in a large *benjo* , with 'the Lizard' watching him from a distance. When the men came in from the line and saw Hiramura, they assumed – incorrectly – that the Korean had ordered Weary to do this work. Their hatred for him increased ten-fold from that day.

In fact, Weary chose to do it, but it offended the Japanese sense of what was fitting for a commanding officer. 'No. 1 not work *benjo* . No good,' they decided, and gave him a squad of six men but no tools. 'Use hands!' they replied when Weary asked for shovels.

Hiramura was 'always exquisitely polite' about supplying a fixed number of men for the engineers, but no amount of cigarettes, coffee and food lavished upon Weary in an effort to extract more workers softened him. He kept an accurate tally of the sick men he was forced to send out, and supplied damning evidence to the War Crimes Tribunal in 1946.[5]

Jack Hands appeared and reported similar treatment at Kinsayok and a rising death toll amongst the English and Dutch. When Smits walked in some time later, wearing the mask of an eager conspirator, Weary was 'too busy and upset to see him'.

The Japanese ordered the officers to form wood and water parties and dig the *benjos*. Weary told the others frankly that they must pull their weight, but it was usually Weary, Woods, Clarke and Wearne who took over the hard and filthy job of digging latrines or firing them in a futile attempt to reduce the swarms of maggots.

Capt. Allen and his canteen staff had remained at the river to intercept the barges and unload stores, while Lieut. Smedley ranged back and forth between the two camps portering canteen stores to the top of the hill. Usuki and 'the Lizard' consistently refused to supply men for this heavy job.

The Dutch had scratched a small dam out of the gritty red clay near the spring, and the water oozed across the track and down a trickle of a stream. Woods had sketched some ambitious plans, which Ikimoto approved, and with twenty light duty men he had begun enlarging the dam, but Hiroda and 'the Lizard' soon rounded them up and took them out to the line.

On the night of 24 March, a violent storm swept through the forest, uprooting giant teak trees and entire thickets of bamboo which had lain in the path of a tornado that 'cut a belt of destruction' some 200 metres wide between their camp and Konyu, blocking the road. Deafening thunder boomed and reverberated in the hills all around their protected hollow, the forked brilliance of 'almost continuous' lightning turning night into day. 'Probably our situation wedged into the mountain saved us from real trouble.' A group of Thais with their crazy-looking wooden carts and buffaloes huddled in the lee of the bamboo fence by the roadside.

Lorry-loads of sick being transferred next day from Kinsayok to Lieut-Colonel Harvey's hospital at Tarsau were halted by trees and bamboo heaped across the main road near Konyu camp. Parkin was one of a gang of ninety men who took axes and cleared the track from the railway up to the junction so that the elephants could get down with the bamboo chatties of water for the drills. Then they worked back along the Tarsau–Hintok–Kinsayok road, making a passage for the lorries. 'Trees with twelve-foot girths have been snapped like matches.'[6]

Weary was worried about his own sick, whose numbers were increasing steadily. He had 78 in hospital, plus forty-eight who were to be evacuated to Tarsau from the river camp, where they had been in Moon's care since the works' battalions transferred to Hintok K4. Marsden, the SMO at the English camp hospital, had given them bed space.

When the road had been cleared and 190 British and Australian sick from the river reached the top of the hill – 'Speedo, speedo' – Marsden and Moon discovered that they were to hail passing transport which might find space for their patients. 'Hitch-hiking . . . for the sick!'

They sent them off in small groups, bedding the others down for the night at Konyu road camp. The two most senior lieutenant-colonels, More and Hill, went with them. Lieut-Colonel Alan Ferguson Warren now commanded the English works' battalions. They had been there since November 1942, clearing forest from the railway course, but all were now so emaciated that they were useless for heavy work.

Weary and Ferguson Warren sought each other out when they could. Ferguson Warren's kind of war appealed to Weary and his admiration for the man grew daily. Recruited to Intelligence by Sir Roger Keyes after Dunkirk, he was then promoted to lieutenant-colonel in the SOE and sent out to Singapore as GSO I, the liaison officer between all the para-military underground organisations and Malaya Command.

With Spencer Chapman, he had raised and trained private armies of guerillas, gone on raiding parties, been part of the military mission which flew to Chungking to parley with Chiang Kai Shek; and was one of the last two Europeans to leave Penang ahead of the Japanese. Like Weary, Ferguson Warren had elected to stay behind rather than follow almost every other Allied officer who was fleeing the length of Sumatra. He had been disgusted by the behaviour of some of them. At last, Weary heard the details of Coates's bravery and his care of the wounded there.

While the winter monsoon blew from the north, the river had flowed well down in its bed, and chains of men were needed to pass the buckets of water up the bank to the cookhouse or unload the stores from the strings of flat-bottomed barges towed by tiny, diesel-powered 'pom-pom' boats. But from the middle of March, it rained most days.

The 'little rains' (or, as they were also called, the 'bamboo rains'), that overture to the wet season, had begun 'with a vengeance' and the water level began to rise. Overnight, the rustling, dry bamboo broke out in new green leaves and road, tracks and railway course deteriorated into a black, sticky slush. Occasionally, the showers were sharp, heavy, but brief, and the mud crusted and dried when the sun broke through, but mostly men slithered and sank to above the ankles, the 'ski poles' some cut from bamboo being their only means of remaining upright on the walk home in the dark.

On rare, rainless days, cumulus clouds were piled over the rim of the mountain as the humidity climbed. In the landlocked valleys, 'the sun hit you like a burning glass and you could feel the sweat running over your face . . . like those old butchers' windows'. Weary's 'pathetic cloth cap' gave little protection from a sky that dazzled the eyes like polished metal.

The once-gaunt trees flaunted blossoms of scarlet and lilac and yellow. He loved to watch the waves of birds arrive in the cotton trees and swarm voraciously over the branches, tearing the blossoms to pieces until the ground was carpeted in scarlet.

Together with two other ranks, Bob Fox and Steve Wade, Weary and Woods felled trees for the wall of the dam and deepened the stream, 'stark naked, as one becomes covered in mud hacking roots and shovelling in the creek bed'.

Fox and Wade were older and Weary wished to keep them away from the line: 'We didn't want them killed.' They were both 'very good with timber', the mainstay of Jock Clarke's carpenters' shop.

Water was piped almost 200 metres from the dam to a raised platform nine by twelve metres. It flowed through three long bamboo canes, under which a dozen men could shower. Everything was bamboo: pipes, the trestles which supported them, platform, the raised benches round the sides for the men's belongings, the perforated shower pipes. 'To be able to bathe under running water is second only to eating and sleeping,' wrote Parkin.[7]

Long after the war, a British officer who had marched north with 'H'

Force remembered that Hintok was distinguished from other camps by those showers, and the latrines made from wood, 'clean and sixteen feet deep'.[8]

Woods was ingenious. He fabricated a bamboo 'tank' from which drinking bottles could be filled without wasting a drop of precious boiled water; built a stockyard for the starved-looking cattle which arrived periodically; and mended the boots for his battalion, doing a 'most excellent hand-sewn job'. He and Clarke provided their camps with the best designed *benjo* covers along the line.

'Movement is absolutely crazy . . . some of our fellows moving to Konyu one day and back the next.' Apart from the constant confusion 'the Lizard' created with parties of men being shuttled between the three camps in the area, lorry-loads of sick prisoners plied the Kinsayok–Hintok–Tarsau road and more lorries full of Japanese soldiers carrying full equipment moved in both directions.

Then the transit parties began to appear. Lorries jammed with Australians, an early party of 'D' Force with some 8th Division troops from Changi, went through to Kinsayok on 30 March, seeming 'fit and cheerful'. The Good Friday rumours that large groups of prisoners and Japanese were marching up from Tarsau were confirmed on Anzac Day by the arrival of 201 Australians, 'just stumbling along in a strung-out line'.

They were part of S battalion of 'D' Force, the survivors of a party of 500 which had left Tarsau two days beforehand. Their commanding officer, Lieut-Colonel McEachern, was with Usuki at his Konyu headquarters back down the road near the English camp. Two hundred others who could not stagger the extra few kilometres were staging there for the night.

With their arrival, Weary's command expanded again, to 1085 men and three works' battalions: O, P and S. Moon was sent to Kanchanaburi on 28 April to take command of the base hospital at Tamarkan, leaving Weary and Corlette to look after the hospital patients as well as the daily sick parade and the transient sick marching through. Weary found the combined administration and care of the sick almost greater than he could handle, 'a hell of a big job and to get through well over 100 hospital patients in the morning is almost impossible - thus I am working all day and fitting in administration at odd moments'. Wearne's support was invaluable. McEachern was diffident about taking over the camp command, despite being a lieutenant-colonel of seven years standing.

Next day, Weary was warned that around 9000 British soldiers were on their way north. Each party would halt for a day and a night, and must be fed. O and P battalions had to find twenty men for the transit parties' cookhouse.

The first of these appeared on the morning of 27 April, No. 7 Battalion of Manchesters, Gordons and Loyals with Lieut-Colonel Stitt. Stitt's men skilfully pilfered many articles from the bed spaces while the working parties were out on the line. Thereafter, British troops streamed through, as well as occasional parties of Dutch. The latter were even worse: they broke up the men's sleeping platforms for their cooking fires.

Weary always invited the senior officers to the mess for the mid-day meal; it was the only way of exchanging news about events outside their immediate area. He and Corlette also attended to their sick.

'F' Force had begun to leave Changi on 16 April, fed the same nonsense about hospitals and better conditions at their desti-nation – which was, however, kept from them – as their predecessors. Thirteen train-loads of men and equipment pulled out of Singapore Station. It took six of these to move the AIF contingent to Ban Pong, from where they marched northwards, and the first flight of Australians paused for no more than 'a breathing space' on 1 May. Weary listened incredulously when they told him that their heavy baggage, including 'three pianos with band instruments, medical stores and officers' baggage' had been left at Ban Pong and would be sent on.*

Their commander, Lieut-Colonel Kappe, arrived the following evening with 600 of the 2/29th Battalion, AASC, Engineers and Signals. Weary found him 'cheerful but very tired', with a dawning comprehen-sion of the rugged conditions ahead, but clinging to an optimistic faith in the advantage of moving with 'a complete brigade . . . ordnance, AASC, and everything complete'. No one else spoke. Finally, Weary said gently, 'Well sir, I hope that you will remain together, because things are pretty rough up here.'

They moved on in the dark, two hours and twenty minutes later, with

---

* John Stewart, interpreter for the Force and author of *To the River Kwai*, recorded that a piano, band instruments and a church harmonica had been left behind. The piano ended up in the café next to the station.

only ersatz 'coffee' made from hot water and burnt rice to sustain them. Whenever a group arrived, Weary, Wearne and some other senior officers met them with containers of 'coffee'. It was an equal exchange: they brought news of Singapore and the camps they had come through; he warned them of conditions up the line.

For four more nights, the Australians walked in at around 2040 hours and were forced off again approximately two hours later. On 4 May, when Capt. Schwarz and Maj. Bruce Hunt arrived, he heard how Hunt had been savagely beaten up when he fell out 37 sick men which the Japanese MO had agreed were unfit to travel. That night he was in pain, severely bruised and with a bone broken in his hand. Some of the sick had made scarcely a few hundred metres before collapsing and being carried back to Tarsau. 'They are behaving with unreasoning brutality to the sick.'

Like Coates, Hunt was a First World War veteran, a brave doctor who became an inspiration to 'F' Force.

When their escorting guards allowed it, troops on what came to be called the 'Death March' shed their hopelessly sick at Tarsau hospital and camps along the way. Otherwise, they had to support them on the journey, the stronger men carrying the others' belongings. Much movement was by night. They had no torches and the muddy, corduroyed roads caused stumbles, sprains and even broken limbs. Streams, some quite deep, had to be forded. Sandflies and mosquitoes bit savagely. Thai bandits were suspected of robbing, even murdering, the weak and very sick, who straggled far back in the rear. Others suffered painfully from the guards' mistreatment.

Between Anzac Day and 14 May, the movement of troops in transit in and out of the mountain camp seldom ceased, often one or two parties marching in as others departed. One of the last AIF parties on 11 May was Lieut-Colonel Harris, travelling on the roof of a marmon, and his Group Headquarters: they did not stop. Small parties of recovered sick continued to straggle through until the end of the month, dispatched from Chungkai and Kanchanaburi hospitals and moving up to join their original battalions.

Trudging up the road a day behind Harris's party were some Thais with fifty-four bullocks, which, after much haggling between the Thais and Usuki, and a whip-round amongst the officers for funds, Usuki managed to buy. Woods's stockyard was expanded.

Usuki had swaggered in to take over command at Hintok Mountain – now renamed Hintok Camp No. 5 – on 30 April. That evening, when

Weary and McEachern responded to his summons to the guard house, he announced that the duty section had been slashed to seventy all ranks, and that any officers not employed on camp duties would be sent out to the railway course.

During the inevitable lengthy negotiations that characterised any dealings with Usuki, Weary gained three tents for the hospital, 2000 cigarettes for the men, and an extension to 2300 hours for lights out. He also revealed McEachern's seniority to Usuki, but neither man seemed anxious to insist on changes in command.

Camps were proliferating in the area, pointing to a tremendous effort by the engineers to push the line through. Three kilometres along the road towards Konyu were the Australians of T Battalion under Major Quick, with the balance of S Battalion and Major Schneider between them and the coolies camped on the outskirts of Konyu. Sharing the low-lying valley across the creek at Hintok No. 5 were majors Morrison and Gaskill, and many men and officers Weary had commanded in Java, including Captain Rees and F/O Park.

For some curious reason, this last group of 'H' Force was the engineers' responsibility, and like 'F' Force they were under IJA Malayan Command. But although they were outside Usuki's control and the Thailand branch of the IJA, 'we have to surreptitiously feed them and they use our showers'. Later, they were forbidden to have any contact with these men, who starved and died on the hopelessly inadequate rations.

A large party of coolies settled on the fringes of the camp near the engineering lines on 13 May. Weary was unhappy about these Tamils, Malays, Chinese and Thais sharing the showers and water supply, for their area rapidly became filthy with excreta and they 'cheerfully' fouled the stream above the point where the camp drew its water. Worse, rumours of cholera had been drifting down river since February, and these wretched, itinerant masses of men and women were shadowed by the spectre of disease.

The arrival of the two 'prize bastards', Usuki and his 'ill-trained' medical corporal, Okada, heralded the 'speedo, speedo' period. Both men were hounded and bullied by Hiroda to supply a fixed number of workers each day, causing Okada – or 'Doctor Death', as he quickly became known – to snatch men from the hospital to meet these targets in 'mad, unreasonable blitzes'. Weary and Corlette fought him tenaciously. Usuki appeared to cope with the pressure by drinking; Weary's earlier suspicions that he was 'whisky-sodden' turned out to be correct. Hiroda was the worst of the trio, demonstrating a sickening brutality against the men – even stoning them – and this behaviour was aped by his guards in order to gain favour. Frequently, his presence on the line provoked sadistic beatings to the accompaniment of 'ferocious yells' for his edification.

At the end of each day, Weary and Corlette gathered in an increasing harvest of damaged men. The number of sick rose sharply with the onset of the 'bamboo rains', from 349 in March to 549 for April. No table of hospital cases gives a true picture, for 'the majority of admissions had at least three complaints at the one time, e.g. malaria–tropical ulcers–pellagra.' The 'predominating disease' was chosen for the records, but all were treated within the limits of the 'utterly negligible' drugs. Usually, there was a reasonable supply of quinine for malaria, but for septic sores, there were only 'hot foments', and dysentery had to be treated with charcoal ground up by the patients themselves into tablets.

When there were no scraps of cloth, only jungle leaves – and later, the slightly porous banana leaves – were available for the ulcer patients' dressings.

Nutritional disorders fluctuated according to the availability of eggs, meat and vegetables. When eggs were in short supply, which was most of the time, avitaminosis and painful mouths were universal. The greatest number of eggs were apportioned to the hospital patients. Weary never had more than two a week. Few escaped malaria, avitaminosis and beri beri; all suffered septic sores. ' . . . Well-nigh uncontrollable diarrhoea' disturbed their sleep, urging men from their wretched bamboo beds out to the latrines four, five, six times in a night that stretched for seven and three-quarter interrupted hours between lights out and reveille.[9]

No man was fit: by May, even the strong workers 'who throw themselves into work' were 'looking very broken and will obviously not be fit for weeks'.

They got up in the dark and rain at 0645, drew breakfast of watery rice 'pap' and dry rice for their lunch, and endured the interminable counts during which Weary fought on the parade ground for those whom he said were too sick to work. At 0800 hours, the engineer's overseers marched out the day's quota to the terrible ladder up the escarpment.

Twelve hours later, after another wearisome parade, retreat was blown. Then men sluiced the mud from their bodies and washed their rags of clothing, drew their evening rice and thin soup, and huddled round fires in the lines, brewing rice 'coffee'. Sick parade began at five o'clock in the afternoon and continued by the dim light of home-made oil lamps in the rain and slush until around midnight. Sometimes, it took the more unfit up to six hours to stagger back.

Both doctors shrank from adopting the 'disastrous Nipponese standards of fitness' but were forced to send out some unfit men for light duties each morning. If a compromise was not reached, Usuki, Okada and 'the Lizard' would drive the very sick from their hospital bed spaces, yelling and swishing their bamboo canes at patients who could scarcely walk.

Weary and Corlette then began work on the hospital patients and 'fixing discharges' for the following day. On 8 May, Weary spent yet another day 'working almost from dawn to dark', with the sick, for the hospital held 264 men. Lieut-Colonel Ishii, the Commandant of No. 4 Group, arrived from Konyu as a prelude to Major-General Sassa's visit on the tenth, savagely castigating Usuki and Okada for the number of sick, and throwing the two of them into a panic.

Weary was 'sent for, and told to find 700 men for outside work tomorrow'. Enraged, he yelled 'How!' and launched into such a diatribe that both Usuki and the interpreter 'jumped in their chairs'. Only the arrival of McEachern cooled him down.

It was nine days since Weary had advised Usuki of McEachern's rank and combatant status. Next morning, he called a battalion commanders' conference and, without any further ado, 'handed over the camp command to Lieut-Colonel McEachern'. He ignored the other man's reluctance, making it 'clear that I was now too busy with medical work to carry on efficiently with administrative work'.

Okada demanded that Weary discharge forty men from hospital during the notorious Sassa's visit, promising that they would 'not be worked and would come back to hospital later in the day' from their hiding place some few hundred metres away in the bamboo. Reluctantly, he yielded. Everyone was in a high state of excitement, even Ishii, who rushed over a lorry-load of vegetables as 'window dressing'.

Sassa 'halved' the sick figures in Burma that month by 'abolishing' the hospital at the 30 kilometre mark and sending all but twenty of the thousand patients back to work camps.[10] Hintok No. 5 escaped, perhaps partly as a result of Okada's duplicity - but the forty, 'mostly with large ulcers, beri beri and malaria' were forced to roll heavy 44-

gallon oil drums out to the compressor party before struggling back across four kilometres of rocky hillside and negotiating the ladder down the cliff to the camp.

Whether it was Okada or Hiroda who was responsible for 'this . . . the most horrible thing I have seen done as yet, apart from their executions,' Weary was not sure. 'The most primitive of races would scarcely treat sick and starving dogs in this fashion.' He waited for them to return. It was after midnight when he watched the last of them crawl back into hospital.

As soon as Sassa departed, the truck laden with vegetables drove off. No extra food was allowed.

That same day, after walking over to Konyu to see their medical officer, Major Marsden ('most probably a retro-caecal appendicitis' he concluded, after examining him), Weary started the return walk 'in a curious feeling of extreme heat and exhaustion . . . I suspect malaria'. But even 'a temperature of 103°F., a feeling of malaise and weakness of the back, my spleen feeling full and obviously palpable' had failed to curb his cynical amusement at Usuki's negotiations for the scrawny cattle.

He continued to work, visiting Marsden again on 14 May ('considerably improved') and tramping an extra seven kilometres to another camp to 'straighten out one or two worries' of Capt. Millard's, who was uncertain whether his men had dengue fever or malaria. ' . . . Of course they are malaria.' Walking was a tremendous effort. He pushed himself on, talking to himself every step of the way, willing his legs to keep moving. 'Left leg, right leg, left leg, right . . . ' until he was back in Hintok. Sick parades and hospital work awaited him.

' . . . Feeling pretty wretched but spent some time in the evening putting up a severe scald with surgical toilet and Tannafax. I have to keep going somehow.'

His malaria was now complicated by dysentery. 'Obvious blood and mucus.' But he allowed neither that, nor his aching malarial back and head, to stop him going to Tarsau with Okada on 16 May.

Lieut-Colonel Harvey spilled out plenty of wireless news but had no drugs apart from 28 bottles of quinine. McConachie, the surgeon, operated only when there was no alternative, he told Weary, for they had 'no gloves and their wounds always seem to go wrong'. Patients were pouring in from Tonchin, which malaria and amoebic dysentery had turned into 'a real camp of death'. Half the patients admitted to Tarsau in April had arrived from this work camp only eight kilometres or so distant, and the expenses of so many sick caused Harvey grave financial worries. Tarsau itself was 'insanitary – open trench latrines and filth all over the place'.

Maj. Hazelton was SMO to the Australians there, however, and Glyn White had sent him up with as liberal a supply of drugs and stores as could be spared from Singapore. He had decided against pooling them with Harvey. Weary came away the following day with more than he had had since Java: M & B 693, sulphanilamide and plasmoquine tablets, zinc oxide, tannic acid and chlorosol, bandages, cotton wool, lint, magnesium sulphate and mosquito cream. He packed some test tubes and bottles carefully - the journey down had been so rough, even his water bottle being smashed by the jolting, that he had decided against picking up Marsden and taking him to Tarsau for surgery. He was pleased to leave. 'A good place to escape from . . . '

The monsoon swept through Burma and Thailand early that year. He had thought the 'little rains' misnamed, 'shocked' at their severity, but they dwindled into insignificance beside the ferocity of the monsoon rains that speared through the perished canvas of the tents on 19 May, rains of 'extreme violence' that drenched everyone to the bone. Next morning, work parade was held in 'complete obscurity' under an oppressive rolling mass of low, dark clouds. The latrines had over-flowed, washing a thick, stinking tide of fat maggots and excreta across the area. The ground in camp and beneath the tents had been churned into a morass by the men's feet and 'smooth organisation of sick inspection is impossible'.

Roll call was now held under the canvas-covered huts 'in a sea of mud, slush and dripping water'. The hour at which men came in from the line grew later and later; there were more than 200 sick in hospital, but somehow around 690 were marched out each morning. They might be living like pigs, but 'the troops must have hearts like lions . . . '

Greiner and the carrying parties had brought in thousands of eggs. Wearne had found a track down to the river from the embankment, and parties of men were happy to receive two eggs each for portering the stores up after work. A Thai trader, Boon Pong, was making regular trips up from Kanchanaburi, his barges laden with eggs, whitebait, tobacco, salt, peanuts, oil, guala and sugar.

Concealed in these loads were tiny quantities of precious drugs and money supplied by the Thai underground, their carriage organised by John Pearson of 'D' Battalion who had worked for the Borneo Company and spoke fluent Thai.[11] The ravings of their first case of cerebral malaria, Private Lang Fraser, were quietened when Weary 'arranged' for some hyoscine to be procured. Boon Pong's wife assisted her husband back in Kanchanaburi, the threat of torture and death shadowing every excursion she made to buy and package the life-saving substances.

Weary's first contact with Boon Pong had been 'very, very careful and transient', shortly after he arrived at Konyu 3. He had no idea of the depth of the underground organisation at this stage, nor that the immaculate little bespectacled Thai in his white shirt was more than a sympathetic trader. Weary saw him on only two occasions, all the secret and highly dangerous negotiations being carried out by go-between John Pearson.

Eventually, each trip of Boon Pong's furnished three or four thousand tickals for the camp funds and the drugs ordered on the previous trip. Boon Pong brought in the first, precious grains of emetine; while he remained on the barge, Pearson 'smuggled it into the camp with Boon Pong's urgent instructions to get a receipt from a Medical Officer . . . the first MO I met was Colonel Dunlop'.[12] Money came mainly from the civilian internment camp in Bangkok; Boon Pong was one of the agents, distributing the funds and taking orders for drugs. It was 1945 before Weary discovered how everything was set up.

Weary was still shabby with lingering malaria and dysentery, his ankles grossly swollen with oedema. A septic mass on one thigh caused by a fall from a tree when building the dam had never healed; neither had the ulcers on his shins. He chewed his rice slowly and painfully, the skin inside his mouth sloughing with avitaminosis. It was Corlette's turn to shiver with malarial rigors and Weary conducted the sick parades and attended to the hospital patients on his own.

Okada and Hiroda continued to compel him to release men from hospital. Every day they demanded 700; every day he fought to keep some back. Always he succeeded, but the 'state of the sick and the inability to admit many poor wretches to hospital is getting completely on my nerves.' Okada was a coward and never hit him, but Weary was forced to endure bashings regularly from the guards, most of whom barely reached his chest. ' . . . The most humiliating was having to kneel to be hit in the face.' He seethed inwardly, but endured it without any change of expression, standing and bowing to his squat assailants when they finished whilst vowing silently: 'One day, one day . . . '

Worn out one night, he collapsed into bed and 'just didn't feel equal to going out into the wet again' when he learned that the ever-vigilant

Okada had snatched three men from hospital for camp duties. 'I am ashamed of my irritability.'

The men never noticed it. Ivor Jones, who had been captured in Java with other RAF Malaya men and was a member of Dunlop Force, remembered that they all had many personal crises during that speedo period of 1943. They found themselves doing things they had not thought they were capable of, but that in between there were days or weeks of the same grinding discomfort and routine. Whereas, for Weary, every day began with him screwed up to 'crisis point' – 'he had to lift himself every time' – when he fought with Okada and the engineers.[13] And 'he did it every hour, every day, for three and a half years. I just wondered how one man could do it . . . courage, stamina, intellect – he had everything.'

Monday, 24 May, was Empire Day, the fifth anniversary of his departure from Melbourne. The camp had an unexpected *yasume* while Usuki and his guards searched a transit party of English and Dutch who had plundered the camp the previous day while the men were out on the line. Reveille was not until 0900. Weary lay on his soaking wet bedding and thought of the five years since he had kissed Helen goodbye in the cabin full of flowers and waved until the streamers tore apart across the widening gap between ship and wharf.

The Japanese taste for gore and theatre was disappointed when Weary decided against operating on three of the transit party whom he had been allowed to admit to hospital with talk of appendicitis. But since Corlette was back on his feet, Weary decided to operate for a left inguinal hernia and hydrocoele of cord on a machine gunner who was in hospital receiving compensation pay for a lacerated leg.* He had gloves Hazelton had given him at Tarsau; it had stopped raining; and 'the team have to be kept on their toes for emergencies'.

Many of the CCS orderlies were ill, so he decided to give Sgt Bert Lawrence some training. Weary was amused that it turned into a 'chatty party' with the usual spectators. Cpl Sakata, in charge of the camp while Usuki and Okada were down at Tarsau, trotted over for the 'blood letting', but it soon proved to be too much for his stomach.

When Parkin walked into camp at six o'clock that evening, he saw Weary bent over Sgt Stephens's open abdomen, 'swabbing and cutting with quiet, steady concentration', while Corlette held the patient's head

---

* The Japanese paid compensation for injuries received on the line.

between his hands. Corlette had administered 12 cc of percaine as a spinal anaesthetic, and now talked quietly to the man who was looking straight up, his eyes opening and shutting. Scarcely had Weary seen Stephens settled on his stretcher for nursing, than he himself, collapsed with dysentery.

Usuki and Okada returned with cholera vaccine on 28 May. Men portering stores from the barges told of cholera near the Burmese border and at Takanun, and two coolies fleeing south told of men dying, shrunken and unrecognisable, in the 'F' Force and coolie camps up near Three Pagodas' Pass. The entire camp was vaccinated by Corlette and the medical orderlies next afternoon as the men came in from work.

Weary was 'flat out', unable to help, 'properly ill . . . fever, nausea, severe abdominal pain, aching back and weakness ++'. For some time he had suspected that he had amoebic dysentery and after three days, when the M & B 693 tablets every four hours had no apparent effect, he was convinced. 'I have never felt quite so poor in health and full of self-loathing.' He could eat nothing and drank only a little sugared fluid, 'interminably . . . slushing outside in the pouring rain and mud' to the latrines.

Dragging himself out there became increasingly exhausting until, on 1 June, he collapsed under a tree. Unable to walk, he summoned just enough energy to shake his fist feebly at the vultures gathering uncomfortably close on the branches above him. Captain 'Legs' Lee 'arrived from nowhere', helped him back to his bed and over-rode Weary's objections to being given half of Lee's precious supply of emetine. He gave him three tablets. Lee dissolved one on a spoon and Weary injected himself with 1 grain emetine hydrochloric.

By the following day, his stomach pains and the bloody flux had eased. ' . . . Sufficiently improved to throw stones at the vultures.' In the early hours of the morning, one of the machine gunners in hospital with amoebic dysentery had died. 'Perhaps the only difference between myself and this poor lad is a few grains of emetine.'

This was the first death in any of his camps since coming to Thailand, although 'God knows the angel's wing must have been over us in view of the terrible mortality in all the other camps up and down this line'.

Weary read the burial service at the graveside, for there was no padre. McEachern and Greiner were chief mourners, and those of the dead man's comrades who were in camp trailed along behind the body. He agreed with Corlette that Private Edwards 'was killed by the Nipponese just as surely as if he had been shot by them'. It was the first time since Java that Paige's trumpet* had sounded the 'Last Post'.

The cemetery on the bluff above the river at Konyu, shown to Weary so proudly by More on the day they arrived, was now full of English dead, and the coppice of crosses in a new graveyard up by Konyu road camp was thickening. He smelled death when he looked across the creek to Gaskill's camp, for the Englishmen were 'frail stuff . . . skin and bone'. That June, his own sick figure hovered between 260 and 290 per day out of a thousand men; but in Gaskill's camp 250 of the 500 were sick after a fortnight in the area. The engineers drove the sick from the makeshift hospital and at times allowed them only one medical orderly.

Transport was now by river, for the road was impassable, the mud knee deep. Trucks had bogged to the axles. Japanese troops – many of them very young – moved through on foot now, dragging their field guns, or urging on the little Timorese ponies harnessed to the gun carriages.

The wet season produced a new horror: feet injured on the sharp rocks and sodden with unceasing rain and mud turned red-raw, bleeding and swollen with tinea and secondary infection. There was only potassium permanganate - Condy's crystals - solution for treatment. Jones turned up to have his feet looked at one night, and never forgot Weary apologising to him for having nothing else before bathing his feet. Night brought neither relief nor rest, for most men beat a path between the latrines and their tents with diarrhoea and dysentery.

Usuki and Okada appeared back in camp on 7 June after a week at Tarsau. Many men were now finding it difficult to stand; walking was almost impossible. The hospital figure was 261 that morning. Okada was 'savagely ignored' when he demanded that Weary reduce the figure to 200. That day, one of the troops, a dysentery patient who had been bashed by the engineers for not moving fast enough, committed suicide.

When Okada, 'howling like a wolf' for more workmen, refused to allow fifty men to transfer to light duties that evening, Weary's mind snapped. Fatigue, horror at the savage persecution of men he regarded as friends and patients, months of undernourishment and lack of sleep

---

* Paige was a trumpeter. He did not have a bugle.

had pushed him to the edge of sanity. Nothing but the death of the persecutor would satisfy him.

Hiramura had been ordered on a message to Konyu and would return later that night. Weary watched him narrowly, for he planned to slip out of camp and lie in wait where the road bent round a large tree some distance away. He had decided to kill the Korean with a waddy he had made from an iron-hard piece of wood and dump the body in the jungle. Either a tiger would find it, or the Japanese would imagine that Hiramura had been attacked and eaten on his way back.

Clutching his rifle and a torch, obviously terrified, Hiramura walked out of the camp and Weary rose to follow him. He was scarcely fifty metres from the hospital before someone called him back: Usuki wanted to see him with McEachern and De Crespigny immediately.

They found the commandant at the *kempeitai* full of bluster. He had bought 1600 ticals worth of Cat brand cigarettes for the prisoners. Weary calculated swiftly that the 5794 packets, 116 000 cigarettes, made up five months' supply at $2.90 per carton of 200. In no mood to adopt the usual laconic, placatory, pidgin style of speech, he refused them. The money was needed to buy eggs and other necessities. It transpired that Usuki had paid for them with some of the pay due to O, P and S battalions: and he alternated between devious suggestions that if they accepted the cigarettes without fuss (thus saving Usuki from embarrassment), Nippon might be able to pay for the next barge-load of eggs, and threats to close the canteen.

Usuki then raved about the number of sick and the necessity for 'co-operation', while Okada chipped in about the ten men he had been refused earlier in the evening. Weary was past conciliation. He gave the reasons coldly: overlong hours, appalling conditions, lowered resistance to disease through twelve months of inadequate rations and no drugs for treatment, little or no footwear and no change of clothing. When Okada persisted in demanding ten more workers for the morning, Weary swung on him. ' . . . As Okada disagreed with my professional opinion, he could give any orders he liked . . . I was only the doctor.' After this, 'it seemed tactful to take the cigarettes and be diddled gracefully'.

It was fortunate, Weary reflected, that Usuki summoned him when he did; five minutes more and he would have been out of the camp and well along the road behind Hiramura. Had 'the Lizard' disappeared, or been found dead, and Weary not turned up at the *kempeitai* with the others, his head would undoubtedly have been forfeit. It was not beheading which bothered him, but what led up to it: hours – even days – of beating and torture, until one longed for 'execution and a happy release'.

The memory of how close he came to committing murder haunted Weary down the years. ' . . . I was narrowly saved (by chance) from the full realisation of murder's futility,' he wrote twenty-five years later to Gerard Bourke, the Redemptorist priest whom he saved from beheading at Hintok.[14] Weary did not need absolution from Bourke – did not seek it – but the priest was troubled for the soul of the man he admired beyond all others.

'I discussed as a speculative case, the situation . . . The colleague I consulted was a sound moral theologian and had himself had years of experience as a military chaplain . . . Like myself, he came to see the presence of all the reason that would have justified your own judgement . . . re tyrannicide & our being in the state of war. The situation would seem to turn on the question of prudence in view of possible worse reprisal for our own, if there was likelihood of such reprisals being greater than the existing evils. You seemed convinced that this likelihood would not have obtained.'[15]

Weary did not tell anyone else what he had planned for many years. When Bill Belford and Billy Deans had heard him out, they said with one voice: 'We would have done it for you.'

New tactics were necessary. At the edge of the parade ground, alongside the track leading to the ladder, was a large teak log. Next morning, Weary ordered twenty-six men with 'grossly inflamed feet' to sit on the log. Under no circumstances, no matter how much they were shouted at by the guards, were the sick to stand up.

The Japanese Engineer's NCO, 'Billie the pig', roared at the men, attempting to frighten them to their feet. Eventually, thirteen were carried to the hospital tents and the others were driven off to work with the 'special concession' that they would not be bashed for lateness.

Okada appeared and thanked the doctors 'from the bottom of his heart' for their long hours of work and begged Weary to keep down the figures, for otherwise Tarsau would cause trouble. 'This I imagine was sincere in the Nipponese fashion.' Ishii, at Tarsau, was tough and fully supported Usuki in not caring if sick men died: 'Working percentage better.'

Weary never forgave Ishii for laughing loudly when, on hearing that food was withheld for two or three days from Weary's 'emaciated dysentery sufferers, devoid of drugs', he replied: 'In future no food one week, better.'[16]

He decreed that the 'grim log-sitting struggle' be repeated each morning. The men christened the teak log the 'Wailing Wall' and admired Weary's coolness when faced by the engineers' NCO bully boy. 'Now when the Jap bellows, Weary looks at him disarmingly, picks up the man like a baby and stands in front of the Jap with him and says, "This man can't walk, Nippon".'[17]

He was surprised that Okada accepted the log-sitting as a legitimate exercise, justified because it lowered the day's hospital figures and the men could be sent over to the engineers' lines for light duties. Many light sick men were unable to stand, and he carried them over. They were put to work sitting down. Within a week, it was an established procedure, although the classification saved no one from severe bashing.

An extraordinary comic-book travesty of a Japanese doctor appeared without warning, 'a grotesque little figure in appalling clothes with a Hitler moustache and a swinging stethoscope'. He refused to visit the hospital because of the mud, preferring to discuss Weary's wife and seven children – invented in Java for reasons of face and now an established cause of much hissing and teeth-sucking admiration – and 'eventually settled on the real business of trying to change watches with me'. Despite his claim of having graduated from Tokyo University, Weary decided that his medical knowledge was negligible when he watched him at sick parade next morning. He examined nobody, selecting men at random for work parties. Okada held him over Weary and Corlette 'like the sword of Damocles' in order to wring every last man out of hospital.

The daily sick parade now stretched so far into the early hours of the morning that Corlette and Weary took it turn and turn about, working by the dim glow of a crude slush lamp made from oil or pig fat and a scrap of cloth in a tin. Men crawled in on their hands and knees, almost crying with pain, their feet, like 'raw tomatoes', incapable of supporting them. Yet somehow, the death rate in their camp remained lower than their neighbours. More than two-thirds of their works' battalions were out on the line, but of 600 Englishmen at Konyu road, only sixty were working and 32 had died in eleven days. Six men spent all their time digging graves.

Rumour became terrifying fact on 13 June, when cholera took two days to kill 240 coolies camped hard by the Australian officers' battalion a few kilometres from Tarsau. Next day 200 coolies were affected at Konyu and some of the Japanese began to move about Hintok camp clad in masks.

Weary was vaccinated against cholera on 14 June. He ordered the cookhouse to station *cwalis* of boiling water at the head of the meal queues so that everyone could immerse their eating utensils before the food was doled out. He banned raw fruit, unboiled water, Thai cakes and other native food and anything uncooked. Extra Castellani bottles were installed in kitchens and by all the latrines. There were no latrines out on the line, and Bill Warbrick remembers Weary saying bluntly, 'Look soldier, if you don't dig a hole to do your shit in, we are in trouble.'[18]

The Japanese gibbered at the mention of 'chorrera', and handed over the mosquito nets for keeping flies off food, and kerosene and oil for firing the latrines which earlier Usuki had refused.

McEachern lectured the troops about the anti-fly measures. Fat, black flies had bred up prodigiously in the hot, moist conditions and, for over a month, each morning's parade had been conducted below a dark, droning mass that swarmed like bees six metres above the men's heads. The latrines seethed with maggots; they could be scooped in nauseous, crawling handfuls from the seats and the ground about them. Weary moved through dense clouds of flies in the hospital tents, where 'men with sores and such lesions are tormented'. It would have been a miracle if Hintok alone had escaped cholera, for in their miserable jungle camps, at Kanchanaburi, Tonchin and Konyu and all the way up the line to Burma, men purged, vomited, shrivelled and died.

Weary was conducting evening sick parade at 2030 hours on 19 June when a man 'with the most terrible dehydration and no perceptible pulse . . . speechless [but] conscious' was brought in from the railway on an improvised stretcher. When Weary moved over to look at him, he saw all the signs of cholera: 'cyanosed, shrunken, "washerwoman's fingers" . . . severe pains in stomach and cramps in back and legs.' He died shortly after 1 am next morning.

Some hours beforehand, Weary and McEachern had tossed the bomb of 'cholera' casually into the middle of a mahjong game at the *kempeitai*. 'I felt like a small boy with a big cracker in the classroom . . . ' He demanded disinfectants and more vaccine. Usuki and the interpreter were beside themselves with terror, incapable of issuing orders, but Okada recovered sufficiently to promise that he would send to Tarsau for them. 'I would have loved to have yelled 'chorrera' into Korean house guards' sleeping quarters on my way back!'

By breakfast time, the Japanese had marshalled their wits sufficiently to summon all the officers to the hospital, where Weary found Usuki, Hiroda, Okada and a group of masked and nervous soldiers milling about, 'all talking at once'. Okada had supplied potassium permanganate solution and the hospital orderlies were spraying and sloshing it over everything – patients, ground, tents and the Japanese. A panicking Usuki had seized Greiner and another officer and detailed them to carry the body away for cremation 'speedo'.

Weary substituted as bearers the two orderlies who had nursed Harris, Staff Sgt Gibson and Private Lacey. He sent the Australian *shokos* off to build the funeral pyre of bamboo; Okada provided kerosene; and at 1030 hours, Private Harris was buried with simple military honours in the presence of Usuki, Hiroda and Okada.

The tent in which Harris had died was moved to a low-lying part of the camp near the escarpment, well away from the men's lines, and became the first ward in the cholera isolation area.

Hiroda had announced that a certain amount of work was to be completed by the end the month, 'whatever the cost', and he led the guards in an orgy of brutality. Initially, even fear of cholera failed to moderate their violence. Later, as pungent smoke from the cremation pyres rose high above the jungle canopy, men who fell sick on the line were allowed some rest. But if they collapsed with symptoms of cholera, guards would go to insane lengths to avoid contamination. One even felled a victim with blows from sticks and spades and attempted to bury the man and his infection alive. Eventually, he was rescued by his companions. In another camp, an officer was obliged to shoot one of his men because the chosen method of Japanese execution was firing wildly from outside the tent. They were too frightened to go inside.

Light duties' men wore a red armband to indicate that they were exempted from heavy railway work, but Hiroda ignored this, insisting that 'the Lizard' draft them into the working parties each morning. He took a sadistic delight in driving men until they collapsed. These men, few of whom had boots, were usually given the task of felling trees, lopping off the branches, and chopping the trunks into lengths. It took four or five men to haul each de-barked trunk, slippery with sap, through the boulders and bamboo to the bridge-builders.

The men had been working thirty days without a rest when Hiroda beat up a light duties' man with a six-foot sapling because he had protested that his gang was too weak to carry saplings up a slope instead of hauling them up on ropes as they had been doing. That same evening, 22 June, because of discrepancies in the working parties' numbers, a number of men were summoned to the engineers' lines and beaten senseless. One, Sgt Hallam, was dragged out of hospital where he had been admitted earlier with malaria, having collapsed on his way out to the line that morning and returned to camp. He had spent the day on light duties.

'Billie the pig', and his assistant, 'Mollie the monk' - 'a huge, black-haired Japanese . . . of ape-like proportions'[19] - went berserk with fists, feet, wooden clogs and bamboo canes, throwing the men repeatedly to the ground 'with a sort of fireman's lift action, then kicking in the stomach and scrotum and ribs'. Five were carried or assisted to the hospital around 2300 hours. Hallam had a high temperature and gross multiple injuries to neck, chest and limbs.

While Corlette did what he could for them, Weary was in the cholera tent, administering saline to the second cholera patient with apparatus constructed from a record needle, a rubber catheter and a Thompson Walker syringe. After half a litre of Ringer's solution – all he had – he injected Jarvis with the contents of a three-pint saki bottle of saline manufactured from kitchen salt and boiled water. It was late when he walked back to the hospital to look at the injured men. 'Billie the pig' had announced that all of them must work next day. 'This is impossible unless they are to be carried there.'

Four days later, Hallam died, 'slain by these Nipponese sadists more certainly than if they had shot him'. Weary informed Usuki, who agreed to report the findings to Tarsau, that the death was caused by 'contusions to heart causing cardiac arrest as a result of a beating by a Nippon Engineer sgt whilst suffering from malaria'. But privately, Corlette and he thought the causes 'a little vague . . . My theory is Cardiac Beri Beri'.

Weary felt especially bitter about the speech given on the day Hallam died by Colonel Sijue Nakamura when he took over the command of all the Thai prisoner-of-war camps. ' . . . Regret to find seriousness in health matter . . . to my opinion due mainly to . . . absence of firm belief as "Health follows will" . . . Those who fails to reach objective . . . by lack of health, is considered in Japanese Army as most shameful deed . . . you are to remember that your welfare is guarranteed only be obeadience to Imperial Japanese Army.'[20] Nakamura had apparently overlooked 'the fact that we really don't belong to the Imperial Japanese Army'.

Bridges were being thrown up on the Konyu–Hintok section, crazy, multi-tiered affairs built of green timber. The craziest, most dangerous-looking of all, built by the Tamils and nicknamed the 'Pack of Cards' bridge after it collapsed, was near the compressor cutting.

In May, fifty men had been despatched there to make a new camp on the river. The engineers put them to work on compressors and jack hammers, and they fared better than gangs working out of the Hintok and Konyu camps, for the cutting was but a short distance from the camp and light duties men delivered their lunchtime rice and water.

Forty more men were sent there on 5 July after Usuki, McEachern and Wearne had inspected the site and selected an area for the tents. Usuki suggested that everyone would move there 'soon', and the rumours persisted until 18 July when a jubilant Usuki and Okada announced that the two Hintok camps on the road and the river were to remain in the area for railway maintenance on the 'shush pusher'. ' . . . I have no doubt the work will not be light,' responded Weary.

Eventually, some of the fitter Englishmen were to move down to the river, and coolies would take over the Konyu road area. Weary was concerned to hear that coolies working on the bridges had also moved into a site across the creek from which Hintok river camp drew its water.

Usuki, thoroughly rattled by the rising number of patients down in 'Cholera Gulch' and the deaths proliferating in the camps all about them, was making an effort with the rations and 'the evening stew has become a thing to which we hasten home, quite thick with obvious meat'. Wearne, Clarke, Smedley and Brettingham-More all had dysentery, especially trying when the cooks were ladling meat, pumpkin, sweet potatoes and onion gravy into the dixies. It was too late to do much for most of the men; Weary had been haranguing Usuki since January about the Australians' need for fat and protein, particularly meat. He had lost count of the times that he had cited the appalling nutrition as the cause for the rising number of sick.

The men had been working thirty-nine days without a break when Private Jarvis died of cholera on 29 June. He had been unconscious for two days. Anticipating the end, Weary kept Jarvis's brother in camp, admitting him to hospital with a trumped-up illness so that he could accompany the body on its last journey.

The orderlies had sewed the body into its rough, grey blanket shroud and its weight sagged between the bamboo poles of the rice sack stretcher. 'Because of the possibility of infection, I acted as one of the bearers [in] . . . a terrible, sad and dreary procession dragging through the rough jungle tracks between bamboos and gaunt trees in dripping rain . . . '

They lived in a world in which everything was grey: grey monsoon rains, grey skies, grey faces, grey blankets enclosing the dead bodies they carried across the bleak, brief distance to the graveyard.

His eye was caught by a 'bright crimson flower' deep in the undergrowth beside the path, and he had 'an impulse to . . . lay it on the body to add somehow a little touch of beauty'. But the conditioning of his 'stolid British upbringing' was too difficult to cast off in time to halt the burial party and seize the blossom, and it vanished in the lush green tangle about them.

Wearne called the men on evening *tenko* to attention as the 'whisper of the bugle [sic] playing the Last Post and Reveille' drifted across the valley.

Jarvis's and Breen's deaths hit Weary hard, for these two cholera victims had responded well to the doctors' intense work. 'We raised [Jarvis's] intake [of saline] up to 20 pints a day without effect.' They had buried Breen the previous day.

'I simply *must* now try intravenous despite the difficulties of a still and I.V. gear.'

Practical and inventive Jock Clarke came to the rescue. He told Weary, Woods and Wearne what he required, and next day Wearne went to Okada and persuaded him to co-operate in removing a petrol feed pipe secretly from one of the engineer's lorries. This would act as a condenser. Woods cut a large bamboo for a pipe to feed water from the water scheme to the still, then he took a sapling, wrapped a little piece of iron round the end, and bashed it lengthwise through the bamboo to give a steady flow of water. Water was boiled in a four-gallon petrol tin, the steam passing through the petrol feed pipe enclosed in a large jacket of bamboo and cooled by spring water.

Clarke, Wearne and Smedley worked feverishly into the night, stoking the fire and keeping the supply of water constant in the petrol tin and flowing through the jacket. Slowly, drop by drop, the level of distilled water rose in the sake bottles.

One of the orderlies, pharmacist Geoff Wiseman, then made up the saline with rock salt (re-crystallised by boiling for a purer result), filtered it through cotton wool, and sterilised the bottles in a boiling water bath. They produced the first pint and a half of saline soon after midnight and continued to work round the clock.

Weary used the first three pints to give a transfusion to Private Charley Mould. He sacrificed his stethoscope to the intravenous equipment – there was no other source of rubber tubing. A sake bottle, its base removed and the now open end covered with a cloth, was upended on a bamboo framework and the rubber tubing, connectd with bamboo joints, fed the life-giving fluid through a syringe and its needle into a vein.

For three hours, between 0230 and 0530, Weary sat beside him. At first 'apparently unconscious, almost pulseless', the saline appeared to effect a miraculous improvement. ' . . . He . . . partly sat up, looked for a cigarette and began smoking.' He survived a further thirty-seven hours; the intravenous treatment had come just too late.

Mould, 'quiet, efficient', was mourned by all the 2/2nd CCS, for he had been one of the original twenty members. All of the unit who were in camp, including Corlette, Clarke, the NCOs Gibson and Topping, accompanied the body to its cremation and Weary read the burial service.

One of the orderlies poured kerosene over the bundle balanced on top of the bamboo and lit it. The entire party nearly took to their heels when the corpse suddenly sat up 'with the flames all around it'. Weary pulled himself together, his voice sounding unnaturally loud to his ears. 'My God! Tissue tension.'

After a week, Clarke and Smedley moved the still down to a site on the creek and built a mud fireplace, over which the kerosene tins could be more easily balanced. An attap-thatched roof sheltered it. Corlette donated his stethoscope to a second still and another petrol feed pipe was filched.

'Cholera is a major thing in our lives these days.' The officers worked four-hourly shifts and by 10 July they could deliver between forty and sixty pints of saline each day, the means of 'bringing almost moribund men back to some degree of life'. Eventually, three stills worked continuously in a 'flat-out night and day production' of 120 pints over twenty-four hours. Eight crude continuous intravenous sets, manufactured from sake or beer bottles, fragments of rubber tubing, bamboo 'pipes', wooden stoppers and other odds and ends, were hitched up to bamboo frames above the cholera patients' beds.

On one terrible night of storms and beating rain, Weary had scarcely stretched out on his bedframe when he was gripped by 'grinding' bowel cramps and had to dash for the latrines. His boots stuck so fast in the mud that he walked out of them and sprawled on his face, 'losing everything', including the beautiful, sturdy ankle-high half-boots of strong, soft suede made by the Armenian shoemaker, Garabelian, in Jerusalem. They disappeared in the blackness as he floundered towards the special 'thunder box' which Jock Clarke had built for the officers. Miserably, he crouched in the dark and stinking slush all night, purging and vomiting with cholera, examining his shrinking hands with their tell-tale washerwoman's fingers when lightning lit up the clearing.

He convinced himself that he was going to die in the mud, in this squalid Thai camp. But at first light, he found his fingers almost normal and the painful cramps had ceased. Somehow, he had shaken it off.

The wards were grossly understaffed with usually only one orderly to each tent. Patients, such as Ian Wynne and Ernest Niemann, volunteered to hazard death and nurse men reduced to inert, almost unrecognisable bundles of bones with the 'pathetic sunken face of the prematurely born child'.

Eight men, including 'Scorp' Stuart, built bamboo pyres, splashed kerosene over the bodies and collected the ashes in bottles for burial in marked graves. Some members of the cremation parties succumbed and were burned in turn by their successors. In the early days of the epidemic, they burned the bodies one at a time; later, they burned them in fours.

Frequently, Jock Clarke read a funeral service of his own compiling for, as hygiene officer, the disposal of the corpses was his responsibility. He was deeply troubled about burning Catholics – the Church forbade cremation – and could scarcely wait to unburden himself to Bourke when next he saw him. But the Church in the person of its priest was realistic and reassuring.

For the whole of the cholera epidemic, Clarke insisted on cleaning the latrines himself to reduce, if possible, the risk of infection to others.

Across the creek in the English camp, there were so few to dispose of the dead and so many corpses that they were unable to gather enough fuel for the pyres; they buried them instead, in graves too shallow to withstand the rains. Men walked to work through a skeletal under-growth of limbs and rotting flesh. Many years after the war, when his cerebral malaria returned as a recurring nightmare that woke him screaming in a lather of sweat, Lang Fraser painted a ghostly picture of the walk along the track to the escarpment, the bones and bodies of the dead rising from the sodden ground on each side.

At night, Weary and Corlette were called repeatedly to the cluster of low, leaking tents pitched in mud and water as far away as possible from the lines. Cholera Gulch deserved 'a circle in Dante's inferno', for amongst men suffering 'intolerable cramps and abdominal pains and delirium there can be no silence, and the air is full of groans, cries for relief and curses in weak, husky voices'. Few made it to the 'thunder box' in the middle of the tent. Bodies, bedspaces, blankets – if they had them – and ground were fouled and stinking.

Even the life-saving saline caused untold pain and discomfort to cadaverous, severely dehydrated men forced to lie still without displacing the drip in their arm. When they tore the drip out, Corlette and Weary put it back in, again and again. Weary found the appearance of 'cholera sleep' particularly disconcerting. The eyelids of the sleeping men were eerily open, the eyes rolled back into the head 'so that the pearly whites stare from between the lids'. For hours at a time, his tall frame was bent almost double over the sick lying on bamboo platforms slippery with their own excreta resting on the muddy floor. On his feet was rough footwear made from yak hide; he had given his last pair of boots to Geoff Wiseman and the strong and beautiful ankle boots never emerged from the mud.

An ulcer on his shin was growing steadily worse, causing 'miserable, sleepless nights'. He had no relief from the pain that throbbed constantly like a red hot coal, or stabbed like some excruciating 'flounder spear' at any sudden movement. Sleep was impossible. A blanket irritated the 'large, indurated, sloughing, offensive crater', stinking with gangrene, yet if he put his leg outside the cover, he quickly grew tired, for most of the time it was hanging over the edge of the bamboo, unsupported.

Each night, during this worst time on the railway when the sick parades dragged on interminably, Allanson watched Weary deal with the last of the men then sit down with a container of hot water, remove the dressings from his leg, and dress his own ulcer.

He was shabby, haggard, grey, looking ten years older. His thirty-sixth birthday on 12 July passed without comment in the diary. He awoke that morning to see, attached to his blanket, a piece of paper on which was written Byron's 'On this Day I Complete my Thirty-sixth Year'. It made depressing reading. 'Seek out – less often sought then found – /A soldier's grave, for thee the best;/Then look around, and choose thy ground,/And take thy rest.' He suspected Wearne and

Corlette, although neither owned up to it.

Three letters, including one from Helen, were slipped into his pocket while he was attending patients in the cholera tents so that he need not touch them. He wept, briefly, when he read them.

From 26 June, 'Billie the pig' had collected between 40 and 70 men each morning for No. 2 rock-clearing party. They walked out in darkness at seven o'clock and 'dragged their way into camp in the dark again' fourteen hours later. The men dreaded the engineer's NCO and his assistant, for they were the most brutal and sadistic in the area, and tried to avoid being detailed to this gang. Weary could do little to help them, but the 'complete scorn' he continued to hurl at the Japanese and their demands 'built up the camp morale in many ways singlehanded'.[21]

Allanson never saw Weary as 'a natural soldier. He was a doctor, a gentle man, a dreamer, just not suited to giving those harsh military commands.' Heedless of the interpreter, the attitude he adopted was one of 'criticism towards them . . . regardless of his personal safety. It was common for him to refer to them as swine in front of them . . . '[22]

Weary had his own way of addressing the troops and they became accustomed to hearing him preface the day's orders with, 'Gentlemen, I'm sorry that these little swine are causing us such concern, but it seems we are obliged' to supply whatever fresh demands the engineers had made. He may have been neither a regular soldier nor a combatant one, but Duntroon graduates Wearne and Woods found him the more effective commander. After three months of McEachern and another officer co-operating in swindles with the Japanese over the number of working men each day, and how many sick could be taken from the hospital, they suggested to Weary that the sooner Dunlop Force was freed from McEachern's control and had its former identity restored, the better. Self interest amongst the officers was no longer checked.

Usuki had announced that the 'speedo' tactics would cease on 30 June, but the first half of July dragged by with no sign of the pressure easing. On 15 July, men were required to work all night, 'almost out on their feet'. It was the sixty-second day without rest. Only one bridge was unfinished, and the rails were piled on the other side of the 150 kilometre post, waiting to be laid.

Since the war years, the largest cutting they gouged out of the mountainside has come to be called Hell-fire Pass, for it was said that men who looked down on it imagined that the torments of the damned could not be worse than the scene below. But Weary, Jones, Belford and Parkin never knew this name. It is part of a myth which grew up in

Australia after men came home. For those who worked on them, the cuttings had no names.

They drilled and moved and levelled the last of the rock in the orange glare of great, crackling fires and the smoking yellow flare of acetylene torches. Above the rock walls rising sheer into the sky, the light from the fires bounced off the rods of rain. And when the rain squalls ceased, fog swirled about the silhouettes moving stiffly, mechanically with cold and exhaustion, against the flames.

Weary 'thought a good deal' about them out in the foul weather. It was four o'clock in the afternoon when they marched out; over twelve hours later they stumbled back by the dying light of their torches. His concern was infinite. Men knew of this and they, in turn, worried about him. When he went down to the compressor camp, news of his visit flashed round. 'Weary's been down, and he looks well,' Parkin noted in his diary one day. Weary was expert at ignoring his own pain, so all they saw was 'good health and high spirits', which was to all men 'a tonic'. 'He is a symbol and a rock to us.'[23]

Tobacco was their only opiate, deadening the pangs of hunger, offering slight comfort as they dragged the smoke from the strong, black native tobacco into their lungs. Papers were a problem: bibles were the solution. Weary methodically memorised anything he wanted to remember as he tore each page from his bible, rolled the tobacco in it and smoked it. In this most desperate period, he read his *New Testament* and questioned the faith which had served his parents' generation and continued to inspire the padres, Bourke and Thorpe, so well, pondering the teaching in the Sermon on the Mount. This was the only part worth anything, he decided. As he searched for answers, he moved towards articulating his own faith, seeing 'God shining out of all the goodness of men, Christian and non-Christian, and all nature, and interpreted by countless prophets, so that faith comes in varied and extraordinary guises'. He was swept by the conviction that he was closer to 'the kingdom of heaven' in Konyu and Hintok than at any other time. For him, it 'was at hand, not a promise for the future, not dependent on life or death, but here immediately for those who could shed the awful shell of self and start loving their neighbour as thyself – possibly even more than self to the point where death had no terror, only kindliness'.

He was struck by the joy on the faces of dying men reaching out to death. But he was disturbed that his sense of the abiding presence of God could 'co-exist with an implacable hatred of [the] Japanese'.[24]

He came to the conclusion that he could not live by Christ's precepts; they were 'too difficult'.[25] But what he described as his 'barbarous creed' became an inspiration to many, and led to some calling him the 'Christ of the railway'.

Bourke, the priest, concluded that Dunlop the doctor reflected 'Christ-like virtues'. He was a man 'with a definite belief in God, perhaps without any precise affiliation . . . he believed that in serving others it was God he was serving, and that God succours others through our co-operation.'[26]

The work party who returned at 0445 on 16 July reported that a diesel engine rail layer had moved cautiously forward across rails laid by skinny, noisy Tamils and 'a small gang of very well-fed Tommies'. Usuki and Okada were 'jubilant, obviously expecting pats on the back' because the inmates of the Hintok camps were not to leapfrog up the line, but to move to the river on 19 July. Only the sick and those looking after them were to stay at the road.

Weary's ulcer was unhealed and Corlette considered that caring for the cholera patients would be too much for him. But Weary had 'stubborn ideas' of his own. 'I have never handed over the hard end of a job to another fellow yet.' He requested that as many of his unit as possible remain with him, and several of his orderlies were now ill with cholera and dysentery.

The cholera sufferers were to remain in their boggy squalor. Weary's plans to separate them, isolating suspected cases for four days in tents on a clear area of higher ground, were thwarted by Japanese orders that they stay where they were. All the other patients were to lose their tents and move into barracks, even the *kempeitai* and the 'Texaco' barracks formerly occupied by the Koreans being pressed into use, for the tents were needed at the river.

Two men had died the previous night, four the day before, but the Australian mortality was slight compared to the English across the creek. Some days back, Weary had removed an infected eye from one of them and he called over to see how his patient was progressing. 'Rather tactlessly commented . . . that they now had much more space.' He was embarrassed by the smart rejoinder: 'Oh yes, we have thinned ourselves out all right.'

They had lost 100 men in two months, almost a quarter of their strength, and all their sick other than the cholera cases were to be evacuated to Tarsau. He was appalled to learn that only sixty were fit to work and would join O, P and S battalions at the river camp.

'Today and tonight . . . hellish and I had very little sleep at all.' The theft of the English soldier's boots during Weary's operation to remove the eye had depressed him. He was feeling 'inefficient, irritable and not myself' and had argued with McEachern about the men who were not to move. Of the officers, Jock Clarke and Smedley had volunteered to stay with him, but McEachern had been slow to see the necessity for Weary to have a senior officer to assist with the administration. To his 'great delight', McEachern agreed eventually that Wearne should remain as Weary's second-in-command.

He quashed lingering regrets about sharing his set of precious instruments with Corlette, who had been 'doing grand work' assuming a large share of the sick burden while Weary had difficulty walking, and sent him off with one of the stills and two intravenous apparatuses. ' . . . He will probably soon have cholera cases.'

Heavy rain complicated the move on 19 July and seventeen men fell ill with cholera. Since Corlette had not yet had time to set up his hospital, they were sent back on stretchers to the road. Twelve more collapsed the next day and he had the four worst carried up to Weary, for the still was not working.

Weary arranged for Corlette to have a quarter of the saline output. Two runners ranged back and forth between the road and the river, each man carrying two bottles at a time. They boosted these men's diet with liver and blood from beasts killed for the cookhouse, in order to provide them with the energy to make the repeated trips up and down the escarpment.

He had 370 men with him: 342 sick, nine cooks, a duty section of eleven and eight orderlies. Each day, Weary entered the details of the previous night's dead in his records. Repeatedly, he was struck by the incongruities of men who came away in the ranks, yet were 'typical of the well-off Australian landowner'. That such soldiers left peace, comfort and security at home with their wives and children in order 'to go to war and to suffer hunger, hardships and privation along a grim road leading to such a miserable death' filled him with sadness.

Acting on McEachern's report that Usuki had 'entirely written off' Weary and his camp – who would probably be evacuated to Tarsau – Weary promptly discharged a good number from hospital and put them on light duties, in the hope that they would be paid. 'Meantime, no discharged men are to go back to the river camp.'

Contrary to Weary's expectations, he found his work nowhere near as exhausting as he had anticipated when he elected to stay at the road. Despite a 'hard fight' all day with the second case of cerebral malaria, Bombadier Hugh Tully, he played chess with Jock Clarke that night for the first time in months.

For some time, Weary had been worried and puzzled by the increase in the number of patients suffering cardiac arrest. Although he felt that avitaminosis was probably a major contributor, he also considered beri beri, impurities in the quinine and the effects of cerebral malaria.

The orthodox method of resuscitation was to cut open the patients' chest and massage the heart, but Weary dropped onto a new solution with these emaciated men when Tulley's heart stopped, seconds after Weary had given him some quinine intravenously. Desperately, he checked that his air passages were clear and 'pushed his thin chest', yelling to the orderlies for adrenaline. This revived Tully for a short while, but while Weary was watching him, he slipped back 'to no perceptible heart action, collapse and unconsciousness'.

The second injection of adrenaline into the heart muscle and external massage was 'most dramatic in effect.' Weary improvised an intravenous drip with saline and adrenaline. Within hours, and after further quinine, Tully was sweating profusely, his temperature had fallen and he was conscious.

Weary had never heard of anyone being given external cardiac massage, but henceforth, by doubling up his fists, he could massage the heart externally by pumping the chest until an orderly brought adrenaline or coramine. This he injected into the heart, massaging all the while, and it became his standard treatment for victims of Stokes Adam's attacks. Some of them suffered clinical death two or three times. 'I suppose I had a unique experience of . . . getting their hearts going again', bringing dead men back to life.

At the end of July, Usuki announced that he would now command the combined Hintok-Konyu camps from his new headquarters at the river. All fit men in the area, Australian and English, were to be concentrated there. Coolies would occupy Konyu road.

Only the sick and their caretakers remained in the wretched 'H' Force camp across the creek. Their senior officers, Humphries and Newey, had moved to Hintok 3 with the few fit troops, abandoning seventy patients to F/O Park with no money and no stores apart from rice. Unlike the Australians, the English officers there had made no attempt to tithe themselves and support their sick, although they received full pay from Singapore. Newey confessed to Weary that he did 'not quite know how to spend his money' and wondered whether he should save up for a car. Weary looked at him scornfully. 'Ever think of buying a few lives?'

Wearne and Weary decided to share their camp's 'rather meagre' rations with Park and his patients, and Smedley took over the burial of their dead, 'as they cannot cope'. Park messed with Weary, Wearne, Clarke and Smedley. The accumulated remnants of eight battalions, O, P, S, T, E, J, Y and W, were eating well at the river camp, but the Japanese policy of putting the sick on reduced rations meant that only scanty supplies of meat, vegetables and eggs were brought up the hill.

On one of the first fine days in August Weary and Clarke walked to Hintok River camp to see for themselves what was happening. Weary's ulcers were partly healed and he had 'only one . . . of any size . . . shallow and about the size of a shilling piece'. He was enjoying more sleep in a dry and comfortable thatched humpy built by Clarke and Smedley. For the first time since his move from the river, his bedframe was level, at a reasonable height above the ground, and 'free from the constant squeaking and rustle of rats'. (He had had a phobic horror of the latter since the night one had wriggled inside his mosquito net and bitten him on the chest.)

They slid down the elephant pads to the railway line and walked along it for a time, smiling 'with bitter humour at its crude and snake-like course'. The rails might be parallel, but at times sleepers and their attached rails curved up switchback fashion above the ground or rails curved above the sleepers, without making contact, giving the track a 'most disconcerting zig zag'. Nothing was orderly. From above, the sleepers looked as if they had been 'tossed down by a giant hand'.

Their route lay across the curved trestle bridge, now held up by stays. Weary's old height-giddiness reaction almost immobilised him. One glance down through the ricketty rails and sleepers filled him with 'an impulse to crawl on his hands and knees'. Gaps between rails and sleepers had been filled with wooden chocks. Discarded timber was scattered like matchwood amongst stumps and bamboo. Already, eighty of the men he had brought from Singapore had died building this stretch of railway, and 'few trails have been trodden with more suffering'. His pleasure in the unaccustomed sunshine vanished in sombre contemplation of the 'wreckage of humanity, stupidly broken by inefficiency and design'.

In common with every other camp in the area, Hintok No. 3 was wet, boggy and too close to the Tamils. But food, including meat and soya bean sprouts grown in the camp, was plentiful, and Usuki regularly donated pomelos, sugar and eggs.

While Clarke did some dental work, Weary inspected the sick with Corlette and gossiped with the officers. He noted critically that a lack of generosity on the Australian officers' part saw them in roomy, attap-thatched quarters with tables between the beds, while the English inhabited leaking tents. Everyone seemed to be in good spirits, however. Even McEachern, who was shivering with malaria, took it in good part when Weary sat on his bed and broke it.

Usuki was learning English and badgered Weary with questions about the difference between 'perhaps' and 'maybe'. Weary cheerfully explained: 'Perhaps you Japanese win the war, but only maybe.' Weary had been warned of the evacuation of all sick to Tarsau. The movement appeared to be as haphazard as earlier ones, the only difference being that barges had been substituted for the lorries on which men had hitchhiked to hospital earlier in the year.

Clarke and he stocked up on eggs and tobacco and 'slithered . . . home, slipping back nearly as much as forward' before dark.

Four days later, he returned to the mountain camp in a less light-hearted frame of mind after a serious talk with McEachern about finance. Usuki's more liberal ration policy had come too late. Although cholera had declined with the finer weather, the sick figures stayed high with recurring malaria, dysentery and wet beri beri. With so many sick – Corlette now had 400 and Weary 191 – the camps' earnings had been reduced to a point where only 5c a man per day was available for food for the hospital, less than a quarter of the previous expenditure. 'Some sick men will die but . . . this must be faced if the strain on the earners was becoming too great.'

Weary decided that McEachern's control of canteen and men was sloppy. Too many luxuries had been bought; and he had not been nearly tough enough on men dealing privately with the barges, then re-selling to their companions at a profit. 'This practice is to stop.'

Usuki appeared in the mountain camp on 18 August with the unwelcome announcement that on 20 August they must start evacuating all sick other than cholera cases to Tarsau. There would be problems transporting the stretcher cases up the cliff; 'I find it difficult enough to go along the track in daylight without falling.' He dared not look down. Hiroda still demanded every fit man, so the ambulant sick would have to assist the bedridden.

He was consumed by sadness as he watched the first 30 leave on 19 August. ' . . . Nearly all the old 'O' and 'P' men will be going down - terribly broken . . . and I don't think a number of them will see the day of liberation . . .

'Altogether, during the last few weeks, with the absence of the fiendish speedo attentions of Nippon, we have been happy here . . . This happiness is a strange thing.

' . . . My policy of keeping our group of Java party men together was . . . a failure - excellent though the results were for six months - I just didn't quite reckon on the ferocious inhumanity of the last three months - or the cholera . . . Whatever a man has in his body and spirit, it is certain that the last would be extracted here, and he will leave bankrupt.'

They bullocked the stretcher cases up the ladder, rung by rung, the bearers ragged, tattered, mostly barefoot. Others managed to climb with the help of the man behind lifting their legs up, for the beri beri cases could not negotiate steps. He nominated Jock Clarke and Fred Smedley to go as officers with the group, and they went out on the morning of 22 August. 'After an hour or two I felt . . . lonely and restless and decided to carry some medical gear out to the river.' Halfway up the cliff he rescued a man with 'pouring enteritis and a feeble pulse' and helped him back to the hospital as a suspected cholera. When, finally, he was making his way down to the river, he found Topping - very shaky - and a wan Clarke. The patients were lined up at the barge point with no certainty of a prompt passage.

Weary arranged to transfer himself to the river next day with 30 cholera patients. Of the 150 cases of cholera in his camp, 63 had died. But although the deaths which affected him most were the four members of his unit, Findley, Mould, Freeman and Watson, the men could see that he cared about every death, every patient.

Butterworth insisted on taking the valise heavy with surgical instruments and other medical gear, so he had 'no more than an average heavy load' and picked up a cholera patient on the way. ' . . . Arrived looking like Father Christmas' with the patient on his back. Three days later, the 2/2nd CCS and Java Ambulance Car men were still waiting for a barge. Weary worked out that it was their 231st day in the jungle and work on the railway had gone on without a halt for 93 days, for some men had been made to work even on official rest days.

Weary heard the first train steam noisily along the line on 26 August, whistling shrilly and repeatedly as it chugged cautiously through the teak and bamboo. The locomotive pulled only one open truck in which the Japanese top brass were standing as upright as possible in those conditions. Parkin was one of the men working on the line who were ordered to turn their backs as the train passed. Hiroda presided over a noisy celebration and smoke concert in the Engineers' lines: 'cigarettes and beer for all and . . . much sake.'

Australian evacuations had halted temporarily, Okada explained, because some men had arrived at Tarsau with cholera. Weary regarded this as yet another of Okada's face-saving falsehoods: probably, he should have given everyone glass rod tests before sending them down.

Weary was anxious to evacuate all of 'O' and 'P' battalions, and particularly his CCS men, as he feared a move upriver quite soon. He fought fiercely with De Crespigny and McEachern over keeping his CCS personnel in the now combined Australian and English hospital. 'I am willing to send Red Cross personnel out to work to spare sick men, but I do not like the assumption that of necessity they go out just as other men. There are few enough of them left and they are very important to the health of the troops, quite apart from the breach of international law.'

On 1 September there was 'a sudden barge flutter'. By evening, 'chilled to the bone' and beginning to shake with a fresh attack of malaria, he was in Tarsau.

TWENTY-ONE

Stables for the Sick

HAZELTON MET THEM AT THE barge point and stowed the sick in various corners of the hospital barracks. They had been seriously overcrowded since May.

Weary had been anxious to go back to Tarsau, for he had been worried by reports that patients were slow to recover. Many went downhill rapidly once they were evacuated there, particularly the dysentery and ulcer cases. Some of his patients arrived back at Hintok in a worse state than they had gone down. A few, longer-term patients, had been sent to base hospitals at Chungkai or Kanchanaburi, but he could find out very little about them, largely because of the jealousy between the autonomous Japanese administrations of the different areas. Even Arthur Moon at Tamarkan, which was 'very much a prison hospital', had little contact with the outside world and kept in touch by sending an occasional, surreptitious letter back along the line.

Next morning, Weary was not greeted with especial cordiality by Lieut-Colonel Knights when he appeared for breakfast in the mess, run rather formally 'on 4 Royal Norfolk style'. Knights was the commanding officer of Tarsau camp. 'I think he had decided the Australians were a bloody nuisance.'

When Weary began to talk to Harvey, it emerged that there was to be a finance meeting later in the day. He was not invited, since Harvey felt it was 'a camp matter'. Weary disagreed, and announced his intention of representing the Hintok interests.

Until August, it had been the policy of the jungle camps to send money down with patients being evacuated to 4 Group hospital at Tarsau. But Tarsau was also a working camp, which had to care for its own sick as well as those from the jungle camps. Once the cholera and dysentery epidemics took hold in May, and the admissions from the sub-camps escalated, contributions decreased drastically (the sick were not paid). Not all camps could send money with their patients. In desperation, the General Affairs Officer who was in charge of finances at Tarsau, Lieut-Colonel D. Rhys Thomas, began sending accounts to the camps. For the past four months, Tarsau's expenditure had exceeded its income.

Weary had been dismayed when McEachern decided to cease contributing to the upkeep of their sick at Tarsau and to discontinue sending money with new cases being evacuated. He was even more opposed to McEachern abolishing all ranks' subscriptions at Hintok for eggs and other food; 'money collected into funds was much more wisely spent on the whole than by individuals.' Tobacco might deaden the hunger pangs, but eggs would save lives.

McEachern's lax supervision of the canteen purchases rankled with him and, morally, he felt it was wrong to shuffle their sick off to Tarsau and abdicate all responsibility for them. Eventually, Wearne had suggested a compromise: a levy of one-fifth of everyone's earnings; and the sick to be given 2½ ticals plus their canteen credits before departing. The sick in their own camp hospital were to have 5c a day spent on their diet.

The Tarsau Capital Fund had been accumulated, like most other camps' funds, by officers voluntarily contributing their pay; and the hospital working fund was financed with monthly subscriptions from all officers of field rank and above. Other ranks there did not subscribe to the hospital fund, but contributed a proportion of their earnings to the purchase of eggs, sugar, peanuts and so on to supplement their rations from the Japanese. This differed from Weary's camps, where all ranks contributed to the hospital fund.

The finance meeting was useful for the number of people he saw, including his two favourite lieutenant-colonels from Konyu, Ferguson Warren and the balding, humorous McOstritch. Harvey was a pleasant, easy-going colleague, not nearly tough enough, in Weary's view, as SMO. He commanded the hospital and convalescent section of around 2300 patients with a dental officer, Capt. Jim Finnemore AIF, as his registrar, Maj. O'Driscoll RAMC in charge of the convalescent depot, Hazelton representing the AIF interests and taking charge of pathology and McConachie RAMC leading the surgical department. A physician, Capt. Jim Street, ran the dysentery wards.

Boon Pong's deliveries and the underground activities had been a regular feature for some months on the Hintok section, and Weary could elect to have either cash or its equivalent in drugs. Recently, he had acquired a generous supply of emetine for the amoebic dysentery patients and he brushed aside Harvey's worries about the difficulties of obtaining the drug. ' . . . If it was a matter of money I would certainly raise some more.'

Weary had emphasised the usefulness of his trained CCS personnel to Harvey and was relieved when Finnemore and Hazelton favoured using them in the hospital once they had recovered, rather than see them employed on working parties.

Weary's three days at Tarsau were crowded. He had no time to be tactful. He made a thorough and thoughtful reconnaissance of the hospital, inspecting many wards 'superficially by calling on patients'. Those who had come down from Hintok were 'very miserable at the lack of personal attention', particularly in the convalescent area. He decided that both conditions and staff there were a disgrace. Austin Fyffe reported the men's horror at witnessing an English doctor striking a patient. Weary could see no signs of careful care of ulcers and the men confirmed that treatment consisted of a daily application of Eusol. The long wards stank of gangrene; the blackened, sloughing flesh was putrid, often fly-blown.

Two of his amoebic dysentery patients sent down from Hintok some days beforehand had been transferred to O'Driscoll's convalescent section. One of them had been nigh death at Hintok, yet both were required to work. Another 2/2nd CCS man was in a coma, very ill with cerebral malaria and 'obviously failing'. Despite Weary finding a physician to revive him with coramine, he died a few hours later. 'I do not regard this case as well managed.'

Tarsau medical officers had been observing the same complications and sudden death from Stokes Adam's attacks as had caused Weary so much anxiety at Hintok. He accepted their theory that the impure quinine manufactured by the Japanese was the cause, although he did not believe it was quite so simple.

Jock Clarke had returned a negative test to amoebic dysentery, but no sooner was he at Tarsau than he ran a high fever and began to shudder with malarial rigors. It suited Weary that he should stay behind as a battalion representative with Lieut. Piper; Piper and Houston had displayed too much self interest to be trusted with the 'O' and 'P' battalion financial arrangements without supervision.

He spent most of 4 September attempting to return to Hintok. When Usuki appeared unexpectedly, Weary seized the opportunity to suggest that he should go to Chungkai instead and inspect the 'O' and 'P' battalion sick there. Permission was refused. Finally, he ran into

Tadano, now in Tarsau, who promised him a passage on a barge and saw him off next morning.

The quinine had taken effect and Weary's malaria seemed much improved. He lazed in the sun while the string of barges behind their pom-pom boat beat upriver against the strong current. Once the Thais and Japanese on board had given up trying to buy his watch, it was a smooth trip all the way to Hintok. He fed well, topping off 'an excellent lunch' with pomelos and cakes. Five and a half hours after leaving Tarsau, they tied up at the jetty below the camp.

James and McEachern greeted him with the news that a move upstream was mooted and Weary countered with the Tarsau financial arrangements. He had paid the bill for patients treated in June and July and he passed on the meeting's recommendation that if all officers subscribed 5 ticals per month out of their increased pay to a special contingency fund for No. 4 Group, Tarsau could remain solvent. Weary insisted, however, that they must protest immediately if meeting the subscription put their own fund at risk.

They had evacuated 808 Australians from the four battalions between 20 August and 5 September. Nearly a thousand men had been sent to Tarsau once the English sick were included. Now, only 450 Australians and Englishmen remained at Hintok. Dunlop Force had dwindled to 150 other ranks and 7 officers from the 873 men Weary had brought into Konyu, and of the 58 members of his own unit, a mere twenty were still in the jungle.

The Japanese were delighted to see 'No. 1 doctor' back and queued up for medical treatment. Weary did not intend wasting precious drugs on their neurotic complaints – one requested the removal of his appendix, because of his admiration for Weary's jungle operations – and administered revolting but harmless nostrums. 'Yesterday . . . a dose of mixture of mag. sulph., quinine sulphate and other unpleasant ingredients plus permanganate of potash. Today merely sago flour and iodine – a very good colour.' He felt slightly ashamed when one of them slipped him a tin of jam, and donated it to the hospital.

Weary and Corlette elected to indulge in 'much *yasume*', for now that the hospital was run as a combined Australian and English operation, there were medical officers to burn and not much more than a hundred patients. Weary's spleen had enlarged significantly with this bout of malaria, so he put himself on a full course of quinine, atebrin and plasmoquine. The effects of the treatment were not pleasant and now he had bronchitis as well. He spent the days overhauling his surgical instruments, many of which had rusted in the rain and high humidity, and practising his dentistry.

Jock Clarke had given him a demonstration and lent him some dental instruments before he left for Tarsau, but Weary never acquired the knack of extracting teeth cleanly. Rotting teeth fractured and broke off under his administrations, and once he had to leave the roots firmly anchored in the gums, for he substituted brute strength for Jock's precise movements. Some required 'so much rocking that all the bystanders have their mouths open in sympathy'. At one stage, he sent a letter confessing his difficulties and a request for advice down to Tarsau with Lieut-Colonel James.

Nonetheless, he was never short of patients, Japanese, English or Australian, whose jaws he numbed with novocaine supplied by Boon Pong. With practise, his hit-and-miss technique did improve.

The expected move upriver to Kinsayok began on 11 September. Wearne accompanied a draft of twenty sick men and returned the following day to report that Kinsayok camp was a 'fattening paddock . . . A football ground has been prepared and recreation . . . encouraged.' Weary decided to see the camp for himself.

He found Kinsayok full of muddle and inefficiency. It was newly under the command of Lieut-Colonel Lilly, who had arrived only a few days beforehand with Lieut-Colonel Hugonin of the Saigon Battalion, the same who had amazed Weary by leaving all his drugs behind in Indo-China.

The hospital was 'run by a soviet of captains but no common policy, no common stores, no arrangements for diets or special segregation of diseases'. As each group of men arrived, it had set up its own duty section, kitchen and medical arrangements. Hands had been promoted upriver, leaving a number of 'Q' battalion men, but Godlee was still looking after the AIF sick. The camp was ripe for reorganisation.

It was administered by a Korean private, Yamoka, for Hatori – the commander of the camp – appeared to take little active interest these days. The medical sergeant was no less than Okada, promoted to *gunsho*, who welcomed him enthusiastically. After giving Weary a lesson in dressing ulcers, he canvassed ideas for a new hospital. He agreed with all Weary's recommendations and wished him to be medical 'No. 1', replacing Maj. Bennett RAMC.

Over the next three days, James, McEachern, Corlette, Woods and the CCS boys arrived with the rest of the men from Hintok. They had spent the past few days moving vast quantities of fuel down to the river barges for transport to the wood-burning locomotives that now steamed up and down the line.

Sunday was Harvest Thanksgiving and officers had been asked to contribute something for the sick. Weary had been down to the river to complete secret negotiations for medical stores with the 'table tennis man', Boon Pong. No one noticed that he crept in late to the service with two eggs, all he could find.

He called a meeting of the English, Dutch and Australian doctors and proposed a central medical administration for the camp with an appointed staff running the new hospital. Medical stores, until now scattered between the various units, should be pooled; and the hospital should have its own kitchen or special diet arrangements with the cookhouse. He recommended that the 'whole camp contribute uniformly' to camp finances, but left the decision about subscriptions and hospital expenses to Lilly.

Bashing was rife at Kinsayok and the guards were enthusiastic practitioners of the *kere*. Wearne was beaten up by Yamoka for neglecting to arrange accommodation through him when they arrived and suffered episodes of slapping now and again. Neglecting to salute guards was vigorously punished and Weary narrowly avoided a slapping one night 'when performing . . . ablutions in a naked state'. It rose to a *crescendo* with Lieut-Colonel Ishii's visit which, unusually, extended over three days this time and caused great tension amongst the Japanese. Okada hated and feared him and was in his blackest mood, refusing to speak English and insisting that some of the heavy sick be tipped out of hospital and put to work lugging attap up from the barges or carrying bags of rice as a special demonstration in Ishii's presence.

Ishii's inspection was the excuse for various charades. The doctors were to line up with the patients outside the barracks and 'tap tap' (percuss) chests. And the bootless were to be shod. Except that when hundreds of men assembled on parade one evening in the hope of gaining new boots, they were told that only those with 'sunburnt' feet were eligible; anyone who presented himself without this distinguishing characteristic would be punished as a 'deceiver'. Only ninety qualified as having 'sunburnt' feet, all of them Eurasians.

As far as the chests were concerned, Okada relented and agreed that Weary and some of the others might continue working in their MI rooms. (With Okada's blessing, Weary had opened his own MI room featuring an attap shelter for the mud fireplace on which instruments were sterilised.) Tension slackened noticeably once Ishii had departed.

Okada conceded that Weary might decide how many and which heavy sick were to be turned over to him, 'so long as we supply enough'.

The wet season was ending. 'Oh, the relief . . . It has done more to break men's spirits than almost any other factor.' Weary's tropical ulcer was still unhealed, but he was free from malaria and dysentery for the present. Lilly had taken 200 men and moved to a new camp a short distance upriver. Hugonin was now in charge, and they re-grouped into three battalions. That September, O, P, S and T battalions had been renamed *Yama* (River), the English E, J, Y and W *Kawa* , Mountain; in the new organisation they formed one group.

Three days into October, quite unwittingly, Weary ran foul of two Korean guards. On his way back from a meeting with Okada, Weary had not noticed two soldiers soaping themselves in the Japanese bath house until they '*Kurra'd*' him and roughly demanded the reason for his failure to *keré* . Okada came by, 'took in the situation' and rescued him, laughingly saying, 'Colonel Dunropo must remember salute Nippon soldier.'

About two hours later, Weary failed to salute one of the guards outside the office about fifty metres away as he turned into his barrack. They were waiting for him. He was called over and stood to attention. After Weary had saluted, one 'took a swing' at his face with his rifle and nearly fell over 'with shock' when Weary raised his left arm and deflected the blow.

He was ordered to the guard house, where one Korean equipped himself with a length of bamboo around ten centimetres across, stood him to attention and began systematically to beat him up. Weary, 'desperately fed up', finally disarmed his assailant who then embarked on a furious orgy of kicking and beating with whatever lumps of wood came to hand. The other stood watching while Weary caught the wood and hurled it behind him out of their reach.

The commotion attracted Hannimura, the office clerk, who stood both Weary and the Koreans to attention and agreed to Weary's demand to see Hatori, the camp commander.

Weary collected Hugonin and they strode off to report to Hatori. The interpreter was not to be found, so it seemed sensible to seek out Okada. Weary showed him the extensive abrasions, bruises and cuts and Okada then conducted them to the commandant. After Okada had explained in Japanese, Weary made his own 'strong protest' in English, and Hatori half-promised to investigate. The entire incident seemed 'curious' to Weary, who could find no reason for being singled out.

Next morning, Okada suggested that he accompany him to Tarsau with a party of sick being evacuated and 'stay a few days'. The departure was unusually rushed; it was some time before Weary discovered that it was 'a stratagem to get me away from the vengeance of the two . . . soldiers'. On reflection, he decided that he had probably provoked the incident by allowing Okada to help him avoid a humiliating bashing outside the bath house. The Koreans had 'lost face'.

On the trip down, he impulsively presented his Parker fountain pen to the Thai bargee who gave coffee and cigarettes to the sick. Okada was furious; he had coveted that pen for months and Weary refused to sell; now his venality was mortally offended. In a thorough temper, he struck the Thai who appeared quite unconcerned and handed out more cigarettes while Okada glowered. It was not for this that he had agreed with Hatori to remove Weary from Kinsayok.

Tarsau was no better organised than on previous visits. Okada disappeared sulkily and no one met the sick. Finally, one by one, Weary carried nineteen of the men up the steep bank from the barge on his back and waited with them until orderlies transferred them to hospital.

Smedley and Gill fell on him with bitter complaints about the Convalescent Depot and the MI Room arrangements in the lines. Far too many sick men were being sent out to work. The nursing of ulcer patients had not improved – many had now lost their legs or died since his last visit. Knights' reception was a good deal warmer this time and he was satisfied with Weary's explanation that he was down to investigate finances and 'other matters affecting the sick'. After signing the book to signify that he had marched in, he was sent off to report to the Japanese interpreter and formalise his visit. This time, Harvey invited Weary to attend the financial meeting on 6 October.

'O' and 'P' battalions had run up 14 768 patient days in September and, at 8c each day for a hospital patient, their fund would last only two more months. Ross, now in charge of hospital finances, agreed that he should resist the idea of dipping into regimental funds to meet their bills now that Tarsau hospital was on a sound footing and had been operating with a healthy surplus for the past two months.

Thomas, whom he saw next, was also sympathetic to Weary's views, so Weary sought out Ferguson Warren, Ross and McOstritch for a 'council of war' before the meeting. He briefed them on the appalling state of the con. depot and the ulcer wards. The four men agreed to mount a common front. Weary would represent the outside battalions' difficulties in meeting their hospital expenses; McOstritch undertook to deal with the criticisms of the medical arrangements in the con. depot.

On the morning of the meeting, Harvey listened politely to Weary's trenchant criticism of the hospital, particularly O'Driscoll and the convalescent depot. The food and cooking arrangements were poor, but it was the state of the wards and the lack of care for patients that most angered and distressed him.

Conditions in the four ulcer wards were far worse than on his previous visit. The 'sickly sweet and nauseating' stench of gangrene filled the long bamboo huts, where 'huge numbers of men with naked, necrosed bone exposed and sloughing great masses of tendon' lay in terrible pain and clouds of flies. He was shocked by the deterioration of seven of his patients who had been doing well when last he saw them. All were 'in great danger of loss of limb or life'. He had never seen such ulcers: 'they are not limited to the lower legs but include the thighs, buttocks and upper limbs'.

The entire system of treatment was seriously defective. Orderlies were ill-trained and there was no attempt to use sterile instruments, dressings and containers. Cross infection was rife. 'I do not think the orderlies are capable of thorough toilets of ulcers, removing sloughing tissue, even if they had the instruments.' He struggled to control his anger and sadness at the men's 'pale, lined, harassed face[s] and haunted eyes telling of toxaemia, pain and loss of sleep . . . I well remember the pain and sleeplessness myself . . . some have sloughing toes and fingers with exposed bones'.

Apparently, Harvey had not noticed any of this. He declined Weary's offer to move to Tarsau, suggesting that visits similar to his present one would be more useful. They then went in to the meeting. Weary was impressed by the intelligent interest these senior administrative officers took in the hospital. He aired none of the issues he had discussed with Harvey, confining his contribution to the outside battalions' finances and leaving it to McOstritch to criticise the convalescent depot.

Harvey dealt equably with the criticisms. He glossed over the medical side and announced a change in the staff as a solution for the kitchens. He never referred to his meeting with Weary.

Weary spent most of his time in the hospital. McConachie assisted him with an abdominal operation and Weary, in turn, assisted Millard with the amputation of a Dutch soldier's leg. But it was W/O Mepstead's ulcer, 'threatening to ringbark the leg', which worried him most, and he and McConachie decided on amputation. Mepstead was given chloroform as a general anaesthetic, and the operation had scarcely begun before he ceased to breathe. Nothing the anaesthetist did could revive him, so that after around ten minutes, 'he was pronounced dead'.

Weary quickly made an incision over the heart, wide enough to admit four fingers, and administered 'vigorous cardiac massage'.

'Slowly, the grey-white of the face changed and became suffused with some blood . . . and later the dead eyes looked a little more alive. At last, and to my excitement, the heart began to beat . . . Artificial respiration was now continued vigorously and after a seeming age, he began to breathe . . . '

Weary hastily 'and in great nervous tension' closed the abdomen and completed the amputation. He feared that Mepstead had suffered 'extreme damage' to the brain and would not recover consciousness, for his heart had stopped for anything between five and ten minutes. Partly, he blamed the chloroform, whilst realising that ether was unsuitable in the tropics.

The man was a member of Dunlop Force and Weary regarded him as 'really a friend'. He left the operating tent 'depressed and shaken'. 'The nervous strain of the whole business has been extreme . . . ' He caught a barge next morning and returned to Kinsayok 'with a sad heart'.

Weary tried to persuade McEachern and James to approach Knights and the other administrative officers at Tarsau in an effort to solve the deep problems in the hospital. They preferred Weary to go back, armed with a tactful letter from them containing his criticisms and suggesting that as there was no work for him at Kinsayok, his skills would be better employed at Tarsau.

In fact, without Weary's presence, the habitual jungle apathy had prevailed at Kinsayok and none of the hospital reorganisation had gone ahead, although one of the hospital huts built to his design was now complete. Weary drew up a roster for the hospital workers and, intent on unifying the nursing care, appointed as wardmaster Staff Sgt Gibson. Henceforth, the orderlies would report to Gibson, who would supervise all nursing and ensure that the medical officers' instructions were carried out.

Lilly came over for a finance meeting and agreed with Hugonin, McEachern and James that Weary should ask Okada for permission to go to Tarsau. But Weary suspected that it was not so simple, and that

Japanese HQ would have to approve the move. Accordingly, he made himself as objectionable as possible to Okada, 'motivated by a plan to insult him to a degree' that would provoke him into sending Weary to the other camp.

The number of sick increased daily and he refused utterly to reduce their numbers. Finally, when the interpreter repeated Okada's angry request for ten more men and asked, 'Why more sick everyday?' Weary staged an exaggerated exhibition of temper.

'Am I almighty God to answer this question?' he roared. 'Did I make this fever, this unhealthy jungle? Am I responsible that the Nipponese made these men prisoners and then worked them too hard and give them too little food? Look at them with their skin stretched over their bones! The Nipponese are responsible.' He flung out an arm in the direction of the cemetery. 'Why do you not ask why do men die? Look at that cemetery . . . '

Embarrassed, the interpreter mumbled, 'I take it you do not think more men are fit to work.' A 'sulphurous' looking Okada then stalked off, the interpreter scuttling beside him. Thoroughly worked up by now (he had already had a brush that day with one of the English combatant officers over the necessity to employ trained medical personnel in the hospital rather than in work gangs), Weary flung himself into completely reorganising the 'entire Kinsayok POW hospital under my command'. By evening, he had arrived at an organisation chart which satisfied him and he put the scheme into effect next morning.

Okada was always in the hospital these days, giving the impression of working 'very hard in the interests of the sick'. Weary's performance appeared not to have had the desired effect, although Okada's manner had cooled noticeably.

Weary's relentless reorganisation halted when he collapsed with malignant tertian malaria. Several days of malaise led to a 'bone-shaking rigor lasting about two hours'. Shortly before he lost consciousness, he calculated that his temperature was 41° Celsius.

'I . . . [had] a curious delusion of being immovably incarcerated in a block of stone – completely unable to move but with a curious detachment so that I watched my pulse from the throbbing motion transmitted to the mosquito curtain.'

Corlette found him in this state, raving deliriously, and prepared to administer quinine intravenously. To his surprise, Weary suddenly said, 'Ewen, you may think that I don't know what's going on . . . but I've been watching my pulse, which is quite irregular, and if you give me that quinine, I will be dead.'

Staff Sgt Gibson had brought the quinine and was standing alongside Corlette. Corlette, 'perplexed and confused' by this lucid remark amidst all the nonsense, told Gibson to sponge him for an hour in an attempt to bring down his temperature. If he was not better then, 'he must have the quinine'. It took all day to bring it down, but he avoided the danger of having intravenous quinine and took it by mouth.

Two days later, Weary discovered that two or three medical officers were to accompany the next batch of fifty men being evacuated. 'I will have to go.' He was determined to take Gibson and Butterworth also. Okada wished to know why Butterworth should go. 'He is my batman.'

'Batman? Batman? What is Batman?'

After Weary had explained, Okada looked thoughtful. Shortly afterwards, Okada let it be known that he required a batman: 'not very tall, fair hair, clean, young and good looking'. When the next Duty Section was posted, amongst the 53 men appointed, one was to act as Okada's batman.

The day before Weary's departure, a Dutch party staged at Kinsayok on their way downriver. From their medical officer, Stahle, Weary learned of a method of treating ulcers which was beginning to save many men's legs and lives: 'curette, clean and treat with carbolic [acid] applied on cotton wool pledget (just enough to whiten tissues), then dust in Iodoform and close' with dressings. It would smell offensive after a few days, at which point one removed the dressings; and the routine could be repeated if healing had not progressed sufficiently.

Iodoform itself smelled unpleasantly of hospitals. The yellow powder had been used to treat septic wounds in the First World War and the Spanish Civil War and Javanese hospitals used it for ulcers; Stahle assured Weary that pain was quickly relieved when this method was used and that healing was rapid.

Next morning, 25 October, he left Kinsayok, escorted by Okada. Lieut-Colonel Harvey and a bevy of medical officers greeted him at the other end. Hovering in the background were some of Weary's mob. Jock Clarke was back, his malaria better, after working at Tonchin.

In two days time, Harvey informed Weary, he was to take over the hospital and convalescent depot as their commanding officer, reporting to Harvey as Senior Medical Officer.

Weary found around 2400 patients crammed into twenty-four wards: fifteen of these were hospital huts under Hazelton's supervision, the other nine formed O'Driscoll's convalescent depot. About an eighth of the patients were from 'O' and 'P' battalions. He was flattered by the pleasure they showed at the news that he was to stay; but this turned quickly to distress when he was bidden to the bedside of one boy dying from chronic diarrhoea, who greeted him with the words that 'he regarded me as his one hope', but it was ' . . . hopeless . . . just so much ulcerated skin and bone.' Bill Belford insists that the mention of Weary's name and the possibility of seeing him kept Bill Williams alive for ten days.

Iodoform had been acquired and used to treat ulcers, and the patients' condition was markedly improved. When McConachie took Weary round Millard's ulcer wards, he could see that his talk with the two surgeons when last he was in Tarsau had been effective. He had discussed the lack of asepsis and the shortcomings in treatment without a great deal of hope that alone they would be able to check the widespread sloppiness. But Harvey had obviously taken more notice of Weary's outburst than had been apparent at the meeting. 'Ward facilities and staff have all been improved.'

Tarsau would be a different job from anything he had done during these past years in the army. He had set up the hospital in Bandoeng himself, using his own trained and close-knit CCS staff and the RAF doctors. Here, the fifteen medical officers working for him were drawn from the English, Dutch and Australian medical corps and few of the orderlies were trained to Weary's exacting standards. Compared to the resources he had drawn on in Java, they were paupers at Tarsau. But he had been impatient to transfer here, for he could see what ought to be done and he believed he was the person to do it.

He took over the hospital on 27 October and swept through every department, demanding changes and improvement. Harvey was to liaise with the camp authorities and Japanese Headquarters.

He found fault immediately with the hygiene and sanitation. He had remarked the filthiness of the latrines back in May; five months later, they were infinitely worse after the inundation of the wet season. He decided on an ambitious programme of improvement. It began with a 40-gallon drum for a disinfestor; shovels, chunkels, crosscut saws, rope, axes, timber, wire, oil, kerosene, crude disinfectants; *cwalis* for sterilising eating gear; 70 assorted containers and a cart for taking ash, swill and wood to the boilers. He demanded more bamboo stretchers, bed pans, splints, artificial limbs, crutches, and back-rests for beds; a new hut for the medical officers; repairs to ricketty barracks; and 'fresh, deep, covered latrines . . . with flyproof seats . . . special traps should be constructed for soakage and garbage [and] soakage pits for the surgical wards'.

Harvey's head must have reeled at the thought of extracting all this from the Japanese HQ, and these items were only the beginning.

The prospect from the entrance to an ulcer ward was foul. The stinking, ulcerated legs of a hundred men stretched out before him under the constant droning of thousands of flies. Over half the men had scabies and 'some are just covered with impetiginous sores'. Bedding was 'filthy'. He decided to start a training course for orderlies and a 'healing ulcer' ward.

They had run out of iodoform and were reduced to swabbing the infected tissue with potassium permanganate, or scraping out the ulcers before cauterising them with carbolic acid which Weary had brought from Kinsayok.

The Japanese doctor based at Tarsau and in charge of No. 4 Group was Lieutenant Moroko, a 'mild man . . . [of] negligible medical knowledge . . . guilty of utter negligence in that he showed no interest in the . . . thousands who lay in wretched state in his own camp'.[1]

Three days after Weary arrived, a Japanese medical major appeared with two other officers and showed some animation about the more than 700 ulcer patients, asking for details of their treatment. Weary conveyed 'plenty', a shopping list which began with anaesthetic materials, catgut and iodoform and ended with dressings. He needed tulle gras for skin grafts and local anaesthetic, but doubted that anything would come of it.

Nonetheless, he sent a request through an intermediary to Boon Pong for tulle gras and the dentists produced over 400 cc of Novutox, a local anaesthetic. A skin grafting programme for ulcer cases 'would greatly improve not only the rate of healing, but the general morale'. However, it was to be 10 November before he could carry out his first Thiersch graft on a man 'with a large, clean knee ulcer', using a sharpened table knife to cut the graft.

Tarsau was more formally administered than the jungle camps, with parades in the lines night and morning and all numbering and orders given in Japanese.

The *kempis* were everywhere. Most interpreters were members of the *kempeitai* . The sporadic searches for which prior warning was usually given became a thing of the past after the discovery of wireless sets in Kanchanaburi at the end of August. Boon Pong continued to supply illicit money and drugs with the barge loads of food, although Weary wondered how long this could continue now that the Japanese had announced a new scheme. The hospital was to draw up orders for the food they required and they were told this would be delivered by train.

Until now, Weary had led a charmed life in Thailand where the *kempeitai* were concerned; neither Usuki nor Okada had wanted trouble and their timely warnings had allowed him to conceal his contraband.

Eight days after his arrival, he heard that Lieut-Colonel McKellar 'was recently taken from the camp and is detained for some sort of investigation. Nothing is known of him'.

Next day, other officers were questioned, among them a dentist at the hospital. And Lieut-Colonel McEachern was 'seen in the camp under escort'.

The officers held a 'council of war' the evening following McKellar's arrest. After McEachern's disappearance, Weary knew he was 'at risk'.

TWENTY-TWO

We Kempis *do but do our Duty*

WEARY WALKED INTO TARSAU more or less as Okada's prisoner. His plan had succeeded; the little Japanese medical sergeant now wanted nothing further to do with him. Fortunately for Weary, Okada 'pushed him through the *kempis* ' in a high-handed fashion and they did not attempt a search. Had they done so, Weary would have survived only a few days at the outside: just long enough for them to endeavour to extract all the information possible about the illicit wireless sets they knew were possessed by various officers. Since the days in Bandoeng, Weary had never lacked a wireless, called variously his 'mincer', 'sparks' or 'the bird'.

In his pack, he carried far more than a wireless set. There were his diaries, an outspoken and damning record of his captors' behaviour since the fall of Java; the Routine Orders from the Javanese camps and various other official papers; maps; and diaries, watercolours and drawings in which Ray Parkin had recorded their prison camp life to date. The prismatic compass was strapped, as usual, behind his scrotum.

In the camps, they could be hidden in the hollow centres of bamboo, in the false bottom of a table he used for a desk, or distributed over the hospital area. During the cholera epidemic, a *kempi* search failed to turn up the radio, cunningly hidden in a cholera ward. But when Weary moved camps, everything was on his person, sewn into his cap or into the sides of the pack and valise.

It had all been carried from Java to Singapore and concealed during the journey up the line. Only his pistol and ammunition were no longer in his possession: Smits had not returned them.

Before Weary left Bandoeng, John Morris, a wireless expert, told him what to retain; the bulky six-valve set was taken to pieces and sufficient parts were put aside for a set to be reassembled at a later date. These were smuggled out amongst his belongings: a heavy transformer about ten by five centimetres, a fixed condensor around five centimetres long, one valve, various bits and pieces and an earphone.

Once at Konyu, Sgt 'Gus' Cawthron, a signaller who had been with the Garrison Artillery in Timor, built a one-valve set into a battered coffee tin. Cawthron had been a technician with AWA before the war, and he was very nervous indeed about operating the set. 'The aerial was a fine wire up a tree; but it was necessary to work the set on bulky torch batteries always hidden separately' in a biscuit tin.[1] Boon Pong supplied the 'great pack' of batteries. Clarke made a soldering iron, using two pennies and a piece of 8 gauge fencing wire, so that Cawthron could put the set together.

Jock Clarke, Bill Wearne and Allan Woods had also brought parts with them. 'The best place to hide [them] was rolled up in your socks.'[2] Until 'Albert', as they called their set, was operating, they relied on the three lieutenant-colonels at the English camp, Hill, More and Ferguson Warren, and their set for outside news of the war and the world in general. Exchanging wireless news was a sociable but highly secret routine between senior officers whenever one visited another camp.

Information about the sets was kept from everyone but 'the cell', those who owned and operated them, although now and again other ranks tumbled to their presence. Warbrick was part of it because of his Royal Corps of Signals background; Cawthron was the expert. The danger lay in gossip amongst the men overheard by a guard or men like Weary's *bête noire* in the Bandoeng camp, a petty crook named Franklin. He had threatened to tell the Japanese about Weary's wireless set and have him killed if he would not drop some serious charges against him and release him from prison. At the time, Weary had no idea how Franklin had discovered it; perhaps he had overheard the squeal of the set as he tuned in, or the introductory BBC music. But Weary did not give in to blackmail. 'Tell them and be damned . . . I will tell a few reliable men . . . to kill you immediately anything happens to me.'

At first, wireless news was clumsily concealed in the diaries, if at all, with an 'x' indicating information gained this way. He used obvious code names, such as 'Uncle Joe' for Stalin, but most of the time he openly discussed fronts, advances, victories and retreats. The progress of the war on the Russian front, the Eighth Army's defeat of Rommel, the AIF battles in New Guinea and Japanese reverses in the Pacific were all known to the senior officers within days of events occurring. It would have been evident to any *kempi* officer seizing the diaries that this information did not come from Japanese sources.

There were some narrow escapes in the jungle camps. Cawthron was rolled up in the blanket on Weary's bed one night, earphone in place and listening to the BBC, when a guard walked into the tent. Nothing was noticed. Weary had trouble operating the radio: 'technically very difficult', and therefore he tended to leave it to Cawthron. In the evenings, Weary would often be called so that he could transfer the earphone to his ear and hear 'the goods' himself. Ten o'clock at night was the hour to tune in to the BBC Far Eastern Service from New Delhi.

The coffee tin and its bulky batteries were in his pack when he reached Tarsau on 25 October, and he told McOstritch of it when he saw him shortly afterwards. McOstritch, one of the camp intelligence officers, blanched. 'We need that like a hole in the head.' The investigations at Kanchanaburi had flowed out to all the other base camps and every working camp up the line of No. 4 area. A *kempi* team was methodically combing through them.

Kempi supervision was constant and more thorough now than previously in the jungle, where prisoners had benefitted from the fear and distaste with which the Japanese regarded their own military intelligence.

Earlier, when some administrative officers in Kanchanaburi camp had been discovered with wireless sets and maps, two had died after being worked over viciously. Jaws, arms and ribs were broken. They heard in Tarsau that the Japanese continued to beat them even after they were dead, in an orgy of frenzied savagery which went on all night. 'This type of beating to death can scarcely be termed punishment officially and no trial was carried out.'

Weary realised how fortunate he was to be plucked out of Kinsayok. His assailants, transferred to Tarsau – officially for 'attempting' to 'hit Colonel Dunroppo' – had then repeated the performance on someone else. It came to Ishii's attention and he had ordered the guards to ease up on the bashing. But not even a colonel had any influence on the *kempi*. They were beyond an IJA officer's control. They did as they pleased.

After McKellar's arrest, all the senior officers were summoned to an emergency meeting. There was no time for Weary to write up his diary on 4 November: all he entered were the number of sick in the hospital and the figures for 'O' and 'P' battalions. The evening 'was enlivened by some grim accounts of *kempi* tortures'. All agreed that anyone questioned should never admit to the existence of any wireless sets and that camp rumours should be vigorously denied. ' . . . Lie glibly.'

On 5 November, Weary failed to appear at the monthly financial meeting in late morning. The *kempis* had arrested him an hour beforehand. Maj. Williams, also from the Kinsayok area – as was McEachern – and he were thrown into cells. He wondered who had cracked. There had been no time to warn anyone about the contents of his gear.

He was taken to the Japanese lines and shoved into a small cell walled off from one of the huts. The *kempis* had taken over an area of bamboo and attap huts away from the rest of the camp. None of the prisoners in the working camp could see what was going on.

In his shirt pocket was a scrap of paper containing some wireless news which no longer seemed very clever. 'This I chewed up and swallowed.' He was soon taken out of the cell and subjected to patient and prolonged interrogation by a Japanese officer he nicknamed 'Stoneface'. He was accused of having a secret wireless set, of distributing news-sheets. Everything was channelled through an egregious, long-haired interpreter.

After four hours, 'there was a dramatic, violent change'. His interrogator 'pulled down a screen with Japanese characters and a tracery of connecting arrows', the arrows all pointing to a central character whom 'Stoneface' insisted was Weary.

'We know all about you and your set – you will be executed, but first you will talk.'

Weary's wrists were manacled and he was then systematically beaten with heavy lumps of firewood by two guards whenever he gave negative answers to the questions directed at him by 'Stoneface'. He kept his elbows close to his sides to protect his liver and spleen, still much enlarged by malaria, and gritted his teeth, refusing to give them the satisfaction of hearing him cry out. He 'thought of the . . . British officers beaten to death in this way at an adjacent camp where all this had started. I . . . pined for a cyanide pill.'

Weary had no idea how long it was before he was told that he was to die. The guards 'pushed and flogged' him out to a tree, where his arms were manacled behind his back, encircling the trunk. His torso was bared and four soldiers with fixed bayonets began to work themelves up with the 'characteristic belly-grunting, blood-curdling yells'.

He was to have thirty seconds grace. The count down began in Japanese. Weary locked eyes with the 'flinty, impassive face' of the interrogating officer. He felt strangely calm, unable to believe that his life was running out as the seconds were numbered off.

Flashes from his past moved through his mind like the jerky frames of silent films. He recalled with 'ironic amusement . . . a time at school when for an escapade I anticipated expulsion and disgrace'; it had seemed far worse then this. It was difficult to believe he was going to die. ' . . . If you hate people enough, it's a great solace when you're facing death.' He did not feel frightened, 'just a sort of disgust with the whole situation'. Anger had sustained him when beheading seemed imminent in Java; now this feeling of unreality and his 'fixed, absolute resolution . . . never to show fear and [to] try not to flinch' insulated him against a horrible, barbarous, painful death.

'Now ten seconds to go. Have you last message for relatives. I shall try to convey.'

The bayonets were drawn back and poised for the 'last yelling thrust'. Weary flicked his eyes across to the interpreter, then stared straight at 'Stoneface' and spat contemptuously, 'Last message conveyed by thugs like you – no thanks!'

'Stoneface' flushed – the first intimation Weary had that he understood English – raised his hand and yelled, 'Stop! He will suffer a lot more . . . before he dies. Untie him!'

His hands were manacled in front of him once again and the beating began afresh. There was no further interrogation.

Eventually, they pushed him into the cell and forced him to sit cross-legged, his back erect, to contemplate his 'attitude'. Whenever he slumped, a sentry beat him upright with a rifle butt. 'As a ridiculous distraction, I tried to recall Keats' "Ode to a Nightingale".'

He watched a small lizard running across the walls, the one they called a *yasume* lizard because it croaked continuously, ' *Yasume, Yasume* '.

He was barely aware that it was almost evening when they hauled him out to play 'circlos' against the Japanese. His fellow team members were Lieut-Colonel Humphries, Lieut-Colonel McKellar, Padre Headley, two unknown captains, and his old friend fom St Mary's Paddington, Captain John Diver RAMC.

Headley had been with the ill-fated 'H' Force men at Hintok, but Weary had given him sleeping space in the officers' tent there because of the overcrowding across the creek. Diver he had not seen since Singapore.

The game involved throwing a kind of quoit between the two teams; each time it was dropped, the opposing team gained a point. They were ordered to play in 'dead silence', although the Japanese accompanied their performance with 'raucous laughter and derisive yells' at their trembling hands and, in Weary's case, painful bruises and lacerations.

John Diver was in a particularly bad way and the Japanese deliberately kept up the pressure, repeatedly hurling the circlos towards him, jeering when he missed it.

They attempted to speak to each other 'in a stage whisper out of the corner of the mouth' when their faces were temporarily turned away from their tormentors.

Later, Weary wrote cynically in his diary: 'All on friendly terms with the Nipponese guards who were kindly . . . ' The Japanese won 6–5.

Guards pushed him roughly back to his cell. The others were put together in some other area. The manacles were forced back onto Weary's swollen wrists and he was ordered to resume his previous position: legs crossed, back straight, gazing at the cell wall.

He puzzled over whether he would take a cyanide pill if it was available; summoned up a few more fragments of Keats; and thought fleetingly of Helen. But he found it too painful to continue remembering their times together, or to recall his home and past life.

The door opened again and once again he was forced to stumble out to the tree. ' . . . Same grizzly ritual . . . but this time an air of grim finality.' Steady counting, ferocious grunting yells, and now and again the prick of cold steel against his bare skin. He willed himself to die without flinching.

There was a second, surprising, reprieve.

Instead of returning to solitary confinement for the night, he was kicked towards an iron-barred cage like a chicken coop, open to the weather at the top and on all sides. A slender Thai was already inside and there was barely room for the two seated men. Neither could stand up. The Thai greeeted him 'with a gesture of shooting'.

He envied the Thai for his mobile slim wrists and agility when the evening rice was pushed through the bars. By now the manacles had sunk deep into Weary's wrists and it was almost impossible to bend over and scoop the food into his mouth. The *kempis* were experts at humiliation.

He had heard the screams and groans of tortured men. 'I . . . wondered whether I had the fibre to take it.' He dozed briefly and periodically from exhaustion. Intermittently throughout the long dark hours, the Thai made his raised hand into the form of a pistol and pointed at Weary. 'You – bang!' Weary returned the gesture.

He endured another day of swollen wrists, pain, a little rice and contemplation of what they could do to him. ' . . . Handcuffs behind, rope over a beam, standing on a high chair, chair kicked away, dangling with a double dislocation of the shoulders – real torture then begins, eyes, testicles . . . ' But it would not cease with his confessing to the set, for then they would demand where he got it, who operated it with him, who gave him the batteries. The only end for him would be savage death and the knowledge that, Judas-like, he had taken others with him.

In the evening, the Thai was taken out and shot. When the guard reappeared, he decided it must be his turn, faintly relieved that it might be shooting rather than bayonetting and 'almost hoping for a quick, clean end'. But they turned into the interrogator's hut. He was astounded when 'Stoneface' invited him to sit down and began speaking in normal tones, in English. 'Colonel, you must understand that though you have not talked, others have and we know that you are guilty.'

Weary looked at him and replied, slowly, ' . . . They are liars. Why don't you give me a fair trial to throw the lies in their faces?'

The room was silent, the guards motionless by the door.

Weary watched the man's face, saw his expression change to doubt and puzzlement. 'Is it that you really have not done these things, or that you will not talk? He seized this slight advantage and laughed. 'Have I not spent all this time telling you that I know nothing?'

The next words were so astonishing that Weary wondered if he had heard them correctly.

'Colonel, if I were to release you this time, would you have hard feelings against the Japanese, hard feelings against me? We *kempis* do but do our duty . . . '

Choosing his words cautiously, a wild surmise growing within him that there was some curious affinity between them, Weary replied: 'From all I have heard of you *kempis*, I feel that I have been well treated.'

The other man gestured to the guards, who prised the manacles off Weary's wrists. He had no circulation left in them and they were swollen to twice their normal size. As he attempted to smoke a cigarette and drink the beer which was set in front of him, he suddenly realised that other prisoners would be watching. They would interpret this largesse as a reward for squealing. Had he betrayed his fellows in a different way by causing them to think that he had given names and places? 'This dimmed the surge of joy at my release. *Kempi* professionalism to the last.'

Weary returned painfully to the lines around half past nine that evening, much to the relief of his brother officers.

Unexpectedly, Wearne and Hands were there to welcome him. He had missed Wearne badly and was delighted to hear that he would be at Tarsau for a few more days. Stubbornly, shakily, he dragged himself back to work in the hospital that same night.

McEachern was also released on 6 November. Weary conferred with him: he discovered they were the only two officers who had been put in solitary confinement, although McEachern was not beaten. No one knew why Diver had been brought in to Tarsau. He never saw Diver or heard his 'great booming voice' again.

The diary entry for 6 November was written the following evening, almost as if he intended it for the eyes of the *kempis*. Weary and McEachern had a fair idea who had betrayed them.

'I was astounded when the *kempi* authorities said that other officers had made incriminating statements against me, but apparently these misunderstandings must have been cleared up before my release. The interpreter laughed and said I was a hard man to make speak. I guess I don't like manacles as my wrists are big . . . I find now that there has been considerable circulation of news-sheets in this camp and most officers know of them. Kanburi was the source . . . Food was good and treatment reasonable for the type of investigation, but it is good to be out again. The prospect of death is never pleasant . . . '

When Weary was arrested, Jock retrieved the set, wrapped it in a dirty shirt and shoved it under his bedspace. Surprise searches were a feature of Tarsau, and that day he 'perspired a bit' when one was sprung on them. Finnemore lectured the officers about the 'criminal' danger of keeping a radio and jeopardising everyone's safety. Millard was in the bunk next to Jock, nervous of such dangerous contraband so close to his own bed space, but adamant that Jock should take no notice of his more craven colleague. It stayed there some time.

Just before Weary left Tarsau, Major Clive Wallis said he had a use for it, but it was difficult to hide, especially when he thought he, too, was going to move. First, he put it in a water bucket with a false bottom; next, he baked the parts into loaves of bread – but the move did not occur, and the bread went mouldy. Eventually, Wallis decided to dispose of it.

When 'word came to ditch it', Jock recalls that he chose one of his newly dug, deep, dark latrines and heaved it in.

Hands was short of medical supplies, as was the hospital at Tarsau, and Weary immediately proposed to canvass all sources, legitimate and illicit. He had no intention of allowing the drama with the *kempis* to stop him dealing with the underground or delay his reorganisation of the hospital.

His new and 'diplomatic' organisation chart was presented to the weekly heads of departments' meeting a day and a half after the *kempis* released him. He had interposed himself as Commanding Officer of the hospital between Harvey as Camp SMO and Hazelton and O'Driscoll, whose status as department heads was therefore unchallenged, although he was not happy with the semi-autonomous convalescent depot. The medical and surgical departments, in the persons of Vardy and McConachie, continued to report to Hazelton.

Two new departments were established: a central 'A' (Administrative) and 'Q' (Quartermaster branch), to correlate the work of the hospital and convalescent depot and take charge of all works and equipment. In addition to the staff he had inherited, Weary began to call in men whose abilities were known to him.

Weary's energy was prodigious. And one of his greatest gifts was that 'he knew how to choose people . . . and [he] commanded their loyalty at once because he was such an open, trusting person'.[3] Allanson admired his ability to 'delegate wisely', yet 'always retain overall control'.[4] Fifty years later, a patient suggested that he was a 'natural gang leader'.[5]

Two men who were to put Weary's ideas into practice were already in Tarsau: Major John ('Jack') Marsh and Jock Clarke. Weary had met Marsh in early April when he arrived in Hintok with 'Y' Battalion and impressed both Ferguson Warren and Weary with his resourcefulness and handling of men. The son of missionaries, he knew Asia. At seventeen years of age, he had been running the workshops of a bus company in Shanghai: Weary saw him as the ideal quartermaster.

Jock Clarke's brief was as broad as Weary's expectations: there was no time for dental work. Improving hospital hygiene and sanitation was paramount and he was seconded to take charge of this area immediately. Never toppled from his position as 'the *benjo* king', he could be trusted to shake up the kitchens and provide the same 'beautiful, deep, dark latrines' with close-fitting wooden covers which had so distinguished the camp at Hintok. His dental sergeant, Ross, equally pragmatic and efficient, was made the NCO to the new scabies unit and charged with the installation and running of a disinfestor.

Everyone itched with lice and scabies and was covered with scabs and sores, Weary included, for it was extremely infectious. ' . . . As soon as I get the wards clean, a flow of infected scabies . . . comes in.' Weary assembled the wardmasters for a lecture: 'Scabies is a disease of people who do not wash.' And he placed the responsibility for keeping the wards 'spotlessly clean . . . ensur[ing] that all patients wash or are washed daily' squarely before them. 'Warning that I will inspect the hospital and the convalescent depot weekly.'

He continued to be 'busy both with the care of patients and with efforts to improve the hospital hygiene and general management'. Weary never neglected minor details and he followed everything through, putting his 'views strongly to Lieut-Colonel Knights and Lieut-Colonel Harvey' about sterilising containers and dixies, but they showed no interest in helping until a serious outbreak of cholera was traced to the hospital kitchens. 'Damn this closing of stable doors after the horse has bolted!'

Cholera brought Moroko and a group of Japanese officials to the camp for a 'partial inspection'. Weary steered them through the hospital (the cholera patients had been banished to tents in the jungle on the other side of the fence), to the disinfestor and the new, deep latrine with seats which Jock's crew had completed. Moroko was non-committal about providing the wood and other materials required to construct them, he could give them no containers for sterilising the camp's utensils and dixies, but he promised help with tools.

Twenty-nine died from cholera in this epidemic, 'expected in view of the appalling condition of these men before their infection'.

The kitchens were not only the source of infection, but also of friction between the messing officer, John Day, and Marsh.

Marsh's organisational abilities were superb and, like Harvey, he knew how to handle the Japanese. Within three days of becoming quartermaster, he had a fresh supply of matting for the wards and the operating theatre, 300 mats for the bedspaces, and had tacked up the old matting around the walls for protection from the weather and the night-time chill. Encouraged by this, he asked Knights to request blankets and bedding from Japanese HQ for the more than four hundred sick men who had no covering, 'some . . . with practically no other possession than a G-string and a rice sack'. Two hundred and fifty hemp rice sacks arrived for blankets.

Food was another matter. Day had 'too much autonomy'. Weary was not pleased at the independent stance adopted by the hospital and convalescent depot kitchens. He set up a Diet Committee to regulate food purchases, cut out extras with little nutritional value and oversee the preparation and distribution. But Day refused to heed Major Vardy, the head of the committee, Marsh or even Weary. He resented inspections and criticism of the cookhouses and his staff, whom he favoured by allowing them to draw extra food.

A significant feature of Weary's administration in every camp was that expenditure on food in the hospital rose immediately he took over. Where drugs were short, and so many suffered wretchedly from nutritional diarrhoea, he insisted that extra food was essential to build them up and help them recover.

Bludgers and those who did not do their job received short shrift, and the kitchens were in his sights from the day of his first inspection. The efficacy of the special diets he introduced was quickly proven: some men in the dysentery ward put on a kilogram over five days.

Thomas queried the steep rise in costs. Weary showed him the costings of the new diets. His reasoning was sound – his colleagues all recognised that he was 'no bullshitter'[6] – and Thomas promised to support him.

Within a month of his arrival, Weary had stamped his mark on the hospital at Tarsau: new latrines like those which had excited comment at Hintok were in use; filthy kitchens and wards had been cleaned up; a graded diet scheme was operating and the sick were better fed; a central administration was in place; an efficient Q department was co-ordinating all works and services; and new orderlies were being trained and strictly supervised.

First on the agenda at the December financial meeting was Weary's increased expenditure on hospital special diets: 6000 ticals a month. Not only did Weary persuade Knights, Thomas, Ferguson Warren and the others that they must finance the hospital so that it could continue to live beyond its means, he negotiated an extra thousand ticals for what he called his 'therapeutic egg fund . . . to give the patients eggs directly in lieu of drugs'.

'A very satisfactory meeting.'

For the first time since Java, Weary saw an opportunity to organise a 'rather comprehensive entertainment [and] recreation scheme' with concerts and lectures which would benefit the entire camp, not merely the hospital.

He was intrigued that a Maj. Swanton put up many ideas and elected to take charge of the educational and library activities. E. W. Swanton had played cricket for England, and had come to Weary's attention when he developed a paralysed right shoulder. The cause had been puzzling to the medical staff, but in the end Weary immobilised the shoulder and arm in an aeroplane splint.

Although Knights was not encouraging – he felt the Japanese would not approve of concerts – Weary 'roughed out a request' for two concert nights a week for the camp and the hospital. By December, the entertainments were in full swing. When the curtain went up on the Christmas pantomime of *Cinderella* , the audience gasped at the 'ladies' and 'elegantly costumed men'.

'It is simply amazing what can be done . . . [with] mosquito netting and other scraps of cloth, plus silver foil, tinsel and oddments. A most convincing presentation', Weary concluded, despite the 'ladies' unfeminine legs, scarred with scabies sores and ulcers in various stages of healing.

Swanton was proving good at his job; he was now officially hospital amenities officer.

Marsh was accomplishing even greater things in the arts and crafts area. The Japanese agreed to three instructors being appointed to oversee the manufacture of wooden clogs, ice sack stretchers, food containers, bamboo water bottles, bed pans and other ward equipment. Marsh also published a hospital bulletin to make the needs of the hospital known to everyone in the camp and appeal for materials.

Christmas Day in the convalescent depot was not the good-humoured, happy occasion it had been in the hospital. Weary decided that the time had arrived for O'Driscoll and his unco-operative staff to go. ' . . . Their complete autonomy, separate office and either conscious or unconscious obstruction make a single, clear direction of the place impossible.' Harvey agreed that the officers be relieved of duty, and that the NCOs and 'kitchen racketeers' be investigated.

It was Weary's lot to break the news to O'Driscoll. He took it 'well enough'; but some of his staff were 'pipped and angry' at being sent back to the lines.

Their days had been numbered since a group of 300 'F' Force men arrived from Krian Krai by train on 8 December. Weary had arranged for ward space with O'Driscoll, but nothing was done about the men and, 'owing to a shocking mess-up . . . nearly 100 slept in the open'. Three had died on the train journey down; another died after arriving. It was now cold at night. Even in the wards, many men found it impossible to sleep and wandered about seeking fires and warmth.

O'Driscoll appeared to have no control over his staff, who 'live and entertain very well and work a very creditable still to help the conviviality'. Had these officers shown any concern for their patients, Weary might have ignored their after-hours activities, but their unpopularity reached its nadir on Christmas Day when the meals were no good and they did not bother to visit their wards. For Weary, patients were paramount, he had been greatly angered by the neglect of the Krian Krai men, and he was not sorry to see the offenders go.

The way was clear for 'the whole area now to be hospital, with a single office and admin. staff'. Four divisions, medical, surgical, dysentery and infectious, were set up on a heavy and light sick basis. And there were to be no malingerers: 'Discharge of patients to be gingered up.'

Ferguson Warren and he whiled away some of the last afternoon of 1943 together, cooking a snack over a small fire in Warren's area and chatting companionably. Warren had grown to depend on Weary's judgement and company during the grim days in Konyu after More and Hill had abandoned him to the command of the camp, and their friendship had deepened in Tarsau. Weary, in turn, found Warren a 'man of parts, courageous, capable, many-faceted with immense joy of living . . . something of the artist in him'.

The Japanese left them to their New Year celebrations, which were lively and optimistic, 'cheer and songs bursting forth in all the wards and barracks'. Later in the evening, when Weary returned to the mess to join in singing 'sweet, nostalgic, melancholy airs', he was seized by an intense longing for alcohol. Earlier in the day, he had confiscated a still and some alcohol manufactured in the con depot by a Gordon Highlander for Hogmanay. (Some hospital vegetables were discovered in the brew, throwing the ethics 'in doubt'.) Since they could use the spirit medically, he had paid out the 'amazing number' of shareholders and it was now locked in the dispensary.

Now, the 'graveyard' of the six bitter years which had passed since he walked with Helen on the sands at St Kilda suddenly swept him with 'such a dypsomaniac urge. I would have given anything to get so drunk that the pain of memory and twanging of taut nerves would quieten.'

New Year's Day was no better. Even the decrease in the December deaths under his administration failed to cheer him. 'I . . . feel profoundly miserable . . . for the first time really in my POW existence, my nerves are strung to breaking point.'

The cramped and confined conditions of the camp were a breeding ground for dissatisfaction, imagined slights and heightened tempers.

Some days beforehand, Weary had asked Vardy – the mess president – to call a meeting so that some of the niggling complaints expressed to him about food and service could be aired. But a hostile Vardy jumped to his feet and complained to the meeting because the officers had gone to Weary rather than him. He lectured everyone about 'how little we might expect as POWs'.

Sensing that Vardy's diatribe was in danger of splitting the meeting, Weary was 'put in the position of pleading like a child for some reason'.

'I myself care nothing for mess comfort under POW conditions and never say anything on the condition of food, just eat what comes – however nauseating.' Marsh and Capt. John Service, a New Zealander and former rugby player who had taken over as messing officer, introduced some order into the evening eventually.

But Weary went to bed 'in cold fury' at Harvey's lack of support and Vardy's insults. Three days later, he was still smarting. Even plunging into work and a strong rumour that most of the sick would soon be evacuated to Nakom Patom failed to chase away his devils and he decided to confront Harvey with his grievances.

' . . . Although I had played the . . . blunt colonel ignoring all personal considerations or feelings in order to get things done, I was quite sensitive to such considerations and personal issues . . . I was prepared to back him up in any essential matter and . . . I expected him to do the same for me, particularly as my position here was not so strong as his own.

'Further . . . I would never again pass over personal rudeness to me, whether over a mess or hospital matter.

'Thus I got rid of a certain amount of evil spleen which had been weighing me down.'

Throughout all this period, he was frequently lightheaded with malaria ('every fortnight a bit thick'), his blood film 'choked with parasites BT and gametocytes'.

It could reduce him to a shaking, teeth-chattering wreck at any time. 'I was discussing religion and philosophy with Warren when suddenly I shot a fierce malarial rigor.' Whilst walking back to the hospital to do a minor operation, it was necessary 'to stand in the sun until I stopped shaking' before beginning to operate. No sooner had he turned away from the patient than his teeth began to chatter and his hands to shake. Bouts of malaria invariably caused his ulcers to break out afresh. 'I feel wretched.'

The officers had moved into a new hut on the river that November.

Weary enjoyed the luxury of a bay to himself much of the time, although he had a second bed installed for guests. Rats drove him wild, coursing about his bed, wriggling inside the mosquito net, tugging at mouthfuls of his hair and gnawing his greatcoat or clothing. He could tolerate most discomfort, was indifferent to heat and cold, but bugs, lice and rats nearly sent him berserk. At no time in his life could he bear anything crawling on his face.

His sleep was disturbed and disturbing to those about him, for an inner turmoil made him a restless, often violent sleeper, lashing out, muttering, kicking, and tossing to and fro on his nobbly bamboo platform. He was not alone in this; but it was something remarked upon by officers who shared a hut with him through those terrible years. Tormented he may have been, yet he turned a measured calmness to the world during his waking hours, and he enjoyed listening to what was going on in the hut around him.

Religion and philosophy never failed to polarise his hutmates and he was much diverted by the fierce arguments he heard through his bamboo partition between Marsh on one hand, and the Anglo Catholics in the persons of Swanton, Service and Turner, an aspiring British politician, on the other. One night it became a free-for-all, with Marsh particularly critical of the 'Christian Fascists' (as he termed them) using their positions on the hospital welfare committe to proselytise, and heatedly rejecting their portrayal of Franco as 'a knightly soldier of God'. Padre Bourke, the Redemptorist priest from Konyu days, silenced him.

'Seeing that you for months have taken advantage of similar welfare committees to proselytise your own views to troops, I hardly see how you can take exception to others doing it.'

One of Weary's rare and sudden shouts of laughter was heard from his cubbyhole. None of the participants forgot this night: years later, Marsh, Bourke, Weary, Service and McNeilly recalled it to each other.

Like the prophets of old, Bourke and a Church of England colleague named Harry Thorpe had ranged the jungle camps heedless of whether the Japanese approved or not. Bourke's eyes 'burned' out of a thin, lined face beneath greying, dark hair and his extreme thinness made him appear taller than his slightly above medium height. The 'scintillating, brilliant spectacle in scarlet and gold' of Bourke preaching one February Sunday above the Menam Kwai Noi had impressed Weary profoundly. The upright figure in the stained and shabby vestments continued to attest to the presence of the Church Militant throughout the war.

He stood high on the bank in the 'chapel' which another priest of his order, Father John Kennedy, had cleared amongst the tall bamboo. Weary had a further reason to remember that Sunday. He had nearly drowned when swimming ashore with a sack heavy with twenty-four clams. 'It was them or me.'

A week later, he had taken a group of men across to Konyu for a redemptive mission Bourke was conducting, for Usuki had refused the priest permission to come to the Australian camp. Bourke was interested that Weary 'got around that difficulty very simply by leading over the Catholics in the Force himself' and impressed by his 'sensitive [and] . . . practical respect for the religious beliefs of others'.[7] He was even more interested that Weary sat in on the sermon, instead of spending the time with Ferguson Warren. Weary was curious to hear what he had to say, for he had concluded that 'formal religion appeared to have no enhanced appeal in camps of sickness and death.'[8]

Bourke's theme was death. Redemptorists pursue their quarry rigorously, for they are the evangelists of their Church: 'Let one not console himself that we were much more fit in this camp than others. Death always comes like a thief in the night when . . . you are in a complacent state of mind!' He illustrated his sermon with 'numerous precedents of men who had neglected their religious duties only to be caught by death, dying unabsolved', then dived straight for the jugular with a stinging attack on mortal sin.

' . . . Retired with my tail between my legs,' wrote Weary. By this stage of the war, he believed himself to be 'even less a Christian' than he had been in Australia.

Bourke missed little, surmising that the Australian commanding officer 'emerged from the ordeal with head . . . bloody, yet unbowed'.

Bourke and Weary were drawn to each other, and their dialogue and differences about faith, humanity and religion did not cease until Bourke's death some forty-five years later. Each had a profound respect for the other's intellect and Weary spoke to Bourke about matters which he seldom aired, even to his intimates.

Bourke was puzzled by Weary's dismissal of religion as an important force in the camps. 'Could it be that a doctor is primarily concerned with curing and helping his patient to recover and survive?' For Bourke saw his mission as helping them 'face death with peace, especially with hope in what awaited them from a loving and . . . merciful God'.[9]

He had also seen how men who made their peace with God when facing imminent death could be 'sitting up in bed next morning munching their rice', for he and others believed in the 'survival factor' of the last rites for some and saw it demonstrated a number of times. One Dutch medical officer routinely requested that the last rites be administered to the very ill, for he believed the odds were that they would stiffen the man's resolve to live and, whatever happened, leave him in 'great peace'.[10]

Weary, on the other hand, abode by Gordon-Taylor's maxim: 'never operate on the man who seeks to make his will before he enters hospital'. He who faced his surgeon in this frame of mind would soon be greeting his maker.

Bourke returned to this subject twenty-five years later and challenged Weary's statement, published in the *British Medical Journal* immediately after the war. Weary held to his conclusions, although there is evidence that many men were 'converted' during these years in Thailand.

Weary was not alone in concluding that 'the formalities of Christian worship and behaviour seemed . . . to be under merciless challenge' in the prison camps.[11] Jock Clarke, also, had found the more mundane expressions of his faith inadequate. Not all the padres measured up in conditions where 'only sterling silver would do. It was no good being brought up Christian, baptised or even ordained: you have to live and believe the thing'. And, added Weary, 'there were not too many Gerard Bourkes to bring the authentic peace and comfort'.[12]

Thorpe, much younger than Bourke but no less zealous, camped across the creek at Hintok River camp, unhealthily close to the Tamils. He had completed his training in an Anglican seminary, but had not been ordained when war broke out. When he applied to join up as a chaplain, the quota was full, so he enlisted as a private, but the officers agreed that he should follow his vocation. Like Bourke, he was continually in trouble with the Japanese, pushing his parish boundaries as far up and down the river as he could travel. At one time, Weary found him in the guard house at Tarsau for 'jumping a barge . . . to Kanburi' from Hintok.

Bourke was an 'uncompromising zealot' who cared nothing for his personal safety. Weary came upon him when Usuki was about to behead the priest for daring to say that he took his orders from an authority higher than the Imperial Japanese Army. He would not allow Usuki to prevent him discharging his priestly duties and blatantly invited martyrdom. At this juncture, Weary swiftly intervened, tapping his head meaningfully. 'Kistian priests very eccentric men!'

It was amazing how many meanings the word 'eccentric' could assume and how often it could defuse a dangerous situation. It mollified Usuki. 'Ah, "eccentric" man.' He put away his sword.

Yet Bourke only partially conceded Weary's belief that 'the maintenance of strict discipline was the greatest factor in preserving life and maintaining morale, and this was never questioned where officers set an example in unselfish devotion to duty'.[13]

Politician Tom Uren joined Dunlop Force with others of the 2/40th Battalion from Timor. His admiration for Weary, Corlette and Moon, who combined 'medical ingenuity with leadership and comradeship',[14] has been well documented, most notably in his maiden speech to parliament, when he referred to Weary as 'not only a great doctor, but also a great soldier'.[15] Uren saw socialism in action at Hintok and acknowledges Weary as the instigator. 'We lived by the principle of the fit looking after the sick, the young looking afer the old, the rich looking after the poor.' The wisdom of tithing all those who were paid so that the Camp fund could furnish food and drugs was plain and the difference between the Australian and British camps was obvious. 'Only a creek separated [them] . . . but on one the law of the jungle prevailed, and on the other the principles of socialism.'[16]

He did not know of van der Post's proposal to Weary in Java that the officers should 'put everything into the pool and live purely on the men's diet' nor that Weary had rejected his mentor's suggestion because he feared that this 'communism . . . is impractical'. His responsibiity for more than a thousand men wracked by starvation, cholera, dysentery and ulcers had moved Weary closer to van der Post's point of view.

'Uncle Chunkle', the 'nice old interpreter' from Kinsayok, and two Japanese soldiers were put in charge of hospital affairs. They shared a new office with Harvey and Weary not far from the sleeping quarters. Life became relatively civilised. Then, in early January, 'Uncle Chunkle' demanded reams of detailed statistics, adding weight to the rumour that a major move was imminent.

TWENTY-THREE

'Ancient Civilisations'

THE RUMOURS OF movements persisted, for 'it is known that most of the sick will soon be evacuated to Nakom Patom and Chungkai'. Chungkai was an 'ancient civilisation', where most of those who had avoided movement up the line had gone to ground with those 'who speedily tore back', such as 'Mackie' More and 'Hookey' Hill. Nakom Patom was to be a new hospital near Kanchanaburi for around 10 000 sick.

The death rate at Tarsau had fallen (although the sick figure had not), and Weary attributed it to the increased amount of money spent on special diets, 'the greatest single factor in saving life at present'. But Thomas warned him that he would need to show good reason for continuing hospital expenditure at the present rate, as camp finances were again shaky. Once more, Weary eloquently carried the day at the next financial meeting and, with Ferguson Warren (whom he had primed beforehand, together with McOstritch), convinced everyone that they must increase officers' subscriptions.

He left the meeting feeling that he had been 'dealing with some vast city combine or board of directors'. It was a relief to retreat to the theatre and drain a large ileopsoas abscess in the hip of a rugby-playing artillery officer.

No sooner had he written a letter next day explaining his reasons to the officers, than Harvey announced that Weary's next destination was Chungkai. This was not an attractive prospect, for the same rumour mongers who had murmured about the moves, had suggested that the hospital would be for light sick. Moroko informed him that he was to command Chungkai hospital with patients drawn from both 2 and 4 groups. 'How much nicer it would be to start afresh . . . than to tackle the awful business of fixed views and lethargy of long established camps.'

Weary's final hours at Tarsau were preoccupied with settling the

472

financial arrangements of 'O' and 'P' battalions' funds. To his regret, he had 'no time to deal with records affecting tropical ulcers and other matters I was interested in – and will I fear take away nothing of much use for publication'.

Despite the haste with which he had been ordered to get ready the previous evening, there was nothing 'speedo, speedo!' about the journey: just the usual muddle preceding the late morning departure and an uncomfortably hot day penned in open trucks, clanging along the railway line through dense jungle. With his party of 16 officers and 200 men were eight of his CCS orderlies, all of them sick: Gibson, Haddon, Butterworth, Lawrence, Walker, Binns, Brown and Murray. Most of the others were still at Kinsayok.

The march from the station to the camp was a shock, for many of the well-remembered men from 'O' and 'P' battalions who were lining the road lacked a leg. Capt. Jacob Markowitz had carried out 110 amputations; more than thirty of the amputees had died.

He was overjoyed to be reunited with Arthur Moon; not so pleased to witness all kinds of rackets and – as usual – poor hygiene; and astonished to meet a 'massive' Scottish major exactly his height whose name turned out to be Dunlop. He was the hospital registrar.

The commander of this hospital camp of 8000 men was Lieut-Colonel Cary Owtram, the SMO his old acquaintance, Lieut-Colonel Barrett RAMC. The latter appeared to know nothing about Weary's appointment, so after drinking tea and making 'a little polite conversation', Weary retreated to await developments. Four hundred more 4 Group men arrived over the next two days.

On the afternoon of 19 January, Barrett and Markowitz were 'suddenly removed' to another camp by the Japanese. The hospital command was Weary's.

He had already inspected the amputation ward and discovered the same appalling conditions of scabies and skin infections as had prevailed at Tarsau on his arrival. But Markowitz was a talented and innovative physiologist as well as surgeon, and the efficient team in the transfusion centre impressed Weary, as did their work using defibrinated blood. They had given over 300 successful transfusions using this technique of removing the fibre from blood by beating it with a bamboo whisk. The centre was a 'show-piece'.

Immediately Weary arrived, he introduced himself to Owtram. The two men liked each other on sight. ' . . . Here is a man who knows where he is going,' decided Owtram. 'He knew exactly what he wanted

New ward at Chungkai: three rows of bamboo platforms for the sick, 1944

and he was very decisive . . . very pleasant to get on with and I thought, here is a man after my own heart.'[1]

Weary realised that Owtram was 'a very good player' who would support him in his various schemes, and the pattern of Weary's administration quickly became apparent at Chungkai. Expenditure on food rose; with Arthur's willing co-operation the wards were reorganised; and the Camp Sanitation Officer ('the greatest "waffler" I have ever met') discovered that working as Weary's hygiene officer was no sinecure.

Food was better than at Tarsau, many troops being 'quite plump' compared to the skeletons up the line, although the diet of around 2800 calories in value was ill-balanced and deficient – as always – in protein, fat, vitamin B2, calcium and iron.

Five days after his arrival, the hospital finance sub-committee met. Before a further week was out, 'a re-arrangement was . . . made in the management of the camp finances, a comprehensive diet scheme was drawn up and put into force', and it became evident to Maj. Alexander Dunlop RAMC 'that the blackest period was over'.[2]

Weary was 'amazed at the number of long meetings' called to discuss camp finances. Aware that most of the expense of the new, much improved hospital diets was in his area, he avoided being 'the prime mover' in raising the officers' subscriptions, but 'warmly' supported 'the proposal after making it obvious that it is necessary'.

He was despairing about the state of the latrines and the camp's hygiene. He was 'desperate' to see Yasano, the IJA medical sergeant, so that he could put his case for tools for the sanitation workers, who were 'gravely hampered' in repairing latrines, 'making drains and roads, for cleaning soiled ground, for grave digging and the manufacture of wood latrine boxes and disinfectors'.[3]

The medical sergeant was elusive – he spent all his time in the camp gardens – but Sgt Hirota gave Weary and Owtram a hearing. Before leaving Tarsau, Weary had been promised a new operating theatre at Chungkai. He reminded Hirota of this, pleading as well for tools, more water points in the hospital (only one existed to serve 2500 sick), a Q store and a better medical inspection room. Hirota bounced straight back at Weary with a demand for 'scales . . . with amounts needed'.

Weary's letter with attached scales and a plan for new latrines was on the Japanese Commandant's desk next day.

Owtram had put in place a comprehensive entertainment and recreation scheme when he took over the command of the camp in May

1943. Morale under the two previous commanders, Williamson and Sainter (both Indian Army men, 'with no knowledge at all about British troops') had been appalling and it was necessary to do something quickly.[4]

This 'singing colonel' had a fine voice which had been trained by a leading baritone with the Berlin Opera House for some years, and musical comedy, a band and an orchestra played to the troops in an open-air theatre. Weary heard them perform Schubert's 'Unfinished' symphony on 11 March and was amazed at the 'excellent show'. The orchestra was conducted by Eric Cliffe, a lieutenant in the Royal Army Service Corps. Cliffe had begun the orchestra in Changi with instruments drawn from other prisoners and the Red Cross. Some were home-made. He had neither manuscript paper nor music ('had to remember it'[5]), and eight copyists prepared it secretly from the master score he wrote down.

Owtram supported them whole-heartedly by paying the members of the orchestra special rates and making sure that they had their three hours each day for rehearsals. They were unique to Chungkai, for although plays, cabaret acts and dance performances were staged regularly here and elsewhere, nothing was as ambitious as Cliffe's concerts. All entertainment did wonders for the camp atmosphere, for Owtram took concert parties round the hospital as well.[6]

Weary found his relaxation in rugby, swimming and athletics. Usually, Sundays were set aside for sports and the RAMC recruited him enthusiastically. He played five games of rugby here, more than at any other time in Thailand. His namesake, the hospital registrar, also a rugby player, refereed all their seven-a-side matches from the first one on 8 February: 'touch rules'. 'It seemed strange to be running again . . . I scored a try.'

They had been given only a day's warning that parties of 2 Group men were being evacuated from Takanun and would arrive in Chungkai on 1 March. It was growing hotter, with sudden thunder storms, showers, strong winds and dust storms. Six days before the Takanun draft arrived, the amoebic dysentery ward blew down and accommodation was stretched to the limit when 87 of the new arrivals had to be admitted to hospital. Maj. Max Pemberton RAMC, a New Zealander and 'a very sound and thorough fellow', returned with them to the hospital he had commanded for some months until his departure to Takanun in May 1943.

On 2 March, a further 56 new arrivals were squeezed into bed

*Doc Dunlop and his Quacks played Angela Spong and Boyfriends
in the Johnnie Walker Cup Final football, 29 April 1944*

spaces. Most of the sick had to be admitted to the ulcer wards: 'considerable difficulty was experienced crowding them in'. Weary was still very dissatisfied with the state of these and the skin wards.

The 1373 fit men from Takanun, 'red' force, were destined for Japan and were quartered only temporarily at Chungkai, whereas the sick – 'blue' force – would remain. Williamson had come back to Chungkai with them.

Lieut-Colonel A. A. Johnson ('Ackers Crackers') brought Weary news of Bruce Anderson, the former DADMS to the 8th Division whose company he had enjoyed in Changi. In 1943, he had been sent up with 'K' Force and put to work caring for the coolies. It was the first news of Anderson since he passed through Hintok Mountain camp. Now, he was working with the Tamils and burying about thirty a day.

Weary was amused by Johnson, who had intrigued everyone who saw him on his way upriver the previous year, swinging his butterfly net and striding out in front of his party. This ruddy-faced, well set-up man also collected orchids and seemed, to Weary, to 'put on a rather subtle, eccentric act'. He wondered if he was British Intelligence.

The Takanun medical party was absorbed into the staff of the hospital without any charge against 4 Group, since they were already paid by their own HQ. There were now 439 other ranks on the hospital pay roll. Weary was relieved to have the additional medical officers, orderlies, hygiene workers and cooks, for 'hospital work is not going ahead well'. His premonitions about the frustrations of taking charge of an 'ancient civilisation' had been well founded.

Two months after his arrival, the latrines were as unhygienic as ever because of a lack of wood, and the Japanese had ignored his requests for the large drums needed urgently for sterilising hospital equipment and food containers and for disinfestors. Two cases of cholera were admitted on 12 March and Weary protested vehemently when Yasano threatened to confiscate one of their two drums and use it for the pigs. There was already a stack of unused drums in the Japanese lines. Rather unwisely, he lost his temper with the Japanese sergeant and vowed that he would have him hanged if he carried out his threat.

Weary resolved on desperate action. 'With blackened face and hands' and armed with a heavy army torch, he slipped into the Japanese compound and succeeded in removing four drums to the hospital lines. Returning for a fifth, he was suddenly challenged by Ometz, a particularly revolting looking guard 'identified by me by the patchy loss of hair (syphilitic alopecia), and loose, foul, rat-like teeth' when he shone the torch on him. Impulsively, he 'clobbered' Ometz on the head with the torch and sprinted for his hut, head well down, ducking and weaving and 'expecting a bullet'.

Weary dived under his blanket. Heart pounding, he awaited retribution. None came. He fully expected everyone to be hauled out on parade, at which point he would have to confess in order to avoid reprisals against the entire camp, but next day nothing happened.

Two days after his assault, Ometz appeared 'with an obvious lump raising his cap'. Weary had been saved by the 'friendly intervention of retrograde amnesia, the memory loss preceding concussion'. Caution suggested that the drums be introduced into hospital service gradually.

Hospital equipment had been almost non-existent when he arrived, with no bowls or basins, no bedpans, no sterilisers, no irrigators for the ulcer wards, no reasonable supply of hot water, few instruments, no ointments or any inclination amongst the staff to manufacture them from beef or other fats, very little iodoform and no sulphanilamide. Through Capt. G. B. 'Bill' Adams and Private Charles Letts, both of whom spoke fluent Thai, he made his requirements known to the underground, which in the person of Lee Soon, the Chinese who ran the canteen, had been regularly delivering 'pennies from heaven' to the camp. This time, he wanted drugs, for he was 'scratching along with the last dust' in his bottle of iodoform by the end of February.

Much of his ulcer surgery involved skin grafting with what he termed the 'iodoform technique', and he wrote up careful notes on all his patients. The patient was given a chloroform anaesthetic, the edges of the ulcer – usually spreading, the flesh black, necrotic and gangrenous – were excised and the ulcer curetted before cauterising with phenol and sprinkling iodoform over the area. Paraffin dressings were applied and the ulcer left closed for around four days. Generally, the wound was found to be 'clean and granulating' when it was re-dressed, and in due time Reverdin skin grafts were attempted, in nearly every case successfully. Iodoform produced better results than sulphanilamide, but both drugs were scarce until 10 March, when he received the anxiously awaited 500-gram parcel of iodoform from the underground.

Initially, Weary's plans for improving conditions in the ulcer and skin wards were obstructed by a lack of co-operation from those running the Q workshops and the camp scabies clinic and laundry. He recruited his own workers to manufacture sterilisers, portable charcoal-fired stoves and irrigators on the Hintok pattern. Scabies was dealt with by putting clothing and bedding through disinfestors; flaming bug-ridden huts and bed slats; and treating with a sulphur emulsion sludge mixed with coconut oil and beef fat which gave 'good results' when it was rubbed well into clean skin with a shaving brush.

In the more ordered environment of this fixed camp, there was the means to plan his surgical work. Weary appeared to perform only two amputations at Chungkai. The need for amputation receded with improved conditions in the ulcer wards, thorough ulcer toilets by teams of orderlies moving systematically through the wards with their portable sterilisers and irrigating equipment, and the almost miraculous yellow powder. Out of the thirty operations he performed between his arrival and 26 April, 15 were skin grafts on ulcer patients.

As at Tarsau, the death rate fell as the diets improved. When Weary examined the hospital statistics for the previous six months at the end of March, dysentery and avitaminosis had become the chief causes of death; and the convalescent amoebic dysentery wards were the most populated. Deaths declined dramatically from January onwards, the February rate being less than half the January percentage. Throughout his time at Chungkai, the number of patients in hospital hovered just above 2000, except when the 2 Group people from Takanun arrived and pushed the numbers up to over 2200.

Respiratory diseases were never a problem in Thailand, for droplet infection was minimised in the long, well-ventilated huts. Malaria, of course, never left them.

Weary continued John Marsh's initiative of producing a hospital bulletin for the camp so that everyone would be informed and involved in his efforts to improve their hygiene. He needed their 'enthusiastic interest and support'. The wet season was approaching; the small crop of cholera cases in March was disturbing; and he hammered home his message. 'To combat cholera, dysentery and other bowel infections pay particular attention to:- FOOD, FINGERS, FLIES, FAECES, FILTH.'[7]

Weary systematically recorded his work at Chungkai and recruited a number of British artists, Phillip Meninsky, Old, Stanley Gimson and Jack Chalker. Meninsky carefully drew the prototype of the portable steriliser on its mud-frame base that February, the wooden bedpans, crutches, walking sticks and washing boxes. His dated illustrations show the products of the arts and crafts people, whom Weary had encouraged to manufacture hospital equipment, and the new management in the hospital workshop.

Gimson drew the wards, the hut Weary occupied with the padres and other officers, the operating theatre and the cumbersome weighing machine. His sketch of the cookhouse shows a *cwali* on its mud foundations and the precious containers full of boiling water; in another, of the skin wards, an orderly scrubs a patient's back with the sulpher ointment. On the ground beside him is a 'washing box', manufactured as a substitute for the basins they did not have, and a wooden bedpan is abandoned beside the building.

Some men drew and painted for their own pleasure. The more technical work of the artists Weary used adds to our understanding of the conditions, as he intended when he arranged for them to be paid to record what they saw, found them jobs around the hospital and concealed their work until war's end.

Anxious to hurry things along, particularly the manufacture of artificial limbs, Weary appointed Lieut. Bill Bailey to the department, a 'live wire' who 'accomplished more in a single day' than the English officer in charge. As March and April advanced, the items illustrated grow more ambitious: artificial limbs and an amputation retractor in March, skin grafting needles, a mastoid retractor, anaesthetic mask, a

sigmoidoscope and a nasal snare in April. But the most distressing
drawing is of an amputee from the 2 Cambs. Rgt, the skin stretched taut
over his bones in a terrible illustration of their captors' policy of
deliberate starvation.[8]

Wood was short, and bamboo continued to be a versatile material.
An NEI soldier was 'put up in a double Hamilton Russell extension and
a bamboo bed with "Balkan Beams", pulleys made of tin, etc.', a Heath
Robinson-like orthopaedic bed built for a patient suffering from
dysenteric arthritis in the right hip.

The operation which intrigued Weary most at Chungkai was on an
English lance-corporal in the 5th Beds & Herts who had been attacked
by a maddened elephant at Tarsau twelve months beforehand. The
traumatic tusk wounds in his thigh, near his rectum and at the base of
his spine had never healed despite various operations. Weary reopened
the wounds, excised and curetted them. Three months later, they were
almost healed. Old recorded the healing sinus in two vividly coloured
medical illustrations and it was a successful operation in which Weary
took some pride.

The Dutch were a continual irritation. Not only did they run all the
tobacco rackets, which endeared them to no one, but their doctors
consistently saved their 'men from work at the expense' of 2 and 4
groups by classifying them 'C', or 'no work', so that there was no danger
of their being sent to Japan or upriver. Weary was annoyed by this, for
some of his non-medical personnel essential to the running of the
hospital would have to go if no more fit men could be found. At the
Dutch doctors' protest that their troops were 'old men', he threatened
to set up a board drawn from the three forces to identify fit men, and
there was no further trouble.

The Japanese propaganda unit had sent a party of well-fed, well-
dressed Australian, British and Dutch prisoners across from Kanchanaburi on 10 February. Ciné cameras operated by their captors filmed
them working in the Chungkai gardens, then marching and singing
behind 'squeeze boxes and band instruments' before ending the
proceedings with a lustily rendered version of 'Rule Britannia'. This was
observed with some cynicism by Chungkai men (kept well out of camera
range). Weary became part of another exercise a month later.

Forty prisoners-of-war (ordered to be 'well-dressed' and this
accomplished by 'free borrowing') were marched across to a new
concrete monument a few kilometres away at Tamarkan. Complicated
Shinto rites dedicated this cenotaph to those who had died on the

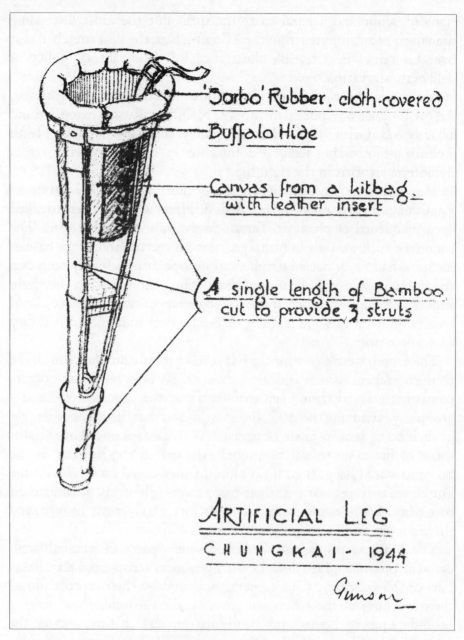

'Sorbo' Rubber. cloth-covered

Buffalo Hide

Canvas from a kitbag.
with leather insert

A single length of Bamboo
cut to provide 3 struts

ARTIFICIAL LEG

CHUNGKAI - 1944

Gimson

*Major F. A. 'Boots' Woods designed ingenious prostheses
for the amputees. Gimson drew them*

railway; and Thai, Muhammadan, Hindu, Buddhist, Chinese and
Christian all took part in turn. He was intrigued and frustrated that he
could find out nothing about most of the religions which informed the
ritual, particularly the Japanese ones. 'I wish I understood more of it.'

After two hours of ceremony and photographs in heat which some suggested was 'around 145° F.', all the men, each clutching a tin of biscuits, were taken to Tamarkan for lunch.

'There I saw Lt Col. Eadie, rather grey and more stooped but quite fat really.' Here, as well, were other 'A' Force medical officers from Burma, Majors A. F. Hobbs, and W. E. Fisher. Weary spent most of his time talking to Brig. Varley, and that night he noted in his diaries detailed mortality figures for 'A' Force up to 31 January 1944.

He blamed the hours out in the sun for his headache, but fever, malaise and a blood film chock-full of 'parasites B.T. and gametocytes' soon announced another bout of malaria. Usually oblivious to heat, Weary was surprised to find himself affected by the rising temperatures with 'an extreme languor and a complete lack of energy in the afternoons'. After two years of starvation he was painfully thin and down to 63 kilos: 'everyone comments . . . scraggy about the neck and thorax and cannot put on weight'. He had acquired more ulcers from knocks received during a rugby game and an earlier, unhealed one had flared up nastily.

The Chungkai Race Meeting was held in the middle of this malaria attack and Weary's performances at 'secret' trials were not particularly good. He was to race in the Officers' Stakes over 100 metres as 'Manfred', with a jockey weighing in at a little over 44 kilos.

'A terrific weight of Australian bookings has . . . pushed my odds down to evens, starting from 5:2.

'As usual, I started to shake with laughter in the middle of the race.' But he won effortlessly with a time of 15.25 seconds and celebrated by becoming 'tiddly on the local brew'.

Had it not been for his close companionship with Arthur Moon and the fun of the weekly 'blood match' of bridge for stakes of an omelette with their partners Bill Taylor and Derek Hirsch (both infinitely better than Moon and Weary), life would have been even more desolate.

Weary does not mention Helen in the diaries now. Two years of prison life had inured him to sudden movement and the loss of friends such as Jock Clarke, Billy Wearne, Ewen Corlette and 'Boots' Woods, but he wondered where they were, for he had heard that Wearne and McEachern were building huts in another large camp. 'I would very much like to see them again.'

He no longer discerned beauty about him, in the flash of a kingfisher's wings or in the sunrises and sunsets which had once brought enchantment. He worried that those at home might have become so accustomed to their absence that the failure of some to return would not cause too much heartbreak. 'I seem to have lost all emotional depths . . . one can't feel much any more. Further, I can't react very much to physical suffering or death . . .

'There is a defensive mechanism in suffering, in that there slowly develops a palsy of the emotions, and a deadness of the imagination.'

But he sympathetically treated the Japanese soldiers who came to him with VD and, after some hesitation, even agreed to circumcise one who dangled a bottle of Thai whisky as a 'big presento' in return for a reparative operation. Overnight, the whisky was quickly consumed by several of them and the operation was accomplished next morning. Akimoto insisted that he would not miss guard duty.

Two hours later Weary was arrested and marched off to the Commandant, Kukubu, whom he found seated cross-legged on a bamboo stool, 'his face dark with wrath like a teak god'. Beside him lay his unsheathed, gleaming samurai sword, 'reputed to have cut down two prisoners'.

After making a faultless *kiotské* and *keré* , Weary stood rigidly and silently to attention. Some minutes later, Kukubu 'dropped his legs to the floor, seized the sword and, pointing an accusing finger, said "Dunrop *chusa*, you despise me – I will kill you." . . . he swung the sword back in a wide arc . . . it then swished down . . . but the blade stopped quivering against my neck'.

Magnanimously, 'disarmingly', he offered the sword to Weary. ' . . . Please honour me by killing yourself.'

Gingerly accepting the sword, Weary began to talk, almost gabbling his reasons for declining to commit *hara-kiri* . His 'eloquent flood' petered out when he saw the incredulous expression in Kukubu's 'fierce brown eyes'.

'You mean, that you are such a great coward that you will not kill yourself?'

Weary was thrown into the 'box house', where Akimoto was already seated disconsolately. 'You rat – no guard duty go!' 'You did not tell me "cut cut" so much pain.'

Two days later, Yasano forbade further treatment of Japanese soldiers without his permission.

In Bandoeng, when Weary wrote an essay for his captors on the private feelings of a prisoner-of-war, he suggested that 'the most surprising thing is how little time one has for detached thinking. As an officer now concerned with Camp administration, the days move busily on. The routine of maintenance of order, cleanliness, hygiene and sanitation, equal distribution of camp comforts and privileges . . . create a small, busy world into which one is drawn away from the realm of previous experience'.[9]

Weary had written this when his study of the Japanese character was in its infancy, yet none of his careful observation during the ensuing two years caused him to revise the ideas expressed so simply and tactfully.

' . . . The most galling cause of anxiety is the almost complete lack of communication with the outside world, and with relatives, friends and loved ones . . . .

'The quality that has come to mean a very great deal in one's relationship with our captors is politeness . . . I have felt when I have met with politeness and courtesy that an unnecessary degradation has been avoided . . . blows delivered do not have the same significance in every country, but to one of my race, to be struck is a painful humiliation.

' . . . World wars bring such universal catastrophe that they cannot be indefinitely prolonged. I believe that it is of importance to the post-war World that we should do our best to understand our opponents whether as captive or prisoner.'[10]

He now understood his captors as well as anyone could and somewhat better than most. His hatred had hardened during the wet season of 1943 and he had enjoyed such revenge as he had been able to wreak on the Japanese. Okada had suffered grave disquiet when Weary 'psyched' him. As the death toll mounted during the cholera epidemic and later, at Kinsayok, Weary had deliberately and obviously stared hard at Okada. When the medical sergeant questioned him uneasily about this intense interest, Weary had eventually replied, pitching his voice solemnly low: 'All men die, Okada. I have been watching you. You, too, will die.'

Okada avoided his eyes after that, but Weary often found him looking nervously in his direction when he thought 'Dunrop *chusa*' was not watching.

Once at Tarsau and Chungkai, Weary was swept along by the relentless routine.

Since January, he had become accustomed to the drone of aircraft overhead, said by the Japanese to be Allied planes, and air raid alarms became common. Anti-aircraft fire was also heard, probably from the aerodrome a few miles outside Kanchanaburi.

The radio set in Chungkai was run by the Webber brothers and moved frequently, so that Weary was well aware of what was happening in Europe, in the Far East and in the Pacific.[11] His experience with the *kempis* at Tarsau had made him cautious, however, and now he carefully kept all radio news out of his diaries. The *kempis* called on him once a month. 'Colonel, how is your health? We know that you are dangerous spy.'

On 6 May, Weary received orders to begin sending 4 Group men by barge to Tamuang the following day. He attempted to persuade Ometz, who was in charge of the movement, to allow him to accompany the sick. Caught between 2 Group and 4 Group Japanese commands, Weary was escorted by a soldier known to the AIF as the 'High Breasted Virgin' to the movement control sergeant, Sukarno, a notorious 'basher' nicknamed 'The Slug'. 'The Slug' was swaddled in his leather jerkin and at bayonet practice, roaring like 'an inflamed rhinoceros' as he charged repeatedly at a straw 'body'.

Weary lost his temper seldom but always at the most inopportune times, and his invariable threat – that of having whoever angered him hanged at the end of the war – provoked 'The Slug' into substituting him for the straw dummy. Had the 'High Breasted Virgin' not coolly placed himself between Weary and the enraged sergeant until they were a comfortable distance away and Sukarno returned to the dummy, Weary would have been transfixed several times by the bayonet.

The 'High Breasted Virgin' had displayed unexpected courage. 'We 4 Group men. 2 Group men very bad. You are unwise to say such things to them. When you come back to 4 Group it will be better.'

He was relieved to be going. 'I have never experienced before the personal antipathy of the Nipponese that I have met within this camp.'

The evacuation of the sick began on 7 May and took sixteen days. That night, the bridge four played their last game in Chungkai, anticipating Moon's birthday by presenting him with a cake and a special card by Old 'with a border of 42 little moons and a picture of 4 silently playing for the weekly omelette'. Four days later, the day the avitaminosis ward crashed down to join the other wrecked hospital huts, Moon took 300 heavy sick upriver to Tamuang.

Weary began to shiver with malaria again, and the petty rivalries between 2 and 4 Group exacerbated his wretchedness. 'I am disgusted with the crazy, parochial, split administration of the place.' Owtram found the 'Red' force commander, Colonel Williamson, 'rather useless', but was nowhere near as irritated by him as was Weary, nursing a painful spleen and a splitting headache.

Red Cross stores arrived for the first time on 16 May. There was food for the men; and the seven cases of medical supplies contained clinical thermometers, syringes, emetine, prontabin, morphia, novocaine and other useful drugs. He was amused to unpack 1000 laxative tablets: 'never were laxative[s] . . . less needed.'

He handed over the hospital command to Pemberton on 21 May and played a final game of rugby on a ground saturated by the 'mango rains', as the bamboo rains were called further south. Weary skidded on the greasy surface, strained his left knee and damaged his back. ' . . . Difficulty in getting up or turning over when lying.'

Five hundred men packed into the open trucks for the rail journey to Tamuang. It was sixteen months since he had driven past the 'semi-civilised' buildings of Kanchanaburi with their shop-house counters piled with tinned goods.

Tamuang camp was a march of three kilometres from the station along a gravelled road with a 'good deal of gear to be carried and . . . two stretcher cases'. (His back was painful, but he helped carry them.) It was in a partly cleared valley of cultivated land rolling gently down to the broad river, well shaded with clumps of tamarind and mango trees and banana groves. To the west, these plains disappeared into a low range of distant hills. Great rafts of vegetation floated downstream and, in spite of the heat, the greenness and patches of shade were easy on the eye after dusty Chungkai. They were now on the eastern bank of the Mae Klong River, below its confluence with the Kwai Noi and 11 kilometres from Kanchanaburi.

Tamuang was full of old friends and enemies. Hatori had moved with them as second-in-command to the commandant, a Captain Susuki. The adjutant was the 'boy *shoko*' (now promoted to *chui*), Usuki; Lieut. Tanaka had responsibility for POW administration and Capt. Hiramatsu, 'The Tiger' from upriver with a better reputation than most for fairness, was in charge of building construction.

Weary's oppressive feelings of isolation and spiritual numbness lifted when he saw the figures of Billy Wearne, Jock Clarke, Allan Woods and Ewen Corlette coming towards him. And with great relief, he saw that his constant preoccupation – hygiene – was 'promising'. 'Everyone here goes in for food container sterilisation . . . the latrines are much the same pattern as Kinsayok – deep trench pattern with bamboo and earth superstructure covered by neat huts and little cubicles made by a lattice fencework of bamboo.' Jock was not so sanguine. He pointed out that the earthen sides had not been reinforced and many were bound to collapse. There was a shortage of bamboo and wood, and the south-west monsoon would soon bring the wet season.

The hospital was at the river end of the camp, but there was still a walk of around three-quarters of a kilometre down slippery tracks to the kitchens and to bathe. Long huts, well constructed from the usual bamboo and attap with continuous bed platforms of rough round bamboo, 'the hardness somewhat countered by bamboo matting', were well laid out. No hut was high enough for Weary: he had to watch that he did not crack his head on the rafters.

Meanwhile, he was to live in the lines and mess with the HQ staff. His acquaintance from Tarsau, Lieut-Colonel Alfred Knights of the Royal Norfolk Regt, was Camp Commandant overall; Lilly was in charge of the British; McEachern commanded the Australians, with Wearne as his second-in-command and Hands as adjutant. Quite like old times.

Also familiar was the 'jungle jealousy and parochialism' which was plaguing Knights and inhibiting the smooth administration of welfare, food and finances. 'There are great possibilities . . . if everyone gets together . . . [but] little sign of this as yet.'

Harvey was SMO. They agreed that Weary should spend a few days talking to people and on a 'general recce'.

Weary handed over the 'O' and 'P' battalion funds to Wearne who, with Woods, McEachern and others, agreed that AIF funds should be held in common. With luck and persuasion, other groups would follow suit and a comprehensive financial scheme could then be worked out. Nonetheless, Weary struck resistance to his ideas amongst the 'jungle lions', the battalion commanders for whom this was the first experience of a large fixed camp and who preferred individual action for their men.

Harvey had put Jack Marsh in charge of the hospital administration, and he and Corlette were anxious for Weary's help. 'I am . . . to keep out of ward work for a week or two.'

He plunged into a major reorganisation for the third time in seven months, his enthusiasm for work restored by being reunited with his companions. They were a tight-knit group; although nothing was said, they fretted for any missing members when they were apart. And all the members of his team were here: Clarke for hygiene, Woods and Marsh for the workshops; the 'good soldier' Wearne for solid advice and a sympathetic ear; Corlette and Moon in the hospital.

There would be cholera during the wet season: he requested vaccine, ordered the construction of two more stills to manufacture saline and told everyone to collect empty bottles for transfusion purposes.

In the midst of his activity, the pathology people discovered strongyloid worms in the blood samples of eight men who were to donate blood to the transfusion centre. Weary took a sample of his own blood and tested it; worms were present in that, also. That night, he slept fitfully, 'contemplating the thought of most of us going home with swollen legs and carrying our scrotums on a barrow'. Next day, it suddenly occurred to him to check the saline solution used to dilute the blood: microfilaria were present. It was the saline, not the blood, which was infested. He breathed again.[12]

Tamuang became memorable for letters, just when he had despaired of feeling emotional warmth ever again. He had had no mail since the day during the cholera epidemic when the letters had been pushed into his pocket to save him touching them in the filth of 'cholera gulch'. Once again, there were three envelopes: one from Helen, written as recently as February; two from his parents, the latest dated May 1943. The Japanese made no attempt to distribute mail – it was piled high in huts in the base camps and doled out occasionally at random.

Conditions were improving very slightly. The Japanese delivered 1000 eggs for the heavy sick and announced that this would be a daily distribution. Earlier, American Red Cross parcels had been distributed, each box of around 22 kilos in weight containing food and cigarettes to be divided between '6½ men'.

Moroko appeared on 30 May to inspect the hospital before the Camp Commander's visit on 1 June and informed them that Nakom Patom was to take a thousand of their heavy sick, lying, sitting, walking and amputation cases. He demanded rolls 'as quickly as possible'.

'Japan parties' of the fit were also being assembled at Tamuang and 900 Australians were to go. Reluctantly, Weary decided that two of his 2/2nd CCS men must accompany it as orderlies and selected Ray Denney and Henry Boys. Padre Harry Thorpe would accompany them. Weary readily wrote a letter testifying to his 'splendid work' in the camps in Thailand.

He drafted a third hospital bulletin along the lines of those he had circulated earlier in Tarsau and Chungkai. When he arrived at Tamuang, he had discerned some criticism of his food policy for the sick amongst the 'jungle lions' and he was determined to present the hospital's case to everyone. More importantly, the sick being sent to Nakom Patom must take adequate hospital equipment with them. Tarsau had already plundered its stocks in order that their sick might depart with their own buckets, bedpans, trays, sterilisers and so forth. Now, the Tamuang sick must be sent off similarly equipped. Weary appealed to the officers for more financial help so that the hospital could buy tools, tins and solder; and he begged everyone to give them their old tins, cloth, bottles, wire and nails. 'Nothing is too old, nothing is too small.'[13]

From sunrise to sunset, his days were busy with reports, diet schemes, meetings and statistics. On top of this, he drew up the lists of sick to be evacuated and co-ordinated their financial arrangements. 'I have done my best for N.P . . . by including as many officers as possible in the party.' Then the axe fell. He was shattered to hear Harvey's reply to a question about which medical officers were to go: ' . . . Only one was known and this was Lt-Col. Dunlop.'

He hoped it was only chatter. Moroko had not mentioned it.

Momentous news swept through the camp on 12 June. The Japanese interpreter confided that the invasion of France had begun six days beforehand. In the west, it was known as D Day.

The secret radios confirmed it. 'No doubt as to the truth of this news!' Weary wrote triumphantly. 'Success to Montgomery and his lads!' Later that day, some other chatter became fact. The Japanese decreed that Dunlop should lead the medical party to Nakom Patom. At least Jock Clarke and his CCS boys would accompany him.

The Great Wat at Nakom Patom could be seen from afar, dominating the flat plains that extended all the way to the coast and the city of Bangkok. It is a holy place to the Thais, the largest stupa in the world. By mid-1944, ragged remnants of camouflage were draped imperfectly over its bell-like dome.

Weary accompanied 500 of the thousand heavy sick to Nakom Patom, arriving at the huge camp in the shadow of the wat on 14 June 1944. The situation for a hospital camp was bad, for they were in low-lying paddy country. He expected the malaria problem to be acute.

The familiar pattern of long hutments met his eye, but there was one important difference: wood was used in their construction. For the first time since Changi, he could stretch out on a firm, smooth, level bed platform over two metres deep. Rain or dry season cold could be kept out by wooden shutters.

That January, with the help of Thai labour, a party of prisoners had begun to build fifty huts a hundred metres long for an expected 10 000 patients. Two hundred men could be housed under each steeply sloping attap roof, with a metre of bed space apiece. Well-drained, level roads ran between the blocks; another encircled the camp. The IJA planned this 'face-saving' camp on a generous scale, with 10 cookhouses, 6 dry ration stores, administrative offices, a wooden floored and walled operating theatre, transfusion clinic, dental clinic, pathology lab., and biological and alcohol factories. Concrete-lined latrines, emptied by POW labour, meant that the danger of latrine walls collapsing through a lack of bamboo revetting was over.

For housing troops, Nakom Patom would have been 'reasonably satisfactory' but its design for the seriously ill was deficient.[14] Still, it was an improvement on all previous hospital accommodation. But it was too late. 'The main battle for men's lives had already been fought in the ghastly conditions of jungle hospital concentrations . . . [at] Kinsayok, Tarsau, Chungkai, Tamuang, Non Pladuc and Kanchanaburi.'*

Weary found his old teacher, Lieut-Colonel Albert Coates, installed as Chief Medical Officer and consulting surgeon with 3998 patients. At its peak in August, 7353 occupied the wards in this base hospital. Coates had been there since March, together with other medical officers and the seriously ill 'A' Force men with whom he had been in Burma. He was 'very glad to see Dunlop arrive'.[15]

The Allied Camp Commander was British, Lieut-Colonel J. D. Sainter, 'the Saint', a notorious and unpopular man who was 'sharply critical' of Weary and opposed to his ideas of using increased contributions from officers' pay and taxing other camps to provide a central fund for the care of the sick. While at Chungkai, his command had been so 'slack' that the camp developed into a 'complete mess . . . people even cutting off the fingers of dying men to get their rings.

---

* Compared to the mortality rate in the construction camps, only 153 deaths occurred at Nakom Patom up till 21 July 1945, wrote Weary to the Australian medical historian after the war. Towards the end of 1943 more men than this died in a single month at jungle base hospitals.

Terrible things went on, all due to [this] wretched commander.'[16]

Owtram had told Weary about his rows with Sainter at Chungkai. '. . . Indian Army . . . useless', like his predecesor, Colonel Williamson. There had been a 'widespread feeling' there that the former HQ staff had been 'too compliant with Japanese demands'.[17] Even the Japanese did not care for Sainter and moved him upriver in May 1943. Before leaving, he appointed Owtram camp commandant in his place. At Nakom Patom, Coates found Sainter and his staff extremely difficult to work with.

Weary's reputation preceded him to Nakom Patom. Before his arrival, Sainter informed van Orden (Weary's block commander) that as a combatant officer he was not to take orders from Dunlop. He, Sainter, would tell him what to do.

Weary was furious to hear this, but van Orden persuaded him not to storm off and confront Sainter immediately. Next morning, he reported to Sainter. 'He came to the door . . . unshaven and in a dirty singlet.' Icily polite, Weary asked why his block commander had been forbidden to take orders from him, and demanded an apology. Sainter burst into a 'torrent of abuse, I had come to this camp to make trouble, I had taken money from officers and done all sorts of irregular things . . . I was nothing but a plague spot and a source of trouble'.

Weary reached forward, 'seized his dirty singlet in the midriff and twisted it slightly and said: "There are several things I do not like about you. I do not like your manners, which are revolting, your discourse which is disgusting, your reputation which is repulsive . . . or your appearance. If you ever come to my section of the camp making trouble again, I shall seize you by your dirty neck and the seat of your pants and throw you out."'[18]

He went immediately to Coates and reported what had happened. Coates believed that Sainter would take no action; nothing more need be said.

Three days after Weary and Jock Clarke arrived, the first group of Headquarters people marched in. There were now medical officers aplenty: to the existing medical executive of Coates, his registrar and medical adjutant Capt. Cyril Vardy and physician and second-in-command Maj. W. E. Fisher, plus the medical officers who had come in with parties of heavy sick, were added four more lieutenant-colonels (Malcolm, Barrett, MacFarlane and the Dutch commander, Larsen), Capt. Markowitz and Lieut. Poh.

Coates made Weary 'Medical Economics Officer', entrusting him with 'the delicate task of handling' money solicited from unspecified 'sources of income'. Keith Bostock, the Australian Red Cross Commissioner, worked with him. Their donations came from group funds; voluntary contributions by officers; salaried Red Cross personnel and anyone else who was 'paid' by the IJA; canteen profits; and what were euphemistically described as 'outside sources' – in other words, the underground.

Weary witnessed friction between Sainter and Coates, for the former held as axiomatic the absolute power of a combatant commander. Medical officers, no matter how senior or distinguished, did not count. But the combatant colonel had underestimated the shrewd, street-wise Coates and his appointment of a clever, tough and tenacious officer experienced in raising money for the sick.

Besides, Sainter and his adjutant, Maj. Finch-White, were very unpopular, but few questioned the importance of the medical officers' selfless and energetic contributions to the corporate survival. Their continued existence was in the hands of these men.

Weary clashed with Sainter over the control of the canteen activities and the 'authorised deductions (i.e. Messing, hairdressing etc.) from all paid personnel'.[19] Sainter insisted that medical personnel should control medical matters, and 'lay people . . . control lay matters'. Sainter had chosen the wrong man for this argument.

Weary was determined to have some control over the canteen's stock, for it was one way of ensuring that men spent their money on foods which would enhance their nutrition, but he was not to achieve this until all the field officers had left the camp. Ultimately, when the canteen was wound up after Weary's and Bostock's careful management, the balance sheet showed '35 984 ticals with a credit balance of 3000 ticals'.

It was some months before the Japanese tumbled to the fact that more money was being spent on general messing and special diets than was emanating from IJA sources – officers' and other ranks' contributions, contributions from outside base camps, IJA contributions, canteen profits and so on. Weary believed that they suspected underground activities but had no proof. They demanded an itemised account of the special diet expenditure, daily lists of menus from the cookhouses extending over seven days, a 'detailed statement of what we ate for each meal' and what extra sum per head was added to the IJA ration issue.[20] This was to be prepared for the entire camp, not just the hospital. Their official reason was that they needed the figures in order to take over financial responsibility for the diets themselves. Nothing eventuated.

For someone whose ambition was to spend as much time as possible in an operating theatre, Weary always found it ironic that so much of his prison camp existence was devoted to financial matters. He did not have a high opinion of accountants.

Three senior British officers who had come down to Nakom Patom were not impressed with Sainter's administration and wished to reorganise the camp along the lines of previous ones they had been in with Weary. Coates had spent his time in Burma and was an unknown quantity to them, whereas Weary's form had been well observed. They suggested that Weary and Coates attend a meeting which they would call; and Sainter would then be forced to retire. But Coates did not care to take any strong action.

Weary would have no part of it once he knew Coates's feelings. He regarded his former teacher as 'immensely my professional superior, a veteran of Gallipoli . . . and whilst my military rank was actually higher as T[emporary]/Col[onel], there was no way that I could be induced to "pull rank" on him'.

Sainter became aware that feelings were running against him in some sections of the camp. He avoided Weary after that. 'He regarded me as too difficult, I think.' He took his revenge on the dissident officers, however. Finch-White, his adjutant, reported to the Japanese that the three of them were not sick men: they had 'come to the camp to make trouble'. The IJA arrested them, 'an appalling action'. The doctors all had to testify that they were seriously ill to save them.[21]

Coates ran an impressive 'medical society' as part of his command, conceding nothing to the unusual circumstances. Clinical meetings of a high order began on 3 May and continued regularly until the last presentation by Maj. Hazelton a week after the war had ended. (Appropriately, since so many lives had been saved by hundreds of thousands of duck eggs during their three and a half years of captivity, this last meeting addressed their success in improving the vision of patients' suffering from 'avitophthalmia', inflammation of the eyes resulting from vitamin deficiency.)[22]

Weary had been in the camp not quite a month when he attended a clinical meeting Coates had called to discuss the place of surgery in treating chronic amoebic or bacillary dysentery. He was interested to see that Higuchi, the Japanese doctor, was present.

All medical officers working in the camps despaired of repairing the ravages of dysentery in those severely starved and broken men afflicted by not one, but a multitude of diseases. Emetine was the drug required,

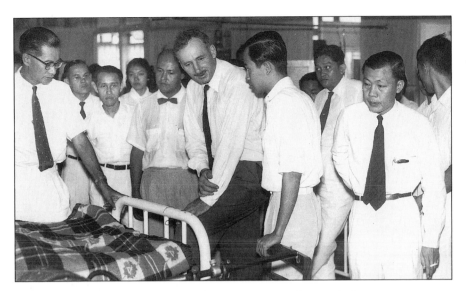

66 *Colombo Plan teaching round, Siriraj Hospital, Bangkok 1952. Dr Kasarn (l.) became President, Royal College of Surgeons of Thailand*

67 *Alexander & John terrorised a neighbouring spinster with bows and cloth-tipped arrows*

68 *John met Dr Sem with Weary in Thailand*

69 *Patiala, India, 1964 with (l. to r.) Prof Manchanda, Weary,*
E. S .R. Hughes and Prof Prakash

70 *New Zealand ex-POWs, overjoyed to see him again, gave him the Freedom of the City of Wanganui*

71 *Weary beat a path back and forth across Victoria to reunions every year, Wagga, 1959*

72 Alexander had trips to India and Thailand with his father

73 Indian President Radikrisnan and Mrs Gandhi thanking him for services to Indian medicine, India Day 1968, New Delhi. Punjabi University conferred an honorary doctorate of science on him that January

74 *A dubbing from Lord Casey, 1969*

75 *Weary worked at Bien Hoa Hospital, South Vietnam, 1969*

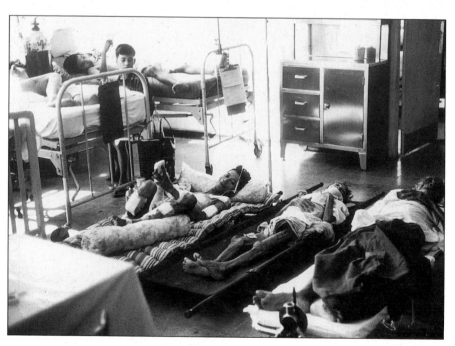

76 *Recovery ward, Bien Hoa Hospital*

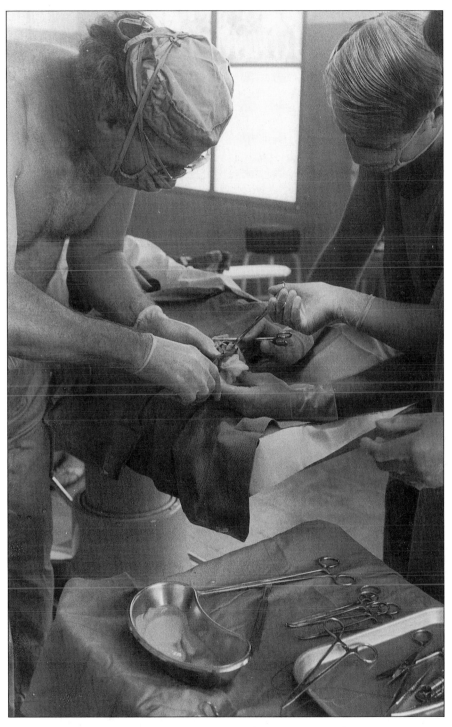

77 *Weary operating, the leprosarium, South Vietnam*

78 *Japanese Marine Defence Force visits Melbourne, 1977. Consul-General Miyakawa and Vice-Admiral Saito seated to Weary's left*

79 This is your Life, *1979, with Bill Griffiths*

but it was rarely available in anything like adequate quantities, very expensive, and clandestinely supplied until late 1944. And now they were seeing patients who were emetine resistant.

In Weary's three months at Chungkai alone, 947 patients had been treated, some surgically. The wards could be places of fearsome suffering, men in the terminal stages of acute dysentery 'conscious and very violent, often hurling themselves around the hut spurting faeces and vomit in their agony . . . '[23]

Where emetine was unobtainable or the patient had failed to respond to it and life was threatened, Weary found appendicostomy – or caecostomy, when the man had already had his appendix out – 'a most effective measure . . . [which] certainly saved a number of lives'.[24]

Quite independently, Pemberton and Weary had both pioneered this procedure. Fisher, cautious as physicians ever are, supported Weary, MacFarlane and the others in the more conservative routine.

Weary also performed a number of ileostomies. Coates, in Burma, had performed the first of these on dysentery patients; and he continued to advocate it as his 'operation of choice', despite being its sole champion during this meeting.[25]

That night, at the dimly lit end of their hut, Weary settled down to play 'a tense rubber of bridge' with Arthur Moon, Bill Taylor and Derek Hirsch. They ignored the lights out bugle. Moon was not down for long – he had accompanied some patients and would return to Tamuang. Outside, they could hear van Orden splashing water over himself.

A Japanese sentry burst in, waving his bayonet, and demanded to know why they were out of bed. In order to give van Orden some extra minutes to slip into his bedspace, Weary took his time in assuming the blame as the senior officer. The guard ordered him to report to the guard house at half past eight next morning.

He reported early, his ulcers protected by thick socks, rendered a 'most respectful *kiotské* and *keré* ', but was ignored by the guard and left to stand rigidly to attention 'for some hours in a boiling sun'.

He became an 'Aunt Sally' for a line of guards and orderly NCOs, the target of kicks, rifle butts, bamboo, sticks or anything else which came to hand. The guard sergeant recited his crimes to all and sundry, until by midday they had become so impossible – 'out of bed almost all night, had come to report nearly a day late, and had been insolent to the guard beyond belief. Really *chusa* , if this goes on you will have to be punished' – that Weary's control snapped.

'God Almighty, do you not think it punishment standing in this sun and being kicked and beaten by a pack of bandy legged baboons?' he yelled.

It took the interpreter a moment to grasp what he had said. Retribution followed swiftly. He was 'belaboured . . . with rifle butts, chairs, boots etc., while I rolled in the dust trying to keep in a ball' in order to protect his spleen, swollen and fragile from recurrent malaria.

' . . . Motionless beyond resistance, lying face down in the dust, conscious of broken ribs and blood from scalp wounds', they gathered him up, 'dazed and rubber-limbed, and trussed and roped backward kneeling with a large log between my seat and my knees.'

They left him there for the rest of the day. Breathing was difficult because of his fractured ribs. The pain in his legs was intense, made intolerable by the rough ground and the weight and pressure of the log; but then numbness set in as circulation in his legs failed. 'How long to gangrene in the tropical heat?'

He squared his shoulders, pulling himself together in a characteristic way that, throughout his life, proclaimed a conscious stiffening of his will to all who saw it.

The sun was low in the western sky when the interpreter delivered his final summation, finishing with: 'If we were so forgiving as to release you, would you have hard feelings against the guard?' Weary considered this warily. His gift for sensing the appropriate response for the circumstances returned to him. 'Hard feelings against what guard?'

'My ropes were released. With a desperate heave, I disengaged from the log, but my legs were functionless.'

When his circulation had returned, he stood to attention, bowed, and in an exaggerated fit of bravado, announced: 'And now, if you will excuse me, I shall amputate the Dutchman's arm who has been waiting all day.'

He could never resist proving that he was tougher than anyone. He made his way – still very painfully – to the operating theatre outside the camp area, scrubbed up, steadied his 'tremulous hands, injected the brachial plexus and removed the totally paralysed, smashed up and infected limb'.

He consigned this occasion to the same plane as some of his choicer rugby adventures. Hearing others tell these stories gave him quiet pleasure. 'I was determined to show them that Australians were tough.'

And despite his by now near-British accent, he was very much an Australian.

Coates was finding Weary to be 'a tower of strength at Nakom Patom, just as he had been in the jungle'.[26] He put Weary in charge of the surgical block when the hospital was reorganised in August, and added the physiotherapy department to his responsibilities in November. From fairly modest beginnings at Tarsau and Chungkai, the masseurs' contribution had become increasingly important, particularly for men whose limbs had been deformed by ulcers or amputated. The masseurs were non-medical men but had been trained by the doctors. In Chungkai, Weary oversaw a group which Barrett had recruited when he was SMO, and many others had learned the techniques in jungle camps. By November 1944, the physiotherapy department was treating 350 cases in its remedial and massage centre in Hut 36 each day, in addition to working with around 700 patients in their wards.

Carpenters had built wooden appliances such as bicycles and a pedalling machine, muscle exercisers, a contraction ladder for the amputees, walking bars and a rowing machine for remedial exercises. The centre had reached the stage where its activities needed medical direction.

Weary was determined to do as much as possible to restore men's limbs so that they could return to an active civilian life. The physiotherapy department worked closely with the orthopaedic workshop run by Allan Woods, where his ingenuity found full expression designing and making artificial limbs for the amputees.

Also with Weary, he adapted Dutch water bottles for fitting to the ileostomy patients and his carpenters turned out splints, leg rests and back rests, a surgical corset and a 'most ingenious little foot suction pump' for the operating theatre. But his true bushman's talents showed in the theatre lamp he conjured out of 'old oil tips and odd pieces of wire'.[27] Four paraffin burners (which used coconut oil in default of paraffin) were arranged on a frame and the counter-balanced light, enabling it to be raised or lowered as required, was suspended above the operating table. The first operation after dark took place the day Woods produced it: 13 November.

Weary was bemused when the masseur who had been with him in Chungkai, and who had illustrated Marcowitz's work with ulcer patients and amputees, wished to sculpt his head in clay. Jack Chalker was talented and Weary's favoured medical illustrator. He was keen to keep him in his orbit, for his well-drawn technical illustrations amplified the case notes he was meticulously writing up with a view to publication after the war.

He gave him a new job as a records clerk in the physiotherapy department, from where he could be summoned to a ward or the operating theatre.

Because of *kempi* supervision and – partly – great shortage of paper, pencils and ink, Weary had not kept his diary since the move from Tamuang to Nakom Patom. But, on 10 November, the sight in his new notebook of a blank page opposite some statistics for his surgical block, tempted him to write pensively: ' . . . The eve of a great armistice . . . I wonder if such an event was as remote to the toiling millions of the last war, some 26 years ago, as it is to me now. Those millions who had become "insentient engines pumping blood". During those appalling days of last year most of us went to some desolate bourn beyond that – to bones. A valley of dried bones.'

Never again would he be free from the remembered pain of those apocalyptic months in 1943, when the south-west monsoon swept the miseries of war up through the green valley of the Menam Kwai Noi.

Hiding his papers had become more difficult. He still possessed all Ray Parkin's diaries and drawings (Parkin had departed from Chungkai in one of the Japan parties), the bulky files and routine orders he had hauled from Java, statistics, reports and letters written in the jungle camps, at Tarsau, Chungkai and Tamuang. How all this was missed during the periodic searches by the *kempis* was a miracle.

The Japanese attitude was changing, 'even asking what we want', issuing drugs and handing over small quantities of Red Cross stores. The wet season had passed, the huts were more or less waterproof, food was more plentiful, and for almost two months he was able to 'return to daily scribbling which I have not been able to do since arriving in this camp'.

Time and the climate had reduced his clothing to rags. Butterworth seized the trench coat bought in Palestine at the end of 1941 and the tailoring shop produced two pairs of shorts for Weary, and 'sundry oddments' made out of the lining for Butterworth and other people. The nights grew colder and he was 'both living and sleeping in all the clothes' he possessed. Until now, he had slept naked on a canvas sheet under a thin blanket, with his greatcoat on top as the temperature dropped (unless he had lent it to a sick man whose need was greater). 'It is hard to see men with almost no bedding . . . One good thing about the cold – the mosquitoes are rapidly fading out.'

Allied bombers were flying regular sorties over the area that November, their approach on these moonlit nights heralded by a rapid tattoo beaten on large gongs hanging in the camp. There were no red crosses to indicate that this was a hospital camp, for the Japanese did not permit them; and neither slit trenches nor air raid shelters were prepared until the escalating raids of December. Non Pladuk, with its railway sidings and workshops, was the target initially, and Weary had operated on casualties brought into Nakom Patom after a severe raid on the night of 6–7 September.

Nights were now disturbed by the crump of bombs and clatter of anti-aircraft fire. Tamarkan was hit on the twenty-ninth. Four nights later, Weary watched 'three waves of giant four-engined bombers [which] flew almost over the camp' and dumped their loads on Non Pladuk, the explosions and fires flaring high in the night sky.

December's activity was the fiercest yet. The very air throbbed on the night of the eighth, as the line was systematically bombed all the way up from Kanchanaburi to the Burmese border. The concrete and steel bridge over the Mae Klong – that bridge which was to be immortalised as the 'Bridge on the River Kwai' – was hit repeatedly that month and the next, until only the wooden structure remained, the one crossed by Weary in 1943. Eventually that, too, went.

He feared for Jack Marsh, who was said to have been on a train that was hit on its way to Tamarkan.

Laughing Colonel Ishii was replaced by the more humane Yanagida in the middle of December. Christmas and the Nakom Patom Race Meeting came and went with 'all the usual merry incongruity of a Thailand race meeting'.

Weary flopped in the 'Colonel's Sprint', as he had feared, losing to Clive Wallis, the major who took over his wireless set and an International rugby player who had captained the Army. ' . . . Never smokes and always fit.' It was Weary's 'first and only horse-racing defeat'. But as Pheidipedes by Marathon out of Greece he triumphed in the Grand National steeplechase, clearing 'the water jump with a foot to spare' and running away from the field. Coates, his delighted owner, took him off for 'two impressive snorts'. That evening, with Billy Wearne and Allan Woods, they 'rose to the dignity of a dinner with table and . . . a cup' concocted from rice distillate. It was the best Christmas yet.

The IJA had contributed one tical in cash, one in kind for the food for each man, lit up the camp until midnight on Christmas Day and distributed free cigarettes and sake. But most remarkable was the feeling of hope for the future: and throughout the hospital, patients 'looked forward to happy release and spending next Xmas at "Home".'[28]

New Year's Day began with Billy Wearne's bombshell that 'all field officers (probably not medical) may be leaving the camp soon'. 'This will be a big blow to me as far as Billy and Allan are concerned. We have long been together and are very close.'

New Year invariably reduced Weary to 'profound depression'. A small party organised by Maj. Sid Krantz on New Year's Eve for the Nakom Patom Clinical Society affected him deeply. 'Somehow the nostalgic songs . . . the pathetic little drinks, the gathering darkness lit by flickering oil lamps, left me with a profound melancholy.' He was swept once more by the 'dipsomaniac urge' which had struck him in Tarsau and sought out his dispenser, Sgt Geoff Wiseman. Wiseman dug around in the dispensary and mixed a potent cocktail of acriflavine and spirit which they found 'tolerable'.

They tossed back their drinks and, full of exhilaration, eventually went to bed. Later that night, Weary 'had cause to ease my bladder and looked up at the brilliant sky . . . written clearly on a saffron coloured heaven was an immortal ode, stanza by stanza'. He stood in the moonlight, suffused by feelings that 'not even Homer, not Shakespeare can equal this. I, too, am immortal'.

Next morning it had vanished. Not a word could be recalled. 'It has been my one experience of the dipsomaniac urge leaving me with some enduring comprehension of the miseries of the spirit and the brief exaltation of the alcoholic.'

The hospital was stunned by the suicide of a patient on 5 January. Weary had had only two other cases in his camps, one at Hintok and the other at Tarsau, when a man who had contracted VD from a Thai village after breaking bounds lay across the line ahead of an oncoming train and was decapitated. The Japanese reaction was typical; in the same way that, earlier, they had refused to recognise typhoid or dysentery as a cause of illness – changing the latter to colitis or 'other conditions of the alimentary tract' – they now insisted that the word 'suicide' be deleted from the man's death certificate.

Life for men sent upriver had not changed. Eight hundred sick were brought in during the first twelve days of 1945, most suffering from severe malaria and gross malnutrition. Away from the base hospitals, hard work, poor diet and a shortage of drugs continued to prevail.

The Japanese demanded that a thousand men be discharged and sent to work up country. In early January, Higuchi ordered Coates to accompany such a party of patients. Hastily, Coates arranged for Weary to take his place in the camp as SMO and left next day with several hundred men. Even Sainter recognised how foolish it would be to move the SMO out with a working party and protested to the IJA commander. Coates was plucked back while only a short distance from camp and a Dutch doctor, Brouwer, was sent in his place.

A bund was being thrown round the camp; and later in January, the hospital was concerned at the random way 'patients are arriving and leaving the camp all times of the day and night without any apparent reason'.

All field officers in the Nakom Patom group were marched out to a Group 7 camp at Kanchanaburi on 23 January and Coates became the Nakom Patom camp commander. Warrant officers and NCOs took over the discipline of the men. Now that Sainter had gone, Coates handed over the canteen administration to Weary, who also chaired the new Finance Committee, and supervised the Q branch and the messing officers. The Group 1 men were the next to depart, all except their heavy sick, leaving on 27 February.

The monotonous weeks crawled by. Once more, the 'mango rains' approached, and the huts which had looked so sturdy the previous May began to fall down. White ants had eaten the posts, the attap roofs were leaking and the matting sides were full of holes.

Weary protested at the fashion in which unfit men were being discharged, sent up country in working parties and 'used up', then returning later to Nakom Patom in a 'dreadful state'. He accused Coates of sending off sick, patched-up men prematurely, particularly the Mergui Road party. In the course of a bitter argument about a group of these men being returned to the jungle, when Weary insisted that Coates and he should confront the Japanese and refuse to send them, Coates accused Weary of 'chicanery'. This 'hurt my feelings a bit'. His protests had no effect. The medical headquarters was reluctant to aggravate the Japanese at this stage. They believed that the end might not be far off, and food and Red Cross stores were appearing in greater quantities.

Weary was in the surgical block when Fyfe, the officer who was assembling the party, rushed in with the unwelcome news that the men had retaliated by throwing Lieut-Colonel MacFarlane into the duck pond and were bent on doing the same to Coates. 'For God's sake,

Austin, where's the bugler?' called Weary as he dashed out the door. 'Put the bugler on . . . '

They called the camp on parade and saved Coates from the humiliation of a ducking. By the following morning, when he came to see Weary, he had put it down to 'high spirits'. Luckily, he never discovered that he was to be the next victim. Tension had been high amongst the men for some time and usually vented itself in violent nightmares. Late one night, Weary was in one of the long huts, restless men moaning and talking in their sleep all about him, when the night was hideously broken by 'screams . . . the whole hut woke up and stampeded out of it' like cattle, wild with communicated fear. It was 'the most terrible thing [he] had ever seen'.[29]

The party on the Mergui Road was in a desperate way by the end of July, few being fit to work – 'it means . . . getting people off their beds directly rigors are over' – in this camp of 300 men. 'There are only half a dozen working for the Japs . . . and the highest figure for work including the lightest camp duties & volunteer medical orderlies has been 49 . . . ' During the time it took to write three-quarters of a page, '3 men have died'.[30] Coates had a very lucky escape. The doctor who was sent in his stead died.

Since the beginning of the year, *kempi* searches had intensified. Weary kept no diary between 3 January and July, when he recorded 'a mounting tension . . . with highly sinister overtones'. The camp was now completely surrounded by the two and a half metre-high bund or earthen embankment. Japanese guards patrolled its flat top. Machine gun emplacements faced inwards at each corner. One of the Korean guards repeatedly and furtively sought him out to pass on news about the progress of the war. 'He was pessimistic as to any hope of our being recovered alive. Invasion [of Thailand], he felt, would be met by massacres and death marches.' Weary agreed.

They knew that Germany had surrendered in May. The war in Europe was over.

On 23 July, the IJA handed over 42 cases of Red Cross medical supplies. These were the first of lorry-loads which began to arrive, part of the 10 000 tonnes reportedly shipped from the US via Japan on a Japanese liner. The IJA alleged that the Americans had inconsiderately sunk it on its return journey; nonetheless, in the 'National spirit of *bushido*' they would keep their promise and deliver the supplies.

Coates and some other senior officers were troubled and anxious. They felt that the Japanese had begun tentatively to observe the Geneva convention and that it was important not to provoke them. Weary was told not to endanger 'this fragile trend' by maintaining his contacts with the underground. 'I am cautioned against seeking even monetary help' in case the IJA's suspicions were aroused again. When the field officers left in January, the talented accountant who faked the figures had gone with them and Coates had found it difficult explaining the discrepancies in the canteen funds.

Even shaving with his forbidden blade razor was regarded as provocation: he made sure Coates did not see him, for he had deliberately concealed it when they were ordered to hand them in. Harsh words were spoken about his 'contraband', the hidden papers and the like. After all, he had been a target for the *kempis*, who continued to watch him. 'I fear that I am regarded as dangerous.'

August arrived. 'Strange things' were spoken of furtively by a Korean guard on 9 August. ' . . . Mysterious, dreadful super bomb destroying cities and 100 000 people.* Weary did not react: it might be a ruse of the *kempis*. But privately he wondered, 'Is this possible?' And next day, amidst the rising tension, he scribbled just six lines.

'The story of not one but two bombs persists. A capitulation of Japan could be our salvation – and for that matter Japan's salvation. Russia said to have entered the war. My hopes are rising.'

The Dutch POW interpreter confirmed the guard's information. But Weary had more insight into the Japanese temperament than some, he recognised their deadly earnestness – 'they play for keeps' – and he worried that the warmongers in Japan would urge a 'fight to the death'. The Korean guard's predictions of a tragic end might still come true. 'This is the moment of truth.'

There were other, 'utterly unusual' signs from the Japanese, when they approved paying 313 heavy sick and issued 300 kilos of soya beans, boxes of milk, soap and clothing from the Red Cross stores. Otherwise, they gave no hint of what was being discussed at their headquarters, remaining 'tight-lipped and admirably controlled'.

Three weeks beforehand, he had discussed his fears with W/O Austin Fyfe. Fyfe had been a major with a Highland regiment in the First World War and been decorated with a DSO and an MC; because his age was above the limit for a commission in 1939, he had enlisted in the AIF as a warrant officer in the 2/3rd Machine Gun Bn. Weary and he had been

---

* The first atomic bomb was dropped on Hiroshima on 6 August, killing around 80 000 people. Nagasaki was bombed three days later.

together since Java and now, in the absence of Wearne's 'professional guidance', he found Fyfe a 'tower of quiet strength and authority'.

Weary had chosen ten NCOs 'of high courage and discretion' and deputed each of them to recruit ten men. Weapons were whatever they could devise, but probably a stone would be all most could muster. His own 'armoury, carefully hidden', consisted of two 'Molotov cocktails' made from saki bottles and petrol, siphoned stealthily from Japanese trucks. Utmost secrecy had been maintained. In the event of a massacre being launched, they had been instructed to rush particular points around the camp. Weary did not intend to escape himself, but he was determined that he would get someone out to tell the world about their treatment by the Japanese.

Coates discussed the situation with Larsen, the Dutch commander, and his adjutant, Vardy, then called a meeting late at night on 14 August. He was gravely concerned to protect the troops, and when Weary told him of his arrangements already in place, he appointed him APM and made Capt. Meldrum RAMC his assistant.* Larsen's opposition was overruled. Vardy, Meldrum and Weary worked out the details. His hundred men were a ready-made force. No longer did he expect to use them in an attempted break-out; their rôle would be as guards, pickets and patrols. The NCOs would guard stores and oversee discipline 'at a time when exuberance, or failure to maintain co-ordination and order, could be fatal'.

He slept little that night. Next morning there were 'wilder rumours' and he clamped his security measures on the camp. 'All at action stations.' The Koreans insisted that the war was over. The officers were told of the probability, but nothing was said to the other ranks.

'Hope is rising in my heart, but who knows to the last minute what the fanatics will decide in Japan?'

---

* The title normally implies control of military police by a senior combatant officer.

TWENTY-FOUR

'Oh Incredible Day!'

'PLACE LIKE XMAS DAY – all men think something big about to come over. Me too. I am convinced.'

So were the Koreans. Many were in tears; all were 'scared'. None of the Japanese officers or NCOs had been seen for four days. A major arrived by motor car early in the afternoon, and all the officers disappeared into their conference room in the Japanese lines.[1]

On a 'hunch', Coates ordered a special dinner: pork *nasi goreng* , a fried egg, one savoury and one jam 'doover' and a beef sandwich for every man in the camp.

The prisoners' headquarters office closed promptly at 6 pm. Weary, Vardy and the others had just reached their bed spaces when one of the Japanese clerks summoned them to a 'dramatic' parade of headquarters staff and hut commanders.

They formed up behind Coates, who led them towards the Japanese compound. A very 'unhappy' Lieut. Wakimatsu, the camp commander, met them at the gate and, almost immediately, Lieut-Colonel Yanagida appeared with the interpreter, Mr Nonaka. Sentence by sentence, Nonaka translated Yanagida's statement into English. 'An Armistice is now being held between all nations. All fronts are at peace . . . we cease to guard you . . . the maintenance of discipline is your own responsibility . . . '

They were words everyone had been longing to hear for forty-one interminable months.

Coates led his staff straight to the theatre area and climbed up on the stage. There were 'unforgettable scenes' as the troops assembled, Australian, British, Dutch and American. Larsen spoke to the Dutch in their own language. Flags, the Union Jack, Australian, Dutch and the Stars and Stripes, were pulled out of hiding places. Cyril Vardy and another stood up and broke into 'Tea for Two' and 'If You Were the Only Girl in the World'. The thirty-five sick Indian prisoners who had been isolated since January, 'very gallant gentlemen' who had been locked up all day without food, were released and 'marched in proudly'.

Sgt Dave Topping knew they would all be going home when he heard the bugle ring out triumphantly.

'Fall in A, fall in B, fall in every company.' Their own call. No more tin-pot Nipponese calls.

'And we knew that was it. Nobody had to tell us another word. We knew the war was over . . . We'd won.'[2]

They shouted, cheered, wept unashamedly. Weary, Meldrum and Fyfe organised the 'pickets . . . out on the bund . . . Extraordinarily good behaviour by all'.

The IJA had handed over responsibility for all internal administration and agreed to release all the Red Cross stores the following day. It was now their turn 'to run around burning papers' in a bonfire which lasted for hours.[3]

Singing and cheering resounded through the camp until 'Lights Out' at one minute to midnight. But the sweetest sound of all was their own 'All Clear', 'Last Post' and 'Reveille'. It was 'an incident-free night', but Weary had 'pract[ically] no sleep . . . mind in a whirl anyway.'

Next morning, the entire camp turned out for a thanksgiving service at eleven o'clock and listened happily to speeches from Coates, Malcolm, Larsen, the Indian, Dr Aziz, and Weary.

Weary went with Coates, Malcolm and Larsen to the Japanese hospital area, where they offered to help with the gravely sick patients sent down from Burma and abandoned in the Japanese lines. It was declined. They also sought rifles, revolvers and ammunition for the camp police. Weary was not surprised when these were refused. Yanagida did not comment when Coates informed him that they needed transport and intended calling on the local Thai officials in order to arrange credit, food more appetising than the usual rice, dried fish and dried vegetables in the IJA stores, and to establish contact with the outside world.

It was an extraordinary feeling to be free. Weary 'felt like a King'. He walked into the township of Nakom Patom with Coates, Vardy, Malcolm, Larsen, CSM Andrews, the Dutch interpreter and the canteen buyer. They needed fresh meat, vegetables, fruit, eggs, but Hashimoto, the Japanese trader, was not co-operative. It seemed that an approach to the Thai district governor might yield better results. As boisterous and elated as schoolboys on an outing, they appropriated a Japanese ration lorry and drove to the governor's house a few kilometres on the other side of town, where they found him with the assistant governor.

Civilly, but not 'over-enthusiastically', they were taken into the council chamber. Even with the interpreter's help, the Thais' understanding of the group's needs seemed slight. Eventually, the governor suggested that a Thai-Chinese trader called Vassana, who had also supplied the camp, would be suitable and he could arrange credit with him for any foodstuffs they needed. A butcher would provide meat.

A request for petrol and a car was refused; even bicycles were difficult – one cost the enormous sum of 3000 ticals – so they rolled merrily back to town, the lorry having just enough petrol in its tank to take them there. 'Vassana was interviewed, our difficulties explained, our requests made known, and all our troubles vanished.'[4] He spread coffee and bananas before them.

Wherever they went, 'friendly Chinese' and Thais lavished 'V for victory [signs], thumb-upping and backslapping heartiness'. Fruit and vegetables were piled in the market in a succulent abundance Weary had not seen since Bandoeng. After a diversion to the temple – he enjoyed being a tourist again – and a visit to Clarke, an elderly missionary who had acted as a conduit for funds from the civilian internees' camp and whose son was in the RAMC, they were escorted by Vassana to a hotel restaurant.

It was a 'free binge with news and beer!' Only Lieut-Colonel Malcom settled for Orange Crush: for everyone else 'the nightly dream over three and a half years became a reality'.[5]

When they rode back to camp on five borrowed bicycles, they were met by the Thai official who had seen them earlier. The IJA had forbidden him to help with their arrangements. 'Flutter of changy, changy – new instructions and we are now under their "safe keeping" and they will arange our supplies . . . We treating them pretty stiffly but agreeing to their proposition as reasonable.' After all, the Japanese were still armed and, until Allied forces took over, still in charge.

Fyfe met Weary with the unwelcome information that ten men had eluded the picket, slipped into town, and were now secured in the camp detention centre in a 'state of blind paralysis'. 'All AIF except one. Hell!'

He recruited Maj. Hazelton and F/O MacDonald to his band so that he would have more time to deal with the camp finances and canteen and whatever else Coates might require. 'Canteen dinner . . . More iced beer!' Vardy spoke for all of them when he said it was 'nectar'.

'Nips looking at us with faces like hams – bad winners, bad players & bad losers.' Weary's diary was now legitimate, but there was little time for contemplation, less for writing. 'Again no sleep tonight to speak of.'

He tightened the picket on 18 August. Pay arrived but was withheld from the troops for twenty-four hours to allow time for the canteen to be stocked up and prevent 'money [being] . . . used in undesirable contacts' outside the camp. In other words, drink and women.

'Much attention to orders but fitting in some operating.' Two appendicectomies were his last operations in a prison camp.

The faithful Staff Sgt Gibson, 'Gibbie', had taken over most of the surgical block organisation. Weary's final entry in the diaries was dated 18 August: he no longer felt any need to record what was happening to them.

Indeed, no one seemed to know what was happening. They had seen no Allied authorities, nor did they hear anything from Bangkok until 20 August, when Maj. de Soldenoff of the RAMC appeared and called the medical officers to a conference. A headquarters was being set up in Bangkok.

Men had begun to arrive from other camps. Packages of tinned food, clothing and drugs were dropped by the US Air Force: not all landed on target – some plummeted into the swamp alongside the camp and had to be fished out.

Weary saw all his patients on the twentieth, entering his usual meticulous case notes, particularly about the ileostomies. These were the last of his medical records, kept under 'great difficulty' since Tarsau. Earlier case notes in the construction camps were written up intermittently and slipped into the diaries. At Chungkai, Tamuang and Nakom Patom, he had found it possible to keep them more systematically in a series of exercise books and on sheets of paper. He warned everyone to begin writing their reports immediately, before moves from the camp began, for these would be required in Bangkok.

McEachern, technically the senior Allied combatant POW officer, was already there, setting up Allied POW Headquarters.[6] He sent Coates a pass; and on 23 August, Coates took Vardy, Larsen and MacFarlane and drove to meet him in his temporary base at Japanese Headquarters.

On 24 August, Vardy returned to Nakom Patom with a message for Weary: he had been appointed Medical Staff Officer for the British and Australian troops and was to report immediately to Bangkok.

Next morning, Weary was wondering how he would get there when a Japanese admiral drove into the camp. Without hesitation, Weary 'commandeered the car and . . . the Japanese driver, kicking out the admiral and the captain'. Butterworth installed himself in the front passenger seat. It looked like being an interesting way to spend his birthday. They both enjoyed watching the admiral and his aide 'bow profoundly' as they drove off.

Weary's exultation was short lived. The bridge was down and, while he was negotiating with the Thai who operated the vehicle ferry, a loud honking prompted him to jump quickly to one side as an IJA lorry drove straight on board. A Japanese officer was sitting with his warrant officer in the cab alongside the driver. 'I suddenly got a rush of blood to the head, to think that these blooming rascals who had been kicking us around all these years . . . assumed the right to drive onto the ferry when we were talking to the Thai ferryman.'

He leaped onto the ferry, dashed up to the lorry, grabbed the little Japanese officer by his tunic, dragged him out of the cab and was about to heave him into the river when he became aware that around forty rifles were trained on his back. ' . . . So I decided to accept his apology and cigarettes.'

By then, the ferry was halfway across the river. He had no choice but to accompany them to the other side then return with the ferryman to pick up his car. Eventually, they were bowling through the paddy and across flat, open country towards Bangkok.

They arrived at dusk. Bangkok sprawled haphazardly along the banks of the Chao Phraya River. Thais squatted by their cooking pots in the flaring yellow lamplight and other figures moved in the shadows. Weary sniffed air fragrant with the scent of charcoal fires, and then wrinkled his nose at the familiar stench of sewage, partially masked by the smoky tang. Next day, he traced it to the *klongs* which criss-crossed the city and ran down to the river, the local people's alternative highways to the churned up mud of the roads. Bombing had damaged the water supply and the sewers; electricity was fitful and its restoration subject to curious, Thai reasons. The Government had collaborated with the Japanese; yet large numbers of the army and the police were said to be part of the Free Siamese movement and had worked with the underground.

They found their way through narrow streets to a bombed building in Tha Prakan. It was now dark and the building appeared to be pretty well deserted. There was no electricity, no food, beds but no bedding. He dispatched Butterworth for lamps, food and beer and went in search of Coates. After knocking on a few doors, Blue bought some kerosene lamps from a rice agent's wife (she threw in for good measure a bottle of wine she had been keeping for peacetime) and was given rations and cigarettes by an English officer in the building. 'The first night was lousy.'[7] They dossed down under their mosquito nets with the bugs, lice and rats.

Next morning, Blue procured two 'Mills bombs' of DDT, pulled the pins, hurriedly shut the door and amused himself elsewhere for the morning. 'When I went back you could shovel them out.' The other nights were comparatively bug free.

Weary located Coates at Allied HQ, which was now in the American Legation building in Sathorn Road. Coates had been attached as Senior Medical Liaison Officer, but he was keen to return to Nakom Patom now that he had acquired a load of medical stores and a vehicle. He handed over to Weary and drove off.

To his great delight, Weary found Ferguson Warren at HQ with another British officer, Lieut-Colonel Douglas Clague. Weary's and Clague's liking for each other was immediate.

'Dougie' Clague had parachuted into a camp in the Thai jungle some time before the end of the war to co-ordinate the members of E group who had been dropped in to organise the Thai resistance 'with these little motor cycles . . . crazy stuff'. When the prospect of an Allied invasion ceased to exist after the bombing of Hiroshima and Nagasaki and the Japanese surrender, they prepared to help, if they could, the prisoners-of-war in the event of the anticipated massacre.

Ferguson Warren he had not seen since mid-1944. It was a happy reunion. That night the three of them went on a binge.

Ever after, Clague and Weary vied at drinking each other under the table. Usually, Weary won. Some weeks later, after one night of furious drinking around the Bangkok bars, he put Dougie to bed and staggered back to HQ. He woke up the following morning, very early and extremely uncomfortable, to find himself bedded down on top of his overflowing in, out and pending trays.

As Force Commander, Clague set up RAPWI (Repatriation of Allied Prisoners of War and Internees), and opened his Advanced Head-quarters on the other side of town in the Tha Prakan building on

Rajavith Road. Medical HQ moved there also. Weary's information about his billet had been correct; it was only that Butterworth and he had arrived two days too early.

RAPWI's headquarters was in Rangoon with General Sir William Slim's ALFSEA headquarters, and the ground rules for evacuating the prisoners of war had been laid down in a fat document dated two days before Emperor Hirohito told the world that the war in the East was over.

Weary was 'amazed at the order which prevailed'. Every detail of 'the treatment and disposal of Recovered Allied Prisoners of War and Civil Internees . . . to their evacuation to India, or their evacuation to country of domicile' had been considered.[8] Clague swung smoothly into action. Coates had already appointed his basic medical staff and made a number of decisions. All prisoners-of-war in camps west of Bangkok were to be evacuated to Rangoon; and the sick west of the bombed bridge over the Mae Klong were to remain in Nakom Patom, where men from other camps would be evacuated, while the more seriously ill in camps east of the bridge were to be admitted to the Red Cross hospital in Bangkok. Weary was to organise the beds.

With de Soldenoff, Weary visited Chulalongkorn Hospital, but the only accommodation reluctantly offered to them was in a run-down and dirty annexe. Coates was furious when he returned on the twenty-seventh; he rang a friend in Twelfth Army and it was fixed in no time.

Next morning, when Weary called on the director of the hospital, they were given a fully-equipped modern block plus three rather inferior wards in a building recently vacated by Thai soldiers. Jack Marsh, now in charge of Welfare at headquarters, promised to procure mattresses, linen, pillows, bedpans, books and all manner of comforts for the expected patients.

Vardy was summoned to take over the day-to-day organisation of the hospital. Weary promised him plenty of Japanese labour to clean up the buildings and grounds and dig latrines. He enjoyed turning the tables on their former captors and requisitioned 600 Japanese soldiers for manual work. (Vardy had expected thirty.)

The RAPWI medical organisation in the persons of Brigadier Wiles and Lieut-Colonel Mackworth flew in from Rangoon on 28 August with 'urgently needed medical stores, comforts and Jeeps for delivery'. Weary was impressed by the 'energy and drive' of the two officers, who pitched in to help transfer the stores.[9]

Mackworth gathered up some of these and left for Nakom Patom with Coates almost immediately to assess the medical situation. By now, Coates was shuttling between points in a V8 prominently marked with the Red Cross and newly acquired from Dr Akouda of the Japanese Medical Corps. Weary had sought out Akouda before Coates returned to Bangkok, arranged daily liaison meetings and collected from him a typewriter and promises of transport. The first ambulance was delivered on 29 August.

Helen was waiting for word. The last card she had received from Weary was dated 10 June 1944, but there had been other news that he was still alive. A woman at Broken Hill had taken down a message from a Tokyo broadcast; in June 1945, a Dutch sergeant whom the Americans had released from Manila in February had called to give her news, but she was out. Tossie poured him tea and retailed his report of Weary's skin-grafting and surgical activities in Chungkai to Helen when she came home.[10] A month later, Helen wrote to Alice that she had 'received two letters from Red Cross recently with news that Weary was seen alive and well' in September 1944 by an English army officer.[11] The three cards and a couple of stilted, typewritten letters, forwarded through the Red Cross and kept in her drawer, were now dog-eared with handling.

She had filled the war years with her degree, with work on penicillin production in the Commonwealth Serum Laboratories at Royal Park, with knitting, lunch, bridge, tennis at Royal South Yarra with her new friend 'Peggles' Gibson, golf and holidays and outings with her parents. She was a dutiful daughter.

An American officer had pursued her; a colleague at CSL was interested; but she had kept everyone at arm's length.

'Peace at last' wrote Helen to James and Alice when she heard 'the momentous news . . . officially confirmed' that the Japanese had accepted the terms of the Potsdam Declaration on 12 August.[12] That night, the telephone rang almost continuously; but no one had any idea whether Weary was alive or dead. 'I still feel that [he] must be well & that nothing alarming can have happened in the past 12 months . . . '[13] Each evening she replied to numbers of letters and cards from friends and acquaintances.

Lieut-Colonel John Williams of the 2/2nd Pioneer Battalion returned. When Weary saw Williams in Bangkok on 28 August and heard he was flying home to Australia, he scrawled yet another brief note in pencil in 'absolutely tearing haste' and gave it to Williams for dispatch to 605 Toorak Road. By the time Williams had slipped it into a letter box on 13 September, the post office delivery boy had already handed over the free cable RAPWI allowed all prisoners-of-war and which Weary sent on 3 September: 'Arrived safely at India hope to be home soon, writing address letters and telegrams to C/o Australian PW Reception Unit Bangalore.'

Helen rushed into the post office and lodged the free reply to which she was entitled.

In fact, he was still in Bangkok, although there had been an attempt to fly him out to hospital in India. For on 29 August, Harvey had turned up at Tha Prakan. Knowing he was coming, Weary had saved two bottles of Fosters' lager, 'keeping them suitably cold'.

That night, he greeted Harvey with a broad grin and 'How would you like a glass of Australian beer, Bill?'

Harvey's eyes 'lit up'. Seizing an army clasp knife, Weary attacked the top of the first bottle with the open blade, only to see it slip and cut most of the tendons across his thumb and the back of his wrist. A fountain of blood from the radial artery spurted over Weary, Harvey, the bottles and glasses.

Coates pounced on him, twisted a tourniquet on his arm and began to hustle him out the door, calling: 'Off to hospital, off to hospital – where's your ambulance?'

It was outside, delivered that day after his second, afternoon reconnoitre of Chulalongkorn Hospital with Brigadier Wiles to check that arrangements to receive the expected 'heavy sick' were shaping up. He had no intention of leaving all the beer to Harvey. He restrained Coates long enough to drain one large glass, before undergoing 'the indignity of getting into the ambulance'. The beer was to be the only approximation of an anaesthetic he would get.

Coates evicted all the Thai staff from an operating theatre when they arrived, fossicked around amongst the bottles, selected an ampoule of 'clear fluid' which he identified as 'probably anaesthetic' and injected it into Weary. With Weary sitting on a chair (and, since the theatre staff had been shut out, filling the rôle of assistant surgeon as well as patient), Coates found a few snub-nosed forceps and 'ghastly instruments', some very coarse cat gut ('not the sort of thing you sew tendons with') and loosened the tourniquet.

' . . . Blood spurted up and hit the light and came down in festoons, dripping . . . '

Seizing one of the pairs of forceps, he plunged towards the wrist and 'put it on [the] radial nerve'. Weary shot upwards with a scream of pain.

'Be all right in six months, all right in six months,' muttered Coates, as consolation.

Weary watched in horror as repeated stabs at his tendons with 'ghastly great needles and . . . cat gut' frayed the ends. He saw all his hopes of a future as a surgeon disappearing. But Coates was resourceful; the frayed ends of the individual tendons were impossible to sew together, so he 'speared three tendons about an inch from the end on both sides' onto one needle and, with Weary pushing up the fingers of his left hand, 'managed to tie like a parcel until the ends came together'. He 'quickly slapped some plaster on . . . and I was handed over to the Thais.' By now, it was after midnight. 'There I was – the first patient.'

Corlette appeared in Bangkok, heard the news and called at the hospital with whisky. 'My first anaesthetic.' Even so, it was an uncomfortable night with one Thai nurse working a fan and another mopping his forehead with cold towels. By morning, Weary had had enough.

He resorted to dumb show since his caretakers had no English. He signalled to one that he was thirsty and next, rubbing his tummy, dispatched the other for food. He put on his trousers – all he had been wearing when he came to hospital – hooked his legs over the window sill, jumped a couple of metres to the ground and hailed a cycle taxi.

Back at headquarters, he found the ambulance – his ambulance – stuck fast in the mud, so he joined the others in dislodging it. Coates, 'taking no notice of my disability . . . was urging me on'. The ambulance was sent on its way and Weary was about to enter the building when he ran into Coates's friend, Brigadier Keith Bush, DDMS Lines of Communication, Twelfth Army. By now Weary was pale, feeling sick and near fainting. Bush took one look at him and decided to fly him out to India with other unfit medical staff. Weary would have none of it. Plaster and all, he was staying in Bangkok. 'I've seen so much . . . with these lads that I do not feel like going ahead of any one of them.'[14]

Coates wrote to Lieut-Colonel Malcolm, now commanding Nakom Patom Hospital: 'Dunlop had an unfortunate accident last night . . . He will be hors de combat for a day or two, until the acute process is over. He has his arm in plaster, but I am sure he will get on with the job soon. Meanwhile, Vardy must carry on Dunlop's work . . . '

Weary was back at work by noon that day, firmly signing innumerable memoranda. He was organising improvised hospital trains, an exercise for which he had gained ample experience in Greece, which he aimed to have running between Kanchanaburi and Bangkok in three days. Thai labour gangs would have to push the coaches across the bombed bridges.

It was only two days since Weary had given Williams his note to Helen. 'Love darling,' it began. 'Working hard on Staff stuff at Bangkok. Quite well. Simply delirious idea seeing you soon . . . love to everyone – Edward.'[15]

On the first day of September, he was handed a bundle of cards 'withheld by the IJA for some months and years', but the immensity of his war in Asia inhibited him when he sat down to reply. 'I can't really find myself capable of telling you all about life in the past few years . . . we have seen the slimy bottom of the well of human suffering at times even though not wishing to groan about oneself . . . I have really been rather lucky, and can't complain . . . have only had about one week in bed altogether. One has to carry on . . . '[16]

No one was certain how many prisoners-of-war were alive in Thailand, although IJA Headquarters offered figures of 29 630 British, 11 334 Dutch, 4662 Australian and New Zealanders and 296 Americans. One of RAPWI's most urgent needs was for the nominal rolls of prisoners-of-war, which Clague had been ordered to send to the War Office 'at the earliest possible moment after recovery'.[17]

The Japanese had destroyed theirs, but in many camps Allied officers were able to produce the rolls they had maintained secretly. Weary had carefully kept his own unit's statistics up to date, as had Woods and Greiner, who had 'maintained most excellent records of the personnel of the working battalions'.[18]

He sent a signal to Pratchai, summoning Dave Topping to HQ with the rolls. Topping reached Weary's headquarters only to discover that the excitement of leaving had addled his wits and he had left the papers by the side of the road. No amount of searching recovered them. Topping had then to sit down and, with Brian Harrison-Lucas, reconstruct the rolls from the master rolls belonging to the British. He was mighty relieved when he typed the last name.[19]

Clague was sending out teams, each of four men, to locate the camps, disarm the Japanese and impose order. Force 136 was eager and efficient. Weary was in Clague's office one day when the radio crackled and one of his teams – a junior officer with a wireless sergeant and a couple of men – reported that they had dropped into an area with '10 000 Japanese . . . proposing to disarm'. 'Dougie snapped back, "Do not, repeat, do not, attempt disarm at this stage. Very few British troops". And the reply [was] "Too late."'

Everyone was being careful, for there were around 40 000 armed Japanese in the vicinity of Bangkok alone, but they were well disciplined and gave no trouble.

The war against starvation and disease had ended; the paper war had begun. Everyone was writing reports. Most medical officers had kept records of their camps and patients against the day of reckoning. A few, like Weary and Pemberton, carried their contraband with them; others had buried it. Varley and his 'A' Force medical officers had buried theirs in graves at Thanbyuzayat and Retpu and directions were given to the recovery party.[20] Now all these were being called in, and typists were transforming the scraps of paper, exercise books, backs of envelopes and pieces of cardboard into neat, foolscap-sized typescripts in triplicate, quadruplicate, quintuplicate.

Weary noticed Jack Chalker's name on a nominal roll of British prisoners-of-war being transferred from Nakom Patom Hospital to a Bangkok staging camp for evacuation. ' . . . Urgently wanted at Medical HQ RAPWI in connection with . . . artistic records,' wrote Weary to the commanding officer of the camp. 'Please arrange that he report to this office.'[21]

He installed Chalker in a corner of the building and told him to paint three sets of illustrations from his working sketches: one for the British, one for the Australians, one for the Dutch. With water-colour paints and flimsy paper, Chalker created an enduring sequence of paintings which takes us into the nightmare of Konyu and Hintok in 1943.

Allan Woods had already completed the photographic record. He took a camera and fifteen spools of film and busied himself in Nakom Patom, Kanchanaburi and Tamuang. Marsh had supplied the equipment on the night of the twenty-seventh and Woods was back in Nakom Patom by the afternoon of the following day. He had no exposure meter and all the film was two years out of date, but he modified the exposure times and issued detailed recommendations about their processing to Kodak Bombay.

He concentrated on men sent up from Tamuang and Nakom Patom between late June and August to Nieke and Songkurai who had arrived back at Tamuang and Kanburi on 24 August 'in a ragged, unkempt state'. Five days of rest and careful feeding had improved their appearance by the time Woods fixed them and their surroundings on film. He was disappointed by the apathy and lack of co-operation from many of the amputatees, particularly since he himself had fitted most of their prostheses, but Weary was not surprised by this.[22] Nor were the psychiatrists sent in with the medical recovery teams by RAPWI, although they found that the doctors in the camp hospitals had anticipated much of the treatment they came in to organise.

Camps all over Thailand were now receiving air drops of food, drugs and clothing in Operation Mastiff. The item at the top of the lists was often the most sought after: cigarettes, Players or Bears – 20 000 packets for a camp of 1566 men.[23] Razor blades, shaving soap and brushes, combs, mirrors, towels and safety razors rained down in great 'bricks' from the skies. With these and new, clean clothing, morale improved. Men fattened quickly on the food and vitamins.

As their condition improved, they sought women in the towns and countryside. Medical HQ took swift action. 'Do not spoil your future health and that of your families at home for the sake of a night's pleasure,' wrote Hamilton, now Australian ADMS at Tha Prakan, in a memo to be read to all patients and troops. 'Overindulgence in alcohol [and] sexual intercourse with native women' were 'medical dangers', for one usually lead to the other.[24] Weary had attended Lieut-Colonel Mackworth's briefing after his return from Nakom Patom, when it was decided to fly in a consignment of condoms and blue light outfits from Rangoon. Now they were distributed to the camps.

Ambulance trains and transport, VD prophylaxis, sick returns and personnel movements, setting up hospitals and evacuating the sick: he was back to the staff routines of the Middle East. Then, he had longed for surgery. Now, it was a relief to be free of it for a time, but 'hectic'. 'I should be skurrying [sic] home with wings on my feet,' he wrote to Helen apologetically, 'but oh Lord this is a busy life.'[25]

Nights were wild with drinking, parties, entertainment by the Thais, talking, eating. 'I just can't get over this not feeling hungry at the end of a meal . . . I'm working with some grand guys blazing with ribbons, who pay calls from the sky in hostile places and play old Hell.' He contrasted their 'young and pink and terrific' appearance with his weather-beaten prison camp skinniness and greying hair. He felt older, but was 'not admitting it and I still play sports designed for tough kids.'[26]

In his letters to Helen, he tried to overcome his reticence about the war years, warning her that he had changed. 'I've taken this war seriously like a life on its own . . . poured everything into it as though five years were one's mortal span – and everything else in life at the moment seems like a bonus or something left over.'[27]

Weary was intensely reserved about himself. He was unable to confide his anxieties about Helen and a post-war life even to Jock Clarke, who was as 'close as anyone' to him. Men could not have lived together in greater intimacy that did Weary, Woods, Wearne, Clarke, Corlette and Moon. Yet, in all Weary's 'interminable monologues', first remarked by Jock in Makasura, he never discussed his family and his earlier life in Australia. Neither did he mention his achievements at university or in London. There were no clues to his background. The information tendered to the men who buoyed him up and whom he supported in turn, centred on anecdotes about his professional life, rugby and people he had met. Anything important he locked up inside.

Don Muang Aerodrome was busy with aircraft. British medical officers were being withdrawn from the camps and evacuated to Rangoon as the Indian Army medical units arrived to relieve them. Both fit and sick men were assembled at staging camps and the airport hospital, to be flown out as soon as the RAF and RAAF signalled their readiness.

On 5 September Lady Louis Mountbatten flew in with an entourage of 'generals . . . I've met them all, but no chance to follow [them] . . . owing to pressure of business.'[28] She disembarked from her aircraft and walked straight into a group of former prisoners-of-war being evacuated. Also drawn up at the airfield was a reception committee of Thais in full court dress at the behest of the Regent of Thailand; and a RAPWI delegation including Coates, which conveyed her to an official luncheon.

Next day, Coates accompanied her to Nakom Patom in a jeep with an Australian soldier 'in slouch hat and rags' at the wheel. Ahead of them was a cavalcade of Allied and Japanese generals and other high-ranking officers.[29] Weary was back in Bangkok, organising the transfer to Chulalongkorn of arriving Indian medical personnel and tonnes of stores. Lady Louis Mountbatten heard about Lieut-Colonel Dunlop; she wished to meet him.

A dispatch rider appeared at Tha Prakan: 'compliments of Lady Mountbatten, would I please come and see her.' Weary hastily assembled his most respectable clothes and presented himself at the gates into the dazzling magnificence of the Royal Palace.

But the Thai guards were unimpressed by Lady Louis' letter and barred the way. Weary promptly swung into his 'When I have seen by Time's fell hand . . . ' act, brushed aside the rifles, strode into the courtyard and through the great doors, only to be stopped by an elderly courtier on the broad flight of stairs. After reading the letter, very politely and in impeccable English, he informed Weary that there were many royal palaces in Bangkok and he was in the wrong one.

A guard escorted him to the right one. Lady Louis had heard about his work in the camps; she also had an eye for personable men. Would Weary join her staff and 'work with her for a few days during her programme in Thailand, and . . . advise her on various matters?' He was too shy to mention that they had met at parties in London before the war with the Porritts and a few others from the St Mary's set. As an impressionable colonial, he remembered all these occasions, whereas for her, he would have been another face in the crowd.

Over the next two days, he travelled with her 'glittering bandwagon' to camps around Bangkok and east of the city. Her sympathy for the men was boundless, and they never forgot her visits and the lift it gave to their drab, uncomfortable hospital lives. They were bowled over by her good humour, her directness and her interest in them. (So was Weary.) She was the first European woman they had seen for years.

Lady Louis, in turn, found it a 'real inspiration to see what had been achieved on the medical and surgical side'[30] and was 'very forcibly' struck by the 'magnificent morale . . . [and] the high degree of discipline which the prisoners-of-war . . . maintained in the camps.'[31] She also liked Edward Dunlop. It was the beginning of a pleasant friendship.

The Australians were restless. Why were they still here? Cynically, they dubbed RAPWI 'Retain All Prisoners-of-war Indefinitely'. Coates had put Maj. W. E. Fisher in charge of evacuations at Nakom Patom and nearly all the British were on their way home. General Tyndall had spoken to many Australians when he accompanied Lady Louis to Nakom Patom. She had been distressed by what she saw. He flew to Rangoon in an attempt to fix the delays and returned to Bangkok on 8 September 'to expedite evacuation'. But even the prompting of the Supreme Commander's wife could not fix complex delays overnight: 'shortage of shipping, minefields, monsoons interfering with the movement of aircraft, Saigon sick being evacuated to Bangkok' and a bottleneck in Rangoon caused by too few hospital beds.[32]

When Lady Louis departed on 9 September, she left behind her aide and St John's Ambulance leader, Mrs Gerouard, and the nursing sister who had accompanied her, Miss Miller, with orders that they were to do what they could for the men in Nakom Patom Hospital. Everyone was very tactful and accommodation was found; but at a RAPWI meeting a fortnight later, Clague recorded in the minutes that 'E Gp/ RAPWI HQ is NOT willing to have further truck with female med personnel'.[33]

With the arrival in Bangkok of the 7 Indian Division Headquarters, their ADMS took over responsibility for all medical matters and Weary, Coates, MacFarlane, Hamilton and Larsen changed their function to an advisory liaison one on 8 September. That day, General Evans disarmed the Japanese Headquarters in Thailand.

On 12 September, a dramatic surrender ceremony took place in Singapore, where Mountbatten made the disarmed Japanese generals hand over their Samurai swords to their opposing numbers in the Allied forces in a calculated passage of humiliation.

The airstrips there were soon repaired and readied for aircraft, and groups of fit Australians began to arrive from Bangkok on the first leg of their journey. Some had already gone, flying into Singapore via Rangoon. Brig. J. E. Lloyd and the 2nd Australian Prisoner of War Reception Group were there to ease their passage home.

Weary signalled Fisher to transfer 320 lying sick from Nakom Patom to Chulalongkorn Hospital. The hospital ship *Dunera* was expected in Bangkok on 20 September. He sent trains and every ambulance and lorry he could summon to Nakom Patom and to Doi Railway Station to collect them.

The waters of Bangkok Harbour and the mouth of the Chao Phraya were strewn with mines. It took an Australian stretcher party of eight squads, the 54 Indian Field Ambulance and a casualty clearing station two days from 21 September to load the sick, for they had a two to three hour trip by motor boat out to the ship. Weary stood by Mitsibui dock and watched the lying and sitting cases transferred from ambulances and lorries. RAPWI signalled Lloyd in Singapore. They needed minesweepers, soon, in order to bring transports in.

Maj-General C. A. Calleghan had flown in on 20 September. Weary enquired about Blackburn, who had been imprisoned in Manchuria and Sian with Calleghan, and 'was immensely relieved' to hear that he was well, despite suffering 'the usual rather miserable time that one associates with these subhuman little brutes'.[34]

Now that the Japanese were disarmed, they became targets for the more unruly of the former prisoners still ranging Bangkok and eager for souvenirs, swords, orders, medals, and a crack at revenge. Lieut-General Hamada's house was burgled; Japanese complained of 'assault and robbery by Allied troops (white)'.[35]

Stray bullets clipped through the bars and street-side eating houses, for the Thais and the Chinese were also settling their differences. But General Evans fixed the blame for roughing up the Japanese squarely on former prisoners-of-war 'or on former PW who escaped and . . . are maintaining themselves by brigandage'.[36] He slapped on a curfew when two Allied POWs were severely wounded during two nights of brawling and gun battles. Everyone, Allies and Japanese, was to remain in their quarters between 7 pm and 6 am until most of the IJA left Bangkok on 23 September. Dance halls and brothels were closed. Patrols were increased.

On the morning of 24 September, Weary paraded everyone at his headquarters and read out Evans's orders. 'NO rpt NO allied personnel will enter any Japanese occupied building or dump . . . in NO . . . circumstances will individual Japanese . . . be ordered to hand over personal property . . . any officer or other rank including ex PW who disobeys these orders will be arrested and will be liable to trial by court martial.'[37] Any transgressors would be clapped into the detention centre at the Chinese Chamber of Commerce. He thought uncomfortably of the Samurai sword Butterworth had presented to him and decided not to ask any questions.

Coates flew out on the twenty-fourth, for his mother was dying. Weary handed him an airletter for Helen and a bulky envelope for Brig. Blackburn in which were copies of the nominal rolls of 'O' and 'P' battalion deaths, a neatly drawn plan of graves in Hintok cemetery and a précis of the terrible months spent 'on one of the technically most difficult bits of the Thailand Burma railway. The rations, working hours and general conditions can not be easily described, and the brutality of the Nips was simply appalling.

'That year of 1943 is just a nightmare of starvation, disease and death . . .

'Our death roll was heavy, but . . . we did ever so much better than anyone else in our area . . . I can genuinely say that the AIF outworked and outsuffered any nationality on that accursed Thailand River Kwa Noi, and . . . your lads from Java showed fortitude beyond anything I could have believed possible. I saw them flogged to work reeling with sickness, and I've carried them to the engineer lines when they could no longer stand up, to do some more work sitting down; but through that long ordeal with sick parades going on in pouring rain into the late hours of the night I hardly ever saw a man refuse to go out in another man's place, nor a man's spirit break until the time came to turn his face to the wall and die. Many of them showed an unselfishness that was truly heroic, and you can be proud to have led them . . . '[38]

Moon and Corlette were still in Thailand. An urgent signal from Weary reached them on 27 September: they must go straight to Tamuang hospital. Boon Pong had been shot late on 26 September and was lying, seriously wounded, in Kanchanaburi. Weary ordered the SMO to 'report upon the condition of Mr Boon Pong, injured Thai civilian, who has done so much for Prisoners of War' and give Moon and Corlette all 'facilities to examine Mr Boon Pong. Ex-POW Headquarters direct that they have full authority to make any arrangements in his interest.'[39]

This was part of the same trouble which was disturbing the streets of Bangkok, 'a little . . . revolution' through which Weary drove one night, 'quite amazed at the amount of shooting without anyone getting knocked'.[40] It fizzled out.

He had had no stomach for the identification parades of war criminals on 28 September. Brutal beyond understanding though most of his former captors were, yet he felt revulsion at the spectacle of men deprived of all dignity, barefoot and holding up their trousers with one hand, having to file out of their cells and along the line of their former prisoners. So many of them were small fry. And he had seen how each level treated the one below it. The Korean guards had been at the very bottom of the heap, despised by their Japanese superiors. Could he condemn a man to hanging by the neck until he was dead? He still shivered at the memory of the executions in Palestine.

In the line was Ishii. Weary grimly identified him, as well as the NCO who had broken the jaws 'of two Australian officers, one of whom was carrying a bucket of water in each hand . . . [and] failed to salute'.[41]

He suddenly saw in front of him the *kempi* officer who had supervised his torture in Tarsau, and then – surprisingly – reprieved him, saying: 'We *kempis* do but do our duty.' Weary allowed no flicker of recognition to cross his face. 'Interesting specimen that,' he said. And moved on.

Weary hated no longer. Hate had dissolved the day he moved forward to help a trainload of wounded Japanese sent back from Burma along the railway whose building had cost so much.

'I paused before a man whose wretchedness equalled the plight of one of my own men – one leg had been hacked off at the mid-thigh and the bone stump projected through gangrenous flesh; his eyes were sunken pools of pain in a haggard, toxic face. With indomitable spirit he had hopped . . . hundreds of suffering miles without care. Some bombs fell and soldiers desperately fought for a place on the moving train. I moved to help him when he was trampled under in the rush, but his hand was limp and dead, and his tortured face was at peace.

'The memory dwelt with me as a lingering nightmare and I was deeply conscious of the Buddhist belief that all men are equal in the face of suffering and death.'[42]

Nearly half a century later, he said sadly: 'They hanged . . . the wrong people.'[43]

'We are concentrated handy for the final move now and it seems very likely to be shipping direct to Australia for the greater numbers.'[44]

RAPWI was winding down. Corlette and Weary filled in an idle Sunday by going to the races on 30 September.

Two hundred fit men, including Arthur Moon, Jock Clarke, Norman Eadie and all the other medical personnel, had been at the airport staging camp from midnight on 29 September awaiting their movement order; and two transports were expected on 8 October to clear another 2500. The harbour had been swept clean of mines. 'Together with [the] air lift, this should clear the country of Australians,' suggested Weary to Ted Fisher, who was to classify the men. As for the lying sick, 'I have arranged accommodation at the Red Cross Hospital'.[45] Boon Pong's accident prompted Weary to discuss the best way of ensuring that the actions of people in the underground be recognised and the money repaid. After conferring with Bill Adams, he suggested to Lieut-Colonel Swinton, the senior UK officer at Ex POW Headquarters in Bangkok: 'In view of the number of lives saved by the organisation and the alleviation of suffering of Prisoners of War, it is hoped that not only will the Governments of the troops concerned accept responsibility for the sums involved, but that those concerned will receive some suitable reward.'[46]

They had risked their lives: Mr and Mrs Boon Pong; the Chinese canteen owner at Chungkai, Lee Soon; the missionary, Clarke; and two men who had been in the Civilian Internees Camp in Bangkok, the head of the 'V' Organisation, Peter Heath, who had been with the Borneo Company and R. D. Hempson of Anglo-Thai. Another Borneo Company employee and a Swiss citizen, Albert Tanner, was the link with the outside.

There was one final letter to write. It was to Dougie Clague.

'It is desired on behalf of the Ex POW Medical Services and as

Australians, in particular the AAMC, to express our warm-hearted appreciation of the efforts made by you and your staff on our behalf, and for the sick in this country . . . we owe you a great debt of gratitude . . . All ex POW Medical personnel cannot speak too highly of the magnificent assistance they have received . . . especially as regards supplies and comforts . . .

' . . . we take leave of you with loyalty and affection and best wishes for a bright and happy future for you all in the post-war world.'[47]

Weary signed as Medical Liaison Officer, RAPWI, and below Hamilton fixed his signature as ADMS, AIF Siam. It was not just for Dougie and his E Group that they wished a bright future – they yearned for one themselves.

Friendship with Dougie and Ferguson Warren was to endure well beyond the war. From his first contact, it had been 'an unforgettable and thrilling experience'.

In Java, he had felt like one speaking from the dead; now he was about to return to life. ' . . . Write and tell me that you are well and that you love me . . . no one could go on loving a grey ghost for 8 years – but say it.'

> She is coming my own, my sweet;
> Were it ever so airy a tread,
> My heart would hear her and beat,
> Were it earth in an earthy bed;
> My dust would hear her and beat,
> Had it lain for a century dead;
> Would start and tremble under her feet,
> And blossom in purple and red.

'I've been thinking over most of the poems I used to like in my head. Good notion when you are doing time.'[48]

Butterworth packed Weary's bags. He was leaving with less than he had brought up the line in 1943, but the valise and suitcase were still heavy with 'practically all my Java records . . . and despite the almost complete absence of paper in this country a good deal of local records'. To Parkin's diary and paintings, he had added his large pile of illustrations by Chalker and others. Butterworth stuffed the battered greatcoat with its rat-gnawed sleeve into the stained and torn valise along with the second set of clothes issued in Bangkok. The Samurai sword was safely in the boot of the car, Butterworth assured him.

They drove to Don Muang and he boarded the aircraft. Then Butterworth dashed up. He had forgotten the sword.

It could not be found. Shamefacedly, Butterworth admitted that after locking it in the boot of the car, he had fallen in with some mates and got drunk. It must have been stolen. Weary felt more comfortable. Much as he desired a Samurai sword, it would have weighed on his conscience.

The plane circled over Bangkok before turning and heading south for Singapore. Below him spread the city, the *klongs* threading their gleaming path between the crowded buildings, his favourite Temple of the Dawn on the east bank of the river, and through the centre of it all the wide, coiling path of the Chao Phraya with its great rafts of green vegetation floating down to the sea from who knew where. He never did work out where they came from. He looked for the tall *chedi* on the plains around Nakom Patom, but a thick haze blanketed anything not immediately below.

He was on the last Australian flight out of Thailand.

TWENTY-FIVE

The Return of Ulysses

THE FLIGHT TO SINGAPORE took seven hours. He was unused to the luxury of so much time for reflection, for there had been no 'rest from work for a single day in three and a half years'.[1] In any case, most contemplation had been painful, 'fragrant memories like a mist in dark, dark valleys', and incessant activity his analgesic.[2]

Helen's first letter and some 'never to be forgotten snapshots' had arrived in Bangkok on 23 September. 'Are we really going to be married?' she asked. 'Old Man Coates', an unlikely but willing Cupid flew out next day with Weary's reply.

Mephan's friend, General Bierwirth, had called on Helen on 9 September, leaving her 'completely dumbfounded' when he told her Weary was in Singapore and would probably be home on the *Duntroon*, sailing on the twenty-fifth. Only the night before 3LR had broadcast a message from a man who had seen Weary 'fit & well on arrival in India'. No one seemed to know where he was. The letters said Bangkok, but telegrams had stated variously Bangalore, Rangoon and Singapore. Everyone was confused by POW mail being sent to these centres for onward distribution.

Alice watched the letter box daily. Helen wrote to her whenever she had a fresh scrap of news. (It never occurred to her to use the telephone: she was careful with money and Benalla was a trunk call.) 'What will he say if he knows he is being featured in the womens papers?' she enquired apprehensively of James and Alice, after Lil rang and asked Helen to take a photograph into the *Women's Weekly* office at 227 Collins Street. She left them a dozen to choose from. Nobody could say what sort of article it would be, for Sydney office was organising it. 'I'm hoping for the best . . . '[3]

When Rohen Rivett returned, the *Argus* had published his praise of Weary and Coates and their work in the camps. Newspapers had reported Weary's 'selflessness and devotion', and Helen recoiled from the horror stories about conditions on the Burma–Thailand Railway which had been appearing in the press since mid-September.

Aunt Lil had Weary's room ready at The Nook. 'Day and night the dear boy is never out of my thoughts . . . '[4] He had more than fulfilled her early expectations when she impressed the importance of the Walpole heritage on her small nephew. Alice and she had comforted each other with assurances about his being 'spared for a great work', Lil suggesting in 1943 that he could be 'doing it even [then]'.[5] They never wavered in their belief that he would return.

Weary's 'first real letter' sending 'oceans of love' reassured Helen when she walked in from work on 17 September. 'I just can't get over the idea of seeing you soon.'[6] Burston had rung only three days beforehand to offer his 'felicitations'. Over the years, John Colebatch, Ron Rome and Benny Rank had sympathised with her insecurity, listened to her anxieties.[7] Of course he would return and marry her, they said. Deep down, Helen was not so sure. She unburdened herself to Peggles, more approachable than Tossie: seven and a half years was a long time. Now, she told Weary, she was 'stunned but very happy'.[8]

Coates spoke to her in early October. As far as he knew, Weary was still in Bangkok and would be there until the last of the Australians were cleared to Singapore. Her question was not answered directly in the letter Coates delivered, but it sufficed. 'You are the sort of dear, loyal, lovable person who would throw away years waiting for a lost fiancé . . . one does want to hear . . . that you can still be in love – with a ghost.'[9]

In Singapore, Brigadier John Lloyd gave him a bed at 2 Half Moon Street in 'a little outhouse' with double doors facing onto the drive. Here, Weary, Hamilton and Lieut-Colonel Charles Anderson VC spent their few days in transit.

Lloyd, Weary and the others lunched early, for Lloyd had been warned that the Supreme Commander was on his way. Mountbatten had arrived in Singapore from Rangoon and, five minutes after his aircraft touched down, Lady Louis flew in from Hong Kong. Weary and his fellow colonels declined Lloyd's invitation to greet the Mountbattens. They returned to their room, opened the doors wide and prepared to while away the sultry afternoon 'spine-bashing in our underpants'.

' . . . Suddenly all hell broke loose . . . coming up the exit drive [were] . . . several gleaming cars.' They had been expected from the opposite direction. Weary jumped up to close the doors when he heard them, 'mindful of John Lloyd's words about keeping out of the way', but Lady Louis' quick eyes spotted him. He retired hastily, 'sweating', to his bed. Scarcely had he stretched out again than a smart NCO knocked on the door. 'Compliments of the Supremo and Lady Mountbatten and will you come out and meet them.'

The cables began to arrive in Australia, thick but not so fast. Weary had been in Singapore two days before wiring Helen: 'Arrived Singapore darling very well job finished leaving by air tomorrow longing see you love precious Edward.'[10] They rang it through from Toorak Post Office two days later, on 15 October. He was already on his way when Victorian Echelon & Records told James and Alice: ' . . . VX259 Major Dunlop E. E. emplaned at Singapore on 14 October for return to Australia . . . '[11]

Helen had wanted to meet him in Sydney: 'Shall I come . . . ? For once I want to be ahead of the family . . . '[12] But he had not replied.

They landed in Borneo and slept that night in the Australian General Hospital at Labuan; then flew to Morotai in the Moluccas. Weary stepped down from the aircraft and saw, drawn up on the airfield, a well-dressed guard of Australian soldiers. As he walked down the line of men, he was 'deeply embarrassed by silent tears coursing down my face'. He slept that night in another hospital. Somewhere off the island of Biak, before landing at the American aerodrome, he glanced at his wrist. His 'prized' gold watch from Simon Artz in Port Said, which he had 'guarded ferociously' through all Okada's covetous attentions, was not there. He must have left it in the shower block at Morotai.

By 17 October he was in Townsville. He sent a telegram to James and Alice. The war had swallowed up 2159 days of his life.

They took off from Higginsfield shortly after dawn next day and arrived in Sydney before lunch. Blue was leaving him here, deaf to Weary's urging that he come with him to Melbourne, that he find a job there. Blue collected his kit, saluted and was then shaken firmly by the hand. Weary watched him walk away. In his pocket, with the extracts from Private Charlie Mould's pay book, one of the first of his unit to die, with Helen's letters and snapshots and telegrams, was a cable from Jim Yeates with his Sydney address. At every airfield, there had been messages from Bierwirth. They were all waiting for him in Melbourne. Cars were laid on. Helen would be there with Mephan and Tossie and

Aunt Lil. Panic rose inside him. He told the duty officer he had changed his mind: he would disembark in Sydney. He retrieved his kit and rang Jim Yeates at 101 Hospital, Punchbowl.

Yeates arrived in a staff car. What did he want to do? He could not say, for Yeates would not understand. He had never been a prisoner. This was the last country he wanted to be in. 'I didn't particularly envisage myself going back to Melbourne . . . the world was wide.' He wanted to return by the most indirect route possible, across Russia, across the USA, across anywhere but the eastern coast of Australia to Melbourne. He felt he 'wasn't fit to come home', that he 'needed to get civilised again'.

They lay in the sunshine on Bondi beach all that afternoon, chatting about old times, while he worried. ' . . . Am I the same person as I was when I left here eight years ago. Will it work out? . . . I had lost my nerve . . . '

He was not alone. Other men resisted the idea of returning to fiancées, wives, children, families, responsibilities and a settled existence. ' . . . They saw this world as an enemy which was going to break up this very precious condition that they had found in prison . . . they lived in packs in London and all over the place and they wouldn't go home.'[13] For they had known a brotherhood in imprisonment. They had cast away unnecessary, material things and reduced their needs to the simplest. They 'lived for one another . . . beyond money . . . [valuing] life for life's sake'.[14] Food, sleep, friendship deeper than most had ever known, a mutual dependency: now they were expected to walk off in different directions towards civilian life, spending their days and nights with people who had no conception of what they had been through. Whatever they did, from now until death, would be shared with the 'dark companion' looking over their shoulder, for 'one can't talk to people about one's war'.[15]

Weary was baffled by his ambivalence. The old saying from his childhood, the one which haunted him in London, was running through his mind once more. 'Hope deferred grows sour, like the apples in the loft'. He did not doubt that he loved Helen. ' . . . Please can we get married soon . . . I can't endure this business any longer without you . . . '[16] Yet he sensed that the jaws of the trap were about to be sprung, leaving him with too much 'unfinished business'. Could he take up where he had left off in 1939 at Hammersmith and then continue his work in the States? Or work as a surgeon in London, where Helen could join him? Dunhill was still there, Grey-Turner, Gordon-Taylor,

Porritt, Dickson Wright and other St Mary's colleagues, men – friends – with influence. He was certain they would welcome him back. Must he deny his urge for new experiences, rule off the page? He felt even more of a rover than when he had left Java. Need it be Australia?

But so many people were waiting for him, anxious 'to pour out loving kindness'. Helen had waited too long already.

Duty always triumphed with Weary. Reluctantly, he decided he must continue to run the course he had begun. Yeates drove him to the airport that night. He rang Melbourne and murmured some excuses; and a civilian was ejected from a seat. Essendon Airport at midnight was a crowd of faces. He kissed every woman in sight. Suddenly, some distance apart from the others, he saw a cool, dark-haired girl regarding him quizzically, a 'whimsical' half smile on her lips. It was Helen.

'I fainted into his arms to find him *exactly* the same, not at all grey, wonderfully well & amazingly English.'[17]

Burston had provided an army staff car to take them back to Toorak. Mephan produced whisky put away for such a day; Peggles Gibson had saved up her coupons and donated a bottle of gin, cigarettes and chocolates. She had filled Helen's room with flowers and the house with lilac and rhododendrons. Rationing had emptied everyone's cupboards. At 605, they laughed and drank and talked until half past three in the morning. Weary buried his doubts deep and enjoyed himself. Weary and Helen stayed up all night. ' . . . No sleep at all.'[18]

There was a sadness underlying his return: quietly, Helen told him that Boyd had been killed in New Guinea. Her father had broken down and 'took days to get over it – he couldn't do any work'. Both parents mourned him deeply.[19]

The wedding must be soon. Weary unfolded metres of Thai brocade from his baggage. He had lost all his money at the races with Corlette, but Blue had been flush with *baht* and readily dealt out enough for the length of heavy, pale green silk. It would make a beautiful wedding dress.

A week afer leaving Morotai, Weary's gold watch was back on his wrist. He had been enjoying a beer in the bar at the Australia Hotel one day, when he heard a voice say, 'Anyone here know a chap named Dunlop?'

One day short of three weeks after Weary's return to Melbourne, the Rev. Alan Watson married them in Toorak Presbyterian Church.

Mephan and Helen were piped out of the house and into the Church at half past three on the afternoon of Thursday, 8 November. The pews were jammed with people. Peggles heard the minister's Scots' voice telling them all what a 'memorable occasion' it was, that 'after all these years of waiting' Weary and Helen were being wed.

Weary and Helen followed Pipe Major MacLennon back down the aisle, through a sea of khaki and red tabs. Only General Blamey was missing from amongst all the friends he had on the staff. Yeates was best man; Blue had arrived to look after 'the chief', to smarten him up and brush him down. Guests had poured in from all the eastern states.

The Fergusons held strong opinions about Roman Catholics, divorce, and scandal. When Mephan saw Blamey's name on the guest list, he insisted that Weary tell him that he could come neither to the wedding nor to the reception. Weary was embarrassed, but he accepted his future father-in-law's ruling. He rang Tom Blamey.

Blamey held that his private life was no one's concern but his. Mephan Ferguson disagreed. The scandal over Blamey when he was Chief of Police, his reputation for womanising and patronising various brothels in the town, his second marriage to Olga: one of these alone would bar him from the Ferguson household. All three put him completely beyond the pale.

Helen stood in the hall in front of the fireplace, 'in another world',[20] the shimmering brocade falling in heavy folds to her feet in their matching shoes, and welcomed the guests streaming in through the glass-paned doors. She was laughing and animated, as many had never seen her before. Weary loomed over her, thin and eager-eyed, his wrist out of plaster, ulcer dressings invisible. Over four hundred people turned up. They filled the vast space downstairs, the ballroom upstairs and spilled out onto the lawns behind the high cypress hedges on that soft, warm, summer's night. Peggles was amazed. 'Weary lost control . . . [said] I'm getting married, come along . . . I don't know how they coped with the catering.'

Weary narrowly escaped having a punch-up with the piper. MacLennon and he sat on the steps outside the house, arguing over their whisky about the Dunlops. 'Thieves and reevers,' insisted MacLennon belligerently. And no-good Lowlanders, to boot. Weary was highly amused, but would not allow the highlander to get away with it. Slowly, it dawned on MacLennon that there was something familiar about the man beside him. 'Ye wouldn't be the bridegroom, by any chance?'

Peggles played waltzes in the ballroom for hours until a crowd of former POWs gathered her up and took her off to St Kilda for a meal. She came back very late but in time to see Weary and Helen leave for the Windsor Hotel. Weary had been enjoying himself far too much to leave early. Wartime conditions still applied: had it not been for Norman Rouse, an ex-POW friend from interstate lending them his room, they would have had to spend their wedding night in someone's house.

It was almost daylight when they reached the Windsor, accompanied by a rowdy crowd of former prisoners. Helen was beside herself with exhaustion by now.

They fled to Olinda in the Dandenongs very late that day, arriving about midnight at a weekend house belonging to a family friend with a complex about security. They located the vast bunch of keys in an old converted tram used for storage in the garden. But every room was locked, as were all the cupboards. They had to unlock every door in the house before they found the switchboard, the sitting room, a bedroom with twin beds and worked out which key unlocked the linen cupboard. Weary had had enough. He made up a bed on the floor, lit the fire and they camped in one room. Helen was 'bemused' by Weary. It was an idyllic time. 'I made love to her all over the garden.'

Weary had twenty-seven days to enjoy his honeymoon. It was interrupted by a letter from the deputy editor of the *British Medical Journal*. He had heard of the work Weary had done in the camps on the Burma–Thailand Railway from some British medical colleagues who had been there. Charles Littlejohn, visiting England, had suggested that the *BMJ* commission something from Weary and and had given Clegg the Melbourne address: could he be persuaded 'to put on record the peculiar experiences of [him] and his colleagues' for the journal? He apologised for interrupting his honeymoon – but might it be finished and in London before December?

Hard on its heels came another: the *Medical Journal of Australia* planned seven 'original articles' on prisoner-of-war related medicine: Colonel Coates had suggested he might prepare one on 'Clinical Lessons from Prisoner of War Hospitals in the Far East'.[21] Marsden, Cotter Harvey, Rose, Stening and Fagan had also been approached. Could he etc. etc.

He retrieved his clinical notes and reports and unpacked the illustrations. Both articles were written before they returned to Melbourne.

Married life began in Marne Street, South Yarra. The flat was let furnished and the landlady insisted that they take it exactly as it was. Reluctantly, she moved a large Buddha off the mantle shelf: Weary 'had had a tummy full of Buddhas'. On 10 December, he began working at Army Headquarters in St Kilda Road with Brigadier Blackburn as ADMS to Blackforce. He was clearing up the business he had begun in Bangkok, 'trying to get some justice for prisoners of war'.

'My hope was that we might have some special consideration [for] all these fellows that contributed above their rank.' Many men working under him had performed duties outside their usual responsibilities, particularly when the combatant officers were removed from Nakom Patom in January 1945. Austin Fyfe and other warrant officers and NCOs had been put in charge of large numbers of men. And throughout their time in Thailand, in the absence of nurses, the nursing orderlies of the 2/2nd CCS willingly undertook tasks far beyond what would usually be expected of them in a casualty clearing station.

Weary had promoted a number of people in Thailand and he hoped to make these promotions stick, but once he was back in Melbourne he ran into trouble. Blackburn, with the powers of a Commander of a Force, 'had a right to say what awards and promotions' he wanted promulgated. But he was a modest man, and tired after his war. Instead, he put them up as recommendations to the 8th Division. Weary went to see Blamey several times to discuss the matter. Blamey had until 31 January to wind up his affairs in the army. 'They wanted to give old Tom a £10 suit and shove him out as quickly as possible.'

He sat across the desk from the general, whose blue eyes were more amiable than they had been in Greece. 'If you can induce 8th Division to give me some recommendations before I go out . . . you will get everything you ask for. But if they stay on . . . shovelling around among themselves, they won't get anything.' Chifley's Labor Government was in power; the Rt Hon. F. M. Forde was Minister for the Army. They encouraged Australians to look forward to a future without war, rather than ponder the sacrifices of the past six years, and this attitude carried over into the treatment of returning men.[22]

Galleghan still smarted at the memory of Weary's memoranda and he had aired his views forcefully. 'You can imagine what happened with the 8th Division after [my] quarrelling fiercely with Black Jack.' None of his promotions went through.

Blackburn was not successful either. A letter from him, unstinting in its praise 'for the magnificent work which you . . . did in looking after the POWs' had greeted Weary on his return. 'I have heard [of it] from dozens and dozens of men . . . Americans, British, Dutch & Australians and in all places from Calcutta & Colombo back to Australia . . . '

He and 'everyone who knew you or had seen the work you did in the early days in Java knew that you would work on unceasingly and in spite of any difficulties . . . looking after the sick and trying generally to alleviate the conditions of the P.O.Ws'.[23] It was another year before Weary discovered Blackburn's intentions.

After a short time, Helen and Weary moved to 66 Walsh Street and their own furniture. Victoria Barracks was an easy journey on the Number 8 tram. Helen was happily cooking, keeping house, playing tennis and bridge, and entertaining.

In his waking hours, Weary was loving, attentive, ardent, making up for all the years they had been apart. But Helen quickly discovered that former prisoners-of-war make unquiet bedfellows. Beds and bedclothes 'engulfed' and 'stifled' him, mattresses and pillows were too soft, and often he finished the night sleeping on the floor. He continued to fight his war in his subconscious, for the inner turmoil which Jock Clarke saw in the camps continued. That streak of violence which the Walpoles share and that once found its outlet in the ring and on the rugby field had been submerged in caring for the men under his command, fuelling his struggle to help them survive. Now the frenzy of his dreams terrified Helen, for he would kick and lash out, and she feared going back to sleep. One night she awoke to find his hands round her throat.

Weary was deeply distressed at frightening her, but it was beyond his control. She knew enough psychology to understand the cause, but was unable to talk of it to anyone else. Much later, she heard other wives speak of similar experiences.

Weary was not a man for confidences, and Helen was too reserved to seek them, but he gradually opened up about the years in Thailand. His ulcers were unhealed and, for six months, changing the dressings was a daily routine. Malaria was under control but the aftermath of dysentery troubled him, and neurological damage affected his sense of place in the dark. Putting on his pants demanded a conscious effort, with his back against a wall, for his balance was affected. Even getting out of a car caused some hesitation: his legs would tremble as he concentrated on swinging them over. The effects of beri beri, pellagra and prolonged vitamin B deficiency were lasting, but he never allowed them to bother him. He worried more about the stiffness in his left wrist and how it would affect his surgical activity.

He was a doctor, a healer, and he dealt with his problems in his own way, scorning drugs or psychiatrists: he threw himself at his work.

Weary presented himself for his final medical board on 16 January. 'Disgusted' by the perfunctory examinations of returning prisoners, he had a bet that he could go through his board in fifteen minutes. He was cynical about 'the way . . . fellows went out marked fit A1 . . . a stone below weight . . . still suffering from malaria or dysentery, all sorts of complaints'; he had seen in Bangkok how quickly a group of debilitated men could 'start looking human again' once they were being well fed. His weight had returned to ninety-eight kilos from its low point in Thailand of sixty-three.

He knew how to bend medical boards to his will: setting them up had been one of his staff jobs in Palestine. He refused a pension, distracted them with talk of stiffness in his wrist and thumb, and won the bet.

The Ranks, the Colebatches, the Boltons and the Dunlops formed an easy group of not-so-young marrieds, although the Ranks and the Colebatches had children and Rank was well established in his career as a plastic surgeon. Like Weary, John Bolton had been a prisoner, but in Germany.

The first time Benny and Barbara Rank invited Weary and Helen to spend an evening with them, Rank listened to Weary and thought of what he had been through. 'I remember thinking, this must look stupid to you. Here's me, living like this . . . doing my elected work for six years and getting an enormous experience. It was a complete contrast . . . [but] he's a chap who never had any malice . . . no jealousy.'[24] Weary had no capital apart from his accumulated war service pay and gratuity. Once he was demobilised, he would be dependent entirely on surgery. And, as Rank pointed out, 'he hadn't been in practice'; he could claim only post-graduate work. He was 38 years of age.

Weary was demobilised on 2 February 1946. He retired as a half-colonel, with £1377 6s 8d to add to his bank account, worrying about how he would support a wife. He appealed to Peggles. How should he set up in practice?

George Swinbourne had been back from the Middle East since 1942 and was now well established as an ear, nose and throat specialist at the Royal Melbourne, with rooms at 85 Spring Street. They shared a background in the Wangaratta district and he offered Weary a place in

his rooms. By 15 February he was installed. The brass plate went up:
E. E. Dunlop MS, FRCS (Eng.).

Four nights after he left the army, he read his article to the Victorian
Branch of the British Medical Association: 'Clinical Lessons from
Prisoner of War Hospitals in the Far East'. Coates and he illustrated
their talks with Chalker's and Meninsky's illustrations and the audience,
including Colonel Allan Walker, the official medical historian, listened
in horrified fascination.

The illustrations were what Walker needed for the Burma–Siam
Railway section of the medical history. Topping came down from
Brisbane to help Weary sort his papers, and Weary passed them over
to Walker. ' . . . While working on the staff in Bangkok I gained a fairly
good idea of all Burma Siam records and know where most of
[them] . . . have got to.'[25] A good number were in the battered suitcase
in Walsh Street.

Older colleagues were generous to doctors returning from the prison
camps. Brigadier Johnston spoke openly of his admiration for the
younger man: 'all of us in the [A]AMC regard you as one of our great
figures – not only of the AMC but of the AIF'. He had not forgotten
'the hectic days in Greece, when you did so much for us', either.[26] Coates
was back at the Royal Melbourne as an Honorary Surgeon to In-
Patients, operating, giving press interviews and already playing a
dominant role on committees. Weary called on him, also on Sir Alan
Newton and Bill Hailes.

But not everyone was welcoming. Animosity from some who had not
been away at the war startled him. And there were others who had and
who were outspoken in their criticism. They resented the attention he
had attracted in the press and the praise from men such as Johnston,
Adey, Burston and Littlejohn.

He was astonished: almost all of it had occurred before he set foot
in Australia and it had come to him as a complete surprise. There had
been ample publicity about Weary, first when Coates returned and
spoke of his work, but mainly from the ordinary returned prisoners,
other ranks, who told everyone who would listen of their regard. The
Women's Weekly article had appeared on the news stands the day after
he touched down in Melbourne, and spread stories about Corlette and
Weary through every town and country district in Australia.

His British colleagues were vastly more generous. Some hours of his
honeymoon had been spent writing to London hospital acquaintances
for references. Arnold K. Henry's glowing tribute to his former

assistant's 'enlightened solid excellence . . . endowed with a humanity and width of outlook' reached him in early December. He hoped that the Board of the Royal Melbourne would not feel inclined to slash him down when they read Henry's opinion of him: 'a type that Cecil Rhodes would choose.'[27] Lord Moran's, Sir Thomas Dunhill's, Sir Gordon Gordon-Taylor's and Arthur Porritt's letters and testimonials reached him in the New Year. Weary felt that he was the only one who lacked confidence in his ability to 'pull the job off'.[28]

Dunhill wrote again to congratulate him on his paper in the late-January issue of the *British Medical Journal* and tell him of the regard in which he was held by medical officers in the UK. But the sweetest praise came at the end of a later letter from his influential mentor. 'You have indeed . . . done a very wonderful job of work – I should think unparalleled in history.'[29]

Weary was appointed Honorary Surgeon to Out-Patients at the Royal Melbourne in 1946, the first new appointment after the war. Difficulties arose immediately. His corresponding Surgeon to In-Patients, Julian Orm Smith, refused to give him beds in his ward, although grace and tradition entitled him to two. He dismissed Weary with harsh words about his jungle surgery. It was not a happy beginning to professional life.

Hailes provided an alternative. ' . . . Come and work with me.' A decade after leaving Hailes at the end of his junior resident's year, he was once more on the team.

Sir Alan Newton also rallied round. Probably 'the most authoritative surgeon in Melbourne', he gave Weary many of his private patients. In doing so, he exposed Weary to the lasting 'enmity' of Henry Searby. Searby was well established, ten years Weary's senior, with his own rooms in the six-storeyed building at 14 Parliament Place which he had built. It was the best medical address in town. Weary felt that he expected to inherit Newton's cases, for he had been his registrar and would be 'aggrieved', but Newton was adamant.

He was out of uniform at last and back 'on the tools'.

PART FOUR

1945 – 1967

'I cannot rest from travel: I will drink
Life to the lees: all times I have enjoy'd
Greatly, have suffer'd greatly, both with those
That loved me, and alone . . .
I am become a name;
For always roaming with a hungry heart . . .'

– *Ulysses*, ALFRED LORD TENNYSON

TWENTY-SIX

Reclaiming the Lost Years

HAILES WAS A GENEROUS MAN and a 'magnificent' friend. Weary kept his rooms in Spring Street for some months into 1946, but attended to Hailes's patients in the latter's rooms at 14 Parliament Place. He was embarrassed that, for the three years he took his cases, 'Allan [Hailes] wouldn't let me give him any of the money that I earned from seeing' his patients. His usual fee in 1947 for assisting Hailes at an operation was three guineas. He never refused Hailes, moving his own patients in order to accommodate the senior man, both at the Royal Melbourne and in the private hospitals.

By 1947, he had moved into G. R. A. (Bob) Syme's suite of rooms on the fourth floor of 14 Parliament Place. He was not short of routine, bread-and-butter jobs. In the first few difficult years, Ray Shatin loyally referred many of his patients to Weary, mainly appendicectomies, varicose veins, gall bladders and hernias, and often assisted him as well. In turn, Weary assisted Hailes and Syme with more challenging procedures: thyroidectomies, gastrectomies, mastectomies and other cancers. Thyroid surgery he had experienced frequently in London with Dunhill, abdominal and oesophageal surgery had been his lot with Grey-Turner and Henry, and at the Brompton Chest Hospital he had observed numerous thoracic procedures.

When Hailes retired, Weary became Syme's corresponding Surgeon to Out-Patients. At first, he spent Monday afternoons and Thursday mornings in the out-patients' clinic of the Royal Melbourne, trying to stem the tide of sick that thronged the waiting rooms and on Friday afternoons, he operated.

Each week, he faced 'up to 80 outpatients, with [only] one or two junior assistants, no secretary, letters hand-written, 6-10 minor procedures in OP theatre, and the hungry students to teach'.[1] One night a week and two weekends a month, he was rostered for emergency work. 'The hospital was always full . . . emergency surgery commonly went all night', with eight to ten operations. They would be exhausted. Rowan Webb was a registrar when first he assisted Weary. He used to remove the cigarette from Weary's mouth when he dropped off to sleep between cases.[2]

Mostly, Dr Gordon Stanton and Dr Gandevia gave the anaesthetics for his private patients; after a couple of years, Stanton was preferred above all others and their partnership continued until 1972.

After a year in practice, his diary was crammed with appointments, for as well as Hailes's cases, a large number of patients were referred to him by Sir Alan. Weekends, he saw Hailes's and Sir Alan's as well as his own, and this routine ended only with Hailes's death in January 1949 and Sir Alan's retirement some months before his death that August. It was 1951 before he dared take more than a week's holiday.

Humdrum cases which paid the rent and expenses were no substitute for the kind of life he had led for six years: he needed to exorcise his war with something more exciting.

' . . . I was always looking out for new things.' Very quickly, he gained a reputation for taking on operations which others would not attempt. He embarked on a course as an 'heroic' surgeon, striking out in the tradition of Edgar King and his pioneering work in gastro-oesophageal cancer surgery, and also focusing on the bowel.

Alf Nathan, the first of the young 'modern-trained anaesthetists in Melbourne' and later a partner in Stanton's practice, began work with Weary in 1949 when he was a registrar at the Royal Melbourne. He called Weary's complex procedures 'pandoodlectomies. To him, no patient was inoperable.'[3] Robert Dickens, another of his residents who became a 'favoured son', saw him as 'a surgeon of last resort'.[4]

Nathan noticed that once the patient was under the anaesthetic, every atom of Weary's concentration was on the case, not the patient: he was 'determined to get that cancer out'. But outside the theatre, to the patient or their families, his empathy with them was unquestionable. 'He would sit by their beds . . . talking to them . . . and they worshipped him.' They believed that with his skills and his indomitable will he 'fought their cancer for them'.[5] One man, dying of cancer of the throat, told of the great comfort he derived from waking at frequent intervals during some long and troubled nights to find Weary sitting silently at his bedside.[6]

Coates commented on Weary's ability to carry over into civilian life the compassion which had been so evident to the men on the railway.

None knew better than he how difficult this was to maintain in the face of years of relentless suffering.

Nancy Murphy has never forgotten how, as a young woman pronounced 'incurable', with an 'inoperable' malignant tumour, her doctor suggested that hope might lie in the hands of a Mr Dunlop. Weary listened to her medical history – the hospital where she had spent the past two years refused to release her records – and suggested that, 'if she was half as bad as she said, he would attempt an operation'. He gave her six months to live if no one operated. But she would have a chance, if he used streptomycin, which he had to have flown in from the United States.*

By now, she was the youngest patient in the Austin Hospital for Incurables. The operation in January 1950 was entirely successful. Grey-Turner's maxim, 'The abyss is worth a leap however wide, if life, sweet life, lies on the other side', had worked for Weary and for Mrs Murphy. Thirty-nine years later, she sought him out at an RSL luncheon and asked for her story to be put on record.[7]

Diagnostic aids such as CT scans are routine today; when Weary began work again after the war, he might not know what he was going to find until he opened up the patient. He was famous with his residents for announcing 'We will make an indeterminate . . . incision', implying that he was 'not sure whether . . . to go up to the top of the stomach or down to [its] bottom'.[8] It could be extended in either direction.

Once, at the Royal Melbourne, Weary was in the middle of a complicated operation on an acute obstructive bowel condition. While removing a length of cancerous bowel, he noticed 'gall stones . . . and a cricket ball lump in the liver. So I thought about this and . . . [removed] his gall bladder'. While he was excising the tumour from the liver, Hailes walked into the theatre during one of his periodic consulting visits, glanced at what Weary was doing, and said 'I see that you have so little to do with your time that you are doing perfectly useless operations'.

' . . . I groaned and admitted that I didn't think [the patient] had much future and, at that stage, fiddling around I found . . . two or three secondaries the size of cherries on the left lobe.' Weary felt even

---

* It was probably what is known as a tuberculoma, which is why he would need streptomycin.

gloomier after this, but the patient recovered, 'lived for five years and . . . died of something else'.

Almost immediately, Weary began to pay his dues to Ormond, where he tutored in pathology and surgery. Later, he attended the anatomy and pathology dpartments at Melbourne University four times a week and examined in this subject with its professor, Edgar King.

Bernard O'Brien faced Coates, King and Weary as examiners. Weary and King examined him for his Master of Surgery, and he found Weary 'fair . . . nothing rough or tough', unlike King, who astonished Weary when he decided to fail George Christie in his pathology *viva* . Christie was Senior Lecturer in King's department: Weary thought it 'the roughest thing ever'.[9]

To O'Brien, a medical student at St Vincent's Hospital in 1949–50, Weary really 'looked the part' of a consultant when he took a round at the Royal Melbourne. ' . . . He was a very impressive figure . . . he was tall and he always had a very nice suit on . . . and he had a red carnation in his buttonhole . . . He talked well . . . on oesophageal and head and neck surgery and upper gastro-intestinal surgery.'[10] Rowan Webb also found Weary in his *tenue de ville* an arresting sight, for he had patterned himself on the London consultants of his pre-war days.[11] Only his homburg, clapped on at a rakish angle like all his headgear, proclaimed the boy from Benalla.

By 1947, he was examining MB BS candidates in clinical surgery. Marking papers ate up precious and all-too-short evenings, for even on the few nights he spent at home, Helen seldom saw him before 10 pm and he was rarely in bed before 2 am.

The household ate at the normal times, and Weary's meals were kept hot for him. Bob Marshall worked as Weary's assistant surgeon at the Royal Melbourne for a year before going overseas in 1955. He once asked Helen if Weary was around. 'I think so,' she replied, 'I haven't seen him for five days, but his dinner keeps disappearing out of the hot box'.[12] (Weary was faintly embarrassed by this story and attempted to deflect it by insisting that he had told it against himself. Not so, said Marshall: it was he who had the conversation with Helen.)

Not that this behaviour was unusual for a surgeon. 'Surgery is a fairly bad matrimonial occupation' according to Donald (Scotty) Macleish. They all work long hours and most neglect their families during the early stage of their professional lives. For some, the pattern becomes fixed; others ease up when they are established. When Marshall arrived back with his English fellowship, he assisted Weary at the Melbourne and privately for another seven years. In that time, he worked seven days a week, doing all the rounds of Weary's public and private patients at the weekends – as Weary had done for Hailes and Sir Alan – and took no holidays with his wife and young family.

Helen discovered she was pregnant early in 1947. They had both been happily coasting along as a couple and the realisation that they would be parents by August took them by surprise. Weary had half hoped she might return to work at the Commonwealth Serum Laboratories, for he was guiltily aware that his long hours away from home left her with time on her hands, but Helen found marriage more interesting than penicillin or employment. They moved to a rented house at 20 Chesterfield Avenue, Malvern.

Alexander Boyd was born on 5 August 1947, Alice's birthday. It was some time before they could agree on his names, so he was referred to as 'Squeaker'; it was even longer before Weary registered the birth. Shortly after greeting his grandson, James Dunlop became seriously ill and died on 14 November.

Helen and Weary found life with the small baby very difficult. All went well while the monthly nurse presided over the nursery with easy efficiency. Her vast bosom – on which she assured Weary that she could balance four babies – caused them great amusement. But once she left, Helen was run ragged by the constant crying of the colicky baby. Peggles came to the rescue many times, after a desperate, telephoned call for help. They used to eat together, for Helen never knew at what hour Weary would walk in. Peggles often stayed the night, walking the floor with the fussing baby while Helen fell into an exhausted sleep. Weary was no use at all. ' . . . He was worn out . . . when he got home. All he wanted was a good meal and to be quiet for a while. He couldn't handle all the drama . . . and Helen was distraught.'[13]

By 1948, Alexander and Helen were more used to each other and she was managing better. Aunt Lil was impressed. 'You are a very lucky person to have such a good wife . . . the way she has tackled her domestic problems single handed is to be greatly admired, more especially as she has not been brought up to doing her own work.'[14]

Around 2 pm on Friday, 17 September, Weary was rung during an operation at the Royal Melbourne. He had been on duty all of Thursday night, and was dog tired. Mephan was ill. He had collapsed during lunch in the Savage Club and when he was stable enough, he would be driven home. ' . . . They weren't quite sure what was wrong.' Weary left his partly-trained assistant to sew up the last appendix and raced to Toorak.

John Bolton was the family physician. Mephan had ruptured his aorta. Next day, Weary operated as usual at Bethesda, then picked up Alexander and called to see his father-in-law.

He put Alexander on the floor and sat on the end of the bed. Suddenly, Alexander pulled himself to his feet and staggered towards his father and grandfather. Mephan gave a great chuckle at the sight of these first hesitant steps and fell back on the pillows.

Weary went out for a walk 'to think things out'. When he returned, Mephan was dead. Helen's younger brother, Jamie, walked back upstairs with Weary and remembers Weary closing his father's eyes. 'He put his little finger on each eyelid, and said "That's it".'[15]

When Jamie married Doreen in March 1950, the family thought the house too large for Tossie on her own. She had grown more frail since Mephan's death, but she refused to give it up. Often, Helen divided her days between Chesterfield Avenue and 605 Toorak Road.

Weary's second son, John, had been born that June and space was tight in the little house under the flowering gums. The nights were no longer peaceful, for he was no easier a baby than Alexander had been. Aunt Lil was concerned about Helen. 'She is a really lovable, lovely girl, unspoiled by the world & I am more than delighted in your choice. I do hope it won't be long before you can get suitable help for the home.'[16] She worried about her 'dearest boy', also. Only Helen, Lil and the Repatriation Department's medical officers realised that he still suffered from amoebic dysentery, varicose veins, and arthritis in his shoulders and knees. He told no one about his arrhythmia or 'soldier's heart'. Any sharp knock could cause ulcers to break out on his shins and ankles. His punishing life did not help and she was relieved to hear that he was on emetine. Lil had surprised Weary on his forty-second birthday with a 'rich cake' – and a generous cheque. She would willingly have given him more: ' . . . You have only got to say the word if you need help . . . I look upon you as a very worthy son, who has done me great credit,' but he refused.[17]

When Syme travelled to Japan for six months in 1950, at the time of the Korean War, Weary looked after all his patients as well as his own, operated for a full day at the Royal Melbourne and experienced his busiest year yet. The diary was jammed with appointments and operations.

Five years after Weary's return, he was operating all over Melbourne and in Victorian country towns: his private patients were installed in St Ives, Bethesda, Freemasons', Epworth, Vimy House, St Benedicts, the Mercy, St Andrews, Mt St Evins, Heidelberg House and Sacred Heart. Anywhere, in fact, he could obtain beds. He had rounds also in the Royal Melbourne and the Eye and Ear Hospital, calling on those patients whom he cared for in an honorary capacity.

Unlike many of his colleagues, who held on to a measure of private life, he was incapable of saying no and 'did more than his fair share of country work . . . [in fact] he would take on more [than] his fair share of any work . . . you care to mention'.[18] Frequently, his nights were spent on the road and in the theatre after responding to an appeal from a doctor in a country town, for by now Weary was driving dangerously all over the state in a large Daimler. He would jump in the car with his theatre sister and instruments at the end of the day – sometimes in the middle of the night – and return to Melbourne in the early hours next morning.* After crawling into bed for a short time, he would be back in the theatre most mornings for an operation scheduled to begin at eight o'clock. Very early, he earned the reputation of being rarely on time.

There are those who suggest that he scarcely waited to be asked, so intent on filling every hour of the day did he appear to be. It was obvious to younger surgeons working with him then that he was driven, but they could not agree on the cause. Certainly, he could not afford to lose any time. A new generation of surgeons who had graduated in the mid- to late-1940s was hard on his heels. Macleish suspected that 'he would never say "No" because he would want all doctors to ask him again . . . and he would give them the very best service he could, at a personal level'.[19] That was only part of the answer.

Hintok 1943 is the key, when he read the Sermon on the Mount in the midst of 'all the misery, the squalor, the grey rain and slush and sick and dying people'. He had never felt more useful. It was then that he was possessed by a 'marvellous, almost religious experience . . . a sort of happiness. I understood what it would mean to love your neighbour more than yourself.'

Weary believed that he did his best work in Thailand, but 'it wasn't . . . surgery. I took over demoralised masses of people and got . . . things moving and organised . . . I was more effective at organising surgery'.

'That was the best job I did.'

---

* Successful surgeons took their personal theatre sisters from hospital to hospital; everyone provided their own instruments.

He resolved to 'make [the] care and welfare' of former prisoners-of-war 'a life-long mission', part of a 'vow when he came back [in 1945], that he would never fail to answer any call that his country . . . made on him in any shape or form . . . [and] he would answer every call from his own community'.[20]

Weary had achieved the senior status of an Honorary Surgeon to In-Patients at the Royal Melbourne in August 1949 and joined the staff of the Royal Victorian Eye and Ear Hospital. In addition to his two half days in out-patients and one afternoon operating at the Royal Melbourne, he was now seeing patients and operating at the Eye and Ear Hospital. By 1956, he had become a Consultant Surgeon to the Peter MacCallum Clinic. Usually, work in their theatres began at 8 am.

In a private hospital it might be earlier. Several mornings a week began with one or two operations (depending on how many beds he could command in a particular private hospital); he might see between ten and fifteen patients in his rooms before leaving Parliament Place around 5 pm to drive all over Melbourne to make his calls.

Since 1946, Tuesday afternoons had been given over to work as medical officer to the Colonial Mutual Fire Insurance Company in Collins Street and frequent appearances in court on litigation connected with the insurance company called him away from the hospital. The working day could wind up with an evening meeting at the Eye and Ear, the Royal Melbourne, Ormond College, the Medico-Legal Society, on Ex-POW business, at a Rugby Union meeting or at a dinner. Increasingly, there were evenings when he would begin major oesophageal operations at 7 pm that could go on until midnight.

Sometimes, Helen was dressed and waiting for an hour or more before Weary appeared, lobbed his homburg onto the hat stand, tore off his short black coat and striped trousers and pulled on a dinner jacket. Life was a good deal more formal then.

As well, there were the POWs, none of whom were charged for their treatment. Not all who called were ill. Some needed to continue a relationship which had meant so much, others shyly brought in their wives and children to introduce them to the man they admired. Wives also came to him, attempting to understand the health problems – the constant diarrhoea, recurrent malaria – and the changes in behaviour in their husbands which only families saw.

Weary's work with former prisoners-of-war extended far beyond their medical care. After the men returned, the Victorian POW Relatives' Association called a public meeting in 1946 and decided to join with former prisoners-of-war to form the Ex-POW and Relatives' Association, rather than support two separate organisations. 'To my horror, we had a great meeting in the Town Hall and I was elected president' with Coates as patron. Weary seldom missed the regular monthly meetings which often ran well into the night.

His concern at the Medical Boards' inadequate investigation of former prisoners on demobilisation had been justified by the problems he and his fellow medical officers continued to see almost daily in their POW patients. He nagged Coates and A. P. Derham about the need to tackle the whole POW health issue.

Coincidentally, *Smiths Weekly* had raised the ire of W. E. (Ted) Fisher and eighteen other Sydney medical officers with sensational sob stories of the difficulties former prisoners of the Japanese and their families were experiencing in finding jobs and living as ordinary Australians. Through the Eighth Division and AIF Malayan Council, they appealed to their Victorian colleagues to join them in affirming their confidence in the Repatriation Commission 'as the proper organisation to provide an adequate medical service for ex-Service personnel'. Apparently, the Australian Legion of ex-Servicemen and Women had decided that Repatriation did not have former prisoners' interests at heart.[21]

Coates convened a meeting on 14 April 1947 of nineteen ex-POW medical officers, and Weary opened the discussion by describing men with complaints which were not being accepted as valid. Few members of the Repatriation assessment tribunals and medical boards had any 'knowledge of the diseases from which P's. W.' had suffered.[22]

They formed a committee of seven, including Alfred Derham as Chairman, Albert Coates, Glyn White, Weary and Howard Eddey (from Weary's year at Ormond), and resolved to offer their expertise diplomatically to the Commission. Nine days after their meeting, his secretary handed him a letter from Maj-General Wootten, Chairman of the Repatriation Commission, inviting him to be one of a national committee of seven which was to tackle the problems faced by former prisoners-of-war in adjusting to civilian life.

Weary accepted immediately, along with Coates, Derham and Glyn White; A. G. G. Carter was to represent the European prisoners-of-war. They were to meet on 13 May as 'The Repatriation Committee on Repatriated Prisoners of War'.

The Australian Red Cross was also anxious 'to discuss the problems of ex-prisoners of war' at their national conference on 2 June. They had had to import extra social workers from England and the United States to deal with the none-too-smooth rehabilitation of former prisoners.

Weary was strongly behind the policy of Red Cross medical and psychiatric social workers helping ex-servicemen and women and their families, for 'health and personality problems [were] still very prominent'.[23] He saw the Repatriation Commission's medical care of the men being complemented by the work of the Red Cross in the community. He cared as little for publicity labelling prisoners-of-war as 'different' as did his fellow medical officers. Nonetheless, he criticised 'the reluctance of government departments and the Australian Red Cross to subscribe wholeheartedly to the policy of clearly earmarking a section of men who have undergone unparalleled trial, for unparalleled measures of help.'[24]

He called for 'a comprehensive survey of all the Ex POW by the Repatriation department, involving medical re-examination and appropriate treatment and adjustment of entitlement and assessment'; and a 'comprehensive social service survey by the Australian Red Cross Society, which should involve contact with every ex-P.O.W. and bereaved dependants of deceased Ps.O.W.'

Weary also took a swipe at the decision by Mr Justice Herring to plough back into general funds the 'millions of pounds' raised by the Red Cross for prisoners-of-war,[25] but not distributed because they were unable to convey comforts to those in Japanese hands. ' . . . At least the sum in question [should be] earmarked by the Red Cross for services to ex POW.'[26] Unlike the Australians, the British Red Cross had regarded such money as a source of repayments to the Chinese and other nationals in Hong Kong, Thailand and Java who had lent money through the underground for the lifesaving drugs and eggs.[27]

The members of the Repatriation Committee put their heads down and by 4 July, the report was finished. Coates did not support the survey, but Derham agreed with Weary and took the idea directly to Wootten. Initially, the recommendations did not go as far as Weary wanted. Rather than all former prisoners-of-war of the Japanese being medically examined, ten per cent were to be surveyed by the Repatriation Commission and the Commonwealth Employment Service. If that yielded valuable information, then all the men would be approached. But at least justice would be done with pension rights at assessment tribunal appeals and medical boards, for an ex-POW (J) doctor was to be present whenever a medical officer was required.

Weary wrote the brochure describing the ailments suffered in the prison camps which was issued to all medical officers involved in examining former prisoners.

Bruce Hunt in Western Australia and Ted Fisher in New South Wales had been better organised than Victoria. Fisher could not resist sniping at Weary: 'I have wondered . . . whether there may not be something in the fact that NSW and Western Australia have physicians on the job . . . '[28]

Weary, Hunt and Glyn White, particularly, were adamant that far more attention must be paid to examining men for bowel parasites, liver problems and the after-effects of dysentery. They suspected that the widespread complaints of 'unnatural fatigue and a sense of personal inadequacy' did not indicate neurosis, but undetected physical ailments.[29] By November that year, the survey was under way. When the results were reported, Weary pressed for the full survey. In May 1949, Wootten instructed his deputy commissioners in each state to launch the 'full medical survey of ex-prisoners of war (J)'.[30]

Weary was convinced that they needed the evidence of this exercise to show the 'total bodily damage done . . . over three and a half years'. When he had paraded his unit in Bangkok for the last time in September 1945, he had suggested that they hold onto their medical records, no matter how scrappy, at all costs. There would be a battle for pensions when they returned. The government would not want to know about their ills. Privately, he believed that they would have 'problems in the future' stretching far beyond the immediate post-war period.

Over the next forty-six years he never flagged in his fight for the rights of his fellow prisoners. He was the right man for these matters, stubborn almost beyond belief. Grandmother Catherine Marie's and Great Grandfather Wattie Dunlop's stern genes sent him back into the fray again and again, whether it was against the Repatriation Commission, the government of the day, or the cancers destroying his patients.

No sooner were the survey details settled, than he turned his attention back to a much more emotional matter: the claim by former prisoners-of-war that they should be paid a subsistence allowance of 3s 0d. for each day that they were imprisoned by the Japanese. The origins of this claim were murky: legend suggested that Weary originated the idea in Java in 1942. In fact, it arose after the war amongst members of the Ex POW & Relatives' Association in Victoria, and the

idea spread through other service organisations. Weary had a good deal
to do with it. 'It is the duty of the country that has you as a prisoner
not only to give you reasonable subsistence, but also to see that you have
pay at the rate of your rank . . . [yet] we lived like dogs on husks . . . in
defiance of international law. So we thought . . . we really must make
a claim about this.' Weary's Victorian organisation threw in its lot with
Fisher's Eighth Division Council in Sydney. Jointly, they fired the
shots.

Questions were first asked in Federal Parliament on 26 June 1946 by
Winton Turnbull, the Member for Wimmera, and the House heard
some heated exchanges over the next three and a half years. Contrary
to Chifley's assertion that the subsistence allowance had been turned
down by Parliament, the question 'was never put to a division'.[31]

The government of the day had hardened its heart against them.
Forde, and later Cyril Chambers who took his place as Minister for the
Army, suggested that they were no worse off than 'troops in the Owen
Stanleys [who] had to exist on 2½ lbs of dry rations per day dropped
from the air'.[32] There, too, 'it rained continuously and they were seldom
dry; and . . . they carried weights up to 90 lbs on their backs but never
grumbled'.[33] Howls of derision greeted this statement.

Chifley was punctilious about replying to the letters from the
Council of the Eighth Division and Service Associates, but he rejected
all claims for a subsistence allowance. He flung a couple of red herrings
to them: the Australian Government would need to consult other
Allied nations about their treatment of recovered prisoners-of-war; and,
surely, if they were eligible for such a payment, why not former prisoners
of the First World War as well? Such attitudes did not endear the
Chifley government to former prisoners and their families. They cut no
ice with Ted Fisher, nor with Weary. When they pulled together, they
were a formidable pair. But they also had their differences.

Smith's Weekly had armed itself with another tear-jerking article
about the plight of former prisoners of the Japanese (gleaned from an
interview with the Secretary of the Ex-POW & Relatives' Association)
and thundered into the lists on their behalf on 24 August. It sent a
frisson through the former captives and their partners with the
suggestion that sterility was another result of their privations and the
bowel infestations common to most. Both presidents felt they could do
without Smith's Weekly. It set Weary's 'teeth on edge', and this
particular issue made him 'feel more grim than usual'.[34] Fisher was
furious and rushed into print.

Weary and 'a deuce of a lot of people . . . [were] damned irritated' with Fisher 'for the intemperate vigour with which you state your views . . . and which appear to imply "why the heck should we worry any more about a bunch of boys who are really doing better than any other service men!".'[35]

He had discerned this attitude in Fisher during their Repatriation Committee meetings, when he waspishly insisted that the effects of imprisonment would not be as lasting as Hunt and Weary believed.

The traditional rivalry between the Sydney and Melbourne medical schools, and the prickly antagonism which could blight relationships between physicians and surgeons, simmered below the surface of many of their exchanges. Weary had found Fisher difficult at Nakom Patom, but latterly, he had admired his dedication to POW health issues and realised that his manner concealed a deep devotion to the men.

An election was coming up. They buried their differences and tackled Robert Menzies, the Leader of the Opposition, and the candidates for the Western District seat of Wannon. Menzies reaffirmed his 1947 call for a 'full and impartial investigating authority so that all the facts may be examined, and a judgment arrived at which is not a cold mathematical judgment, but one which does justice to the enormous, human issues involved'.[36] 'This statement stands, and will be confirmed by me on the public platform.'[37]

Weary saw that they would be better advised to seek assistance on moral grounds rather than legal ones.

The Labor Government had been niggardly in more than one way to the services. Weary had been satisfied at how well his unit had done when the Honours List was published in March 1947. Jock, Corlette and Moon were appointed MBE and various others gained the honours he had put them up for. He was awarded the OBE for his services in Java, and Mentioned in Dispatches. But in May, Blackburn wrote to him. Weary discovered that he, Blackburn, had recommended him 'very strongly for the highest awards which could be given. First for your magnificent work in Java and separately for what you did in . . . Siam'.[38] The former commander of Blackforce was 'utterly disgusted at the inadequacy of the Government's recognition of my recommendations', so disgusted that he spoke to the press. ('No comment,' replied Weary to their questions.)

Blackburn had delayed congratulating Weary in order to let his 'indignation . . . quiet down a bit. It is the rest of us who feel positively insulted over the whole affair . . . every prisoner-of-war with whom you came in contact through those trying years, and every man who has heard of your marvellous work knows that no mere award of a decoration can even begin to express the appreciation and thanks of the many thousands of men who are alive today solely because of your self-sacrificing work.'[39]

Instead of the DSO Blackburn intended, Weary was given another decoration.[40] Falling foul of Brunskill had put paid to Large's recommendation that Weary be awarded a DSO for his work in Greece: he had been fobbed off with Mentioned in Dispatches. The 8th Division dealt with him the same way. His sharp tongue was his worst enemy. Fisher would have agreed.

Weary and he concocted a letter to the press summarising the various political parties' stands on the 'three bob a day' issue so that 'the present situation . . . should be . . . widely known to the general public.[41] Labor had to go and they intended the maximum number of former prisoners-of-war to know why.

Menzies and Fadden swept into power in the 1949 elections in a United Australia Party and Country Party coalition.

Menzies kept his promise. He set up a tribunal to investigate and report upon their claim and it met in the Commonwealth Arbitration Court in Sydney on 14 June 1950. Mr Justice Owen was the Chairman; with him sat 'that marvellous old soldier' Sir Stanley Savage and Ted Fisher.[42] 'The prisoner-of-war organisation took it to Sydney, but they were supported by the ex-service organisations and . . . the RSL . . . who met with us like the lion with the lamb.'

The decision was two to one against, because their treatment had been the responsibility of the detaining power, not the Australian government. Fisher did not give up easily. He wrote a minority report to Menzies. The Prime Minister was sympathetic. In 1952, the government granted £250 000 to set up a fund for 'special hardship'. It was called the Prisoners of War Trust Fund and all prisoners-of-war 'suffering distress or hardship as a result of disabilities arising from the conditions of their captivity, or as a result of any material prejudice directly related to those conditions' were eligible to apply for financial assistance.[43] It was advertised in all newspapers and ex-Service publications. Proformas were sent out all over Australia.

The Fund was barely launched, when the Melbourne *Herald* suggested that the money was not being used effectively: it would be frittered away on administration. Immediately Weary saw the afternoon paper, he rang Keith Murdoch 'in high anger' and marched straight over to Flinders Street. An urbane Murdoch gave him tea while Weary 'poured out the story of this terrible article'. Murdoch agreed with him blandly. 'Even I do not control the policy of the paper. We must get Williams up.' To Weary's astonishment, after Williams had heard him out, he said 'Yes, as a matter of fact, it would entirely suit our political platform at the moment . . . we'll give it the full blast.'

They were 'never molested' by the Murdoch press again.

In January 1949, an old friend from his staff days on I Aust. Corps in the Middle East, Brigadier Lloyd Elliott, was leafing through some files when he came across Weary's name amongst a list of promotions made by Blackburn in Java. As he later told Weary, it was 'outrageous that Blackburn had the powers of a GOC and . . . made these promotions' which were not recognised. Elliott raised the matter with the Military Board. The first Weary knew of his improved status, was a letter from Southern Command advising him that he had been granted the rank of temporary colonel from 8 March 1942.[44] He collected another £640 in very welcome back pay. But 'the thing that really pleasd me was that all the promotions . . . I had made were honoured, Moon and Corlette were raised to lieutenant-colonels and . . . everyone I had put up got their back pay'.

By 1952, Tossie's health had worsened and the solution seemed to be that Helen and Weary should move in with her. As far as Weary was concerned, 'I can't say it was entirely my idea', but Helen was comfortable with it, she would have her mother for company and support, and Toorak was an excellent address for a surgeon. Weary would need to buy a house at some time; he might as well buy half of 605 from Tossie.

Even though it had been Helen's home, it was a difficult, rambling house to run, with a huge garden. The responsibilities of the two small boys – John was also a handful and much favoured by his grand-mother – the increased housework, the constantly ringing telephone with a stream of messages for Weary and the uncertainties of his movements made Helen extremely anxious. Alexander was a roamer, with a remarkable gift for disappearing. Helen resorted to pinning a label displaying his name, address and telephone number to the back of his overalls. On one nerve-wracking occasion, when he lost himself, he made his way to the police station and enjoyed a grand tour in a Black Maria before being delivered to his distraught mother and grandmother.

Not even his incarceration at Little St Margaret's, the nursery school down the road, gave her freedom from anxiety, because he was into everything. Both boys loved their time there. Weary did his best to take time off at weekends now. And Tossie was a willing grandmother who 'adored the children and that enabled us to go out together quite a lot'.

TWENTY-SEVEN

The Solace of Surgery

EXTRA-CURRICULAR ACTIVITIES gobbled up an enormous amount of time. He spent hours, pen in hand, writing: reports for workers' compensation claims connected with his insurance work; letters to his patients' physicians or general practitioners who had referred cases; and letters to men who had been prisoners with him or reports on POW patients for appeals against a ruling on their pensions. He had also to keep his case notes and results in order, for publication was important.

Weary had submitted his first medical paper to the *Australian and New Zealand Journal of Surgery* in 1938 about a patient whom he treated while a house surgeon at the Children's Hospital under the supervision of Dr H. Douglas Stephens.[1] It was Stephens' son who had given the dinner party for him in Tobruk. His paper was accepted for publication the day the *Ormande* set sail across the Indian Ocean.

Weary wrote his second paper with his Parsee friend and colleague at Hammersmith on intramuscular administration of fluids, but he was in Jerusalem by the time it was published. Bomy Billimoria's letter and the reprint from *The Lancet* did not reach him until November 1946.[2]

Billimoria had traced him through the *British Medical Journal*, after reading Weary's two articles about his time in Thailand. The latter one, 'Medical Experiences in Japanese Captivity', reveals a depth and restrained passion that make it a memorable report of wartime medical experiences. The reader needs no clinical background: the message is plain.

Weary did not publish a large number of papers in his lifetime, but their contents open a window on the man he had become.

John Hayward was the only specialist surgeon in Australia trained in thoracic work, and he was appointed to the Royal Melbourne in March 1946 to set up the new Thoracic Surgical Unit. He was released from the army in May. It seemed aeons since Weary had stood in for him at the Brompton Chest Hospital. Their interests were complementary:

Weary wanted to learn more about the chest (from the neck to the diaphragm), and Hayward desired abdominal experience. They had both assisted Edgar King as residents at the Royal Melbourne. Now, they decided to work as a team on oesophageal surgery. 'With [Weary's] background and heroic spirit, it is not surprising that he chose . . . one of the most challenging of the new post-war developments . . . '3

The concept of a team working together regularly was relatively new in Melbourne, although by now common in the USA. Each surgeon had his preferred anaesthetist: Stanton (or later his partner, Nathan) for Weary and Margaret McClelland or Lionel Bridges-Webb if the case on the table was Hayward's. Ian McConchie, who had worked with Hayward in New Guinea during the war and was being trained by him as a chest surgeon, became Hayward's favoured assistant; John Zwar or Ian Ogilvie were often his counterparts on Weary's team in the early days, although Weary's assistants varied and he trained no one formally; he preferred to do everything himself.

No matter which surgeon was in charge of the operation and post-operative care, the other one would always be included in the rounds, because both men were vitally interested in the patient's progress.

Together, they struck out into tiger country. Hayward was a 'pernickety, rather slow sort of surgeon in a way [who] was careful not to get into trouble . . . whereas Weary was so busy on the job . . . It was like going into a scrum, getting to that ball'. The partnership worked 'perfectly'. 'We were both positive . . . people . . . [who] liked and respected [each] other.'4 They published their first results in 1948.5 So little had been reported about the subject, that 'even a tiny series' of twelve was 'worth publishing'.6

Radical surgery was the only hope for the emaciated and usually elderly patients, unable to eat or drink comfortably. Diagnosis was late: by the time these people reached Weary's or Hayward's consulting rooms, their cancers were very advanced. ' . . . The diameter of the narrowed area [the gullet] may be less than that of a lead pencil'.7 Cancers in this area were 'usually fatal in outcome, and . . . associated with appalling distress'.8 His compassion was aroused by the sad picture these men and women presented.

Oesophageal or pharyngeal cancer surgery was, indeed, a 'grave assault' upon the body.9 It encompassed removing malignant tumours of the upper alimentary canal from the pharynx (throat), and including the larynx, to the stomach. In a number of cases, the spleen, the pancreas, the liver or all three might be involved; in others, the stomach or part of it had to be excised, along with a substantial portion of the gullet. The high mortality attending these operations deterred those surgeons who were anxious about how their results would appear to their colleagues: not so Weary. The sight of 'human suffering' and the prospect of its relief reduced 'survival rates to secondary importance in appraising the results of treatment'.[10]

Their first case was in August 1946; the last of this series took Weary six and a half hours in the operating theatre at the Royal Melbourne in January 1948.

Hailes was most interested that, after operation, all the patients could take food in the mouth and swallow it. They were complicated procedures and became more so as the 1950s advanced, some of them involving many 'skin reconstructions . . . we reconstructed . . . at all levels'. The patients were taken back to theatre again and again. Some repeatedly tore the complex skin grafts and reconstructions off. But Weary was more stubborn than they, and he continued to replace them until the patient yielded to the sterner will of the surgeon.

Those whose larynxes had been removed had to learn to speak in an entirely different manner. Weary's friends were interested in what they were doing. Rank sent him the transcript of a talk by a speech therapist in 1950 on pharyngeal speech, apparently a marked improvement on oesophageal speech. Weary gently bullied those patients who insisted on clinging to their pads and pencils and would not persevere with relearning the art of speech.

By 1952, both surgeons had become so busy that they could no longer find much time to work together. Sometimes, the best they could do was arrange to be in neighbouring theatres at a hospital, so that one could slip in and observe something interesting while the other was operating.

By now, Weary had a further twenty-five patients in his series, and he reported the results in the first of 'two classical papers'.[11] He was conscious of the criticisms of his colleagues, but unrepentant. 'The justification of mutilating surgery is the absence of a satisfactory alternative, but it can only be faced with equanimity when attended by a low operative mortality, and reasonable prospects of alleviation or cure.'[12]

Those who accused him of ignoring the quality of life which his patients enjoyed after surgery were wrong. They looked at the bold and radical surgery – what Marshall has called the 'high, wide and hand-some' approach – and failed to see that his motivation was a belief that he could reduce pain and suffering and give them further years of useful and enjoyable life.

Weary was never afraid of taking risks: 'Surgical interventions of great magnitude may be necessary . . . '[13] The twin spectres of open ether or chloroform anaesthetics and infection, which had hovered over operating theatres before the war, had been banished, but until E. B. Drevermann entered the arena, resuscitation techniques were still imperfect. The patients might die – but they would die anyway, if he did not operate. 'He always hoped they'd be better in every sense . . . not just . . . physically better, but feel better and enjoy the extra life his efforts had given them.'[14] Many of them did. His second paper in 1960 reported a case series of 170 patients, 'including every person who has sought treatment for carcinoma of the oesophagus in the period after the end of the Second World War in 1945 to August 1959'.[15]

In this, he included his own personal series of 91 patients seen and treated five years or more previously. Of these, 18 to 20 per cent survived three years or more, and 14 were still living for five to ten years. When the results were compared with those of other world clinics, 'his five and ten-year survival figures for laryngectomy were easily the best in the world'.[16]

The mortality was still high, for 'at the heart of our difficulties rests the age and frailty of the patients together with the formidable nature of the disease.'[17] The daunting prospect spurred him on. 'I think my reputation at the Melbourne was that I was prepared to give an operation a go when there wasn't any alternative, however great the risk might be. I don't think one should ever apologise for that.'

Weary's detractors accuse him of insensitivity. Julian Orm Smith and he never recovered the camaraderie enjoyed in the Middle East. Weary's tendency to go over time in the theatre annoyed Orm Smith intensely, particularly since he may have started late – and Orm Smith knew it. Sisters and surgeons in the Royal Melbourne one day complained to Orm Smith, the Senior Surgeon, that Weary was still in the theatre where others were due to operate. Orm Smith barged in and said, 'Weary, you might have been Christ on the Burma Railway, but you are not God almighty here. Get out!'[18] Macleish saw this as a 'terrible public . . . encounter'. And it was only one in a long chain of disagreements. But Hayward, perhaps the only surgeon now alive who trained and worked with Weary both before and after the war because of their apprenticeship with King and their shared interest, rejects the common view. He was amused by Weary's 'quirks, whereas other people got very angry'. Some thought Weary's expectations were unreasonable.

'It wasn't that he was selfish, or deliberately unreasonable . . . but once he was on a job, that was the *only* thing that was in his mind. Time, our assistants, what was happening to anybody else, his wife, his family – for practical purposes (he'd started an operation, say, or he was doing a consultation) . . . nothing else in the world mattered. He had a mind that could be absolutely focused . . . The clock ticking round was of no consequence whatever.'[19]

Not all the staff complained. Sister Elizabeth Potter was training theatre staff at the Royal Melbourne in the late 1950s when Weary's surgery truly earned its designation of 'heroic'. Neither she nor another sister, Audrey Anderson, drank anything after their evening meal the night before operating with Weary. They would be at the hospital by 7.30 the next morning; they might not finish the day until 11 pm or midnight after only two or three cases. The surgeons could leave the theatre during a case while an assistant carried on, but only one theatre sister was on duty, and she needed a cast-iron bladder.

Weary was not unique in the length of time his operations took. Anderson was involved in the early heart surgery, in sessions continuing for sixteen hours. None of Weary's were this long, but his tendency to exceed his allotted time riled some people. The Royal Melbourne gave him a full day instead of two half days during Potter's last year or so. 'But it didn't work. [He] didn't cut down the hours at all.'[20] They found it exciting, 'new – it was a challenge to us, it was team work, and this was what we enjoyed'.[21] Potter scrubbed for just two surgeons: Rank and Weary. She thought very highly of both. Neither ever asked her for an instrument. 'They just stretched out their hand.'[22]

Weary asked her to scrub for him only on major cases. 'It was tiring surgery.' Her presence made all the difference to 'a man who never asked for what he wanted'.[23] There is no substitute for a highly intelligent sister who knows her surgeon; she understands the operation, she anticipates his wants, and senses when he is in trouble 'by instinct . . . '[24]

Weary's operations were challenging, all right. 'You had to have every instrument that you could . . . possibly need [which] could mean several trays.' Everything had to be ready on the trolleys. 'You were always prepared for the worst.'

One of Weary's favourite instruments was unique to him. Macleish called it the 'knife and fork', but it was more like a rake, with a scalpel at the other end. In surgery, there is sharp dissection, and blunt dissection. Where another surgeon might use his fingers, Weary would use the rake to pull the tissues slowly back. It was useful, but it caused some nerve-wracking moments, particularly when a vein got in the way. And he was not good at extricating himself from a mess. 'Weary's technique of operating was very interesting, in that he would do a dissection by fiddling with his fingers . . . things that he ought not to do.'[25]

Marshall consistently observed Weary operating across eight years, and he often wondered if Weary had defective vision caused by malnutrition during the war. In 1957, when Weary was being tested for eye glasses, he was shocked to discover that the vision in one eye was 6/60. He had a central scotoma which could not be corrected. It was not his custom to tell anyone about his problems. 'He just got on with it.'[26]

If Weary was given the wrong instrument, he dropped it gently on the floor, unlike others, who might hurl it the width of the room. Once, Potter was startled by Weary dropping a scalpel which speared her shoe to the floor between two toes. 'All I could do was stand and look at him. He leaned over and looked at the floor – he used to wear these little glasses that sat on the end of his nose and he had these beautiful blue eyes that used to blink at you over the glasses – and said: "Oh, I couldn't have done that if I'd tried".'[27] But he was very concerned. The 'dirty nurse' unpinned her. The operation continued.

Theatre staff are exposed to a cross section of surgical techniques; their verdicts can differ from a surgeon's peers. Potter thought Weary 'was unique'. Whereas another surgeon might be stylised and do everything exactly by the book, he evolved his own methods. 'I think he worked it out in his mind as he went along . . . what he was going to do', once he had opened up the patient. She believed his 'innovative ideas' allowed him to do the operations that he did, 'because he used to bypass things, anything to . . . make it work . . . It wasn't necessarily curing anything, but it [would] make the patient comfortable'. They recognised that this last was important to him.

Professor Gabriel Kune considers that Weary's operations at the time, 'keeping in mind the stage of the disease of the person', constituted intellectually 'a paradigm jump'. Whereas he was not the greatest surgeon technically, he took the treatment of these cancers of the gullet and put 'the technical aspects of [their] surgery on a . . . new plane'.[28]

If Weary had had his four or five hours sleep the previous night, there was a good atmosphere in the theatre. He chatted to the residents, talked about his war experiences, told such long and convoluted funny stories that Potter 'lost track . . . and tuned out'. But if he had gone short on rest, Hayward noticed that he 'got the slows' as the operation and the night advanced. He would be exhausted, but 'he had a drive that wouldn't stop for anything . . . he just didn't seem to realise that he was getting slower and slower.'

He could be very forgetful. Potter answered the telephone in Theatre A one day. It was Helen. Would she mind asking Weary what he'd done with the children? When he left home, they were in the back of the Daimler.

' . . . He had to think for quite some time to realise that he'd parked the [car] outside Myer with the children in it and . . . caught a taxi to the hospital.' She thought 'he forgot that he . . . had children unless someone reminded him'.

Hayward suggests that Weary reached his peak in the 1950s. His stature as a surgeon was unquestioned: 'There's no doubt about that.' Like Coates and some other pre-war surgeons who had to get in and out quickly because of the limitations of anaesthetics when they were training, 'he was always a little bit rough, always very enterprising . . . [and] would stop at nothing . . .

'At the beginning his surgery was very good indeed. None of the theatres would have [tolerated] him going on forever and a day . . . if the surgery wasn't good. And the patients did well. The very fact that the nursing staff and anaesthetists did put up with him is proof that he was a bloody good surgeon, judged on results . . . ' They were all proud. 'They're not going to put up with a surgeon whose patients aren't doing well.'

Hayward and Weary were both too busy to write up all their results. Hayward believes they were the first to use jejunum, that part of the small intestine between the duodenum and the ileum, to bridge the gap between a short gullet, and the stomach which they had moved down into the chest, of a young boy with an hiatal hernia. Although by 1952, the partnership was withering, they retained a lively interest in each other's work for many years.

Weary's fascination with the gut did not stop at the duodenum. His attention was constantly focused on the bowel while he continued to treat ex-POW patients suffering from lingering dysentery. It was but a short step to treat his ulcerative colitis patients by ileostomy, whose genesis lay in the Thai camps and his operations for amoebic dysentery. 'I was the first . . . who took on the very serious people with ulcerative colitis to remove the colon and do ileostomies.' Initially, it was difficult to find the bags and the fittings. Ansell, the rubber glove firm, made some under Weary's supervision. He experimented with various sorts of bags and belts, made to his designs by local manufacturers. These were adequate until the smarter, US-made accessories arrived.

Weary inclined increasingly towards ileostomy, for he believed that it enabled his patients to regain 'a cheerful and vigorous attitude of mind', allowing them eventually to return to their normal occupations and 'live full lives'.[29]

He read his second paper on the subject to the Australasian Medical Congress in Perth in August 1948. Weary was forced to squeeze in his paper between someone who went over time, and morning tea, which was announced ten minutes early by the President. He was not pleased.

Many found the idea of ileostomy objectionable, refusing to believe that 'with modern management a . . . useful economic and social existence is possible'. E. S. R. Hughes accused him in an open discussion of 'chaining patients to the lavatory'.

Weary wrote a paper about the pioneering procedure he developed for colectomy with ileo-rectal-anastomosis and submitted it to the *BMJ*. Unfortunately, it became caught up in internal politics when the two editors, Naunton-Morgan and Hugh Lett, quarrelled. 'My paper was not published for three years'; in the meantime, Aylett's paper was published, and the procedure became known as 'Aylett's operation'.

Weary rarely lost sleep through worrying about what others thought of him, but he was 'disconcerted' when he was criticised 'for saving lives of appallingly sick people' with these procedures, especially when his surgery was conservative and Hughes' was radical. He believed absolutely in the rightness of what he was doing. But at least he was now a fellow and included in the congress. When Henry Searby had invited him to present a paper on an earlier occasion in Melbourne, the College had treated him like some member of a 'foreign legion', admitted to the lecture theatre immediately before his paper and afterwards 'completely ostracised'. Only fellows were invited to attend the other sessions.

At the time, he had not been a fellow of the Australasian college, although his FRCS gave him the first part of the examination. Soon after the war, Hailes suggested that he sit for the second part. There was a snag: it was no longer a *viva* , but written papers. Weary had been out of touch with modern research and academic life for six years. 'I would hate to sit as an old chap in Out-Patients and fail!' he told Hailes, Censor-in-Chief for the College. Finally, the College conceded that those who had been away at the war be allowed to sit a special *viva*.

Out of a dozen candidates, only two passed: Weary, and his old friend from Sydney (and Barts), Frank Mills. They were admitted as fellows on 27 January 1948.

After this, he participated in everything, but the response to his papers was not always warm. He was particularly angered by a surgeon from another state who queried his series of resections of pharyngeal pouches at a congress. This condition was so rare, that the number he reported was disbelieved. Operations on pharyngeal pouches were difficult, with a high complication rate. Patients were sent to Weary because it was known that he was willing to take them on. What no one seemed to consider, was that it would be 'quite out of character' for Weary to falsify figures.[30]

The following year, in Tasmania, he spoke on another rare condition, warning his audience that it was 'a disarming series of one'.[31] The Adelaide surgeon who had called Weary's integrity into question was present. Weary looked straight at him. Then he called in the eleven-year-old patient and had her confirm her name and that she was his patient on whom he had operated. She replied to all his questions and left the lecture theatre. Weary, and honour, were satisfied.

Eventually, he felt 'squeezed . . . out' by Hughes, one of his earlier, severe critics, who developed surgery of the bowel (including ileostomy) as his main interest and was the accepted authority by the mid–1950s. Weary was cynically entertained by his championing those very procedures that earlier he had felt so squeamish about.

Weary abandoned the area 'gratefully' and concentrated on the oesophagus. The Peter MacCallum Cancer Clinic offered him a richer lode of experience. He found the whole field of 'the mouth and throat and jaw, mouth cancer and reconstruction . . . all very satisfying'. During the 1950s and the 1960s, when the Peter MacCallum largely treated people with radiotherapy, Weary would operate on selected patients at the Eye and Ear Hospital where facilities were better.

Working twenty hours out of twenty-four had not stilled his restlessness and, professionally, he wished to see what was happening in such centres as the Mayo and Lahey clinics in North America. In 1952, he decided to take three months off to visit the United States and his many friends in England. Helen had no opportunity to accompany him. She was totally absorbed in caring for the two little boys.

Weary flew to Sydney on 16 September. Some months beforehand, the government had announced that each former prisoner-of-war of the Japanese would receive compensation of £32 from Japanese reparations. The Eighth Division and Service Associates' Council proposed to appeal to all recipients for £5, to be donated to a special trust fund for their benefit. Weary was asked to be one of the trustees, and that afternoon Gordon Bennett, Sydney Smith and he set up the Prisoners-of-War Trust Fund.

Next morning, he took off for the USA. Three days later, he was in San Francisco and by 22 September, he was in Toronto, chatting to Jacob Markowitz about old times, poetry, 'Marko's' experimental surgery at the University of Toronto and his own fascination with the oesophagus. Marko took him to dine with Gordon Murray, whose Hunterian Lecture on his experiments with the drug heparin, blood vessel surgery and grafts he had attended in June 1939 at the Royal College of Surgeons in Lincoln's Inn Fields. He was interested to hear from Murray of his use of heparin with venous arterial grafts; the articles describing this were published during the war and he had missed them.

He spent more than five stimulating weeks in the USA, shuttling between Rochester, Chicago, Washington, Baltimore, Boston and New York. He was 'very impressed' by the Mayo Clinic. Rochester was a smaller and more tight-knit community than the other cities, with a welcoming atmosphere for their international visitors. Charlie Mayo was a wonderful host.

Weary first met O. T. 'Jim' Clagett during his visit to Australia in 1950. To watch him on his home ground was amazing. He found Clagett 'a marvellous surgeon [and] a very human man', but his relationship to his patients was foreign to Weary's nature. He saw his patients at their physicians' rooms, explaining that 'you never want to let them into your consulting rooms. You can't get them out'.

When Gabriel Kune acted *in locum tenens* for Weary at various times, he discovered that Weary's patients would arrive at his consulting rooms and settle in for the day, 'waiting for Weary to turn up . . . talking . . . virtually with the thermos'. Kune took his responsibilities seriously and he was a punctual young man. They 'were displeased by my promptness' and Weary's absence.[32]

Weary believed in personal involvement with his patients. They 'came to talk about themselves . . . I think it was part of the treatment'.[33]

Now, witnessing the impersonal team approach to surgery prevailing at the Mayo Clinic, Weary decided that 'it brought something into medicine that was very much like the big store'. Nonetheless, he decided that it would be a good place in which to work, for both their record system and the back-up was superb. Clagett, 'one of the people you just had to see', was an 'operating machine . . . He operated nearly all day for about three or four days a week, doing about ten or twelve cases'.

Thousands of patients and visiting surgeons from all over the world came every month to the tall, grey stone wedding-cake of a building in Rochester, Minneapolis. Visitors were collected from their accommodation around half past six in the morning and kept busy all day with lectures, seminars and operations. The theatres were set up for observers with a large gallery. More favoured visitors joined the operating team on the same level. Weary quickly became a friend of Clagett's and was 'always on the floor when he was operating'.

Weary was much amused to hear Clagett speak very slowly and distinctly to a quiet Japanese up in the gallery: 'Do – you – do – this – oper – ation – in Japan?' The little man snapped out, 'Yes, but very much better, slicker and quicker than that.' It was K. Nakayama, famous for his oesophageal surgery.

He visited Frank Lahey, Richard Cattell and Kenneth Warren at the Lahey Clinic in Boston, a large institution entirely for private patients. The three wonderfully equipped and staffed hospitals, the Massachusetts General, the Peter Bent Brigham and the Boston City were impressive, but like their counterparts in Chicago, Baltimore and New York, he found them vast and impersonal. Once again, he envied the surgeons their conditions and the facilities for research.

On 5 November, he boarded his BOAC flight for London, London House and a world of ration books and public transport. The contrast on the other side of the Atlantic was marked. Weary's first call was on Ken Starr, then sharing rooms in Harley Street. For the next six weeks, he combined surgery and a meeting of the Gastroenterological Society with happy reunions, lunches, dinners, dances, parties, theatre, and weekends in the country. He also dined with Richard Doll, whose theories about the connection between smoking and lung cancer would prove so influential and which impressed Weary.

Porritt, now knighted and surgeon to the king, invited him to St Mary's; Maltby was Sergeant-at-Arms in the House of Lords; E. W. Swanton worked for the *Daily Telegraph*; Billy Wearne was a lieutenant-colonel at the Combined Operations Centre in Devonshire; Laurens van der Post was in Aldeburgh; and Jack Marsh, the founder and number one member of FEPOW, the Far Eastern Prisoners-of-war Association, was the Director of the Industrial Welfare Society in Bryanston Square.

It was a vastly more civilised and entertaining existence than Melbourne, Australia. Even Hector MacQuarie was still at Angus & Robertson and lavish with hospitality at Bank Farm in Bucks. There was theatre with Arthur and Kay Porritt (for he had been divorced and remarried), and luncheon with Edwina Mountbatten at 2 Wilton Crescent.

In 1945, he had traced Mickey Borgmann Brouwer, in an effort to retrieve the papers he gave her in May 1942. She replied briefly. The papers had been found by the Japanese and she had spent the war years in prisons and internment camps. Weary felt responsible, and he wished to hear the full story. On 21 November, he flew to Schiphol and took the train to Zeist, where she was looking after her parents.

Whilst she was working with the underground in Java, the Japanese had found the papers, arrested, tortured and imprisoned her. She was lucky to be alive. Andrew Crichton was living in Amsterdam; John Disse was now in Medan, in Sumatra. Mickey had shed her husband and returned to her maiden name of de Jonge.

'People were his life,' Tom Kemp pointed out. Weary never willingly let someone go. He flew to Dublin to renew his bond with Arnold K. Henry and to Edinburgh to see his 'Falstaffian' friend, surgeon John Bruce and the artist from Chungkai, Stanley Gimson.

By Christmas Eve, he was back at 605 Toorak Road with presents for everyone and all the items on Helen's shopping list, including twenty pairs of stockings, a very expensive bedjacket and shoes for her hard-to-fit feet.

He also returned charged with fresh confidence in his oesophageal surgery and with some new notions about vascular surgery and the replacement of arteries from Murray in Toronto and Gross in Boston, Mass. He had found the exchange of ideas vastly beneficial.

Early in 1953, his corresponding Surgeon to Out-Patients, Douglas Leslie, went up to Ward 8 East after an out-patients' session at the Melbourne to find Weary and a group of students standing by the bed of an injured wharf labourer with his left thigh 'so crushed by compression between a crane load and the wharf that his major blood vessels were disrupted. His leg below was greyish white, cold and lifeless'.[34] Weary was silent for some time, staring down at the man and obviously deep in thought. Eventually, he told Leslie that he was going to do an arterial graft and told him what he required.

Leslie went to the post-mortem room, 'harvested a femoral artery', and returned to the theatre where Weary had already begun operating. The man's femoral artery was too damaged for the severed ends to be joined. With Leslie assisting him, Weary 'sewed across the gap', grafting a section of the artery Leslie brought him to the damaged left femoral artery in the man's thigh.

It was the first time the operation had been performed in the southern hemisphere.[35]

TWENTY-EIGHT

Surgeon Ambassador

SOME PATIENTS BECAME FRIENDS. One who did so was a member of Menzies' government, the Rt Hon. Richard Casey, Minister for External Affairs.

Casey had spent the war years successively as Australian Minister in Washington, where in 1940 he opened the first Australian diplomatic mission in a foreign country, United Kingdom Minister of State in the Middle East (for which appointment he could thank Churchill's high regard for him) and Governor of Bengal. His wife, Maie, was the daughter of Sir Charles 'Plevna' Ryan, a surgeon-politician who had earned his medical spurs in the Balkans at the Battle of Plevna, and attended Ned Kelly after the shooting at Glenrowan. She was articulate, widely travelled, a writer and artist. During their postings abroad, the Caseys had moved in the highest circles. She was also a friend of Edwina Mountbatten's.

Casey and Weary enjoyed each other's company. He put him up for the Melbourne Club in 1949 and it formed the apex of a triangle drawn between Weary's rooms in Parliament Place and Casey's office in Treasury Place, where he could be found when Parliament was not sitting in Canberra. Weary was invariably late for engagements. 'I know what you bloody medical men are like,' Casey would complain. If it was a dinner he wanted Weary and Helen to attend, he used to book them up well in advance and hound Weary mercilessly about the date and time.

Much later in Casey's life, a serious car accident confined him to Edrington, their house in Berwick. Weary spent many convivial Friday evenings with his beloved Dick and Maie, drinking and talking the night away. Helen was never part of those occasions.

Casey believed firmly that Australia must play a central rôle in the affairs of her Asian neighbours and, in order to do so, she must work at understanding them. Communism was a perceived threat. The war had not brought prosperity to those nations north of Australia and they were struggling to find their identity in the post-war world. They were impatient to become self-sufficient, to improve their living standards and to acquire technical skills; and Communism was seen as an efficient way of modernising backward countries quickly.

In 1950, at a Commonwealth conference of Foreign Ministers in Colombo, the idea was born for a different kind of economic aid which would counter the trend to Communism: the Colombo Plan for Co-operative Economic Development in South and South-East Asia.

By 1956, Casey had succeeded Spender as Minister for External Affairs. Weary's interest in the Colombo Plan was aroused by Casey's enthusiasm 'about the goodwill resulting from exchanges in the medical field' and Rank's account of his visit to Singapore, Malaya, India and Pakistan.

By now, Weary's feelings about his professional life were ambivalent. He enjoyed the contact with his patients, his surgical work was fulfilling, yet he 'never found the cut and thrust of life in Melbourne . . . entirely to [his] satisfaction', never regained the 'exhilaration' of his earlier days. 'I think that in these great teaching hospitals, there are . . . antagonisms and jealousies . . . that you have constantly got to push aside.' As Hayward observed, 'Weary could influence people, but not necessarily make friends.'[1]

The Fifth International Congress of Gastroenterology was to be held in London in July 1956. Was he planning to attend and did he wish to read a paper? enquired Avery-Jones, the Secretary of the Scientific Committee.

Weary submitted a summary for the section on 'Pre-malignant Conditions of the Gastro-Intestinal Tract' and confirmed that he would be there. Then he suggested to Casey that he would like to combine his trip to England with operating and teaching for the Colombo Plan in Thailand and Ceylon.

Casey asked Weary to put his reasons in writing. Weary was persuasive, and he knew from Professor Milroy Paul in Colombo that a surgeon specialising in oesophageal surgery would be welcomed. He was unable to predict Thailand's reaction, but the Minister was convinced.

There was a flurry of activity in June, for he had decided to travel to London by way of South Africa so that he could stay with Tony and Marjorie Scott and his godson, Anthony, whom he had never seen. The news of Anthony's birth had been one of the few letters to reach him in Thailand during the war.

Gordon Stanton was to join him in Thailand in August: External Affairs advised Weary to take his own anaesthetist, for Rank had found this valuable. Casey briefed Weary personally before he departed in late June. Stanton and he would be the first Royal Melbourne hospital experts under the technical assistance sector of the Colombo Plan to visit these two countries.

The congress occupied only four days in July, but the contacts made there spread out across his time in England. The paper was well received.[2] His programme was 'strenuous and a month proved all too short to see something of surgical and other friends'.[3]

He parted from Edwina Mountbatten on bad terms. She had placed him beside her at a luncheon party she gave in Wilton Crescent that July. Capital punishment was being debated in England at the time and Edwina was strongly opposed to hanging. Unwisely, and misjudging how intensely she felt about the issue, Weary decided to play devil's advocate for no better reason than to hear her arguments. She was furious and the luncheon was ruined. Weary wrote her a trite little apologetic note that evening, and her reply revealed that he had hurt her deeply. He felt bad about this for years, for they never met again before her death in February 1960.

Weary found his arrival at Don Muang early on the morning of 9 August more emotional than he had anticipated. Nearly eleven years had elapsed since he flew out of Bangkok with that last plane-load of Australians. 'Even at 5.45 am, the well-remembered steamy heat of the wet season was very evident.'[4] Standing in the airport beside the official from the Australian Embassy was a Thai surgeon who had visited him in his operating theatre at the Royal Melbourne, Dr Sem Pring Puang Geo, surgeon and Director of the Women's and Children's Hospital in Bangkok. Stanton had arrived the previous day with a great deal of excess baggage: Weary's personal operating gear, weighing sixty kilos in all.

Weary had to conceal his impatience at the amount of protocol which prevailed during their first week in Thailand. He gleaned much useful information for Casey during the formal calls and sightseeing, through which he was expertly steered by the Australian ambassador, David Hay, and his embassy staff, or Dr Sem.

The latter was a well-informed reporter on the country's 'threadbare' medical services. Eighteen million people spread over 71 provinces were the responsibility of around 300 doctors. Not only did they need to train more doctors, nurses and technical support people: they were in desperate need of far more basic services – sanitation, plumbing, less erratic water and electricity supplies and a vast public health programme.

The USA and WHO were pouring in money and aid. He decided that the most practical help which Australia could provide would be to train doctors, nurses and technical support people at both under-graduate and post-graduate level; and to 'take graduates and nurses or technicians of proven capacity and give them at least two years in Australia for training as key personnel'.[5]

That Sunday, he made a pilgrimage to the cemeteries at Kanchanaburi and Chungkai and wandered along the lines of gravestones of 'friends who rested in the quietness and beauty'. The sight of their names, of the mountains rising ever higher above the Kwai Noi River, of 'the jungle grown thick and green to hide the scars of camps where living and dead skeletons used to be so plentiful', filled him with a dragging sadness. There were just 'too many ghosts' amongst those 'men of all the Allied Nations . . . intermingled in the strange comradeship, which is perpetuated in death'.[6]

Weary had one piece of private business. Boon Pong Sirivejjaphand had recovered from the bullets in his chest and was running a bus company from his Bangkok headquarters near the stadium. 'He now looks a little older and I suspect that business is not flourishing, but he is still the same pleasant, friendly Boon Pong.'[7] It was years before he had any recognition of his bravery from the British government. Because all sterling in Thailand was frozen after the war, he had not been allowed to use the funds he had accumulated up until August 1945. Former British prisoners-of-war thought this was poor compensation for the risks he had taken on their behalf; they clubbed together and bought him a tractor. The Borneo Company and Anglo-Thai Corporation had also helped. Finally he was given a British decoration. Weary intervened in Australia and the government donated a modest sum of money. He never felt that Boon Pong was treated generously, considering the grave risks he had run, the piles of promissory notes he had accepted and the cheques he had cashed during the war.

Although Weary 'stressed as tactfully as possible that work was our principal objective', he was not let loose in an operating theatre until they flew north to Chiangmai.[8] The two Australians were installed in a luxurious house belonging to the Minister of Public Health. As they drove in, Weary remarked a bevy of Thai beauties driving out; Stanton and he were given a bunch of respectable elderly women servants to look after their needs. That afternoon, Weary launched into a sub-total gastrectomy at Nakorn Chiangmai Hospital without Stanton, who had succumbed to gastro-enteritis. ' . . . The ether anaesthetics . . . were given quite efficiently by the Thai anaesthetist'. He was startled to learn that the only cuffed tube (used in anaesthesia) in Thailand was in Bangkok.

He lectured, operated and conducted ward rounds while rising flood waters swirled through the streets and about the buildings. Some hospitals on their programme were cut off. By Friday they were back in Bangkok facing a further week of operations, teaching and ward rounds, lectures and luncheons at the two medical schools at Siriraj and Chulalongkorn hospitals.

The seventeen days spent in Thailand generated a great deal of goodwill. Many of the staff at the two teaching hospitals had trained in England or the United States. They were articulate, able and experienced. He decided that Thais 'took to surgery like ducks to water'.[9]

Weary found 'fascinating surgical problems' on his ward rounds at both hospitals and his lectures were received with 'rapt attention'. Occasionally, he was slightly baffled by this last, unable to decide whether the subject was of special interest, or whether they had difficulty understanding him. Lively discussion followed his lecture on cancer of the pharynx, for a number of the surgeons had treated this themselves. Oesophageal cancer was common in the region.

Weary performed Thailand's first operation for portal hypertension at Siriraj Hospital on 20 August. He had undertaken the first operation at the Royal Melbourne, also, although his early efforts had 'disappointed' him. On the Saturday morning, Kasarn Chatikavanij, the thoracic surgeon, and he selected the case for operation: a teenage boy with a congenital malformation in his portal vein, cirrhosis of the liver and a huge spleen. Weary then delivered a lecture on the problems of oesophageal surgery.

By Monday morning, he was dismayed to find that the boy had bled so badly during the night that he was unrouseable. Kasarn was extremely anxious that he not operate, but Weary was determined 'to give it a go', even though on such 'goodwill tours, the death of a patient would be a serious blow'. It was the boy's only chance of life. Assisted by a young Thai surgeon, Sira Bunyaratavij,* Weary removed the spleen and 'did the necessary [spleno-renal] shunt', as it is called, with 'the most satisfactory lowering of venous pressure'. Not only did the patient survive – he 'lived for years'.

After a long day operating and teaching in both hospitals, and a final dinner at Hoi Thien Lao restaurant, Weary spent the night writing his reports and packing. The 'indefatigable Dr Sem', who seemed to sleep even less than Weary, accompanied them to the airport at 4 am on 26 August for their flight to Colombo.

He had found Thailand a 'stimulating and happy experience'.[10] Dr Sem told Casey that the visit was a 'grand success', for everything went well, 'professionally and socially'.[11] The Australian Embassy also praised them. 'I am quite sure that visits such as [this] . . . are of real value both from the technical knowledge you can impart and in the goodwill you foster,' wrote Casey.[12] Weary agreed. ' . . . A life saved by the spontaneous, freely given exertions of western doctors represents an impressive gesture, and such gestures are badly needed.'[13]

Ceylon had taken them at their word. Work began at a lively pace a few hours after they arrived. The political situation here was tricky. The Suez Canal crisis was at its height and the sympathies of the people lay with Egypt rather than their colonial master, Great Britain. Casey had warned Weary of the intensely nationalistic feelings and Ceylon's desire for independence. Weary and the Australian High Commission were careful to stress to the pressmen waiting at the airport that they were there 'to exchange ideas'. This fooled nobody. 'Aussie surgeon will show how', clamoured the *Daily News*.

By 2.30 pm Weary was in the wards of Colombo General Hospital, surrounded by many doctors and students. He found the wards, facilities and equipment in the hospitals more up-to-date than Thailand, but the same grave shortage of trained people. All the surgeons were FRCS (England). Over a period of seventeen days, he performed twenty-nine major operations in five hospitals and fulfilled a punishing programme of ward rounds, teaching and lectures in Colombo, Kandy and Galle.

Nine days after their arrival, Weary and Stanton drove to Kandy,

---

* Now Emeritus Professor of Neurosurgery, Ramathipodi Hospital, Bangkok.

higher and cooler than the cities on the coast. Here, the senior surgeon was K. G. Jayasekera. It was a busy hospital with a wealth of clinical material, 'rare tumours, liver abscesses etc.' Jayasekera himself had performed around 2200 operations over the past year.

He assisted Weary, finding it educational and Weary 'tremendous – a breath of fresh air'. Weary did not 'waste time on trivialities – he went for the big stuff'. They shared an intense interest in oesophageal cases. Weary, with his vibrant personality, 'instilled a great deal of confidence in [one] . . . and for me that was . . . remarkable'.[14] Jayasekera had not enjoyed such stimulation since his time in London at Guy's and the Royal Cancer Hospital.

After their days 'pulling out oesophaguses and goitres', the two surgeons retreated to the golf club, where Jayasekera was captain.[15] He was a better player than Weary, who employed the same 'high, wide and handsome' approach to golf as he did to surgery. Weary almost met his 'Waterloo' in Kandy with a full day spent on two long and difficult operations. 'On the whole it was a relief to emerge on the golf links to be soundly trounced by Mr Jayasekera.' His luck held: both patients survived.

His last day in Ceylon was long, with a morning of operations beginning at 8 am, no lunch, a demonstration of numerous oesophageal patients to a crowd of doctors and students, ward rounds and a formal lecture to the Ceylon Medical Society on cancers of the pharynx and cervical oesophagus. Later that night, he was dining at Milroy Paul's when he was rung and asked to 'undertake an operation for a most distressing and advanced cancer of the pharynx in a young woman whose condition was considered to be beyond hope . . . '[16] It was impossible to refuse.

With an attentive audience of surgeons, he completed the procedure around 3 am with only an hour to pack and drive to the airport. On returning to his hotel, he was dismayed to find that his cases had been ransacked and over £50 worth of gear was missing. He said nothing.

Many of the operations had been 'most testing' and some were 'appalling'. Yet 'it has been astonishing to me the way my acceptance of extreme odds and hazards has been favoured by fortune and every case in Colombo is doing well'.[17]

Ceylon was a great contrast to Thailand. ' . . . The surgical programme of operations, demonstrations and lectures has been so heavy that there has been very limited opportunity to enquire into the wider fields of medical organisation and the general scope of health measures.'

He was not complaining. It was a pleasure to have so much use made of his specialised knowledge and technical skills.

It was impossible for Ceylon to train the number of people needed. He recommended to Casey that Australia contribute by attracting 'students and graduates seeking advancement in special fields, as well as help to train some of the nurses and technicians required'.[18]

The Australian Commissioner in Singapore gave him dinner. By then Weary was past wanting to sleep and found himself incapable of stopping talking, although conscious that his host was tired. He subjected the man to an interminable monologue until the early hours of the morning.

To Weary's surprise, flashbulbs popped when he arrived in Perth Airport that night: the press were waiting for him. 'Well, if it's not old "Weary" Dunlop!' they printed over his photograph in the *Weekend Mail*. 'He Repays his Helpers,' said the *West Australian*. But by then, he was on his way home to Melbourne, looking forward to sharing his enthusiasm with Casey.

His months away with the Colombo Plan had been a highlight in his life, 'satisfying . . . very exciting indeed'. The visit had awoken in him a desire to do whatever he could to advance Casey's plans, whom he believed to be far 'beyond the thinking of his time' in his determination to encourage *détente* between the essentially British community in Australia and Asia, where he believed the future lay.[19]

In 1957, with five other Australian doctors, Weary was invited to spend some of July and August in the Soviet Union visiting hospitals and medical institutions. But Helen's collapse and subsequent hysterectomy put an end to his long-held desire to explore the heartland of Communism. There was no trip abroad that year.

To his great sadness, Aunt Lil died in August. Alice had preceded her in 1955; the last of the trio, Aunt Violet, continued to live at the house in Elsternwick. Tossie, whose frailty had been the reason they moved to Toorak five years beforehand, was still in excellent health, accompanying them on jaunts throughout the state when Weary had speaking engagements or was guest-of-honour at Anzac Day ceremonies in country towns.

Weary sometimes found it difficult to fit time with the boys into his life, but he often put them in the car when he had calls to make at weekends. Staff in the various hospitals regarded them as 'terrors'. Travelling with Dad could be fraught with problems. He was often deaf to pleas for ice creams, sweets and drinks, but one day, after they had pestered him for some distance on the way to Frankston, he swerved off the tarmac and headed for an empty parking space. Weary was never particularly successful at parking and it took some backing and filling to position the Daimler. Just as he was slowly reversing in, a smart Aleck zipped in behind him. Little did he realise what he was taking on.

Weary jumped out, strode over to the other car, opened the door and yanked the driver out in his favourite fashion – by the scruff of the neck and the waist of his pants. Holding him high in the air and threatening the same treatment as he had meted out to the Arabs, he gave him a piece of his mind. Then he dumped the man on the ground, released the handbrake, and rolled the car out of the parking space, the terrified girlfriend still in the passenger's seat. No longer cocky, the interloper jumped into his car and drove off. Weary reversed in majestically. The boys, who had been utterly silent in the back seat, suggested that they would not bother about ice creams. After all this trouble, said Weary, 'You'll bloody well eat them.'

In 1956, he had been appointed a consultant surgeon to the Repatriation Department and to the Peter MacCallum Clinic for Cancer. Marshall, who had assisted him for a year at the Royal Melbourne from 1954, had returned from England in late 1956 to an appointment as an assistant surgeon. He also assisted Weary privately and did his weekend visiting, allowing him time with Helen and the boys, for 'Life was excessively busy'.

By 1959, Weary was doing well enough financially to contemplate a longer trip than usual away from Australia. Helen was eager to go: Alexander and John were both being educated at Scotch College and could become boarders there. They were too much of a handful to leave with Tossie. Peggles Gibson promised to keep an eye on them.

'Dear Dickie,' wrote Weary in August. 'I feel hungry for a sight of Europe and the British Isles again, and have a fancy to go travelling with my wife.'[20] When Dickson Wright had visited Melbourne, they had discussed another matter. 'I have a long cherished ambition to . . . give a Hunterian Lecture at the Royal College . . . ' He had 'gathered up quite a lot of useful stuff in a personal series of 170 patients with oesophageal cancers treated by a wide variety of methods . . . '[21]

The project nearly foundered, because Weary was late putting in his synopsis, but Dickson Wright promised to put matters to rights with the Council. 'I will be able to help it through should it need any which I doubt because the subject matter is of great interest.'[22] It was to take place in the summer of 1960.

Weary also spoke to Casey. The Colombo Plan had been extended to 1966, beyond its original span. It was agreed that he would visit India, teaching, lecturing and demonstrating.

The Professor of Clinical Surgery at Patiala, Dr R. L. Manchanda, had gained his Fellowship of the Australasian College in 1958, after coming to Australia as a post-graduate student on the Colombo Plan. Rank and Weary were 'horrified . . . that they should send a middle-aged man' as a student, but later they realised that someone of his seniority would exert greater influence when he returned to India.[23] Weary had welcomed his wife and him to 605 Toorak Road. Helen and Weary were keen on Scottish dancing and the grave Indian couple soon lost their inhibitions and spent some Friday evenings breathlessly attempting to master Highland reels in the ballroom.

Manchanda wished Weary to visit Patiala: 'I am arranging to send a request from this side for your proposed visit to our country . . . ' He had been appointed to the chair of Clinical Surgery in May 1959, the day he returned to the Medical College at Patiala.[24]

Weary fired off a volley of letters to the United States, for he needed to take substantial funds out of Australia to finance his travels and had to persuade the government that he was 'a truly bone fide traveller'. Offers of visiting professorships to Pittsburgh and Yale convinced the bureaucrats of the usefulness of Weary's tour; and the lecture fees would help with the expenses of two months in North America. By the time Weary and Helen settled into their seats on their Qantas flight to San Francisco on 29 April, he had arranged a whistle-stop itinerary of lectures and visits from the west coast to the eastern seaboard. They were also dropping into Toronto to see Marko and Gordon Murray, and anyone dealing 'in the oesophagus and mouth and throat surgery'.[25]

In all, he had six lectures arranged: two on hiatal hernia in Los Angeles at the Veterans' Administration Centre and in Long Beach at their hospital, and four on oesophageal cancer at the Kaiser Foundation in Los Angeles, the University of Pittsburgh, and the V. A. Hospital, Hines.

Weary's slides were a source of worry and irritation to both Dunlops, but for different reasons. More than once, Helen was known to tell him to 'bring a dilly bag but *no* slides' on a trip. They were already seated on board the plane when Weary's slides arrived for his American and English lectures: the late Neil Bromberger 'rushed out to Essendon and across the tarmac' to hand them to a member of the crew.[26]

Charles Puestow of Hines, the University of Illinois, was impressed by Weary's figures for cancer of the oesophagus – 'your statistics are far better than ours, and my associates will be anxious to discuss techniques with you'[27] – and Jim Clagett warned him that he and others at the Mayo Clinic would 'pick your brains as thoroughly as possible' about his results. He was delighted to be paid an unexpected honorarium of US$50 for a lecture he gave in Rochester.

Weary's fascination with vascular surgery had strengthened since 1952 as his penchant for performing ileostomies waned, although he never gave up anything entirely and nothing overtook his primary interest in gastro-oesophageal surgery. His work was extremely varied. 'He was one of the true general surgeons when surgeons did more or less everything . . . [His] philosophy . . . and his personality [was] such that he would do arterial surgery, oesophageal surgery, bowel surgery, bone surgery'.[28]

Macleish, who was looking after Weary's practice during his absence, had only recently returned from post-graduate work with one of the leading vascular surgeons in the world, Michael DeBakey, at the Texas Medical Centre in Houston. Weary juggled his dates so that he could visit DeBakey's department, but he muddled the arrangements made so carefully for him by Macleish. He arrived late and was peeved to find himself in the observers' room, rather than on the floor, from which he could see little. It was his own fault that the visit was 'a great disappointment' compared to his time with Al Humphries at the Cleveland Clinic. Watching Humphries and other leading vascular surgeons at work inspired him afresh when he returned to Australia.

Helen was relieved to reach New York after the stress of flying from city to city every three or four days. Sometimes, Weary had arranged not much more than twenty-four hours in a place, and he was quite ready to stay up till all hours dining and talking. New York was pure pleasure for her and she revelled in all the city offered, much to Weary's amazement. For twelve days, they plunged into visits to the theatre, to Radio City, concerts, dining and sightseeing. She was more outgoing than he had ever seen her, ready to amuse herself while he called on hospitals, doctors and surgical instrument firms.

Weary had warned Dickson Wright that his campaign to treat cancer with major surgical procedures might arouse controversy in England, where radiotherapy was favoured, but he regarded the kind of surgery he saw in New York with distaste. 'I didn't like the medical climate . . . nor the work they were doing in the Cancer Memorial Hospital . . . vast mutilating operations.'

His objections were not confined to New York. He was equally critical of the Peter MacCallum's methods in Melbourne, 'their total misuse and overuse of radiotherapy'. He saw the bias towards radiotherapy as 'like the Nabateans preying on the caravans' on the way to Petra. 'And what's more, they sent their people out all over the state, proselytising. I operated on people who had [dead] bone right through to the back of the skull. One man with cancer of the throat, when I opened him up there was just a gap – he had no gullet.'

Weary was more approving of the work at the M. D. Anderson Cancer Hospital in Houston. 'They showed a bit of restraint . . . they weren't trying to cure people by cutting them in half.'

By the time Helen and he were with Marco and Ruth Markowitz in Toronto, he had visited twelve cities, the Mayo, Cleveland and Lahey clinics, and a number of large teaching hospitals. Weary was now up to date with current North American research and techniques and had widened his circle of professional friends still further at meetings of the Illinois Surgical Society and the Surgeons' Club in Rochester.

By 1 July they had crossed the Atlantic and were ensconced in the Junior Army and Navy Club in Horse Guards Avenue, London. Helen complained to Peggles that her shopping and sightseeing expeditions were interrupted by trips to the typing agency and other messages for Weary, who was short tempered and working on the final stages of his paper. After a fortnight in Scotland, he was to deliver the Cecil Joll Lecture to the Royal College of Surgeons on 28 July.

Weary took Helen with him to his rehearsal for the lecture the day beforehand and showed her over the College. The room at the bend in the stairs where he had awaited the announcement of his results in 1938 was no longer there, a victim of enemy bombing raids during the war, but the Hunterian Museum enthralled her. Then she sat patiently amongst the portraits and the panelling in the Edward Lumley Hall while he ran through the routine with the technician.

Next day, Helen seemed oblivious to his tension and irritated Weary by trying to persuade him to fit in a few more days in Scotland. Shortly before he was to leave for the College, she picked up his carefully organised slides and accidentally dropped the lot on the floor.

Promptly at the appointed hour, the President and Weary entered the rear doors at the head of the long procession of England's eminent surgeons who bore office in the College. Helen had repaired her tear-stained face and was in her place in the audience. Weary walked to the lectern.

He had seen Cecil Joll operate one summer's afternoon in 1939 and 'the memory of that leonine feast' was described to his listeners. ' . . . The list began with four subtotal thyroidectomies, followed by a total thyroidectomy, a total gastrectomy, a total hysterectomy, then moved through three less arduous abdominal procedures to a precise unhurried close at 7.30 pm.

'That tall immaculate figure, with the elegant carnation in the buttonhole . . . savoured an excellent cigar, and seemingly as fresh as when the day began, passed on to dine . . . His frame contained some source of prodigious energy, and was driven relentlessly by a mind which demanded intense purposive activity, and a passion for detail.'[29]

Joll, Grey-Turner, Dunhill, Gordon-Taylor: these were the men who had made a deep impression on the young Australian surgeon when he worked in London hospitals more than twenty years before he received the Cecil Joll Prize. Dunhill had won the same prize. No other lecture would ever give him the same sense of recognition.

They moved into the visitors' flat in Nuffield House next door to the college for a couple of weeks while Weary whirled Helen around on visits to his friends between Fridays and Mondays. During the week, she continued to beat a path between the typist's and the College, for now the lecture had to be prepared for publication. In mid-August, they left London for a month on the Continent. Once the manuscript had been delivered to the journal, Helen's plans did not include watching surgical operations or listening to talk of surgery or the war over interminable dinners.

They returned from Rome in September. By now, Helen had attended countless functions in Australia for former prisoners-of-war, but it was only when she accompanied Weary to the annual FEPOW Reunion at the Festival Hall that she realised how revered he was by so many of the British. When he was introduced, a great cheer went up from the thousands of men and women in the audience, far greater than they gave General Percival, Brigadier Toosey or Sir Paul Maltby.

Weary was to be in New Delhi by 14 October. They broke the journey in Athens and in Beirut. Their room in the Grande Bretagne Hotel looked out across Syntagma Square to the Parthenon; and in Beirut, he insisted that they take a room in the Hotel Royal, where he had stayed with the rugby team in 1940. By the middle of October they were reunited with the Manchandas in Patiala, almost overwhelmed by Indian hospitality.

Weary spent a month operating and teaching in India at the Patiala Medical College in the Punjab, in Bombay, Madras, Vellore and Calcutta. From Madras, they flew to Madurai and drove up to Vellore, the hospital in South India founded by Ida Scudder where his old tutor, Ted Gault, was Professor of Pathology. As in Ceylon and Thailand, there was great interest in oesophageal surgery and he was presented with patients suffering from rare conditions. At first, he found the crowds of students and staff around him unnerving, especially since 'they trotted out their most difficult problems'.

Patiala was the only place where a patient of his died 'with an aneurysm of the aorta . . . they [had] no blood to speak of, and that was . . . difficult . . . I tried everything'.

Their last five days were spent on holiday in Kashmir. Srinagar seemed quiet, but it was not until they were on their way to Gulmarg, that Weary realised they had arrived in the middle of a cholera epidemic. All the way up, they met the corpses of cholera victims being brought down on horseback. Weary brushed aside Helen's anxious questions about whether their inoculations were up-to-date. But when they regained Srinagar and he looked at their certificates, he saw that they had expired: he had forgotten to check them before leaving London. Neither wished to be put in quarantine in New Delhi. All their airline bookings had to be changed. Helen did not relax until they were on their way to Hong Kong. By the end of November, they were home. Helen was exhausted. Weary never skipped a beat.

His latest paper had just been published in the *Australian and New Zealand Journal of Surgery*: 'Carcinoma of the Oesophagus with Survival'. Not only had he pioneered the technology 'of how to remove and join up the gut better' he had been the first 'to amass a large experience of surgery of the gullet . . . probably the most extensive surgery undertaken [then] . . . and he made it work'.[30]

He had been gratified by the praise for his work and generous acknowledgement of his achievements from those men in the USA whom he regarded as pre-eminent in their field, and by the way he had been received in London.

In Melbourne, he was referred to as 'a high mortality surgeon' and he was 'bitter' about what he saw as unjustified criticism from some of his peers. 'For example, I operated on five hundred goitres before I had a death . . . when it comes to cancer of the oesophagus, you can't have a low mortality.'

Weary was not the most attentive father. During their early years, Alexander and John were usually asleep when Weary arrived home and they caught but fleeting glimpses of him in the mornings, but once Weary bought the farm at St Andrews in the late 1950s and the Smith's Gully property a few years later, more time was spent together in the country. He encouraged them to help out with the farm work, marking calves, baling and stacking hay.

When they were teenagers, he began to take them with him on his travels if surgical conferences coincided with school holidays. He took Alexander to New Zealand in 1962, and both boys scored a trip to India in 1964. That year, Weary enjoyed a busy year of travelling, leaving his practice in Marshall's care. Accompanied by Alexander, he was in Chandigarh in January with E. S. R. Hughes at the Second Asian Congress of Gastroenterology, before embarking on a further grand tour of hospitals and surgical friends in Bombay, Madras, Vellore and Calcutta, then renewing his links with Ceylon; he was at a conference in Philadelphia in May; and in December he returned to India for the Silver Jubilee Meeting of the Association of Surgeons of India.[31] This time, John went with him.

It was Christmas Day when they arrived in New Delhi and they flew on to Bombay on Boxing Day for the Silver Jubilee. They were in Madras when the New Year honours list was published in Australia and Weary was awarded a CMG, engineered by Sir Robert Menzies because of a general feeling that the OBE and MID after the war did not attach sufficient merit to his contributions in Java and Thailand. Elsie Noble, his secretary, suggested he would need a week to plough through the pile of congratulatory letters.

After Weary had given his paper and shown a film made by the Royal Melbourne on oesophageal surgery at the seminar in Bombay, they criss-crossed the sub-continent on Indian Airlines to his usual haunts, Madras, Madurai, Vellore and New Delhi. His Indian friends welcomed them joyfully into their homes and their hospitals. Everyone wanted to hear him lecture and to see the film made by the Royal Melbourne which he had shown in Bombay. Inevitably, there were ward rounds, operating, teaching and discussion, yet this time Weary paid for the trip himself without any support from the Colombo Plan. In his baggage he carried a personal gift of instruments unobtainable in India for Krishnamurthi of the Cancer Institute in Madras.

'Dear wandering boys,' wrote Helen. They might be having a thoroughly enjoyable time in India, but nothing was going well at home in Melbourne. Tossie's sister, Great Aunt Briddy, died in January and Alexander failed his matriculation examinations (but retrieved chemistry on a recount, after driving Helen to distraction because he had lost the slip with his examination number).

In early December, shortly before Weary left Australia, Hughes had visited South Vietnam and sent word to Weary: ' . . . You simply must go to visit the team.'[32] Macleish was just ending his tour of duty as leader of the Australian surgical team in the civilian hospital there. Weary had decided that he must 'jolly the staff we had [from the Royal Melbourne] at Long Xuyen' and obtained two-day visas. His timing was impeccable; he gave John an adventure which made everyone else's summer holidays look very tame indeed. They arrived in Saigon by way of Bangkok, Kuala Lumpur and Singapore.

When Pan American flight 2 from Singapore touched down on 26 January, Weary and John walked straight into one of the coups engineered by Air Vice-Marshall Nguyen Cao Ky and General Nguyen Can Thieu. The atmosphere in Saigon was 'charged with tension . . . student riots, hunger-striking buddhists [and] a buddhist nun [immolated] herself during the afternoon', setting a match to her petrol-soaked clothing.[33] Anderson, the Australian Ambassador, was not all that pleased to see John: no one had realised Weary was bringing a fourteen-year-old with him.

They flew off across the Delta next morning in an eight-seater Beechcraft and landed at Long Xuyen forty-five minutes later. The hospital was a few hundred metres from the strongly fortified American base, although there was only sporadic Viet Cong activity in the area at the time, since it was Tet – the Vietnamese New Year.

Weary looked over the hospital, ceremonially removed an appendix to mark the occasion, and they then moved off to inspect the American army base. No sooner had they arrived than there were a few shots with the answering chatter of machine guns. 'It was absolutely fascinating for John to see . . . all the Americans standing by their weapons.' Weary enjoyed it also, the fortified area, 'machine guns posted' and the odd mortar going off.

They arrived back in Saigon in the nick of time to appease the ambassador, who feared trouble if they exceeded their visas. A few days shopping in Hong Kong and reminiscing with Dougie Clague was very small beer after that.

Casey could see that Weary was vastly stimulated by these international visits. More to the point, his reports were sharp and well informed and he gathered friends for Australia around him wherever he travelled and taught. Quite informally, Casey suggested one day that he had been considering his friend's growing dissatisfaction with surgery. Weary had maturity, personality, breadth of experience and intelligence. Perhaps his activities could become more general? Not all the diplomatic corps need be career diplomats.

Weary welcomed the idea, but Helen was horrified. She was devoted to Weary and the children; she enjoyed her life of golf, the Lyceum Club and her friends; she was happy entertaining in her own home and travelling as the wife of a successful surgeon. But, essentially, she was a private person, quiet, reserved and more comfortable in circles of her choosing, rather than breasting the billows of official life amongst strangers abroad. Weary took official dinners, parties, balls and conventions in his stride. Helen accompanied him, but while her exuberant husband danced the night away, many noticed her sitting quietly at a table, waiting. 'I was often naughty about that. Her feet hurt and she would want to go home.' More than once, John Blunt saw her at dinner dances and similar functions where former prisoners-of-war gathered, seated at a table, rolling pieces of bread into little balls and piling them on a plate.[34]

The suggestion went no further.

Through the Colombo Plan, the Royal Melbourne Hospital, the Australian-Asian Association and privately, he became a great friend of Indian medicine. Surgeons and post-graduate students from the institutions he visited in India were placed in Melbourne hospitals, funded either by the Colombo Plan or privately. He had friends all over Asia: Lieut-Colonel Dargao Singh at the military hospital in Pune; Manchanda at Patiala; Professor Santokh Singh Anand, the Director and Professor of Surgery at the Post Graduate Institute of Medical Education & Research at Chandigarh; Bomy Billimoria, Arthur de Sa and P. K. Sen in Bombay; L. B. M. Joseph at Vellore. To those early Colombo Plan friends, Dr Sem, Professor Karsarn and Dr Smarn in Bangkok, he added men met at the regular international meetings in his field of gastroenterology: G. B. Ong of Hong Kong (whom he met this year), and, after Helen and he travelled to Tokyo for the Third World Congress of Gastroenterology in 1966, Shinichi Kawashima.

The 'little bread' which Weary cast upon the waters by smoothing the professional paths of his Indian friends in Australia, folding them into his family and devoting his time to operating and teaching throughout the sub-continent, 'came back as currant loaves' when he was awarded an honorary doctorate by the University of the Punjab in January 1966 'for services to Indian medicine'. More precious to him than academic honours was the deep affection of his Indian friends.

His international activities absorbed an increasing amount of time during the 1960s. When Hughes and he were in Chandigarh, they had diffidently offered Melbourne as the home for the Third Asian-Pacific Congress of Gastroenterology in 1968. Their 'diffidence was in no way lessened' by the superb Japanese organisation of the world congress in Tokyo in 1966, but the Melbourne congress met their expectations. Casey, by now Governor-General of Australia, opened the proceedings; Weary was a Vice-President and the organiser of the panel discussion of Diseases of the Oesophagus, dividing the duties of moderator with G. B. Ong.

Weary shared with Casey a disregard for race, creed and colour and spent a great deal of energy furthering the causes of his Asian colleagues. In 1971, when Ceylon was beset by serious political troubles, Jayasekera wrote him a desperate letter. Their house had narrowly escaped being blown up by a terrorist bomb. He had to leave, and bring his family with him, for he could see no future for his children there.

Over the next four months, Weary wrote letters, pulled strings and did everything he could. Jayasekera could bring no money out, even though he owned considerable assets, but friends and relations sent money to Australia for air tickets and the family's expenses. Weary sponsored the family and insisted that Jaya must stay at 605 Toorak Road until he was established. Letters were intercepted and telephones were tapped in Colombo, for someone of Jaya's seniority in the government service would not be allowed to leave permanently. They had to use a code to conceal the remittance of funds: £500 was a 'wallaby'.

Jaya arrived on 11 August, four days before Weary was to leave for Moscow. Weary organised for him to register in Sydney with the Medical Board of NSW, since new legislation prevented him registering in Victoria without examination, despite his FRCS (England), and wrote letters of introduction to Frank Mills and Professor John Loewenthal ahead of Jaya's arrival so that he would have friends at court. Two months later, he was registered both as a doctor and a specialist and had a job with a group practice in Melbourne. One more month, and his wife and five children had joined him.

Weary and Jaya thought alike: 'One's calling to medicine comes before one's personal needs. Surgery has to take absolute precedence over everything else.'[35]

Leaving Helen to look after Jaya at 605 Toorak Road, Weary flew to Moscow with his Australian co-delegate and professor of cardio-thoracic surgery Rowan Nicks, to an International Society of Surgeons' congress.

Rowan and Weary had met at the Australasian College meetings. They discovered a shared experience of war (although Rowan's casualty clearing station in the Royal Navy was vastly different from Weary's), a love of poetry and ideas, of whisky and of sheer good fun. More than any other man, Weary would say of Rowan and he 'How often you and I/ Have tired the sun of talking/And talked him down the sky'.

Japan was in the throes of a currency crisis when they stopped there overnight on their way to Moscow. The American dollar had plum-meted and the Imperial Hotel refused to cash their travellers' cheques. Weary was equally determined that they would, and neither he nor the manager would risk losing face by backing down. Nicks could see that 'in some curious way, the manager had become in Weary's mind like one of his former enemies'. He suggested a solution. Why not entertain their Japanese friends to dinner in one of the hotel's restaurants and charge it?

They ate lavishly, course after course with wine, liqueurs and cigars. When no one but Weary's party and the exhausted-looking band remained in the restaurant, he signed the bill with a flourish.

Next morning, Weary took an interminable time getting up and the airport bus was already waiting when they reached the lobby. The manager's expression was grim when he saw the sheaf of chits on Weary's room bill. With great loss of face and very ill grace, he had to accept the travellers' cheques. Nicks was becoming agitated, for Weary showed no sign of boarding the bus, even though a flunkey told them several times that it was ready to leave. He merely observed to Nicks, 'The longer we keep it waiting, the more "face" we gain.'

Eventually, he sauntered out. He was quite right: two front seats had been kept for them.

Congresses were occasions for relaxation unless Weary was giving a paper, and Nicks and he saw as much of Moscow and the countryside surrounding it as possible. Their Russian tour almost came to a premature end late one night when Nicks imitated the Russian guards 'goose-stepping' in Red Square. Soldiers erupted from everywhere and seized him by both arms. Weary, in a hurried pantomime, managed to convey that they had both drunk a great deal of vodka and that Nicks – tapping his forehead – was 'nuts'.

The international scene absorbed them as the Australasian College failed to do. Weary was a strong leader, but he was of too independent a bent to begin lower down the ladder and steadily work his way up to greater office amongst men who let him know that he had been given rather more publicity about his prisoner-of-war activities than was considered acceptable. Had Hailes lived longer, he would have persevered, but he was impatient of a life spent 'playing politics' in Melbourne. The International Society of Surgeons and the James IV Association of Surgeons, a select society of 100 members to which he was elected in 1971, satisfied his love for travel and variety and offered a broader intellectual platform.

The International Society of Surgeons is the oldest of its kind in the world. The two men set up the Australian chapter of the Society in 1977, with Weary as Chairman and Rowan as Secretary, and brought in two younger men, Bernard O'Brien and Graham Copland, to take their places as delegates when it was time to retire. The Bicentenary of European settlement in Australia was ten years away. Weary suggested that they propose Sydney for the 1987 international congress.

They attended the San Francisco congress the following year and, at Montreux in 1981, Weary was appointed a vice-president. By then, Weary and O'Brien had secured the 1987 Congress for Sydney and Weary retired gracefully from the international scene. He remained Chairman of the Australian chapter for a number of years. O'Brien noticed how he was 'known all over the world in that Society and greatly respected'.[36]

PART FIVE

1967 – 1993

O Lord God,
   when thou givest to thy servants
      to endeavour any great matter,
   grant us to know
   that it is not the beginning
      but the continuing of the same unto the end,
   until it be thoroughly finished,
   which yieldeth the true glory . . .

                    – from SIR FRANCIS DRAKE'S prayer

TWENTY-NINE

'The Influence of Weary'

WHEN WEARY RETIRED from the Royal Melbourne Hospital in 1967, his former residents presented him with a bound volume of their research reports and papers. Firmly stamped on the spine were four words in gold leaf: 'The Influence of Weary.'

Weary 'thoroughly enjoyed being a general surgeon', but latterly he concluded that 'if he had to be a surgeon again, the time had come to be a professor: the day had gone . . . in which you could do everything'. He insisted on 'doing everything', not only in terms of the range of operations – 'he would pin a hip, take a mole off, do an oesophagec-tomy . . . anything that came in' – but in the operation itself.[1] During all the years that Marshall was his assistant at the Royal Melbourne and privately, until he went to an appointment at Prince Henry in 1963, 'Weary would do the whole operation down to the last skin stitch . . . I never did an operation when Weary was there.'[2]

Even in a procedure where it was usual to employ two surgeons (in this case a combined synchronous abdomino-perineal resection of the rectum), Weary did it all on his own in about three and a half hours one day at Epworth. He could have completed it in forty-five minutes to an hour if Marshall had been allowed to play an equal part instead of the supporting rôle. Stanton had given the anaesthetic and, afterwards, he asked Weary if he had ever considered doing a combined synchronous operation. Weary looked at him. 'Well, I suppose if you have two surgeons of more or less equal ability and experience, there is something to be said for that . . . '[3]

Marshall was stunned. Here he was, nearly forty and with his fellowship – the same age as Weary had been when appointed Surgeon to Out-Patients – and he was still being treated as the young resident. Weary, when taxed with this, merely looked surprised. 'I couldn't let an assistant operate like that on a private patient.'

His peers agree that Marshall is 'an extremely good surgeon',[4] the archetype 'of the guy who learnt how to operate by watching and learning often how not to do it'.[5]

As junior residents, Michael Long, Brian Buxton and Robert Dickens chose to work for Weary in the early 1960s, because they wanted the breadth of experience he offered. ' . . . In the other units where there were specialised surgical teams . . . there wasn't that sort of general cover and you didn't get . . . as much exposure.'[6]

Dickens's first experience after graduating was three months of working with Weary. 'Marvellous, marvellous time . . . it was very exciting . . . it struck me that surgery was my game after that.'[7]

Mindful of his teaching responsibilities, Weary was more generous to them. Dickens found that even though he was quite junior, it was a 'marvellous opportunity to do some operating . . . pin hips, take out appendices . . . I did one or two gall bladders'.[8] For Michael Long, 'the best thing I ever did was select to go to Weary's unit'. Most of Long's colleagues did not wish to join Weary 'because it involved too much work'. As students, they had seen him as 'someone who worked extremely long hours . . . did incredibly big operations that often finished at midnight, had a lot of staff who fell apart and couldn't keep up'.

Dickens recognised a 'killer instinct in him . . . I watched this one night, operating until about 11 pm, and I think he almost got a feeling of satisfaction out of seeing one of us on his team faint. He was stronger, he was still able to operate and the young junior couldn't stand the pace . . . ' He always ignored his own discomfort and 'he loved people who were in there with him', no matter who they were.[9]

While Long was a student working with Weary at the Royal Melbourne, he was on Ward 7 North, then the general surgical ward. Although its function has changed, he never walks into it without thinking of Weary. 'We would assemble . . . and he would invariably be late . . . '[10] Long remembered what he taught because he 'livened it up', and now, teaching students himself, it sometimes goes through his mind, 'I learned this from Weary'.

He had high expectations of students. His unpunctuality frequently meant they gave up waiting and returned to their quarters. Weary would summon them back to the theatre or the ward. 'Now you mutinous dogs . . . ' he would say, 'and keep us there for hours . . . You had to work quite hard to be taught . . . but what he [said] was gem-like.'[11]

Dickens's first ward round was for two o'clock in the afternoon. He arrived in the ward, having boned up on every patient there 'so that I would be ready to work wonders when I ran around the ward with him', but Weary was almost eight hours late. The medical students had given up and gone home. 'We went round all the patients waking them up so that he could see how they were . . . '[12]

Lateness became part of the legend. Most private patients visiting his rooms took it in their stride. So did his staff, eventually. 'The worst thing that happened was if he turned up early.' His operating started at 8 am 'but no one would get there until 9 am'. If, one day, 'he turned up at 8.15 instead of his usual nine o'clock there would be total disarray'.[13]

At first, Dickens expected the nursing staff to find Weary frustrating, because of his unpunctuality and the length of time his cases took, but 'never did I see a problem. The whole bunch would stay down there and work. They realised that when Weary was operating, it might go on to eleven or twelve o'clock, so they just cancelled everything . . . ' As Potter pointed out, he always treated them well, and Dickens noticed how 'terribly gentle' he was: 'the nurses never did any wrong.'

Once he ceased to operate, surgeons would ask him to assist. Peter Nelson was one of the last to do so. 'He was so good to me . . . it [was] my pleasure to ask him along . . . a sort of reciprocal thing'. Weary was 'extraordinarily pleasant to operate with . . . because he [had] a sense of humour'.[14] Over the years, Nelson and Weary entertained each other with poetry. One would quote a line and the other would be expected to finish the stanza or sometimes the entire poem. Nelson never produced a line Weary could not complete, but Weary often had him stumped.

When he was assisting, 'one of the problems was to keep his hands off'. But there was never friction. Gabriel Kune did several locums for Weary after 'escapades in which cars seemed to run into [Weary's] car'. He found operating with Weary 'breathing down my neck . . . nerve-wracking'.[15]

Often, patients referred to another surgeon by Weary would request that he be there, they had such faith in him. Nelson says this was well-founded. 'It was very useful to have him . . . I can recall just two or three people in town whom . . . you would like to have on a difficult case, and he was one.'[16] Long agrees that he was a better clinician than a technical surgeon and there was consensus that 'you could get no better opinion' than Weary's.

By 1960, with the rise of specialisation and the influence of the vast teaching hospitals and private clinics in the USA on visiting Australian surgeons, it was plain to all that the days of the true general surgeon were over. Weary never accepted that, although he saw himself as 'a general surgeon with hobbies, and my hobbies were very specialised'. Macleish, who assisted Weary for five years from 1962 at the Royal Victorian Eye and Ear hospital, saw that 'Weary was never prepared to give up what he had trained in and he did well at covering a wide field . . . '[17]

Nelson was Orm Smith's houseman. Weary might be upstairs operating with his Chinese registrar from Malaysia, Geoffrey Chiam, 'doing horrendous upper gastric and oesophageal operations', malignancies that no one else would touch because of the difficulty. 'He just kept working until it was finished.'[18] When the patients came down from theatre, if Nelson rather than one of Weary's housemen was on duty, he would put in the drips and look after them through the early hours of the morning.

Dickens can 'remember so many of those patients to this day, people who died post-operatively'. He used to ring Weary when their condition deteriorated. 'Mr So-and-So has started to leak from his oesophagectomy and anastomosis.' There would be a very long silence on the other end of the line, and eventually the houseman would hear Weary say, 'Unfortunately, my experience . . . is that invariably it is fatal.'

'You just had to make the patient as comfortable as you could.'[19]

Weary became 'emotionally involved' with his patients suffering from advanced cancer. He used to lie awake at night, worrying, and 'you would find yourself getting up at two or three o'clock in the morning and going to see the patient'. This was particularly so at private hospitals, which lacked the facilities of the large teaching hospitals. In those days there was no intensive care.

Patients found his appearance by their beds in the early hours of the morning in kilt and velvet jacket, a froth of lace at his throat and wrists and *skean dhu* tucked into his stocking top, much more surprising, when he came straight from a Scottish dancing night, or a Melbourne Scots dinner.

Two things about Weary stood out for Kune. 'His humanity, his real warmth towards a person and their family . . . ' Weary was a good listener and a close observer. He talked to people to find out what they did and how they felt, in order to suit the care to the patient. 'That was something I am sure I copied . . . ' Kune was also influenced by the example of his 'complete commitment to that person as a patient' and 'his doggedness to pursue what is best . . . for that particular person . . . '[20]

Patients understood instinctively that 'he was doing the best for them'. He told them as much as he thought they needed to know and would avoid committing himself to a prognosis, 'for one can be very wrong'.

'Well, you do what you think, sir,' Dickens heard them say. These days, he says, patients 'expect you to spend hours explaining in minute detail'. Then, they didn't. Long found it amazing that 'all these people would go off to theatre knowing they were being operated on by this great man, all entirely happy, and some of them died with smiles on their faces'.

Most of Weary's residents found him helpful during their early careers. Women surgeons were rare; he gave Lorna Sisely great support, encouragement, and work assisting him. He was instrumental in Nelson going to a job at Hammersmith Hospital in London and was one of the referees for his appointment to the Royal Melbourne. Weary extended the same practical help to Nelson as Hailes had given him in the 1940s: the younger man used his rooms and secretary and assisted him. Nelson's father-in-law was Guy Moore, who had shared the 'Tomcats' House' with Weary during the early days in Jerusalem.

When Kune was appointed one of the foundation professors at the University of Melbourne, he found him 'really terrific . . . one of my mentors [but] not in a direct way . . . [more] behind the scenes in supporting things that I have done. I became interested in cancer and [its] causes and prevention and he . . . stimulated me quite a lot with his . . . ideas.'[21] Kune also worked for Repatriation and gained a close understanding of Weary's frustrations in the pensions field.

In Melbourne, and later, as a post-graduate student in London, Weary had determined he would be an excellent surgeon. He saw surgery then as a profession at the very 'top of the tree . . . no mere craftsman's hand'. His belief in himself was unshakeable and he never doubted his ability, but at the end of his life, he concluded that he had not pursued excellence as ruthlessly as he should have done; he had allowed himself to be side-tracked 'and the achievements of a lifetime seem . . . trivial'. The insight which rarely failed him did not reveal the remarkable qualities which he passed on to others and which pervaded the institution he worked in.

Every surgeon who has worked with Weary as a resident, registrar or assistant mentions his humanity, his compassion and his dedication to his patients. Anyone who had contact with Weary 'can relate to young people, they are good teachers and [have] this tremendous responsibility to patients . . . He was one of the main reasons for it.' These were part of his legacy, 'very infectious. It has been like a bushfire throughout this hospital, to anyone who has had contact with him'.[22]

Weary was no saint. 'The beauty about Weary [was] that he was a person with whom you could identify because he had good and bad points . . . '[23]

His patients may have seen him as a god-like figure, but his residents and his friends saw the wild streak in him which 'Helen never understood'.[24] Most of them wonder how she survived it all.

Weary was enormously hospitable to his residents and registrars. He would take them out for drinks, drop over to the mess for a few beers after operating. 'I think he loved . . . having a drink with us.'[25] He often picked up Long in the Daimler and the two of them would spend the late afternoon rabbit shooting at Smith's Gully. On their way back to the car, he would call his cows over to talk to them: they were all named. Back in Toorak, Alexander and John would be taught how to skin the rabbits and stretch the skins on fencing wire. After they had been hung up in the garden shed, Helen would feed everyone, and the night would be spent 'with Weary regaling you with stories . . . you couldn't outdrink him . . . then he would drive you back to the hospital'.[26]

Every year he took one of his registrars to the Melbourne Scots dinner. That was an 'eye-opener' for someone like Dickens, for they would be seated next to the head table on which would be Sir Robert Menzies, captains of industry, important men.

Dickens was taken to a rugby dinner in St Kilda which was the only known occasion on which Helen stood up publicly to her very dominating partner. Weary invited everyone back to Toorak for a drink afterwards, and when they were milling noisily around in the front garden in the early hours of the morning, she rang the police. Weary was at the door when they arrived. As he was explaining that there was no need for them to call, Helen appeared.

'Do you know this man, madam?' asked the sergeant politely.

Helen stared straight at Weary. 'I've never seen him before in my life,' she replied.

He was free with his fists when he thought injustice had been done or in self defence. ' . . . He would get into all sorts of alterca-

tions . . . there would be yelling . . . punching, things like that.'[27]
Macleish was in an adjoining theatre at Epworth Hospital one morning
when Weary appeared with a bloodied face and shirt front. Weary had
been driving to the hospital, probably in his usual cavalier fashion: no
signals, sudden bursts of speed, cutting in and out of the traffic, tearing
across intersections as the lights changed, horns blaring, brakes
squealing. As he came up to an intersection, another car zipped in front
of him and beat him to the lights. He gave the driver a blast on the horn.
The man leapt out of his car at the lights, dashed back to Weary and
punched him on the nose through the open window.

No one ever bargained on Weary's reflexes being so fast. In no time
at all, he was out of his car and had given the fellow a 'shirt full of ribs'
to remember him by. Streaming blood and mucus, Weary walked into
the hospital, rang Helen and told her to bring him a clean shirt, and
marched up to the operating theatre. Rejecting Macleish's offers of help
or a call to Rank to look at his damaged face, he cleaned himself up,
stuffed his nostrils with cotton wool, put on three masks, scrubbed up
and did his case.

The colleague he consulted suggested that they wait for the bruising
and swelling to subside before setting the nose. Weary decided to take
care of it himself. Some days later, he set it by poking a toothbrush
handle up each nostril.

Macleish was also in the hospital the night a very dishevelled Weary
appeared, carrying his two operating bags and reporting that he had
rolled his Daimler over a bank on the way home from operating in a
country town. 'I remember [that] to get out of the car, I had to push
the door upwards.' Dazed and bruised, he managed to hitch a ride back
to Melbourne. He had dropped in to leave his instruments to be
sterilised for the next day and for a cup of tea, but 'Sister Scott, the night
sister . . . put him to bed in the nurses' ward' where he managed three
or four hours sleep. He was in the theatre on time that morning.[28] The
police called and politely informed Weary that they had found his car.
Had he any idea how it had ended up near the Kororoit Creek? Weary
thanked them for their trouble. He had no idea.

Weary drove as if he owned the road. He loved speed. Helen was a
timorous driver and often a petrified passenger. John remembers family
outings with Weary at the wheel, the journey punctuated by grumbles
('Bloody fool, shouldn't be on the road!') and the sharp hiss of Helen's
indrawn breath as she pushed her foot flat to the floor on imaginary
brakes. Weary never believed himself to be in the wrong, but when the

situation demanded it, he would leap out of his car and march across to the other one. If his transgressions provoked only swearing and fist-shaking, he would raise his hat politely and drive majestically on.

Weary believed that he seldom drove into people: they drove into him, and his insurance claims are masterpieces of logical reconstruction. His secretaries kept files labelled 'Car Accidents'. Often, he had to drive Helen's Austin because the Daimler (and, later, the Ford) was in dock. This would be not only from accidents: plugs and pins mysteriously sheered off, transmissions packed up, involving copious correspondence and threats of court action.

Nathan was to give an anaesthetic for him one morning and came over to pick him up because Weary, in backing his car out of the garage, had successfully put both Helen's and his off the road. Nathan decided that his colleague had a malevolent influence on other people's vehicles: as he surveyed the wreckage in the drive at 605, there was a loud bang, and his own car blew up. With no change of expression, Weary murmured, 'Looks like you're in trouble also.' They drove to the hospital in a taxi.

One Daimler had a detachable steering wheel. There would not have been many drivers who managed to shoot backwards into the rear seat holding the steering wheel, connected to the column only by a cable. Weary plunged forward, re-engaged the wheel on the steering column, and clambered back into the driver's seat.

The Daimlers were an expensive hobby, and Weary was quick with litigation if agents or garages tried to wriggle out of their responsibilities. But even minor problems were treated seriously, his pen scoring the paper as he berated someone who did not measure up. Whether it was an insufficient trade-in price on a new car for Helen or the failure of the newsagent to deliver the correct newspapers, they received an irascible response by the next post.

Overcharging always provoked him into caustic correspondence and threats of removing his business.

In Gordon Stanton, Weary was blessed with a gifted anaesthetist possessing the patience of a saint. 'He was an integral part of the whole era',[29] and had given Weary's anaesthetics since 1947. As the years rolled by, Weary's inability to arrive anywhere on time worsened, but he could be intolerant of unpunctuality in others and extremely bad-tempered. Stanton ended an association of twenty-five years on the day that Weary dressed him down for being a few minutes late. 'You can go to hell!' he snapped and walked out.[30] He never gave another anaesthetic for Weary after May 1972. It was fifteen years before Weary's theatre sister, Shirley

Hah (who saw a deep affection between the two men during their working lives), engineered their reconciliation and snapped the two of them shaking hands at Weary's eightieth birthday party. Both men were happy to bury their differences, but neither would make the first approach.

Stanton's partner, Nathan, fell out with Weary at much the same time. Weary's generation of surgeons regarded anaesthetists as 'lackeys'. Surgeons were gods of the theatre and treated as such; Nathan once watched Norman James, the most senior anaesthetist in Melbourne, wait by the door of the theatre while Coates strolled out of the tea room, down the corridor and through the door held open by James. Only then would the anaesthetist enter.

Surgeons are translated warriors, and whereas one war finished for Weary in 1945, another began with his return to Melbourne and his revitalised interest in cancer. In his earliest imaginary games at Summerlea, he always had a clear image of the kind of person he wanted to be. Weary never seemed to need to refer to anything in order to know how he should behave: Kune thinks it was 'programmed into him . . . it has to do with his DNA'. It was inevitable that with this genetic blueprint for behaviour, he should pick up the gauntlet and do battle against some of the most formidable and challenging cancers.

Even the vocabulary suited his heroic ideas. Weary did about 150 'commando' operations for cancer, 'an operation on the mouth in which you remove the jaw and dissect the neck as a clean sweep' from the ear down to the collarbone'. In Weary's day, the reconstruction involved was complicated by the difficulty of keeping the blood supply intact; now, there are 'marvellous facilities to put in a chunk of bone, muscle and skin and revascularise'. Nelson found this upper facial oral surgery, 'opening up jaws, taking out tongues and making grafts from various parts of the body' memorable.[31]

One needed a special kind of courage to concentrate in a field where the mortality was so high, for 'he was ahead of his time, attempting surgery too great for his era and behind in anaesthetics. Today, I think he would be accepted as a very good surgeon.'[32] Only someone possessing great gifts of resilience of spirit, dogged persistence and deep compassion for his patients could 'sit by their beds for hours talking to them' and conquer the depression of seeing one's patients die.[33]

In 1964, Weary became the Senior Consultant at the RMH. He 'hated bureaucracy and administration' and, throughout the 1960s, there was increasing pressure on surgeons to conform to timetables and labour laws.[34] Long sensed that 'he was becoming unhappy in a place like this'.

Then, surgeons retired from the hospital at the age of 60. By July 1967, Dickens was Weary's surgical registrar and he arranged the last operating list. Tradition decreed that it be typical of the surgeon's career. 'A large and respectful crowd' of nursing staff and students had gathered for his ward round on Monday 10 July,[35] when Weary arrived to carry out his last official duties in the hospital where he had worked as student, houseman and surgeon for twenty-eight of his sixty years.

Weary found it 'an emotional occasion. I . . . gave my last lecture and forgot my slides . . . '

All sorts of people who would not normally be there were in the theatre for his final list. It 'was the greatest *potpourri* . . . nothing complicated: just pinned a hip and did a laryngectomy, an appendicectomy, a cholecystectomy . . . just like Weary's standard list. Weary did everything . . . He was the last, truly great, general surgeon.'[36]

80 *Weary and Helen at 605 Toorak Road, 1980*

81 *Les Tanner often baked scones for Weary; for the 80th birthday he sent a card*

You've taken the cake! so have a scone

80th

Happy birthday Sir Weary

Les Tanner with gratitude and affection

82 *Young John, Weary, Andrew and John admire the 80th birthday cake*

83 *Australian–Asian Association China Seminar, 1980. Weary*
with HE the Ambassador for the People's Republic of China
& Dr John Colebatch

84 *Launceston cenotaph. Year after year, on Anzac Days and at*
reunions, Weary always laid a wreath

85 *He spoke at many British FEPOW reunions in the Festival Hall, London*

86 *With 'hammer and tap man' Bill Haskill, looking at a drill hole, Hellfire Pass, Thailand*

87 *Weary in Hellfire Pass, Anzac Day 1991*

88 *Blue Butterworth in Hellfire Pass*

89 *Hellfire Pass, 1943*

90 *Yi Hak-Nae (Hiramura or 'The Lizard') met Weary*
    in Canberra, 1991

91 *Melbourne University honoured him: LL.D (Hon.), April 1988*

92 *Weary was made an honorary Fellow of the Royal College of Surgeons (Edin), 1991*

93 *Kanchanaburi Cemetery, April 1987. 'I see so many names I know.'*

94 *Jack Flannery was on the Railway. Voluntarily, he drove Weary all over Victoria during his last years*

95 *The last Anzac Day, 1993*

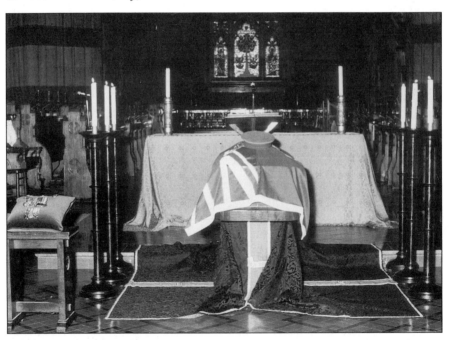

96 *Weary would have been 86 on the day his country gave him a State Funeral, St Paul's Cathedral, Melbourne*

THIRTY

The Life-long Mission

WEARY CONTINUED TO EMPLOY his own theatre sister, although only very successful surgeons could afford to do so by the 1960s. In 1966 Shirley Hah came to work at 14 Parliament Place after scrubbing for him at the Royal Melbourne and St Andrew's. He christened her, 'Honourable Theatre Sister'; for Shirley, he was 'Boss'.

Shirley enjoyed organising his patients and operating in country hospitals with him, particularly with his old friend Dr Cyril Checchi at Willaura, the last in which he operated regularly. But she was not comfortable with his driving. 'Slow down, slow down, cars coming,' she used to say. 'I don't think he liked it.'[1]

Shirley reminded him of the devoted sisters of his younger days: quick, intelligent and able to anticipate his needs while he was operating. She was efficient with the patients' records and brought a Chinese pragmatism to the accounts; she also chivied him into being more punctual. Weary 'could be bad-tempered when things went wrong', but Shirley knew how to handle him. 'We never had a row. He respected me and I respected him.'

Shirley was fiercely proud of 'Boss', and after his retirement from the Royal Melbourne, she felt it was time he received a knighthood. Lady Casey often called in to the rooms for a chat; one afternoon, Shirley backed her into a corner of the office. She was astonished when Maie Casey told her that a knighthood had been offered to him already, and he had refused. 'He thought that he didn't deserve it.'

Shirley was determined. 'Now it is time. He should have a knighthood.' Maie Casey agreed.

When the letter arrived, Weary discussed it with Helen: she was not enthusiastic. He did nothing. Some days later, the telephone rang in the operating theatre and it was Lord Casey; Weary interrupted his operating and took the call. Casey cut through his objections and told him not to be 'bloody stupid'. He was 'putting him in'.

On the morning of 1 January 1969, Maie Casey rang up. 'Shirley, did you see the paper?'

'Yes, thank you Lady Casey.'[2]

The boy from the farm on Sheepwash Creek was now Sir Edward Dunlop, Kt.

In 1969, Alexander (or Zeke, as his friends began to call him) was studying medicine at Monash University after sailing through his second attempt at Matriculation with high marks, and John was at Ormond College, having won a Commonwealth scholarship to do an engineering degree at Melbourne.

Both boys had the look, the height and the stamina of the Dunlops. Sons of famous men begin life with a grave handicap. John inherited his father's love of poetry, but otherwise his interests developed in fields where he was not competing with Weary, such as mountaineering, and his decision to become a mining engineer removed him further from his father's influence. Alexander's choice of medicine met with his father's approval but also attracted his criticism. He also painted. Curiously, in view of Weary's own hidden, imaginative life as a child, this artistic facet of Zander's character was not something his father understood.

For all James's fine and traditional Scottish virtues, he had been a poor rôle model for Weary as a father in the second half of the twentieth century. Weary decided to counteract what he saw as a regrettable materialism amongst the boys' generation in the eastern suburbs by making them 'tough', and he succeeded admirably. They played rugby, went trout fishing, climbing and bushwalking. He was usually on the sidelines at rugby matches, where coaches tended to consult him at half-time, and he readily gave whichever team John or Alexander was playing on a rousing 'pep-talk'. It could be confusing when they were on opposing teams.

But he was seldom at home when they needed him, either during their early years or later, as they moved through adolescence to manhood. Helen never reproached him for his absences or mentioned her own emotions; and Weary never told her how 'hurt and shut out' he had felt during the boys' early childhood, when she became so absorbed in them. Incessant activity had been his solace and he found it impossible to break the habits of many years.

She took the day-by-day responsibility for their sons' upbringing. They grew up loving their mother – she could be as forthright as Weary about drinking and behaviour – but with little emotional warmth for Weary. He found it impossible to establish the same easy, companionable relationships he enjoyed with his young residents with his sons.

Sibling rivalry decreed that each boy try to outdo the other. On one notable occasion, Alexander and his friends were walking in rugged country in the Victorian alps, when out of the blue appeared John. When he consulted his brother about his goal on the map, Alexander sent him off across twenty kilometres of punishing country in the wrong direction. Without John noticing, he put a rolled-up dead snake in his rucksack.

The year at boarding school had made John the more independent and killed any desire to spend time at home. By the time he left Scotch College, he had hitch-hiked around Australia three times, and held down holiday jobs working in the mines in North-western Australia, on an off-shore oil rig and fruit-picking. The proceeds bought him a motorbike which became the envy of his contemporaries; and the exhilaration and adventure of working in the West confirmed his wish to be a mining engineer.

Weary's only comment was that John was to go to Ormond College. There was no argument. Alexander continued to live at home, throw wild and memorable parties and study at Monash.

Early in 1969, Tossie died. She had had a coronary in January 1968 when Weary and Alexander were in India. Helen had expected her to live only a few more weeks, but she hung on rather miserably for another year. John had been her 'dear lamb', and he missed her very much, as did Helen. With both boys away from home by now, Helen spent some lonely evenings with only Blake, the cat, for company.

Since Weary's visit to Long Xuyen, he had kept himself informed about the work being done in South Vietnam. In 1966, he managed another two days there on his way to Tokyo for the 3rd World Congress of Gastroenterology. Operation Attleboro was underway in heavily forested terrain north and west of Saigon, and he was unable to take a civilian flight to Long Xuyen. He spent the whole day 'dusting' over the Delta in a Caribou on the 'milk run', ending up at Can Tho for the night. Next day, he reached Long Xuyen on a convoy. Weary enjoyed being amongst the combat troops, and he found the journey more appealing than the few hours in the hospital.

Professor Sydney Sunderland, Dean of the Faculty of Medicine at the University of Melbourne, returned from there in March 1969. He had been sent by the Department of External Affairs to evaluate the

Australian medical teams' contribution and to investigate how Australia might help teach Vietnamese medical students. Apparently some teams had exceeded their brief and upset the local doctors. In Australia, the press had been quick to pick up criticisms by returning team members and suggested that 'the Australian aid programme in its present form is inefficient and a waste of tax-payers' money'.[3]

Sunderland recommended modifying the Australian contribution. More significant, as far as Weary was concerned, was his suggestion that 'the most useful doctor is an experienced and resourceful general surgeon'.[4] Shortly afterwards, a colleague rang and handed him the means of breaking out of his 'mundane . . . life'.[5] Would he lead the Alfred Hospital team which was going up in July? He contacted External Affairs. The prospect of doing useful surgery spiced with adventure was irresistible.

By early July, his appointment as Team Leader and Surgeon was confirmed and the departure date set for Sunday, 20 July. Over the next ten days, he was briefed by the department, met the new team members, took some lessons in Vietnamese, arranged for Peter Nelson and Carl Schneider to look after his patients, and amazed everyone by being the first to arrive at Essendon Airport on the morning of their departure. He even beat 'Honourable Theatre Sister' to the terminal. She fired last-minute instructions at him about contacting her family in Singapore. She would supervise the practice while he was away.

Tan Son Nhut Airport and 'shabby, war-pitted' Saigon were masked by sheets of rain when they arrived two days later after a stopover in Singapore. Weary was sceptical about the optimistic briefing they received from Ambassador J. A. Harry. 'Everything rosy.'

With the hospital administrator, John Flynn, they drove to Bien Hoa. Within twenty-four hours, he had decided the ambassador's briefing was 'bullshit'. From what he heard at the base, there was no sign of the Americans winning the war.

Bien Hoa was a grubby town in the delta and the civilian hospital was in its centre. The Australians occupied part of the 'exceedingly squalid' buildings, in which the beds were packed so close together in the concrete floored wards, one could scarcely move between them. The grounds were drab and badly drained, the water supply and the sewage system inadequate.

The team was housed in a heavily guarded residence as dreary and lacking in amenities as the hospital; Weary found it merely 'adequate' and he was relieved to move upstairs into the air conditioned team leader's quarters five days after his arrival. He had no difficulty sleeping – Michael Long watched him sleep in the middle of a crowd of vendors in an Indian airport once, while trading went on around him – but the others found the 'incessant din and chatter of helicopters and jets day and night', the small arms fire and grenade 'pops' disturbing. Night skies were 'brilliant with all the aircraft, flares and tracer displays'.[6] They were close to an American air base, the largest in the country and, at that time, the busiest in the world. Everything was surrounded by sandbags and armed sentries, 'most of these sleepy and scarcely . . . effective'.

His three-month tour of duty overlapped his predecessor's by four days. Brian Smith handed over after a farewell cocktail party for the outgoing staff which left Weary incapable of returning to his room without help – 'disastrous mixtures'. It was one of the very rare occasions in his life when he was flattened by alcohol.

'The days are utterly full and interesting . . . especially as the war activity has flared . . . '[7] Hugh Dudley, Professor of Surgery at Monash, worked with him at Bien Hoa for a fortnight before leaving for the 1st Australian Field Hospital RAAMC at Vung Tao. Weary discovered 'a great tempo of work' at Bien Hoa and was impressed by the surgical load Dudley had carried. First, Don Sidey arrived from Adelaide to replace Dudley, then Brian Buxton flew in from New Guinea to join his old chief.

Casualties came in from all over the country. As well as cancers, abcesses and infections and 'every sort of surgical problem to be solved' they dealt with a stream of injured civilians suffering from multiple fractures and head injuries from traffic accidents or grave, septic wounds inflicted by bombs and exploding mines.

Weary discovered captured Viet Cong, some of them paraplegic, others with phosphorous wounds, dumped on the concrete floor of an outhouse. After 'an appalling row' about this with the Vietnamese Army administration, he admitted them to the Australian wards. Under protest, they sent soldiers 'with fixed bayonets' to sit by the beds. But when Weary asked his Vietnamese nurses to attend to the VCs – many of whom were very young boys – they refused. Nursing devolved on the Australian staff. It was a battle he could not win.

Most Thursday mornings he made a 'lovely, swooping flight across the rivers' by helicopter to the leprosarium at Ban San to operate on patients, and he was back and forth between Saigon, Bien Hoa and the Australian hospitals at Long Xuyen and Vung Tau.

Lectures, clinical meetings and dinners with US army medical staff broke the routine of operating. The 93rd and 24th Evacuation hospitals filled him with admiration. At Long Binh he watched the wounded come off the 'choppers'; it was 'the surgical dream come true' with every investigational and resuscitation facility. They reached hospital within an hour of wounding. 'Not so the poor civilian victims who come in at all . . . times with every sort of lethal fragment in their . . . body' to the Australian operating suite.

Sunderland had reported that the Vietnamese doctors resented Australian efforts to train staff in western ways and avoided working with the team. Weary concluded that this was nonsense, for he witnessed the same urgent desire to modernise which he had seen in other Asian countries. Team members who returned for a second tour of duty were greeted with 'real joy'. 'We now have not only Dr Duc as a regular surgical team member, and the two anaesthetists, Mr Phuoc and Mr Quy, but two Vietnamese nurses who have commenced duties in the surgical suite. Also we have two post-graduate North Vietnamese doctors who became disillusioned with service in the NVA.'

Weary's first *News Bulletin* from Bien Hoa said something positive about everyone. Upsets were inevitable when teams changed over, so he kept his qualms to himself for a time. He was disturbed by the friction between two Vietnamese assistants and a few of the Australian staff in the theatre. 'I don't think . . . [some] are very popular with the Vietnamese girls with whom they work – only the rare ones like Sue Terry, who have a special tenderness for them.'[8]

He was also unhappy about the team spending too much time with the Americans, neglecting to mix socially with the Vietnamese. He gave them all a 'tough talk' after two of the men had a 'glorious prang' in a team vehicle early one morning and were brought to the hospital by a US military police patrol. Even more worrying was the 'obvious problem . . . that a few European women [dropped] into a sea of virile combat mission . . . males soon become preoccupied with . . . drink parties that pass for entertainment in these parts. Result: they don't have much time or energy to spare for cultivating the Vietnamese which is the whole purpose of their being here'. He reminded everyone that it was their 'job to promote friendship with the Vietnamese . . . they should be above loathing and desire'. By September, they had settled into well-knit efficiency.

A sketchy diary he kept reveals how disturbed he was by some aspects of his administration. Being team leader was a solitary task. ' *Je suis si seul*,' he wrote one weekend, echoing his long-ago French girlfriend's lament when he left her to return to London in 1938.

He was eager to see as much of Vietnam as possible, for 'I may well find this the last of [my] adventurous assignments and enterprises.'[9] The Americans flew him all over the country. They were generous with hospitality, particularly the US Air Force's oldest and most famous squadron, the 'Pair-O-Dice' or 90th Tactical Fighter Squadron at the nearby base. After repeated nights of hard drinking and tall stories, he was initiated into the squadron by being dumped 'bum first' in a rain barrel and won the right to wear the famous 'pair-o-dice': 'for proficiency I fear in other activities . . . than flying'.[10] The friendship he struck up with Colonel Dexter lasted for the rest of his life.

He explored a good deal of the province by road with Ed Vanderhof of USAID, the Director of Medical Services for the region. Vanderhof was a cool customer who thought Australian security was 'much too stuffy' and Weary did not like to be thought timid.

Weary drove from the residence to the hospital or the air base by jeep. The rules stated that at night they might drive only between Bien Hoa and the local base; when driving to parties or dinner at Long Binh, the large logistic military base spread over an area many kilometres square, a military escort must 'ride shotgun'. Anywhere else was out of bounds after curfew. It was a court martial offence for a serviceman to drink in the bars in Bien Hoa. Viet Cong were everywhere, murder or kidnapping by bandits had occurred and the roads were often mined.

'Wars have the same general patterns . . . large chunks of boredom and drink,' and evenings spent at the bases palled.[11] He accepted an invitation from a South Vietnamese officer to dine at Tan Hiep a few kilometres away, aware that they would be out after curfew and probably the target of sniper fire. Weary was uneasy when he had to park the jeep conspicuously in the main street and continue on foot down a maze of narrow alleys.

It was a long evening of greasy, unpalatable food and numerous tumblers of whisky which had to be drained each time, Asian style. Weary began to worry about driving back, but the other two resisted his attempts to finish the evening. When everyone except the interpreter and the officer who had brought him was asleep, he suggested returning to the Mess for an Australian beer and they wound their way unsteadily back to the main street.

A bullet whizzed across the top of his head as they reached the jeep. There was no time to check for bombs. Heaving the other two in, he dived behind the wheel. 'Fortunately, for once, it started immediately.' Keeping his head low to avoid any more bullets, he drove 'hell for leather' back to the hospital. He was not afraid of being shot; but he was 'terrified' of being taken prisoner. The incident drove home the realisation that he was growing older. He was 62. He felt, and looked, in his prime, but no longer could he take such escapades in his stride.

He found the Vietnamese 'absolutely lovable . . . one of the most charming peoples in the world. The children nearly tear your heart out'. Their stoicism and tolerance of pain and suffering astonished him. 'Two small brothers sat talking quite brightly the other evening whilst waiting for me to deal with multiple mortar wounds – just like a casual visit to the dentist.'[12]

While working under the Colombo Plan, he had become accustomed to the sick being nursed largely by their relations. They 'used to watch the clinical condition of the patient very closely'. But more than once in Bien Hoa, he was frustrated by a mother removing her child from hospital when death was near. He begged one to let him do a tracheotomy on her daughter, for the girl's life would be saved, but the woman insisted on taking her home. Losing his temper and refusing to sign the documents to release the patient had no effect. Later, he learned why. The mother feared that her daughter 'would die in this terrible place . . . She must die in her own home, otherwise she might become a lost and wandering soul forever down the centuries'.

This was in his mind one night, when he put a badly injured young boy, afraid of dying in hospital, in the jeep and drove him back to his village. He knew it was 'very dangerous' and an ambush by the Viet Cong was a 'distinct possibility' on the dark dirt road, but his desire to still the boy's misery and terror eclipsed his own fear of capture.

Weary found his months in 'the awful tragedy' of Vietnam 'very moving'. He was baffled by the actions of the Viet Cong, attacking the homes of civilians, killing and maiming women and children. But the US presence there saddened him far more. He concluded that they 'didn't fight [the war] as a serious business', that 'thunder and fire from the sky' were no substitute for efficient fighting on the ground. Australian troops trained in guerilla warfare by men who had fought in the Malaysian insurgency played the same game as the Viet Cong, fighting, dispersing, then striking back unexpectedly. They trained Montagnards and Nungs, tribal people in the mountains, as mercenaries. 'After one or two showdowns with the Viet Cong, the Australians in Phuoc Thui province never had another major engagement.'

Helen's letters from Melbourne were bright and businesslike, but a note from John at the end of September revealed that she was lonely, bored and unhappy. He was relieved that his father was going to 'give her a decent holiday'. Helen was to meet Weary in Saigon on 22 October. It would be the first time she had been away since Tossie's death.

Three months had flashed by since he drove up to a hospital displaying squalid conditions 'rarely seen apart from prison camps'. By 30 September, an Australian construction team financed by the Adelaide Jaycees had transformed it, repairing the sewage system, renovating the buildings and paving the grounds. The Ambassador handed over the greatly improved facilities to the Vietnamese Government before a crowd of dignitaries. Despite all the back-patting, Weary decided that some of the morale problems suffered by Australian surgical teams were due to the changed attitude of External Affairs since Casey's retirement in 1960, when he was elevated to the peerage and became Lord Casey of Berwick. No longer were they treated as an elite, with introductions to diplomatic staff in the host government; and insufficient acknowledgement was given to the sacrifices many team members made in volunteering for service on their country's behalf. Whereas Casey had briefed and debriefed senior technical advisors to the Colombo Plan personally, the present Minister did not seem so interested.

He suggested to the Department that surgeons of some standing would hardly volunteer three months out of their busy lives if they thought the government attached little value to their contribution.

Weary spent his last weekend amongst the mountains at Dalat, where 'the salient impression is of quietness'. The Vietnam of the Delta assaulted the ears with the roar of Hondas, Suzukis and Lambrettas 'and the eternal clatter and din of war'. Yet the Dalat Palace Hotel with its 'lofty ceilings, dark massive beams . . . and terraces flooded with light' overlooking the lake brought him no peace. Every room seemed to be occupied by couples, mostly Americans with their girlfriends. He felt more alone than ever.

Helen had a gentle introduction to her two days in Vietnam. They drove through sixty kilometres of lush, rolling country to Xuan Loc, where a French doctor lived amongst the rubber plantations in a colonial villa modified for the times: two 'ports' at the top of the covered stairway allowed him to drop grenades on intruders. His surgery was raided constantly by the Viet Cong.

Not only was life with Weary unpredictable, it could also be very uncomfortable. Early next morning, unsuitably clad and at barely an hour's notice, they flew to Song Bé on the 'chopper' with the stores. No one thought to tell Helen how long the journey would take or what she would meet when she arrived. 'The noise . . . and the . . . wind made conversation impossible.'[13] Strapped in, feet braced on metal cross-pieces because the helicopter was floorless, they flew at 350 metres, well within the range of Viet Cong fire. Two armed scouts and a rear machine gunner rode with them. As they came in to land, they could see great bomb craters from the B52 raids and the central fortress area of Song Bé with its concrete pill-boxes, criss-cross trenches, mortars, claymore mines and massed barbed wire.

The base camp was close to the Cambodian border, an area of strategic hamlets occupied by slim, dark, Montagnards, the 'Ghurkhas' of Vietnam. Colonel Dexter organised combat dress for them and they drove to Bu doc, an entrenchment seven metres underground. This was Weary's second trip; he was fascinated by the place with its crows-nest lookout and sophisticated electronic detection devices. The effect of the 175 mm guns was 'positively ear-shattering'.

By the time they arrived back at Bien Hoa for their farewell party, Helen was stiff, cold and deaf. Next morning they were virtually unidentifiable as they drove to Saigon under a mass of files, souvenirs, suitcases, operating bags, presents and Weary's omnipresent boxes of slides. He was to lecture in Singapore before whisking in to Bali for a few days holiday.

He left South Vietnam 'filled with wild rage . . . that the West had gone in . . . We were surrounded by nice people who were going to be devoured by wolves'.[14] He was also afflicted by 'the most ghastly depression. I felt that European civilisation had been tried in the balance and found wanting . . . I felt very, very, very sad'.

Three days in Cambodia eased his return to the workaday world. Weary gazed on the ruins of Ankhor Wat and Ankhor Thom and their exquisite bas reliefs in amazement. He drew strength from 'the beautiful compassionate face of Buddha facing four ways' at Ankhor Thom, and that night, they sat in the floodlit splendour of Ankhor Wat, entranced by a timeless performance of classical dancing.

His practice always dropped off quickly in his absence, but the diary filled up just as fast when he returned. A backbone of insurance and medico-legal work provided a steady income over the years, but the reports which ate up the greatest amount of his time yielded none. He never charged former prisoners or veterans.

The 'bamboo radio' broadcast Weary's movements and activities world wide. The London FEPOW Club always knew within days of Weary's writing to a FEPOW when he would be in Great Britain. In Melbourne, not a morning passed but at least one letter arrived on Weary's desk from a former prisoner-of-war. If someone was ill or needed help, the 'bamboo' told him. Bill Belford, the rangy sergeant-pilot who had been captured with Ron Ramsay-Rae in Java, kept tabs on all the hammer-and-tap men in Queensland and despatched word of them regularly. 'Dear Colonel' begin his articulate and newsy letters. Plenty of others continued to use his army rank. 'It pleases me to address you thus. To others you may be "Weary" . . . but I always remember you as I knew you most indelibly in those climactic days of 1943.'[15]

The man who had stood between them and the Japanese as a 'shield, a bulwark to us all'[16] became their most knowledgeable advocate.

Men he had not met, or their widows, sent bulky files with pleas which never went unanswered: would he assist them in appealing against a ruling made about their pension entitlements by an asessment tribunal or the Repatriation Commission? The volume of written material supporting these applications and appeals would have been an almost impossible burden for most people. Weary never complained and never refused, although the pressure became almost impossible, for his private practice took up much time. The space left by his retirement from the Royal Melbourne and the Eye and Ear hospitals had been quickly filled.

A decade after the original Repatriation Commission research was published, Weary had pressed for a follow-up study, but the department refused. That 'very extensive' survey of around 12 000 former prisoners 'had a good deal to do with pension justice' during the years immediately afterwards, influencing the attitudes of the assessment tribunals and the department. But as veterans aged and knowledgeable departmental staff retired, the struggle for fair pensions intensified.

Weary fought the Repatriation Commission and its administrative body, which later became the Department of Veterans' Affairs, with the same bulldog-like tenacity with which he tackled his patients' cancers. He did not limit his exertions to Australia. Ex-Prisoners-of-War Associations in New Zealand, Canada and the USA, Stanley Gimson, now Scotland's President of the Pension Appeals Committee, the British Legion and a range of physicians in England wrote seeking information about men who had been treated by him in Java and Thailand or opinions on cases they were handling. His wartime case notes were referred to repeatedly, his memory of men and their ailments was astonishing. No one was turned away; many were helped; and they reported their successes jubilantly and gratefully.

Gimson and Weary had a particularly easy correspondence because of a mutual affection and regard and their shared passion for fair play on pensions. 'Like you, I have been disgusted by departmental attitudes as related to early breakdown and death. It affects particularly those individuals who were self-reliant and proudly independent and who scorned various pensions and entitlements . . . I find that file by file I have to fight each case separately and that precedents established by the appeal tribunals are never taken into account thereafter. To my mind the enormous rebound from years of starvation so that many men doubled their weight in a matter of months is a metabolic disturbance of immense significance.'[17]

Weary believed beyond all possible doubt that the 'complex of starvation and multiple deficiencies including . . . many vitamins . . . gross protein . . . and mineral deficiency' contributed to 'postwar disability, premature age, and death.'[18]

A key sentence in the Australian Soldiers' Repatriation Act of 1920 spelled out quite clearly that, in case of doubt, the benefit was to go to the veteran, yet Weary saw a new generation of career public service medical officers taking the opposite view. Time and again, his letters supporting claims ended: 'Surely he should receive the "benefit of the doubt" which is stated to operate?'

Fights could be bitter as the claimants moved painfully through the cumbersome stages of appeal. Sometimes, it took years. His prophetic words to his men in Bangkok had come true.

When the department was set up earlier in the century with responsibility for the medical care of returned servicemen and women, its aims had seemed 'imaginative and generous'. But the Second World War produced a different crop of health problems, particularly amongst the former prisoners of the Japanese. The man who had lost limbs was granted a pension; at his death, his wife became a war widow. On the other hand, those who claimed during the 1970s that their ateriosclerosis or cancer was caused by captivity and starvation, could meet with an unsympathetic reception. Results were inconsistent: 'There was a time . . . when 72 per cent of smokers who started smoking in the army were being rejected for compensation for lung cancer and 28 per cent were being accepted.'[19]

It seemed almost impossible to persuade the Commission that cancers could be war-caused. Weary marshalled his facts, describing the conditions in the camps, explaining how the strong, high-tar, native tobacco was the only substance which made constant hunger pangs halfway bearable. Sir Macfarlane Burnet provided him with ammunition: 'severe hardship, debilitating diseases and malnutrition damage the immune mechanism which protects the body. Thus, if this protective mechanism (which he thinks could well be centred on the thymus gland) should suffer damage, then a premature aging and diseases of old age take over. This of course includes cancer.'[20]

In the early 1970s he 'went to some pains' to collect his conclusions in a submission to the Returned Services' League on 'The Acceptance of Cancer as War-caused.' They did not accept it at the time, although it 'speedily gained interest overseas'. Indeed, at one time the RSL suggested that no exceptions should be made for prisoners-of-war of the Japanese: all veterans should be treated equally. Weary did not agree. But neither did he 'advocate blanket acceptance of all cancers in veterans . . . each case requires separate examination' by the medical officer.[21]

He mobilised all his friends and supporters in his long-running battle against the Repatriation Commission, 'anyone who was likely to be authoritative', such as Sir Macfarlane Burnet, Dr Nigel Gray of the Anti-Cancer Council and Dr Donald Metcalf, the senior cancer research worker at the Walter & Eliza Hall Institute.

The history of this decade is one of his increasing frustration at a refusal to acknowledge that the conditions of imprisonment by the Japanese could cause premature breakdown in health, or death. Case after case was knocked back. It is even alleged that members of the old Repatriation Boards and Tribunals were quietly told that they should disregard his medical advice 'because of his affiliation and bias towards the veteran community'.[22]

As Federal President of the Ex-POW Association of Australia, and as an individual who had dedicated himself to acting as watchdog over the health of former prisoners-of-war, Weary never let up in his campaign for pension justice and benefits. There was one gleam of hope in the 1974 budget: the government granted free medical care to all former prisoners-of-war for any disabilities, whether war-caused or not.

By the 1980s, however, he began to see some notable victories: the Law case in 1981 and the Morecombe case in 1983. Weary appeared as an expert witness in both. With his 'mind like a steel trap'[23] allied to his sense of theatre, and years of experience appearing as a witness in court, he was stimulated by the challenge. After the latter case, he met with Dr M. M. Kehoe, the Chief Director (Medical Services) of the Department of Veterans' Affairs to discuss his paper. It had taken twelve years for this to come about.

By 1972 he was full in the public gaze as Chairman of the Executive Committee of the Anti-Cancer Council of Victoria and President of the Victorian Foundation on Alcoholism and Drug Dependence.

John Rossiter, the Victorian Minister for Health, persuaded a reluctant Weary in November 1970 that he should become the VFADD president in place of Sir Philip Phillips, who had died suddenly. Rossiter's confidence in Weary was justified. Whilst he protested that he was no expert in the field, he was a tireless worker who knew how to capture the attention of the press at a time when the organisation was broadening its brief to include drug dependence. Weary was a very visible president; he travelled throughout the state to gain public support for the idea that alcoholism and drug addiction were diseases in the community that must be fought.

When the Anti-Cancer Council wanted a new Chairman for their Executive in 1972, they looked no further than Weary. 'In the 1960s and 1970s, he was a senior surgeon at the Number One hospital, and . . . an active force in the political life of all the institutions around town.'[24]

Weary had been involved with the Council one way and another for some years as a surgical representative from the Royal Melbourne Hospital. The community knew him as a cancer specialist. Apart from that, he had a high profile with the press because of his earlier sporting career and the war. Reporters always turned up if a press release mentioned Weary would be speaking at a function or holding a press conference, and it was rare for them not to mention rugby and the Railway, even in stories about drugs, drink, smoking, cancer and heart disease.

Weary was a 'marvellous resource' to these two organisations.

He became President in the middle of the struggle to include health warnings that cigarettes were harmful in all advertising matter and on cigarette packets. In retrospect, Nigel Gray sees this as his own 'blooding as a political tactician', and he found Weary a 'Rock of Gibraltar . . . always supportive', whose instinct was always 'to take the tough course'. It was rewarding for Gray 'to work with a Chairman who was behind me with a heavy hammer ready to hit anybody who attacked you'.[25]

Weary had given up smoking in the 1950s after meeting Richard Doll in London. He did it 'cold turkey' – from sixty a day to nothing – and never smoked again. He perceived then what many others in his profession did not: the era of prevention had arrived and it was time for the Anti-Cancer Council to educate the public about the links between smoking and lung cancer, and heart disease. Later in the 1970s, they changed Australian thinking about the effects of the sun and skin cancer with their inspired campaign, 'Slip, Slap, Slop'. Weary led the Council through this era, and when he wished to scale down his involvement, Gray says 'he was much too valuable to be allowed to disappear, so we made him President and then Patron' in 1982.

Weary was never a mere figurehead. He always supported any organisation to which he lent his name by attending their meetings and turning up at functions. The size and importance of the organisation did not signify: his contribution did not vary. Sir Reginald Swartz, a former Minister for Repatriation, prisoner-of-war in Malaysia and latterly Chairman of the AIF Malayan Nursing Scholarship, found Weary's energy and thoroughness amazing when he became their Patron. 'How he did it, I can't comprehend. Whatever was put to him, he replied personally; he came to meetings, he was very helpful with funding and went out of his way to assist.'[26] At one time, he was involved with forty organisations, either as office bearer, committee member or patron, and he actively supported them all. He was available to the press if it was required and he enjoyed talking to everyone, from the clerical staff to the dignitaries.

His appointment diaries for these years were filled with an astonishing array of activities. Up until the early 1980s, around twenty patients would be booked to see him on days he was not operating, and most week nights featured an early evening meeting and at least one other engagement, often two or three. If he was operating in the morning, the number of appointments in his rooms dropped back to ten or so. Pencilled at the top of many pages are reminders that a workers' compensation or Veterans' Review Board case was coming up that day. He could be called away to the former at any time, often at great inconvenience, especially if – as often happened – he arrived only to

618 | Weary 1967 – 1993

hear that the lawyers had called for an adjournment on some technicality and his presence was now required on another day entirely.

'I am the man who can never say no,' Weary replied to a friend one day, when it was obvious he was exhausted and unwell and should not attempt to keep the engagements filling the pages of his diary. Somehow, he always found a reserve of energy and met his commitments.

He lived most of his life in the public arena, yet there were contradictions in his character which puzzled some observers. For such an approachable man, 'He always stood apart . . . seemed different.'[27] To those who worked for him he 'did not give out a great deal'.[28] He revealed his private side to very few, and most of them remained observers rather than participants. Weary could withdraw into himself whenever he chose. It would be obvious to someone watching him immersed in reading poetry – one of his favourite relaxations – biography or history, that he had retreated into this private world and was oblivious to everything around him.

He loved parties. Helen and he enjoyed opening their house to the associations they supported – and some their friends supported – for dances, recitals, cocktail and garden parties, fashion parades, wine and whisky tastings. Japanese, Malaysian, Indian and Sri Lankan students stayed with them, came for dinner, lunch and Christmas Day. ('Please have no worry about a place to stay when you arrive . . . you can always stay with me.') Visiting surgeons were wined and dined and taken to the farm at Smith's Gully when the new house was completed in the mid-1960s. Helen was a willing, gentle, charming partner in all of this.

Any former prisoners who arrived at the door, no matter what time of the day or night, were welcomed, often given a drink or included in a meal with other guests. If Weary thought the man was short of money, he was sent on his way with the taxi fare. When they came to an appointment at his rooms, patients from the country whom he knew had a struggle to survive on their pensions would have their train fare pressed upon them.

Successive governments had topped up the Prisoners' of War Trust Fund endowered by Sir Robert Menzies' first post-war administration, and nearly seven thousand former prisoners had benefitted from its grants. Weary had succeeded Colonel Allan Spowers as Chairman, but since the end of 1970, the number of applicants had declined and the Prime Minister, John Gorton, informed them that it would be phased out by 30 June 1977. The Labor Party was in power in 1977. When the fund was wound up, $864 000 had been distributed: nothing like the three bob a day subsistence allowance which had been sought, but it had relieved many of the less fortunate of hardship.

'Cobbler's children are the worst shod,' was another of Alice's old saws which Weary quoted. He gave so much of his time and loving attention to other people, that those closest to him had to make do with the leavings. Dunhill's words had come true, but when Weary realised it, it was too late. The boys had grown up and left home to make their own lives, Alexander to practise medicine in the country, John to Tasmania.

John had married Heather Beshara in 1970 whilst they were both studying. After graduation, he joined BHP and they crossed Bass Strait to live in Rosebury, where he worked as a mining engineer. By the middle of 1972, Heather and he had two little boys, John and Andrew. Weary was uncertain how to behave with babies, but Helen was delighted with her grandsons.

Now that she was free to travel, over the next eight years Helen accompanied Weary to medical congresses all over the world. By 1972, she was relishing her new-found independence and spent three months driving round England and Scotland and visiting friends. Towards the end of her stay, she was counting the days until Weary joined her in London. Helen had a reputation for not liking to spend money, but this time she ordered her spouse to bring *very little* in a *large*, half-empty suitcase for all the shopping. She issued an embargo on slides. There was once a tremendous drama and much bad-tempered muttering on Weary's part when he deposited his slides in the left-luggage room at Victoria Station and they disappeared.

Very little of 1974 was spent in Australia. He was appointed Chief Medical officer to the British Phosphate Commission that year and expanded his bailiwick to embrace Nauru, Christmas Island and the Gilbert and Ellis Islands, giving Helen some lovely Indian summers of travel in tropical seas. He very nearly did not return from Christmas Island one year. Whilst swimming far off shore, his heart began to play up, causing him great distress. At one stage he doubted that he could regain the beach, but he returned cautiously and reached their quarters, only to discover that he had forgotten to bring the drug he took for episodes of arrhythmia. There were no suitable drugs in the island dispensary and it took him a day to recover. He found these attacks temporarily distressing. They had begun in Thailand and continued throughout his life.

When, that April, he accompanied his patient, the dying Japanese Consul-General, Mr Yamanaka, back to Japan and handed him over to his family, he fulfilled Buddha's saying from *The Dhammapada* that he had locked away in his desk: 'Never in this world can hatred be stilled by hatred; it will be stilled only by non-hatred. This is the Law Eternal.'

Before he became a patient, Mr Yamanaka was a staunch supporter of the Australian-Asian Association, as were all the members of the Asian Diplomatic Corps. The association was one of Lord Casey's 'brain children', formed in 1956 as a non-political body to help Asian students arriving in Australia. In turn, through various activities, they would convey an understanding of their rich and different cultures to Australians. Weary had succeeded Sir Charles Lowe as President in 1965, and his home became almost an open house to the association. He saw it as a trust vested in him by Casey, and he vetoed attempts to change its non-political charter. Weary's lively mind and curiosity propelled the association into organising three major seminars on China, India and Thailand during the 1980s. These satisfied both the intellect and the senses, with lectures, dinners, dance and musical performances and art exhibitions.

Weary never lost his desire for new experiences. Those who judged him slow and bear-like because of his stance and size and voice seriously misjudged the man. He could be quick and quiet on his feet with a boxer's agility. His gaze missed nothing, even when age sunk his eyes deeper into his head so that one had to look closer for the bright, alert spark which was one of his most striking characteristics for many years. This shows up plainly in photographs of him as Australian of the Year in January 1977 at the age of sixty-nine.

He was surprised to learn of his selection when he stepped off the plane from India, where he had been a guest lecturer at a surgical conference, and told the reporters, 1976 must have been 'a very lean vintage'. He thought they were 'pulling his leg'.[29] Not at all, they replied. The Australia Day Council had chosen him because he had been Chairman at the congress plenary sessions on cancers of the oesophagus and stomach at the 5th Asian Pacific Congress of Gastroenterology.

.Weary gave the Sir Gordon Gordon-Taylor Memorial Lecture at the Royal Australasian College of Surgeon's meeting in Kuala Lumpur in 1978. This time, Helen was not required to shuttle between Weary and a typist. Weary had a new secretary, Valda Street, and the lecture was crisply typed before they left Melbourne. Although he gave a few brief scientific papers at congresses in later years, this and his introduction to the Grey-Turner Lecture at the International College of Surgeons' congress in Montreux in 1981 were his last major medical addresses to his international peers. No longer scouting on the frontier of his speciality, he had become part of the history of Australian surgery.

In 1980, he was openly acknowledged by the Department of Veterans' Affairs as eminent and expert. Weary's medical reputation had risen steadily with the Department from its nadir in the mid-1970s. He had regained his stature of the 1950s when he was the prime mover and an important part of the enquiry into the health of prisoners-of-war. Once again, his affinity with the veteran community was seen as an advantage. On the advice of the Minister for Repatriation, the Department welcomed his appointment as the RSL representative on the Scientific Advisory Committee investigating the effects of Agent Orange on veterans of the Vietnam War.

The attributes which clinched Weary's appointment and which made him admired by his fellow members were his compassion, intellect and realism. 'It meant that those of us who are rationalists [were] not allowed to run away too far from the human angle',[30] for he was a 'forceful and influential champion of veterans' rights.[31]

Weary chaired the first meeting of the Committee and helped them focus on the main issues, for no one knew where to go, where to start: the Government had set it up in a 'panic move . . . heads were on the block'.[32] Over the next four years, Nick Letts, the Head of the Taskforce on Vietnam Veterans' Health problems, found him a 'force for balance . . . possessed of broad vision, clarity and integrity . . . yet with a capacity for detail',[33] who maintained their momentum until the mortality study report was finally endorsed at the Committee's last meeting on 16 August 1984. Without Weary, they would 'not have got to where they were'. He was a 'leaven' amongst the epidemiologists and other scientists, whose view was narrow compared to Weary's 'down-to-earth, practical knowledge of soldiers overall': Letts found it 'sobering' that Weary should be the only Committee member to have served in South Vietnam. Like Nigel Gray and the Anti-Cancer Council, he found Weary strongly supportive, not at all frightened of the bitter media campaign which waged throughout these years, and an 'advocate for the absolute truth . . . informed, not prepared to be speculative'.[34]

The epidemiological studies which were produced on birth defects and mortality positioned Australia at the forefront in this research world-wide. Even so, it was not sufficent compensation for Weary, who still regretted Australia dropping back in the field after establishing such a fine base line with the 1950 prisoners-of-war survey.

Hindsight suggests that he underestimated his influence on government when he battled with the department down the years. So intent was he on proving scientifically, case by case, that former prisoners of the Japanese had been grossly damaged and therefore qualified for pensions, that it never occurred to him to throw all his energy behind the Ex-Prisoners-of-War Association's claim in 1969 that *all* of those men were entitled to pensions *as of right* , whether well or ill. Tony Ashford, National Program Director (Benefits) for the Department of Veterans' Affairs in Canberra, suggested that he should have gone higher than the Minister for Repatriation. When Ashford was a deputy commissioner in Victoria, he saw Weary frequently, both professionally and socially, and he believes it would have happened if Weary had chased it as forcefully as he pursued the cases of individuals.

Weary never lived to see the most important concession in more than twenty years granted to former prisoners-of-war. Legislation was passed in the Australian parliament on 18 August 1992 giving all widows of ex-prisoners-of-war war widow status on the death of their husbands. It ended for all time the bitter, humiliating, time-consuming arguments by widows and their advocates to prove that the privations of imprisonment had shortened and blighted their husband's lives.

Henceforward, they would have their pensions as of right.

THIRTY-ONE

Almonds to those who have no Teeth

FRUSTRATION, LONELINESS AND SADNESS haunted Weary during these latter years. The Friday nights at Edrington had ceased when Casey died in June 1976, the same year that Michael Long noticed how 'vague' Helen was becoming when he accompanied Weary and her to an international congress in Mexico. Familiar suburbs and streets became uncharted territory. Barbara Lofts, whom she had met in Sydney just after Boyd was killed, and befriended when Barbara married and moved to Melbourne in 1946, began to receive telephone calls from Helen confessing that she had set out to drive to Barbara's house in Balwyn, but had returned home because she 'couldn't remember the way'.[1] Friends never knew if she would turn up to their weekly game of golf. Meals were uncertain. At first, Weary became impatient when he found no food prepared and little in the refrigerator, for confusion enveloped her so gradually that he was unaware of its seriousness until friends pointed it out. His professional life was demanding, the years 'flying by like telegraph poles seen from an express train', and he was one of the last to notice that Helen was suffering from mental failure.

By 1979, when Weary and Rowan Nicks represented the Australian chapter of the International Society of Surgeons at the congress in San Francisco, her Alzheimer's Disease was plain to her companions and Jaya and Nicks were much saddened by her condition. Weary and she went on from here to join a Melbourne Scots' tour of Scotland. Helen's joy at being there again was great, but it was obvious that extensive travel was now beyond her. Weary took her overseas with him for the last time in 1980, to New Zealand, after which she deteriorated rapidly.

That year, he found their usual large Christmas luncheon and dinner 'like a second job' and, by March 1981, when John came down to

623

Melbourne to graduate as a Master of Engineering Science, the family decided that Helen should spend August and September in Groote Eylandt with the younger Dunlops when Weary travelled to England and Europe. The ISC had invited him to Montreux to give the introduction to the Grey-Turner Lecture that September.

Housekeeping was a nightmare, for she could not shop, drive or cook. Weary would arrive home in the evenings to find the day's post distributed all over the house, cheques and bills in the rubbish bin. At first, friends helped, delivering groceries and meals. Eventually, Sister Betty Thompson moved in to nurse her. It was a 'black pain at the heart'.

He revealed none of this sadness, and to the casual observer his life changed very little. The appointment diaries were as crammed as ever with patients, meetings and functions. Weary felt 'terribly over-committed with semi-public life . . . [and] a large practice' but was quite incapable of calling a halt. He included Helen in many engagements, and at home she went through the motions of playing hostess, even if she was past comprehension of her activities. This troubled Alexander, who had returned to Melbourne and begun to assist Weary in the operating theatre; he suggested his father was too hard on his mother, and friends remarked the younger man's 'gentle, loving manner, his understanding, thoughtfulness and readiness to help' when the world bewildered Helen and she clung to his arm or to Weary's 'like a child lost in the darkness'.[2]

Rather than insensitivity to Helen's illness, it was a stubborn resolve not to cut her off from the warmth of human companionship that prompted Weary to continue taking her out when she could no longer cope. He never had paid much attention to what other people thought.

Dougie Clague died of cancer in 1981; he had not been the same old Dougie since 1975, when his beloved Hutchison fell victim to the stock-market crash and the company had to be rescued by the Hong Kong Bank and Bill Wyllie. Then, Weary and Dougie had sat all night in Dougie's kitchen in Hong Kong, drinking whisky and eating bacon and eggs until it was time for the October meeting at which Wyllie took control. Two months after that, Alan Ferguson-Warren had died, 'the closest to me in spirit and in affection', and Weary mourned him 'like a favourite brother'.[3] In Bangkok in 1945, he had compared the 'young, pink and terrific' physique of Clague and his fellow officers to his own grey skinniness; now the two he admired most were dead and he, the older man, was very much alive even if he did chafe at doing the 'same bloody pottering things'[4] in a life he suggested was full of 'trivia'.

For the first year since the war, he kept a diary spasmodically, beginning it on Ash Wednesday 1983, when the horrors of the bushfires which devastated Victoria filled the Parliament Place rooms with acrid, choking smoke. He drove home through smoke, dust and whirling leaves as thick as fog and worried about Gumberwil and his cattle at Smith's Gully. That Friday, 18 February, he noticed that the heads of the Armed Services were present at the POW ceremony at the Shrine commemorating the Fall of Singapore for the 'first time in years'.

The high points in these years became the overseas trips to International College meetings with Rowan Nicks, when he could escape the dead hand of routine. 'I have asked nothing more of life than to go on working and being useful until the end. It is with immeasurable disgust that I find myself like that aged character in Tennyson's 'Ulysses' – "among these barren crags,/Matched with an aged wife" and with no prospect of any worthwhile surgical activity . . . medico-legal stuff I find totally degrading'. Nicks was frequently in India, Asia or Africa, teaching and operating. 'Compared to you, I feel like Prometheus chained to a rock in the Caucasus.'[5] But with Betty Thompson in residence, he could travel more often and the Hong Kong meeting in March, followed by an Australasian College visit to Edinburgh, Glasgow and Dublin, gave him three weeks of freedom. Later that year, it was a relief to visit England and Hamburg, for the 'crucial sadness' of having to cease operating that August had cast him adrift and only minor 'office' surgery remained. St Andrews had been the last hospital to give him beds. He felt that the new breed of nursing administration made 'surgery difficult when over 70, and beyond human dignity over 75'.[6] His grief was deep and his pride was lacerated. Only the role of assistant was now available to him.

But even when sunk in depression, his ironic sense of humour did not desert him: 'Maybe some cultivation of the art of fly fishing is the answer . . .' he suggested to Rowan. Weary's casting was a standing joke with his sons, with Rowan and with Charles Janson in Scotland, who likened it to 'swatting wasps'.

After Hamburg that September, he joined Janson in Sutherland for three days stalking and salmon fishing in the Highlands at Ben Armine. Stalking was tougher than he had anticipated and his right 'rugby' knee, damaged forty-four years ago at St Mary's, played up. He had had no problems with it since the 1950s when it 'gave out, surfing at Jan Juc', but now it caused him constant pain, and he was relieved to be taken fishing next day.

Rowan's friendship meant a great deal to him during Helen's decline. His 'spirits were at a low ebb' while he was in Europe, for the decision to stop operating had come on top of the break-up of John and Heather's marriage. It was always intended that Heather should move south with the boys, for young John was to start at Scotch College in 1983 and Andy to join him there a year later. Unfortunately, the marriage did not survive the separation and Weary worried constantly. 'There are more problems in life than solutions . . .'[7] His own 'abundant energy' was one of them; he longed 'to find some outlet which satisfies my longing to be of use'.[8]

Helen was unable to communicate effectively by 1984: she could not even write her name. Weary could scarcely bear to be in the house, for it was 'heartbreaking to see her weep in frustration at her inability to dress herself, turn on a shower or tap'. He fought back feelings of guilt, wondering if her complete and unselfish devotion to him had contributed to her condition. 'She gave up her own career and interests so completely.'[9] For so much of her life, she had been caught between his own dominating personality and Tossie's.

On Sunday 20 May, up at the farm, he slipped and fell heavily onto some rocks, smashing his femur, with a spiral fracture running down the bone. No one heard his calls for some hours. 'I got the leg straight by getting onto my back and pushing it down with my good leg and right hand . . . My only movement an agonising thrust backwards on my buttocks pushing, with the unstable leg dragging after me.'

It was dark when John and Andy came looking for him; Hamish, John's Gordon Setter, reaching him first. Andy stayed beside his grandfather, who ignored his pain and pointed out the constellations overhead, while John fetched the ambulance.

Now, for the first time in forty years, he was 'abed and on my back like a large turtle' in the Freemason's, after an operation lasting two and a half hours.[10] 'I have a nail and a large plate, very many screws . . .' His orthopaedic surgeon was astonished at the strength of his thigh muscles and 'bone good enough for a buffalo'.

Judy Sewell, Pam Nicholson and the other sisters found him a good patient, 'not at all difficult'. His main problems were pain and sleeplessness, 'the nights a horror', and they used to drop in and chat. They enjoyed nursing Weary, almost invisible under masses of flowers, fruit, sweets, books, telegrams and visitors'. '. . . An endless deluge of letters' arrived from all over the world.

Former prisoners wrote – 'Dear Colonel', 'Dear Friend', 'Respected comrade' – quoting poetry, giving news of men and their families, 'for the bond and magic remained',[11] fuelling their concern for the man who had done so much for them. Valda appeared to type the replies; and some of his patients even pursued him into hospital.

The Microsurgery Foundation was holding a fundraising dinner on 9 June. Weary had been a director since its inception in 1971 and he was not going to allow a broken leg to prevent him attending. Bernard O'Brien, a fellow director, dropped in to see him and discuss the plans for the dinner, and Weary announced that he would be there.

His dinner jacket was sent into the hospital and on the night, they wheeled him down to a large hired car. 'And out he comes on his crutches' three weeks after suffering a major fracture. As the night wore on, Weary murmured to O'Brien, 'I feel an irresistible urge to talk.' Onto the dance floor and up to the microphone he swung on his crutches and gave 'a rousing, inspirational address'. They raised $150 000 that night: 'a big sum'. He even managed to dance a little and 'had a fair bit to drink . . . it was quite a performance.'[12] Next day he was 'not the best'.

A month after the accident, Weary discharged himself from hospital. By the beginning of July, 'with the aid of crutches', he was negotiating stairs and driving himself daily to the physiotherapist, the swimming pool and his rooms. He tossed away the crutches at the end of the month. When anyone enquired what he would say to a patient who had done likewise when three months on crutches was the accepted time, he replied: 'If they are over 70, I tell them to do what they bloody well like.'[13]

Financial worries preoccupied him increasingly: expenses were mounting and Helen needed to go into a nursing home. Rich in assets but poor in cash, reluctantly he considered the possibility of living off his savings. He was not a man to go readily into overdraft. That August, Thomas Nelson, a Melbourne-based publishing company, suggested that they publish his war diaries. Another company had begun work on them during the 1970s, but financial difficulties had caused them to abandon the attempt. Now, he decided, the diaries should come out of their dark drawer, for they might succeed in focussing attention on the problems of aging, former prisoners-of-war and gain some pension justice. Royalties from sales of the book would help him, also, for his practice, though busy with patients, ran at a loss. However, a dwindling income never affected his generosity to charities; and he marked his debt to Ormond College by setting aside money for a scholarship commemorating Sir Victor Hurley. He also showed his gratitude to the Thais by making over a percentage of future royalty earnings to a project very close to his heart: the Weary Dunlop-Boon Pong Exchange Fellowship, whose details he was to discuss with Professor Kasarn and Dr Thira Limsila when he returned with a group of former prisoners-of-war to Java and Thailand for Anzac Day 1985.

This meeting set in train a vigorous medical exchange programme between the two countries. The idea arose out of his friendship and correspondence with John Marsh some years beforehand, for Weary desired to mark his gratitude to Boon Pong and other members of the Thai resistance.

The attention given by the press to the tour of Java and the Burma-Thailand Railway in April 1985 surprised him, and the publicity generated 'a spate of speaking engagements'.[14] Later that year, the Department of Veterans' Affairs established the Sir Edward Dunlop Medical Research Foundation and asked Weary to be Patron. It was to carry out research into the aging and health problems of veterans which, ultimately, would benefit the entire population. Weary consented, although initially he believed that Veterans' Affairs should fund all the research. Later, he realised that it was an advantage to be independent of a government department. He announced that the government should at least match funds raised dollar for dollar.

Weary wanted the Foundation to continue the work begun on former prisoners-of-war of the Japanese in 1950 by re-surveying for cancers, hypertension, stress, psychiatric disorders and the effects of avitaminosis; and co-ordinate the research done in Canada, the USA, the UK and Norway on the long-term effects on all body systems of captivity, starvation, stress, untreated injuries and diseases. But he was discouraged by the failure to reach their target of 2 million dollars. Wherever he spoke from now on, he gave a strong plug for the Foundation and for the Weary Dunlop-Boon Pong Exchange Fellowship, which was launched during Anzac week 1986 in Perth through the efforts of a group of former prisoners-of-war.

Since only Weary could decipher much of the faint, tiny handwriting in the notebooks and on sheets of paper, the preparation of the diaries for publication occupied many hours. He had not read them since they were written, and some passages were deeply distressing. Night after night, he sat in his chair or at the dining-room table until the early hours of the morning, dictating them onto tapes. Valda helped with the typing, but eventually a medical secretary staying in the house, Caroline Bagworth, transcribed the remainder. They were to be published in October 1986. 'I think it will be an awful sweat . . .' to finish on time.[15]

The diaries were launched on 18 October 1986 by the Governor-General, Sir Ninian Stephen, at a national reunion of former prisoners-of-war in Queensland. Weary was bemused by the fuss. 'TV and press . . . to turn my poor head . . . they seem to have gone through the first print of 10 000+ in the first week . . .'[16] He hoped they would help pay his 'enormous bills for a year or two. I don't know just how long I can inhabit 605; but Helen still seems to react to it as home when we bring her there . . . I can't imagine anything I have contributed to life to make me worthy of the love that she has poured upon me all these years.'[17]

It was a considerable time before he took the book seriously, believing that demand could dry up as suddenly as the surge of interest in him and his war had swept him into 'a spate of travel, TV, radio, press, receptions and speaking engagements more appropriate to one half my age'. This was entirely different from the kind of publicity he had been used to. 'I have been quite surprised, even puzzled as to the success of my book which seems even to have had appeal to the young.'[18] Schools clamoured for him to speak at prizegiving ceremonies, founders' nights and at special assemblies. But the adulation, whilst flattering at a time when he felt crushed by his 'wretched' family situation, also made him very uneasy, 'concerned as to the plaudits which paint one as a national hero . . . The best pathway to a peaceful old age is found by low posture and a neck well pulled in.'[19]

The book took him out into the community in a way quite different from his previous experience. He was groping towards some sort of 'philosophy adequate to ensure a peaceful decline towards decrepitude of mind and body which must accompany most old age', for although he attempted to ignore his own aging, he watched Rowan moving stiffly in the mornings when they were on holiday in the Snowy Mountains and wondered when he would be affected similarly.

As he brooded over Helen, 'a sweet, lingering, lost ghost', Weary's own personality softened. He also found it increasingly difficult to keep pace with correspondence, reports and other responsibilities. Speaking engagements assumed a greater part of his life; he continued to see patients, but 'one of the sad things about old age is you can't be bothered to gird yourself up for action – you say to yourself, "Oh, What the hell!"'

Even though Weary believed he had 'no great gift for self-analysis', he recognised that age had brought him a bonus. 'One of the good things . . . is the gentleness – you lose the desire to squash the ants.'[20] By the 1980s, he was amused to see himself avoiding the punch-ups that once formed part of his make-up. In Brisbane for a medical meeting, he was jumped on by a young thug demanding money. Weary resisted the urge to hit him, reminding himself that such action usually resulted in broken spectacles, 'broken hands and the knee out of a suit'. Instead, he 'swiped him' with his satchel, 'pushed him off' and moved warily backwards, whilst he and his assailant eyed each other 'like panthers'. He was saved by the approach of another couple. 'What a pathetic story of elderly caution. I still ache for the abandon of a quick one-two.'[21]

Increasingly, in the hundreds of speeches and addresses he gave between 1986 and 1993, he was reworking the themes of service and sacrifice which had formed the nucleus of his Anzac addresses in the 1940s and 1950s. Then, fresh from the war, intent on helping men adjust to civilian conditions after the traumatic experiences of 1939 to 1945, he comforted the survivors in heroic language, showing them their war as 'courageous', their behaviour in captivity 'an unsurpassed example of discipline, courage and endurance . . . I yield to none in my admiration of the qualities of British soldiers, but I take special pride in the fact that Australian soldiers under those conditions outsuffered and outendured all others.'[22]

Latterly, he illustrated these themes with incidents from his own life, not only at war and in the prison camps, but in India, Thailand, Sri Lanka and South Vietnam. Weary came late to the realisation that he had something precious to pass on to future generations, that he was speaking to them of the human condition, and of values which a nation needs if it is to go forward confidently into the twenty-first century. With no precise religious affiliation, he suggested that the afterlife was 'immaterial'; what was important was to 'rise above self', losing oneself 'in the happiness of service to others', for one's best is achieved only when 'at full stretch'.[23] His energy had found a cause, yet he did not seem to recognise it until his last few years.

Weary's message was simple, for in many ways he was a simple and modest man, ever conscious of his origins and grateful for his success. 'It is nice to think of life's progress from barefoot kid and impoverished youth to reasonable affluence – and reflect, well, I have lived . . . '[24] It was not unusual to see tears on the cheeks of his audiences. He never thought tears unmanly. In 1993, two weeks before he died, he wept uncontrollably for the men he had known: 'in the prison camps they were the best . . . they were survivors.'[25]

In April 1987, Weary returned to Thailand to dedicate the memorial at Hellfire Pass to the men who died on the Burma-Thailand Railway and the Thais who had conveyed the barge-loads of eggs, other foodstuffs and drugs upriver. The Australian Government granted money towards the project conceived by J. G. (Tom) Morris and co-ordinated by the Australian-Thai Chamber of Commerce, financing the steep pathways down to the Konyu or 'Hammer and Tap' Cutting, whose construction had began on Anzac Day, 1943.

Weary was troubled by the increasing publicity and shrank inwardly from the exposure which increased as the years went by, for three separate documentaries were made about this journey. He could act on behalf of others, but was strangely impotent at halting or reversing events affecting himself or those closest to him and bewildered by the attention. 'I am continually at a complete loss to understand how in this funny little world of "Oz" I seem to get blown up into something of a public figure. I have little taste for heroics, and feel that I am a light-weight in any of the dimensions of the great . . .'[26]

On his return from Thailand, Weary was astonished to learn that he was to be made a Companion of the Order of Australia, and it was announced in the Queen's Birthday Honours List on 8 June. Mail continued to arrive by the bagfull as his eightieth birthday approached and, by 12 July, 'having soldiered through my AC correspondence, I am stricken with hundreds of telegrams, letters and . . . cards'. Valda Street and Heather organised the largest party he had ever given, an 'open house to which between 750 and 1000 people turned up'.

His fellow surgeons threw a dinner for him at the Melbourne Cricket Club, awarded him the medal for service to the Australasian College and raised around $8000 for the Weary Dunlop-Boon Pong Fellowship. The ex-POWs also gave him a dinner; the RSL held an evening reception; and Sir Bernard Callinan officially launched the Sir Edward Dunlop Medical Research Foundation at a Legacy luncheon. 'Dear me, this is a crowded year for ego tripping,' he wrote, about to leave for yet another luncheon, this time one given by the RAAF.[27]

Alexander, Heather and Andrew accompanied him to Canberra for the investiture in August. Weary often found it difficult to decide on the appropriate dress for an occasion and 'wavered between morning dress, lounge suit and uniform'. He settled for a lounge suit, but 'because "investees" don't wear decorations for the ceremony – forgot my evening gongs for dinner.' He found his medals tricky to pin on and they made a mess of his suits.

In one week 'of peripatetic yapping' in September, he spoke to retired businessmen and women; the Savage Club; the Children's Hospital Auxilliary; the Ormond College Students' Dinner in Hall; and gave a major address: the John Henry Newman Lecture at Monash University. There was just time for him to attend the International Society of Surgeons' Congress in Sydney (which he and Rowan had gained for Australia as their Bicentennial gesture) before Qantas bore him off to London for the publication of the diaries. They were launched on 27 September at London University's Dixon Gallery, with an exhibition of Jack Chalker's drawings and paintings of the Railway, by Laurens van der Post. Next evening, Weary's fellow FEPOWs acclaimed him at the Festival Hall and he signed books for over two hours. He was upset that the publishers, a small English firm, put only 2500 books on the market, for the stock was quickly exhausted and many people could not buy copies. But 'the hell with all that. I have been to Somerset, Brighton, West Sussex, Aldershot Command [where he spoke 'to a large audience and a nest of generals'] and go to Oxford tomorrow to have lunch with Zelman Cowan', the former Australian Governor-General now at Oriel.[28] By 7 October Weary was on his way to the United States and nine days after that, he flew to Thailand on business connected with the exchange fellowship.

Australia's Bicentennial in 1988 saw Weary named as one of the 200 great Australians. He felt 'shocked and inappropriate'[29] about being singled out in this way: 'How the hell could they put me in ahead of nearly all the 15 000 000?'[30] But he enjoyed the excitement of the great dinner in January, despite having 'not the faintest idea' how he became one of the approximately 160 guests.[31]

Throughout the early months of 1988, Helen was fading. She had not recognised John and Alexander, nor her brother Jamie, for some time, although until now she had always given Weary the 'sweetest' smile whenever he walked into her room. On Saturday 9 April, as she was sinking deeper into unconsciousness, Weary's old university conferred an honorary doctorate of laws on him. He moved through the ceremony as in a dream, robed in scarlet, the mediaeval scholars' black cap on his head. That discipline which ever governed his life helped him write his address and take him through an occasion reminiscent of another day forty-two years earlier, when he had sat 'in the Chancellor's chair in the old Wilson Hall' to address the 'Blues' at their presentation ceremony, and was rewarded by a verse in 'The Song that never dies'. Now, he spoke particularly to the graduating students of the day about their obligation to this 'cherished' institution which had 'nurtured and moulded' them and him and of his treasured memories. 'I once questioned Lord Bruce . . . which [honours] he prized as the three high peaks of his career . . . '[32] Weary's own were his presidency of the Ormond College Students' Club, his first Australian cap at Rugby Union, and the 'unofficial title given to me by ex-prisoners of the Japanese, "King of the River" . . . the Menam Kwai Noi . . . a sad kingdom of suffering and death'.[33]

Helen was dying 'day by day'. Weary spent a great deal of time sitting by her bed, just as he had sat by so many patients' beds across the years, but this time feeling 'that awful inadequacy, conscious of all the questions never asked'.[34] He had no heart for the opening night of *Tosca* on 20 April. Jim Donaldson, the minister at Toorak Uniting Church and a companion of many late-night sessions at Weary's fireside, was away on his honeymoon ('I just hope he will be back in time to help.'[35]); the Rev. Gordon Powell, an Ormond Man and Weary's contemporary, was standing by.

On 21 April, Weary spent most of the day beside her, returning to his rooms in the late afternoon. Shortly before he was to leave for a reception at Anzac House he was sitting with Valda in her office at Parliament Place when the telephone rang. Helen was dead.

Alexander came home and John, with his new wife Chantal, flew over from Perth. Not even his deep sadness, however, stopped Weary, in his 'old London heavy barathea uniform and scarlet tabs and cap with a rather untidy arrangement of 14 medals',[36] from taking his place at the head of the 8th Division on Anzac Day. They had asked him to lead them, and 'What I say, I do', but there was no bounce in his step on the twenty-fifth. 'I rather hoped that my uniform would disguise me, but apparently I was clearly identified' by the television cameras. Neither did he miss the Reception given for the Queen.

He saw Helen last on the morning of the funeral on 28 April and 'inside the casket . . . placed, with tears, a spray of huge purple orchids'.[37] Helen 'departed as she came in, to her beloved pipes – "The Flowers of the Forest" and "Amazing Grace".' A church packed with people, and many more standing outside, sang 'Jerusalem', just as it had been sung at their wedding in 1945, and Weary was 'left reflecting that her simple goodness in the long haul outweighs my own more complex life'.[38]

During long hours of silence and self-examination following Helen's death, 'the more I contemplate my own life, the more the unease, the banal[ity], the convergence of mediocrity'.[39] He was filled with dread at the prospect of the thousands of cards, letters, telegrams and messages which must be acknowledged, and at the two papers (as yet unwritten) which he was to present at the military session of the Australasian College meeting in Cairns in May. Cancelling the next fortnight's engagements in Brisbane, Cairns and Canberra, or backing out of giving the papers never occured to him.

'*Je suis si triste, je suis si triste – un moment; j'ai du courage* . . . I must move towards shedding 605 . . . '[40]

The marketing of his house attracted far too much publicity for Weary's liking. He hated the idea of leaving. 'I slink past the sale board on my fence . . . ' He was deeply embarrassed by an interview published on the front page of the evening paper, which suggested he was selling up because he could no longer afford to live there, and he felt 'fit for ritual hara kiri . . . Whatever happens in life, I am not one to squeal or cry poor – and that is not the issue.'[41] The house sold at auction and he bought a unit 'rather like a coffin which is probably good training'.[42] Appalled at the prospect of moving the accumulated possessions of years, he was saved by the recession: the buyer reneged and Weary stayed.

The British Lions played Australia and New Zealand in Brisbane in July 1989; Weary, an official guest of the Australian Rugby Union, ended up more battered than the players after plunging from the catwalk onto its iron supports whilst returning from the microphone to his seat. He smashed his nose and 'split my forehead . . . for about 10 cm.'[43] A second-row forward pushed his nose back towards the centre of his face. Weary refused to go to hospital, so he was given extra whisky, the team doctor 'produced an amazing bag and sewed me up on the spot'. He missed only one course of the dinner. A few days later, he drove himself from Melbourne airport to the rooms, somewhat handicapped by a headache, 'slit-like vision and two black eyes out to the ear'.[44]

Scarcely had he recovered from this than he came off second best in a car accident. With massive bruising, broken ribs and concussion, he refused to cancel his trip to North America and the United Kingdom, for he was to lecture at the Uniformed Services University of the Health Sciences in Bethesda, Maryland that August; attend the 4th World

Congress of the International Society for Diseases of the Oesophagus; and join Rowan in Toronto for the 33rd World Congress of Surgery.

'Frozen with pain in the right side of my chest and with no interest in food', he moved out of his seat only once during the flight from Australia to the USA, to discover on arriving that the airline had changed his schedule and destination. A timely call brought Colonel Bob Dexter to his rescue to drive him to Bethesda where, feeling like a 'ghost with pain, sleeplessness and abandoned time rhythm', he gave his two lectures before retreating thankfully to Dexter's home.

It was a full programme for someone in good health; for Weary, aching all over and deprived of sleep, it was an ordeal. During the day, he 'did his best to dissemble', but the nights were miserable. Changing position was impossible, and he could only lie flat on his back. Getting up was a slow, shaking, exercise of his will. When the gastroentero-logical congress began on 6 September, however, he was moving a little less gingerly following some lazy golden summer days spent with friends in East Hampton and with Ken Warren in New Hampshire.

After a week-long surgical congress and three days at Niagara Falls at the American Ex-Prisoners-of-War National Convention, he flew to Ireland for a weekend, spent the week in London and joined the Scottish FEPOWs in Glasgow for twenty-four hours before flying home to Melbourne via Bangkok and a meeting with Kasarn about the fellow-ship. The Royal College of Surgeons of Thailand had conferred an honorary fellowship upon him in July 1988, for he was universally revered in that country for his work there. It was the first time ever that an Australian had been so distinguished.

A group of former prisoners-of-wars led by Jim Boyle and Ivor Jones of the RAF Malaya, plus film-maker Quentin Fogarty, organised a variety evening at the Melbourne Concert Hall in October 1989 as a tribute to Weary and to raise money for his Medical Foundation. Weary took none of these demonstrations for granted and never failed to be surprised at the enthusiasm he aroused. Guests filled his house, including Bill and Alice Griffiths who had flown out from England especially; the organisers produced a telegram from the Queen; and he enjoyed the occasion greatly. But he was also 'humbled' by the packed concert hall and the crowds, 'deeply moved and quite unworthy of the generosity of it all' and concerned at the mounting adulation with which he was being greeted by both public and media. ' . . . The exposure tends to go on in a way that frankly amazes me . . . '[45]

The New Year of 1990 depressed him anew, for at the cricket that

January, he realised his good eye had failed. Tests confirmed his worst fears; nothing could be done. ' . . . My vision hangs on at the last functioning level. Can read and drive, but the future is uncertain.' He envied Rowan his work: 'Oh to be doing something useful, arduous and sweat-producing . . . Alas, for me no Africa to fly to . . . Shakespeare's seventh age – ugh!' He refused to give up driving, although Jack Flannery had taken over that duty when he attended reunions, and Valda insisted that Weary be driven to and from many speaking engagements. The household was now in the capable care of a new housekeeper and excellent cook, Melvie Barter, and he re-discovered the pleasure of giving frequent dinner parties.

The winter of 1991 produced the usual crop of colds to which he had become susceptible. The previous winter, his influenza had developed into mild pneumonia, so this year he gave himself a precautionary 'flu injection, but to no avail. In the winter rain and chill one Friday night that August, running a temperature and head spinning with 'flu, his foot caught on the accelerator and he smashed his car into the brick wall of the car park behind his rooms. His right knee hit the steering column and the floor of the joint was fractured, then, 'tense with blood', seized up completely after walking up and down the stairs to the telephone to summon the RACV.

Weary 'lost two whole weeks in wandering, aching delusion . . . in a shivering void aching in every pore and devoid of the least shred of energy'. His bed was moved to the tiny downstairs bedroom and a nurse was called in. Eventually, feeling at a 'near-time low', he insisted on returning to his own bedroom, and negotiated the broad stairs 'on his bottom'. He decided that he was 'diseased, accident-prone . . . maybe in the finals! . . . God, how I hate and despair personal disability. How much better the sudden out.'[46]

He struggled out of bed and flew to Canberra to participate in a seminar at the Australian National University later in the month with other survivors of the Burma-Thailand Railway and Australian and Japanese historians. Frail, far from well, in pain, his leg in a splint and 'a mountain of bandages', he refused to cancel the trip, although he 'was reluctant to continue to present myself as an object'.[47] In Canberra was Hiramura, 'The Lizard', or as he was called in Korean, Yi Hak-Nae. Weary was 'embarrassed . . . by his assistance to help me stand' and quite shattered by his gift of a gold fob watch and chain, 'deeply inscribed' to Edward Dunlop.

Many were incensed at Weary attending the occasion, for they believed that he had been manipulated, but he shook his head at his doctor, David Kings, when he reported it. 'You don't understand,' he replied. He was deeply affected by Hiramura's gesture and his pilgrimage to apologise publicly to the former Australian prisoners. Weary saw this as yet another instance of the 'little bit of God in every man', for he had been responsible for Hiramura being sentenced to death as a war criminal. Although he was reprieved and the sentence commuted to 20 years imprisonment (10 of which the Korean served before being released), Weary felt immeasureably humbled by the man's capacity for forgiveness.

'Everything' was still a 'a great travail . . . whilst I can now walk fairly freely I pay for it with an aching knee . . . ' In October he was to be made an Honorary Fellow of the Imperial College of London, an Honorary Fellow of the Royal College of Surgeons of Edinburgh and President of the Scottish FEPOWs. Ten kilos underweight, with 'an agonising short circuit in energy and performance', he flew in wretched discomfort to London at the end of September.

Weary's old friend and contemporary Sir Michael Woodruff presented him to the Edinburgh College of Surgeons on Friday, 11 October 1991 and recalled a quality of Weary's which he felt contributed to the nickname: 'Dunlop concealed a formidable intelligence and great physical strength behind a facade of . . . *aequanimitas* – which can be translated roughly as unflappability . . .'[48]

Thirteen days later, he stood 'dazed', proud and puzzled as to his admittance to the distinguished group of Fellows of the Imperial College of Science, Technology and Medicine. Amidst the glowing magnificence of the Royal Albert Hall, he listened to his citation. 'God knows how I got amongst that high-powered science mob bristling with FRSs.'[49] It must be his connection with that 'charmed circle' of St Mary's Paddington, he decided. He felt that he had gained far more from St Mary's than they had enjoyed from him, despite his contribution to the rugby. ' . . . Perhaps from a sense of pity the poor bastard from the "colonies" was given quite an ovation.'[50]

That night, he took the train to Scotland and next day in 'that lovely Glasgow Town Hall' was installed as President of the Scottish FEPOW Association. Tom Kemp had taken him to the Committee Room at Twickenham earlier in the month, where he watched New Zealand defeat England in the opening match of the World Cup, but he missed out on tickets to Murrayfield on the twenty-fifth. He had to settle for watching that match on television in Edinburgh.

Weary had always been proud of his entry in *Who's Who*, but these latest achievements amazed him. He quoted an old Chinese proverb, 'Almonds come to those who have no teeth', and suggested that he was 'all honours and little substance'.[51] Still, his pleasure was evident when he showed his citation from the Imperial College to a few friends, and he wore his tie with its gold suns from the Royal College of Surgeons 'proudly' to the very last. It became his favourite.

The last great international honour came to him from his beloved Thailand in April 1993. With Donald 'Scotty' Macleish, he flew to Bangkok and was installed as a Knight Grand Cross (1st Class) of the Most Noble Order of the Royal Crown of Thailand. 'Eight fellowships seems rather a lot to carry and with my two hon. doctorates a train of baggage after my name.'[52] Now, he had two knighthoods as well.

The last years of life were brightened by his granddaughter, Isabelle, who captivated him with her graceful feminimity and quick intelligence. This was the first time he had had anything to do with small girls and in Bangkok that April, he had chosen a myriad tiny figures and animals for her birthday. She was entranced by the many parcels. His trip to Thailand had been the high point of the year, although the 'trivial round' of endless talks and more formal addresses to organisations in Victoria continued, and the number of letters and cards to be acknowledged never lessened.

In 1992, the ABC had approached him about a documentary for a series which would include the lives of Sir Sydney Nolan and Sir Mark Oliphant. Weary had 'no wish or desire for publicity, but equally as a reasonably obliging person I always find it difficult to refuse'.[53] It was filmed in Rowan's flat in Sydney, Weary feeling 'reluctant to get into programmes in which the subject is dissected as to man's precise relationship to God . . . I who believe that there are as many ways to God as there are faiths and religions – still don't want to remove that mustard seed of faith from anyone else . . . I must be guarded against any *ex-cathedra* assumptions of authority'.[54] He was not pleased with the results. 'They never ask the right questions.'

He was 'fed up with war stuff' and never having felt the need to 'huddle together with the prisoners-of-war', increasingly he had to 'steel' himself 'to do this again'.[55]

Weary was tired. He had first felt the cold fingers of old age in Scotland in 1983, when he was attempting to deal with Helen's illness, and either accidents or malaise had cast him down at least once a year since 1987. India in 1990 weakened him with amoebic dysentery and his back caused intermittent pain from 1991. By 1993, the naps which he had always taken became more frequent and he grew increasingly introspective about life and death. Weary was not afraid of death. 'I care little about the "grim reaper" lurking behind each year, each passing landmark . . . Death is a thing I've looked in the face before without flinching, and many companions of the way have been "gathered unto their fathers".'[56] But he did not feel ready to follow them. 'I ought to be wrapped in an aura of silver grey, but I aint. I still want to cast lances in the sun . . .'[57]

On 25 June 1993, Weary flew to Sydney to speak at a Commandos dinner. Next day, he returned to Melbourne and drove to Numurkah for POW reunion which he attended most years. As was his wont, he stopped off at Gert Hutchins' house for tea and a snack. The car gave trouble and they arrived back in Melbourne during the early hours of Sunday morning. After very little sleep, he put on his kilt and was taken to Aspendale/Edithvale RSL for 'an afternoon of Scottish music and song'. The slight cold of Thursday became worse during the long afternoon in the chill wind and he regained 605 Toorak Road with an aching throat and a headache, but he stayed up until 2.30 am on Monday writing letters and pottering about.

By Tuesday he was gravely ill, although he insisted on driving himself home from his rooms, where he was the last tenant in the echoing, run-down building. An alarmed Melvie called David Kings, who diagnosed pneumonia and prescribed massive doses of antibiotics. By Thursday morning, his throat was more painful than he had ever known with thrush (a reaction to the antibiotics), his voice almost unrecognisable. He knew how serious was his condition and he rang Hong Kong to speak for the last time to Isabelle, who was on her way to France with Chantal.

Kings had seen him that morning and announced that he was on the mend, but Melvie was dubious. During the afternoon, Doreen and Jim Ferguson watched him stump downstairs to fetch the newspaper, wearing his green and gold 'Anzac' jersey given him in 1989. Later, Melvie took him up some chicken soup, changed the wringing-wet bedding and left him alone, as he wished. Shortly after 10.30 pm there was a crash upstairs: Weary had struggled out of bed, collapsed on a chair and appeared to be unconscious. She rang Jim Donaldson next door and he and his wife sat with Weary while she rang the ambulance and tried to contact Kings.

They worked through the night at the Alfred Hospital in an attempt to resuscitate him, but around 3.30 am on Friday, 2 July, his heart stopped and he could not be revived.

Born on a Friday while Edward VII was on the throne, he died on another wintry Friday morning, ten days short of his eighty-sixth birthday. His life had spanned the reigns of four monarchs. Friday's child had indeed been loving and giving, but he had also worked hard for a living; and inspired a nation.

Within a few hours of his death, the 'Bamboo Radio' carried word to Singapore, Hong Kong, New York, London, Blackpool, Edinburgh and The Hague. Not only his friends wept. People whom he had never met stopped still, as they heard the announcements on radio and television, recognising that something precious had passed from their world. That 'St Crispin's' band of brothers whom he had led emotionally and spiritually for more than fifty years since their captivity by the Japanese was bereft.

When Professor Fred Hollows had died earlier in the year and was given a State Funeral, a friend had suggested that he, too, would be accorded one. 'Nonsense. I wouldn't allow it,' he retorted.

'Then you will have to put it in writing, because otherwise you will have no choice.'[58] He laughed, and turned the conversation aside to other matters.

On Monday, 12 July 1993, crowds began gathering outside St Paul's Cathedral in Melbourne. By eleven o'clock, around 10 000 stood silently in the bleak, grey streets. Friends had flown in from all over the world. Bill Griffiths, whom he had refused to put out of his misery with morphine in 1942 was there. At the family's request, in the front row of the cathedral sat a long line of former prisoners-of-war. The Prime Minister of Australia, Paul Keating; the Leader of the Opposition, John Hewson; members of state and federal parliaments, the diplomatic corps and thousands of ordinary people stood in deference to a great humanitarian.

The first notes of the anthem floated through the cathedral like the wind in the trees on a dark night.

His body was taken on a gun carriage to the Shrine in St Kilda Road where he had stood so often down the years on Anzac Days, Remembrance Days and that February day marking the fall of Singapore.

Farm boy, scholar, sportsman, surgeon, soldier, diplomat, statesman, greater in total than all the heroes of his youth who had motivated him to reach out for the glittering prizes: in the end, his stature was greater than theirs, his influence more profound. He gave his country a vision of sacrifice, compassion and service. Race and creed had been no barrier to his understanding. The Melbourne Buddhist community had 'sung him up to heaven' that Sunday, for to them he was 'an enlightened soul'.

As the funeral cortege drove slowly out to the crematorium at Springvale, people stood at the roadside and watched it go by. A postman stood beside his bicycle, mothers held children by the hand and gazed. A sad group of men lined the road outside a pub along the route, each standing as they stood on Anzac Days.

The day following the funeral, his friend, Sir Zelman Cowan, suggested that 'the experience . . . was altogether remarkable and it is surely one which will remain in the collective life of the nation as a celebration of human worth.'[59]

Weary would have been more astonished at all of this than at any other event in his life.

ACKNOWLEDGEMENTS

My principle source of information was my subject, Sir Edward Dunlop, and I am grateful that he was able to read most of the manuscript before he died. He was ever generous with his time and encouragement, once he became used to the idea of a biography: for he had a well-developed ego, but very little vanity. He was always frank about his life and clear-eyed about himself. His one stipulation was that no one should be hurt by revelations: disloyalty was the ultimate crime. I had unlimited access to his papers, and I was encouraged by his own sense of discovery as he watched his life unfold on paper. Over the years, events had sometimes become muddled, and he was pleased to see them placed in their correct context. This stimulated his memory and some of my best material came very late in his life. He never attempted to influence my interpretation of events. Like Nick Letts, who was involved with the Scientific Advisory Committee on the Agent Orange Enquiry, I found that Sir Edward was only interested in the truth, and I have written the book with this in the forefront of my mind at all times.

Sir Edward's family has been very supportive during the seven years this has taken. Many people helped me; some did not wish to be singled out for thanks – it was sufficient for them to know that they contributed to the total picture. I must thank particularly my great friend, Patsy Adam-Smith, whose house was always open to me. I could walk in at any time and find a bed, copious cups of tea, laughter and understanding. Sir Edward felt comfortable there and was able to relax away from the public eye. We three spent many congenial hours discussing war and the way the world wags.

In London, I am grateful to the staff of the British Library, India Office Library Records, the Imperial War Museum, the Royal College of Surgeons and the Public Records Office, Kew; in Canberra, the Australian War Memorial; in Melbourne, the Australian Archives, the University of Melbourne Archives: Strathfieldsaye Estate Collection,

643

the Latrobe Library, the Royal Australasian College of Surgeons and
the Public Records Office of Victoria; and the National Library in
Singapore. I must also thank the surviving men of Dunlop Force and
the many former prisoners-of-war who sought me out when they knew
that I was writing Sir Edward's story. My life has been enriched by these
years.

The following supplied letters, interviews, assistance of one sort or
another, hospitality and information: D. C. Ainsworth, Rod Allanson,
L. J. Allison, Audrey Anderson, Tony Ashford, National Program
Director Benefits, Bruce Manning and Mike Smith, Director (Health
Statistics), Dept of Veterans' Affairs, Melvie Barter, Bill and Joan
Belford, Eric Beverley, Professor Geoffrey Blainey, John Blanch, the late
John Blunt, Jim Boyle, Reg and Beverley Bradshaw, Jack and Helene
Bridger-Chalker, Milton 'Blue' Butterworth, Brian Buxton, researcher
Jenny Carew, Graham Chase and Film Australia, Professor Kasarn and
Tan Puying Sumalee Chatinkanovij, Geoffrey and Margaret Chiam,
Jock Clarke, John Colebatch, Neil Collinson, Julie Anne Cox, James
Daly, Billy Deans, John Denman, Robert Dickens, The Rev. James
Donaldson, R. E. Douglas, Graham Dow, Alexander and Amanda
Dunlop, James Dunlop, John and Chantal Dunlop, Robert Dunlop,
Jack Ella, Dean Ellis, J. Mephan and Doreen Ferguson, Keith Flanna-
gan, Jack Flannery, Ann Fleming, Keeper of Film, Imperial War
Museum, Sibella Jane Flower, A. W. Frankland, William Fraser, the
late Miss Margaret 'Peggles' Gibson, Ron Gilchrist of the Australian
War Memorial, the late Don and Jess Gillies, Stanley Gimson, Sir
Archibald Glenn, Bert Gogoll, Dorothy Gracie, Nigel Gray and the
Anti-Cancer Council, Dorothy Green, Bill and Alice Griffiths, James
and Simonette Guest, Charles Guest, Shirley Hah, Carol Harrison, Bill
Haskill, John Hayward, Brenda Heageney, Direktor Hendarman,
Lembaga Pemasyarakatan, Bandung, Indonesia, R. W. Jarvis, Frank
C. Johnson, David B. Johnston, the late Charles Hopkins, Gert
Hutchins, Mr and Mrs Jayasekera, The Rt Hon. Earl Jellicoe PC, KBE,
DSO, MC, FRS, Ivor Jones, the late M. A. de Jonge, Tom and Ruth
Kemp, David Kings, Professor Gabriel Kune, Ruth Lack, Mr and Mrs
Leslie Le Souef, Douglas Leslie, Nick Letts, Dr Thira Limsala, Barbara
Lofts, the Warden, London House, Anthony Lucas, Professor Stuart
Macintyre, Donald Macleish, Arnold K. Mann, the late John Marsh,
Robert Marshall, Sir Carol Mather MC, Professor Gavan McCormack
and Hank Nelson, Research School of Pacific Studies, ANU, Davis
McCaughey, Gp Capt J. McCulloch and Sgt P. Ryan, Office of the

Defence Attache, Australian Embassy, Jakarta, Major M. K. McGregor, Central Army Records Office, Yvonne McLaren, Neil McQualter, John Mitchell, Fr Gonzalez Munoz, Nancy Murphy, the late Dr Alf Nathan, Peter Nelson, Rowan Nicks, the late Bernard O'Brien, Ben O'Connor, the late Col. Cary Owtram, Elise Padreny, Vida Parker, Ray Parkin (who also drew the maps of the Railway, contributed information and illustrations, and was happy for brief quotations to be used from his own book about the war, *Into the Smother*), Harold Payne, A. N. H. and Mrs Peach, the Lord Porritt, Col Sir Laurens van der Post, Elizabeth Potter, Bill Power, Air Vice Marshal and Mrs Ronald Ramsay Rae, Sir Benjamin Rank, A. G. Robertson, the late Ronald McK. Rome, Bruce Ruxton, Lionel Sapsford, Bronwyn Self, Judy Sewell, N. Shaw, Dorothy Shea, Miss Lorna Siseley, Colin Smith, Archivist at the Royal Australasian College of Surgeons, Margaret Smith, Olga Steele, Douglas Stephens, George Stirling, Janet Stott, who patiently typed transcript after transcript, Frank Strachan, Archivist at the University of Melbourne Archives, A. H. Stevenson, Valda Street, Roderick Suddaby, Keeper of Documents, Imperial War Museum, Sir Reginald Swartz, Les Tanner, Wayne Thomas, Colonel L. A. Thomson, Lindsay Timms, Barbara Todd, Dave Topping, the Hon. Tom Uren, Margaret Walkum, Robert and Elizabeth Walpole, Bill Warbrick, Jean Wardle, Bill and Elizabeth Wearne, the late Rowan Webb, Dorothy White, Robert Williams, Elizabeth Willmott, Alice Wilson, Molly Woodhouse, Dale Wright, who took the portrait for the jacket of the Australian edition of the book, Tom Young.

Most illustrations were taken from Sir Edward's collection. The portraits of Sir Thomas Dunhill, Sir Gordon Gordon-Taylor (SB6/1/7) and W. A. Hailes (SE25/74), illustrations 12, 26 and 39 are from the Royal Australasian College of Surgeons Archive, Melbourne; that of George Grey-Turner operating (24) was given to Sir Edward by his son, Dr E. Grey-Turner; the Australian War Memorial: A. Seary Collection hold illustrations 51, 58 and 59; Stanley Gimson drew illustrations on pages 393, 474, 482 and illustration 54; Jack Bridger-Chalker painted illustration 52; and J. H. G. Jelley sent illustrations 53, 55, 56, 57 and 89 to Sir Edward shortly after the war. Illustration 62 is reproduced by permission of the Imperial War Museum, as are illustrations 41 and 46; illustration 86 is reproduced by permission of the *West Australian*.

I am grateful to the Australian War Memorial for permission to reproduce the maps on pp. 153, 205, and 304. Ray Parkin drew the maps on pp. 327, 380 and 399, the Konyu-Hintok section being based on a map prepared by Ken Bradley, although we differ from his map in some important points. The lines from 'A Shropshire Lad' were taken from *The Collected Poems of A. E. Housman*, published by Jonathan Cape, 1945 by arrangement with The Richards Press Ltd.; and John Masefield's poem, 'A Consecration' came from *The Collected Poems of John Masefield* published by William Heinemann, London, 1934.

Any infringement of copyright has been unintentional and I would welcome corrections if mistakes have been made.

I thank my editor, Linda Ristow, and the book's designer, George Dale, and the staff at Penguin Books Australia. I would also like to thank Russell Brooks, a superb indexer.

Lastly, I must thank three people whose lives have been most affected by my pre-occupations and absences over the past seven years: Malani Pandithage, my daughter Georgina Grosvenor, and my husband, Francis.

AAMC	Australian Army Medical Corps
AASC	Australian Army Service Corps
ADC	Aide-de-camp
ADMS	Assistant Director Medical Services
ADS	Advanced Dressing Station
AGH	Australian General Hospital
AIF	Australian Imperial Forces
ALFSEA	Allied Land Forces South-East Asia
APM	Assistant Provost Marshal
AQMG	Assistant Quartermaster General
ATS	Australian Transport Service
Bn	Battalion
CCS	Casualty Clearing Station
CO	Commanding Officer
DADMS	Deputy Assistant Director Medical Services
DA&QMG	Deputy Adjutant & Quartermaster General
DDMS	Deputy Director Medical Services
DGMS	Director General Medical Services
DMS	Director Medical Services
DR	Dispatch rider
EMO	Embarkation Medical Officer
EPIP	European personnel, Indian pattern (tent)
ESO	Embarkation Ship's Officer
F/O	Flying Officer
GCM	General Court Martial
GOC	General Officer Commanding
GSO1	General Staff Officer 1
G Staff	General Staff
GHQ	General Headquarters
HQ	Headquarters

IJA	Imperial Japanese Army
J	Japan
LO	Liaison Officer
MAC	Motor Ambulance Corps
MC	Military Cross
MI Room	Medical Inspection Room
MLA	Medical Liaison Officer
MP	Military Police
MO	Medical Officer
MT	Motor Transport
N	Nippon, Nipponese
NCO	Non-commissioned Officer
NEI	Netherlands East Indies
OR	Other Rank
PAC	Prophylactic Ablution Centre
QM	Quarter Master
RAAF	Royal Australian Air Force
RAF	Royal Air Force
RAMC	Royal Army Medical Corps
RAP	Regimental Aid Post
RMO	Regimental Medical Officer
SMO	Senior Medical Officer
SOE	Special Operations Executive
US5A	Convoy number
WOI	Warrant Officer, Class 1
WOII	Warrant Officer, Class 2

Japanese words

bango number
ichi, ni, san one, two, three
keré salute
kiotské attention
yasumé stand at ease
benjo latrine
Chusa Lieutenant-colonel
Chui Lieutenant

Keicho Lance-corporal
kempeitai Command post, guard house
kempis military police
shoko officer
socho officer
tenko parade

All unsourced quotations in this book are taken from the many hours of tape-recorded interviews which I did with Sir Edward, from numerous conversations and from the original hand-written diaries of 1942–1945. These last were abridged for publication and published as *The War Diaries of Weary Dunlop* in 1986. For the sake of accuracy, and because information which a reader might find uninteresting is invaluable to a biographer, I preferred to use the uncut originals. The book would have contained far too many notes if every quotation had been attributed.

Sir Edward gave many scientific papers at medical congresses throughout the world. These were not always published, although his speaking notes and rough drafts and many slides have survived. These, together with the numerous addresses he gave latterly, and the many forewords he was asked to write for various publications, offer valuable glimpses of the man. Attributions to published and unpublished material are readily identified.

Reports, letters, memoranda etc. relating to the war and to his post-war life without a call number from the Australian Archives, the Australian War Memorial, the Imperial War Museum, London or the Public Records Office, Kew, form part of Sir Edward's papers, presently held by the author pending their presentation to an appropriate institution.

A major secondary source has been interviews and correspondence with people who knew Sir Edward, and these are attributed in the relevant chapter(s).

There were some lucky finds: particularly the 'lost' letters he wrote to Helen Ferguson between 1938 and October 1945. Lady Dunlop was said always to burn letters, but these she kept, hidden in a cupboard, where they were found over a year after her death. Until that day, Sir Edward never knew that they had survived – perhaps she had forgotten them herself.

Eventually, my papers and the tapes used to write this book will be deposited in the Australian War Memorial, for I do not doubt that others will wish to examine the life of this remarkable man.

The following collections were consulted:

AWM Australian War Memorial, Canberra

Disher papers. These are held in the University of Melbourne Archives, Strathfieldsaye Estate Collection: Official War Correspondence, 1940–42

Dunlop papers

IOLR India Office Library Records

PRO Public Records Office (Kew, England & Vic.)

ONE: *Beginnings*

1 Milton ('Blue') Butterworth to SE, interview 6 November 1987.
2 IOLR, N/2/17/131.
3 IOLR, L/MIL/10/125.
4 IOLR, N/2/17/131; N/1/50/198; N/1/60/138; L/MIL/10/125; L/MIL/10/166 & 167.
5 Conversation with Mrs Jess Gillies, Catherine Marie's granddaughter, Benalla, 25 June 1989.
6 *Wangaratta Chronicle*, 28 September 1889, p. 2.
7 *Official Post Office Directory & Gazetteer*, Victoria, 1868, p. 659.
8 VPRS 640/1986, PRO Vic.
9 Conversation with Ruth Lack, a Walpole cousin, 22 July 1993.

TWO: *Friday's Child*

1 Alan Dunlop, *Little Sticks*, published by the author, 1985.
2 Ruth Lack to SE, 22 July 1993. Ruth Lack saw a great deal of the Payne sisters.
3 E. E. Dunlop, 'The Asian Pacific Scene – a Surgeon's Viewpoint', Newman Address given at Monash University, Melbourne, 1987.
4 R. S. McConachy, Sermon preached at memorial service, Benalla Methodist Church, and reported in the *Benalla Standard*, 8 January 1948.

5 *Benalla Standard*, n.d. but probably 1923, in Alice's scrapbook of newspaper clippings.
6 A. Dunlop.
7 ibid.
8 EED to Father Gerard Bourke CSSR, 20 February and 7 November 1978.
9 A. Dunlop.
10 ibid.

THREE: *The Philosopher's Stone*

1 Gertrude Hutchins to SE, interview 12 December 1986.
2 Alice Dunlop to Mary Ferguson, May 1940.
3 Pharmacy Board of Victoria, Certificate of Exemption No. 421 dated 3 May 1924.
4 Conversation between EED and SE, date not noted.

FOUR: *Men of Ormond*

1 David Kennedy Picken to EED, 4 February 1930.
2 E. E. Dunlop, Occasional Address to Melbourne University on the Conferring of LL.D (Hon.), April 1988.
3 Stuart Macintyre, 'War and Peace: a History of College Initiation', p. 97 in Stuart Macintyre (ed.), *Ormond College Centenary Essays*, Melbourne University Press, Melbourne, 1984. Macintyre quotes this from *Ormond Chronicle*, 30, 1950, p. 9, reporting Archie Anderson at a 1950 Club Dinner.
4 Stuart Macintyre (ed.), *Ormond College Centenary Essays*, Melbourne University Press, Melbourne, 1984.
5 C. McT. Hopkins, *How you Take It*, Neptune Press, Geelong, 1985.
6 Macintyre (ed.), op. cit., p. x.
7 Graham McInnes, *Humping my Bluey*, Hamish Hamilton, London, 1966, p. 99.
8 Macintyre, op. cit., p. 85.
9 McInnes, op. cit., pp. 96-7.
10 E. W. Gault to EED, 21 November 1930.
11 Jack Pollard, *Australian Rugby Union: the Game and the Players*, ABC Enterprises, 1984, pp. 190-1.

12 Dr E. Wilmott to SE, 6 July 1993.
13 Unidentified newspaper clipping from EED's collection.

FIVE: *Dunlop of Benalla*

1 Colin Lowndes to ? Jack Pollard (ref. on letter CRL/AGB) re the history of Australian Rugby Union.
2 Melbourne University *v.* Sydney University 11–3 to Melbourne; Queensland University *v.* Melbourne University 23–21 to Melbourne.
3 The Sir Wallace Kyle Memorial Oration delivered by Sir Edward Dunlop on Monday 13 March 1989 at the University of Western Australia.
4 Don Maddocks, 'The Doctors', in Macintyre (ed.) *Ormond College Centenary Essays. . .*
5 McInnes, *Humping my Bluey*, pp. 151–2. And EED to SE.
6 Hopkins, *How you Take it*, pp. 7–8.
7 That mistakes were made is evident in the previous year's results, where a second class honours mark has been altered to first class by the University's administration; and with second place in the class, it is likely that his memory was correct.
8 *Ormond Chronicle*, 1934, p. 4.
9 *Sun*, Sunday 12 August 1934, p. 1.
10 A. H. Spencer to EED, 3 October 1934.

SIX: *'Nulla Vestigia Retrorsum'*

1 Rowan Nicks, *Surgeons All: the Story of Cardiothoracic Surgery in Australia and New Zealand*, Hale & Iremonger, Sydney, 1984.
2 Alice's book: unidentified newspaper clipping.
3 EED to James and Alice Dunlop, n.d. but postmarked 21 January 1932.
4 Reference dated 19 December 1935, signed Sidney Sewell MD, Physician, Melbourne Hospital. Examiner for MD in the universities of Melbourne & New Zealand.
5 *Argus*, n.d. on cutting in Alice's book.
6 Sir Benjamin Rank to SE, interview 27 June 1989.
7 Alice Dunlop to Mary Ferguson, May 1940.

8 Mephan James William Ferguson (Jamie) to SE, interview 1 November 1989.
9 MJWF to SE, 1 November 1989.
10 MJWF to SE, interview 26 June 1992.
11 AAMC Christmas card to Helen Ferguson from 'Ray', Children's Hospital Carlton, with note signed 'Weary' on inside back cover, n.d.

SEVEN: *Journey to the Promised Land*

1 Unidentified newspaper clipping in Alice's book. 'A Traveller Abroad. Letters from Dr E. Dunlop.' n.d. but written in 1938.
2 Fragment of diary kept during 1937–8.
3 EED to HLRF, 13 November 1938, EED to the family, 23 November 1938.

EIGHT: *Mr E. E. Dunlop MS, FRCS*

1 Anne de Courcy, *1939 The Last Season*, Thames and Hudson, London, 1989.
2 Testimonial dated 30 January 1939 and signed Thomas Dunhill.
3 E. E. Dunlop, 'Great Men are like Mountains. Introduction to Grey-Turner Memorial Lecture', International Society of Surgeons' Conference, Montreux, Switzerland, 1981, 8 pp typescript.
4 E. E. Dunlop, 'The Whole Earth is the Sepulchre of Heroic Men. In memorium Gordon Gordon-Taylor', Memorial Lecture given to a combined meeting of the Australasian College of Surgeons and Malaysian surgeons at Kuala Lumpur, 1978.
5 EED to HLRF, 23 September 1945.

NINE: *War by any Means*

1 E. R. Chamberlain, *Life in Wartime Britain*, Batsford, London, 1972.
2 ibid.
3 Lord Porritt to SE, interview 22 February 1988.
4 ibid.
5 Dr Tom Kemp to SE, interview 12 February 1988.

6 *The Times*, 27 November 1939.
7 Allan S. Walker, *Middle East and Far East, Australia in the War of 1939–1945*, Series 5 Medical, Australian War Memorial, Canberra, reprinted 1962, p. 27.
8 Gavin Long, *To Benghazi, Australia in the War of 1939–1945*, Series 1 Army, Vol I, Australian War Memorial, Canberra, 1961, p. 68.
9 Disher papers, Colonel H. C. Disher to Major-General Rupert Downes, 13 January 1940; Rupert Downes to H. C. Disher 27 January 1940.
10 From documents held in Central Army Records Office, Melbourne, Victoria.

TEN: *Unholy Holy Land*

1 Memorandum to Headquarters, Southern Command, Victoria Barracks, Melbourne from Military Liaison Officer, London, 4 January 1940.
2 Disher papers, R. M. Downes to H. C. Disher, 27 January 1940.
3 E. E. Dunlop, 'An Australian in Palestine', Letter dated 6 February 1940, reprinted as an article in *Benalla Standard*, n.d.
4 Disher papers, Accommodation plan – southern zone, CR/Pal/15811/0, Force HQ, 7 Dec. 1939.
5 Disher papers, HCD to Rupert Downes, 24 January 1940.
6 ibid.
7 Disher papers, HCD to Rupert Downes, 27 February 1940.
8 Gavin Long, *To Benghazi, Australia in the War of 1939–1945*.
9 Disher papers, HCD to Rupert Downes 26 January 1940 in letter dated 24 January 1940.
10 Disher papers, HCD to Rupert Downes, later entry dated 29 February 1940 in letter dated 28 February 1940.
11 EED to HLRF, 2 February 1940.
12 E. E. Dunlop, 'An Australian in Palestine', Letter to Alice Dunlop which she passed on to the *Benalla Standard*, as was her wont.
13 EED to HLRF, 2 February 1940.
14 E. E. Dunlop, 'An Australian in Palestine'.
15 Disher papers, HCD to Rupert Downes, later entry dated 15 February 1940 in letter dated 11 February 1940.
16 Disher papers, HCD to Rupert Downes, 21 April 1940.
17 EED to HLRF, 2 February 1940.

18 EED to HLRF, postscript dated 23 March 1940 to letter dated 20 March 1940.
19 EED to Lily Dutton, [February 1940].
20 Disher papers, HCD to Rupert Downes, 27 February 1940.
21 ibid.
22 Disher papers, HCD to Rupert Downes, 30 March 1940 in letter dated 28 March 1940.
23 Disher papers, HCD to Rupert Downes, 19 March 1940.
24 ibid.
25 David Horner, *General Vasey's War*, Melbourne University Press, Melbourne, 1992, p. 56.
26 Disher papers, HCD to Rupert Downes, 21 April 1940.
27 The AIF rugby team to play the French Army on 27 April 1940 was: Maxwell, Hassett, McElhone, McVicker, Feathertonehaugh, Basil 'Jika' Travers (captain), Matchett, Wand, Long, Campbell, Loughran, Teunbar, Jackson, Dunlop (vice-captain). One man is unknown.
28 Hetherington despatched his story from 'Beyrouth' on Sunday 27 April 1940.
29 Disher papers, HCD to Rupert Downes, 20 May 1940.
30 Alice Dunlop to Mary Ferguson, 30 May 1940.
31 ibid.
32 EED to HLRF, 18 June 1940.
33 AWM, 2/1st AGH War Diary, 16 June 1940, 27 June 1940.
34 EED to HLRF, 25 June 1940.
35 EED to HLRF, n.d. but probably week of 15 July 1940. The promotion and appointment were published in the Government Gazette in May, without EED being aware of it.
36 ibid.
37 EED to HLRF, 27 July 1940.

ELEVEN: *Scarlet Major at the Base*

1 Disher papers, S. R. Burston to HCD, 11 September 1940.
2 Barrie Pitt, *The Crucible of War 1: Wavell's Command*, Papermac, Macmillan, London, 1986, p. 50.
3 Disher papers, Burston to HCD, handwritten postscript dated 29 October 1940 to letter 28 October 1940 from 1 Aust. Corps, Gaza.
4 Officers Record of Service dates his transfer from Overseas Base to

2/2 AGH as 1 July 1940.

5 Disher papers, Burston to HCD, 8 November 1940; EED to HLRF, 11 November 1940.
6 Disher papers, Burston to HCD, 8 November 1940.
7 AWM 52 11/1/45, Nov/Dec 1940, Appendix 33, p. 2.
8 ibid., Appendix 33, Visit DDMS 1 Aust Corps, DADMS do to GHQ Cairo, 12–15 Nov. 1940.
9 Disher papers, Burston to HCD, 5 December 1940.
10 Disher papers, Burston to HCD, 9 December 1940.
11 Disher papers, Burston to HCD, 6 January 1941.
12 AWM 52 11/1/45, Nov/Dec 1940, Appendix 33, p. 2.
13 Gavin Long, *Greece, Crete and Syria*, *Australia in the War of 1939–1945*, Series 1 Army, Vol. II, AWM, Canberra, 1953, p. 1.
14 W. S. Churchill, *The Grand Alliance, The Second World War*, Vol. III, Penguin Books, Harmondsworth, 1965, p. 13.
15 Churchill, op. cit., p. 17. Telegram drafted 10 January 1941 by W. S. Churchill for dispatch by the Chief of the General Staff to General Wavell and Air Chief Marshall Longmore.
16 Colonel N. Hamilton Fairley was also Consultant in Tropical Diseases to the British Forces in the Middle East.
17 Corelli Barnett, *The Desert Generals*, Pan Books, London, 1983, p. 57.
18 Barnett, op. cit., p. 60.
19 Long, op. cit., p. 9.
20 AWM 52 41/72/51, Report on Visit to Cairo, Suez and Palestine 11–17 March, 1941 by DMS AIF HQ ME, SRB.
21 Sir Benjamin Rank to SE, interview 27 June 1989.
22 Disher papers, Burston to HCD, 20 January 1941.

TWELVE: *Across the Wine-dark Seas*

1 AWM 52 11/1/6, Dec 40–Mar 41, DMS HQ AIF ME.
2 ibid.
3 Gavin Long, *Greece, Crete and Syria*, p. 23.
4 HQ, BTG, Report by Medical Liaison Officer, AIF to DMS AIF, No. 1, 31 March 1941.
5 Norman D. Carlyon, *I Remember Blamey*, Macmillan, Melbourne, 1980, p. 38.
6 AWM 52 11/1/45, Apr/41, DDMS 1 Aust Corps, 'Inspection of Site for Con. Depot, Athens', 7 April 1941. Colonel Johnston has

become confused about the name of the Vouliagmeni site, calling it 'Karviza'. Varkiza was the bay next to Vouliagmeni.

7   AWM 52 11/1/45, MLO, Apr/41.
8   ibid.
9   ibid.
10 AWM 52 11/1/45, Report by Medical Liaison Officer.
11 ibid.
12 PRO W0177/96, XC151673, HQ BTG, DDMS War Diary Apr/41, Appendix 7, 9 April 1941.
13 AWM 52 11/1/45, Report by Medical Liaison Officer.
14 Allan S. Walker, *Middle East and Far East*, p. 237.
15 AWM 52 11/1/45, Apr/41, Appendix 4, Report upon Hospital Site Reconnaissance Stylis and Region.
16 The account of the bombing of Piraeus is taken from Weary's field notebook, which he carried with him from April onwards.
17 EED to Johnston, DDMS, I Aust Corps, 9/4/41.
18 AWM 52 11/1/45, MLO HQ BTG, Serial 4, 10/4/41.
19 Long, *Greece, Crete and Syria*, p. 70.
20 Disher papers, War Diary, ADMS 6 Aust. Division, 12 April 1941.
21 AWM 52 11/1/45, No. 7.
22 PRO WO177/96, XC151673, HQ, BTG, DDMS War Diary, Appendix 14, Message given to Colonel Money, OC No. 6 Aust. Gen. Hosp., 15 April 1941.
23 PRO op. cit., Appendix 13, R. H. Alexander to OC No. 1 New Zealand General Hospital, 0130 hrs 15 April 1941.
24 AWM 52 11/1/45, No. 7, 15 April 1941.
25 ibid.
26 Carlyon, op. cit., p. 41.
27 AWM 52, AIF HQ, Rear Echelon AIF, ME, 27 April 1941. Report of visit of DMS AIF to Greece 10–23 April 1941, entry for 17 April 1941.
28 Leslie Le Souef, *To War without a Gun, Artlook*, Perth, 1980.
29 op. cit., p. 97.
30 EED to HLRF, 18 April 1941.
31 EED to HLRF, [6 May 1941], letter written in Egypt.
32 AWM 52 11/1/45, 17 April 1941.
33 AWM 52, Medical Arrangements Covering period 13/20 April, Report by DDMS 1 Aust. Corps, 20 April 1941.
34 Disher papers, War Diary 17 April 1941.
35 ibid.

36 AIF 52, AIF HQ, Rear Echelon AIF, ME, 27/4/41. Report of Visit of DMS AIF to Greece . . . 18 April 1941.

37 EED to HLRF, 18 April 1941.

38 AWM 52 11/1/45, 18 April 1941.

39 Le Souef, op. cit., p. 97.

40 AWM 52 11/1/45, 18 April 1941.

41 PRO WO177/96, XC151673, Signal to DQMG, MIDEAST from Brunskill BRAMG, War Diaries, Appendix 19, n.d.

42 AWM 52 11/1/45, 19 April 1941.

43 EED to HLRF, 18 April 1941.

44 Roald Dahl, *Going Solo*, Penguin Books, Harmondsworth, 1988. Dahl was a pilot in 80 Squadron and flew one of the Hurricanes in the Battle of Athens. His logbook shows that seven planes and eight pilots remained at the end of the day. They then lost two more and five Hurricanes were flown to Crete on 22 April.

45 Carlyon, op. cit., p. 43.

46 AWM 52 11/1/89, 21 April 1941.

47 AWM 52 11/1/89, Comments Upon Medical Aspects of the Campaign in Greece, by Medical Liaison Officer, AIF.

48 EED to HLRF, 18 April 1941.

49 Field notebook, 22 April 1941.

50 AWM 52 11/1/89, 22 April 1941.

51 Field notebook, 22 April 1941.

52 Walker, op. cit., p. 261.

53 Milton ('Blue') Butterworth to SE, interview 6 November 1987.

54 The war diary has been classified in two parts by the AWM, despite their both being one record of EED's time as MLO to HQ BTG. The handwritten diary to 0900 hours 21 April is 11/1/45, whereas the typed portion of the document is 11/1/89.

Colonel Starr has annotated and initialled the first page of the typed part: 'Duplicate also received for April.' I have not seen the duplicate, which may be a handwritten copy prepared by EED from his field notebook, but it seems that the typewritten section was done at HQ in Egypt after EED's return from Crete.

55 Field notebook 22 April 1941.

56 EED to HLRF, 24 April 1941.

57 AWM 52 11/1/89, 23 April 1941.

58 AWM 52 11/1/89 and field notebook for 23 April 1941.

59 EED to HLRF, 24 April 1941.

60 AWM 52 11/1/89 and field notebook, 24 April 1941; Carlyon p. 46.

61 AWM 52 11/1/89, n.d., but field notebook has as 25 April 1941.
62 EED to HLRF, [6 May 1941].
63 PRO WO177/96, XC151673, Appendix 21, Lt M. E. M. Hurford RAMC. Statement showing how he was evacuated.
64 EED to HLRF, [6 May 1941].

THIRTEEN: *Grey Ships Waiting*

1 PRO WO17796, XC151673, p. 9.
2 Milton 'Blue' Butterworth to SE, interview 6 November 1987.
3 ibid.
4 ibid.
5 EED to HLRF, [6 May 1941].
6 AWM 52 11/1/89, 25 April 1941, [Actually 26 April 1941, for evidence see this chapter.]
7 EED to HLRF, [6 May 1941].
8 Field notebook.
9 NZ Film Unit. Cameraman: Capt. Massey-Collier. Location: Greece–Nauplion. Date: 26/4/41. No. A125, Imperial War Museum.
10 Field notebook.
11 One of the most evocatively written accounts of the rôle played by the Navy in the Greek Campaign is in Vice-Admiral H. T. Baillie-Grohman's papers, held at the National Maritime Museum, Greenwich. These include reports of Operation Demon written by beach-masters, officers-in-charge of embarkation craft and cäiques, captains of the ships, and the vice-admiral's own two volumes of typescript memoirs entitled 'Flashlights on the Past'. With A. Heckstall-Smith, he wrote *Greek Tragedy '41*.
12 Long, *Greece, Crete and Syria*.
13 EED to HLRF, 24 April 1941 and [6 May 1941].
14 Disher papers, War Diary, 28 April 1941.

FOURTEEN: *'Sorry, Gone to Tobruk'*

1 Churchill, *Grand Alliance*, p. 239.
2 Clement Semmler (ed.) *War Despatches of Kenneth Slessor*, UQP, Brisbane, 1987, p. 177.

3 Disher papers, 24 May 1941.

4 Report on the Battle for Crete by Freyberg to the New Zealand Minister of Defence, 1941, quoted in Paul Freyberg, *Bernard Freyberg VC*, Hodder & Stoughton, London, 1991, p. 297.

5 Verbal testimony of Marika Markantonaki, Canea, quoted in Costas Hadjipateras & Maria Fafalios, *Crete 1941 Eyewitnessed*. Efstathiadis, Athens, 1989, p. 80.

6 AWM 52 DMS War Diary, Notes on Reorganisation of the Army Medical Services, 15 May 1941.

7 AWM 52 11/1/89, Comments upon Medical Aspects of the Campaign in Greece, by Medical Liaison Officer, AIF, p. 6.

8 AWM 52 11/1/89, op. cit., pp. 5–6.

9 John Devine, *Rats of Tobruk*, Angus & Robertson, Sydney, 1943, p. 88.

10 Devine, op. cit., p. 89.

11 Barton Maughan, *Tobruk and El Alamein, Australia in the War of 1939–1945*, Series 1 (Army), vol. III, AWM, Canberra, p. 279.

12 ibid., p. 279.

13 J. E. R. Clarke to SE, interview 4 July 1992.

14 Maughan, pp. 316–7.

15 *Tobruk, Libya*, Army Film Unit, recorded 17 July 1941 by Capt. Borradaile, Imperial War Museum, Ref. A148.

16 Charles Littlejohn DSO, MC, CBE had been a Rhodes Scholar, had served with the British Army in the First World War and was the first orthopaedic specialist at the Royal Melbourne Hospital. Weary much admired him.

17 AWM 52 11/2/4, 2/4th AGH War Diary, Apr–Jul. 1941.

18 AWM 52 11/6/2, 2/2 CCS, 20 July 1941. J. E. R. Clarke to SE, interview 4 July 1992.

19 AWM 52 11/6/2, 3 July 1941.

20 Field notebook.

21 AWM 52 11/6/2, 1 July 1941.

22 Milton Butterworth to SE, interview 6 November 1987.

23 ibid.

24 J. E. R. Clarke to SE, interview 4 July 1992.

25 AWM 52 11/6/2, Appendix 1, Function of 2/2 Aust. CCS, Tobruk, Sub-Area.

26 AWM 52 11/6/2, 24–5 July 1941.

FIFTEEN: *The Back Garden of Allah*

1   EED to James and Alice Dunlop, 7 September 1941.
2   AWM 52 11/6/2, 2/2nd Aust. War Diary, CCS, 1 August 1941.
3   EED to HLRF, dated 8 August 1941 but internal evidence suggests 9 August.
4   Maughan, p. 309.
5   Carlyon, *I Remember Blamey*, p. 69.
6   EED to SE, interview 2 October 1988.
7   Lord Porritt to SE, interview 22 February 1988.
8   EED to HLRF, undated but postmarked 22 September 1941.
9   AWM 52 11/6/2, 2/2 nd Aust. CCS War Diary, 29 September 1941.
10 Blamey to the Minister for the Army, Percy Spender, 8 September 1941. Quoted in Carlyon, p. 70.
11 [Rank?] J. Monro, consulting surgeon to the British Army in Cairo.
12 AWM 52 11/6/2, 2/2nd Aust. CCS War Diary, Appendix 8A.
13 op. cit., Appendix 8B.
14 op. cit., Appendix 8C.
15 op. cit., Appendix 7C, Conference of Officers and Sergeants, 2/2 Aust. CCS on Saturday, 1 Nov. 41.
16 Churchill, *The Grand Alliance*, p. 157.
17 ibid.
18 Report by Sir John Dill, CIGS, 6 May 1941, 'The Relation of the Middle East to the Security of the United Kingdom', quoted in Winston S. Churchill *The Grand Alliance, The Second World War*, Vol. III, Penguin Books, 1965, p. 375.
19 Martin Gilbert, *Second World War*, Weidenfeld & Nicolson, London, 1989, p. 262.

SIXTEEN: *Fastest Ship of the Convoy*

1   Australian Archives, 55/422/10, Despatch dated 11 January 1942, Cairo, from Official War Correspondent Kenneth Slessor.
2   Lionel Wigmore, *The Japanese Thrust, Australia in the War of 1939–1945*, Series 1 Army, Vol. IV, AWM, Canberra, 1957.
3   AWM 54 559/1/2, Notes on conferences held at HQ 1 Aust. Corps, Tjisaroea, 7 February 1942.
4   Dave Topping to SE, interview 9 March 1993.
5   AWM 54 559/1/2, 16 February 1942.

6 J. E. R. Clarke, Diary, 18 February 1942.
7 J. E. R. Clarke, op. cit., 18 February 1942. Captain MacNamara was accompanying his unit's personal baggage.
8 Allan S. Walker, *Middle East and Far East*.
9 Dunlop papers, Report Upon 2/2 Aust. CCS Personnel Following Embarkation of HMT *Orcades* 31 Jan 42 and 1 Allied General Hospital Java 26 February 1942–18 April 1942.

SEVENTEEN: *Into the Bag*

1 Vida Parker to SE, interview 9 March 1993.
2 EED to SE, interview 17 February 1993.
3 AWM 54 559/2/4, Major General H. D. W. Sitwell, MC, Dispatch on Operations in Java – February to March 1942, p. 3.
4 Sitwell, op. cit., p. 2.
5 AWM 54 559/2/2, Brigadier A. S. Blackburn VC, Report on Operations of the AIF in Java – Feb/Mar 1942, p. 2.
6 Blackburn, op. cit., p. 3.
7 E. E. Dunlop, Black-covered diary. This date differs from that given in Report upon 2/2 Aust. CCS Personnel Following Embarkation on HMT *Orcades* 1 Jan 42 and 1 Allied General Hospital Java 26 Feb 1942–18 April 1942, upon which Allan S. Walker based the account in the official medical history, *Middle East and Far East*. I prefer to accept the diary note made by EED at the time, as anecdotal and other evidence, including the report to Lieut-Colonel C. W. Maisey made by the British hospital's senior medical officer, Fl/Lieut. Nowell Peach, points to the later date.
8 AWM 54 559/2/2, p. 8.
9 AWM 54 559/2/4, p. 16.
10 AWM 54 559/2/2, p. 8.
11 M. A. de Jonge, Second World War Memoirs, Ts., 1948, p. 13, Imperial War Museum, London.
12 op. cit., p. 14.
13 M. A. de Jonge to SE, interview 26 September 1991.
14 E. E. Dunlop, 'Report upon 2/2 Aust. CCS Personnel Following Embarkation on HMT *Orcades* 1 Jan 42 and 1 Allied General Hospital Java 26 Feb 1942–18 April 1942', p. 7.
15 E. E. Dunlop, *War Diaries of Weary Dunlop*, Nelson, 1986, p. xxviii. Eric Beverley outlived Weary.

16 Dunlop, Report, p. 10.
17 ibid., p. 14.
18 J. E. R. Clarke, Diary, 7 March 1943.
19 Dunlop, Report, p. 11.
20 ibid.
21 Walker, *Middle East and Far East*, p. 440.
22 Dunlop, Report, p. 11.
23 ibid.
24 EED to SE, interview 1 February 1992.
25 Clarke, Diary, 7 March 1942.
26 Dunlop, Report, p. 12.
27 op. cit., p. 13.
28 ibid.
29 Clarke, 9 March 1942.
30 ibid.
31 Dunlop, Report, p. 14.
32 ibid.
33 Australian Archives Victoria, Department of the Army, Classified correspondence files, multiple number series, 1940–42, 42/421/500.
34 M. A. de Jonge to SE, interview 26 September 1991.
35 Dave Topping to SE, interview 9 March 1993.
36 Clarke, 9 April 1942.
37 de Jonge, Memoirs, p. 22.
38 A. Nowell H. Peach, Report dated 2 September 1945, to Lt. Col. C. W. Maisey [from] P.O.W. Camp, Batavia, Java, Imperial War Museum, London, H. 91/18/1.
39 John Denman to SE, interview 25 February 1988.
40 Dunlop, *War Diaries . . .* p. 5.

EIGHTEEN: *Singing and Games Forbidden*

1 Black diary, 18 April 1942.
2 M. A. de Jonge to SE, interview 26 September 1991.
3 Clarke, Diary, 20 April 1942.
4 This incident has been reconstructed from the Black Diary, the published diaries and conversations with EED.
5 Clarke, Diary, 21 April 1942.
6 Black diary, 22 April 1942.
7 J. E. R. Clarke to SE, interview 17 September 1992.

8 Sir Laurens van der Post to SE, interview 11 February 1988.
9 ibid.
10 Sir Laurens van der Post in E. E. Dunlop, *War Diaries of Weary Dunlop*, p. xi.
11 Clarke, Diary, 15 June 1942.
12 Air Vice Marshall Ronald Ramsay Rae to SE, interview 25 February 1988.
13 Sir Laurens van der Post to SE, ibid.
14 Donald Stuart, *I Think I'll Live*, Georgian House, Melbourne, 1981.
15 Sir Laurens van der Post to SE, ibid.
16 Stuart, op. cit., p. 164.
17 Clarke, Diary, 21 December 1942.
18 ibid.

NINETEEN: *Via Dolorosa*

1 Rod Allanson to SE, interview, 24 November 1987.
2 Walker, *Middle East and Far East*, p. 674.
3 EED to SE, 26 November 1990.
4 EED to SE, ibid.
5 Ray Parkin, *Into the Smother*, Hogarth Press, London, 1963, pp. 18–19.
6 Dunlop papers, Memorandum from E. E. Dunlop, Comd, AIF Troops, Transit Area to Comd Southern Area and copies to Comd AIF Area, 15 January 1943.
7 Dunlop papers, Memorandum to HQ, Southern Area from Lt-Col E. E. Dunlop, Comd AIF Troops Transit Area, Footwear AIF Troops, Transit Area, 15 January 1943.
8 Dunlop papers, E. E. Dunlop to Comd HQ Malaya COMD, 19 January 1943.
9 Dunlop papers, Memoranda from F. G. Galleghan, Comd AIF Malaya, 20 January 1943.
10 EED to SE, ibid.
11 Walker, op cit., p. 571.
12 Tim Bowden, *Changi Photographer. George Aspinall's Record of Captivity*, ABC Enterprises and Sun Books, Melbourne, 1989, p. 115.
13 Tom Young to SE, 20 January 1992.

14 Merton Woods, 'British and Japs called him "King of the river",' *Australian Women's Weekly*, 20 October 1945, p. 17.

15 E. W. Whincup, Speedo, Speedo, Unpublished Ts. in Documents Section, Imperial War Museum, London, n.d. No call number.

16 'Had the railway followed the road it would have obviated the need for the construction of the two bridges at Tamarkan (over the River Mae Klong), the Chungkai cutting and embankment and the two Wampoo viaducts.' from J. Coast, *Railroad of Death*, Commodore Press, London, 1946, p. 279.

17 E. E. Dunlop, Medical Report Upon Ps.O.W. in Burma and Siam – 1942 to 1945, RAPWI, Bangkok, 5 October 1945, p. 1.

18 J. Coast, *Railroad of Death*, p. 104, quoted in Wigmore, *The Japanese Thrust*, p. 566.

19 Parkin, op cit., p. 50.

20 Rod Allanson to SE, ibid.

21 Bill Haskill to SE, 12 December 1986.

22 Father Gerard Bourke CSSR, Untitled typescript describing *This is your Life*, programme on Sir Edward Dunlop, 1979, dated 27 June 1979.

23 Parkin, op cit., p. 51.

TWENTY: *Valley of the Shadow*

1 From Map of the Burma–Thailand Railway Line, Konyu–Hintok section, compiled by Ken Bradley ATCC, January 1989. Ray Parkin, Jock Clarke, Weary and SE have changed some features to what they believe is a more accurate representation of 1943.

2 J. E. R. Clarke to SE, interview 3 November 1992.

3 Parkin, *Into the Smother*, p. 2.

4 E. E. Dunlop, Evidence given under oath, Melbourne, 29 August 1946.

5 War Crimes investigations: Hintok Camp, E. E. Dunlop, Affidavit sworn 29 August 1946.

6 Parkin, op. cit., p. 75.

7 Parkin, op. cit., p. 71.

8 J. Coast, *Railroad of Death*, p. 104.

9 E. E. Dunlop, Medical Report upon Ps.O.W. in Burma and Siam – 1943 to 1945, RAPWI, Bangkok, 5 October 1945.

10 T. Hamilton, Report on Conditions and Life and Work of P.O.W.

in Burma & Siam 1942–1945, Medical Liaison Office, Civilian Internee Camp, Bangkok, 12 September 1945. Lieut-Colonel Hamilton AAMC was the OC, 2/4th CCS. He included in his report information from Capt. E. Newton Lee, who had moved with Lieut-Colonel Anderson's battalion to the 18 kilo camp in October 1942, where he was the only doctor. The 30 kilo camp was opened at the beginning of May.

11 Sibylla Jane Flower to SE, 11 November 1993, quoting a letter from John Pearson to S. J. Flower, 2 September 1992.

12 ibid.

13 Ivor Jones to SE, 8 November 1989.

14 EED to Father Gerard Bourke CSSR, 20 February 1978.

15 Father Gerard Bourke CSSR to EED, 16 February 1978.

16 E. E. Dunlop, 'Medical Experiences in Japanese Captivity', *BMJ*, Vol. ii, 5 October 1946, p. 482.

17 Parkin, op. cit., p. 149.

18 Interview with Bill Warbrick, ex Royal Corps of Signals, at Kranji War Memorial, February 1992.

19 Parkin, op. cit., p. 163.

20 Dunlop papers, Sijue Nakamura, Instructions given to P.O.W. on my assuming the command, 26 June 1943.

21 Rod Allanson to SE, 24 November 1987.

22 ibid.

23 Parkin, op. cit., p. 188.

24 EED to Father Gerard Bourke CSSR, 20 February 1978.

25 EED to SE, day of conversation not noted [February 1993].

26 Bourke, Untitled typescript, 27 June 1979. This appears to be a draft of a letter, possibly written to Bourke's family after he appeared on the Channel Seven television programme *This is your Life* devoted to Dunlop.

TWENTY-ONE: *Stables for the Sick*

1 E. E. Dunlop, Medical Report on Ps.O.W. in Burma and Siam – 1942 to 1945, RAPWI report, Bangkok, 5 October 1945.

TWENTY-TWO: *We* Kempis *do but do our Duty*

1   E. E. Dunlop, 'The Spirit of Survival', p. 2, Address to Ian Gawlor Symposium, 'Surviving in the 90s', Dallas Brookes Hall, 14 November 1992.
2   J. E. R. Clarke to SE, interview 3 November 1992.
3   John Marsh to SE, interview 9 February 1988.
4   Rod Allanson to SE, interview November 1987.
5   Les Tanner to SE, interview 26 April 1991.
6   John Marsh to SE, ibid.
7   Father Gerard Bourke CSSR, untitled typescript, 27 June 1979.
8   E. E. Dunlop, 'Medical Experiences in Japanese Captivity', *BMJ*, vol. ii, 5 October 1946, p. 485.
9   Father Gerard Bourke CSSR to EED, 16 February 1978.
10 ibid.
11 EED to Father Gerard Bourke, 20 February 1978.
12 ibid.
13 E. E. Dunlop, *BMJ*, p. 485.
14 T. Uren, Passage from autobiography (in press), quoted in Gavan McCormack and Hank Nelson (eds), *The Burma–Thailand Railway: memory and history*, Allan & Unwin, Sydney, 1993, p. 54.
15 Parliament of Australia, *Hansard Parliamentary Debates*, House of Representatives, Canberra, 26 February 1959, pp. 358–61.
16 ibid.

TWENTY-THREE: *'Ancient Civilisations'*

1   Colonel H. Cary Owtram to SE, interview 15 February 1988.
2   AWM 54 554/5/4, Brief History Chungkai POW Camp Hospital, p. 3.
3   AWM 54 554/5/2, E. E. Dunlop, Letter to the Camp Commandant, Nippon Army HQ, Chungkai, Hygiene & Sanitation Chungkai Camp & Hospital, 10 February 1944.
4   Colonel H. Carey Owtram to SE, ibid.
5   Percy Eric Cliffe, Japanese concerto, Ms. Imperial War Museum, documents section, London.
6   Colonel H. Carey Owtram to SE, ibid.
7   Dunlop papers, E. E. Dunlop, Chungkai Hospital Bulletin, Jan., Feb., March 1944, Facts and Figures about your Hospital, March 1944.

8 Dunlop papers, Old: 5933487, Pte Foster, F. J., 2 Cambs. Amputation 20 October 1943, Tropical ulcers, malnutrition, 15 March 1944.

9 Dunlop papers, E. E. Dunlop, The Private Feelings of a Prisoner of War, Tjimahi, 1942, Ts., 2 pp.

10 ibid.

11 Colonel H. Carey Owtram to SE, ibid.

12 Many prisoners of war of the Japanese are probably host to strongyloid worms, Weary decided much later. Infestation can be very dangerous indeed. He decided that he most likely had them himself.

13 Dunlop papers, Chungkai Hospital Bulletin, ibid.

14 Dunlop papers, R. C. Wright and B. W. Andrews, Report of the QM Department at Nakompatom P.O.W. Hospital Camp, Departmental Reports and Statistics, Nakom Patom, 29 August 1945, p. .4

15 A. Coates & N. Rosenthal, The Albert Coates Story, Hyland House, Melbourne, 1977, p. 126.

16 EED to SE, March 1992.

17 Robert Hardie, The Burma–Siam Railway. The Secret Diary of Dr Robert Hardie 1942-1945, Imperial War Museum, London, 1984, p. 54.

18 EED to SE, March 1992.

19 Dunlop papers, Memorandum from Lieut-Colonel J. D. Sainter to all Group Commanders and Chief Medical Officer, Nakom Patom Camp re Red Cross Administration of Funds. In appendices to War Diary, Nakom Patom Camp, POW Hospital, 14 June 1944.

20 Dunlop papers, Nakom Patom Camp, POW Hospital War Diary, 29 November 1944.

21 EED to SE, March 1992.

22 Dunlop papers, Nakom Patom Hospital Medical Society, Clinical Meetings, 22 August 1945.

23 L. R. S. MacFarlane, 'Unusual Aspects and Therapy in Amoebic Dysentery, Royal Army Medical Corps Journal, Vol. LXXXIX, no. 5, pp. 223-4 and no. 6, pp. 255-73.

24 Dunlop papers, E. E. Dunlop, The Surgical Treatment of Dysenteric Lesions of the Bowel amongst Allied Prisoners of War, Burma and Thailand. Interim report presented to Medical Society, Nakom Patom POW Hospital, n.d. but ts. prepared in Bangkok, 8 September 1945.

25 Dunlop papers, Report on meeting held to discuss the place of surgery in chronic disease of the large bowel on 20th July 1944, Nakom Patom Hospital Medical Society, Clinical Meetings, 20 July 1944.

26 A. Coates & N. Rosenthal, ibid.

27 Dunlop papers, Nakom Patom Camp POW Hospital, War Diary, 13 November 1944.

28 Dunlop papers, Impressions of Cpl Foster (Australian Journalist) on 24/12/44 and 25/12/44 at the N'Patom Base Hospital, Nakom Patom Camp POW Hospital Diary, 27 December 1944.

29 EED to SE, conversation 22 September 1992.

30 Dunlop papers, D. P. Dewey to A. Coates, dated 31 July 1945 and completed 10 August 1945. Coates was the chief witness for the prosecution at the sessions of the War Crimes Tribunal.

TWENTY-FOUR: *'Oh Incredible Day!'*

1 Dunlop papers, Nakom Patom Camp POW Hospital Diary, 16 August 1945.

2 Dave Topping to SE, interview 9 March 1993.

3 Dunlop papers, Nakom Patom Camp POW Hospital, War Diary, ibid.

4 ibid.

5 ibid.

6 Colonel Douglas Clague and Colonel Alan Ferguson Warren told Weary that McEachern insisted it was his duty to take command. 'Duty, McEachern? And what would you know about a thing like that?' retorted Clague.

7 Blue Butterworth to SE, conversation 5 July 1993.

8 HQ Allied Land Forces South East Asia Command, 'Directive. The Treatment and Evacuation of Recovered Allied Prisoners of War and Civil Internees', No. 21815 A.1, 13 August 1945.

9 Medical HQ War Diary, 28 September 1945.

10 HLRF to Alice Dunlop, 3 June 1945.

11 ibid.

12 HLRF to James and Alice Dunlop, 12 August 1945.

13 ibid.

14 EED to HLRF, 20 September 1945.

15 EED to HLRF, 28 August 1945.

16 EED to HLRF, 1 September 1945.

17 HQ ALFSEA Command. 'Directive . . .', p. 5.

18 Dunlop papers, EED to Brig. A. Blackburn VC, n.d. but written 23 September 1945. Taken by Coates to Australia.

19 Dave Topping to SE, interview 9 March 1993.

20 Dunlop papers, Memorandum from A. E. Coates to OC, Advanced Base, RAPWI, 31 August 1945.

21 Dunlop papers, Memorandum to OC, Law University Camp, Bangkok dated 6 September 1945.

22 Dunlop papers, Report to Senior Medical Liaison Officer, Allied HQ, Bangkok, by F. A. Woods, 'Photography – Cases and Eqpt – Kanburi, Tamuan and Nakom Patom 29 Aug '45 – 1 Sept '45, 2 September 1945.

23 Dunlop papers, List of supplies dropped by plane 1000 hrs 1 Sep 45, E & S, Takuri (Taka Buti).

24 Memorandum from Lieut-Colonel T. Hamilton AAMC to OC, Allied HQ, 'Prevention of Venereal Disease', 4 September 1945.

25 EED to HLRF, 20 September 1945.

26 ibid.

27 ibid.

28 ibid.

29 A. Coates & N. Rosenthal, ibid.

30 A. E. Coates to Lieut-Colonel Malcolm, 16 September 1945, quoting from a letter written to him by Lady Louis Mountbatten.

31. 'Short Report by Lady Louis Mountbatten on the Recent Work Undertaken in Connection with the Recovery, Care and Repatriation of Allied Prisoners of War and Civilian Internees in the South East Asia Command', Singapore, 21 November 1945.

32 Memorandum to all SMOs, ADsMS, Commander Nakom Patom Hospital from A. E. Coates re 'Instructions and Information by Col. Leaning ADMS 7 Ind. Div., 9 September 1945.

33 Minutes of Meeting No. 4 held at HQ E Gp/RAPWI, Bangkok, 1100 hrs 23 September 1945.

34 EED to Brig. A. Blackburn VC, ibid.

35 Minutes of meeting No. 3 held at E Gp/RAPWI HQ 1100 hrs 22 September 1945.

36 ibid.

37 03103 to All units from HQ 455 Sub Area, 24 September 1945.

38 EED to Brig. Blackburn, ibid.

39 Memoranda from EED to SMO Kanburi, 26 September 1945; to SMO Tamuang, 28 September 1945.
40 EED to HLRF, 1 October 1945.
41 Australian Associated Press, 23 September 1945.
42 Dunlop, *The War Diaries* . . . p. xxii.
43 EED to SE, 28 January 1993.
44 EED to Brig. Blackburn, ibid.
45 Memorandum from EED to Maj. W. E. Fisher, SMO Nakom Patom, 19 September 1945.
46 EED to Lt. Col. Swinton, 27 September 1945.
47 Memorandum to Lt. Col. J. D. Clague OBE, MC, RA, OC E Group, RAPWI, from E. E. Dunlop, Medical Liaison Officer, RAPWI, and T. Hamilton, ADMS, AIF, Siam, 8 October 1945.
48 EED to HLRF, 20 September 1945. The stanzas are from Alfred Lord Tennyson, *Maud*, Part I, xx:xi.

TWENTY-FIVE: *The Return of Ulysses*

1 EED to HLRF, 23 September 1945.
2 EED to HLRF, 20 September 1945.
3 HLRF to James and Alice Dunlop, [10 October 1945].
4 Lily Payne to [Alice] Maude Dunlop, 24 March 1943.
5 ibid.
6 EED to HLRF, 1 September 1945.
7 Interviews with Dr J. Colebatch, Sir Benjamin Rank and Mr R. McK. Rome, November 1987.
8 HLRF to EED, 17 September 1945.
9 EED to HLRF, 23 September 1945.
10 EED to HLRF, cable 1057, 13 October 1945.
11 Telegram from Victorian Echelon & Records to Mr J. H. Dunlop, 16 October 1945.
12 HLRF to EED, 6 September 1945.
13 Sir Laurens van der Post to SE, 11 February 1988.
14 ibid.
15 ibid.
16 EED to HLRF, 1 October 1945.
17 Helen Ferguson to Margaret 'Peggles' Gibson, 19 October 1946.
18 ibid.
19 Margaret Gibson to SE, 10 May 1991.

20 ibid.
21 Read at a meeting of the Victorian Branch of the British Medical Association on 6 February 1946.
22 Paul Hasluck, *The government and the People 1942–1945*, *Australians in the war of 1939–1945*, series 4 (Civil), Australian War Memorial, Canberra, 1970, p. 618 & p. 624.
23 Arthur S. Blackburn to EED, 12 October 1945.
24 Sir Benjamin Rank to SE, interview, 27 June 1989.
25 Disher papers, EED to Colonel Allan Walker, 15 February 1946.
26 W. W. S. Johnston to EED, 9 March 1947.
27 Arnold K. Henry to EED, 29 November 1945.
28 Arthur E. Porritt to EED, 21 January 1946.
29 Sir Thomas Dunhill to EED, n.d. but probably February–March 1946.

Twenty-six: *Reclaiming the Lost Years*

1 EED to Rowan Nicks, 23 September 1990.
2 Rowan Webb to SE, interview 4 December 1987.
3 Alf Nathan to SE, interview 30 November 1987.
4 Robert Dickens to SE, interview 15 June 1992.
5 Donald Macleish to SE, interview 5 December 1990.
6 Dr David McCaughey to John Dunlop, 12 July 1993. Re a mutual friend of Weary's and his, on whom Weary had operated.
7 Nancy Murphy to SE, East Keilor RSL, October 1987.
8 Donald Macleish to SE, ibid.
9 Bernard O'Brien to SE, interview 16 June 1992.
10 ibid.
11 Rowan Webb to SE, ibid.
12 Robert Marshall to SE, interview 26th November 1987
13 Margaret Gibson to SE, interview 10 May 1991.
14 Lil Dutton to EED, 21 April 1949.
15 James Mephan Ferguson to SE, 11 September 1993
16 Lil Dutton to EED, 21 July 1949.
17 ibid.
18 Donald Macleish to SE, ibid.
19 ibid.
20 Bernard O'Brien to SE, ibid.
21 W. Cotter Harvey, W. A. Bye and W. E. Fisher to the President,

8 Div and AIF Malayan Council, 29 April 1947; W. E. Fisher to Alfred Derham, 30 April 1947.

22 Minutes of Meeting of ex P.O.W. Medical Officers at the Medical Society Hall, 436 Albert Street, Melbourne, Monday, 14th April 1947 at 8.15 pm.

23 ibid.

24 Red Cross Conference, Address by E. E. Dunlop, representing the Ex-POW & Relatives' Association, 2 June 1947.

25 Council of the Eighth Division and Service Associates, 'Report of the Sub-Committee of Council Appointed to inquire into Payment of Subsistence to Ex-Ps.O.W. (J)', Sydney, 10 February 1949.

26 ibid.

27 War Office, W. Gardner to Lieut-Colonel Sharp, AIF, 28 December 1945.

28 W. E. Fisher to EED, 6 September 1949.

29 Submission by E. E. Dunlop to the Chairman, Repatriation Committee on Repatriated Prisoners of War, Appendix A, n.d.

30 Maj-General G. F. Wootten, Chairman, Repatriation Commission, Memorandum G. 1846 to Deputy Commissioners, all states, 23 May 1949.

31 Pro forma letter written by Eighth Division and Service Associates to the press, n.d. [?November 1949].

32 Hansard, Vol. 188, p. 4210, 9 August 1946.

33 ibid.

34 EED to W. E. Fisher, 1 September 1949.

35 ibid.

36 The Rt Hon. R. G. Menzies to W. E. Fisher, 24 October 1949.

37 ibid.

38 Arthur S. Blackburn to EED, 8 May 1947.

39 ibid.

40 Citation by Brigadier A. S. Blackburn, GOC AIF Java for Maj (T/ Lt-Col) Ernest Edward Dunlop, 2/2 Aust CCS.

41 Letter to the press from the Council of the Eighth Division and Service Associates, n.d. [?November 1949].

42 Commonwealth of Australia, 'Preliminary public sitting of committee appointed to investigate and report upon the claim made by certain organizations of ex-servicemen that a subsistence allowance should be paid to ex-prisoners of war', Sydney, 14 June 1950.

43 Commonwealth of Australia, Hansard, Question No. 1476, 26 November 1974.

44 Australian Military Forces: Southern Command to E. E. Dunlop, 14 January 1949.

TWENTY-SEVEN: *The Solace of Surgery*

1 E. E. Dunlop, 'Slipped Upper Femoral Epiphysis, with a Report on a Case Treated by Skeletal Traction', *Aust. & NZ Jnl Surgery*, Vol. 9, pp. 279–86, 1940.

2 B. R. Billimoria and E. E. Dunlop, 'Intramuscular Administration of Fluids', *The Lancet*, 20 July 1940, pp. 65–8.

3 Rowan Nicks to SE, 3 August 1993.

4 John Hayward to SE, interview 9 September 1993.

5 E. E. Dunlop and J. I. Hayward, 'Malignant Tumours of the Oesophagus and Upper End of the Stomach', *Royal Melbourne Hospital Clinical Reports: 1848–1948*, August 1948, pp. 72–83.

6 John Hayward to SE, ibid.

7 E. E. Dunlop, 'Some Observations and Reflections upon the Surgical Pathology of Oesophageal Malignancy,' *Studies in pathology presented to Peter MacCallum*, Melbourne University Press, 1950, pp. 259–77.

8 ——, 'Surgery of the Laryngo-Pharynx and Cervical Oesophagus,' *Aust. and NZ Jnl Surgery*, vol. xxii, no. 2, 1952 pp. 81–99.

9 ——, 'Some Observations and Reflections . . .', p. 276.

10 op. cit., p. 259.

11 Rowan Nicks to SE, ibid.

12 Dunlop, 'Surgery of the Laryngo-Pharynx . . .'

13 ibid.

14 John Hayward to SE, ibid.

15 E. E. Dunlop, 'Carcinoma of the Oesophagus with Survival', *Aust. and NZ Jnl Surgery*, vol. 30, no. 2, November 1960, pp. 81–91.

16 R. D. Marshall, 'Weary Dunlop – Surgeon, *RACS Journal*, in press.

17 ibid.

18 Donald Macleish to SE, interview 5 December 1990.

19 John Hayward to SE, ibid.

20 Sister Elizabeth Potter to SE, interview 5 December 1990.

21 Matron Audrey Anderson to SE, interview 5 December 1990.

22 Sister Elizabeth Potter to SE, ibid.

23 ibid.

24 ibid.
25 Robert Marshall to SE, interview 26 November 1987.
26 Donald Macleish to SE, ibid.
27 ibid.
28 Gabriel Kune to SE, interview 17 June 1992.
29 E. E. Dunlop, 'Ulcerative Colitis: the Ileostomy Life', *Medical Journal of Australia*, 26 March 1949, pp. 399–403.
30 Arnold Mann to SE, interview 20 June 1989.
31 E. E. Dunlop, 'Congenital Haemangiona of Colon', RACS General Scientific Meeting, Hobart, 19–22 May 1964.
32 Gabriel Kune to SE, ibid.
33 ibid.
34 E. E. Dunlop, 'An Idea for Australia's Future – Change the Human Brain', in 'Australia Tomorrow', draft manuscript for seminar held in Melbourne, n.d.
35 Douglas Leslie to SE, conversation 20 September 1993.

TWENTY-EIGHT: *Surgeon Ambassador*

1 John Hayward to SE, interview 9 September 1993.
2 E. E. Dunlop, 'Problems in the Treatment of Reflux Oesophagitis', *Gastroenterologia*, Vol. 86, No. 3, 1956, pp. 287–391.
3 ——, Report upon Colombo Plan Visit to Thailand, n.d. [August 1956].
4 ibid.
5 E. E. Dunlop, 'General Impressions of our Visit to Thailand', 24 August 1956.
6 ibid., Sunday 12 August 1956.
7 E. E. Dunlop, 'Report upon Colombo Plan Visit to Thailand' . . .
8 ibid.
9 E. E. Dunlop to Dr Ben Eiseman, 9 October 1956. Eiseman was Associate Professor of Surgery at the University of Colorado and spent a good deal of time in Thailand.
10 E. E. Dunlop to the Rt Hon. R. G. Casey, 6 October 1956.
11 Dr Sem Pring-puang-geo to H. E. Mr R. G. Casey [sic], 10 September 1956.
12 R. G. Casey to EED, 4 October 1956.
13 E. E. Dunlop, Draft of report to Department of External Affairs, Canberra, n.d.

14 Dr K. .G Jayasekera to SE, interview November 1990.

15 K. G. Jayasekera to EED, 27 April 1971.

16 E. E. Dunlop, 'Report on Colombo Plan Visit to Ceylon . . , n.d.

17 ——, Diary notes for report on Ceylon, [11 September 1956].

18 ——, 'Ceylon', n.d. [September 1956].

19 Australian–Asian Association of Victoria, 'Lord Casey – a Tribute by Sir Edward Dunlop', *Newsletter*, September 1976.

20 EED to A. Dickson Wright, 25 August 1959.

21 ibid.

22 A. Dickson Wright to EED, 19 September 1959.

23 Sir Benjamin Rank to SE, 27 June 1989.

24 R. L. Manchanda to EED, 13 May 1959.

25 EED to Ruth and Marco Markowitch [sic], 28 March 1960.

26 Donald Macleish, conversation 4 October 1993.

27 Charles B. Puestow to EED, 2 March 1960.

28 Donald Macleish, conversation 4 October 1993.

29 E. E. Dunlop, 'Carcinoma of the Oesophagus: Reflections upon Surgical Treatment', Cecil Joll Lecture delivered at the Royal College of Surgeons of England, 28 July 1960, *Annals of the Royal College of Surgeons of England*, Vol. 29, July 1961, pp. 28–53.

30 Donald MacLeish to SE, interview 5 December 1990.

31 The lecture he gave, 'Malignant lesions of head and neck', and the film *High Oesophageal Surgery*, were repeated in each city he visited. In Madras, for instance, he gave three lectures to three different medical colleges.

32 E. S. R. Hughes per Jean Lister to EED, 14 December 1964.

33 E. E. Dunlop, Draft report on Visit to Vietnam, incomplete, [January 1965].

34 John Blunt to SE, interview 26 November 1987.

35 K. G. Jayasekera to SE, November 1990.

36 Bernard O'Brien to SE, interview 16 June 1992.

TWENTY-NINE: *'The Influence of Weary'*

1 Robert Dickens to SE, interview 15 June 1992.

2 Robert Marshall to SE, interview 26 November 1987.

3 Marshall, ibid.

4 Michael Long to SE, interview 17 June 1992.

5 Marshall, ibid.

6   ibid.
7   Dickens, ibid.
8   ibid.
9   ibid.
10   Long, ibid.
11   ibid.
12   Dickens, ibid.
13   ibid.
14   Peter Nelson to SE, interview 19 June 1992.
15   Gabriel Kune, ibid.
16   Nelson, ibid.
17   Donald Macleish to SE, interview 5 December 1990.
18   Nelson, ibid.
19   Dickens, ibid.
20   Kune, ibid.
21   ibid.
22   Long, ibid.
23   ibid.
24   EED to SE, interview 2 July 1990.
25   Dickens, ibid.
26   Long, ibid.
27   ibid.
28   Macleish, ibid.
29   Dickens, ibid.
30   Marshall, ibid.
31   Nelson, ibid.
32   Alf Nathan to SE, interview 30 November 1987.
33   ibid.
34   Long, ibid.
35   Peter Little to SE, conversation 6 June 1990.
36   Dickens, ibid.

THIRTY: *The Life-long Mission*

1   Shirley Hah to SE, interview 3 May 1991.
2   ibid.
3   *Courier Mail*, 4 February 1969.
4   Department of External Affairs, 'Australian Civilian Medical Aid
     to Viet-Nam', report by Professor Sydney Sunderland, Faculty of

Medicine, University of Melbourne, March 1969.

5 EED to Dr Cyril Cecchi, 20 October 1969.
6 EED to Alan Dunlop, 21 September 1969.
7 EED to Cyril Checchi, 19 August 1969.
8 EED to Cyril Checchi, 20 September 1969.
9 EED to Alan Dunlop, 21 September 1969.
10 EED to Cyril Checchi, 19 August 1969.
11 ibid.
12 EED to Cyril Checchi, 20 September 1969.
13 Helen Dunlop, 'Two Days in South Vietnam', *Newsletter*, Australian–Asian Association, July 1970.
14 EED to SE, 22 September 1992.
15 Arch Flanagan to EED, 17 January 1990.
16 Bill Belford to SE, 10 March 1993.
17 EED to Stanley Gimson, 20 April 1974.
18 E. E. Dunlop, Submission to the Repatriation Commission re granting a widow's pension to the wife of [name withheld] MX-48315.
19 Dr Nigel Gray, Anti-Cancer Council of Victoria, to SE, 7 September 1993.
20 EED to Tom McDermott, National Prisoners of War Assn, Canada, 30 July 1972.
21 EED to Dr M. M. Kehoe, Commonwealth Department of Veterans' Affairs, 6 January 1984.
22 Bruce Ruxton to SE, conversation 4 October 1993.
23 Robert Marshall to SE, interview 26 November 1987.
24 Nigel Gray to SE, interview 4 July 1992.
25 ibid.
26 Sir Reginald Swartz to SE, conversation 10 October 1993.
27 Tony Ashford to SE, interview 12 October 1993.
28 Valda Street to SE, conversation 13 October 1993.
29 *Age*, 18 January 1977.
30 Bruce Manning, Department of Veterans' Affairs, to SE, conversation 15 October 1993.
31 E. E. Letts to SE, 29 October 1993. Mr Letts was 1st Assistant Secretary, Dept. of Veterans' Affairs, and headed the Taskforce on Vietnam Veterans' Health Problems.
32 ibid.
33 ibid.
34 ibid.

THIRTY-ONE: *Almonds to those who have no Teeth*

1 Barbara Lofts to SE, conversation 29 October 1989.
2 Tribute to Lady Dunlop by Dr John Colebatch, Toorak Uniting Church, 28 April 1988.
3 E. E. Dunlop, tribute to Col. A. G. Ferguson-Warren, published in *Globe & Land*, March–April 1976, p. 127.
4 EED to Rowan Nicks, 4 September 1982.
5 ibid.
6 EED to Rowan Nicks, 17 October 1983.
7 EED to Rowan Nicks, 16 November 1983.
8 EED to Rowan Nicks, 17 October 1983.
9 EED to Rowan Nicks, 5 April 1984.
10 EED to Rowan Nicks, 29 May 1984.
11 W. Belford to EED, June 1984.
12 Bernard O'Brien to SE, interview 16 June 1992.
13 EED to Rowan Nicks, 22 July 1984.
14 EED to Rowan Nicks, 1 August 1985.
15 EED to Rowan Nicks, 31 March 1986.
16 EED to Rowan Nicks, 21 October 1986.
17 ibid.
18 EED to Rowan Nicks, 10 January 1987.
19 ibid.
20 EED to SE, 9 May 1991.
21 EED to SE, 4 June 1988.
22 E. E. Dunlop, Address to 2/29th Bn, n.d. but before 1952.
23 EED to Susan Braithewaite, 6 January 1989.
24 EED to Rowan Nicks, 31 March 1986.
25 EED to SE, 18 June 1993.
26 EED to SE, 16 June 1990.
27 EED to SE, 17 July 1987.
28 EED to Rowan Nicks, 24 February 1987.
29 EED to Susan Braithewaite, 6 January 1989.
30 EED to SE, 31 October 1988, after attending a luncheon in Canberra for the 'chosen 200 of the Bicentenary'.
31 EED to SE, 7 January 1988.
32 E. E. Dunlop, Occasional Address on Conferring of Doctor of Laws (Hon. Causa), Melbourne University, 9 April 1988.
33 ibid.
34 EED to SE, 20 April 1988.

35 ibid.
36 EED to SE, 29 April 1988.
37 EED to Rowan Nicks, 8 May 1988.
38 ibid.
39 EED to SE, 10 January 1992.
40 EED to Rowan Nicks, 8 May 1988.
41 EED to SE, 26 October 1988.
42 EED to Rowan Nicks, 20 April 1989.
43 EED to SE, 24 July 1989.
44 ibid.
45 EED to Rowan Nicks, 9 January 1990.
46 EED to SE, letter dated 11 September 1991, but actually August.
47 EED to SE, 2 September 1991.
48 Address by Sir Michael Woodruff on presenting Sir Edward Dunlop to the Royal College of Surgeons, Edinburgh, for an honorary fellowship, 11 October 1991.
49 EED to Rowan Nicks, 3 November 1991.
50 EED to Rowan Nicks, 15 November 1991.
51 ibid.
52 EED to SE, 6 January 1992.
53 EED to SE, 17 August 1992.
54 ibid.
55 EED to SE, 16 January 1992.
56 EED to SE, 29 September 1990.
57 EED to SE, conversation 24 June 1993.
58 SE to EED, date of conversation not noted, but following the funeral of Professor Fred Hollows.
59 Sir Zelman Cowan to John Dunlop, 13 July 1993.

Ackland, John & Richard (eds), *Word from John*, Cassell, 1944.

Allanson, Rod, The Lost Legion, unpublished Ts.

Barnett, Corelli, *The Desert Generals*, Pan, London, 1983.

Barber, Noel, *Sinister Twilight: the Fall of Singapore*, Arrow, London, 1988.

Beevor, Antony, *Crete: the Battle and the Resistance*, John Murray, London, 1991.

Bellair, John, *Amateur Soldier: An Australian Machine Gunner's Memories of World War II*, Spectrum, Melbourne, 1984.

——, *From Snow to Jungle: a History of the 2/3rd Australian Machine Gun Battalion*, Allen & Unwin, Sydney, 1987.

Bowden, Tim, *Changi Photographer. George Aspinall's Record of Captivity*, ABC Enterprises and Sun Books, Melbourne, 1989.

Boyle, J., *Railroad to Burma*, Allen & Unwin, Sydney, 1990.

Bradley, James, *Towards the Setting Sun*, J. M. L. Fuller, Wellington, NSW, 1982.

Calvocoressi, Peter, Wint, Guy, & Pritchard, John, *Total War: the Causes and Courses of the Second World War*, vol. I: *The Western Hemisphere*, 2nd edn, Penguin, Harmondsworth, 1989.

——, vol. II, *The Greater East Asia and Pacific Conflict*, 2nd edn, Penguin, Harmondsworth, 1989.

Carlyon, Norman D., *I Remember Blamey*, Macmillan, Melbourne, 1980.

Chamberlain, E. R., *Life in Wartime Britain*, Batsford, London, 1972.

Churchill, W. S., *Second World War*, vol. III, *The Grand Alliance*, Penguin, Harmondsworth, 1985.

——, *Second World War*, vol. IV, *The Hinge of Fate*, Penguin, Harmondsworth, 1985.

Clarke, Hugh, *A Life for every Sleeper*, Allen & Unwin, Sydney, 1986.

Clarke, P. *The Governesses: Letters from the Colonies 1862–1882*, Hutchinson, Melbourne, 1985.

Clune, Frank, *Tobruk to Turkey with the Army of the Nile*, Hawthorn Press, Melbourne, 1949.

Coast, J., *Railroad of Death*, Commodore Press, London, 1946.

682

Coates, Albert & Rosenthal, Newman, *The Albert Coates Story: the Will that found the Way*, Hyland House, Melbourne, 1977.

Cooper, Artemis, *Cairo in the War 1939–1945*, Hamish Hamilton, London, 1989.

Cope, Zachary, *The History of St Mary's Hospital Medical School*, Heinemann, London, 1954.

Corrie, E. C. W., *Survival against Odds*, published by the author, n.d.

Cruickshank, Charles, *SOE in the Far East*, Osford, 1983.

Devine, John, *The Rats of Tobruk*, Angus & Robertson, Sydney, 1943.

Dunlop, Alan J., *Little Sticks*, published by the author, Melbourne, 1985.

Earlwood, E. C. Gurney (ed.), *The First at War: the Story of the 2/1st Australian Infantry Battalion 1939–45, The City of Sydney Regiment*, Association of First Infantry Battalion, Sydney, 1987.

Foster, Frank, *Comrades in Bondage*, Skeffington, London, n.d.

Freyberg, Paul, *Bernard Freyberg VC: Soldier of Two Nations*, Hodder & Stoughton, London, 1991.

Gardner, Brian, *The East India Company*, Rupert Hart-Davis, London, 1971.

Gilbert, Martin, *Second World War*, Weidenfeld & Nicolson, London, 1989.

Gough, Richard, *Special Operations Singapore 1941–42*, Heinemann, Singapore, 1987.

Griffiths, Bill, *Blind to Misfortune*, as told to Hugh Popham, Leo Cooper, London, 1989.

Hadjipateras, C. & Fafalios, M., *Crete 1941 Eyewitnessed*, Efstathiadis Group, Athens, 1989.

Hall, E. R. (Bon), *Railway of Death*, Graphic Books, 1981.

Hardie, Robert, *The Burma–Siam Railway: the Secret Diary of Dr Robert Hardie*, Collins, Sydney, 1983.

Hasluck, Paul, *The Government and the People 1939–41*, vol. I of *Australia in the War of 1939–1945* series 4 (Civil), AWM, Canberra, 1952.

——, *The Government and the People 1942–45*, vol. II of *Australia in the War of 1939–1945* series 4 (Civil), AWM, Canberra, 1970.

Heathcott, T. A., *The Indian Army*, David & Charles, Newton Abbott, 1974.

Hopkins, Charles, *How you take it*, Neptune Press, Geelong, 1985.

Horner, David, *General Vasey's War*, Melbourne University Press, Melbourne, 1992.

Innes, P. R., *The History of the Bangal European Regiment now the Royal Munster Fusiliers, and how it helped to win India*, Simpkin Marshall, London, 1885.

Irving, David, *Hitler's War*, Hodder & Stoughton, London, 1977.

Kinder, Hermann & Hilgemann, Werner, *Penguin Atlas of World History*, vol. II, *From the French Revolution to the Present*, Penguin, Harmondsworth, 1988.

Kinvig, Clifford, *River Kwai Railway: the Story of the Burma–Siam Railroad*, Brasseys, London, 1992.

Kiriakopoulos, G. C., *Ten Days to Destiny: the Battle for Crete 1941*, Avon Books, New York, 1985.

Le Souef, Leslie, *To War without a Gun*, Artlook, Perth, 1980.

Long, Gavin, *To Benghazi*, vol. I of *Australia in the War of 1939–1945*, series 1 (Army), AWM, Canberra, 1961.

——, *Greece, Crete and Syria*, vol. II of *Australia in the War of 1939–1945*, series 1 (Army), AWM, Canberra, 1953.

Lunn, Hugh, *Vietnam: Reporter's War*, UQP, 1985.

McCormack, Gavan & Nelson, Hank, *The Burma–Thailand Railway*, Allen & Unwin, Sydney, 1993.

McGrath, R. & Oliver, K., *History of Baddaginnie School*, privately published, 1971.

McInnes, Graham, *The Road to Gundagai*, Hamish Hamilton, London, 1965.

——, *Humping my Bluey*, Hamish Hamilton, London, 1966.

Macintyre, Stuart (ed.), *Ormond College Centenary Essays*, Melbourne University Press, Melbourne, 1984.

MacLear, Michael, *The Ten Thousand Day War*, Thames Methuen, London, 1981.

Maughan, Barton, *Tobruk and El Alamein*, vol. III of *Australia in the War of 1939–1945*, series 1 (Army), AWM, Canberra, 1966.

Nelson, Hank, *Prisoners of War: Australians under Nippon*, ABC, Sydney, 1985.

Nicks, Rowan, *Surgeons All: the Story of Cardiothoracic Surgery in Australia and New Zealand*, Hale & Iremonger, Sydney, 1984.

Official Post Office Directory and Gazetteer, 1865, 1868, 1871–2, 1875.

Owen, Sep, (ed.), *10-Course Wags: Stories of the Wireless Air Gunners*, F. S. Owen, Newcastle, 1986.

Parkin, Ray, *Out of the Smoke*, Hogarth Press, London, 1960.

——, *Into the Smother*, Hogarth Press, London, 1963.

Pavillard, S., *Bamboo Doctor*, Macmillan, London, 1960.

Pepper, Peter, *A Place to Remember: the History of London House . . .*, Ernest Benn, London, 1972.

Pitt, Barrie, *Wavell's Command*, vol 1 of *The Crucible of War*, Papermac, London, 1986.

——, vol 2, *Auckinleck's Command*, Papermac, London, 1986.

Pollard, Jack, *Australian Rugby Union: the Game and the Players*, ABC Enterprises, 1984.

Post, Laurens van der, *The Seed and the Sower*, Penguin, Harmondsworth, 1985.

Rank, Benjamin K., *Heads and Hands: an era of Plastic Surgery*, Harper & Row, Sydney, 1987.

Ricks, Christopher (ed.) *A. E. Housman: Collected Poems & Selected Prose*, Allen Lane, Harmondsworth, 1988.

Rivett, Rohan, *Behind Bamboo*, Angus & Robertson, Sydney, 1946.

Royal Melbourne Hospital, *Clinical Reports 1848–1948*, Royal Melbourne Hospital Old Students Assn, August 1948.

Skidmore, Ian, *Marines Don't Hold their Horses*, W. H. Allen, London, 1981.

Stuart, Donald, *I Think I'll Live*, Georgian House, Melbourne, 1981.

Terry, Susan, *House of Love*, Lansdowne Press, Melbourne, 1966.

Thorne, Christopher, *The Far Eastern War: States and Societies 1941–45*, Counterpoint, Hemel Hempstead, 1986.

Victoria Land Conservation Council, *Report on the Ballarat Area*, Melbourne, June 1980.

Victorian Gazetteer, 1865, 1871.

Victorian Government Gazette, vol. 2, 1854.

Walker, Allan S., *Clinical Problems of War*, vol. I of *Australia in the War of 1939–1945*, series 5 (Medical), AWM, Canberra, 1956.

——, *Middle East and Far East*, vol. II of *Australia in the War of 1939–1945* series 5 (Medical), AWM, Canberra, 1953.

Wigmore, Lionel, *The Japanese Thrust*, vol. IV of *Australia in the War of 1939–1945*, series 1 (Army), AWM, Canberra, 1968.

OTHER SOURCES

Newspapers:

Age, Argus, Benalla Standard, NSW Rugby Union News, Ormond Chronicle, 1930–1935, *The Referee*, 1932–1935, *Sun*, 1932–1935, *Telegraph*, 1932–1935

Articles and papers:

Cliffe, Percy Eric, 'Orchestras in Captivity', *Music Journal*, December 1945, p. 5.

Dunlop, E. E., 'Surgery and Surgical Pioneers', the 37th Dr Mackay Pioneer Memorial Oration, *North-Eastern Historical Society Newsletter*, vol. 19, nos. 3–5, 1980.

Ferguson, G. T., 'Wattie Dunlop: a Dumphries Clerical Humorist', *Gallovidian*, 1904, pp. 54–8.

Guest, Charles & Venn, Alison, *Studies of Morbidity and Mortality of Former Prisoners of War and Other Australian Veterans*, Sir Edward Dunlop Medical Research Foundation report, Dept. of Community Medicine, University of Melbourne, 1990, 147pp.

Waller, R. P., 'With the 1st Armoured Brigade in Greece', *Jnl of the Royal Artillery* vol. LXII, no. 3, July 1945.

Wavell, Field Marshall Earl, 'The British Expedition to Greece, 1941', *Army Quarterly*, January 1950, pp. 178–85.

Unpublished Sources:

Reports, diaries, war diaries and letters in Sir Edward Dunlop's papers and in private collections. Sir Edward's papers contain, *inter alia*, in addition to his personal war diary kept from the eve of capitulation to the end of the war and the letters he wrote to Helen Ferguson and his family, official papers relating to the 2/2nd Aust. Casualty Clearing Station; Routine Orders parts I and II for the camps he commanded in Java; a mass of memoranda and reports issued or compiled during the war and at RAPWI Headquarters in Bangkok at war's end; meticulously kept medical records of operations performed in the prisoner-of-war camps; an almost complete set of the original illustrations painted by Jack Chalker at medical headquarters in Bangkok; correspondence, newspaper cuttings and photographs relating to all his interests; medical papers and research material from which he spoke, together with many 35 mm slides.

Australian Archives

MP 729/7:42/421/500, 38/421/21, 38/421/210, 33/421/18, 33/421/21, 42/421/642, 42/421/500, 55/422/10
MP 742: War Crimes Trials, Affidavits

Australian War Memorial

AWM 52 AIF & Militia War Diaries 1939–1945 War: 11/1/6, 11/1/18, 11/1/32, 11/1/33, 11/1/34, 11/1/37, 11/1/45, 11/1/59, 11/1/71, 11/1/72, 11/1/78, 11/1/89, 11/2/1, 11/2/2, 11/2/4, 11/6/2, 41/72/51, 41/92/27
AWM 54: 163/2/1, 173/1/1, 173/2/1, 173/4/2, 403/3/5, 403/3/6, 403/3/12, 405/75, 423/11/44, 481/1/22, 534/5/8, 534/5/13, 554/5/7, 554/5/13, 559/1/2, 559/2/2, 559/2/4
AWM 75/217; AWM 76

British Library, India Office Library & Records

Medal Rolls for Punjab War
Town Major's Lists
N/1/50/198; N/1/60/138; N/2/17/131; L/MIL/10/125, 166, 167.

Church of Scotland, Edinburgh headquarters

History of the Congregations of the Presbyterian Church 1733–1900.

Imperial War Museum

Baillie-Grohman, Vice-Admiral H. T., Flashlights on the Past, Ts., 2 vols.

Brunskill, G. S., The Memoirs of Brigadier G. S. Brunskill CBE, MC, Ts. entitled 'A Soldier's Yesterdays', PP/MCR/136.

——, 'Administrative Aspects of the Campaign in Greece in 1941', Ts., Imperial War Museum, original report dated 19 June 1941. This and the following report were published in altered form in the *Army Quarterly*, April 1947.

——, 'Administrative Aspects of the Campaign in Crete', Ts, Imperial War Museum, 19 June 1941.

de Jonge, Maria A., The Second World War Memoirs of Mrs M. A. de Jonge MBE, Ts., 152pp, 1948.

Kano, Tosh, The Other Side of the Fence, Ts., PP/MCR/160.

Peach, A. Nowell H., Report dated 2/9/45 and diary, 91/18/1.

Whincup, E. W., Speedo, Speedo, unpublished Ts. in Documents section, n.d.

Films

A112/1, Location: Greece, 13 March 1941; A125, Location: Greece–Nauplion, 26 April 1941; A129, Location: Crete and Alexandria, 31 May 1941; A138/3, Location: Greece, 16 April 1941; A148, Location: Tobruk, Libya, 17 July 1941; A186A, Location: Tobruk, 12 July 1941.

National Maritime Museum, Greenwich

Vice-Admiral H. T. Baillie-Grohman's papers.

Public Record Office, Kew

WO201/2737, 2744, 2745, WO177/46, 94, 96, 1596, WO169/174, 590

Public Record Office of Victoria

VPRS 14, VPRS 626/48, VPRS 626/468, VPRS 626/518, VPRS 640/986, VPRS 640/1877, VPRS 795/654, VPRS 795/846, VPRS 7396/P1, VPRS 7397/P1, VPRS 7410/P1,

Map of Parish of Dean, Counties of Talbot & Granit, showing blocks selected by H. N. Walpole and T. R. W. Walpole 1869, 1871.

State Library of Victoria

University of Melbourne Archives

Strathfieldsaye Estate Collection: H. C. Disher papers

n denotes endnote
text illustrations in italic